THEODORE DREISER

Theodore Dreiser, circa 1893 (UP)

THEODORE DREISER

AT THE GATES OF THE CITY
1871–1907

Richard Lingeman

G. P. PUTNAM'S SONS / NEW YORK

Photo credits will be found on pages 425–26.

The text of this book is set in Caslon 540
Designed by Anthea Lingeman

Library of Congress Cataloging-in-Publication Data

Lingeman, Richard R.
Theodore Dreiser: at the gates of the city, 1871–1907.

Bibliography: p.
Includes index.
1. Dreiser, Theodore, 1871–1945—Biography.
2. Novelists, American—20th century—Biography.
I. Title.
PS3507.R55Z664   1986   813'.52 [B]   86-9380
ISBN 0-399-13147-7

Printed in the United States of America
1   2   3   4   5   6   7   8   9   10

To Anthea

CONTENTS

Prologue

The career of Theodore Dreiser was one of the most obstacle-ridden in American letters. As a transitional figure between the genteel era dominated by William Dean Howells, Mark Twain, and Henry James, and the rebels of the twenties, he was a messenger picking his way through a minefield of censorship, prejudice, and snobbery, clearing a path for the generation that went over the top after him and took the literary high ground.

At first his mission was a lonely one, his only allies a handful of mentors in his youth, a few friends, two or three sympathetic editors, a worshiping wife; he was driven by naive, undisciplined genius and a passion for truth that was like a natural force. Although he had learned his craft in the raucous Tenderloin of late-nineteenth-century journalism and ten-cent mass magazines, his innate honesty remained intact, uncorruptible. In his first novel, *Sister Carrie*, he sought to provide a true picture of social conditions, of the way the world works, "of the game as it is played."

He was no self-conscious rebel, though, no literary anarchist setting off bombs in a literary Haymarket Square. In many ways he was a conventional young man with a vague idealism about art and literature that cut him off from the commercial hustle of the Gilded Age, though he was not immune to the success virus by any means. Born in 1871 to a poor family headed by a fanatically religious German immigrant father and a "pagan," indulgent mother, he was, like most second-generation children, full of American dreams of power, sex, affluence, and status. He had cut his teeth on Horatio Alger as a boy, and like many in his generation he envisioned himself becoming another Andrew Carnegie or John D. Rockefeller. But he regarded money as the key to a finer sphere, naively envisioned in terms of beauty, luxury, fame, and the love of women. Lacking the discipline for the traditional slow Algerine climb up the clerical ladder, throwing away the chance for a university education, and sensing from his childhood immersion in poverty that the race was unequal, he drifted into journalism and there his seedling literary ambitions took root.

In adolescence and young manhood, he was introspective, awkward, prudish. Sex mesmerized him, a hot flame he feared getting too close to. Burning, he married. She was a gentle, small-town girl from Missouri, Sara Osborne White; it was a prolonged courtship fueled by romantic agonies of thwarted desire. He placed literary fame on the same pedestal that he had put his fiancée, abandoning a lucrative career grinding out "specials" for popular magazines. He had a simple faith that if he wrote something good, true, and artistic, he would win the favors of the dream goddess, just as he had won his wife, and continue his days as a literary gentleman, neither a high-paid confectioner of popular society romances nor a hack pandering to "low" tastes.

But there was a rebellious streak in his makeup; he had a voluptuous, sensual temperament, a love for dreamy idleness, that lured him even as he was straining on the success treadmill; he also had an iron stubbornness with a cynical, perverse (some would say evil) twist. Something in him—resentment, distrust—instinctively rebelled against the reigning genteel tradition. In the light of his background, it seemed false, irrelevant to everything he had experienced, beginning as a boy in Terre Haute, Indiana. While he paid obeisance to the establishment figures like novelist William Dean Howells and poet Edmund Clarence Stedman, and sought their patronage, they sensed something not "right" about the tall, voluble, awkward Hoosier with a cast in one eye and edged away.

That was perhaps for the best, for he was a natural who had to go his own way. Until his first novel was published, he sought to placate the dominant morality with compromises, but he had gone much too far along the road to the new literature—a democratic novel, its pages open to characters previously considered vulgar, which spoke unselfconsciously in the flat tones of Middle Western speech and focused on life as it is rather than as it ought to be.

Dreiser's early life, the subject of this volume, is a remarkable story of failure and victory. He saw the most brilliant truth-telling young writers of his generation struck down by illness, drink, or despair, and for a time, in the early 1900s, it was a near thing whether he himself would live or die, or if he did live, whether he would ever write again. His battle to survive was the crucial period of his life, and the story has never been fully told. My window to that troubled time was the holograph manuscript of a then-unpublished work called *An Amateur Laborer*, written only a year after he suffered a nervous breakdown following the failure of *Sister Carrie*. Sitting in the clublike reading room of the University of Pennsylvania library's Rare Books Collection, I puzzled out Dreiser's tiny, faint penciled scrawl on yellow half sheets. The pages seemed to emanate a faint lambency, a pulsing of the energy and suffering that created it eighty years before. *An Amateur Laborer*, which he never completed, was my introduction to Dreiser, and it set me on the path of trying to understand what had led him to the situation he wrote about—and more important how he survived it and was able, seven years later, to resume his writing career, which ultimately would culminate in the writing of his masterpiece in the 1920s, *An American Tragedy*.

Looked at in retrospect, his life towers like a lonely mesa, striated with layers of American time, beginning in nineteenth-century Indiana and encompassing those epical social temblors that altered the landscape—the mass migration to the cities, the widening fissure between rich and poor, the rise of industry, the centralization of economic (and political) power in the corporations and trusts. It offers many glimpses of journalism in the pre-Yellow and Yellow eras, of New York City in the Mauve Decade, of America in the age of enterprise and the age of progressivism; of the optimism and budding imperialism of the early 1900s, as reflected in the popular magazines of the day; and of the literary tides and crosscurrents that boiled up in the twentieth century.

Dreiser's story begins with a newspaper item from a compilation in the Sullivan, Indiana, public library which I happened on almost by chance, given the haphazard organization of the material by its compiler, a local historian named Dr. Maple. The event described in the Sullivan *Democrat* of May 3, 1866, occurred five years before Theodore Dreiser was born, yet the family legend that grew out of it would throw a long shadow over his childhood: "We learn that man named Paul Dresser [sic], engaged at Jewett Brothers' Woolen Factory, near the depot, was seriously injured last Saturday. In erecting a scaffold for finishing the cornice of the building, a piece of timber fell, striking Mr. Dresser on the head and knocking him senseless. His injuries are not fatal."

In family legend John Paul Dreiser's failure in America, which dragged his large brood down into poverty, had its germ in the incident described in the clipping. As a result of the injuries he suffered from the blow to the head, his son Theodore later wrote, repeating what he had heard, he became "queer" and obsessed with religion. Disabled by the accident, he lost the managership of a prosperous woolen mill and was cheated by his partners. Because of an obsessive belief that he must either pay off his debts or face an eternity in purgatory, and the mentally warping effects of his fanatical Catholicism, he was never able to recoup.

So went the story—at least as Theodore heard and believed it. As a result of the accident, John Paul Dreiser lost his chance for financial success and became a "morose and dour figure, forlorn and despondent, tramping about the house, his hands behind his back and occasionally talking to himself." His spirits traced a pendulum course between the torments of hell and the faint hope of heaven.

Like many legends, this one contains a core of truth, but it was colored and distorted by the tellers, and Dreiser added his own embroidery when, in his fifties, he set it down in his autobiography, *Dawn*. One of the most truthful autobiographies ever written, it is still the work of a novelist, who shaped and rearranged the facts available to him.

Part One

BOYHOOD

1. The Immigrant

I will not say this is a true record. What I have written is probably
no more than accumulated and assorted heresy, collated and
arranged after the facts. . . . One does not make one's relatives
or oneself or the world. The most interesting thing one can do
is to observe or rearrange or explain, if possible.

—Dreiser, *Dawn* (1931)

Johann Paul Dreiser debarked at Castle Garden in 1844, one of
thousands of young Germans escaping the Prussian military
draft, whose tentacles had stretched to his birthplace, Mayen,
an ancient provincial town of some four thousand people near
Koblenz in Alsace-Lorraine that had grown up around a feudal
castle. A prominent landmark was St. Clemens Catholic church, which
had an odd, twisted spire, the result of a structural flaw when it was built
in the fourteenth century. The populace was overwhelmingly Catholic
(4291 out of 4395 people in 1843). Dreisers had lived in the Mayen area
for centuries; the name means "of Dreis," a neighboring village where
the family originated in the Middle Ages. Theodore Dreiser always believed that his German ancestors were "of no great standing." Actually,
they were solid burghers; the family home was a large stone structure in
the center of town near the church. Six Dreisers had served as mayor,
and a street bore the family name. Paul Dreiser's father, also Johann, was
a farmer and a strict, almost saintly man, according to another son, Henry:
"I have never met a man so honorable and straightforward. . . . I do not
know why he did go to confessional as . . . even in his thoughts [he]
committed no sin; he was charitable, he was good, although he was a
Disciplinarian and very severe with his children. I had many beatings
from him, which I have not forgotten to this day."

Since Johann had twenty-two children to chastise, his arm must have
been oaken. He had married three times, and Paul, who was born in 1821,
was raised by two stepmothers. Such a home situation was not calculated

to hold an ambitious young man either emotionally or economically. Since only the oldest son would inherit his father's land, Paul took up a trade, becoming a weaver and dyer of wool. The region was noted for its woolen industry, but in the early 1840s it fell on hard times and mills were closing down. Given all these factors, the Prussian impressment was simply the precipitating factor in his decision to emigrate to America. A number of his brothers left as well, many of them ending up in France and one, the aforementioned Henry, landing in London.

Although he abandoned his father's Christian name, Paul Dreiser seems to have brought with him the older man's vision of an implacable, punitive God who demanded nothing less than perfection. He clung to the conservative rituals and stern morality of the Church in the Old Country—a gnarled, tortuous belief like the twisted spire of St. Clemens. A family friend recalled him as an old man saying to her on the way home from Mass: "There is no real faith in this country. On the other side— *there* is the real faith."

But upon his arrival in the United States, Paul Dreiser seemed eager to get ahead and did not settle in one of the German enclaves in the cities. He had a fierce ambition to succeed and made his way to Somerville, Massachusetts, where he found work in the woolen mills. Around 1849, accompanied by a *Landsmann* named George Heinemann, he struck out for the West. Peddling housewares to farmers' wives to pay their expenses, the two men made it to Middletown, Ohio, where Dreiser obtained a job in George Ellis's woolen mills, located near the lock of the Miami Canal just south of Dayton. Ellis, a seasoned wool man from Leeds, England, had moved to the state fifteen years earlier after learning the American end of the trade in Philadelphia.

Paul's skill and industriousness won him a patron in Ellis. When the latter moved to Terre Haute in 1853 to found the Ellis Woolen Factory, he sent for Paul, who came accompanied by a wife, the former Sarah Mary Schänäb, whom he had married on New Year's Day, 1851. A strong, pretty farm girl with a radiant smile, Sarah was of German-Moravian ancestry. Her father, Henry Schänäb, had trekked to Ohio from Pennsylvania Dutch country and settled six miles west of Dayton, where Sarah was born in a log cabin on May 8, 1833. Nine years later, the family moved on to Kosciusko County, Indiana. Henry took up a parcel of land near the village of Silver Lake, stuck out the lean years, and became a prosperous farmer. Around 1850 Paul Dreiser worked in a woolen mill in Fort Wayne, and somehow met Sarah, with whom he fell "madly in love," he told Theodore years later.

There was a serious obstacle, however. Sarah's parents were Mennonites—"plain people"—who were deeply opposed to the Church of Rome in particular and to intermarriage in general. The Mennonites (the name comes from the sect's founder, Menno Simons) represented a schism in the Lutheran Church. They preached simplicity of worship in the style of the early Christians, plain dress (Theodore remembered Sarah wearing black shawls and a Mennonite bonnet), and opposition to war and secular authority. They had fled from Switzerland to Germany, where they made numerous converts, and those who came on to America clung to their language and beliefs through successive migrations to Pennsylvania, Ohio, and Indiana (the more otherworldly Amish are an offshoot of the Mennonites).

Not surprisingly, when Sarah fell in love with the wiry, devoutly Catholic immigrant twelve years her senior, her father was adamantly opposed to the match. But Paul Dreiser was a determined man who hungered for a wife and home after seven years spent bouncing about his new country, and Sarah was a rebellious and headstrong girl. The couple eloped to Piqua, Ohio, where they were married on New Year's Day 1851 by the Reverend Edward Faller. Her father promptly disowned her, but she kept in touch with her brothers and sisters after they left the family homestead. Two years or so later, they moved to Terre Haute. They had three children, but two died in 1854 and the third in the following year.

In later years, Sarah liked to recount the sad story of those three babies. In her version a young mother of barely twenty rebels against her fate. One evening, standing behind her brother's farmhouse, she wishes her children were dead. Immediately, three ghostly lights appear at the base of the meadow and begin bobbing toward the house in single file, until they are almost upon her. Then they vanish into the dark woods. In time her three babies died, and Sarah was so stricken with remorse for making the fateful wish that she vowed to God that if He gave her more children, she would never complain again, no matter how many there were. God was bountiful, and gave her ten more children, all of whom lived.

Family lore was filled with such stories, all originating with Sarah, who entertained (and sometimes frightened) the children with them. Just before she met Paul, another went, she had seen thirteen bobbing lights, a sign she would have that many children. The Virgin Mary once appeared in her garden; and on the day of Theodore's birth, three Maytime graces materialized in their house. Paul, whose supernatural beliefs were confined to the Church, believed the house where Theodore was born was haunted and called in a priest to sprinkle holy water about. And after

Theodore was born, he was so sickly that a local conjure woman was consulted. She advised measuring the baby from head to toe and fingertip to fingertip. If his arms were as long as his body, he would not die. Theodore measured up, but as insurance Sarah took him outside on three consecutive nights, held him so that the light of the full moon would strike his eyes and forehead obliquely, and recited the following incantation: *Was ich hab' nehm' ab; was ich thu, nehm' zu!*—Take away that which ails me; let that which I undertake prosper.

Her love of the supernatural led Dreiser to proclaim his mother a "pagan," the antithesis of his rigidly religious father. Actually, she too must have been brought up in a strict religious household (two of her brothers, who Americanized their names to Snepp, became ministers in the United Brethren Church, the American offshoot of the Mennonites), and retained vestiges of her childhood faith. Sarah converted to Catholicism upon her marriage, but probably never wholeheartedly embraced it. She was an independent spirit who was impatient with dogma, and this attitude would become mixed up with her later opposition to Paul's harsh discipline and his insistence on sending the children to Catholic schools. By all accounts an intelligent woman, she was more "American"—certainly less tradition-bound—than Paul. In the early years of marriage, however, she would have deferred to him; Paul was older and probably better educated (a product of irregular pioneer schools in Ohio, Sarah could read but was unable to write until her children taught her).

As for the fairy tales, they were part of her German heritage, and the children remembered her as a wonderful storyteller and raconteuse. But she seems to have made her stories didactic, using them as subtle methods of asserting her dominance over her children, whether by scaring them or by glorifying her own role as the person who had given them life. The tale of the three bobbing lights has an implicit moral: the rebellious young wife learns that children are God's to give or take away, and she must not question her duty to care for them. As a Catholic, Sarah's husband would have agreed with such a moral, regarding himself as God's instrument. But the story has a subtext: unconsciously, Sarah rebelled against having no choice in the matter of children, against submitting to God's— the father's—will.

In 1857 Sarah conceived again, and this baby—John Paul, Jr.—lived. They were residing on First Street near Walnut, less than a block from the Ellis mill. Paul was working as a spinner, but his employer had better things in mind for him. The following year Ellis made a downpayment of three hundred dollars on a lot for the couple, at Second and Poplar streets, and Sarah sewed for the garment makers on Wabash Avenue to help pay for the house. By 1863, Paul was foreman at the Ellis mill, which was enjoying flush times as a result of the Civil War and the government's demand for soldiers' clothing.

That same year, Ellis purchased and completely refitted the Sullivan Wool Manufactory in Sullivan, Indiana, a hamlet of about eight hundred souls located twenty-five miles south of Terre Haute. In March, however, he sold the mill to the brothers D. M. and E. D. Jewett, of Terre Haute, and they hired Paul to manage it. That July Dreiser sold his Terre Haute house for $375 and moved to Sullivan. The Jewetts' father, the Reverend Merrick A. Jewett, had business interests and may have put up the purchase money for the mill, but it was generally believed that Chauncey Rose, Terre Haute's wealthiest businessman, was the major investor. In the same month they bought the establishment, the brothers took out an advertisement in the Sullivan *Democrat* announcing they had "employed a man as Foreman who has had many years experience both in Europe and this country—" undoubtedly Paul Dreiser.

The Jewetts' venture was ill-starred, however. In June of the following year the factory burned to the ground. The loss on the building and machinery was set at $10,000, the value of stocks on hand, $10,000. Insurance covered only $4000 of that loss; nevertheless the brothers bounced back, announcing in October that they planned to build a three-story brick building on a new site, which was purchased in March 1866. It was during the construction of the new mill that their German foreman suffered the accident that reverberated through Theodore's early years.

The family version of the accident compresses its aftermath considerably. Paul's decline was not nearly so precipitous as the legend had it. How long he was disabled is not known, but the belief of Theodore's oldest sister, Mary Frances, that the Jewett brothers "ruined the business during Father's illness," and Theodore's repeated hearsay that they made off with some deeds while his father was incapacitated, are inaccurate. For, in March 1867, apparently fully recovered, Paul entered into a partnership with the Jewett brothers. That same year he purchased two lots in town—adding a third in 1869—and erected a house that was larger than the small cottage near the depot and the old mill the family had previously occupied.

Also in 1867, Paul helped build a church for the five or six Catholic families then living in Sullivan, most of them poor Irish immigrants. He probably did not endow the church, as Theodore believed, but he did take the lead in raising the money for it, soliciting contributions from the mostly Protestant townspeople. Paul did purchase the land, however, and his name was inscribed as a patron on one of the stained-glass windows. It was a tiny church with a visiting priest. In the Dreisers' time, Father Herman Joseph Alerding performed the holy offices part time and stayed with the Dreisers while he was in Sullivan. Later, he would have occasion to repay their kindness. Sarah, who had a soft heart, was active in charitable work among the parishioners. Years later, local merchants recalled her as a kindly and intelligent woman. One family that never forgot her benefactions was the Bulgers, a large, impoverished Irish clan that would also reappear in Sarah's life.

All in all, then, the Sullivan years were good ones for the Dreisers despite the accident. Mary Frances, known as Mame, remembered "a little home amid large trees, flowers of every description, dear little brothers and sisters for playmates, a pet pig much loved and bathed every day, likewise a dog loved by all." (It should be said that Mame, a sentimental soul, was in her eighties when she set down her Sullivan recollections for her niece.) Every evening the family would gather to hear their father's "earnest voice" raised in prayer, "noting the spiritual glow in his face as he would state with conviction, 'Grosser Got Were Zobendech [sic].' For years he asked God's blessing for the day and the night." Two more children were born in Sullivan to Paul and Sarah, bringing the total to eight—Theodore's older brothers and sisters. Since one of them came in 1867, there was apparently no interruption in marital relations between Paul and Sarah after the accident. Summing up those years through a pink haze of memory, Mame portrays her parents as "happy with their brood about them. Father was an expert woolen man with a good business making blankets and woolen clothes, and was a generous provider."

Clearly Paul was becoming a man of substance in the community. A local resident remembered "the large family seated in church as so many peas in a pod . . . they were an impressive spectacle . . . a devout Catholic family." Their house, on North Broad Street, was in "one of the best residential sections in town," a former neighbor said.

Paul's partnership with the Jewett brothers was also a propitious sign. He was manager and had a share of the profits, while they put up the money and handled financial matters. The mill was a typical local operation. The farmers brought in their wool, selling it for cash or bartering it for finished goods or merchandise. The raw materials were turned into "custom"—shawls, "cassimere," jeans, flannels, blankets, and yarns.

By 1869, however, legend and reality begin to converge. The brothers announced that the partnership with Paul Dreiser had been dissolved, the latter "withdrawing from the firm." Mame believed her father had been a victim of "Yankee treachery." Paul was, after all, an immigrant. It appears that the partners had a falling out, and perhaps Paul was angered by some kind of sharp practices on the Jewetts' part. Nevertheless, a notice in the April 15, 1869, issue of the Sullivan *Democrat* states that the brothers would continue business at the old stand and would "pay all indebtedness on the old firm." So it seems that the debts Mame and Theodore spoke of were on the shoulders of the Jewetts at this stage of Paul's woolmaking career. And then, in May 1870, Chauncey Rose purchased the mill for more than $10,000, belying Mame's memory that the Jewetts had "ruined the business." What is more, Rose installed Paul as his manager. An advertisement in the *Democrat* announcing "Highest Cash Price Paid for Wool" was signed "Paul Dreiser, Proprietor." The ad was contracted to run until September 28. And in the 1870 census roll, dated August 30, John Paul Dreiser is identified as a "wool manufacturer," the owner of real estate valued at $1750, and a personal estate worth $500. Although he was scarcely a wealthy man, he was modestly prosperous.

Still, sometime that fall or winter, Paul lost his position. The immediate cause was a storm that blew away the mill's top story. In February 1871 Rose sold the mill to Peter Hill and Eli and Anthony Milner for $7000. The $3000 markdown was probably owing to the damage wrought by the storm. Now Paul Dreiser's downward spiral was beginning. In March 1871 he sold his home for $1400, and on April 17 he conveyed a tract, known as the "millowner's lot" to Hill and the Milners for $125.

In the *Democrat* for May, Paul Dreiser, "formerly of the Sullivan Woolen Mills," advertises: "Wool! Wool! Wool! Wool Wanted! . . . for cash or exchange for goods." In the same issue appeared an ad placed by Hill and the Milner brothers, who were at the new stand, announcing "Great reductions in prices." Was Paul trying to make a comeback with the capital he raised from the sale of his house? If so, the attempt was a failure, for the announcement appeared only once, and by September the family was back in Terre Haute. Paul and Sarah Dreiser purchased a large house on the southwest corner of Twelfth and Walnut streets for $1200, paying $200 down and assuming a mortgage of $1000. At least he had sufficient standing in Terre Haute to qualify for a mortgage. The listing in the 1872 Terre Haute directory is ominous, however. The occupation of Paul Dreiser is given as "laborer."

Within the space of two years he had sunk from manager of a mill to laborer. The cause of Paul's sudden drop remains obscure, but nothing on the record suggests that he was either cheated out of his rightful share or that the blow on the head had made him mentally unstable. In truth, the Sullivan mill, built in the immediate afterglow of Civil War prosperity, had in a few years become a loser; the storm damage was the coup de grace. Chauncey Rose, Terre Haute's shrewdest businessman, got out from under rather than repair the place, which he could well afford to do. And the mill's subsequent history—it limped along but never resumed full-scale operations—suggests he was right about its prospects. Paul had been caught in a business reverse, and had neither the capital nor the financial acumen to recover. As one of his former neighbors summed up his Sullivan career, "He was a good citizen but a poor businessman and his family suffered at times." The stories of his being mentally unbalanced or cheated are the rationalizations of a son with ambivalent feelings toward his father, and a loving daughter. Theodore said it was all Paul's fault; Mame, not his fault at all. Theodore attributed much of his father's failure to qualities in him that he disliked, primarily his religiosity, which allegedly drove him to pay off sizable debts and made him unfit for the world of business. To Mame, a loyal daughter, he had been cheated by bad men—conniving Yankees.

The central truth is that Paul Dreiser's failure in Sullivan was the family's fall from grace, their expulsion from the Eden of middle-class respectability. Never again would their status in the community be so assured, and at times it would be precarious indeed. The memory of belonging to that elevated sphere caused Theodore and the other children, with Sarah as chief propagandist, always to consider themselves better than their fallen state, but it left him in a state of chronic foreboding echoing the primal disaster. It also made him identify with the heroes in so many melodramas and dime novels of the nineteenth century: the young man or woman of good birth who is plunged into poverty as a child but who rises by hard work or virtue and whose true nobility is revealed in the dénouement. The Horatio Alger dreams of recovering his rightful place mingled with the fear that failure—disaster—would be his lot.

John Paul Dreiser faced a bleak prospect in the new home in Terre Haute. The outlook was not helped by the arrival of his ninth child on August 27, 1871, a boy who was christened Herman Theodore Dreiser at St. Benedict's Catholic Church on September 10—the day before the final papers were signed for the family's new home.

2. Dawn

All this industry we see about us is man's response to man's increasing desires. The utter savage has no more wants than the brute—the *partially* perfected man wants not only the earth but the infinite, and the one man dreams, another thinks, and all work, and the whirligig of time, and the rush and whir of the busy struggling generations go hand in hand through the centuries and the eons.

—H. W. Beckwith, *History of Vigo and Parke Countys* [sic] (1880)

Terre Haute at that time was beginning its industrial takeoff. The old Yankee pioneers were still very much alive, notably Chauncey Rose, land speculator and railroad builder, who lived with Scottish frugality in a large, plain house, and doled out dimes to the worthy poor and business loans to hard-working young men. There were even a few descendants of the original French *voyageurs* about, who had heard accounts from their fathers of rounding the bend in the Wabash and being the first white men to gaze on the pleasant breast of rolling green hills on the Indiana side, the salubrious "high ground," where they set up a trading post. The town had been founded in 1816, and the early arrivals from New England (with a sprinkling of Germans) would take up the best farm, forest, and grazing land. Rose's fortune was founded on the land.

Even in the relatively pastoral pre–Civil War era the distant rumble of industry could be sensed by visionary businessmen. Abundant coal and some iron ore were to be found nearby, and dreams began to swell like iridescent bubbles: Terre Haute would be the Pittsburgh of the Middle West. Chauncey Rose raised the capital for the first railroads that linked the town with Indianapolis, St. Louis, and eventually Chicago. Then came the postwar boom. The population mushroomed from twenty thousand to seventy thousand in three decades, as immigrants, largely from Germany and Ireland, streamed in to perform the heavy labor. The Terre

Haute *Gazette* predicted a city of one hundred thousand by 1890. Thirteen railroad lines radiated out from it; the smoke of heavy industry smudged the sky—the Phoenix Foundry and Machine Works, the Wabash Iron Company, the Terre Haute Car Manufacturing Company. Hulman's wholesale grocery concern supplied the region's staples as it had since pioneer days, and another holdover from the agricultural era, the Terre Haute Distillery, had grown to be the second largest such concern in the nation. It had a broad inclined roadway up which farmers could drive their wagons and dump their loads of corn into huge bins without unhitching their horses; hundreds of wagonloads a day could be accommodated.

In the 1870s and 1880s, the town completed its shuddering metamorphosis into a city. The heady gas of boosterism filled the air, but old-timers felt that something had been lost in the rush to industrialize—a spirit of fellowship, egalitarianism, cooperation. An old-style Yankee businessman like Chauncey Rose, though grasping and shrewd, felt some obligation to the community—hence his beneficences ranging from homes for orphans to a polytechnic college that would train the engineers for the new age. Rose sought no publicity and it was said of him that "he contrived to carry to his grave the secret of most of his charities." But the generation of industrialists that came after him vied with one another in assembling manufacturing corporations founded on patents, labor, machines, and capital. A fissure was opening up between management and labor, and the new entrepreneurs flaunted their pre-eminence by segregating themselves in enclaves of mansions surrounded by high cast-iron fences. The barriers of class clicked silently into place.

Those who had grown up during Terre Haute's prewar years remembered the vanished era with a keen nostalgia, strengthened by the contrast between it and the smoky, bustling city. Theodore's eldest brother, Paul, Jr., would cling to the pastoral image, as would the labor leader and socialist Eugene Victor Debs, who knew Paul when both were boys. Debs would later extol his hometown as "that sacred little spot," that "beloved little community . . . where all were neighbors and all friends," that "enchanting little village."

Theodore would spend his first six years in the large house his father had purchased on Twelfth and Walnut, though in later accounts Theodore gave the impression that he had been shuttled about among five abodes. The Dreisers' neighbors were decent, lower-middle-class folk—shopkeepers, respectable workingmen, small-time officials. Two years after

Theodore arrived, Sarah gave birth to her tenth child, completing the family. She was forty, and all her children were healthy. Sarah Dreiser produced a vigorous brood, most of whom lived long lives. To run down the roster in order of appearance, giving first the German names they were christened with:

> Johann Paul, born 1858 (John Paul, Jr., Paul)
> Markus Romanus, 1860 (Rome)
> Maria Franziska, 1861 (Mary Frances, Mame)
> Emma Wilhelmina, 1863 (Em)
> Mary Theresa, 1865 (Theresa, Terese, Tres)
> Cacilia, 1866 (Sylvia, Syl)
> Alphons Joachim, 1867 (Al)
> Clara Clothilde, 1869 (Claire, Tillie)
> Herman Theodore, 1871 (Theo, Thee, Dorsh, Teddy)
> Eduard Minerod, 1873 (Edward Meinrad, Ed)

Those names were what would be expected in a devout German-Catholic family, derived from saints or the Old Country. Many of them were Dreiser family names, showing that the pull of Mayen was still strong within Paul. As the Americanizations and nicknames show, the foreign appellations were summarily discarded.

Sarah, who was after all American-born, may have had a hand in that process. Her strong maternal presence dominated the children's lives, particularly Theodore's, who perhaps because he had been, in Mame's words, "puny beyond belief, all ribs and hollow eyes and ailing and whimpering," at birth received special solicitude. He remembered being rocked in Sarah's arms and confessed, "I was always a mother child, hanging to her skirts as much as I was permitted until I was seven or eight years old." And for the rest of his life he clung to her idealized memory—her "velvety hand" whose touch was like balm, her "sweetness and grace of mind," her "genial smile," her "natural understanding . . . tolerance . . . charity for all," her "glamour—the pearly radiance of romance and tenderness" she cast "over everything she did, said, thought," the "comfort of the mere presence of her"—such tributes gush on in an unpublished essay he wrote, "Sarah Schanab," curiously using her maiden name as if to erase her marriage. He was not alone in his mother worship. Paul, Jr., as the songwriter Paul Dresser, had no rivals as the chief exponent of the "mother song" in the 1890s; Mame simply wrote, "My Mother beyond doubt was one of the greatest women of all times."

To Theodore "her body, sheltering knees," were "home, shelter, blessedness, perfection, peace, delight," a refuge in a world whose terrors the imaginative child magnified. Once, to keep him from venturing into the cellar, Sarah told him a "cat man" lurked in the darkness to pounce on small boys and eat them. The figure became omnipresent in his mind, and when Theodore heard the monotonous rasp of the locusts, he conceived they were cat men perched in the trees. Terrified, he ran to his mother, "enfolding her legs in my fright, crying, pressing my face against her body." When the youngest were mischievous Sarah would announce she was going to leave them forever, pack a bag, don her black shawl and Mennonite bonnet, and stride out the door to a growing chorus of wails from the frightened children (sometimes the older ones chimed in, even though they were innocent bystanders). Once Theodore was so wrought up that he fainted.

This tactic left its mark: fears of abandonment that haunted Theodore the rest of his life. It was as though his mother conditioned him to feel that her absence was the worst possible disaster ("Oh years later, when she was really gone, I knew why I cried!" he exclaims in *Dawn*.) As he wrote in the 1920s: "Long after I had passed my thirtieth year and when she had already been dead for years, I still used to dream of her as being alive but away, threatening to go off and leave me and awoke to find myself in fear. Even to this day dreams of her inevitably evoke a great sadness and longing in me—the result I presume of the psychic impact of those other terrors of long ago."

Sarah Dreiser conveyed to her children in a hundred subtle and not so subtle ways her sacrifices, even her martyrdom, for them; she manipulated their emotions in myriad ways. She had a "form of brooding affection which would not let her cease thinking of them wherever they were, day in and day out. . . . Her thoughts, like bands or chains, were reaching out to them, binding them to her. They were bound to her by these psychic chains—as each confessed—always thinking of her or going back to her in thought and wondering how she was getting along." For all the miraculous healing power of her tenderness, her emotional claims could be exorbitant, for what greater power is there than sweet, sacrificial abnegation—the velvety hand that conceals "hooks of steel"?

Ed's daughter, Vera Dreiser, a child psychologist, concludes that Sarah exercised control through "charm and seductivity." Her children were extensions of herself, almost "disassociated implements." This woman, who had married while still a girl, who had borne children over a span of two decades, cared for a large family, and acceded to a dogmatic, older husband, made her children the objects of her thwarted possessive desires. As Vera Dreiser writes, "I am convinced from the stories my father has told me (confirmed by Mame, Sylvia, and Rome) that she was a sweet charming woman, and a passively controlling woman who unfortunately had a disturbing influence on most of her children."

The upshot in Theodore's case was a fixation on his mother and a deep ambivalence toward his father. He worshiped the former and alternately despised or feared the latter. In his attitude toward his father, Theodore was reflecting Sarah's own resentment of her marriage, which she communicated to him. Ed, who managed to extricate himself from Sarah's dominance, always remembered his father warmly and never felt the bitterness toward him that Theodore did.

A vivid childhood memory shows Sarah making Theodore an accomplice against the father. She is sitting in the parlor in a white dressing gown, a faint light filtering through the curtains. The little boy crawls to her and begins stroking her toes, protruding through a hole in her shabby shoes. "See poor mother's shoes?" she croons. "Aren't you sorry she has to wear such torn shoes? See the hole there?" Her voice, which "could make me cry at any time," upset him.

"Are you going to grow up to be a big man and work and bring me nice shoes?"

"Work, work, yes, I work," the little boy stammers.

Finally, "a sudden swelling sense of pity that ended in tears. I smothered her shoes and cried." In the dimly lit room, a sobbing child, a mother bent over him, wed in shared sorrow. "That was the birth of sympathy and tenderness in me," Dreiser wrote in *Dawn*.

He attended St. Benedict's parochial school on Ninth and Walnut, although the Fourth Ward School, a brand-new square structure with a cupola, was only a block away from their home. Paul, of course, insisted on religious indoctrination for his offspring despite the extra expense. The school was established for children of St. Joseph's German congregation. German was spoken, and lessons, including grammar, were rudimentary. The boys were required to doff their caps and say, "Praise be Jesus Christ!" to the grim-faced priests patrolling the halls, who barked "Amen!"

The rote learning of parochial school did not nip the child's budding curiosity. "When friends called at the Dreiser home," a friend of the family recalled, "the little wise-looking child drew up a chair and listened to everything with a knowing air." Freud might have called him a scopophiliac child—always looking, absorbing, grasping. When a watchman who had given the boy candy every day on his way to work died, Theodore was taken to the funeral and lifted up to peer in the coffin. He tried to snatch the gleaming coins that covered the corpse's eyes. Death was a mystery: what had departed that once vibrant body that was now like the shell of a locust?

Sunday Mass was another mystery. When someone—his father perhaps—explained to him that God was present in the communion wine and wafers, the child cried, "Give me God! Give me God!"

3. *"The Damndest Family"*

> At the same time, this city of my birth was identified with so much struggle on the part of my parents, so many dramas and tragedies in connection with relatives and friends, that by now it seemed quite wonderful as the scene of almost an epic. . . . I will only say that from the time the mill burned until, after various futile attempts to right ourselves . . . we finally left this part of the country for good, it was one unbroken stretch of privation and misery.
>
> —Dreiser, *A Hoosier Holiday* (1916)

> The more I think of my father, and the more I consider the religious and fearful type of mind in general, the more certain I am that mere breeding of lives (raising a family without the skill to engineer it through the difficulties of infancy and youth) is one of the most pathetic, albeit humanly essential, blunders which the world contains.
>
> —Ibid.

lowering cloud hung over John Paul Dreiser's economic prospects during the years the family lived at Twelfth and Walnut. The Directory lists him variously as "laborer," "spinner," and "sorter"—and once as a "blacksmith." "Father worked at anything available," Mame recalled. Ellis's mill and the others in town operated irregularly now. The great depression of 1873, triggered by the failure of the Jay Cooke banking concern, swept west like an economic tornado, ravaging businesses in its path (six thousand firms toppled in 1874). The storm raged for four years, and at its height three million men were out of work, their families hungry, even starving. Thousands of displaced workers took to the road searching for jobs, and the gaunt, ragged figure of the tramp entered the consciousness of respectable folk, a specter of failure and degeneracy, in the words of the dean of the Yale Law School, of "a lazy, incorrigible, cowardly utterly depraved savage."

On top of the national recession, Terre Haute was hit hard in 1875 by "a great business depression as a result of flood and high water," according to a local historian. And the wool business was undergoing structural changes that would make small concerns like the Ellis mill and skilled craftsmen like Paul Dreiser obsolete. Paul started out with Ellis as a spinner, the aristocrat of the mills, making the highest pay. But the mechanization sweeping American industry in the postwar years (which had been prefigured in the wool industry in the 1830s) had altered the job. Ellis's mill had two self-activating spinners ("mules"), which made the job that of a machine tender and supervisor. John Paul was qualified as a dyer as well, and also a sorter, the least mechanizable of all the tasks, since it called for judging the quality of the fiber before it was spun.

Given John Paul's skills and experience, Theodore could not understand why his father drudged along in temporary positions rather than managing another mill. In *Dawn* he writes, "He could still have borrowed money and secured control of a mill if he had had the courage." Supposedly (family legend again) Chauncey Rose offered to advance him the necessary capital, but Paul's unreasoning fear of going into debt caused him to decline, and Theodore theorizes that "by now he was so depressed by various ills that he could not bestir himself in the proper way."

Possibly the Sullivan failure—or the blow on the head, come to that—had shaken his self-esteem. But, even if he retained the driving ambition of his earlier years in America, the economic cards were stacked against him. In the first place, Ellis's son Edwin was now superintendent of his factory, so John Paul was no longer his protégé. As for Paul's borrowing money and opening a mill of his own, that was not a realistic option, given the state of the wool trade in Terre Haute.

When Dreiser visited Terre Haute in 1915, he looked up Edwin and found him operating a feed store. He had been out of the wool business for years; in 1885 he'd converted the mill's water-driven machinery to generating electric power. "All the woolen mills in this section died out long ago," he told Dreiser. "Your father foresaw that. . . . This was no country for woolen manufacture. We couldn't compete with the East. Why, I read here not long ago that two hundred mills in Indiana, Ohio and Illinois had closed up in twenty years—two hundred!"

Industrialization had transformed an activity conducted by hundreds of small separate mills turning out "custom" to one dominated by large establishments centered in New England and Pennsylvania, manufacturing mass-produced clothing for wholesalers and large urban department stores. The hordes of factory workers swarming to the cities provided an expanding market for cheap, tough work clothes, while white-collar workers had come to prefer ready-made suits of serge and worsted to those woven of heavier, bulkier custom fabrics. The development of techniques for weaving cloth from cheaper, short-fiber wool also made such apparel much more economical.

Paul's only alternative would have been to move to one of the new wool-manufacturing centers—Boston, Providence, Philadelphia, or Chicago. But at his age and with his large family, he must have lacked the heart to pull up stakes. (Shortly before his death he was offered a job as a wool buyer with a large eastern firm at a munificent salary; by then, however, it was too late.) And so the family stayed on, clawing for a handhold on middle-class respectability but skidding down the slippery slope to hunger and want. Dreiser remembered "long, dreary, gray, cold days: meager meals, only fried potatoes or fried mush at times." Sarah, who had grown up on a prosperous farm with a well-stocked larder, was hard pressed to put food on the table and began to question her husband's authority for the first time.

He was being challenged from another quarter as well—his children. The oldest ones were now in the full heat of adolescent blood. The first to rebel was Paul, Jr. Fourteen years old when the family moved back to Terre Haute, he had grown into a big, husky boy with a knockabout sense of humor and an appetite for pranks. Such antics angered his austere father, who decided, in Mame's words, "to devote his eldest son to the service of God." He could not have picked a more unlikely candidate for the priesthood. Perhaps he merely hoped that exposure to the discipline of the seminary would sober the boy up; repeated beatings seemed to have had no effect on him. In 1872 the young Paul was shipped off to the St. Meinrad Seminary in southern Indiana, which offered a preparatory course leading to the study of the priesthood.

Paul, Jr., lasted about two years. During the summer between terms he was packed off to work for Jesse Rector, a family friend who owned a farm near Switz City, about fifteen miles from Sullivan. That fall he came home atop a wagon loaded with potatoes, vegetables, and ham, which sustained the family through a lean winter. During his second year, Paul was placed in charge of a group of younger boys whom he taught dance steps and jokes, picked up while watching minstrel shows. By now infected by the show-business virus, he left St. Meinrad in 1874, voluntarily or otherwise, and hung out with a group of would-be thespians. The group graduated from impromptu song and dance performances in the streets; then Paul joined a minstrel show known as the Lemon Brothers which toured the surrounding small towns. But business was poor and their money ran out. Stranded, Paul headed for the Rector farm, hoping for work as a hired hand. He remained there awhile, then lit out for Cambridge City in search of Father Alerding, the visiting priest at Sullivan who had stayed with the Dreisers. But Alerding had recently been appointed rector of St. Joseph's in Indianapolis, and Paul had to tramp on through the bitter winter. He showed up at Father Alerding's doorstep a cold, hungry, and tired lad.

St. Joseph's was in a poor neighborhood, and many of the parishioners were out of work because of the depression. Nevertheless, Father Alerding was trying to raise money to build a new church and had organized a series of fund-raising events—debates, literary evenings, and entertainment shows. Encouraged by his friend, Paul put his experience to work staging minstrel shows.

Eventually Father Alerding persuaded the boy to go home and face the music—probably interceding with John Paul, Sr., beforehand. The father took him back and attempted to teach him and Rome the wool trade. Young Paul toiled for a time at the Ellis mill, but as Mame primly recalled, "Paul never worked hard at anything requiring manual labor." Soon he was in trouble with the law. The Sullivan *Democrat* picked up the story: "A young man named Paul Dresser was arrested at Terre Haute last Monday (2-21-76) and fully convicted by the mayor on the charge of burglary. His father formerly resided here." According to the Terre Haute *Express*, the target of the attempted burglary was Miller's Saloon. Paul, Sr., had to borrow money to post the three-hundred-dollar bond, adding to the family woes.

The next-oldest boy, Rome, was also heading down the primrose path. He had a regular job with the *Journal* as a press feeder, but at night he donned loud clothes and joined the sports in front of the Terre Haute House, known as the "Terrible Hot House," a toothpick dangling from his mouth to give the impression he had just eaten in the dining room. Rome had grown into a husky, handsome youth, but Theodore remembered his white "wolfish" teeth and his "guttural, sinister laugh." Rome seemed indifferent to the family's precarious position in the community, living entirely for himself with "vainglory, indifference, colossal selfishness." When Mame became involved with a wealthy citizen whom Dreiser calls Colonel Silsby, Rome sought to profit from it. Sarah had found out about Mame's admirer when her daughter asked if she could keep ten dollars Silsby had given her to buy a hat. Surprisingly, Sarah said yes, and when the Colonel came up with further gifts, she was too hard pressed financially to refuse. Sarah seems not to have warned Mame about the compromising nature of the relationship. And like most Victorian mothers she was reluctant to instruct her daughters about sex. Dreiser admitted

And so the precociously observant little boy sensed a primal battle being waged. Ultimately, though, Paul's authority depended not on tradition or righteousness but on his ability as a provider. As Dreiser put it:

They fought over how the children should be regulated, who should correct them, what should be said or done. At the time I came into the world, the battle had already been practically won by my mother . . . for I saw only the tail end of the storm. She could not stand to see the children beaten or abused and to his charge that they were plunging straight to hell under her too yielding supervision, her reply was that he could not make a decent living for them, that he was too narrow and hard and she did not propose to see them governed by his theories. Let him first provide a good living and then talk.

But Paul had sacrificed his pride as a skilled craftsman—his manhood—to work at whatever job he could get. Once he took Theodore to the mill where he was working as a handyman. The boy was impressed by his father's knowledge of all aspects of the manufacturing process as Paul showed him how the wool was blown and cleaned, then taken to sheds to be washed, then to the spinning mules and weaving looms and finally the dye vats. The dark oily place seemed "a wonder world," and perhaps for the first time Theodore saw his father as a human being: "a grave thoughtful man of about 55 or 6, spare, brown-eyed with heavy overhanging eyebrows and dark reddish brown hair." His father seemed to take an interest in him too. Theodore's abnormally inquiring mind appealed to him. Yet the final impression the son took away that day was that his father "seemed even then to be doing things beneath our dignity."

One can imagine Sarah's social terrors as their poverty deepened and she sensed the neighbors' gossip about her children's various delinquencies. When Paul, Sr., was sick and there was no money, she had to send the oldest ones to the railroad tracks to gather lumps of coal that had spilled out of the tenders. "It was during this time," Dreiser recalled in later years, "that the severe phases of poverty which so impressed me occurred."

In May 1878 Paul, Sr., sold the house on Twelfth and Walnut for $1400—$200 more than he had paid for it but subject to an outstanding mortgage on which he had been unable to keep up the payments. Their next address was 533 North Seventh Street, a much smaller place, near a lumberyard and the railroad tracks. For a time Sarah tried running a boardinghouse, but she spent more on food than the guests paid.

Now Sarah put into effect a curious plan: she and the three youngest children—Claire, Theodore, and Ed—would move to Sullivan. There they would live cheaply in a little house with a garden where they would grow vegetables. To earn money they would take in boarders, perhaps. Paul and the older girls would set up a household in Terre Haute, with Paul, Jr., and Rome coming and going. Al would be packed off to live on her brother's farm near Manchester, Indiana.

The plan was justified as an economy measure, but there was probably more involved. Her disagreement with her husband over the children's discipline and education (she favored public schools for them) had hardened. By now the oldest children—Paul, Jr., Rome, and Mame—were beyond help, so far as she was concerned, but at least she might save the youngest three. At some deeper level, though, Sarah was taking flight—from the strains of her marriage, from her husband's sexual demands (and having more children), from the disgrace of their poverty—some or all of these psychological factors entered into her decision. Her life had been fearfully hard the past five years, and the thought of returning to Sullivan, where she had been happy and the family had been respected, must have been seductive. The ostensible economic reason seems tenuous. The family's fortunes had temporarily improved; Paul had a job as foreman at a carpet factory, and he planned for the girls either to work there or to enter domestic service. The girls needed their mother more than ever, it would seem, yet here she was abandoning them—not to mention poor Al. She seemed to be saying, Let *him* take over their upbringing. They would come to visit her to be sure, but it would be at her own house, where she was in charge.

Ed always remembered the sadness the children felt over the separation. The night before they left, Paul assembled them in the parlor and sang a German folk song:

> Now we are about to travel out of the gate of the city,
> I sit down to say good-bye, good-bye, good-bye, good-bye, farewell!

Theodore blotted the song out of his memory until Ed sang it for him half a century later. The parting was more painful than he knew. Nor could he appreciate that the song, a relic of medieval times, expressed regret for leaving the security of the city. To go outside the gate meant that one was either a traveler, with all the attendant perils, or an outcast.

4. Her Wandering Boy

Over the hill to the poor-house—my childr'n dear, good-bye!
Many a night I've watched you when only God was nigh;
And God'll judge between us, but I will al'ays pray
That you shall never suffer the half I do to-day.
>—Will E. Carleton

'Twas not thro' word of anger, 'twas not thro' love of gold,
'Twas not through pangs of hunger, he wandered from the fold,
But just a restless nature that none could understand . . .
Next eve there came a knocking, upon the homestead door,
"Your last words, mother, saved me, I won't leave you any more."
>—Paul Dresser, "You're Going Far Away,
>Lad; or I'm Still Your Mother, Dear" (1897)

 arah's scheme almost collapsed at the outset. She wrote to the Bulgers, the Irish family she had patronized in better days, and was told that economic conditions were not favorable to her boardinghouse venture. Determined to leave anyhow, she impulsively wrote to a woman named Sue Bellette, another stray, an orphan she had befriended in Terre Haute who had married a fireman in Vincennes, thirty miles to the south. Sue replied that there would be plenty of room for them all in the firehouse where she lived, and urged her to come. Sarah seized on the offer, even though it made her beholden to a woman she disapproved of and considered "bold and bad."

It was an unwise move. It turned out that the firehouse, a large building with several floors and numerous beds, served as the town brothel as well. Sarah stuck it out for a while, since she had enrolled the children in the local parochial school. Ed and Theodore found the firehouse an exciting place to live. The clang of the bell galvanized the place into frenetic activity: the men shrugged on their waterproofs, slid down the brass pole, and climbed onto the gleaming red engine hitched to a team of pawing, snorting horses straining in their traces. Another wonder was the new telephone—the first in Vincennes. Theodore remembered Sue's husband hoisting him up to the receiver and hearing a faint, tinny voice crying, "Hello! Hello!"

As soon as Sarah determined that conditions were a bit more propitious in Sullivan, she packed their things and they boarded the train. The place of their former glory was still a placid county seat with a population of about twenty-two hundred. It had little industry, though there were a few coal mines in the vicinity. The prominent structures were the courthouse on the square, a few stores, a roundhouse where coal cars were loaded, a new depot, and one hotel, the Sullivan House. The woolen factory, reliquary of the ashes of Paul Dreiser's ambition, operated only intermittently now; Hill and the Milners had sold it to J. W. Brunger and W. E. Adelotte.

Sarah found that the Bulgers had moved up in the world; indeed, now it was they who were the benefactors and Sarah the poor relation. James Bulger was section boss on the railroad. As devout a Catholic as Paul Dreiser, he marched his large family to the little church every Sunday in a column. His son Jimmy, a friend of Paul, Jr.'s, was well launched on a career of small-town devilment; his father's frequent resort to a horsehide whip had proved as futile as Paul Dreiser's chastisements of his eldest. In later life, Jimmy would continue down what Paul, in a song, called "The Path That Leads the Other Way," at the end of which the electric chair waited.

Sarah found a small house at the edge of town, on the wrong side of the Evansville and Terre Haute Railroad tracks. Green fields of corn and wheat stretched to the east, and to the west was a common covered with a rank growth of weeds and with a slaughterhouse in one corner. The rent was only seven dollars a month, and they moved in with no furniture other than a couple of straw mattresses and a chair borrowed from the Bulgers. The place was well located from the standpoint of Sarah's scheme: it was near the roundhouse and within walking distance of the coal mines, two facilities from which she hoped to draw her boarders. But first she had to furnish the house, and for a time they survived on what the Bulgers lent them and credit from storekeepers who remembered Sarah from better days. Full of enthusiasm, she scrubbed down the house and made it into a bare but comfortable abode. To earn immediate money she took in washing—the traditional small-town occupation for impoverished widows and abandoned wives.

Although full of the euphoria the drug of change always produced in her (like her pioneer forebears she believed in the great good place just over the next hill), Sarah must have had some misgivings about her social position in this town where a decade before she had been the mill manager's wife. As was her way, she communicated her doubts to the children. Theodore, at least, sensed them, for he remembered being deeply ashamed of having to deliver the baskets of clothes and making his rounds via back-street routes. He also remembered going to school barefoot and being told to get some shoes when the weather got cold. Since there was no money to buy them, he and Ed dropped out for a time, then went back. Ed later said Theodore exaggerated; they had gone barefoot in summertime as was the small-town custom and had shoes when winter came. But Theodore was acutely self-conscious and imagined that everyone in town looked down on them. His solution was to hold himself aloof, clinging to an imagined superiority. Sarah had managed to instill in them a sense of the family's vanished glory; their present lowly state was merely temporary and better days were ahead.

But she had to lavish affection on him constantly; he cried easily and had bad dreams about the slaughterhouse. Twice a week, Spilky, the owner, would herd the hapless animals from an adjacent field into the shed that served as his charnel house, and the boy could hear their frightened bleats and squeals. Afterward, Spilky would emerge and toss bloody chunks of meat into a wagon. In his nightmares Theodore saw ghostly pigs and steers with lolling tongues and wide, panicky eyes racing frenziedly about.

He could escape from his fears in rambles about the countryside, rising early when the horizon was streaked with pink and orange and the grass on the common beaded with dew, with a mongrel dog named Snap as his companion. Together they might follow a bee on its rounds or watch a chicken hawk wheel against the sky. He imagined the sky was a sea within a larger sea—a different, greater sphere beyond the earthly one, where God dwelled—the Catholic heaven.

He remembered sitting on the porch on summer nights, his mother rocking, inhaling the fragrance of the roses she had planted and telling them stories or gazing up at the stars. Sarah was alone now, in a kind of exile, waiting for the restoration of the happiness of the old days. Still, she found neighbors even poorer than they were to help. This place was Sullivan's end of the line, a social boneyard. There was nothing she could do but wait and hope.

Not that they were entirely cut off from the others. Paul, Sr., sent them money and visited occasionally. In time the girls returned one by one, drawn by Sarah's psychic chains. Paul's Terre Haute household had lasted less than a year. He had rented a place at 205 North Thirteenth, and for a time all the children lived with him. The Directory reports that Paul, Jr., was pursuing the trade of "lightning rod agent." That was either one of his pranks or the surveyor was hard of hearing (Rome is called "Corwin"); actually, he was performing in a traveling medicine show for the Lightning Liniment Company. His local theatrical career was picking up. As early as 1878, the Terre Haute *Mail* reported, "Paul Dresser, another of Terre Haute's musical composers, has just written a song and dance entitled 'Where the Orange Blossoms Grow,' which is said to have much merit." The young composer (who had adopted the Americanized spelling of his surname) performed his composition before George Primrose, a leading minstrel. He asked Paul what he wanted for the song. The latter said "nothing," so Primrose "sent the author a fine diamond ring as a token of his appreciation." The 1878 Directory gives Paul's address as the National House and his occupation as "musician." By 1880 he vanishes from the Directory, and Terre Haute, for good.

Rome had also pulled out of the ménage on Thirteenth, running off to become a candy butcher, selling sweets, peanuts, and newspapers on the trains (a job Paul also held) and then heading west. The girls went their various ways, unable to stand their father's constant lectures and his nagging to go to Mass and Vespers.

The first to turn up in Sullivan was Sylvia, who later told Theodore she had hoped that life would be "easier and somehow safer . . . she would look after me." Syl had bloomed into a beauty—the prettiest of his sisters, Theodore always thought—and spent her time lolling about the house, despite Sarah's lectures.

She was soon followed by Emma, who had quit her job at the mill. The two of them spent most of their time dressing up in their best clothes, then promenading around the courthouse square, ogled by the local dudes. After some near disastrous flirtations—Sylvia almost ran off with a traveling salesman—they became bored and decided to go to Chicago, which a friend of Emma's had been extolling as a place of glamour and excitement. At the last minute Sylvia had to back out—the ticket agent she cajoled into giving her a free fare changed his mind, so Emma went alone, dreaming of the fine clothes she would someday buy and the handsome, wealthy men she would meet.

Next Mame arrived bearing more troubles than all the others combined: she was pregnant, perhaps by the old but still vigorous Colonel Silsby. The man, whoever he was, had directed her to a country doctor who was reputed to perform abortions, but when she arrived she discovered that he was dead. So she slunk back to Sarah and confessed the worst—she was not even married. Her mother took charge, comforting Mame ("Perhaps you will be a better girl for it"), keeping her out of sight until the baby came. Sarah delivered it herself, and when it turned out to be stillborn, she buried the tiny corpse in the yard under cover of darkness. (Many years later, Mame had a medium contact her lost child and claimed she talked with it.)

Eventually these extra boarders moved on, and after about a year Sarah replaced them with the paying kind. In addition to a taciturn man who was, it turned out when detectives came to arrest him, an escaped convict, there were a few miners and railroad workers. The most distinguished guest was Professor Solax, a dapper book agent. He was peddling *Hill's Manual of Social and Business Forms*, an eclectic compendium of useful information on etiquette, letter writing, composition, U.S. history, literature, and poetry. Sarah bought a copy for Theodore, who devoured it, finding it the door to a finer world of polite swains who wrote stiff courtship letters to highly proper young ladies, who either accepted their suits or rejected them for character flaws ("Observation proves that, while many men use tobacco and are not drunkards, almost every drunkard is a user of tobacco").

The professor made mellow eyes at Sylvia while reciting in a resonant voice poems from *Hill's*, including Will Carleton's highly popular ballad "Over the Hill to the Poor-House," the heart-wrenching tale of an old lady whose children put her "on the county." Sentimental and melodramatic, the poem conveys accurately the awful fear many Americans of that time had of becoming a ward of charity, a feeling that touched a nerve when the old republican virtues of self-reliance and individualism were being swept aside by the new industrialism which made men dependent on factory wages rather than the land. The poem always reminded Dreiser of Paul, Jr.'s, attitude toward Sarah—or rather his guilt feelings about her.

During their second winter, Sarah must have felt that the poorhouse had become a real possibility. The boardinghouse languished and she took up washing again. Paul, Sr., was laid off, so his contributions stopped. As wintry gusts rattled the windows, Sarah felt the icy breath of failure. The children were sent to the mines to gather lose chunks of coal to keep the fire going in the stove. There were days when there was nothing to eat but cornmeal, and Dreiser remembered walking to the gristmill in order to save a few pennies. For years after, the onset of winter or the sight of a poor neighborhood filled him "with an indefinable and highly

oppressive dread . . . thoughts and emotions which had a close kinship
to actual and severe physical pain."

What deepened the trauma of this time was Sarah's discouragement.
She sank into a "dumb despair," plodding listlessly about her tasks or
sitting in her chair rocking. With no idea what to do, she could only hope
something would turn up. The effect of her attitude must have been
psychologically devastating to Theodore, who was so dependent upon
her. His painful memories of dark, cold days in Terre Haute and the
haunting dread that some disaster was about to strike—took on exaggerated proportions amid this latest crisis.

But the Dreiser family fortunes followed the script of popular melodrama rather than tragedy. In a sequel to his poem, written because of
popular demand, Carleton has the black-sheep son return from the West,
where he has conveniently struck gold, to rescue his mother from her
disgrace. One day in February 1882, a loud rapping was heard at the door
of the Sullivan cottage. When Sarah opened it, young Paul burst in and
swept her into his arms. To the children, who barely knew him, he seemed
an emissary from some higher, finer sphere, dressed in a thick fur coat
and silk hat and carrying a walking stick. His presence lit up the room,
"like the sun, or a warm cheering fire."

As far as Sarah and the children were concerned, Paul might as well
have struck gold out West. He passed out presents and pressed soft green
bills in his mother's hand. They sat mesmerized as he told them his adventures over the past three years. For a time, he traveled with the Lightning Liniment troupe, appearing frequently in Terre Haute and Evansville.
He performed in blackface, sang, danced, told jokes, and played the
elaborate pipe organ on the wagon (his mother somehow had started him
out with piano lessons). When he and his fellow performers had put the
crowd in a good mood, the pitchman would appear to extol the virtues
of Lightning Liniment for aching muscles and a host of other ills.

Next he joined the bill at the Evansville Apollo Theater, an open-air
beer garden where the city's large German population spent summer evenings and Sunday afternoons soaking up Würzburger and *Gemütlichkeit*.
Paul's comic blackface routines were well received, and he moved up to
a star turn at the Opera House. On the side, he wrote a column of quips
and doggerel for a weekly paper called the *Argus*. He was also composing
songs, and he passed out copies of *The Paul Dresser Songster*.

A big man, around six feet tall and weighing two hundred pounds, Paul
was nonetheless light on his feet. His routine consisted of broad, shame-
lessly corny pratfalls, jokes, and comic songs, which went over well with

the entertainment-starved rural audiences to whom the arrival of the medicine show was a major event. He often poked fun at dudes—the young swells who affected the airs of gentlemen despite their empty pocketbooks. One of the songs went:

> The festive dudelet
> With his poodlet
> Took a walklet
> Down the streetlet

He also had great success with a popular ditty called "Lardy Dah," according to someone who heard him sing it in Cumberland, Maryland. Paul wore a high starched collar that protruded over the brim of his derby, and at each "Lardy dah" would tug at his coat, pulling the collar down and tipping his hat. The number provided plenty of opportunities for this business:

> Let me introduce a fella, Lardy dah! Lardy dah!
> A fellah who's a swell, ah, Lardy dah!
> To observe him is a treat, Lardy dah! Lardy dah!
> Though of cash he lacks complete, Lardy dah!

He also wrote a send-up of former President Ulysses S. Grant's 1879 Grand Tour to meet the crowned heads of Europe and points east: "I'm General Grant and I've Been Around the World."

In Evansville he was popular for his "big smile . . . and his great big happy ways," one old-timer recalled. "I do not believe he had an enemy in the world. He . . . was never at a loss for an answer so that it became a common expression, 'You can't get ahead of Paul.' " A man who worked with him on the *Argus* remembered him as "big and good natured, with a disposition that was always sunny."

But he had a serious side that was usually hidden. A bartender at Wierbacher's, a saloon near the Apollo where Paul hung out with the local dudes, remembered, "You hardly ever saw him but what he was scribbling verses." When his friends kidded him about it, Paul uncharacteristically withdrew into himself. He was beginning to write more "serious" ballads that told a sentimental, melodramatic story, yet were rooted in his own experiences. Under the minstrel's blackface was his mother's boy, a sensitive soul, easily moved to tears. In Evansville he was well remembered for his generosity. Once he gave his last dollar to a beggar, telling a friend: "It looks as if that old man has no friend in the whole world but now with my dollar he has a friend . . . and even if I get cold and hungry I am happy that temporarily I made it better for him."

At one point he decided to have a try at New York. Green as a sassafras shoot but brimming with self-confidence, he attempted to get an interview with Augustin Daly, author of the hit melodrama of the 1860s, *Under the Gaslight*, and now the owner of a palatial theater on Broadway with a resident stock company that featured John Drew, Mrs. Scott-Siddons, Ada Rehan, and other leading thespians. After haunting the stage door for days, he managed to speak to a supercilious functionary who told him, "No mah deah boy; we have all the talent we desiah." Undaunted, Paul had some cards printed up reading: MR PAUL DRESSER/DALY'S THEATER/ STAGE ENTRANCE—NO FURTHER. After being deluged with those cards, Daly sent for him and gave him a place in one of his road companies.

Paul found other work during his New York sojourn. In September 1891 a theatrical paper ran the announcement that "Paul Dresser, eccentric comedian and vocalist" would open at Miner's New Theater in the Bowery. "He gives his address care of his office," the paper adds, suggesting that Paul was living out of his suitcase. The following month he is listed second on the bill of the National Theater, his "Mirthful Morsels, Songs and Parodies" preceding such headliners as Parker and His Dogs, the Lanier Sisters, and Emerson & Clark. Earlier that year he was featured at the Buckingham Theater in Louisville, Kentucky, where a local press agent dubbed him "the sensational comique."

He also put in a stint with the Thatcher, Primrose and West Minstrel Show. Perhaps he got the job by reminding George (Prim) Primrose of the song he had written for him in Evansville. During his minstrel-show career Paul mainly worked as an end man—the comic who provides the punchlines to jokes set up by the interlocutor's questions. Although past its heyday, the minstrel show provided an unparalleled opportunity to study the basic categories of popular music, all pioneered by Stephen Foster, who composed for "Daddy" Rice's original troupe, and others. These were: sentimental ballads (always sung by the resident tenor) that related sad stories of unrequited love, dishonored maidens, and dying tots; "end songs"—comic ditties—with a rowdy flavor featuring stereotyped Negro characters with a craving for 'possum and watermelon; the march or "walkaround," which served as a finale and featured the entire cast; and manly, dramatic songs tailored for the company's bass singer, such as "Asleep in the Deep" and "The Bell in the Lighthouse."

Such was the résumé Paul recited for Sarah and the children. Undoubtedly he left out some of his racier adventures on the road, for he was already acquiring a taste for women and whiskey, and exploited the itinerant actor's power to arouse the buried passions of small-town girls. Nor, probably, did he tell them much about his new Evansville friend, Sallie Walker, other than to say she would call on them. Sallie was the main reason for his mooring in Evansville.

When she did arrive a few days later, Sallie turned out to be a beautiful, dark-haired woman, well-dressed, refined, and several years older than Paul. She stayed for the space of one train (as they said in that era of ten or twelve trains a day), discussing Paul's and her intention to move the family to Evansville. Soon after she left, boxes of groceries and fruit arrived. For Sarah and Claire there were also some secondhand dresses of a rather flamboyant cut.

What Paul probably did not tell his mother was that Sallie Walker (real name: Annie Brace) was a madame, the proprietor of Evansville's most elegant brothel. Sarah must have guessed that Sallie was no Sunday school teacher, but she was not one to inquire too deeply into the background of her children's friends. The important thing was that the family was saved; the good life had returned.

5. City Lights

In 1889 Chicago had the peculiar qualifications of growth which made such adventuresome pilgrimages, even on the part of young girls, plausible.

—*Sister Carrie* (1900)

In late spring 1882 Paul, Jr., came and put Sarah, Claire, Theodore, and Ed aboard a train for Evansville. Late that night, when they emerged in the street, Theodore gazed with sleepy eyes at the crowds of people and the rumbling wagons, lit up by rows of gas lamps. After the somnolence of Sullivan, they had been plunged into the hurly-burly of a small city of about twenty-five thousand people. It seemed like a "fairy land" to Theodore.

Paul piled their luggage into a jitney and they clopped out Main Street to 1415 East Franklin, located in a new addition at the edge of town. The house was spanking new—a half-story brick cottage set in a large yard and surrounded by a picket fence. When Theodore, the next morning, ran out to explore, he discovered a barn, a garden, a chicken run in the back, and open country beyond. To Sarah it was a palace—new furniture, carpets on the floors, and a well-appointed kitchen. The sight of such luxury brought tears to her eyes, causing Paul to cry too. The wandering boy and the mother who kept the light burning in the window—it was the stuff of a sentimental ballad, and Paul would write it often in the coming years.

Evansville is located on high ground at a point where the viscid brown Ohio River makes a sharp bend to the south. Main Street ran down to a stone levee, where white steamboats docked, their tall chimneys belching black smoke, their paddle wheels churning up a boiling wake. Cotton bales, boxes, and barrels were piled about in front of great warehouses and black roustabouts lounged or labored. Along Water Street—as the levee was known—was also located the vice district. And not long after their arrival, Sarah sent Theodore with a basket of preserves to Sallie's establishment, an imposing mansion of gray stone with white marble trim.

He had been told to leave the basket at the front door, but a Negro maid beckoned him inside and led him down a long hall with doors on either side. Some were open and he could see beds, chairs, and dressing tables. In one cubicle, a woman sat before a mirror, languidly brushing her blond hair, clad only in a white chemise. One strap had slipped down to expose a white, pink-tipped globe. The boy gawked a moment, then hurried on.

The maid ushered him inside Sallie's private apartment, which was furnished with airy white wicker furniture; awnings over the windows made the room dim and cool. Paul, dapper in silk shirtsleeves and light summer trousers, greeted him, while Sallie, in a sheer, frilly peignoir, watched them, a faint smile playing about her lips. After some banter with Paul, he was led out, past the same doors. The odor of perspiration mingled with perfume and powder hung in the hall. There was a fleshy warmth in the air that was pleasant and vaguely stirring.

On weekends Paul would journey out to the house on East Franklin with gifts for Sarah and the children. He spent hours chatting with his mother in the kitchen, playing comic songs on the piano or hitting flies to Theodore and Ed, whom he had equipped with gloves and bats to go with the Evansville team uniforms their mother had sewed for them.

His younger brothers had become such inseparable companions that Paul dubbed them "Frassus" and "Fitus." With the other boys in the neighborhood, they sometimes put on plays, inspired by performances they had seen at the Opera House on passes donated by Paul. Al, who had rejoined the family, was always the villain. He was a husky youth now, toughened by hard work, and together with Ed, who excelled in sports, they were a contrast to Theodore, who had little aptitude for such things, though he joined in. Theodore preferred to take long walks or read. Sometimes Ed accompanied him on those rambles, and he later recalled,

[Theodore] would do most of the talking, but he was always interested in my questions and answers. . . . Theo would suggest we pick a subject, any subject under the sun, and talk about it. We talked and talked for hours. It was amazing the way everything and everyone in the world interested him. He wasn't aggressive or anxious in the same way [most] children are. His manner was earnest and gentle; and in place of a random curiosity quickly satisfied, he was interested strongly in people, what they were doing and thinking . . . everything.

Once, when they were playing with some other boys on the riverfront, jumping from barge to barge, Theodore slipped and fell in. Just as he was about to be swept away, Ed and another boy pulled him out. This narrow escape confirmed a fear of water Theodore had already developed and which he retained all his life. The seed was planted when he and Rome were in a boat on the Wabash. A small steamboat passed by, rocking them with its waves. When Theodore began to scream, Rome rocked harder, laughing his guttural, sinister laugh. "For some four or five years thereafter," Dreiser writes in *Dawn*, "I could not view any considerable body of water without having brought back to me most clearly that particular sensation of something that could and might destroy me . . . with almost personal violence."

But in the manuscript of *Dawn* Dreiser also describes paddling on a plank across a slough swollen with rainwater. In the published version, the incident is a normal boyish adventure, but in the manuscript he describes the "yellowish" water as "deep enough to drown a child" and remembers "an intense sense of possible disaster . . . a kind of terror [not only] of dying but of offending the mythical God, whose espionage and wrath were constantly being drummed into me now." Somehow the fear of death by water had merged in his mind with the terrors of hell as described by his father—or was it that all his fears seeped down into a single preconscious pool of dread?

The oppressive fears associated with Catholicism became more deeply rooted during the years Theodore lived in Evansville. Though Sarah would have preferred that the children go to public school, Paul, Sr., came down from Terre Haute to make sure they were enrolled in the Holy Trinity parochial school near Third and Vine. Ed evinced a normal aversion to book learning, but came around when he discovered the joys of after-school play; Theodore resented the rote learning, which consisted of a little grammar, arithmetic, and spelling and mainly indoctrination in Church history. The object was to prepare the students for first communion at age twelve; after that it was assumed they would be put out to work in a factory.

Most of his education Theodore picked up on his own, wandering about the city, observing people at work—a potter shaping a formless mound of glistening white clay on his wheel, or men in a foundry feeding scrap into the furnace's fiery maw. He also read avidly in the books he found in their new house—Gray's "Elegy," Oliver Goldsmith's "The Deserted Village," Ouida's *Wanda* and Bulwer-Lytton's *Ernest Maltravers*. More interesting, though, were the illustrated weeklies and dime novels he purchased with nickels from Paul (the price of most "dime" novels was five cents). He became addicted to the tales in such publications as *The*

Family Story Paper, *The Fireside Companion*, and *The New York Weekly*.
Many of these stories had urban settings, and they served to instruct
America's predominantly rural and small-town populace in the wonders
and pitfalls of the city. Dangers, moral and otherwise, there were aplenty,
but success and happiness crowned the efforts of the virtuous shopgirl
or clerk who adhered to simple moral code learned at mother's knee. A
favorite genre was the working girl who was kidnapped or otherwise lured
by villainous thugs for unmentionable purposes. Trapped, she would buckle
on the armor of righteousness, as does the heroine of *Night Scenes in New
York: In Darkness and by Gaslight:* "Hear me, Lyman Treadwell; I am but
a poor shopgirl; my present life is a struggle for a scanty existence; my
future a life of toil; but over my present life of suffering there extends
a rainbow of hope . . . the grave is but the entrance to eternity. And you,
villain, ask me to change my present peace for a life of horror with you.
No, monster, rather may I die at once!"

The premier urban hero appeared in the Horatio Alger stories—always
poor but honest (and often well-born) lads. Theodore sampled the volumes in Alger's proliferating library—*Luck and Pluck*, *Wait and Win*, and
several others, learning that industry, frugality, and saving the boss's
daughter from a runaway horse were the routes to modest but solid prosperity.

But he had an even better running drama closer to hand—the ongoing
Dreiser family saga that had more stormy exits and surprise entrances
than an Augustin Daly melodrama:

> *Mame and Theresa move to Chicago, where they find male friends. Emma and
> Sylvia leave the city and come to Evansville, where they work in a candy store and
> a ten-cent store, respectively. Rome, the "family Nemesis," arrives in his cups. After
> begging Sarah's forgiveness and a few dry days, he hurries to the nearest saloon.
> Having no money, he forges a check with Paul's name and lands in jail. Paul
> springs him, but he promptly steals a buggy and goes for a joy ride. Arrested again,
> he is let off with a warning to leave town. Exeunt Rome, with only an occasional
> postcard from Wyoming, Texas, or Mexico to tell them he is still on the earth.*

Actually, with Paul's financial support, and Sylvia, Emma, Al, and Paul,
Sr., adding their mites, the Evansville branch of the family was fairly
prosperous. The trouble was, the whole arrangement rested on Paul's
relationship with Sallie. Apparently she put up most of the money for
the household, probably regarding it as a way of insuring her young lover's affections. Later, Paul explained to Theodore that Sallie had purchased the house and that he contributed money for expenses, but deed

records show it belonged to Edward F. Goecke and was rented to Paul,
who made the payments. Since Paul had a taste for high life and could
not have been earning too large a salary at the Opera House, the money
probably ultimately came from Sallie.

In *Dawn*, Dreiser writes that Paul was an "unregenerate sex enthusiast," and in a passage he cut from the final book he writes that after
one escapade his brother contracted syphilis, which he cured with the
standard mercury treatments. However, a lesion erupted on his nose,
leaving a pitted scar which Paul always covered with a small piece of
flesh-colored tape. Once he ran off with one of Sallie's girls but returned
and begged her forgiveness. She took him back and fired the girl, but
when he launched an affair with a respectable woman from a wealthy
local family, she kicked him out for good. Respectability was something
Sallie couldn't fight; also, as a professional, she must have felt contempt
for a man who would put pleasure before business.

Deprived of Sallie's financial assistance, Paul joined a minstrel company and later moved on to New York City, where he established himself
as a blackface comedian at Tony Pastor's nightclub on Fourteenth Street
and then played at the London Varieties.

As for Sarah, she pulled herself together and planned the next move.
This time she set her sights on Chicago, about which she had been hearing a lot from Rome, Mame, and Theresa. All the children, save Al, who
had a girlfriend and a steady job in a furniture factory, were gravitating
there. Its rapid growth was the wonder of the Middle West, and there
were said to be jobs for the asking. Paul, Sr., was working again at the
Ellis mill and did not want to join them; at sixty-two, he was too old to
give up a position in hand.

The idea was for all of them to share an apartment in the city; everyone
would be expected to contribute a portion of his or her earnings to the
family pot. If for some reason that didn't work out, Sarah had a fallback
plan. Ninety miles from Chicago, near Silver Lake, she owned a five-
acre plot of land, inherited from her father, perhaps as a deathbed pardon.
This land had assumed an outsize importance in her mind; after over
thirty years of marriage, it was the only thing she owned, and she romantically envisioned their living on it, perhaps operating a truck farm.
After all, if you have land, you can't starve. . . .

So they packed once again, and once again boarded the train. Theodore had acquired some of his mother's blind faith in the good place over
the next hill, and he had heard the enthusiastic tales about the magic of
city lights from his older brothers and sisters. But these constant up-

rootings and the dizzying rise and fall of their fortunes instilled in him a deep anxiety, so that in later life he could never leave a place (or a person he was close to) without a sickening sense of doom and disaster. Perhaps it was not the simple fact of constant moves that caused this, but rather the larger cloud of insecurity that hung over them. With an absent father and a mother who seemed at the mercy of the whims of chance, he could never develop a faith in a stable, parent-dominated cosmos that most children have. His family, he sensed, was exposed to the elements.

First signs of Chicago hove into view through the train window; the flat prairie broken by a line of telegraph poles marching to the horizon; houses set on raw earth in a gridwork of unpaved streets, signs already in place—new developments. Then the houses grew more numerous and gave way to blocks of flats, factories, grain elevators. Looming against the sky were two ten-story buildings—Burnham and Root's Montauk Block and William Le Baron Jenney's just completed Home Insurance Building, the first iron-and-steel-framed structure and precursor of the "skyscraper." Finally, the locomotive entered the Dearborn Street Station, with its tall clock tower, and they clambered off inside the great shed and plunged into a maelstrom of novel sights, sounds, and smells.

To Theodore the city was the ultimate wonder of his life. By the time they reached their new home, a six-room, third-floor rear flat on the corner of West Madison and Throop, he was drunk on it. He hung out the apartment window, gaping at the crush of people and horses and wagons on the street below. In the beer garden atop the Waverly Theater across the street, he could hear a band playing and see pennants flapping in the breeze. Peddlers with pushcarts sold vegetables or purchased rags, iron, and bones. As night fell, the clamor subsided and new sounds wafted through the window—music and laughter from the beer garden, the plinking of a mandolin, the hum of voices from the throngs of pleasure-seekers. Gaslights dripped pools of radiance, and in the windows of the flats across the way figures swam in and out of view in the yellow glow of oil lamps. Theodore watched the spectacle until he fell asleep, exhausted, at the window.

In 1884 Chicago was bursting with new arrivals like an overripe melon. It had risen from the ashes of the 1871 fire more vital and energetic than ever. In the two decades from 1870 to 1890, its population increased five-fold, from 368,000 to 1.3 million, and its area from 35 to 185 square miles. Great grain elevators towered over the tangled ganglia of tracks, and factory chimneys belched black smoke, the votive incense of prosperity. By

1890 there would be ten thousand manufacturing establishments turning out $64.5 million worth of goods—foundries making steel, stockyards with sprawling mazes of open pens where herds of cattle waited to be butchered. On the dirty, noisome Chicago River, intestine of the city's wastes, a fleet of barges and scows hauled coal and produce. The vibrant hum of commerce, the promise of fortunes to be made, hung in the air. "It is the only great city in the world to which all its citizens have come with the one common, avowed object of making money," remarks a character in Henry B. Fuller's novel *With the Procession*.

Prominent among those recent arrivals was Charles T. Yerkes, a lone wolf from Philadelphia who had cornered the transit system. Regarding the little people who spent their nickels to ride in his crowded, rickety cars, Yerkes had this assessment: "Tush! It's the straphangers who pay the dividends."

To titans like Potter Palmer, Chicago was a grand Monopoly board. In the 1860s Palmer, a financier and real estate speculator, decided that the city's development, which up until then had been along an east-west axis should take a half turn and proceed in a north-south direction along Lake Michigan, with State Street as the main thoroughfare. He built a huge brick castle on the North Shore, then an empty tract of marshland, bought up State Street tracts at less than a dollar a square foot and, lo, the city turned. Other entrepreneurs were equally bold—Marshall Field, pioneer in the idea of a great store with a number of departments selling a variety of quality goods under one roof; the Armours and the Swifts, who mechanized the slaughter of animals in the stockyards; William Ogden, the railroad magnate who as mayor had almost single-handedly given the city its first railroad, and who became president of the Union Pacific; George Pullman, whose eponymous sleeping cars dominated the nation's tracks; Cyrus McCormick, inventor and manufacturer of the mechanical reaper, which swept across the wheat fields of the Great Plains like hordes of locusts. These moguls and their armies of lawyers, accountants, and clerks, expanded their holdings, watered their stock, and consolidated their companies into trusts and corporations, pyramiding their profits and operating unchecked by law or custom. They elbowed aside the old New England merchants and landowners who had dominated the city's early years, and erected huge stone mansions on the Lake Shore Drive and Prairie Avenue.

In the business heart great office buildings rose up to house these commercial empires. Manning the fortresses was an army of clerks that moved paper around and translated the flow of goods into columns of figures.

The average wage of the white-collar worker was twice that of a semi-skilled blue-collar worker, reflecting the growing division between capital and its bureaucratic satrapy and wage labor. Male office workers averaged $1000 a year (women half this); semiskilled laborers about $450 to $500 (barely above the poverty line), and the miserable denizens of the sweatshops between $200 and 240. The ambitious young man naturally aimed for the clerical ranks; after all, hadn't Marshall Field started as a clerk?

The appetite for unskilled labor was voracious. Young women were needed as shopgirls in the department stores like Mandel Brothers; Field; Schlesinger and Mayer; Carson, Pirie, Scott; and The Fair, or as machine tenders in the shoe factories and garment-making concerns at four to ten dollars a week. Untrained young men fresh from the farm or the boat performed heavy labor in the factories, stockyards, foundries, mills, train yards, grain elevators, and warehouses, and in thousands of smaller tributary concerns.

Lured by the promise of work, the newcomers poured in, and in such numbers—fifty thousand a year—that wages were chronically depressed. The American-born farmers among them had been driven off the land by plummeting commodity prices; forced in part by the overproduction made possible by new machines such as McCormick's reapers. Further impetus was provided by inflated freight rates rigged by Chicago railway magnates, which ate away farmers' profits, and by deflated currency and high interest rates, set by the city's bankers, which made it impossible for them to pay off their mortgages.

To the greenhorn and the rustic, the city pulsed like a beacon of hope, promising not only economic opportunity but excitement, sociability, glamour, comfort, and ease. In the rich brogue of his fictitious Irish saloonkeeper Mr. Dooley, the Chicago *Sunday Post* columnist Finley Peter Dunne summed up the attractions of the city:

"But I must go back," I says, "to th' city," I says, "where there is nawthin' to eat but what ye want an nawthin' to drink but what ye can buy," I says. "Where the dust is laid be th' sprinkler cart, where th' iceman comes reglar an' th' roof garden is in bloom an' ye're waked not be th' sun but be th' milkman," I says. "I want to be near a doctor whin I'm sick an' near eatable food whin I'm hungry, an' where I can put me hand out early in the mornin' an' hook in a newspaper," says I.

Theodore had a chance to explore this metropolis when his father, out of work again, arrived for an extended visit, and they took long walks together. On those excursions their mutual awe at Chicago's furious growth formed a bond between them. Everywhere there were new buildings going up. Locomotives exhaling plumes of steam, the clang of machinery, the acrid odor of coal smoke in the air emblemized unleashed forces. Sometimes they walked east on Madison all the way to the business heart, crossing the river, passing factories and mills, shanties and abandoned warehouses and coal yards. Peering through the new plate-glass windows of the great office buildings, Theodore could see the men at desks and boys scurrying to and fro, and he wondered about the mysteries of commerce.

During those walks, Theodore had another of his rare glimpses of his father as a person. He had seen little of him in the past five years and he noticed subtle changes. In his low-crowned derby and shabby alpaca cloak, his once-reddish hair now grizzled, Paul Dreiser, Sr., looked old and worn. When he got off the subject of religion, he discoursed knowledgeably about his travels in France and Europe before coming to America. He had a shrewd eye for character and human frailties. Yet he seemed a beaten, depressed man, and Theodore began to pity him. After forty years of labor, all Paul had to look forward to was more toil and nights in his lonely room reading the Bible and praying to his harsh God for absolution. His family had left him behind in its rush to the city; now he saw his children only when he was idle.

The neighborhood where the Dreisers lived was on the borderline of a bastion of respectability known as Union Park. Once an elegant upper-class neighborhood, it was rebuilt after the fire, and was now largely middle class. The clerks, shopkeepers, and skilled workingmen who moved in had constructed a distinctly antiurban culture in which each family was a tight little island of respectability, fearful and contemptuous of the poor and envious and resentful of the wealthy and their "immoral" ways, wary of the city's temptations and suspicious of its opportunities.

The neighborhood the Dreisers lived in presented a more mixed and vivid social canvas than Union Park. A cataract of shouts, laughter, and quarrels spilled down the dumbwaiter shaft in their building. The apartment above was occupied by a woman with a drunken husband, a musician, and once Paul, Sr., was forced to call a policeman after he had beaten her into insensibility. Eventually he abandoned her, and Sarah temporarily adopted their child until the wife could get back on her feet.

They had not been in Chicago long before Theodore began to overhear scraps of conversation that had a familiar ring. The gist of them was that the family economy was again shaky. They were paying thirty-five dollars a month for their apartment, and also buying furniture on time, which meant an additional monthly outlay of twenty-five dollars; beyond that there was the cost of food and clothing. The males of the family were contributing little to offset this outlay. The father was unemployed, and Rome, now twenty-four, was incommunicado. Paul, Jr., twenty-six, had recently stopped sending money because of romantic problems. Theodore and Ed sold newspapers—daringly clambering aboard Yerkes' trolley cars and working the packed crowd of homebound commuters until the conductor kicked them off—but sank their profits into licorice whips and cream caramels.

That left the girls, but they were flying off on romantic tangents. Mame had become involved with a genial casketware salesman named Austin Brennan, who was nearly twenty years older than she. Although Brennan had a good income and hailed from a socially prominent Irish family in Rochester, New York, he was a playboy and bon vivant. Mame had met him while she was working at a boardinghouse, which operated a gambling room on the side. He became fond of Mame, now a tall, striking young woman of twenty-three with a full figure and a warm smile, and lavished clothes and jewels on her.

The twenty-year-old Theresa was keeping company with an aging, wealthy widower to whom Brennan had introduced her and whom the ever-hopeful Sarah treated as a bona fide suitor. Emma, twenty-one, also had an affair perking with an older man, a cultivated, prominent architect. He had set her up in a hotel on South Halstead Street. Theodore had visited her there once, and she showed off her silver toilet articles and a closet full of dresses.

His sister's apparent success impressed him, but was also confusing. In his head he reflected his father's portrayal of them as hell-bent harlots, but in his heart he felt vaguely ashamed because, as his father complained, they "were selling themselves too cheaply, that men were using them as mere playthings." Yet they seemed happy and prosperous and independent. Where, exactly, was the immorality?

None of their illicit prosperity made its way to Sarah, however. As the family fell behind on rent and furniture payments, she decided it was time to move to Warsaw, Indiana, which had the virtue of being near her plot of land. More important, she had brothers and sisters living in the area. Warsaw was the seat of Kosciusko County and was considered a pleasant town with good schools. By now Sarah was determined that Theodore, Ed, and Claire would have a public education.

Sarah had conceived the idea she could take the furniture along, even though it was not fully paid for. But just as Theresa and Theodore were preparing to leave, a representative of the company appeared and threatened to have them arrested for illegally taking unpaid-for goods out of the state. Theresa confessed that the furniture was at the Railway Express office, and the three of them went to collect it. After he had recovered the furniture the collector became friendly, asking Theresa for a date. About a year later she happened to see him in church passing the collection plate, a picture of Christian piety. She was outraged: "What a pity such wretches should be permitted to rob the poor all week and go to church on Sunday."

That was a very Dreiserian reaction, the view of Union Park from Madison and Throop, by a family that had clung to the margin of the middle class but had come to identify with the poor, and that found itself outside the pale of official sanctimony (though, in the case of Theresa, not beyond the amorous advances of a churchgoer).

6. Awakenings

I was raised in Warsaw, Indiana, but it would be more truthful
if my early life were ascribed not so much to one place as to
the whole state. All my life I have been a traveler.
                                        —Dreiser to Richard Duffy (1901)

From contemplating most of the small towns with which I have
come in contact . . . I have come to dread the conventional point
of view. The small mind of the townsmen is anti-polar to that
of the larger, more sophisticated wisdom of the city. . . . I never
was in such a place for any period of time without feeling cab-
ined, cribbed, confined intellectually if not emotionally.
                                        —Dreiser, *A Hoosier Holiday* (1916)

arsaw was a pretty town in 1884. In summer it seemed to
be washed by brilliant Alpine light. The flat green terrain
was the opposite of Alpine, but it was dotted with lakes;
two were near the town and one, Center Lake, was right
at its edge. The relaxed gaiety of arriving vacationers (for
the town was something of a resort), the bright-colored sailboats and
canoes on the gleaming blue lake, the bathers on the shore—gave it a
festive air. Contributing to this atmosphere was the new white-limestone
courthouse in the square, which was built in a cheery rococo style. It
featured a tall tower with a clock that chimed the hours and gave the
structure a vague resemblance to a European town hall.

The population then was around thirty-three hundred, and while there
was no large industry or wealthy few, a "good" society of sorts existed.
The manners and morals of the thin upper crust were set by the wives
of the town's successful grocers, landlords of office blocks, owners of the
biggest hardware store and meat market, chiefs of the flour and planing
mills, and assorted lawyers, doctors, and politicians. This provincial "400's"
doings were faithfully chronicled in the society pages of the *Daily Times*.
The ladies led twin crusades for temperance and culture. The Zerelda

Club, a reading circle, combined both; it was named after Zerelda Wallace, a leader in the antiliquor cause. The Thespians presented annual productions of Gilbert and Sullivan, and the Opera House imported such attractions as the Townshend Dramatic Company with Shakespeare, Abbey's Double Mammoth Company in *Uncle Tom's Cabin*, and the Myrtle Ferns troupe in *Love and Honor*. Relatives of Ambrose Bierce, the San Francisco satirist, resided in the town, and James Whitcomb Riley, the popular Hoosier poet, had passed through in his sign-painting days. The lettering for Marcus Phillipson's dry goods store was authoritatively attributed to him.

The sons and daughters of the town's leading families had their own parties and excursions, which were duly chronicled in the *Daily Times*—dances, skating, and cutter (sleighing) parties in winter and canoeing and masquerade balls in the summer. The bal masqué held by young Bram Funk, son of W. B., president of the Lake City Bank, on his family's new veranda was the highlight of the recent season.

Into these social waters, placid on the surface, but full of concealed snags, plunged Sarah and her three youngest children in hot pursuit of a normal existence. To the mother that meant a "simple, conservative, well-mannered" way of life. For a time it looked as if she would achieve it. She settled them in a large old brick house, known as the Grant Place. With living cheaper, and both Pauls resuming their financial contributions, the family's situation was stabilized. Theodore, for the first time, felt a sense of belonging. Didn't his mother's people come from around here?

The public school was next door, and the children were enrolled soon after their arrival (there were tirades from Paul, Sr., later, but Sarah held firm). After the authoritarian Catholic schools, the place seemed like heaven to Theodore. His seventh-grade teacher was a kindly woman named May Calvert, who had warm blue eyes and long blond hair and was only twenty. He fell in love with her, and she, sensing he was a "mother boy," gave him special attention, coaching him in grammar, which was his weakest subject. Despite her efforts he failed it, but she promoted him anyway, saying he was too bright to be held back. He bloomed under her attention and for the first time found school interesting.

Also interesting were the girls in his class. Among the beauties were Augusta Phillipson; Myrtle Weimar; Carrie (Cad) Tuttle, who had thick tawny hair; her sister, Maud, who was plump and blond; and Berta Moon, with jet-black hair and a slim figure. He was too shy to speak to them at first, for he had formed the idea that he was unattractive and unlikable.

At Miss Calvert's urging Theodore obtained a card at the town's small public library and rifled its shelves. There he discovered Hawthorne's *The House of the Seven Gables* and *The Scarlet Letter,* fellow Hoosier Lew Wallace's *Ben-Hur,* Charles Kingsley's *The Water Babies* (a kind of Darwinian fable for children that strangely fascinated him), the novels of James Fenimore Cooper, the poetry of Longfellow, Bryant, Whittier, and Poe (whom he liked best of all). He also read the romantic effusions of popular writers such as Laura Jean Libbey, who supplied "some phase of impossible sentimentalism which my nature seemed to crave."

After about a year the family moved to the old Thralls mansion, a rambling, twelve-room brick structure built fifty years ago by a prominent judge but now in a state of decrepitude. There was a pond in back, where logs for the planing mill were massed, and Theodore, Ed, and their friends jumped about on them, lumberjack style. The place also had an orchard, several chestnut trees, a large garden, and a grove of ash trees from which they took firewood. Tall pines surrounded the house, and in spring Sarah made cauldrons of apple butter over a pine-cone fire in the yard. The land sloped down to a marsh where in the spring flocks of red-winged blackbirds fed on the wild rice. Beyond, through woods and fields, flowed the Tippecanoe River, a serpentine silver band.

Theodore made a few friends, including the Shoup brothers, whose father was co-owner of the flour mill and whose mother was Sarah's niece, but it didn't escape his notice that he and Ed were never invited to their homes. He sensed an invisible line which his family could not cross.

The boys spent hours loafing and talking in the woods, with sex, a subject about which the thirteen-year-old Theodore was becoming curious, the chief topic: "legs, breasts, thighs, underclothing, stories of encounters, of seeing things through windows or key holes—of boys and girls lying together in the depths of the woods. . . ." A boy named Gavin McNutt gossiped knowingly about Warsaw's sexual underground; he knew which young woman was in trouble and which young rake would have to leave town. Theodore's closest friend, Harry Croxton, served as scientific consultant by dint of his having attended a "sex hygiene" lecture by an itinerant savant, who solved the mystery with the aid of a pointer and male and female anatomy charts. Croxton passed on the professor's lurid warnings about the horrors of venereal disease and the awful consequences of masturbation: pimples, sterility, madness, death.

Such talk inflamed Theodore. He reread the lustier passages of Shakespeare and Fielding; a picture of an actress in tights turned him into a quivering jelly of adolescent lust. He began fantasizing about the girls in his class, though when he confronted them he was painfully shy and averted his eyes, lest they divine his desires. He formed a kind of idealized passion for the mousy, ethereal Myrtle Weimar—she reminded him of pictures of Quaker maids he had seen in books—while the sensuous-looking Carrie Tuttle stirred him in a physical way. Myrtle had no connection with the seething inside him. All he hoped for was a chaste kiss.

His chance came when Theo, Ed, and Claire were invited by Myrtle to a party, at which a game of post office would be the main event. Theodore escorted Claire "instead of some other youth's sister," as he oddly puts it in *Dawn*. It was an important party: the "elite of the seventh grade at three different schools" would be present. His mother was overjoyed; at last, it seemed, they were being drawn into the social stream. The party turned out to be the Dreiser family's social high-water mark in Warsaw. He always remembered sitting with Ed in the ash grove the next day, trying "to recall how wonderful it had been and how we felt."

The evening's high point, as far as he was concerned, came when as "postmaster" he announced a letter for Myrtle. After what seemed an hour, he saw her slight figure next to him, a "shy mouse of a girl." His throat was dry, his body numb. He bent down and pecked her as she averted her head; the experience left him weak and trembling. Theodore would also long remember how Cad Tuttle, trailing perfume and laughter, boldly pressed her soft warm lips against his.

But in the following weeks and months he progressed no further with Myrtle or Carrie or any of the other girls. His only sexual experience came with the baker's daughter, who was about his age and already known as a town pump. As he walked by the shop one day, she called him and they talked. Suddenly she cried, "Bet you can't catch me!" and ran to the back, with Theodore in pursuit. He followed her into a shed, where she turned to him, panting faintly, a half-smile curling her lips. After a brief mock struggle, they sank to the floor, and in a chaotic blur of sensations, his pent-up desires found a sudden, blinding release. Afterward, however, he could only think of Croxton's warning about a horrible pox known as the clap, and he never went back to her.

He knew that he had no chance with the "nice" girls, and never even dared a kiss, convinced that because he was homely and lacked "money, daring, this and that, [they] would never permit . . . such familiarities as the baker's daughter. . . ."

While Theodore was anguishing over his shyness, Ed slipped easily into the social swim. "I never had much luck getting Theo to come with me to call on a girl," he recalled. "He didn't dislike girls but he found other things more interesting." Apparently Ed little knew that his brother was being consumed by the temptations of St. Anthony. Before long Theodore found the inevitable outlet—the "ridiculous and unsatisfactory practice of masturbation." Already ashamed of his secret desires, he acquired a habit that was condemned in every pulpit and pseudo-scientific pamphlet in the land.

In a passage Dreiser expurgated from the published version of *Dawn* as too risqué, he tells of sitting on his bed and fantasizing about Carrie Tuttle and the other girls in his class; an erection ensued and he manipulated it. The ejaculation was intensely pleasurable but also terrifying. He jumped up, thinking he had injured himself. A few days later, the fantasies recurred, and he repeated the process. "A kind of wild rapture of mind accompanied it, a heavy reaction of mood followed it." He resolved to stop, but the urge would seize him and he would hurry to his room or the bathroom and "in a kind of fury and excess of passion and delight give myself over to this form of self ab-use [sic]."

After some months of this he began to notice alarming physical symptoms. Harry Croxton asked him, "What are you doing to yourself, Ted—jerking off? Your face is all covered with pimples." One night, at the dinner table, he felt a whirring sensation in his head and a ringing in his ears, followed moments later by a wave of vertigo so severe that he would have fallen had he not been sitting down. He hallucinated spinning red, yellow, green, and blue lights; his heart raced, then beat feebly. He had to excuse himself and go to his room and lie down.

Theodore decided he was having a nervous breakdown, which was nature's way of restoring his system to "parity." He had been overtaxing his body, or, as he put it, "paying out of one treasury by drawing too swiftly and too heavily on others." Nearly fifty years later he retained the Victorian belief that excessive emissions of semen represent a sort of overdraft on one's "energy bank." This was the prevailing medical opinion. The British physician William Acton wrote in *The Functions and Disorders of the Reproductive System* that sexual intercourse and masturbation were equally harmful because of "the large expenditure of semen," which "is a highly organized fluid, requiring the expenditure of much vital force in its elaboration and in its expulsion."

In the ensuing months Theodore worried that he was wasting away. Desperate for advice but too shy to ask, he copied a prescription from a home medical guide and a friendly pharmacist filled it. When his mother received the bill, she asked him about it. He stammered incoherently but she did not press him, suggesting, in a voice "as soft and pleasing as that of a sweetheart," that he see Dr. Wooley, the family physician. He never did, but he also never forgot what he sensed (however she intended it) as the seductive undercurrent in her voice, implicating her permanently in his sexual awakening.

Like a bad omen, Rome reeled into town. As usual he tearfully begged Sarah's forgiveness, but she had heard this old song too often and berated him for endangering their position in Warsaw. Later, when he was fishing on Center Lake with Theodore, Rome scoffed at her deference to local opinion. "Who the hell are they? A lot of cattle and jays!"

As though Rome were a harbinger of a social disaster, Emma and Sylvia arrived, both of them voluptuous and spoiling for romance. They promenaded around the square in flashy city clothes, Emma in patent leather shoes with white tips, and Sylvia in rings and furs. Paul, Sr., who was temporarily in residence, called them "shameless creatures." After trolling their allures, they landed two sports from the upper crust: the son of the bank president and of the leading butcher. In their naiveté, Syl and Em did not realize that going out with such boys branded them as loose women. One night, when they came home after 2:00 A.M., Paul was waiting up for them. He announced he was throwing them out: the door was closed to them forever. Sylvia wailed, Emma screamed, and Sarah shouted, "You are too rough! You always were! What will the neighbors think!"

The next day at school a boy who lived in the neighborhood asked Theodore if someone had been sick the previous night. A few days later another boy slyly referred to Emma and Sylvia as the "Ticket sisters," using the last name of one of their swains. The innuendo was clear: only fast girls went out with Harry Ticket. Theodore was reminded of the time in Evansville when some locals teased him about Paul's relationship with Sallie Walker. He had a premonition that "scandal hung over our household—a household . . . darkened by doubts as to its own validity and decency."

The family's fortunes went downhill after that. Emma was banished to Chicago, but Sylvia remained, bored and sulky. Later that winter the trouble that Emma was courting fell on her like a load of hay. She was smitten by a forty-year-old clerk named L. A. Hopkins, a slight, dapper man with a mustache who was nicknamed "Grove" because of his resemblance to Grover Cleveland and his amorous proclivities. He worked for Chapin and Gore, a chain of saloons that catered to a working-class clientele, and had a wife and an eighteen-year-old daughter living on the West Side.

Mrs. Hopkins got wind of her husband's adultery and hired a private detective to trail him to the apartment on the South Side that Emma shared with Theresa. Determined to catch Hopkins in flagrante delicto, she, the detective, and some friends went to the love nest at one o'clock in the morning. According to the Chicago *Mail*, Mrs. Hopkins climbed in the front window and spied the guilty pair asleep:

> She watched the sleeping couple for a moment, and then called him by name. He was awake in a moment, and upon beholding his wife's white face at the window, he exclaimed:
> "My God! ma (he sometimes called her ma), is that you!"
> He jumped from the bed, and, rushing to the window, he prayed to his wife to forgive him. The moment the Treigh woman [Emma] heard Hopkins call to his wife she ran into the back parlor where Mrs. Nelson [Theresa] was sleeping.

A reporter had talked to Theresa at the South Morgan Street address, and it was she, apparently, who invented the false names—calling herself "Mrs. Nelson" and Emma "Minnie Frazier" in one interview and "Mamie Tracy Treigh" in another. "Mamie Tracy Treigh" seems a word salad, uttered in panic, an amalgam of Mame and her own nickname (Tres).

What made the story a three-day wonder in Chicago journalism was the fact that Hopkins absconded with $3500 in cash and $200 worth of jewelry from his employer's safe. After taking the money, he and Emma boarded a train to Montreal (Canada had no extradition treaty with the United States at that time). Once there, Hopkins got cold feet or had a change of heart and returned all but $800 of the money to Chapin and Gore, who declined to press charges. He and Emma then went on to New York City for a new life. A reporter covering the incident concluded that the theft was planned in advance. Hopkins was responsible for closing the warehouse every other Sunday night, the day he fled. Two days before the theft, neighbors said, a letter had arrived for Emma. Shortly after receiving it, she summoned an American Express truck to pick up her trunk and take it to Hopkins's office. In other words, the smitten clerk was not acting on a drunken impulse.

Two detectives came to Warsaw to question Sarah about her daughter (Mrs. Hopkins had told police about the Dreiser sisters' involvement). At least their real names never appeared in the stories in the Chicago papers with their lurid headlines (A WOMAN IN THE CASE, A DASHING BLONDE,

and EMBEZZLER HOPKINS HAD A FAIR COMPANION WHEN HE SKIPPED FOR CAN-
ADA). However, Sarah was shaken, and she never dared tell her husband
about the affair.

But another scandal occurred that could not be covered up. Bored and
lonely, Sylvia threw herself at Don Ashley (as Dreiser calls him), a well-
off young man-about-town with a reputation as a gambler and a womanizer. Sarah had the naive idea that her daughter was moving up in the
world and permitted Syl to entertain Ashley in their home before meeting
him (her complaisance when her daughter's marriage prospects were involved was seemingly boundless). That fall, however, Theodore noticed
his sister acting strangely. He sometimes compulsively went into the girls'
rooms when they were out, drawn to the hothouse of female scents—
hair, perfume, powder—and stole some small token. He wanted to penetrate this intimate, musky sphere; the tendrils of desire he would have
normally sent out to girls his own age turned back on him, becoming
ingrown, incestuous. But on that occasion, Sylvia was there. He noticed
a bottle marked "poison" on her bureau and queried her about it. She
mumbled that it was medicine. Then she shut herself in her room weeping, refusing to eat. Sarah coaxed her secret from her: she was pregnant
and Ashley was the father.

Sarah thought of bringing a paternity suit against the young man, but
the lawyer she hired was beholden to the Ashley family and stalled her.
Finally, Sylvia was sent to Emma's in New York City to have the baby.
Sarah had heard that Emma was prospering but probably did not know
the source of their money: she and Hopkins were running a bedhouse,
to which streetwalkers brought their clients. Hopkins had ingratiated
himself with Tammany Hall and had an arrangement with the local pre-
cinct. As a result, Emma was living high—lavish clothes, carriage rides
in Central Park, and sumptuous dinners at Delmonico's. She was glad
to take in her sister.

After Sylvia gave birth, she refused to keep the baby, and once again
Sarah was stuck. She took the little boy, who was named Carl, and his
presence in their house sealed their doom in Warsaw society. The child
was passed off as a relative, but Warsaw's moral guardians were not fooled.
For Theodore it was a dismal period, a gloom from which he never completely emerged. "I was more or less in a state of doldrums concerning
us," he recalled. "We were just naturally bad perhaps and could not be
made much better." He, Ed, and Claire were now outside the pale. Claire
had only one friend, a girl in similar circumstances. They could only yearn
for the other world in Warsaw—that of the superior social set one read

about in the society pages of the *Daily Times*, the young people who sailed in bright-painted boats on Center Lake and went to garden parties lit by strings of Chinese lanterns, like soft pastel moons. He envied them: "They were constantly going off somewhere on weekend excursions. . . . They were better clothed and carried themselves with an air of ease and sufficiency to which I did not feel I was entitled."

The sense of being an outcast oppressed him terribly. Torn between his father's religious morality, which he rejected even though he feared it, and his mother's gentleness and compassion, which he preferred but which seemed linked to one family disaster after another, he was in a quandary. He resented having to bear the obloquy of Sylvia's transgression, yet "seeing what my own sex feelings were I could not be very hard on her." Unlike Claire (who was closer to Paul, Sr., than any of them and already something of a prig), he could not condemn Sylvia. But he was in no position to flout convention. Like any child his age, Theodore wanted to be liked and accepted. He had been thrust into a state of nonconformity he had not chosen and scarcely understood.

He became increasingly solitary—reading, taking long walks, lying in a hammock watching the birds wheeling against the sky. School provided his only happy times. His latest teacher, Miss Fielding, had taken a shine to him and encouraged him to cultivate his mind as a way of achieving success. She had come from a poor background and risen by sheer grit, making herself over into an attractive woman by dressing well and having her protruding upper teeth straightened. She urged him not to pay any heed to small-town gossip; he could make something of himself. The superintendent of schools had also become interested in Theodore after reading a composition he had written about discovering a dead Jewish peddler in the woods. May Calvert had already put him on to Samuel Smiles's success primer, *Self-Help*, and the superintendent urged him to study the rise of the German empire and read Shakespeare.

Even in bucolic Warsaw the virus of commercial ambition was in the air. The town was abuzz with schemes for growth, none of which panned out. Theodore sensed "a keen rivalry among tradesmen and people of all walks and stations for place." *Place*—that was what he must have, "to be something, to have some money and to get out of this state of fear, cowardice, and bashfulness." Here he was nothing. Only boys whose fathers owned established businesses could hope to rise. And was a businessman's career what he really wanted? A poem he wrote around this time—the first he ever wrote, according to Ed—revealed an idealistic side:

I would not give the bells that ring
For all the world of bartering
Nor yet the whispering of the leaves
For all the Gold that Greed conceives
To me, the grass that grows in Spring
Is sweeter than Fame's offering
An Ah! the smile of kindly worth—
Than all the wealth of all the earth.

The Dreiser family left few traces of their sojourn in Warsaw. The county historian, George A. Nye, an otherwise assiduous recorder of local trivia, makes this passing reference to them: "In the old brick house built in the 1850s by George Thralls lived the Dreiser family, a very poor family. Miss Clothilde, Theodore, and Paul were some of this family. Theodore became more or less famous as an author after leaving Warsaw and wrote a story in which the old house is mentioned." There is also on record the adult recollection of a contemporary which gives a brief, painful glimpse: "We knew Dreiser . . . in his high school days in Indiana. He was a gawk then; kept to himself, had no dealings with the other boys; went along the street with his head down as if afraid to look anyone in the eye. We boys thought he was 'queer,' and in the main were as ready to avoid him as he was to keep away from all companionship."

In the summer of 1887, not long before his sixteenth birthday, Theodore read an account in a Chicago Sunday supplement describing the raucous, vibrant, pushcart life on Halstead Street, which brought back vividly the sights of the metropolis. "If only we could return to the city," he thought. "There our neighbors would not care what we were." He went to Sarah and announced, "Ma, I'm going to Chicago."

She was wary, but not one to step on her children's dreams. So attuned were their psyches that Sarah had probably been feeling a similar desire. She protested feebly that she wanted him to finish school and make something of himself, but Theodore argued he would get an education somehow. "I don't want to sit around this place any longer," he said. "We can't get anywhere here. People only talk about us." Sarah could make no argument to that. Her hopes of winning respectability in Warsaw lay in ruins.

She gave him three dollars and packed a shoebox with a cold chicken, half a pie, and some apples. Theodore left that same day on the Nickel Plate line, without even saying goodbye to Ed and Claire.

7. A Start in Life

Ah the horror of the commonplace, of disgrace, of shame, of being shut out, ignored, forgotten, left to wander friendless and by myself. How often have my hands beaten in spirit at least at those doors and windows on the other side of which I fancied joy or a hope of beauty to be. How often have I stood outside and looked in wishing and longing with a too full heart.

—Dreiser, *Dawn* (1931)

As the now familiar environs of Chicago rushed past the train window, Theodore felt an infusion of hope. He had sworn he wouldn't look up his sisters when he arrived; he intended to prove himself—this bashful, skinny boy whose most recent job had been picking vegetables on a farm near Warsaw (he lasted one day) and who had no visible talents other than reading and daydreaming.

In a pleasant neighborhood that reminded him of the small town he had just left, he found a boardinghouse, run by a motherly old lady called Mrs. Pilcher. Immediately guessing that he was trying to "make a start in the world," she offered him a small front bedroom for only $1.50 a week. She understood how it was with young men; she had a son starting out in Kansas City.

The next morning he was up early and out tramping the streets. He made the rounds of shops in the neighborhood but it was always the same: "No Help Wanted." He purchased a copy of the *Daily News* and scanned the "Boy Wanted" columns, but when he went to the addresses, he found that he was not what was needed—too puny or lacking the required skill.

Soon he was down to his last two dollars. He rationed the contents of the shoebox his mother had packed, but when it was gone he had to lay out eighty-five cents for food. Then an encouraging letter arrived from Sarah with two dollars enclosed. She wrote that if Theodore could find work, and if Al, Theresa, and Mame could be induced to contribute their shares, she would join them and set up a new household. That galvanized him into renewing his search. Spotting a DISHWASHER WANTED sign in the window of a Greek restaurant, he went in, and the proprietor, John Paradiso, a dark man in a greasy apron, hired him on the spot; he was used to rapid turnover on this job.

Eventually Theodore looked up Theresa but, too embarrassed to say where he was working, he told her he was clerking in a Halstead Street haberdashery at the respectable sum of seven dollars a week. The two of them immediately discussed how to put Sarah's plan into action. Theresa, "a shadowy, self-effacing girl" blessed with the common sense her sisters lacked and closest of all to her mother, began looking that same afternoon and found a suitable flat on Ogden Avenue. The rent was thirty-five dollars a month, but with Al, Mame, Theodore, Theresa (who was working as a dentist's assistant), and Paul contributing, in addition to what Ed and Claire would bring in once they got jobs, survival seemed possible.

Sarah was summoned immediately, and Theodore and Theresa met her at the station, a commanding figure leading a safari of fellow travelers carrying her boxes and trunks. Al joined them a day or so later. While in Warsaw he had tried a stage career in amateur minstrel productions and displayed a talent for writing comic songs. But now he was anxious to find a trade. Mame had been living in a North Side love nest. Now she bustled about suggesting various improvements that would make the flat appropriate to her newly elevated social level.

When Al said he wouldn't mind a cushy position in a gent's emporium too, Theodore was forced to confess where he was actually working. Al asked him to quit so they could make the rounds together.

Telling his mother he had been laid off by the haberdashery, Theodore plunged once more into the economic storm. At a hardware company, he was put to work cleaning stoves, but a sadistic co-worker kicked him after he balked at lifting a heavy stove. Brandishing a stove leg, Theodore was angry enough, for once, to fight. Next he worked as assistant to Theresa's boyfriend, Davis, a painter of stage sets and backgrounds for photographers. Davis made the mistake of recommending authors to read—Walt Whitman and Christopher Marlowe, among others—which encouraged Theodore to engage him in endless philosophical discussions. So Theodore was tactfully eased out in favor of the less intellectual Ed.

Then Rome blew in from parts unknown and, between drinking bouts, took Theodore in hand. He had a railroad buddy with the Chicago, Burlington and Quincy who would fix up his brother with a job as a freight-car tracer. Rome's friend said the job paid forty-five dollars a month—eleven dollars a week! But Theodore would have to commute to the Hegewisch Yard, ten miles outside of the city, on the 6:40 A.M. train.

Rome convoyed him the first day. He had had a few eye-openers, and during the ride launched into a diatribe against rich men like Armour and Pullman, who were amassing great fortunes while most poor slobs toiled for pittances to support the magnates' "sissy sons and daughters." As Theodore watched in horror, Rome repeatedly stabbed the velvet plush on the seats with a penknife, saying, "Oh, the company's rich. It can afford it."

The job of tracer consisted of locating freight cars scheduled for shipment. Theodore scampered about the huge railyard looking for tags that corresponded to the cabalistic notations on a sheaf of slips given him by the foreman. A kindly brakeman volunteered some advice, but even so, Theodore finished his stint in a state of total confusion. Still, he found beauty in that unlikely setting: "The shadows, the red, white, blue, green and yellow switch lights winking and glowing like flowers, the suggestion of distant cities. . . ."

On the train home, he observed his fellow laborers, most of them foreigners, silent, toil-worn men, clutching their lunch buckets with cracked, grimy hands: "inured to a lean and meager life which horrified me and yet made me sad." He wondered if they were a foreshadowing of his own future. Would he be a workingman like them—like his father? The thought filled him with "a morbidity that was almost devastating."

Running around in the freezing December drizzle, he had caught cold, and the next morning he was too sick to go to work. The pity in his mother's eyes as he described the job made him feel sorry for himself, and when he was better he did not go back. Soon he was tramping the streets again. The family was living on such a tight margin that Theodore's six or seven dollars a week spelled the difference between solvency and eviction. Their combined monthly earnings during this period never came to much more than seventy dollars. After rent, furniture payments, and food, there was nothing left. Sarah, the family rock, was, as usual, planted on shifting sands.

After days of fruitless search, Theodore found a place as a box-rustler and stockpiler at Hibbard, Spencer, Bartlett & Company, a huge wholesale hardware concern. In the cavernous warehouse, shelf after shelf was filled with ironware, tinware, bolts, nails, brooms, mops, razors, mugs, spoons, coal scuttles, and kitchenware. Each seemed to cry out, "You need me! You need me!"

As the days went by, Theodore noticed two well-dressed young men from the East, sons of friends of the owners who were learning the business. By their condescending airs they made it clear to the others that their sojourn here was a mere interlude before they assumed their rightful positions. Their arrogance made him conscious of the unfairness of a society in which well-born boys had a head start in the battle for place.

But the co-worker who made the deepest impression on him was a Dane named Christian Aaberg, a "shambling man with a wrinkled, emaciated, obviously emotion-scarred face." Looking well over forty, Aaberg bore the stigmata of alcoholic martyrdom. On Monday mornings, shaky and puffy-eyed from a hangover, he would moan, "My gott, how drunk I was yesterday! Oh these women! These devils of women!" He had a *manqué* air about him, hinting of an aristocratic upbringing, which he subsequently confirmed. Now, however, he was poor, making ten dollars a week and drinking up most of it. His talk was sprinkled with allusions to heretic philosophers and writers he had read—Ibsen, Nietzsche, Schopenhauer, Strindberg, and they would discuss intellectual matters as they sorted bolts or stacked pots and pans. His message echoed Miss Fielding's in Warsaw: "Mind and mind alone, makes the essential difference between the masses and the classes."

Aaberg saw a spark of brilliance in his young disciple, and in a letter he wrote Dreiser thirty years later, reporting he had "conquered the [liquor] habit that ruined my life," he recalled Theodore's "intense interest in matters of the mind" and "extensive knowledge of the best literature of the world . . . at an age when boys of the ordinary type only think of sport."

When not sitting at Aaberg's feet, Theodore spent a good deal of time gazing out the window at the crowds below: little humans bending into the bitter wind swirling off the lake or forming masses of bobbing black umbrellas. Or he gazed at the new structures thrusting up, avatars of the city's brawny ambitions. Chicago hummed with the frenetic trading at the wheat pit, the talk of a world's fair in 1893, John D. Rockefeller's plans for the University of Chicago. Theodore's head was filled with "buzzing dreams of leaving Chicago and becoming a great man." He thought of the fine mansions the owners of the hardware company must live in on Michigan or Dearborn avenues: "How beautiful it must be this life they led! . . . How wonderful! Think of the glory of being rich— horses and carriages and servants. Ah—if it could only be so—if I could only take a carriage and ride home to one of their wonderful lamplit mansions that lined the great streets of the city." (Dreiser's biographer Dorothy Dudley, who grew up in Chicago and played with Hibbard's grandchildren, recalled the "enormous red brick house" with a stone fountain and the drawing room "dressed in pale green and gold brocade" with marble statues and black teakwood cabinets and a baronial dining room with elk heads and mounted trout on the walls and dark pictures everywhere.)

Though he needed the job, it was harming his health. The dust he breathed daily was playing havoc with his lungs. He also had a nervous stomach and suffered from constipation. He was tortured by the fear that his sexual excesses had rendered him impotent. With all this turmoil in mind and body, he became languid, rising with difficulty each morning, dragging through the day, and returning home exhausted.

But then Miss Fielding turned up at Hibbard, Spencer. She had left her job in Warsaw to become principal of a school in a Chicago suburb. Having saved some money, she wanted to use it to give Theodore a year at Indiana University. This was to be an experiment; perhaps he had an aptitude for something better, which college training would help him discover; perhaps not. At any rate, she wanted him to try. Theodore snatched at the lifeline. He had little idea of what college was like and read books like *Dink Stover at Yale* to find out. Miss Fielding knew the president of Indiana University and arranged for Theodore to be admitted as a special student. She would pay his two-hundred-dollar tuition and provide him with a monthly allowance of fifty dollars for room, board, and expenses.

He had no idea of what he would study (there were no courses for Great Men, after all), only a vague notion that in an industrializing, commercial society a young man who wanted to get ahead should acquire "technique"—a professional skill.

The time came to say goodbye to his fellow hardware stackers and box rustlers. They envied him his escape from drudgery. Aaberg would miss his disciple most of all: "I am glad for you, but that leaves me here with no one to talk to but these swine! God damn!"

8. The Freshman

I attended the state university at Bloomington for several years, acquiring nothing save a disrespect for cut and dried methods of imparting information. This is not wholly true, however, for the beauty—natural and architectural—which invested the scene carried me to mental heights not previously attained.

—Dreiser to Richard Duffy (1901)

Bloomington in 1889 was a country village of a few hundred souls—a "charming place," Dreiser called it in a letter to a friend a few years later, probably gilding memory. When he got off the train he carried a single suitcase and wore one of Paul's cast-off suits cut down for him. He had three hundred dollars in his pocket, two hundred of which was earmarked for tuition.

From the train he could see the limestone quarries for which the area was famous—huge, rough-cut amphitheaters pitting the countryside, some filled with milky green water. Wagons hauled the enormous white blocks to the railroad spur, where they were piled on flatcars and hauled away by straining little locomotives. In the rich bottomland were small farms, and the hills roundabout were honeycombed with caves and underground rivers.

After years of dreary jobs, Bloomington was a peaceful haven. The campus had groves of trees and a creek winding through. Several modest stone and brick buildings housed classrooms and the library, and the six hundred students either lived in fraternity or sorority houses or boarded at private homes near campus. The university was a "social" school, attracting the sons and daughters of some of Indiana's most prosperous citizens: substantial bankers and hardware merchants, lawyers, manufacturers, and well-to-do farmers. A continuous whirl of parties and dances centered around the secret societies to which the elite youth belonged—the young men who would go into their fathers' businesses or pursue careers in law and politics, and the young women who would become their wives and doyennes of small-town society.

The faculty was top drawer. Heading the mathematics department were William Gifford Swain (later president of Swarthmore) and Rufus L. Green, who would achieve national prominence as an astronomer. Jeremiah Jenks, later at Cornell, taught sociology and political economy; Edward Howard Griggs, literature; and Von Holst, who headed the department at the University of Chicago, history.

During his three terms at I.U., Theodore never studied under these scholars, however. Although he was a special student and presumably could have selected a variety of courses, he chose the required freshman subjects, suggesting that he was aiming for a degree. He did not get off to a blazing start, receiving an incomplete in Anglo-Saxon, an X (passed without grade) in Latin, and a 1 (fair) in geometry. The second trimester, he received another X in Latin, a 1 in philosophy, and a conditional in freshman geometry. His third and final term he received his third X in Latin, a 2 (good) in something called "the study of words," and a 1 in freshman algebra. Dreiser's mediocre showing was probably due in part to his poor preparation but also to his lack of interest. As he later recalled: "I never learned, all the time I was there, quite what it was all about. I heard much talk of -ologies and -tries without grasping quite the fundamental fact that they were really dealing with plain, ordinary, everyday life—the forces about us. Somehow I had the vague uncertain notion that they did not concern ordinary life at all."

But Theodore's university year gave him the leisure to think and dream, and enabled him to associate with a kind of youth he never would have met otherwise. Some were as poor as he was, but wealthier boys also befriended him with the innate democracy of their small towns. He was an outsider, but not to the extent he later described. He joined Philomathean for example, the leading literary society, and was elected secretary.

Theodore boarded with a widow and made friends with Will Yakey, a young man who was his social opposite. Yakey came from a well-off family and was an athlete and lady's man. Why he was drawn to the gawky, painfully shy freshman is hard to fathom. Perhaps it was only proximity (they slept in the same bed); also, Yakey seems to have felt sorry for Dreiser and became his protector, finding him girls and urging him to do exercises to strengthen himself. But Theodore rebelled whenever the other overstepped the invisible line between friendliness and condescension. When Yakey became the star halfback on the Cream and Crimson eleven and insisted that Theodore attend the games as a sort of mascot, they drifted apart. Dreiser's resentment of Yakey's condescension was still fresh two years later when he complained, in a letter to a childhood friend, of Yakey's "belligerent attitude on all questions and a dominant desire to rule."

He promptly found another patron, a wealthy sophomore named Day Allen Willy, who also made an effort to fix him up with girls. The efforts proved fruitless because of Theodore's shyness and belief that he was homely. Whenever Willy found him a putatively willing coed, Theodore's fears of impotence prevented him from seducing her. When Eva Casper, another of Willy's sexual charities, played the aggressor and led Theodore to the point of consummation, he panicked—with the predictable result. He was so embarrassed that he never saw her again and avoided Willy for fear Eva had told him of his failure and everyone would laugh at him.

Imagining himself a complete gawk with women, Dreiser developed an idealized passion for a fifteen-year-old girl whom he saw walking to school one day. She was a pale, ethereal beauty, the image of Myrtle Weimar. Too shy to speak to her, he slipped her a note, asking her to meet him at the campus stile. She took it and scurried off like a frightened faun.

"Never in my life have I been more heart hungry—or sex-hungry if you will—than I was then," he remembered, "and never . . . was I so completely out of almost everything." An exaggeration; but everywhere, it seemed, youth and love were in ferment, while he stood in a corner and watched. Theodore sensed he didn't belong in the social whirl, and he was neglecting his studies. He moved out of the room he shared with Yakey, found another boardinghouse inhabited by young men who were as déclassé as he was, and buried himself in his studies.

At the new place he made friends of a different sort. One was a cheerful boy named Howard Hall, who was puny like Theodore. The two of them pursued fitness in hikes, exploring the caves in the hills outside Bloomington. Another was Russell Ratliff, who was working his way through school by running a student laundry service. They were drawn to each other by a mutual interest in philosophy. Together they read and discussed the writings of the contemporary thinkers who were revising philosophy in light of Charles Darwin's theory of evolution—Herbert Spencer, Thomas Huxley, Alfred Russell Wallace. Ratliff agonized over the Darwinist interpretation of society. What relevance had it to the growing disparities between rich and poor, the running warfare between capital and labor, the prevalence of vice and crime? Ratliff introduced Theodore to Tolstoy's *What to Do?*, which called for men to return to simple physical labor, each working only to provide for his own needs, eliminating exploitation of the poor by the rich. But Darwinism seemed to deny the possibility of altruism. Weren't most men selfish, grasping, driven blindly by instincts? The two were unable to reconcile their views (unlike Tolstoy, who simply rejected Darwinism and sociological positivism).

So they talked and studied into the warm spring nights, Theodore's attention constantly straying to the sounds of singing and gaiety wafting in the window from the fraternity houses. Here he was, a well-read young man with a good, if untrained mind, of a philosophical bent, who if he had concentrated on his studies (which in fits and starts he did), might have accomplished something; instead his work bored him and he chose to moon over what he couldn't have.

He visited his family during the Christmas holiday, a stay enlivened when Willy blew in and took him for a tour of the city's red-light district. Theodore refused to let his friend buy him a prostitute, however; he was too fearful of the reality of the sex he dreamed of. Taking stock of himself during the Christmas break, he decided that college had brought him no closer to acquiring the *technique* one needed to rise; his scientific inclination was thwarted by his poor record in geometry, a prerequisite to further study. He had no interest in business or law. Somehow he would rise, but college seemed too dry, too bookish. It was all very well for youths like Yakey and Willy, who would return to their small towns, where their way would be smoothed by family connections. For him, however, the future was opaque.

Back on campus the oaks and maples and the arbutus vines on campus soon burst into green, and the lazy buzz of preparations for commencement hung in the air. Theodore did not attend the customary bonfire at which the freshmen ceremonially burned their books. Instead, he walked by the home of the girl with the ethereal face, hoping to catch a glimpse of her. In vain.

In later years Dreiser emphasized his failure at the university, while playing down his modest successes. What really seemed to irk him was his social failure, the same exclusion that had plagued him in Warsaw, the thwarted yearning to move among the glittering youths. Actually he had had a respectable freshman year. True, his grades were not stellar, but he probably could have improved them in his sophomore year. Socially, he found a niche, even if it wasn't the one his outlandish dreams called for; he belonged, as mentioned, to the literary society, which was where his interests lay, and a contemporary group photograph shows that he also joined a spelunkers club.

Certainly Theodore liked the prestige of being able to call himself a "college man," and on occasion claimed to have spent "several years" at the university. To another friend (a young woman he was trying to impress) he wrote nostalgically of "those dear old college days" that "made every cloud a silver legend." He also felt superior to his brothers and sisters, a feeling he already had in a vague way, as a result of his reading, but now given the stamp of academic experience. In truth he liked the dream of college, but had no patience with the boring realities of it. He was too much in a hurry, with little idea of where he was going or how to get there. At the time his thoughts about returning were more ambivalent than he later let on, and Miss Fielding would probably have staked him to another year. Still, when he returned to Chicago, his omnipresent family soon overshadowed the evanescent joys of college life, and they became silver legend. Upon his arrival home in June 1890, Theodore found his family still precariously together. Economic pressures had eased temporarily, but the clashes of these sharply individualistic temperaments raged on. It was a remarkable brood. Though most of them, for want of a good education, had not developed their talents to the fullest, their temperaments had bloomed riotously. They were driven this way and that by strong emotions, but Sarah remained their center of gravity.

As the summer drew on, they all noticed changes in her. She had grown unusually stout, and the added pounds slowed her down. Theodore would always remember his mother padding heavily about her daily rounds: up at 4:00 or 5:00 in the morning to prepare breakfast, washing dishes, cleaning, sweeping, sewing, resting awhile and telling stories to whoever gathered around. Now her bottomless well of strength was going dry, and the spectacle of her deterioration threw terror into their hearts. One day she could drag herself around no longer; a heavy lassitude seemed to have settled on her, reminding Theodore of that winter in Sullivan.

He had taken a job with a real estate promoter named Asa Conklin, a Civil War pensioner who had inherited five hundred dollars and intended to parlay it into a fortune in the city's rampant land boom. Theodore's job was to call on prospects, and he was given the use of a horse and buggy so he could take his mother for rides. But the excursions did little good. By now Sarah had turned over the housekeeping to the girls, who, chastened by her illness, could not do enough for her. Theresa became a fanatically devoted nurse, while Mame, confronted with the unspeakable, dropped her airs and vied with Theresa in running the house. Theodore sat with his mother by the hour, playing songs on a mandolin he had bought in college, talking "profound nonsense." Arrogating to himself the status of college man, he considered himself "a kind of patron-philosophic stoic, the hope of all the family."

Sarah's health continued to deteriorate. One day in October, when Theodore took her for a drive to view the autumnal foliage, she told him, "You know, I feel so strange these days, I hate to see the leaves turning. I'm afraid I won't see them again."

"Oh, ma, how you talk!" he said. "You're just feeling blue now because you're sick."

"You think so? Well, maybe. But I have such strange dreams. Last night I dreamed my father and mother were near me and motioning to me."

Remembering the great store she put in such portents, Theodore's heart sank. He begged his sisters to call another doctor, who told them nothing more could be done for Sarah. She slipped in and out of a coma.

One day Theodore came home at lunchtime to check on her. Theresa told him she was feeling better and seemed cheerful. When he entered the bedroom, Sarah asked him to help her sit up. Theresa insisted she lie back and rest, but Sarah refused. She began to struggle, kicking off the covers. Theodore rushed to the bed and with great difficulty hoisted her into a sitting position. He went out for a moment, and when he came back, she was on the side of the bed. Then she strained forward as though trying to walk, shuddered, and collapsed. Theodore rushed to her side and supported her soft bulk as she sank to the floor. Her deeply weary eyes stared blankly for a moment, then glowed with a preternatural light. But the light clicked out; a veil closed over.

"Mamma! Mamma!" Theodore cried. Theresa was at his side in an instant, clasping Sarah, chafing her hands, breaking into a spasm of uncontrollable sobs. Rushing in, Paul, Sr., saw his wife lying on the floor and knelt beside her. "I'm old. I should have gone first!" he moaned.

Soon the others came in, one by one—all save Sylvia, and Em, who were in New York; Rome, who was wandering; and young Paul, who at that moment was giving a matinee performance in Chicago. Ed had to fetch Al and met him on his way home. "She's dead! She's dead!" Ed called the moment he saw his brother.

Al looked at him strangely a moment, then said, "Well, that's the end of our home."

9. An End and a Beginning

It always seemed to me that no one ever wanted me *enough,* unless it was my mother.

—Dreiser, *Dawn* (1931)

hey were a family rocked by a catastrophe. Old Paul sagged in a chair, mumbling to himself. Al was numb. "I can't cry," he said. "I don't know what's the matter with me but I can't." The girls—a shattered Theresa and a subdued Mame—were sobbing quietly. Ed could not bring himself to look at the body. But Paul, who had rushed home after finishing his matinee performance, sat alone with his mother for a long time; when he finally emerged he was shaken and weeping.

Each in his or her own way grasped the truth Al had uttered. It was the end of the family. The woman who had woven an emotional web of tenderness that enmeshed them all was gone, leaving an emptiness at the center.

To Theodore his mother's death was a seismic shock. "The earth seemed truly black and rent," he said later. "The ground shook under me. I dreamed sad, racking dreams for years." In those dreams Sarah was alive, but about to abandon him forever, as she had threatened to do when he was a child. Sometimes she was in a boat, drifting slowly away through a woolly fog.

The family went about the preparations for her burial like automatons. Old Paul had summoned a priest as soon as his grief gave way to fear for her immortal soul. But when the little Bavarian cleric arrived, he was appalled to learn that Sarah had not been to church in many months and demanded to know why he had not been summoned earlier. Old Paul wrung his hands, while the children looked on with growing anger. Sarah had drifted away from the Church, and her husband had let the matter of her salvation slide. The old quarrel between them had lost its fire.

Paul had abandoned messianism and retreated into some private monastic cell in his mind. When Sarah's vitality began to ebb, he simply refused to believe she would die. It was unthinkable; they all depended on her so much.

But the officious priest was insensitive to the heartbeat of this family. All he knew was that the rules had been broken, and for this the punishment prescribed was burial in unconsecrated ground. Old Paul was devastated—the everlasting shame of it! While he pleaded, the others, led by a spirited Theresa, screamed at the pastor. Finally a compromise was hammered out whereby the family pledged to pay for Masses and burn candles in Sarah's name, and the priest said he would allow her to be buried in a Catholic cemetery.

Before Sarah was laid to rest in St. Boniface Cemetery, the fissures in the family began to reopen. The other sisters disapproved of Sylvia— and by extension her protector, Emma—because Sylvia had abandoned little Carl. Emma was prospering, however. Arriving from New York, she made a grand entrance decked out in fine dresses and furs, and old Paul fussed over her. But his hostility toward Sylvia was adamantine. When she offered him her lips in a penitential gesture, he gave them a perfunctory brush. Sylvia's chief critic was Mame, but given Mame's own slips from virtue, Theodore thought, her moralizing was hypocritical.

Shortly after the funeral, Rome turned up. No one had notified him because no one knew where he was. But he had had a dream, he told Theodore, in which Sarah appeared on a black horse. Rome took this as an omen that she was ill and hurried home. When he learned he was too late, he wept long, drank deep, and disappeared once more.

Old Paul tried to assume the leadership of the family, but it was no use. The soul of this household was gone, leaving only the residue of rivalries and centrifugal ambition. As was his wont, Paul insisted on paying his debts on the mark, including the $2.50 a week for Masses and candles for Sarah. The children grumbled about this levy—particularly Theodore, who was hard pressed for cash at this point. Asa Conklin, his employer at the real estate office, was an ineffectual businessman and so little money was coming in to the firm that Theodore's wages were in arrears. Conklin's wife was actually the shrewder of the two, but she spent her time running a religious mission for the poor and homeless. Asa, white bearded and still wearing his blue Union uniform with gold buttons, came to the office each day and dozed away the hours at his desk. When Theodore took the job he had been fired with ambition, and he scoured the streets for likely rentals and houses for sale. He succeeded in snaring a number of clients, but not enough of them to make the business pay.

When he told his father why he could no longer contribute to the family fund, old Paul stormed into Conklin's office and demanded that his son be paid. Deeply embarrassed, the pensioner offered to let Theodore use his credit at a clothing store to buy a blue chinchilla suit. In his new finery, Theodore cut a dandyish figure dashing about in the borrowed buggy, but with no money coming in he had to seek another job.

He hated tramping the streets again, "asking cool, indifferent men who cared no more for me than they did for the dust and paper in the street if they would give me something to do." He saw himself as a failure; after nineteen years of life he had no skills, no place, no prospects. In the grim light of his situation he regretted not returning to Indiana University; when the student newspaper queried him about his plans, he supplied them with the following item for the January 1891 issue: "Theodore Dreiser, through Freshman last year, is working in Chicago at present, where his home is. He expects to return to I.U. next year." The expectation was no more than a wistful hope; Dreiser was too proud to admit that he was unemployed and near penniless.

His ambition to succeed still burned, but the only path open to him seemed to lie in the world of commerce, where his rise thus far had been glacial. In his dreams the upper class was the "one to which I properly belonged." Poverty was a black hole, the lives of common working people brutish, grinding with drudgery (though they enjoyed greater sexual freedom that the middle class). His mother had always aspired to a niche in the middle classes for her brood, but after their Warsaw experience, Theodore was repelled by the bourgeois proprieties even though he admired the "stable virtues, order, care" which middle-class life represented: the stable home life he had rarely known. But the moneyed aristocracy lived the truly glamorous life in America, and the press gave them idolatrous coverage, as though they were American royalty—which in a way they were, lacking only the hereditary security of Europe's nobility.

With inflated dreams (and his own mother's favoritism to give him an added push), he could not settle on a conventional career, could not set his foot stolidly on the bottom rung of the clerical ladder, work diligently, live frugally, and save up for the day when opportunity knocked. In that incapacity he was not alone; all the Dreiser children, save Ed and Claire, were similarly lacking in "character." Mame had gone from Colonel Silsby to snaring the wealthy Brennan (who doted on her) and had adopted the airs of his class even though she was not accepted by his family. Em and

Sylvia had tried the backstreet route to social success in Warsaw, and then bartered their youth to rich older men in return for the trappings of luxury without the legitimization of marriage. (When Emma finally did marry, it was to a thief turned ward heeler, so respectability continued to elude her. Sylvia settled down after "years and years of an insatiate sex life.") Then there was the family bright angel, young Paul, who, defying his father, had taken the vaguely wicked theater route which led to celebrity and wealth, though not necessarily social acceptance. And the dark angel, Rome, who in his violent, inarticulate way, demanded to know why he shouldn't be as rich as Vanderbilt and who fled from conventional ties. Sarah had encouraged them to dream of regaining the lost Sullivan, yet she had never showed them the way to achieve it.

Claire and Ed would never travel by such devious paths and would end up as solid bourgeoisie (Ed after a detour as an actor). Significantly, both identified most strongly with their father. Ed never remembered old Paul with the bitterness Theodore did, and toward the end of his life Claire worshiped her father as a saint. Theodore, the most sensitive and imaginative of the triumvirate, had been wounded most deeply by the poverty of the Terre Haute and Sullivan years, and the picture of the return of Paul, Jr., like the hero of a melodrama to save them, was etched indelibly on his brain. He sensed the contrasts of wealth and poverty more keenly than did Ed and Claire. As a result, he was more skittish and high-strung, more prone to pendulum swings of mood, often prompted by changes in the family's circumstances (and, later, his own). And Theodore's faith in the potency of money to fulfill dreams was the strongest of all. His dreams effortlessly carried him where he did not know the way.

Now he was shaken by the glandular storms of adolescence and harried by the necessity of earning a living—most likely doing work he hated. So the dreaming part of his brain worked double overtime in compensation, blowing bubbles of sexual fulfillment with beautiful women, of riches and ease, of himself as the head of a "thrashing great business," or as a famous writer or philosopher, or the consort of a rich woman— or even as an ordinary Union Park businessman coming home to a cozy flat, the aroma of dinner cooking on the stove, a wife and child greeting him lovingly.

Sustained by his dreams, even though they could treacherously, suddenly, throw him into the pit of despair, mocking him with their improbability, he tramped the streets and finally found a place as a driver for a large laundry. It was hard work—twelve hours a day, including Saturdays, when he did not get home until midnight. Nevertheless, he throve. The job kept him out in the open air and his health improved. It was an adventure to drive his wagon through the raucous, clogged streets, and making deliveries and pickups gave him entrée into a cross section of homes, from the mansions of the wealthy to the cottages of the poor.

The female workers at the laundry inflamed him. They toiled in a large, low-ceilinged room, over huge vats and tubs of steaming soapy water, centrifuges that spun the sheets and towels dry, and great rotary irons. Most of them were immigrants—German, Irish, Polish. With their plump arms bared, their skirts tucked in to expose smooth white calves, and their faces pink from the steam, they exuded a coarse sensuality. Upstairs, other, more genteel women handled the skilled labor—ironing shirt collars or doing delicate piecework. These were prim old maids or young girls, dainty in shirtwaists and long skirts.

He became friendly with a dark-haired cashier named Nellie Anderson. Born to Scottish immigrant parents, she was two years older than he. Their flirtation soon evolved to furtive kisses at the end of the day. Although Nellie was shy and genteel, she was no prude, and gradually permitted more serious kisses and hugs, though she never allowed his avidly groping hands to stroke her breasts and body. He liked her parents, but when he sensed that they were eyeing him as a likely son-in-law, he got cold feet. He feared entrapment in marriage, and Nellie was too conventional for him. Too fond of her to break it off, however, he let matters drift, secretly going out with other women, and slowly emerging from the chrysalis of adolescence.

His career at the laundry flourished. When a rival firm dangled a two-dollar raise before him, Theodore snapped at it. His new employers were three Jewish brothers, who thought Theodore might bring his old customers with him. They assigned him to a new route, however, which took him into the business heart, where the congestion was fierce. The brothers were never satisfied with his performance, accusing him of laziness; he found them vulgar and dishonest. The culmination of his dislike for them came when he collided with another wagon, damaging his new vehicle beyond repair. The accident had been the other driver's fault, but the brothers blamed him and he was summarily fired. Afterward their uncle slyly suggested to him that all would be forgiven if he would testify in a lawsuit against the other driver's company. Theodore refused.

Now he was tramping the streets again, wondering if he "would always be getting poor places and losing them." But one of his women customers, who had been impressed by his energy and efficiency, recommended him to her husband, Frank Nesbit, whose business was selling clocks, rugs, lampshades, and other bric-a-brac of garish taste and shoddy workmanship on the installment plan. In need of a collector, Nesbit sent for Theodore, liked his looks, and hired him on the spot. The work was enjoyable, for it enabled him to study exotic species of humanity in their native habitats. His duties were simple: he and a half dozen other collectors fanned out through the meaner streets, picking up weekly payments from the purchasers of Nesbit's gimcracks. Most paid up, though occasionally a hulking man would answer the door and dare him to collect. Hard cases like these Theodore wrote off as bad debts. He found he could complete his rounds by two in the afternoon, leaving him the rest of the day to spend at the library or the art museums.

The job took him to slums where he knocked at the doors of mean shanties with rubble-strewn yards. Fat black women leered invitingly at him; blowsy widows told him how lonely they were; strumpets rose naked from their beds and slouched, yawning, to the mantel to get the money to pay him—or offered him their services instead. He walked down streets paved with cedar blocks that had splintered and rotted, emblems of the city's heedless growth. In middle-class neighborhoods housewives sometimes signaled him to go around to the back door so their neighbors wouldn't see they were buying on time. Pictures registered in his brain: "The palls of heavy manufacturing smoke that hung low over the city like impending hurricanes; the storms of wintry snow or sleety rain; the glow of yellow lights in little shops at evening; mile after mile, where people were stirring and bustling over potatoes, flour, cabbages. . . . " Scenes like Goose Island in the Chicago River, its black muck littered with abandoned boats and shanties; the new Masonic Temple, which at twenty-two stories was the tallest building in the world; the vulcanic din of factories, such as the vast Pullman yards, where grimy workers toiled like ants, fabricating the machines of this new, dynamic age.

He began to paint word portraits in his mind of what he saw. Sometimes he would chant these "word-dreams" as he walked, fancying himself an orator like the Reverend Frank W. Gunsaulus, a prominent evangelist spellbinder of the day. He began writing them down, and when he had a respectable number of them, sent them to Eugene Field, whose "Sharps & Flats" column in the Chicago *Daily News* printed verse and short items by outside contributors. Field never replied, but Theodore hardly expected him to: the act of sending them was communication enough.

Although his college days seemed a dream, the intellectual interests kindled there were still vibrant. Miss Fielding invited him to visit her in Highland Park, the suburb where she was principal, and on those occasions she dinned into him the importance of developing his mind. Mind—that was the passport to the world of wealth, fame, and love. His college friend Ratliff had turned up, still an idealist and a Tolstoyan. Ratliff had been doing charitable work among the poor, and was becoming convinced that the Tolstoyan model of one who gives up his wealth and seeks to change poor people was wrong. Such efforts had little effect over the long run; they were just tinkering with one part of the social engine. Rather, one should devote one's efforts to overhauling the engine completely by working for sound reform measures.

As it happened, Theodore was searching for a religious faith that was relevant to the modern world, an alternative to his father's ingrown Catholic dogmatism. The social gospel—a movement to engage Christianity in the solution of contemporary problems—appealed to his idealistic side. He read the best-selling novels of Mrs. Humphry Ward, particularly *Robert Elsmere*, which described a minister's crisis of faith which leads him to challenge the comfortable pieties of his parishioners. The message could be found in popular novels like William T. Stead's *If Christ Came to Chicago!* and Charles M. Sheldon's *In His Steps*, which asked what would happen if people applied Christ's teachings in their everyday lives. The settlement house movement, which Jane Addams had sparked in Chicago in the nineties, reflected these religious concerns. The city also spawned a notable group of dissident preachers—men like Gunsaulus and H. W. Thomas, a fiery old man who had been expelled from the Methodist ministry for his radical views. They demonstrated to Theodore the possibility of a nondoctrinal, rational religion. He listened to Thomas's sermons at McVickar's Theater and attended meetings of the Ethical Culture Society.

Accompanying him to these affairs was a new love, a friend of Claire's at The Fair named Lois Zahn. Claire had brought her home at Christmastime, and although Lois was seeing another man regularly, a thirty-five-year-old clerk with a steady job who wanted to marry her, she was attracted to Theodore and flirted with him. She admired his height, now a gangling six feet, and his soft, light brown hair which he combed in a pompadour.

During that Christmas of 1891, Theodore felt a growing pressure to make some decision about his future, to choose some profession in which he was at least interested, rather than continue working at jobs he loathed. What precipitated these thoughts was the loss of his position with the

Nesbit company. His growing prosperity had made him desire more of the little luxuries. He had varied the routine of fifteen-cent meals of ham and beans at little restaurants frequented by other clerks with one-dollar-fifty-cent feasts at fancy places like Delmonico's. He also longed for better clothes, a necessity for impressing the girls he would someday meet, and settled his aspirations on a new overcoat. When one of Nesbit's customers paid off her bill in full, to save the trouble of making weekly payments, he was struck by an idea. Other customers had paid him in full. Why not keep the money the next time it happened and give Nesbit the thirty-five-cent installment? He would eventually pay off the entire debt, so he was not really cheating his boss.

The scheme seemed foolproof; soon he had accumulated twenty-five dollars, with which he bought a handsome woolen overcoat that would protect him from the frigid gales off Lake Michigan. But he had overestimated the docility of his clients. A woman complained that her clock was not working. When told that collector Dreiser's records showed she still owed money, she insisted she had paid him in full. Nesbit, who had probably seen this trick before, summoned Theodore immediately and demanded to know where the money was. Unable to brazen it out, he confessed. Nesbit had taken a liking to him and shook his head sadly. "Theodore," he said, "if you're going to begin anything like this, you know, you're on the straight road to hell, and I can't keep you." Deeply ashamed, Theodore went home and wrote a letter of apology, promising to pay back the money. He never did, but he never again stole from an employer.

While he was between jobs at Christmastime, he took a temporary post doling out toys for the Chicago *Herald*'s help-the-neediest campaign. Although he was disillusioned to learn that the toys were shoddy and secondhand, he stuck it out because the ad had promised "promotion possible," meaning, he hoped, a reporter's job. This turned out to be a false hope, but the boy's ambition was set ablaze. The *Herald*'s offices, with their marble floors and bronze decorations at the entrance, proclaimed important matters were taking place. What reporters actually did, he could only imagine. They were sent out to write up a story about a traffic accident or a murder, he supposed, and that seemed easy and exciting. Whenever he saw a minor collision on his daily rounds, Theodore would compose an account in his mind.

He also imagined that newspapermen consorted on a daily basis with the great, the wealthy, and the famous. Their press cards were tickets to the grand world, and he envisioned himself exchanging sage observations with some magnate and then setting them down in his mahogany-paneled office. After which he would adjourn to a fine restaurant and regale his fellow scriveners with cynical observations. If he could not be a millionaire, this was the next best thing, and it did not require a long, arduous climb up the commercial ladder. In April 1891, having saved sixty-five dollars, Theodore quit a collector's job he had obtained in the mean-time, vowing he would become a reporter or starve.

It was a time of endings and beginnings. The beginnings were barely begun, but the ending had a sonorous finality to it. He and Claire, in rare agreement, decided to move and Ed agreed to come along. When the three youngest announced their intention to leave, old Paul became distraught, pleading with them to stay, but Theodore was implacable. He delivered an ultimatum: they would stay only if Mame's airs were curbed. But their father's authority had been eroded by a thousand little rebellions among his fissiparous brood over the years.

Paul said goodbye at the doorway, looking old and frail. "I'm sorry, Dorsch," he told Theodore. "I done the best I could. The girls they won't ever agree, it seems. I try, but I don't seem to do any good. I have prayed these last few days. . . . I hope you don't ever feel sorry."

It was an ending. Youth was over. Looking back, Theodore said, "Well might I write above the gravestone of my youth, 'He yearned.' "

Part Two

APPRENTICESHIP

10. The Cub

Goaded by the knowledge that only sixty-five dollars stood between him and the streets, Theodore began to lay siege to the offices of Chicago's papers, making the rounds at noon and again in the evening for a solid week. Always he met rebuffs, but at least he was used to these by now, and it was exciting just to be outside looking in. Then he hit upon the idea of staking out one office until his face became so familiar that he would be hired. He selected the *Globe,* the smallest and least prosperous of the city's dailies and the black sheep of Chicago journalism. Its owner was a man named Mike McDonald, who had made his money as Chicago's gambling czar. While serving his fellowman in this fashion, Mike drew the notice of the reform element in town and became its favorite target. The great organs of Victor F. Lawson (the *Morning News,* later the *Record*) and Joseph Medill (the *Tribune*) thundered against him. The criticism got under McDonald's skin, and he decided to buy a paper and hit back at the reformers and police brass (harsh treatment from the press had also moved Charles Yerkes, Chicago's "traction king," to found his own newspaper, the *Inter-Ocean*). It was an era of personal journalism, and every owner freely injected his biases into his news and editorials. Medill, a foe of horse racing, once led a successful crusade to close Washington Park, a favorite turf venue for Chicago society to see and be seen. When his sports page reported the general unhappiness among the haut monde, Medill fired the entire staff. McDonald's favorite exposés were of police corruption and the fail-ures of reform administrations to curb vice.

Theodore began his siege by sitting near a door opening into an alley. From his post he could watch the reporters at their desks. At one end of the room, behind a railing, like Quakers on the facing bench, were the desks of the editors, including the city editor, who ritually told him, "Nothing today. There's not a thing in sight." His tone was not unkind, though, and Theodore did not lose hope. Theodore became a familiar face to the six or seven reporters who made up the *Globe*'s staff, and some of them tossed him scraps of advice on the staff situation at their paper and tips on potential jobs at other places.

After he had kept a faithful vigil for two weeks, John Maxwell, the copy editor, a corpulent man with cynical eyes, asked him what he was doing there. When Theodore told him he wanted a job, Maxwell said, "Why did you pick the *Globe*? Don't you know it's the poorest paper in Chicago?"

Theodore explained that was why he had chosen it, on the theory it would have a faster turnover. Maxwell nodded approvingly and advised him to hang around. In June the Democratic National Convention would convene in the city to choose its presidential candidate, and the *Globe* was sure to hire some part-timers as it expanded its coverage.

After a month or so, his chance came. Gissel, the *Globe*'s single editorial writer, a "squeak," a house mastiff who mauled McDonald's enemies, had written a novel—a nostalgic tale of boyhood in the popular *Tom Saw-yer* vein, and had the idea that his former high school classmates would buy copies because of their fond memories of him. He proposed that Theodore call on every one of them, and if he did a good job, he could have a tryout on the paper. Since he was an experienced door-to-door man of sorts already, Theodore jumped at the offer and managed to sell more than a hundred.

Having done his job and relayed to Gissel exaggerated reports of his ex-classmates' enduring love for him (most hardly remembered him), he confidently awaited his elevation to the staff. Nothing happened, until Maxwell insisted he be hired as one of the extra reporters the paper was taking on for the convention. Theodore got the job at fifteen dollars a week, with the guarantee of at least two weeks' work.

And so, decked out in new clothes—light check trousers, a bright blue coat and vest, a brown fedora, and squeaky yellow shoes—the new cub began his assignment. Theodore's knowledge of politics was vague; he read the newspapers and had ingested a smattering of John Stuart Mill,

Tolstoy, and other social philosophers, but he had not the slightest grasp of the intricacies of Tammany Hall, free silver, and patronage.

The reporter heading the *Globe*'s election team told him to hang around the lobbies of the hotels where the delegates were staying. With his nickel-plated press star pinned on his lapel, Theodore importuned whoever was warming a chair, feeling a rush of self-importance when he said the magic words, "I'm a reporter from the *Globe*." On his first day he collared Senator "Pitchfork Ben" Tillman, who said he didn't want to be bothered. Clutching this inscrutable fragment, and his firsthand impressions of the Richelieu Hotel lobby during a political convention, Theodore hurried back to the office and filled nine pages of foolscap on both sides with vague speculations on the Democratic Party and the future of the Republic. His violation of the most elementary rule of journalism—don't write on both sides of the paper—was only the first of the sins he had committed. The city editor turned him over to John Maxwell for salvage. Maxwell asked Theodore to tell him exactly what he had seen, and listened for a time to the torrent of incoherent impressions before saying, "No, no! . . . It's not news."

When Theodore recounted his abortive interview with Pitchfork Ben, Maxwell said, "Very good! You haven't anything to write." And then he proceeded to explain what news was, adding that the *Globe* had a political reporter who would sketch the big picture. Theodore's job was to pick up bits of news that his betters could fit into that larger mosaic. He suggested that Theodore concentrate on discovering the name of the party's likely nominee, since there was no obvious front-runner.

He returned to the hotel and buttonholed Tammany Hall boss Richard Croker, who brushed him off. Then it happened—the lucky break that sometimes comes to drunks and cub reporters. Gossiping in the bar with some fellow journalists, he bruited the name of a southern dark horse, Senator McEntee, who happened to be standing nearby and tipped him off to an important meeting of the party leaders in progress. Theodore got his story. Rewritten by Maxwell, it made the front page:

CLEVELAND AND GRAY THE TICKET

Cleveland and Gray will be the ticket. This was decided upon last night at a meeting of the leaders of the party held at the Richelieu hotel in the apartments of ex-Secretary [of the Navy William Collins] Whitney.

This momentous result was achieved almost solely by the efforts of Mr. Whitney, who has been moving heaven and earth to destroy the last vestige of opposition to Mr. Cleveland.

It is a concession to the Tammany men, who dictated the nomination of ex-Gov. [of Indiana Isaac Pusey] Gray for second place. Gray was [New York Governor David Bennett] Hill's choice for the tail end of the ticket should the latter have been nominated, but as the Tammany men learned that this was impossible, they took what they could get—the second place.

Save for the fact that Adlai E. Stevenson ultimately was the convention's choice for the second slot on the ticket, it was a solid scoop.

Grateful for Maxwell's help on the story, Theodore placed his hand on his shoulder. The other stiffened. "Cut the gentle con work," he snapped. "Life is a Goddamned stinking, treacherous game, and nine hundred and ninety-nine men out of every thousand are bastards. . . . Don't think I'm not one, or that I'm a genial ass that can be worked by every Tom, Dick and Harry."

Despite his misanthropy, Maxwell liked Theodore and was a valuable ally, persuading the *Globe*'s management to hire him as a full-time reporter when the convention was over. He covered small fires, arrests, and assorted mayhem, dreaming of one day joining his idol, Eugene Field, on the journalistic heights. Field had become a national celebrity (and considerably richer) through the popular children's verse he wrote—including "Little Boy Blue" and "Wynken, Blynken, and Nod." (Less well known was the bawdy doggerel he recited at stag parties.)

Other journalists with a literary bent—notably George Ade, whose column in the *Record*, "Stories of the Streets and the Town," was beginning to be noticed, and Finley Peter Dunne, whose Irish saloonkeeper Mr. Dooley was dispensing shrewd political wit—were following the trail Field had broken. All of them had developed a distinctive style of commentary on city life. Field satirized the cultural pretensions of the packinghouse aristocracy, Dunne skewered the corruption and bombast of contemporary politics, and Ade had an unerring ear for the vernacular of Chicago's newly arrived. All of them affirmed ethnic or small-town values, while poking fun at the rich, the greenhorn, the solemn young clerk from a small town. Together with Brand Whitlock, a reporter and aspiring novelist who later left to work for Governor John P. Altgeld, Opie Read, publisher of *The Arkansas Traveler*, Melvin E. Stone of the *Daily News*, and other literarily inclined journalists (including a political reporter for the *Herald* named Arthur Henry, whom Theodore may have met), they formed a literary circle of sorts called the Whitechapel Club, which met in a dimly lit room off an alley near the *News* office. There they sat around a coffin, which served as a table, amid a decor of hangman's nooses, murder weapons, skulls made into lamps, and other *memento mori* and talked of books and concocted elaborate practical jokes.

A more reclusive figure in Chicago's literary world was the novelist Henry B. Fuller, who came from an old, wealthy family and in 1892 had published *The Cliff-Dwellers*, which portrayed with uncommon realism and gentle satire the city's old and new rich. He materialized irregularly at the Little Room, the generic name given to Friday studio gatherings of artists and writers. Among the latter were Harriet Monroe, a vibrant young woman from an old Chicago family, who would found *Poetry;* George Barr McCutcheon, a journalist who would win popular success with his best-selling romance *Graustark*, and Hamlin Garland, author of the grim *Main-Traveled Roads*.

Many of Chicago's reporters and editors had scholarly credentials. Field translated Horace. Dr. Frank Reilly, managing editor of the *Daily News*, a Civil War surgeon, was an expert in public health and sanitation. Charles N. Wheeler was a Greek scholar and political pundit, and Sherman Duffy, who knew Greek and Latin, was made sports editor after Medill's purge and went on to hold that post on the *Journal*. Several Chicago reporters became prominent in politics—Ray Stannard Baker, muckraker and press secretary to Woodrow Wilson; George B. Harvey, editor and ambassador to England; Brand Whitlock, mayor of Toledo, and Robert W. Wooly, director of the United States Mint.

At the *Globe*, however, Theodore was on the far side of the tracks from these luminaries; the paper drew from the sludge of Chicago's journalistic pool. The most prominent name on the staff was typical of these castoffs. He was John T. McEnnis, who took over as city editor after Theodore had been on the job several months. McEnnis was a brilliant writer but he had a headline-sized thirst. After losing a succession of jobs because of drinking, he had sunk to the *Globe*. Raucous and uncouth-looking, clad in a long frock coat and a pair of shiny black trousers that were perpetually caked with tobacco, food, and liquor, he had a bulbous red nose like J. P. Morgan's.

As it turned out, McEnnis took a fatherly interest in Theodore, giving him encouragement and useful advice, then borrowing a dollar for whiskey. Part of the attraction, perhaps, was that he liked Theodore's writing and saw in him a reflection of his own youthful promise. Reporting had tapped a "nosing and speculative tendency" in Theodore. Now he had a license to roam the streets, collecting swatches of colorful material and basting them into articles. McEnnis assigned him to do a feature article for the Sunday edition about a vile slum known as Cheyenne, bounded by Van Buren, State, and Sixteenth streets and by the river. Such neighborhoods weren't new to him, but now he had the duty of getting them down on paper. Coming upon Cheyenne on a hot summer night, he noted the denizens, most of them immigrants, sleeping on the sidewalks, in doorways, and on the roofs. The area was unutterably filthy—

> From surrounding basements issue the sickening heat of laundries, or equally as bad, the fumes of whisky and the odors from the underground restaurant. The alleys reek with decaying garbage and human filth, the vile odors carrying disease and death to those already weakened and enervated by such environment. No really healthy face greets the eye. No ray of intelligence beams from the faces of the wandering, jaded inhabitants.

He closes the piece by asking what can be done for these unfortunates: "They nestle in the very arms of free education and are not aroused. Let the wise of the world ponder. Let human pity extend a helping hand."

Dreiser, of course, had no solutions, but he was fascinated and moved by the spectacle. Maxwell applauded his effort and told him, "Maybe you're cut out to be a writer after all, not just an ordinary newspaper man." Soon Theodore was touring the morgue, pondering the fate of the unidentified dead:

> A cheap coffin, six feet of earth, a headstone bearing a number only and the potter's field has gained an addition.
> The morgue-keeper was asked for some stories of unidentified bodies. He replied:
> "An unknown has no story."

Maxwell and McEnnis preferred straight news stories, but such personal journalism was popular at the time, and Theodore showed a knack for it, though he also did a notable exposé of fake auction shops that caused a considerable stir. But he liked doing Sunday supplement features, full of color and lurid details. Charles Dickens was the model, and the idea was to give readers a roller-coaster ride from the lower depths to the haut monde, employing the free-roaming gaze of the novelist and ending on a moral note, lest it be thought that the newspaper was sanctioning the vice portrayed in such loving detail. This kind of writing could be called sensationalism, but it unleashed the imaginations—and pens— of tyro novelists. Many writers of the nineties and early 1900s—Stephen Crane, David Graham Phillips, Richard Harding Davis, Brand Whitlock, Harold Frederic—served literary internships in the city rooms. As Phillips wrote: "The daily newspaper sustains the same relation to the young writer as the hospital to the medical student. It is the first great school of practical experience."

Theodore also published his first piece of fiction in the *Globe,* a fable headed "The Return of Genius." The author used the pseudonym "Carl Dreiser" at Maxwell's behest. (Maxwell had nicknamed him Carl, but Theodore told his family he wanted to credit his nephew, Sylvia's unwanted child, who was still living with them.) The story tells of a young writer "whose younger years were spent in poverty and sorrow" and who longs for fame, riches, and pleasure. The God of Genius appears and offers him "glory and an undying fame" on one condition: that he never know of them on earth. The Genius agrees and is whisked to a fabulous palace where he enjoys every luxury. But at last he begins to miss the admiration and praise of men. The god appears once more and sends him back to the world, where he is stripped of his immortality. "In thine own hand is the power—the strength," a voice whispers to him. "Achieve thine own glory. It is for thee alone to do this. In effort, will thy genius be sharpened. Aid from the gods would but destroy thee."

His own life among men—and women—was in better shape. He had taken a pleasant room in Ogden Place, overlooking Union Park, with its green lawns surrounding a small lagoon. His affair with Lois was progressing favorably. He was half in love with her and she more than that with him, though she continued to see her faithful Harry as insurance. But he continued to court her, driven by his sexual yearnings. One night Dreiser persuaded her to accompany him to a cheap room on Halstead Street. It was his first experience with taking a woman to bed, and his old fears of impotence welled up. After penetrating her partially, he had a premature ejaculation. The excitement and her gentle remonstrances— "I don't mean to cry. I can't help it"—were probably the causes, but Theodore regarded it as another defeat. They met again, but he could not bring himself to take her virginity and contented himself with emissions into his handkerchief. Although Lois was a virgin, she was willing, and he could have taken her. When he did not, she was frustrated and told him, "Dorse, I think you're the most bashful man I ever knew."

It was a measure of how tightly the old bugaboos about masturbation gripped him that years later Dreiser thought of his precipitousness as "impotence." In a passage later expurgated from *Newspaper Days,* he writes, "though I ejaculated copiously, I still imagined I was impotent due to youthful errors and bordering on senility." Inexperience and an inordinate fear of making Lois pregnant—not only because a child would tie him down to her but because of his memories of his sisters' experiences—

probably go far in explaining his unsatisfactory performance. He considered "potency" equivalent to ejaculating inside a woman, which created the risk of impregnation, and he seems not to have known about contraceptives. It could almost be said that Dreiser's anxiety served as a psychic coitus interruptus. It induced a compulsion to withhold that was overridden by his strong desire, with the result that he "spent" uncontrollably.

His retentiveness was reinforced by the prevailing sexology which, as we have seen, held that to "spend" meant "overdrawing" one's account. In the expurgated passage Dreiser goes on to compare himself to "the religionist who imagines he is close to heaven yet is a cold narrow grasping skinflint." He realized he had been a sexual miser, inhibited by the puritanical mores of the time from consummating his desire in the fullest sense. Had the affair progressed, he would have felt obligated to "do right" by Lois even if they didn't have a child, and he didn't want to marry her. In his heart of hearts he felt superior to her: his boundless ambitions included some vague, ineffably beautiful and wealthy feminine figure who would embody all his dreams of success. Against such a fantasy Lois seemed commonplace.

Theodore's "buzzing dreams of living in Chicago and becoming a great man" left little room for her, and his eyes constantly roved to others. One day, as they were about to go to an Ethical Culture Society lecture, she told him, "You don't care any more. I'm going back to Harry." Theodore halfheartedly protested his affection, but he knew she was right; he didn't care enough to give Lois what she really wanted—marriage, or at least living together.

Perhaps it is wrong to attribute too much significance to a first sexual experience—and these trysts with Lois were his first with a woman he cared about. But at least until his marriage eight years later, the act of sexual intercourse was a furtive, almost mechanical affair. With Lois, Theodore had an opportunity to enter into a fuller relationship, but his ambitions and fears that she might entrap him prevented this. From then on, this earliest imprinting conflicted strongly with his yearnings for a romantic, loving relationship, and he could rarely be satisfied.

Meanwhile, events in his life were moving at such a pace that Lois was already receding into the past. Impressed by the job he had done on the auction-shop series, McEnnis urged him to seek a position on a larger paper, where he could get the training he needed. The editor suggested as a likely possibility the St. Louis *Globe-Democrat*, which, under the editorship of the great Joseph McCullagh, was one of the best papers in the West. The *Globe-Democrat*'s traveling correspondent, who was a friend of McEnnis's, was in Chicago to cover the preparations for the 1893 World's Fair and dropped by to see his old colleague. McEnnis suggested that Theodore work for him on a free-lance basis as a legman, conducting man-in-the-street interviews. This served as a tryout, and when Theodore completed the work successfully, McEnnis told the *Globe-Democrat* man to ask McCullagh to take him on. In a few weeks a wire came offering a reporter's job at twenty dollars per week, and on October 29, 1892, Theodore drew his last pay envelope from the Chicago *Globe*.

There remained only Lois, whom he could have won back from Harry just by saying the word. Theodore thought of telling her about the job, but procrastinated until the night before he was to leave. After a farewell dinner with McEnnis, he went to her house but found she was out with Harry. Angered, he decided to punish her by not saying goodbye. The next morning, as the train passed by her house, Theodore felt a keen pang of sadness. Another desertion: parting, change, pained him, always.

11. St. Louis Days

> I went into newspaper work . . . and from that time dates my
> real contact with life—murders, arson, rape, sodomy, bribery,
> corruption, trickery and false witness in every conceivable form.
> The cards were put down so fast before me for a while that I
> was rather stunned. Finally, I got used to the game and rather
> liked it.
> —Dreiser to H. L. Mencken (1916)

> What reporters know and don't report is news—not from the
> newspaper's point of view, but from the sociologists' and the
> novelists'.
> —Lincoln Steffens

S t. Louis in 1892 was "busy, rich, substantial," recalled Henry
Burke, a newspaper editor at the time. Its largely German and
southern population of four hundred fifty thousand was hard-
working and prosperous. The city's papers were full of talk about
a world's fair in 1903 to commemorate the Louisiana Purchase—a counterblast to Chicago's World Columbian Exposition, scheduled to open in 1893.

The city had a lively press, with four major dailies of regional, if not
national, stature: William Hyde's *Republic*, small and struggling; W. E.
Scripps's *Chronicle;* the *Globe-Democrat*, edited by McCullagh, "Little Mac"
in Eugene Field's poem; and the *Post-Dispatch*, which had exploded into
prominence in the 1880s under the brilliant, neurasthenic Joseph Pulitzer,
who boosted circulation with his crusades against municipal corruption.
That and spiritualism, because of the large number of Swedenborgians
living in the city, were the number-one topics. By the time Theodore
arrived, Pulitzer had moved on to New York, purchased the ailing *World*,
and used his patented editorial mix of sensation and crusading journalism
to drive its readership to the top of the city's papers.

Perhaps it was best that Theodore was unaware of the intensely competitive journalistic world he was entering, or he might have taken the

train back to Chicago. But he was consumed by a desire to rise—"ambitious, until my very heart aches . . . ," he wrote his childhood friend Emma Rector. One day he thought of becoming a business magnate, the next a newspaper publisher. His first meeting with Little Mac turned his fancies in still another direction: he would become a great editor.

McCullagh was a short, solid man, who inhabited a tiny office piled to the ceiling with newspapers. Painfully shy and introverted, he kept the only three chairs covered so visitors would not be encouraged to linger. Under his editorship the *Globe-Democrat* had prospered. It concentrated on presenting world, national, and regional news in a sober, almost stodgy style, but its editorials were crisp and sometimes whimsical. When the "old man" wrote one, his mordant wit crackled through every paragraph. McCullagh had won his spurs as a correspondent in the Civil War, and now he was a venerated figure in the city, especially among the farmers and small-town people of the region, who made pilgrimages to the *Globe-Democrat* and stood outside his office in attitudes of hushed reverence. But reporters considered him a remote and chilling figure. When another paper scooped him, he would wait at the water cooler and fire the first reporter who appeared (and rehire him a few days later).

McCullagh barely spoke to his new man, merely shaking hands and mumbling, while continuing to chew a cigar, "Um, yuss! Um, yuss! See Mr. Mitchell in the city room, Mr. Mitchell—um, yuss."

Mitchell, a large, chunky man with a perpetual scowl, took an instant dislike to Theodore and dispatched him to a phony address. When Theodore returned, the assistant city editor, a mousy man named Hartung, said it was just like Mitchell to break in a new man in that way. For the next several days Theodore drew routine assignments. The city seemed a backwater compared to Chicago, and the reporters were cowed by their bosses. "I despised St. Louis at first," Dreiser wrote Emma Rector. Reporters arrived around noon, checked the assignment book, and if their name was in it, went out to cover the story indicated. They might write up two or three "sticks," short news items of about one hundred fifty words, a day. (McCullagh had pioneered the human-interest story that ended on a note of pathos. And oddly, for such a shy man, he stressed articles about personalities—celebrity interviews in particular.) Finally, at 11:30, Mitchell would scowl at them and say, "You boys can go now."

Those first weeks in St. Louis were lonely ones. When Theodore went home to his small hall bedroom, the walls seemed bare and cold. He missed an enveloping feminine presence—his mother, his sisters. He had an "intensely uxorious nature" and needed "feminine ministrations," so he gravitated to boardinghouses run by widows, who maintained the homelike atmosphere he craved. After a time, he was drawn to the landladies themselves. His first boardinghouse was run by a fat and fortyish woman who wasted little time in confiding that her husband was consumptive and neglected her. When she became bolder and touched him suggestively he "flushed like a girl." But her overripe coyness sickened him, and one night he sneaked out.

He found another room in a neighborhood near Broadway and the theatrical and restaurant district. His new landlady was Mrs. Zernouse, a stocky, attractive, Slavic widow with two young children. She provided a clean, spacious room with high windows, which Theodore decorated in what he conceived as a bohemian style—tapestry-cloth curtains, a bookshelf for his few volumes, and a plaster statue of Venus on the mantel. The nude fascinated Mrs. Zernouse, who took it as a sign that he was a devilish fellow. Unlike his previous landlady, she was attractive in a coarse, peasant way. She teased him constantly about the statuette, which embarrassed him.

While covering a church revival meeting, Theodore picked up a girl his own age. Emboldened when she let him hold her hand, he invited her to his rooms. He began kissing her and then undressed her, negotiating over each article of clothing, until she balked finally at one last flimsy, token undergarment. But by then he had won, and they spent a delicious night together. It was his first full sexual experience, and she seemed to enjoy their lovemaking. She left at dawn without giving him her address, and he never saw her again.

When Mrs. Zernouse came in to clean, she spotted a hairpin on the sheets. Rather than being shocked, she made bawdy remarks, and soon they tumbled into the still unmade bed. She was passionate in her transports, uttering abandoned cries and achieving a climax quickly. Theodore, in his inexperience, took her ardor as a sign of abnormality. This liaison continued until he tired of her, feeling she was beneath him socially and intellectually. Too cowardly to make a clean break, he rented another room, gradually moved his things, and tiptoed out late one night for good.

Again his landlady was a widow who was drawn to Theodore's stripling charm. Petite and prettier than the others, she was also more socially acceptable and owned a large brick house on Chestnut Street with windows trimmed in white stone. The affair proceeded like the previous one. When Theodore returned after midnight, she would come up and slip into his bed; or he would go to her bedroom. She was demonstrative, giving him little love bites, coiling her legs tightly about him, and uttering muffled cries. "Do you like that? Do you like to do it to me?" Her behavior shocked Theodore; he thought "the mere act of silent, secretive friction was enough." Although his doubts about his ability to perform had been vanquished, in the aftermath he was filled with black remorse, scoring himself as a "wastrel," a criminal fornicator.

Dreiser's sexual nature was split: one part of him was drawn to women of experience who were openly sensual and took the lead in the affair ("made their way" with him). But another part sought an ideal, which meant fresh, young girls with petal-smooth faces and innocent eyes, like the nymph in the painting "September Morn." In contrast to the sexually demanding older women, these visions were sweet, shy, and demure. As he wrote Emma Rector, "I adore the womanly traits, when confined and not roughened by the world." But only the women of a certain age were available, while the dream girls eluded him.

He found a few male friends of his own age, two mainly, artists at the *Globe-Democrat* named Peter B. McCord and Dick Wood, who affected a bohemian life-style and liked to talk long into the night about art and life over growlers of beer. Wood dressed like a *fin-de-siècle* dandy—flowing black tie, loose linen shirt, soft felt hat, cape, and boutonniere of violets, like the character Des Esseintes in Huysmans's novel *A Rebours*. His "studio" was furnished with pictures, hangings, and curious *objets d'art*, and was intended to resemble a Latin Quarter atelier. Actually, Wood's illustrations in the paper showed him to be a mediocre artist: his real interest lay in writing. A highlight of their evenings was a reading from his latest work in progress. Too fine for the world of journalism, Wood aspired to marry a wealthy woman who would finance his literary career. He complained continually about the chalk dust he breathed (newspaper artists etched their drawings on plates through a film of chalk dust) and predicted that he would die of tuberculosis.

Like Wood, McCord was a small-town boy from the Middle West. He wore practical work clothes and an unkempt black beard, and there was nothing affected about him. His wide-ranging curiosity led him to works of natural philosophy. He collected information about primitive sexual rites from forbidden books purchased at dusty secondhand shops. He loved to perpetrate elaborate hoaxes, often assuming a false identity. Though brought up a Catholic, McCord seemed to Theodore a true pagan, a free spirit who had sloughed off the constricting skin of convention and come to an acceptance of life in all its grim and pleasurable facets.

Tiring of amorous landladies, Theodore had moved to bachelor's quar-

ters in a large building at 12 South Broadway, inhabited by other reporters. He was not as close to his other co-workers as to Wood and McCord,
but they made a lasting impression on him. Like most newsrooms, the
Globe-Democrat's held a number of reporters with literary ambitions, whose
example made Theodore think seriously of becoming a writer of some
kind. Several former newsmen from St. Louis had achieved commercial
success in New York, notably the playwright Augustus Thomas, who had
put in a short stint as a reporter on the *Post-Dispatch*. Though Thomas
had probably spent more time with local theater troupes than in journalism, he was a beacon to St. Louis reporters who dreamed of fame and
fortune in New York.

Two of the oddest fish in American journalism were also spawned in
the Queen City's newsrooms. One was William Cowper Brann, who went
on to found a monthly Texas newspaper called *The Iconoclast*, which
preached atheism and antipuritanism. Unfortunately, Brann also followed
Pulitzer's lead in exposing political corruption and was fatally shot by the
object of one of his crusades.

The other notable figure, who had acquired only a local reputation in
Theodore's day—and that a bad one—was William Marion Reedy. In
the 1880s, Reedy had been a star feature writer on the *Republic* and the
Globe-Democrat, but drink, the curse of the working press, almost felled
him. After McCullagh rusticated him, he was reduced to toiling for a
gossip sheet called *Star Sayings*. In 1890 he joined forces with two other
St. Louisans (one of them, a tough investigative reporter named Red Gal-
vin, became something of a nemesis to Theodore, beating him out of
several scoops by superior cunning), to found a weekly called the *Sunday
Mirror*. Reedy, a paunchy Irishman with a cherubic face and bulging eyes,
was an insider par excellence and knew St. Louis politics intimately. But
he continued to scandalize propriety with his alcoholic escapades and,
later, his marriages to a prostitute and a madam.

An autodidact but formidably well read, Reedy would quote Herod-
otus to a fellow reporter on the police beat, Vincent Beyars, a linguist
and a scholar who chanted verses from the ancient *Edda* in reply. At this
time Reedy was caught up in the Decadent movement in literature. He
had interviewed Oscar Wilde when the playwright visited St. Louis in
1882 and discovered a sound thinker underneath the dandified exterior.
Wilde led him to European writers like Huysmans, whose protest against
convention and exploration of hitherto taboo literary subjects intrigued
the unconventional Reedy. He next came under the spell of an American
follower of the Decadent school named Francis Saltus, a minor versifier

of more pretension than talent. Saltus's half-brother Edgar had imported Schopenhauerian pessimism to American shores with his book *The Philosophy of Disenchantment*. But Decadence was an aesthetic way-station to Reedy; his next stop would be realism in literature, of which he would become the leading champion in Theodore's generation.

The realism in the air in St. Louis at this time was distinctly foreign in origin; called "naturalism," it was signed by names like Emile Zola and Guy de Maupassant. There was an acolyte of the Parisian school at the *Globe-Democrat*, a jovial young reporter named Bob Hazard, who had been dining out for years on an unpublished novel he had written with a fellow journalist named Grubb, who was later murdered in an opium den. Hazard's story was reputed to be too daring to be published in the United States, but many of the younger reporters, who were writing their own callow novels or bad poetry in imitation of Swinburne or Rossetti, had read it and pronounced it fine.

Theodore longed to join Hazard's coterie but was too timid to introduce himself. One night, however, they met under proper literary auspices. As Theodore was working on a story, he was handed a letter from Lois. She wrote that she understood his feelings had changed and asked him to return her letters. She closed with a postscript that deeply moved him: "I stood by the window last night and looked out on the street. The moon was shining and those dead trees over the way were waving in the wind. I saw the moon on that little pool of water over in the field. It looked like silver. Oh, Theo, I wish I were dead."

Plunged into a deep, poetic melancholy, Dreiser stared out the window awhile, then took some clean sheets of copy paper and began writing, almost automatically. The words spilled onto the page, arranging themselves in what resembled stanzas of poetry.

At that moment, Hazard passed by, paused, and asked him what he was doing. When Theodore explained, Hazard gave him some professional advice: there's no money in poetry, write a play. Theodore countered that being a famous poet seemed a glorious destiny, but Hazard, with the seasoning of his twenty-six years and the confidence of the city room's most famous unpublished novelist, conjured up visions of the luxurious life a playwright like Augustus Thomas must lead. Hazard had switched his literary ambitions to the theater.

His novel was a pastiche of Zola and Balzac and was set in Paris, which its authors had probably visited only in the works of their literary models. The plot involved an actress-heroine named Theo, whose lover, a newspaperman, is wrongly accused of murder and goes to the guillotine despite her efforts to save him. This tragic tale was spiced with midnight suppers and other sinful Parisian diversions. In one daring scene Theo has a fight with a rival and spanks her with a hairbrush. It seemed to Dreiser strong stuff.

That Hazard and Grubb's novel was unpublishable in the United States made Dreiser aware of the gulf between what American contemporary novels portrayed as life and what he had seen as a reporter. One night, dressed in evening clothes, he might cover the Veiled Prophets Ball, assiduously reporting the feminine fashions on display, and then rush to a shabby slum dwelling where a father had just murdered his children. The pitiful story was good for a stick to titillate readers at breakfasttime. However, when he obtained information on a compromising relationship between a visiting medium and a local society woman, which the man's landlady had viewed through the keyhole, he was told it was unprintable, though the amorous spiritualist was confronted with the information and strongly advised to leave town.

A similar schism existed in Theodore's own nature. He continued to see life in terms of poetic yearnings, romantic ambitions, and dreamy, far-off vistas. His attitude toward women was that of a young romantic, yet he knew from experience that women too had desires. He watched the whores who worked near his office, lolling on the front steps or sashaying languidly down the street—and sometimes he hired their services or just talked to them. (Office rumor had it that he procured girls for Mitchell, though Dreiser does not mention this in his autobiography.)

Following Hazard's advice, he wrote a comic opera about an Indiana farmer who is transported back in time to the Aztec empire and is acclaimed as a god. (The plot owed something to Mark Twain's novel *A Connecticut Yankee in King Arthur's Court*.) The Hoosier hero is corrupted by his absolute power and becomes a tyrant, but a beautiful Aztec maiden teaches him mercy and compassion, and he transforms his domain into a republic. Theodore timidly read the libretto to Wood and McCord, who, to his relief, pronounced it promising.

While Theodore was thus addling his brain with dreams of Broadway glory by night, by day he was pursuing an apprenticeship for his real vocation. The expectation was beginning to form in some literary circles that the great American novel—a realistic one that Told the Truth About Life—would be written by a reporter. In 1893, the year that a young, sallow-faced free-lance journalist named Stephen Crane had privately published a novel about the slums called *Maggie: A Girl of the Streets*, James L. Ford, a critic, had prophesied:

The enduring novel of New York will be written . . . by [a] very young man from Park Row or Herald Square. . . . When this young man sits down to write that novel it will be because he is so full of his subjects, so thoroughly in sympathy with his characters—no matter whether he takes them from an opium-joint in Mott Street or a ball at Delmonico's—and so familiar with the various influences which have shaped their destinies that he will set about his task with the firm conviction that he has a story to tell the world.

With his energy, inquisitiveness, and powers of observation, Theodore was a natural reporter. In the noise and confusion of the newsroom, under the pressure of the daily deadline, he acquired the habits of speed and concentration. Description and narrative force, not style, were his strong points. When getting the facts bored him, he let his imagination do his legwork.

One of his copy editors, Captain Webb, remembered him as "a splendid writer," but "better as a writer than in getting news."

Though you sent him for a "story" and he might not get it, he always, as I recall, brought back some story. He had an inventive fictional mind. But you must watch his copy. On a good "story" he might get carried away from the facts by his own emotion. Or again, he might come in with a yarn you just knew didn't happen.

Once, Webb recalled, Theodore handed in a description of four old men's daily card game. Each of them, he wrote, played a different game, yet somehow they came up with a winner for every hand. Suspecting a tall tale, Webb used the story as a feature rather than a news item.

Perhaps in tribute to his inventive powers, Theodore was assigned to write a column of hotel news called "Heard in the Corridors." He might interview visiting celebrities, like Annie Besant, the Theosophist and Hindu mystic, whom he asked if greater progress might be achieved when self-interest was replaced by concern for the welfare of others. She told him that it would: "Men set up before themselves a false God; they follow a misleading standard. Though they achieve every honor that this world can bestow and everlasting fame they are still unhappy." Ambitious as he was, Theodore was drawn to such idealistic sentiments.

Hazard, who had previously written the column, told Theodore that when there were no visiting firemen, he could invent talks with imaginary people. Dreiser reported, for example, a story related to him by "Olney Wade of Elizabeth, New Jersey." It is a highly fictionalized account of the life of Christian Aaberg, the cynical Dane at Hibbard, Spencer, and

Bartlett. As "Wade" tells it, Aaberg, the son of a nobleman, squandered his annuity on drink and was reduced to running an elevator. Then he inherited seventy thousand dollars and bought a country place, where he devoted himself to full-time debauchery. He died young, surrounded by "books and fine wines." In another item, "F. T. Croyden," a former bill collector, deplores easy-payment plans because they encourage people to buy luxuries they cannot afford. A fictitious businessman advises, "If you want to be successful and immensely wealthy, you can only do it one way and that is to manufacture something." The "Reverend J. B. Lemill" deplored the immorality of contemporary literature and music— the trend toward the "realistic and the luxurious." There is also a report of a poets' convention in Warsaw, in which Theodore satirizes his boy-hood abode's cultural aridity.

"Heard in the Corridors" was something he did with his left hand while continuing to handle general assignments. In the city's rough-and-tumble journalistic life, he learned that to lie and cheat was all right: the only sin was to be scooped. His dreams had undergone a severe overhauling during his spell in St. Louis, he later wrote Emma Rector. "Worldly experience" had "shattered the ideals" of youth, and he looked back on "the years of labor I have endured . . . with a feeling akin to sorrow and almost disgust." Corresponding with Emma filled him with halcyon memories of the Sullivan days, when they had played together on the Rector farm, which was about eight miles from the town. He recalled "the gorgeous sun rising over one of the neighboring hill crests bathed with that early dew which is pearly and casting its molten arrows aslant the meadow and the stream that ran near your house." Now, however, he rarely saw the sun rise, since "I never get up until 10 A.M."

He was, he confessed, "of a gloomy disposition, and a dreamer, to whom everything romantic appeals, and everything (in fact nothing but the) natural in real action, satisfies." In other words, Theodore sought escape into a world of fantasy but remained fascinated by the color and variety of the urban scene. Poetry was one escape—the door to "a world of beauty and light where sorrow and want could never be."

There was a certain amount of preening in his flirtatious letters to Emma, but also a surprising amount of candor. He provided a romanticized but probably accurate portrait of himself at age twenty-two:

When you look at [my picture], you will see egotism written in every lineament; a strong presentiment of self love in every expression. I have a semi-Roman nose, a high forehead and an Austrian lip, with the edges of my teeth always showing. I wear my hair long, and part it in the middle, only to brush it roughly back from the temples. Then I'm six feet tall, but never look it, and very frail of physique. I always feel ill, and people say I look cold and distant. I dislike companionship, as far as numbers go, and care only for a few friends, who like what I like. I prefer writing to reading and would rather see for myself, than hear or read all the knowledge of the world. You will not like me, I'm sure.

The cynicism he half-boasted of was the protective coating over a sensitive nature that was lacerated by the horrors he had seen as a reporter. Some were so shocking he could not veil them in "colorful" writing or shape them into fiction—for example, a train wreck he covered.

One Sunday afternoon he was idling at the *Globe-Democrat* office when a man burst in and told him excitedly that a passenger train had run through an open switch and crashed into some tanker cars filled with oil on a spur track three miles from Alton, Illinois. None of the editors were in at the time, so Theodore hurried to the scene on his own initiative, planning to telegraph his copy from the station. Shortly after he arrived there was a tremendous explosion. Flames burning around the tanks had caused two unruptured tanks to heat up, turning them into huge bombs which hurled a fiendish shrapnel—jagged chunks of white-hot metal and scalding gobbets of oil—onto the crowd of bystanders: "Many forms were instantly transformed to blazing, screaming, running, rolling bodies, crying loudly for mercy and aid. These tortured souls threw themselves to the ground and rolled about on the earth. They threw their burning hands to tortured, flame-lit faces. . . . They clawed and bit the earth, and then, with an agonizing gasp, sunk, faint and dying, into a deathly stillness."

Goyaesque scenes of horror passed before his eyes; he tore off his coat and tried to beat out the flames on one shrieking human torch, to no avail.

All the while his mind was recording the carnage, thinking how to describe it. When a train bringing doctors and nurses arrived from Alton, he hurried to the depot where the dead and dying were taken. He watched physicians bend briefly over the charred figures on the litters. Most of them were beyond help. He automatically recorded the name of each doctor and other details. An "accommodation" (local) train was commandeered and the victims were placed aboard. Theodore came along and rode to Alton, where waiting wagons carried the sufferers to St. Joseph's hospital. He saw dirty, oil-soaked rags being cut away from bodies, laying bare scorched skin, swollen lips and noses, and "eyes that were either burned out or were flame-eaten and encrusted with blood and dust."

A throng of relatives wandered about vainly seeking a recognizable face among the seared masks, whispering comforting words in their ears when they found a loved one. A group of parents, whose children had gone to the site of the wreck, milled in the hall asking for information. Theodore decided to act. He went from stretcher to stretcher, asking the occupant his or her name and address, telling those who protested, "Someone will want to know about you."

> To those inquiring the list was read, and as the last name was spoken and "that's all" ejaculated a score of sighs were heard, for many an anxious heart knew that the loved one was not in the list.

Later in the afternoon another train arrived bearing more victims. Some begged the doctors to kill them. "I'm blind," moaned one. "Oh, to be without eyes, to have the light shut out forever, that is too much. I want to die! I want to die!" Then, "a loving mother bowed low over the moaning form and buried her tear-stained face and misery-convulsed form in the clothing that shielded her son."

By then Dick Wood had arrived to sketch the scene, but he was in a state of shock and kept muttering, "It's hell, I tell you." Theodore sent him to gather additional details and returned to the explosion site to interview eyewitnesses, who told of narrow escapes or of futilely trying to assist agonized victims. A man aiding one human torch cut away the man's clothes; in pulling off the sleeve of his coat, the skin of the victim's hand stuck to it and came off like a glove: "I tried . . . to console him in his awful plight. . . . He recognized my voice, and, with his burned and sightless eyes turned toward me, he managed to inform me that he was my old friend, James Murray."

Finally, the city desk ordered Theodore to return and write up his story. When he arrived at the newsroom, reporters who had already read his brief telegraphed dispatches were talking excitedly. He went straight to his desk; as he finished each page, a boy would snatch it away and run it to the copy desk. A knot of reporters gathered around him. At last it was done, and the next morning's front-page headlines proclaimed:

BURNED TO DEATH
One of the Most Disastrous Railroad Casualties Ever Recorded
Six People Killed Outright and a Score of Others Will Die
The Fearful Holocaust Brought About by an Open Switch
—Total Destruction of the Big Four's Southwestern
Limited Express—Heartrending Scenes

The next day Theodore went out again to compile further grisly details and to cover the coroner's investigation that was in progress. The two accounts add up to a remarkable job of reporting—long, vivid, gruesome (in the style of the times), yet ballasted with facts. Such was Theodore's lack of confidence in himself, however, that in the aftermath he was seized by a fear that he had been wrong to chase after the story without getting permission. Mitchell, who disliked him, might think he had a swelled head; perhaps he would be fired. He was so late returning from his second trip that he missed his daily assignment, so when Mitchell told him that McCullagh wanted to see him right away, his heart sank.

"You called for me, Mr. McCullagh?" Theodore said timidly.

"Mmm, yuss, yuss!" the editor replied, not looking at him. "I wanted to say that I liked that story you wrote, very much indeed. A fine piece of work, a fine piece of work!" He reached into his pocket, extracted a thick roll, and peeled off a twenty-dollar bill. "I like to recognize a good piece of work when I see it. I have raised your salary five dollars, and I would like to give you this."

Theodore took the bill, muttered his thanks, and stumbled out the door a reporter.

12. Love in the White City

I went to Jackson Park and saw what is left of the dear old World's Fair where I learned to love you.

—Dreiser to Sara Osborne White (1898)

Dreiser took advantage of McCullagh's patronage to request a job he coveted—that of theater critic. It was a part-time post, but at least it would give him some respite from stories of death and poverty. As he ruefully recalled, the theater was "a world of unreality which unfortunately fell in with the wildest of my youthful imaginings." Although part of him recognized the falsity of the stage illusions—the glamorous drawing rooms, all plush and gilt, fairy tales of mythical kingdoms inhabited by fat comedians and pretty soubrettes in sexy knee-length dresses or tights—he succumbed to them nevertheless.

His reviews consisted mainly of a recitation of the plot and the names of the players, garnished with a few complimentary phrases. He favored the romantic action and realistic settings of plays like *Paul Kauvar:* "Those who are interested in the exciting times of the great French revolution, with its streams of blood and mountains of dead bodies, can get an inkling of the dramatic realism of it all. . . ." Plays with compelling love scenes also elicited rhapsodies from the *Globe-Democrat*'s critic. Theodore's predilection for gushing tributes got him into trouble, however, when in a review of a performance by Mme. Sissieretta Jones, known as "the black Patti," he wrote that her voice "brings back visions of the still glassy water and soft-swaying branches of some drowsy nook in summertime." The applause was "wild and long." He didn't know that to praise a black person without condescension in language traditionally used for whites was an unforgivable trespass of the color barrier in St. Louis.

A rival Democratic paper (despite its name, the *Globe-Democrat* was Republican) pounced on the review in a snide editorial that attributed the sentiments to McCullagh and twitted him for his admiration of "the colored lady, name of Jones," his "fervid tribute to this chocolate-hued diva." It was another example of Mac's "black Republicanism." Another paper, without referring to Theodore's notice, set him straight on the facts: "The African temperament is essentially and hopelessly inartistic."

But Theodore's worst gaffe as theater critic was yet to come. The city editor had resented Theodore's appealing over his head to Little Mac for the critic's job, and was doing everything he could to pay him back. One night, when Theodore looked forward to covering the openings of three plays, stopping briefly at each and sampling the performance before writing his notices, Mitchell ordered him to cover a streetcar holdup. Theodore hastily wrote his reviews from the press releases (a common practice among reviewers) and hurried off to his assignment. Unfortunately, heavy rain across the river in Illinois had washed out sections of the track, and the actors in two of the shows did not arrive. McCullagh was again the butt of jokes among the wiseacres who gathered at such journalists' watering places as the La Clede and Phil Hackett's bar, and again the Democratic editorialists went after him in full cry. General descriptions of the shows would have been bad enough, but Theodore had ventured some criticism of the acting. For example, on the prizefighter Peter Jackson, who was starring in *Uncle Tom's Cabin*, he commented that while he could be judged only by the standard of James J. Corbett, John L. Sullivan, and other pugilists who were then the rage as theatrical-circuit performers, "he is even better than the standard, and manages to lay aside that very suggestive, not to say sluggestive, air of trouble-picking which accompanies constantly his guild brothers." Theodore was probably remembering Sullivan's performance a few months previously, before which the ex-champ had "dallied with the 'black bottle' as only John L. can dally with it." When a man in the balcony laughed at his drunken antics, Sullivan challenged him to a fight and then shambled through the performance, handling his leading lady "so carelessly that the paint on her left cheek was rubbed off, giving the woman much pain and embarrassment."

The other papers were not impressed by the critic's sage observations on fighters as actors. After alluding to Mac's alleged praise for "the colored Patti," the *Chronicle* quoted the words about Jackson and those about Lewis, an actor in the other missing show. It concluded: "McCullagh is becoming a faddist in the phenomena of the occult. Was it a manifestation springing from an unknown, unseen beyond that inspired his criticism on Peter Jackson and Jeffrey Lewis?"

When this disaster blew up in his face, Theodore realized he was in for a severe reprimand or worse from Little Mac, whom he revered. To save his editor the trouble, he left a letter of resignation and slunk away without a word to any of his colleagues. For several days he remained in his room, afraid he might meet someone he knew on the street. When his money ran low, he obtained a job at the *Republic*, the smallest and shakiest of the city's dailies, for only eighteen dollars a week. The city editor, H. B. Wandell, was a small, birdlike man with piercing eyes who drove his reporters hard, demanding sensational stories that would enable the *Republic* to beat the *Globe-Democrat*. A connoisseur of news, he tucked into a good story like a gourmet devouring a soufflé. He demanded novelistic touches of color and atmosphere. "Remember Zola and Balzac, my boy, remember Zola and Balzac," he exhorted.

Theodore was assigned to writing Sunday specials and acted as a traveling correspondent, a job that took him on short junkets outside St. Louis. On one of these assignments he covered a story that haunted him for years. It was a typical border-state occurrence: the lynching of a Negro for raping a white woman. This particular assault was a brutal one; an ex-convict named John Buckner had ravaged two women, one white and one black, near the village of Valley Park, fifteen miles from St. Louis. A posse was quickly formed and he was arrested at his family's home and taken to the jail in Manchester.

Theodore's first dispatch from the scene told of Buckner's (referred to as the "brute" and the "demon") "fiendish brutality"; in keeping with the contemporary style the word "rape" was never mentioned, however, though the description of his assaults left no doubts as to his intentions. The first story closes with a mention of the possibility of a lynching, and as if egging the townsfolk on, the editors at the *Republic* headlined it:

THIS CALLS FOR HEMP
St. Louis County the Scene of a Shocking Outrage

A NEGRO'S DOUBLE CRIME
Two Women Criminally Assaulted . . . One Being Colored and the Other White—Desperate Struggle of the Latter for Her Honor—The Brute Captured and in a Fair Way to Be Summarily Dealt With

That night a mob formed and headed for the jail, where they brushed by complaisant guards and abducted the prisoner. In a lengthy follow-up story the next day, Theodore described the scene. The moon had gone down but in the light of the yellow flames of lanterns the Negro's face could be seen, "distorted with all the fear of a hunted beast . . . waiting more like an animal than a human being." He was taken to a bridge in a cart, and a rope tied round his neck. Then, "with a swish and a plunge his great hulking body strained at the cord." Later, Theodore, who may or may not have been present at the lynching, visited the dead man's home, and described the scene: "Through the broken panes of a miserable log window the pale, cloudbroken moonlight cast its sheen and shadow on the gaunt form of the dead, while near it, in a dark corner, wept the mother of the erring boy alone."

Here a glint of compassion breaks through like the moon through the clouds in a story that otherwise reflects the racist point of view of the lynchers, who are described, in a low-keyed way, as ridding the community of a dangerous criminal. A hastily called coroner's jury found that Buckner "came to his death at the hands of a person or persons unknown" and the *Republic* headlined Theodore's second account approvingly:

TEN-FOOT DROP

The Brute Who Assaulted Mrs. Al Mungo and Miss Alice Harrison Is Taken From His Home by a Band of Quiet, Determined Men and Sent Into Eternity Before the Dawn of the Day Following His Fiendish Outrages

That story was not the one that won him his spurs at the *Republic* however. What caught Wandell's—and, more important, the publisher's—fancy was a humorous account Theodore wrote about the preparations for an annual charity baseball game between the Owls and the Elk lodges, sponsored by the paper. Here Theodore tapped a hitherto unknown talent for low comedy, as well as bringing to bear his proven ability to fictionalize. He invented a do-or-die rivalry between the principals, as this excerpt shows: "Mr. Joy said he had not kicked in anybody's rib for some time and Mr. Melchin said that the taste of the last ear he chewed off had completely faded away, so that both are pining for the enemy and the enemy is equally pining for them. The contest is to be for nine innings only and no gouging. Any kind of bat from a rail to a board fence is permissible, and no one will be permitted to hit the ball twice at the same time."

He found he could dash off each article in an hour, leaving him time to dally with his current landlady. What is more, the series brought him more local celebrity than anything he had previously written. Local gentry would clap him on the back in the bar at the La Clede or in hotel lobbies. But Dreiser had a sneaking suspicion of this talent; it was all too easy, too superficial—the writing as well as the fame, and later he decided that the comic approach was not for him. "Mere humor, such as I could achieve when I chose, seemed always to require for its foundation the most trivial of incidents, whereas huge and massive conditions underlay tragedy and all the more forceful aspects of life."

At the *Republic*, with Wandell's encouragement, Theodore also was able to inject more colorful descriptions into his stories. He wandered the streets as a roving reporter, taking note of the sights and sounds, and using them to pump up a routine "colored people's murder" into a sympathetic "Catfish Row" epic of Negro life, evocative of "the hot river waterfronts . . . the sing-song sleepiness of the levee boat-landings . . . the idle, dreamy character of the slow-moving boats," the trinket peddler's cry—"Eyah—Rings, Pins, Buckles, Ribbons!"

The popularity of his series on the charity baseball game led to another choice assignment—escorting a group of prize-winning schoolteachers to the World's Columbian Exposition in Chicago, which had just opened. The contest was sponsored by the *Republic*, and Theodore was supposed to record the young women's reactions to the fair's wonders.

He was at this time a presentable enough young man, with a taste in clothing that ran to the outré. "Jock" Belairs, a police reporter for the *Republic*, later recalled Dreiser as "the best dressed newspaperman I ever knew . . . a classy dresser," who liked to don evening wear when the assignment called for it. Theodore affected soft collars and flowing ties like Dick Wood wore. Another colleague, however, thought he had "a genius for overdressing. Just the wrong touch in his effort to be altogether correct . . . he was so ambitious, so anxious to appear as one 'to the manner born.' " Dreiser's description of himself as a youth was more succinct: "a parvenu."

After the initial awkwardness, Theodore introduced himself to the schoolmarms on the train and found himself a caliph in a harem of Middle Western beauties who vied for his attention. Only one of the girls held back, and for this reason she interested him. She was tiny and sweet-faced, with eyes like a startled doe's and long auburn hair, which she wore in braids pulled together in a bun. He sensed in her "an intense something . . . that was concealed by an air of supreme innocence and maidenly reserve." She somehow seemed older, more mature, than the others. Perhaps her reserve conveyed that, perhaps it was her eyes, alternately pensive and vulnerable. Her hair was the color of his mother's, and her first name, he learned, was the same, though she had dropped the "h"—Sara White. She was from Danville, Missouri, but taught at a grade school in Pattonville, a village near St. Louis. Called Sallie by her friends, her family nickname was "Jug," a sobriquet given her by a beau named Bob Rogers because she wore brown so often that she resembled the little brown jug of the song.

The Chicago World's Fair was the wonder of the 1890s, a great festival of low and high art, technology, science, and commerce presented to audiences of some twenty-seven million visitors who came from every corner of the nation. Built at a cost of upward of ten million dollars, it was Chicago's celebration of its preeminence among Middle Western cities. The design was conceived by local architect Daniel Hudson Burnham, who took over after his more brilliant partner, John Root, died of pneumonia brought on by his labors to create a miracle on the sandy, weed-grown soil of Jackson Park beside the lake. Burnham had quickly abandoned Root's preliminary ideas, which were groping toward a vision of modern technology. Rather than enlisting the Chicago school of architects, some of whom—notably Louis Sullivan—were revolutionizing the cityscape, he hired Charles B. Atwood, a fashionable New York builder, to oversee the planning. Burnham also solicited the patronage of the city's social, political, and business elite (as he told Sullivan, he intended to "work up a big business, to handle big things, deal with big businessmen").

The landscaping and the lagoons, bridges, and canals dotting the setting were by Frederick Law Olmsted, designer of Central Park in New York City. The buildings, most of them by New Yorkers, followed the stately Beaux Arts style decreed by Burnham and Atwood.

The result was undeniably impressive. Visitors were dazzled by the Court of Honor, the central complex of exhibition pavilions arrayed around Grand Basin, at one end of which towered a statue of the Republic—all constructed of a plaster-fiber mixture called staff, which was painted white to simulate marble. Because of their color, the buildings were collectively dubbed the White City.

Sophisticates like the New York heiress Adele Sloane noted, "It is too ideally beautiful to be real," but to a raw young reporter from St. Louis the "lightness and airiness" of it all caused him "to be swept into a dream from which I did not recover for months." In one of his daily dispatches to the *Republic*, Theodore declared out of his considerable architectural ignorance, that the White City was the incarnation of Athens: "One can understand . . . why the Grecians were proud and how it came that men

could meditate the sublime philosophy that characterized the mythic age."
Most Americans regarded Burnham's creation as the apotheosis of the
city, a utopian vision of urbanism cleansed of all its present flaws, em-
bodying the highest ideals of the age.

As far as the business, political, and social elite who underwrote the
cost of the fair were concerned, Burnham and Company had built well;
those ornate structures were safely "beautiful" by European standards,
which were the only ones that counted. The neoclassical aesthetic also
corresponded to the reigning high culture in the universities, which called
for idealism, a style from which the mean, sordid facts of America in its
industrial birth throes were excluded. Idealistic art, the professors said,
should by definition inspire and edify.

Some nonacademic intellectuals were more ambivalent about the White
City, though they found much to praise in it. Plump, sad-eyed William
Dean Howells, America's most influential novelist and critic, wrote lyr-
ically of the reflections of the ten thousand sputtering arc lights in the
black waters of the lagoon, but he was equally interested in the fair's
social message. He considered it an optimistic one of fruitful collaboration
between businessmen and artists. The historian Henry Adams, a slight,
stooped man with a domed forehead and a mustache that drooped like
tragedy's mouth, stood in Machinery Hall and brooded on the hulking,
dully gleaming black forms of the dynamos, seeing in them the deities
of the new age. William T. Stead, a visiting British journalist and reformer who in 1895 would write his exposé of the Black City, *If Christ
Came to Chicago!*, comtemplated the Court of Honor at night, finding it
as "beautiful as a poet's dream, silent as a city of the dead." To Stead,
the "ivory city" was more compelling when viewed "in the silence
and solitude with no one near except the lonely sightseers fleeting
like wandering ghosts across the electric lighted square" than when
it was filled with the three-quarters of a million visitors who came on
Chicago Day.

Two cultures jostled at the fair—the reigning high culture and the up-
start popular culture of the multitudes who streamed to Chicago for an
experience they would remember the rest of their lives. They rode to
Jackson Park in transit magnate Charles T. Yerkes' streetcars and ate their
box lunches around the fountain he had endowed with its replicas of the
Niña, the Pinta, and the Santa María; or rode the Ferris Wheel, America's
first, with its large gondolas holding twenty-five people (one of them carried members of John Philip Sousa's band, playing repeatedly "After the
Ball," the hit of the fair); or toured the art exhibits and were shocked by
the nudes; or heard a black man named Scott Joplin play ragtime piano

music; or glimpsed the future at the Electricity Building with its stoves, fans, and dishwashers; or thronged the Midway Plaisance to watch Little Egypt and her troupe gyrating in what was politely called *la danse du ventre.*

Theodore saw the fair through the people's eyes. In a description of a night scene he wired to the *Republic,* he restored humanity to the dreamscape—"a massive crowd, a surging throng," which came "in droves— armies, thousands" to see a display of the illuminated fountains:

> They made one black and motionless mass. From such a ground-work of humanity, up sprang the waters. High they leaped, rolled, rushed and then curved and gracefully descended to the surface below. . . . It was only when the whistle wailed out its reminder of the lateness of the hour that the fountain ceased. . . . Then the great enthusiastic mass tramped its way out and rejoiced that it had been fortunate enough of all the world's children to have seen such a display.

Idealism and realism clashed in many venues. At the Congress on Literature a young writer from the West named Hamlin Garland, whose collection of short stories, *Main-Traveled Roads,* had recently been praised by Howells, called for a new kind of literature, which Garland alternately termed "veritism" and "local color"—a literature that was authentically American rather than imitative of Europe and that used homespun American speech. In his column Eugene Field kidded Garland for preferring fictional heroes "who sweat and do not wear socks."

Oblivious to the debate, Theodore inhaled the sights, often escorting Miss White and her pretty younger sister, Rose. He found in Rose a liveliness that the older girl lacked and was attracted to her, but Sallie White held him with a stronger magnetism. She was quiet and genteel, complementing Theodore's egoism and gaucheness. Her earnestness and intelligence drew him out, yet made him temper a little his usual stammering volubility. In keeping with her gentleness of manner, Sallie had a delicate constitution and spent the hot part of the days in the hotel parlor. When Theodore tried to kiss her, she begged him not to be "sentimental," so he courted less inhibited girls in the party. But Sallie White intrigued him, and he resolved to write her when he returned to St. Louis.

During Theodore's Chicago excursion, he visited his father, whom he found living alone and querulously complaining that the other children neglected him. Theodore took him to the fair several times, and old Paul enjoyed coffee and little cakes with caraway seeds at the German Village, which featured a romantic Rhine castle. When Paul asked Theodore if he still attended church, Theodore told a merely venial lie to comfort him. Although he no longer believed in Catholicism, he did not begrudge the comfort that old Paul's faith provided him in his last years. The gloomy, ranting figure who had loomed over his childhood was now, he saw, a forlorn old man.

Back in St. Louis, Theodore called on some of the schoolteachers he had met at the fair, but the memory of Sallie White's almond eyes and auburn hair persisted. Finally he wrote her, and she replied after a decent interval, telling him that she was planning to visit relatives in the city and that he might call on her. The thought of seeing Sallie again set Theodore's desire ablaze. He bought a new suit for the occasion—"a heavy military coat of the most disturbing length, a wide-brimmed stetson hat, Southern style, gloves, a cane, soft pleated shirt." He also wangled press passes to the latest shows, determined to sweep Sallie off her feet by exposing her to a whirl of urban sights. He took her to the best restaurants, and for afternoon strolls in the park, attired in his finery, which he changed before returning to the newsroom.

The more he saw her, the more he desired her. Sallie entertained him in the parlor of the home where she was staying, playing the piano while he eyed her petite, perfectly formed figure. Afterward, they would hold hands and he would beg her to let down her luxuriant hair. Sometimes she agreed, but she resisted his pleas to sit on his lap. Her coolness had the effect of inflaming Theodore all the more. His desire was so intense that he decided he must be in love with her, and began to think of becoming engaged. He wrote her long letters, which, she later said, made her love him. The courtship grew serious, and Sallie agreed to an informal engagement.

Around that time John Maxwell barged into town, looking for work. When Theodore showed him Sallie's picture, Maxwell remarked that she appeared to be a churchgoer and warned, "If you marry now—and a conventional and narrow woman at that, one older than you—you're gone . . . . Run with the girls if you want to, but don't marry." Theodore was not averse to running with the girls. There were two sisters from a German family who encouraged him. The family reminded him of his own—a stern German father and rebellious daughters seeking pleasure. But when he reached the brink of an interesting relationship with both of them, Theodore drew back, remembering Sallie, sweet and trusting in Pattonville.

Then Paul came to town, as lead comedian in a farce called *The Danger*

Signal. He was fatter than ever, and dressed in the height of Broadway fashion. When he met Jug he was genial and considerate, but afterward he pointedly advised Theodore not to get tied down with a girl. He must come to New York! He could not go on forever working in these slow Middle Western towns. New York was the place for a writer and a news-paperman. Paul had friends at the big papers who could get him a job. "You should see Broadway, sport," he would say. "The theaters, Del-monico's, Madison Square, the Metropole bar, where the actors hang out." Paul's descriptions intensified a desire that Theodore had been feeling for some time.

Before Paul left, Theodore invited all the prominent editors he knew to a late supper in his brother's honor. He thought the evening was a flop. He had told his friends to wear evening dress, but Paul came in a business suit and told jokes and theatrical anecdotes. Others who were present did not share Theodore's view. They found Paul a funny fellow and enjoyed his repartee. Theodore's attitude toward his brother had al-ready acquired an ambivalence. He envied Paul's success, yet thought him vulgar; he assumed others felt the same way.

Theodore was growing restless. If he continued on his present course, he might at best eventually become an editor on one of the city's papers, or at least a prominent local reporter, settling down to a home and family with Jug. But the thought of such a conventional future seemed stifling (he could not admit to himself that perhaps the idea of marriage itself was oppressing him). With subconscious purpose, he began making moves that would ensure that he had no future in St. Louis. He turned down a chance to return to the *Globe-Democrat* at a higher salary than he was making at the *Republic.* But he also came and went as he pleased, so Wandell, who had made him something of a pet, sent him some stiff letters. In one he warned, "Your habit of walking in and out of the office at your own pleasure does not suit me. . . . If you don't want to comply with the rules of the *Republic* office your resignation will be accepted."

In December 1893 Dreiser wrote to Emma Rector: "New York's the place for special writers and literary effusions are my strong 'fast ball' . . . so that I must go. Not now however. I'm a newspaper man at present with all the untoward instincts of one and not until I have achieved a certain status of perfection will I be able to throw off the shell as they say and spring out into that other much desired sphere."

Then a reporter friend from Chicago named Hutchinson, who had moved to St. Louis, told him of his plan to buy a country newspaper near his home in Ohio and asked Theodore to be his partner. To Theodore the pretext was as good as any. He half-dreamed of becoming an influential small-town editor, commenting sagely on local politics. But this dream was a quixotic one to say the least, for it meant throwing up a good job in the depths of the financial panic of 1893. When Dreiser gave notice to his employers, they tardily offered him a raise, but he was too proud to accept. His motives were an impossibly contradictory mix of wander-lust and yearning for the stability of small-town homelife. Also, the jour-nalistic grind was wearing him down; he felt constantly tired and couldn't sleep. In early March 1894 he said goodbye to his comrades at the *Republic* and took the train. Ostensibly it was bound for Ohio; actually, it was taking him on the first leg of a journey to a destination he was still afraid of reaching: New York, the ultimate city.

13. Wanderjahre

I was of the wandering tribe of newspapermen. . . . I passed bright windows of many splendid mansions and saw through the half drawn curtains the blaze of genial fires. . . . Others had their delights I observed, while I was . . . always on the outside, in the snow and cold.

— Dreiser, Letter to Sara Osborne White (September 21, 1896)

I was more interested in moving on and in seeing everything than in staying anywhere. I was constantly speculating as to my permanent abode. When, if ever, was I to have a home of my own.

— Dreiser, *Newspaper Days* (1931)

His immediate destination, however, was a tiny village called Grand Rapids. A main street, some slatternly shops, and a few houses—that was it. Not a human form in sight. The stationmaster pointed the way to the Hutchinson farm, and Theodore picked up his grip and started walking along Main Street. Soon he was in open country, striding past fields in which sere brown cornstalks stabbed through the thin carpet of snow. At last he came upon a rambling old farmhouse with a large barn and a lean-to kitchen, smoke curling from its small chimney.

The next day Hutchinson took him to the nearby town of Weston, where the office of the *Wood County Herald,* the paper he wanted to buy, was located. Their capital consisted of the hundred dollars Theodore had saved and the little that Hutchinson could borrow. The paper, Hutchinson told him, could be had for two hundred, which seemed a lot after they saw the office. The press was in bad shape and the type was worn. The names of about five hundred subscribers were listed in a dusty old ledger.

The thought of investing in such a rickety enterprise and trying to please an audience of narrow-minded merchants and farmers was appalling, and

Theodore dissolved the partnership on the spot. Hutchinson didn't seem surprised and said he might still have a go at it. (He did, but was soon forced to fold. Afterward, Hutchinson drifted from one small-town paper to another, writing unpublished short stories on the side. He ended up selling automobiles, and when Dreiser saw him years later, he seemed as "hollow as a dream.")

Now that he had given up his safe berth in St. Louis, Theodore chose to be a tramp reporter, and so began a period of Wanderjahre. But he had no prosperous father to subsidize his peregrinations; he was, he wrote Emma, "brushed around" from town to town. He was haunted by the fear of slipping off the economic treadmill, of becoming one of the cast-offs like the unemployed men in Jacob Coxey's "army" who were at that time marching across Ohio on their way to Washington.

In his loneliness he wrote Jug long letters—some of them running to fifty or sixty pages—in which he poured out his feelings. This was the first truly expressive writing he had ever done; he disgorged "all the surging and seething emotions and ideas which had hitherto been locked up in me," for which reporting offered no outlet. Only in his poem to Lois had he so fully vented his emotions. From the start, his creative drive was powered by erotic energy.

After a few days of relaxation, he decided it was time to move on, and he chose nearby Toledo as his next way station. There he tramped the streets, gazing longingly at the comfortable homes in which people lived happy lives: would he always be alone, outside looking in? Finally screwing up his courage, he entered the office of the *Blade* to inquire if they needed a reporter. They didn't—at least on a full-time basis, but he hit it off with the city editor, a plump, apple-cheeked young man named Arthur Henry, who had worked for the Chicago *Herald* while Theodore was on the *Globe*. As it happened, a streetcar strike was in progress, and the company was running a car manned by scabs. Violence was expected, and Henry needed a reporter to ride in the car. It could be a dangerous assignment. Theodore took it, and was soon on his way to the car barns to find out what was happening. That evening he returned with his story—there had been no violence—and Henry thought it so good he personally shepherded it through the typesetters and proofreaders, making certain no one would tell the publisher, who was antilabor.

Theodore recalled being told to stay neutral, but his sympathies were with the workers. To show that the company's intention was to break the union, he posed as a union man from St. Louis looking for a job and was told that no union men were wanted. Actually, Henry's wife, Maude, a strong feminist who had badgered the paper until it hired her, wrote the main story, while Theodore wrote sidebars such as the item about the union man.

Dreiser handed in a couple of other trivial pieces. In one he described the countryside in poetic terms, and Henry, recognizing a kindred literary spirit, took him to lunch. They talked for three hours. Henry had ambitions of being a novelist and a poet, and dreamed of going to New York. He had written a book of fairy tales for children, and he and Maude performed plays with other members of Toledo's bohemian set at their old mansion on the Maumee River. That night, when Theodore and Arthur reconvened for dinner, they were bonded as soulmates. As Dreiser later wrote, "If he had been a girl, I would have married him."

Theodore hung around a few more days and took a boat ride on the river with Henry. But his new friend had nothing to offer him save an occasional free-lance assignment, so Dreiser decided to move on. Henry urged him not to go too far—Cleveland, or Buffalo, say—for perhaps a job would open up on the *Blade* and he would telegraph him immediately. Theodore agreed, and that night he wrote Emma Rector describing his outing on the Maumee, which "hurrys [sic] along over the coolest and mossiest of all stones." He felt "ever so rested" and said he was heading for Cleveland and then Buffalo—or perhaps Pittsburgh and Philadelphia. Forgetting Jug for the nonce, he told Emma to write him care of Henry in Toledo, promising her that when he returned to St. Louis he would stop off and see her. (He never did; nor did he write Emma again.)

In Cleveland, Theodore tried his luck at the *Plain Dealer*. But the job prospects were even worse there than in Toledo. He did wangle a few Sunday supplement assignments—a piece on a chicken farm and an interview with the captain of one of the new "turtle-back" grain ships. He spent his spare time in pilgrimages to the homes of the wealthy, with John D. Rockefeller's mansion on Euclid Avenue the highlight. His awe was now qualified by questions about the power of a man like Rockefeller and his Standard Oil Trust. He strolled along the shores of Lake Erie, wrote Jug voluminous letters, and read Laurence Sterne's *A Sentimental Journey*, which Henry had recommended.

All told, Theodore earned only $7.50 for his free-lance work, and decided he had better head for Buffalo. He stayed there ten days, poking about the poorer sections, which did not help his morale. He received one tentative job offer—for six weeks hence—but he did not have enough money to wait. Before leaving, he made a side trip to Niagara Falls, and, standing on a rock near the falls, he experienced a sudden wave of vertigo, as though the roaring waters were drawing him in.

Passing the railroad station one day, he noticed a ticket broker's sign advertising cut-rate fares to Pittsburgh, and decided on the spot to make that city his next stop. By 10:00 that same morning he was on the train speeding south, and by 7:00 he was in Pittsburgh.

14. The Young Man From the Provinces

Just about then, in Pittsburgh, where I was working as a newspaper man, I came across Balzac and then I saw what life was—a rich, gorgeous, showy spectacle. It was beautiful, dramatic, sad, delightful, and epic—all those things combined.

—Dreiser, interview (1911)

The City of Pittsburgh is surely exceptional. In spite of the wealth which it has created for certain individuals it is almost always in trouble. If it is not a steel strike it is a [railroad] car famine, and if it is not a car famine it is a society scandal, which is almost as bad. . . . Poverty, filth, wretched laboring conditions on one hand, and, set over against this, great wealth and great display.

—Dreiser, "Pittsburgh" (1909)

s Dreiser crossed the steel-arch bridge over the Monongahela leading from the station to the business district, the black waters below were suddenly suffused with a febrile glow. He looked up and saw a row of perhaps fifty great smokestacks extruding bright orange tongues of flame into the sky.

The next day he studied the local papers to get a line on what sort of journalism was practiced in Pittsburgh. He noted that the news columns were filled with brief reports of industrial accidents, a litany of maimings and deaths. He was also struck by the obsequious way the press chronicled the doings of the local industrial aristocracy. Junkets to New York for theatergoing and shopping, jaunts to shooting lodges in Virginia for the duck season, sailings to Europe, dinner parties, balls and fetes were slavishly reported. Juxtaposed with the stories of industrial carnage, these society notes made the world of the rich seem an empire built on pain.

Later, he explored those disparate worlds, taking a trolley to Homestead, site of the great strike of 1892, during which the workers occupied Andrew Carnegie's steel plant and fought off boatloads of imported Pinkerton detectives. After four months the people of Homestead were starving, and the state militia was patrolling the Carnegie works. Many workers were blacklisted; the rest returned to their jobs. Henry Frick had won. As Secretary of the Treasury Charles Foster observed about the Homestead strikers, "They were talking about . . . Carnegie being too rich, while they were poor." Revolutionary talk—a fissure had opened between capital and labor.

Now, in Homestead, Theodore explored a defeated city. The young veritist Hamlin Garland also visited Homestead in the spring of 1894, on an assignment for *McClure's Magazine,* and he recorded these impressions:

> Higher up the tenement houses stood in dingy rows, alternating with vacant lots. The streets of the town were horrible. The buildings were poor; the sidewalks were sunken, swaying and full of holes. . . . Everywhere the yellow mud of the street lay kneaded into a sticky mass, through which groups of pale lean men slouched in faded garments, grimy with soot and grease of the mills.

The next day Theodore followed Fifth Avenue out to the East Side, his destination Schenley Park. He soon found himself in another world— one of clean, tree-lined streets, shiny streetlamps, imposing homes surrounded by green lawns, formal gardens, and tall iron fences. In the park was a great glass-domed conservatory in which brightly colored flowers bloomed in lush profusion. Not far away stood one of Andrew Carnegie's libraries, an imposing five-story limestone building. All of this, he thought— the conservatory, the library, the mansions—had been built with profits squeezed from underpaid workers by Olivers, Thaws, Phippses, Fricks, Thompsons, who could hardly find ways to spend them.

He looked for a job. At the *Dispatch* he found an editor who responded to his application with studied indifference. Come back in ten days, he said; there might be something. Upon his return to his boardinghouse, Theodore found a telegram from Henry offering him a position with the *Blade* at eighteen dollars a week. Toledo seemed tame now, but Henry's telegram proved useful. Taking a pen, Theodore changed the eighteen dollars to twenty-five and then showed it to the editor at the *Dispatch,* who was impressed and hired him at the higher figure.

That night Theodore rode the cable car up Mt. Washington and surveyed the city lights spread out below like strands of pearls on black velvet. He had treated himself to a large dinner and felt warm and content. Now his dreams of wealth seemed callow; his life up to now had been a farrago—all his hopes of success shrank into insignificance before the looming power of coal, steel, and money in this city. He decided that the best he could do "was to think and dream, standing aloof as a spectator." A reporter was at least granted that privilege; one could go through life as a traveling correspondent, observing the passions and sorrows of humanity but avoiding the grief of disappointed hopes.

When Theodore reported for work the next morning, the city editor briefed him on the ground rules: no stories on labor relations (the labor reporter handled those considered printable), nothing derogatory about religion, nothing critical of society, no scandals in high places. "I'd rather have some simple little feature any time," he told Theodore, "a story about some old fellow with eccentric habits, than any of those scandals or tragedies."

One of his first assignments was an interview with Speaker of the House Thomas B. Reed. Theodore was curious to know what the congressman, considered one of the greatest to wield the gavel in American history, thought of Coxey's "Industrial Army," the raggle-taggle band of unemployed men that was marching on Washington to present a petition of grievances under a banner reading, "Peace on Earth Good Will to Men, He Hath Risen, but Death to Interest on Bonds." Actually, Coxey was a well-to-do businessman from Massilon, Ohio, and his army was composed largely of unemployed workingmen who wanted the government to give them jobs. Reed, who was in a hurry, thought the subject "too serious" for a brief interview. But he opined that the movement showed "the general unrest of the people," adding that unfortunately the administration in Washington did not seem to appreciate its significance. (In his autobiography *Newspaper Days*, Dreiser unfairly portrays Reed as a mossback who branded the men "revolutionaries.")

The labor reporter, a stocky, soft-spoken young man named Martyn, explained to Theodore how the owners imported cheap foreign labor to displace the union men, and how, after the Homestead strike, wages had gone down 25 percent while the workday was increased from eight to twelve hours. He took Dreiser on a tour of the "courts" where the workers lived—ramshackle tenements surrounding an open courtyard, where the women did the laundry, drawing their washing and drinking water from the same hydrant. As many as twelve people were packed into the two-room flats, and one outdoor wooden latrine served the entire building; its twelve stools emptied into a single septic tank, which was flushed out periodically with laundry water. Of course Martyn never wrote about those things; he had a wife and a child, and needed his job. The gap between what the reporter knew and what he wrote seemed, if anything, wider here in Pittsburgh than in St. Louis.

For a time, Theodore was assigned to the police beat in the city of Allegheny, just across the river. Every morning he checked in at the courthouse to see if anything of interest was brewing. Usually there was nothing, so he was free to spend the rest of the day gossiping with the other reporters and the municipal functionaries, or reading at the library, another monument to Carnegie's philanthropy. The steel magnate had donated a similar building to Homestead, but, as a worker there told a visiting journalist, "After working twelve hours, how can a man go to the library?"

Theodore had plenty of time, though; the library became his university. It was there that he discovered Balzac, one of the writers Wandell had urged him to emulate. Taking down a volume entitled *The Wild Ass's Skin* one day, he settled into one of the comfortable alcoves. Soon he was lost in the story of Raphael, the idealistic young man from the provinces who comes to Paris. The shock of recognition was profound: they dreamed the same dreams of conquering the city and suffered the same rebuffs.

Another novel, *The Great Man From the Provinces*, spoke even more directly to his own life, with its tale of Lucien de Rubempré, the naive young poet who is sucked into the mephitic swamp of Parisian journalism where cynical reporters sell their principles to the highest bidder. As he devoured other volumes of *La Comédie Humaine*, Theodore was filled with awe at Balzac's teeming mural of Parisian life. All those grasping, greedy people were so dispassionately scrutinized: no attempt was made to idealize them. Their fates were determined by the dice of chance; some rose, others fell, but all hungered for the same glittering prizes—wealth, fame, position. Society was like a night-blooming flower, crawling with insects trying to gorge themselves on its sticky nectar.

This view of life hit Theodore with the force of a revelation. Now all the world looked Balzacian to him. Pittsburgh's bridges became *ponts* of the Seine. Why couldn't a young novelist anatomize an American city as Balzac did Paris?

When the city editor suggested he do humorous feature stories about eccentric old men and the like, Theodore took as his inspiration Lucien's column of observations on Parisian life, "The Man in the Street." His first effort was well received, and he was turned loose to roam around the city and write about whatever struck his fancy. Sometimes he reported what he saw; sometimes he engaged in pure fancy; and sometimes—rather, most of the time—there was a bit of both. The talent for humor Dreiser had unleashed on the Owls-Elks baseball game in St. Louis was revived. But now there was a faint undertone of morbidity. An amusing bit of whimsy about a housefly describes the insect as "a suicide by inheritance. Unnatural and untimely death is his delight." One such specimen, deciding every man's hand is against him, what with flypaper and people constantly shooing him off tasty morsels, chooses to end it all in the vinegar jug; another prefers the gravy bowl. In a more serious piece, "Hospital Violet Day," Theodore displays considerable charm in describing the death of an old man named Fritz in a hospital ward amid the jokes of the other patients and the perfume of spring flowers. Another article is a sustained flight on the many ramifications of blue Monday, from the cranky magistrate who hands out a stiff sentence, to the housewife facing piles of washing. But wait—there is a "little heap" awaiting one good woman, the childish wearer of the clothes gone forever. The little garments are to be washed and then "stowed away with heartaches and teardrops, the real symbols of life's greatest pain." In an urban montage, he describes the music to be heard on the city's streets, starting with the trill of a penny whistle and the thwang of a Jew's harp and ending with a funeral dirge. A recurrent motif is a lonely grave in which one of the city's anonymous throng is laid, epitomizing the urban dweller's fear of dying alone and unmourned. "An unknown has no story."

Balzac had broadened Dreiser's sympathies perceptibly. Another author who galvanized his imagination was George du Maurier, whose *Trilby*, a tale of artists in the Latin Quarter, was appearing, somewhat bowdlerized, as a serial in *Harper's* and causing a sensation. The novel later became a mad best seller, touching off Trilby fashions in clothes and speech. The heroine, an artist's model, had beautiful feet (a fetish that provided an erotic substitute for descriptions of her nude body, which might have baited the censors). Women's feet were nicknamed "trilbies."

But *Trilby* had a more urgent personal message: it turned Theodore's thoughts yearningly to Jug. The story of Little Billee's love for Trilby and his devastating loss when she is lured away by the evil mesmerizing Svengali set Dreiser imagining that he would lose Jug. Not that he was entirely faithful. Emma Rector was probably not the only girl with whom he carried on a flirtation; his desires tormented him. And there were prostitutes, many of them immigrants' daughters from the courts of Homestead. Sometimes he liked to pick up a streetwalker just to talk, but usually it was physical release, the secret friction, he sought. One woman delighted him with the "words and expressions she used when rutting . . . or positions she was willing to take."

More memorable, though, was the hard-bitten whore whose bare arm was covered with needle scars. When Theodore lectured her on the evils of morphine, she exclaimed in a flat, tired voice: "Oh great God! What do you know about life?" Very little, he was coming to see. But he was learning.

15. A Moth to the Lamp

> Your home which I had never seen was always some silvery
> cottage that swam in a soft vista of my imagination. There were
> nothing but murmurs and soft odours about it.
>
> —Dreiser to Sara Osborne White (1896)

> New York . . . had the feeling of gross and blissful and parading
> self-indulgence. . . . Here . . . were huge dreams and lusts and
> vanities being gratified hourly. I wanted to know the worst and
> the best.
>
> —Dreiser, *Newspaper Days* (1931)

Theodore's anxiety about Jug's fidelity was fueled by a recurrence of his panicky fear that life was sliding through his fingers. Surely she had already tired of waiting for him and found someone else. Desperate to see her, he took a vacation in the summer of 1894 and journeyed to Missouri.

Jug was living at her father's home near Danville, a village really, that clung to the title of county seat but felt it slipping from its grasp under the strong pull of nearby Montgomery City, a place of some fifteen hundred people which had become the terminus for the Wabash Railroad. In the battle for survival among towns, being bypassed by the railroad meant sure decline, and that would be Danville's fate.

Whites had been living in the county since 1824, when Morgan B. White, Sr., arrived from Kentucky to take up a large plot of land and become, according to the county history, "a man of some consideration." The family traced its origins to Virginia, and people in the county used another word to sum them up: "aristocrats."

Jug's father, Archibald Herndon White, son of Morgan B., Sr., was a prominent farmer and politician. He was elected county sheriff in 1885 and was active in the local Democratic Party. However, he was considered too honest ever to go very far in politics, though he was much loved by his fellow citizens. He regarded every poor person in the area as his personal ward. Once when he saw an attendant at the county poor farm beating a retarded man because he would not carry in some wood, White intervened, then strode to the courthouse and swore out a complaint against the functionary. After he had finished what was more oration than deposition, the clerk suggested that it might be harmful to the Democratic party, of which the offending attendant was a wheelhorse, if too much were made of the affair. To which White replied, "What's this got to do with it? Do you want the Democratic Party to starve the poor and beat the insane?"

In a story, "A True Patriarch," Dreiser described his future father-in-law as "tall, white-haired, stout in body and mind. . . . One might take him to be the genial Walt Whitman, of whom he is the living counterpart." From Dreiser's portrait of him it seems that Arch White adopted many of the traits of Morgan B., as set down by the county historian. He was a farmer and only "moderately successful"; he was "not a man whose highest conception of life was to accumulate a fortune," preferring "mental improvement." He read deeply in history, government, and the Scriptures, and "few men of this part of the country were better informed in politics, history and religion than he." Although Morgan B. served in the state legislature, it was at the urging of his fellow citizens rather than out of political ambition. He and his wife, Mary A. White, had thirteen children. The historian sums up his legacy in this way: "He believed that the treasures of the mind were to be prized far more than material wealth, and that the father who left his children provided with good educations and integrity of character transmitted to them a richer inheritance than he who leaves broad acres and large possessions."

Arch White, now in his sixties, and his wife, Ann Drace White, had reared an extremely close-knit family of three sons and seven daughters, all of whom Theodore was sure would amount to something. Like their mother before them, the girls had gone to Danville Academy, "a very successful and good school attended by daughters of prominent families from all parts of Missouri as well as other states." Jug's sisters Linnie and Minnie White, and possibly Rose, taught school as a way station before marriage. Of the sons, Richard Drace White would have a successful career in the navy. Missouri's first appointee to the Naval Academy, from which he graduated in 1899, he served in the Spanish-American War; was wounded in World War I and received the Navy Cross; served as a naval attaché between the wars; retired with the rank of captain; and returned to active duty in World War II, becoming an admiral. Arch White, Jr., moved to Colorado in 1895 for his health and served as clerk of the State

Supreme Court there. F. V. (Pete) White departed for Texas in the early 1900s and was considered a financial failure, a man who "never had two nickels to rub together." Oddly (or not), he seems to have been the brother who admired Theodore the most.

This attractive homestead was a jarring contrast to the courts of Homestead—not to mention Theodore's own anarchic kin, who had been dogged by economic insecurity and social condemnation. He could not help but compare the White family's rocklike stability, its honored place in the community, its superior "breeding" (though not wealth) with his own impoverished, itinerant childhood. He was beguiled by the picturesque rural setting, and Jug seemed more desirable than ever.

The summer heat, the humid air, the drone of the bees in the honeysuckle vines, stirred potent desires in both of them. When they met in the hall or an empty room, they would urgently kiss; now she was as ardent as he was. One humid night, when the heat lightning flickered on the horizon and the distant thunder rumbled, their lovemaking spilled over the old bounds. As fat raindrops began spattering the leaves, they hurried inside. The rest of the family was asleep, and they met in the sitting room after Jug had changed into a flimsy nightdress through which Theodore could feel the soft contours of her body. As the rain drummed against the French windows, they sank into a stupor of passion, she half-fainting. He carried her to her room, and only Jug's pleas for him to protect her because she could not help herself prevented him from taking her.

After a week, Theodore tore himself away. A stopover in St. Louis to visit McCord and Wood depressed him, though, as change always did. There were new faces in the newsroom, a sense of lives going on without him, of time passing. He left as soon as he could. He had some vacation time remaining, and in a recent letter Paul had again urged him to come to New York. After a winter on the road, his brother was boarding with Emma and Hopkins and looking forward to an idle, pleasant summer. He promised to show Theodore the city, and to introduce him to journalist cronies who could help him get a job on a great paper like the *Sun* or the *World*.

Theodore stopped over in Pittsburgh only long enough to pick up a change of clothes at his rooming house and to telegraph Paul that he was coming, then caught the New York express. When he got off the train in Jersey City the next morning, Paul was there to meet him in the huge, glass-roofed train shed, from which they took the Hudson River ferry to Manhattan. They landed at Cortlandt Street in Lower Manhattan, and

Paul hailed a carriage. Theodore's first view of the city was of the narrow alleys and drab tenements along the East River. Paul told him not to judge prematurely. Wait until he had seen *his* New York.

They went directly to Emma's place at 215 West 15th Street, near Seventh Avenue. Theodore found his sister much changed. The plump, delectable beauty of her youth had faded; she was now stout and worn-looking. Still, she was the same uncomplicated, affectionate Em, who would always be his favorite sister. She made a huge breakfast for them—steak, biscuits, and gravy. Paul, after alleging he was on a diet, tucked in with gusto—in honor of Thee's arrival, of course.

Emma, Theodore would learn, was now enduring the drab aftermath of her love story with Hopkins, who had been ousted from his Tammany Hall sinecure as a result of the Lexow Committee's investigations of political corruption, and was unemployed. Emma had taken in roomers for a time—that is, bona fide roomers, Hopkins having also lost his police protection—but now Paul was subsidizing the household.

Not only had Hopkins failed as a provider, he had turned to other women. Emma had resigned herself to this behavior and stuck by him. Subdued after her early flings, she was a proper homebody, slavishly devoted to her two children, Gertrude and George. Theodore thought her a wonderful mother. Inside her thickened body the ingenuous desires of her youth still pulsed.

The next day Paul took Theodore for a walk up Broadway. They began at Fourteenth Street and Union Square, once the heart of the theater district. Paul pointed out some of the landmarks from his earliest days in the city—Niblo's and Miner's New Theater, where he had got one of his first jobs as an "eccentric comedian and vocalist"; the original Rialto—the stretch of Fourteenth Street where the out-of-work actors used to loaf after making the rounds; Tony Pastor's nightclub; and a few blocks farther downtown, the notorious Bowery. Theodore grew impatient with Paul's thespian nostalgia; enough of the old—he wanted to see the new. He knew that the theater district, like the city, was surging uptown.

Broadway above Fourteenth Street was a fashionable thoroughfare, a glittering channel cut across the grid pattern of streets, lined with theaters, fancy emporiums, and luxury hotels. At Fourteenth Street it swept around "Dead Man's Curve," skirting the equestrian statue of Washington at the southwest corner of Union Square, and then headed uptown. Cable cars, which the year before had replaced the horsecars (the new line—the Broadway Surface Railway Company—had won the franchise by lining the pockets of the Tweed ring), careered perilously around this bend, threatening to jump the track at any moment. Paul thought it too hot to walk and hailed a hansom cab, and they were borne slowly uptown on the sluggish current of traffic. Buildings of ten or even twelve stories, with ornate façades and jutting cornices, loomed on either side. Like a tour guide, Paul called out the names of their famous occupants—Tiffany's at Fifteenth Street, Park and Tilford's fancy grocery, and the studio of Sarony, photographer of actresses and society women. Theodore gaped at the crowds surging along the sidewalk—the Broadway "parade." The men were all nattily dressed in silk hats, frock coats, and spats. Women in voluminous skirts and mutton-chop sleeves formed small, chattering flocks that were ogled by the sports standing in little knots on each street corner.

At Nineteenth Street they passed the Goelet mansion, with its peacocks strutting about in the garden. (When May Goelet was married to an English duke ten years later, thousands of excited women rioted outside the church and had to be repelled by club-swinging police.) At Twentieth, Paul pointed out the offices of Howley, Haviland, the song publishing firm in which he was a silent partner. The area had become the center of the infant sheet-music business, anchored by the old, established firm of Oliver Ditson Company, which had its offices on Eighteenth and Broadway. Of more interest to Theodore were the fancy department stores—Lord & Taylor, Arnold, Constable and Company; Sloan's; and Brooks Brothers, the gentlemen's clothing emporium.

At Twenty-third Street they came upon Madison Square Park, on which fronted palatial hotels like the Bartholdi and the Fifth Avenue, where presidents stayed and where influential politicians gathered in the bar at the Amen Corner. Dominating the north side of the square was the Garden, with its soaring tower capped by the gold statue of Diana and her bow. Continuing up the street, they passed luxury hotels like the Albermarle and Gilsey House, home to "Diamond Jim" Brady and theater folk, including, at times, Paul. To the west, on Sixth Avenue, his brother told him, was the Tenderloin, a district of dance halls and brothels, now nailed shut by the Reverend Charles Parkhurst's antivice crusade, which had put a reform administration in City Hall. They stopped for a drink in the barroom of the Hoffmann House Café, with its huge painting, "Nymphs and Satyrs," by Bourguereau.

After finishing their drinks, they walked the rest of the way, past more luxury hotels—the Broadway Central, the Marlborough, the Grand, the Imperial—and theaters—Koster and Bial's Music Hall, Keith and Proctor's, the Garrick, Augustin Daly's (where as an unknown song and dance man Paul had laid siege to the stage door ten years before), the Metropolitan Opera House and the Empire. At Forty-second Street they reached the northernmost outpost of Paul's world—the Hotel Metropole.

Inside was a huge lounge with a long, darkly gleaming mahogany bar and brass rail and leather banquettes around the wall. Paul led him to a table, scattering greetings like papal blessings. A stream of cronies came up to his table to pay their respects, and Paul had a joke or an anecdote for each, smiling, gladhanding, calling them "sport" and "old fellow," introducing his brother as "a writer from out West." Theodore later learned that Paul's bonhomie was in part motivated by business concerns. In addition to writing songs, he was "outside man" for Howley, Haviland, his job to charm composers into joining the firm, and to cajole tenors and soubrettes into plugging its songs. It was "good old Paul" and glasses of whiskey and booming laughter. Occasionally a long-haired, out-of-work thespian would touch him for a "V" or a "tenner." Retired prospectors who had made a strike in the West, or gamblers who had taken all the pots, mingled with actors, vaudevillians, rounders, and salesmen. They talked in a colorful lingo about people who were "dogs" and "swine" or "God's own salt."

The remainder of Theodore's week was a blur of impressions. Almost daily Paul would make a ceremonial progress up Broadway, retailing along the way the latest funny story, giving it a full performance at each stopping place, with appropriate gestures and accent. This was Paul's element, Theodore realized; the laughter and backslapping were as much nourishment to him as his heavy breakfasts at Emma's.

Sex was another appetite, and Paul satisfied it as greedily as he ate. One day when they were standing with a group of sports on a Broadway corner, Paul suggested they nip over to a special brothel he knew, a "French" place. When Theodore mumbled some excuse, Paul explained, "Don't you know what people mean when they say 'French,' sport? It's not just that they're French girls. It's the different way of doing it. They go down on you—blow the pipe—play the flute. Aren't you on?" Under Paul's prodding, he agreed, and the group headed en masse for the Tenderloin, with Theodore feeling he was "undertaking a dreadful, perilous and shameful adventure."

The girl he chose, pretty and dark and seemingly genuinely French, laughed at his shyness, and he undressed and submitted to her ministrations, which sent him into paroxysms of groaning delirium. But in the immediate aftermath he was plunged into a black depression, as if he had committed a crime against nature.

When Paul was preoccupied with business matters, Theodore made forays on his own. He journeyed to upper Fifth Avenue, where brownstone mansions squatted in haughty splendor, two or three to a block, now boarded up for the summer while their occupants cavorted in Newport or Saratoga. He toured Wall Street and slum areas; the contrasts between rich and poor in New York seemed even more glaring than in Pittsburgh. Here the poor appeared more hopeless and the rich more arrogant.

His final Sunday in the city, he accompanied Paul on an excursion to Manhattan Beach, a fashionable resort for the urban upper middle class and the group just below them that looked up to them as a model. Businessmen, politicians, clerks, and their wives and girls, were headed for this pleasure dome; the trains and ferries were packed with smiling people, the women in lace-trimmed summer frocks and the men in white flannels and striped blazers.

Strolling along the boardwalk, the brothers passed two huge hotels, the Manhattan and the Oriental, where well-boodled politicians and the latest millionaires summered. From a large bandstand in the distance came the strains of a Sousa march. When dusk fell, they sat on the broad veranda of the Manhattan and watched the fireworks display over the water. As the dull booms intoned, the sky was lit by silver starbursts that rained liquid fire on the dark ocean. The scene filled Theodore with a wistful longing for a place of ineffable sweetness just beyond his grasp, like the toys in his childhood dreams, as evanescent as the arabesques of fire lighting up the sky. He envied Paul, so sleek and confident and superbly equipped for success in such a world, which Theodore could observe only from the fringe. He sensed the vulgarity of all this prosperity around him, founded on trade and speculation and political corruption, yet he admired it. Out of the moil of cupidity, lust, and vanity that made up the city's seething energies had come this fabulous spectacle—Manhattan Beach. He thought: "I have never lived until now."

The next morning, with the scenes of the previous night still incandescent in his mind, Theodore boarded the Limited for Pittsburgh, determined to return as soon as he could save enough money to stake him to a gamble on this city.

Ringing in his ears were the words Paul had spoken to him that first day on Broadway: "Sometime you ought to write about these things, Thee. . . . The people out West don't know yet what is going on, but the rich are getting control. They'll own the country pretty soon. A writer like you could make 'em see that."

16. First Principles in Pittsburgh

To understand how science and religion express opposite sides of the same fact—the one its near or visible side, and the other its remote or invisible side—this it is which we must attempt. . . . We see good reason to conclude that the most abstract truth contained in religion and the most abstract truth contained in science must be the one in which the two coalesce. . . .

For every religion setting out though it does with the tacit assertion of a mystery, forth with proceeds to give some solution of the mystery, and so asserts that it is not a mystery passing human comprehension. But an examination of the solutions they severally propound show them to be uniformly invalid.

—Herbert Spencer, *First Principles* (1862)

Now that he had seen New York, Theodore knew he must leave Pittsburgh as soon as possible. For the next three months he scrimped, spending a nickel for a breakfast of coffee and a doughnut and fifteen cents for dinner, his only substantial meal, at a greasy spoon. Still thin and gangling, his 140 pounds distributed sparingly over his six-foot-one-inch frame, he almost succeeded in ruining his health by the time he had accumulated two hundred and forty dollars.

He read avidly magazines like *Town Topics*, which retailed smart gossip about the "400." *Munsey's Magazine*, which had recently lowered its price to ten cents and boosted its circulation as a result, stirred his desires with its risqué portraits of beautiful actresses in "artistic" *tableaux vivants*. Then there was Town Topics, with its society gossip and *The Standard & Vanity Fair*, whose stories of the demimonde—the Tenderloin and the "white-light" world of Broadway—hinted of parlor scandals and decadent pleasures.

The decision to try New York City also marked the end of Theodore's Wanderjahre. His peregrinations had shown him America "in the furnace stage of its existence." He had begun to understand that the trusts were gaining control of the country—a process of centralization that according to journalist Ida M. Tarbell, who would expose the Rockefeller octopus for *McClure's* in 1903, "left the country consolidated in vast economic units." And he had learned enough about the labor movement to know that he was not in complete solidarity with the unionists or the ragged "soldiers" of Coxey's army; still they represented a counterforce to the power of the trusts, an organization to fight for their members' livelihoods in self-defense. Having seen the demoralized state into which labor in Pittsburgh had sunk, Theodore's attitude was one of pity toward the weak on whom the strong fed. But at the same time, he admired the titans of business who were building factories and mines and railroads.

He was unfamiliar with the writings of the dissenters thrust up by the economic turmoil of the 1880s—Edward Bellamy, the socialist who in *Looking Backward* proposed a benign, citizen-owned trust to govern the country; Henry George, who advocated a single tax on land, which he considered the basis of all wealth, and who harked back to a simpler, Jeffersonian vision of America when there was free soil for all (in 1890 the Bureau of the Census announced the closing of the frontier); the Populist agitators of the West and South, like Ignatius Donnelly, Mary Elizabeth Lease, "Pitchfork Ben" Tillman, Tom Watson, "Sockless Jerry" Simpson; the urban radicals like the socialist Eugene Debs, the anarchist Johann Most, and the Marxist Daniel De Leon, head of the Socialist Labor Party; or the Christian socialists, like William Dean Howells. The protest movements spawned by social unrest in the eighties and nineties produced a torrent of violent rhetoric that mixed the anathemas of Biblical prophets with modern talk of class struggle. (Donnelly had charged, "There are really but two parties in this state today—the people and their plunderers.")

But American radicalism was such a cacophony of voices that it is doubtful Theodore could have gained much certitude even if he had read its manifestos. He remained a detached, unemotional observer of the spectacle. The most enduring impression his wanderings leave was of a young man seeking a place, yet uncertain of how to achieve it and lacking in education and skills—face pressed against the window, gazing with desirous eyes at the mansions of the wealthy. As he later told Jug, he was "an ambitious young man without a competence . . . working for a place and a name."

More important than Dreiser's inability to find his place in society was his perplexity about his—and all humankind's—role in the cosmic scheme. A single book that he read in Pittsburgh did more to shape his political and philosophical ideas than any other. That was Herbert Spencer's *First Principles*. As he wrote later, it "quite blew me, intellectually, to bits," though his copy of the book contains marginalia—"not true," "nonsense," "yeah!"—that suggest that Dreiser did not swallow it whole. Spencer had been a revelation to an entire generation of British and American intellectuals, and though his vogue in America was beginning to wane, its reverberations would continue in American literature until well into the twentieth century. And, of course, Spencer's ideas on the "survival of the fittest," a phrase he coined, found favor among industrialists to whom it was a license for ruthless acquisitiveness.

Spencer packaged moral philosophy as science. He synthesized Darwin's theory of evolution, Malthus's demography with its iron law of population, Ricardo's economics with its iron law of wages, and Lamarck's biology with its doctrine of the inheritability of acquired characteristics, into a great, overarching theory.

Spencer was a brilliant spinner of theories, proceeding magisterially in books like *Social Statics*, *The Principles of Sociology*, and *Synthetic Philosophy* to construct a vast edifice that comprehended all human knowledge. The trouble was that he preferred theorizing to evidence. In this he was the polar opposite of Charles Darwin, the patient grubber of facts. (Darwin once wrote of Spencer, "his conclusions never convinced, and over and over again I have said to myself, after reading one of his discussions, 'Here would be a fine subject for half-a-dozen years' work.' ")

Spencer's friend and increasingly exasperated critic, the great polemicist and evolutionist Thomas Huxley, once said, "Spencer's idea of a tragedy is a deduction killed by a fact." Spencer spent most of his life avoiding such tragedies, just as he avoided overwork by cultivating an array of psychosomatic illnesses. During the last forty years of his life he limited his writing time to a few hours, and finally a few minutes, a day.

Though Spencer's prose style was ponderous, it was lucid, and the grand sweep of his generalizations and the laws he propounded carried an aura of authority that won him converts among writers, intellectuals, autodidacts, and village atheists in nineteenth-century America. Economic distress, social upheaval, and rapid change had propelled many of them into a crisis of faith. Spencer came along at the right time to fill the vacuum, and socialists as well as capitalists drew solace from his calm omniscience, his tranquil belief in the ultimate moral and material progress of the race.

Some of his readers experienced a revelation akin to a religious conversion. Andrew Carnegie, Spencer's most famous American disciple, said, "I remember that light came as in a flood and all was clear. Not only had I got rid of theology and the supernatural but I had found the truth of evolution."

Paradoxically, the man who inspired these conversions was a radical materialist. Trained as an engineer, he envisioned the universe as a great machine driven by divine hydraulic power. Force was the basis of motion and matter. Force persisted through all time; it had been triggered by something—an uncaused cause, which Spencer called the Unknowable. Force was the propellant of Evolution; translated into motion and matter, the basic entities of the universe, it traced out the Unknowable's inscrutable plan. Spencer believed that evolution—in animals, human beings, and human society—moves from the homogenous to the heterogeneous, from the simple to the complex, from cell to organism, from nebula to universe.

More important, evolution was progress. Out of the inchoate flux and "undulations" of matter and motion, of action and reaction, came specialization and complexity. Humanity evolved from the primitive to the civilized, becoming ever more virtuous, altruistic, and happy. The end product of evolution was equilibrium—in the case of humankind a state of perfect harmony between desire and environment, supply and demand, population and resources. Individuals are moved by the force of desire, not ideals or ethics. In maximizing his own satisfaction and happiness, the strong individual necessarily displaces the weak in the competition for the earth's scarce goods—the survival of the fittest. When all are equally strong, one man's desire will be checked by another's.

Spencer seemed to settle the boundary dispute between science and religion. The material universe, ever undulating and evolving, decaying and renewing, was the domain of science, but beyond the limits of knowledge was the Unknowable—God if you liked. Spencer left a blank space on the ballot, and the religiously inclined could write in the deity of their choice. Religion was not ousted from human affairs, but it no longer had a corner on truth. It was no wonder that many liberal theologians welcomed Spencer. Evolution, which taught that humans were descended from the lower animals, was no longer the enemy: it was God's plan, a divine momentum propelling humankind ever upward and on, lifting it out of the mire of brutishness to the heights of peace, prosperity, and virtue.

This cosmic optimism in Spencer appealed strongly to converts like Andrew Carnegie, who wrote: " 'All is well since all grows better,' became my motto, my true source of comfort. Man was not created with an instinct for his own degradation but from the lower he had risen to the higher forms. Nor is there any conceivable end to his march to perfection. His face is turned to the light; he stands in the light and looks upward."

Spencer taught that all should be free to pursue happiness, but he never asked if all were equal at the start. He implied not that we get what we deserve but that we deserve what we get. Traits of character were inherited; character determined fate, and a bad fate meant a bad character. The fittest survived; the unfit were culled for the sake of the betterment of the race.

Theodore was chastened by the precept that his failures in life were determined, that he was a mere atom in the great void. Now he understood the things he had seen as a journalist—the venalities, the suicides, the murders, the inhumanities. All were explained, Spencer taught, by the fact that desires—"nascent excitations"—were the spark plugs of the human engine; they ignited consciousness into action, propelling men and women along the lines of least resistance to seek pleasure. There was no free will; virture was avoidance of pain; "the correspondence of certain inner physico-chemical actions with certain outer physico-chemical actions."

Life rewarded the strong: "Personal ends must be pursued with little regard to the evils entailed on unsuccessful competitors." This message confirmed Theodore's observations in Pittsburgh of the strong battening on the weak. And he also took comfort from Spencer that the desires that tormented him had been bred into him; they were a fact of nature. Finally, instead of the implacable Catholic God, there was the abstract, aloof Unknowable, acting out His own inscrutable purposes through puny humanity. What did that mean for Theodore's grand destiny? Why, he could be cast out in the evolutionary boneyard (like butcher Spilky's in Sullivan) at any time. He was a blindly whirling atom, his ambitions mere fragile bubbles of desire. What the individual tried to do mattered little, and his morality or lack of it mattered not at all.

In furnace-stage America, in the crucibles of its premier steelmaking city, the novelist was formed. Balzac made Dreiser see "for the first time how a book should be written. . . . I did not expect to write like Balzac but to use his method of giving a complete picture of life from beginning to end." Reporting had opened a window on the real world, and the view had convinced him that the lives of the great mass of men and women were hard and brutish, mirroring the ceaseless struggle in nature. Life was far from what it was represented to be by the priests and ministers; by the good, solid people like the Whites who lived in their dream world, the great American rural homestead; by the novels of sentiment and idealism; or by copybook maximists like Professor Hill, whose *Manual* Theodore had read in his boyhood. All those people were spinners of illusions.

But reporting had also showed him that nature had endowed him with a talent, writing, with which he could express his chaotic feelings. Reading Balzac, he had sensed that a novelist could write about what he saw, about life as it was lived. The rise and fall of individuals was a paradigm of the undulations of the Spencerian universe. In literature one could reenact the defeats of one's own dreams—and attain wealth, fame, and immortality in the process. Miss Fielding had told Theodore that *mind* was the touchstone of success, and now he had heroes who exemplified her advice—Spencer and Balzac. Philosophy and art were the royal roads to power. Two years later, he would call Spencer an intellectual Napoleon ("At the approach of his victorious mentality all living things bowed in vassalage, and he exacted the tribute of their reason and meaning from all") and Balzac "the Alexander of literature," whose conquering imagination penetrated into every corner of society and every guarded niche of the human heart.

The road ahead of him clearly led to New York. One night in late November 1894, perhaps after writing a story about the Salvation Army leader William Booth's last appearance in Pittsburgh, "General Booth Says Farewell," he stopped at the Press Club and fell into a conversation with the *Dispatch*'s political editor, who asked Theodore why he stayed in Pittsburgh. He was young and unencumbered—why didn't he go up to New York? Theodore blurted out that he hoped to. They talked about the welcome recently given to Rudyard Kipling by his New York admirers. Kipling's collection of short stories and poems—*Barrack-Room Ballads, Plain Tales From the Hills*—and his novel, *The Light That Failed*, were causing a stir, and he was the toast of the city. More to the point, Kipling was a former newspaperman, in India, a man of little education and no family connections who had made a literary success.

The next day Theodore gave his notice to the city editor, who did not seem surprised. The following Saturday he drew his final paycheck and at four o'clock that afternoon, with a bag and the two hundred and forty dollars he had saved, he boarded the express for New York. (His life, he might have thought, had been a series of train journeys—Terre Haute to Sullivan, Sullivan to Evansville, to Chicago, to Warsaw, to Chicago again, to St. Louis, Toledo, Cleveland, Buffalo, Pittsburgh . . . journeys without arrival.) As he was drawn into the future the locomotive's pistons seemed to chant, "change, change, change."

17. Fear of the City

New York in November 1894 was not the summertime city he had last seen. Paul was on the road, and Theodore missed his brother's bolstering presence. Emma's household was in a gloomy state. Hopkins was still unemployed, and he seemed to have given up trying to find a job. Emma greeted Theodore joyfully—relieved, he later learned, because she counted on his taking up the financial slack left by Paul's departure.

New York had sunk into an economic slump that cast a pall over his own prospects. Paul's newspaper connections might have helped him, but he was too proud (or naive) to exploit them. The papers reported that unemployment was severe. There were one hundred thousand men out of work in the city, and as Theodore passed the Sisters of Mercy Convent on Fifteenth Street he could see lines of shabbily dressed men stamping their feet to keep warm as they waited for admission to the soup kitchen the sisters ran.

One damp, chilly day he boarded the Sixth Avenue elevated and traveled downtown to Park Row, where the offices of all the city's major newspapers were located. He planned to start job hunting at the *World*— Joseph Pulitzer's paper, where a former St. Louis reporter might receive extra consideration, since Pulitzer had begun his rise to power in St. Louis.

As he walked through City Hall Park, Dreiser could see the *World* building at 32 Park Row, towering sixteen stories above him, capped by a golden dome. It was by far the tallest of the newspaper offices on the block (indeed the second tallest building in the city, next to the twenty-story American Surety building), dwarfing the *Tribune*'s nine-story redstone structure with its slender clock tower. It seemed calculated to make him feel insignificant. Nerving himself, Theodore entered the large doors and took the elevator to the city room on the eleventh floor. Immediately he was set upon by a pack of hostile office boys who refused to take his card identifying him as a correspondent for the St. Louis *Republic*.

Repulsed by the phalanx of sentinels, Theodore tried the other papers along the Row. At each he was greeted with indifference or contempt. It soon became clear that no paper in the city was hiring: he was only one of hundreds of out-of-work newspapermen. The confidence in his ability, the pride in the standing he had earned, whooshed out of him.

He sat awhile in the park, gazing up at the imposing row of newspaper offices, their windows staring back blankly. The park was full of bums and tramps, known as "benchers." He felt a kinship with them, which changed to cold fear. In what way was he superior? He too was unknown and jobless, a face in the crowd. While he was sitting with the bums of City Hall Park, looking at no one in particular, "the idea of *Hurstwood* was born," Dreiser wrote in *Newspaper Days*. He did not mean the fully developed George Hurstwood of *Sister Carrie*, the saloon-greeter who falls in love with Carrie Meeber, the pretty small-town girl adrift in Chicago. Rather, it was a vision of a shabby bum—the *fate* of Hurstwood—that suddenly flashed before his eyes.

Back at the warm apartment, he sat in the dark parlor, rocking. Finally Emma came in and placed an affectionate hand on his shoulder. "Paul says you can write wonderfully," she said. "You've only been here a day or two. . . . New York isn't so bad, only you have to get started." Once again, he mused, he must make a start in life.

In the ensuing days and weeks, Theodore toured the newspaper offices, meeting stony indifference. Finally, angered by the arrogance of the office boys at the *World*, he bulled past them into the city room. As the pack closed in, he stared in awe at the huge room, full of reporters scribbling stories and copy editors working at desks on a platform in the center. Cries of "Coppee!" rent the air (but no clatter of typewriters or ringing of telephones; those journalistic tools were still rarities).

As the watchdogs tried to drag him off, a tall, slender young man noticed the commotion. Handsome, his brow lined with premature wrinkles, Arthur Brisbane would, in 1895, become Sunday editor of the *World*, leading Pulitzer's army in the yellow journalism war against William Randolph Hearst's *Journal*. Brisbane calmly asked the now beleaguered hopeful who he was and what he wanted. When Theodore told him, Brisbane escorted him to the city editor's desk. "This young man wants a job," he said. "I wish you would give him one." With a quick nod, he was off.

After Brisbane left, the city editor eyed Theodore fishily and told him to wait for an assignment. An hour later, Dreiser was sent to Elizabeth, New Jersey, to investigate reports of ghostly emanations in a cemetery. "Where is Elizabeth?" he asked his new chief, who snarled, "Back of the directory!" meaning the city directory. After much effort Theodore was able to find the graveyard, but the reports turned out to be false: he had been sent on the customary journalistic snipe hunt.

After he returned from his fruitless quest to Elizabeth, the city editor told him he would be taken on as a space-rate reporter. He would be paid $7.50 per column (twenty-one inches of newsprint) or a proportion thereof, depending on how long his article ran, plus expenses and fifty cents an hour while out on assignment. His first published story—an account of a meeting on "How to Improve Tenement Life"—was boiled down to a few inches, and he received $1.86 for his efforts.

That sum should have signaled him that space-rate reporting was a losing game, for him at least. In his best week he made only $12.50—a bit more than what a skilled steelworker got, but well below the rate for beginning reporters, which was $15 to $20 a week. Actually, Dreiser seems not to have realized that most reporters at the *World* worked on space, and top performers, like David Graham Phillips and Albert Payson Terhune at the *World*, Stephen Crane at the *Herald*, and Lincoln Steffens at the *Evening Post*, earned up to $75 a week at it.

Most space-raters, however, were part of the labor pool the publishers maintained to keep wages down. The field of journalism was overcrowded and intensely competitive because so many newsmen were drawn to the city. The *World* was known as a journalistic jungle, a simulacrum of Pulitzer's driving, neurotic personality. The chief was now directing the paper in absentia, from his yacht off Cap-Martin, France, where he was recuperating from overwork. His trusted managing editor, Colonel

Cockerill, who had shot a man in St. Louis, drove the staff mercilessly while the chief hurled thunderbolts in the form of lengthy telegrams full of detailed instructions. The reporters worked long hours, and space men were required to put in the same office hours as everyone else. When Theodore was on the late watch, he had to stay until the first edition was put to bed, at 3:00 A.M.

The *World* had beaten out Charles A. Dana's *Sun* in circulation after Pulitzer's arrival in the 1880s. The *Sun*, somewhat more staid, was a writer's paper, and went in for long, elegantly crafted features. Dana was obsessed with good writing, and was known to fire a reporter at the drop of a solecism. His staff people were encouraged to take their time with their stories, and turn out a finished essay. Pulitzer's motto, posted prominently in the city room, was "Terseness—Accuracy—Terseness." When Hearst took over at the *Journal*, his byword was speed, speed, speed, and when he challenged Pulitzer to a circulation war, the final stage of devolution was reached: "Sensation, sensation, sensation."

It was into this milieu that Theodore dipped a tentative toe—a world of ruthless newspaper barons, thoroughbred reporters, and whiskey-drinking hacks, glamorous figures like Richard Harding Davis and David Graham Phillips, and sleazy types like Frank Butler, a flabby man in food-stained clothes who looked like "a dropsical eagle that had spent the night in a coal bin."

Reporters flaunted a bohemian life-style, spending their leisure hours in saloons like Hess & Loeb's and the back room of Perry's Drug Store, though most of them eventually acquired wives and children and houses in the suburbs. A few were celebrities, like the elegant Davis, glamour boy of the era and model for Charles Dana Gibson's lantern-jawed Gibson Man, who escorted society belles and actresses to Delmonico's and was a regular at the Waldorf bar (when he was not off on some foreign assignment). The equally handsome Phillips wore dandyish suits and shirts of startling hues, but was known as something of a prig among his colleagues. Davis was considered a snob. Both had started out at Dana's *Sun*, writing stories about the prostitutes who were herded into the Jefferson Market Courthouse every day for revolving-door justice, then graduating to more ambitious pieces about con men, murderers, suicides, and terminally ill little girls.

Theodore nursed a resentment toward Davis and Phillips and their kind—those well-groomed young college men in fine clothes who seemed the favored ones and who spoke familiarly of high governmental and society figures. He resented their glib talk of "reform," a word coming into vogue, sensing in it the condescending charity of the rich to the worthy poor. His experience with reform was that it had cost Hopkins his job, leaving his sister Emma hard up. Always, it seemed, the Dreisers were the victims of the forces of respectability.

Lacking Davis's and Phillips's self-confidence and panache (or Stephen Crane's precocious genius, for that matter), Theodore was condemned to sit on the bench with the other space-raters, treated like a cub, a nobody—he who had been a star in St. Louis. Now he could not seem to hit upon a story that would catch the city editor's glazed eye. His first assignment finally came when he embroidered a routine fight in the tenements. Headlined "Mrs. Moriarty Knocks Out Healy," it was a stereotypical account of a drunken Irish laborer who brawled with some female co-tenants on East Twenty-ninth Street. The city editor, on the lookout for color and "josh," liked the item and quickly assigned Theodore to look into an altercation at the Hoffman House between the manager and a young Vanderbilt. But when Theodore arrived at the scene, all the parties clammed up. He was intimidated by the haughty employees of the hotel and by the supercilious butler at the youth's home. Finding no one would talk with him, he reported to his chief that there was no story. The city editor was angry, probably expecting that, interviews or no, Theodore would concoct something. That was the last plum assignment he gave the new man. Thereafter, even when Dreiser brought in a good story, it was passed to one of the staff reporters to write up. Theodore was paid only for his time and expenses (which he had learned to pad).

During the endless hours he spent in the reporters' room, he met other hangers-on from the West. One of them, a reporter from Pittsburgh, was trying to support a family on "space" and finding it impossible. Another told him about a mutual friend, a city editor they had known in St. Louis, who had committed suicide in a West Street hotel.

"What was the trouble?" Theodore asked.

"Tired of the game, I guess," was the reply. "He didn't get along down here as well as he had out there. I guess he felt that he was going downhill."

Going downhill was an occupational hazard of the newspaperman's life, and Theodore remembered the crack reporters in St. Louis who had become bums and drug addicts. The vision of the derelict that came to him in City Hall Park lurked in the back of his mind. How was he any better than the other hopefuls drawn to New York?

Meanwhile, life at Emma's had grown more uncomfortable. Hopkins spent most of his days lounging dispiritedly around the house, "waiting for something to turn up," and Theodore watched him (seeing him through Em's eyes) progressively going to seed, not shaving, wearing old clothes, refusing to take the odd jobs his political cronies offered him out of charity. "He had turned fifty and he came to feel life was over for him," Dreiser later wrote. With Christmas approaching, Emma was desperate. There was no money for presents, and her husband was proposing that they rent rooms to transient lovers again.

The idea of Em operating a bedhouse outraged Theodore. When it came to his blood sister, of whom he was fond, his attitude was protective like Paul's. Moreover, she was a mother, and therefore sacred. Hopkins wanted to exploit her because he was too lazy to work. Theodore could not stand the idea of any of his sisters being used. Branded in his memory was the humiliation of the Warsaw and Chicago days when Em and Theresa were playthings for rich men.

He had developed a strong antipathy to Hopkins. There was something vulpine about the man, something predatory in his eyes that reminded Theodore of Rome's feral selfishness. But there was also something there that mirrored what Theodore was also feeling: fear. They were "suffering from the same terror of life or New York." This fear, causally linked with failure, was in the eyes of the derelicts in City Hall Park. It was like a contagious disease—the disease of poverty.

Theodore had by now concluded that Em's marriage was intolerable; she and the children must leave Hopkins. When he broached the idea to her, however, she broke into tears. She told him how much she had loved Hopkins in Chicago—had been insane about him really. And she had been partially to blame for the affair, she confessed. She had been so wild then—a flirtatious girl, sympathizing with Hopkins when he told her how miserable his life was with his first wife. Now that her youth was gone, it was no wonder he was indifferent. The fire had gone cold. And Emma had no training; it would be hard for her to survive on her own, though maybe Paul would help. Keeping house was all she knew.

Gradually, however, Theodore wore down her resistance. With the family talent for evading the issue, they devised an elaborate ruse. Sometime after Christmas—which Theodore had made a good one for the children with money from his shrinking savings—the plan was put into motion. Telling Hopkins he was going back to Pittsburgh, Theodore took a room near the Bowery. Not long after he moved in, a policeman banged on his door and demanded to know who he was; it turned out that the place was a bedhouse. He quickly found new lodgings. Next, he wrote a letter and had a friend on the *Dispatch* mail it from Pittsburgh. Emma showed the letter to Hopkins and told him that she was going to join her brother and that he would have to look out for himself. Hopkins was sufficiently roused by this ultimatum to find a job as a hotel clerk in Brooklyn. After he had gone, Em had the furniture moved to a new apartment she had taken on West Seventeenth Street. The two once-notorious lovers never saw each other again. Hopkins died a year or so later. Theodore had seen him once in Brooklyn, a ruin of a man. (By another account, Hopkins had returned to his wife in Chicago.)

Theodore continued to warm the bench in the reporters' room at the *World*. Now he was just a legman, obtaining facts for others to write. He covered a streetcar strike in Brooklyn, as part of a team of *World* reporters—an experience that provided him with background for *Sister Carrie*. Often he went to the city morgue to check out a report of a suicide. If there was some colorful angle, or (even better) the victim was a pretty young girl, a suicide story was worth a few inches. (Richard Harding Davis's epitaph for such cases—striking the correct note of pity and irony—was, "At least she'll never get to the Haymarket [a notorious dance hall]." Dreiser was also assigned to Bellevue Hospital, a charnel house; going home late at night, he passed girls who had got to the Haymarket, and men lying unconscious on the street, their pockets rifled.

New York seemed a welter of corruption and venality: the political hacks who presided indifferently over the wards at Bellevue, the little man at the morgue whom he regularly bribed with a pouch of tobacco when he needed to view some pale corpse. At a higher remove of society, he sensed a grander corruption—the arrogance and cruelty of the wealthy. The hugeness and force and heartlessness of the great city oppressed him. He felt the mortal chill of poverty as he trudged streets piled with dirty snow and saw the shabby men shivering in breadlines.

Yet the day came when he could take no more of the indifference with which he was treated at the *World*. When he brought in a story—about one of the waxen maidens of the morgue—the city editor told him perfunctorily to give it to a rewrite man. Something in Theodore snapped and he protested: "I don't see why I should have to do this. I'm not a beginner in this game. I wrote stories and big ones before I ever came to this paper."

"Maybe you did," the editor replied, "but we have the feeling that you haven't proved to be of much use to us."

Sensing his imminent firing (the blue slips informing a reporter he was sacked were a common sight in the mail pigeonholes), Dreiser quit. He paid a last visit to Brisbane, hoping that the man who had intervened by chance to get him this job would now help him again. Brisbane was courteous but noncommittal; he read Theodore's *Dispatch* clips and suggested he try the *Sun*, where they were more interested in feature stories. Or he should become a magazinist; daily journalism wasn't his game.

After drawing his last meager check and then walking out the city room door, past the watchdogs, who had been right—he belonged on the streets with the rest of the "hams"—Theodore swore he would starve rather than work for a newspaper again. His chances were reasonably good of doing just that.

18. Street Scenes

Not much is known about Theodore's movements during the next months. He still had some of his savings left, and could afford to free-lance for a while. He was becoming accustomed to living frugally.

Having failed at journalism, he decided to heed Brisbane's suggestion and become a magazinist. He first tried penning short stories for distinguished publications like *Harper's Monthly*, *The Atlantic Monthly*, the *Century*, and *Scribner's Magazine*. But after studying them assiduously, he concluded they had only the remotest connection to life as he knew it. So smoothly written and delicately wrought in their observations, they showed faithful love rewarded and dreams always coming true. The female characters exemplified the highest ideals of chastity. The men were either drooling satyrs to be vanquished by a stern look of blue-eyed rectitude or else misguided boys to be redeemed by the superior power of feminine virtue.

Wandering the streets, he stored up impressions in the honeycombs of his subconscious. The exotic corners of the city and their teeming humanity were what he really wanted to write about, but the kind of word pictures in his head did not translate readily into newspaper copy. When Dreiser suggested doing stories about the great contrasts between wealth and poverty, editors would say, "Old stuff! Old stuff! Think up something that everybody doesn't know about." Once he encountered Mark Twain strolling along Doyers Street in Chinatown, elegantly clad in a fur-collared overcoat and a top hat, tapping the sidewalk with a gold-headed cane. Having read that Twain was scheduled to meet with his lawyers to untangle the bankruptcy of a publishing company in which the humorist had an interest, and knowing that the papers were interested in "old authors who were about to fail," Theodore tried to get an interview. Twain, however, shooed him away, saying, "I'm not to be interviewed in this way. I don't mind you newspapermen interviewing me—and saying that you saw me. But no more than that. Otherwise I'll have to deny it." Cowed, Theodore muttered that he understood, then cursed himself for missing his big chance.

No other story so salable came his way; perhaps he didn't look very hard. Rather, he explored the side streets and stared at the strolling girls, "of the painted cohorts of the city," in Stephen Crane's phrase. Their pimps, dressed in high Bowery fashion—tight pants, silk hat, black scarf, polished boots—hovered in the background, waiting for them to lure marks into a back room, where they could roll them. At night the "jays" would descend on the area looking for excitement in notorious saloons like Ahearn's or the Atlantic Gardens. The origin of the term jay was the phrase "naked as a jaybird"; that's what those country boys would be after the toughs picked them clean.

Bums were everywhere, drawn to the saloons, where for the price of a schooner of beer—a nickel—they could nurse a bowl of hot, greasy soup at the free-lunch counter. According to Jacob Riis, the Danish-born police reporter who had, four years previously, written a book on New York's poor, *How the Other Half Lives*, ten thousand homeless men descended upon the Bowery every night, seeking a place to sleep in the cheap lodging houses. For a quarter, they could purchase the luxury of a partitioned room; fifteen cents got them a dormitory bed; and, for a nickel, they could sleep on the floor crammed between other unwashed bodies. Riis reported that sanitary police inspecting one such inn of the homeless found twelve adults in a room measuring thirteen by thirteen feet—three of them in bunks and the rest on the floor; three others were sprawled in the hallway. It was in such a flophouse that Stephen Crane stayed when he wrote his sketch "An Experiment in Misery," which appeared in the New York *Press* in April 1894. When he entered, Crane "felt his liver turn white . . . there came to his nostrils strange and unspeakable odors that assailed him like malignant diseases with wings. They seemed to be from human bodies closely packed in dens; the exhalations from a hundred pairs of reeking lips; the fumes from a thousand bygone debauches; the expression of a thousand present miseries."

After Riis published his book, young journalists regarded the Bowery as a testing ground. Lincoln Steffens, a Californian of respectable upbringing just arrived in the city, wrote excitedly to his parents that he was going to "the vilest part of the horrible East Side amid poverty, sin and depravity. Will it degrade me? Will it make a man of me? Here is my field, my chance."

A similar sense of quest may have stimulated Theodore. He watched bums gathered in Chatham Square, waiting for the flops to open; the breadline (here the term was coined) of hungry men that formed every night at Fleischmann's Vienna Model Bakery on Tenth and Broadway, waiting for employees to distribute the day's leftovers; the foundling home where unwed mothers stole up to leave their babies in an anonymous crib; the crowd of men jamming the door of a mission soup kitchen.

When he wandered over to the Italian neighborhood around Mulberry Street, site of the famous "Bend" that Riis pinpointed as the nadir of the other half's misery before its noisome tenements were torn down, Theodore was more enthralled by the teeming, vivid life spilling out on the streets than by the statistics of poverty. He saw clots of gossiping old women in black dresses, mothers breast-feeding their infants on the stoops, girls leaning out the windows to flirt with pushcart men selling cut-rate bruised vegetables and decaying chickens. Riis had eavesdropped on the hidden dramas inside those sagging brick structures—the "sweater [sweat] shops" on Hester and Bayard streets, where pale Jewish girls toiled; tiny, fetid rooms in which large families lived in squalor; courts like those at Homestead, with stinking privies hard by the single hydrants from which the residents took their drinking and washing water; narrow alleys that led to stale-beer dives where the dregs of the poor could buy a tomato can of the rancid stuff for a penny: "A room perhaps a dozen feet square, with walls and ceiling that might once have been clean—assuredly the floor had not in the memory of man, if indeed there was other floor than hard-trodden mud—but were now covered with a brown dust that, touched with the end of a club, came off in shuddering showers of crawling bugs, revealing the blacker filth beneath."

Sometimes "conditions" became too much for these people. Riis relates the story of one family whose members all took poison: they were "tired," neighbors said. They had lived "in the attic with a sloping ceiling and a single window so far out on the roof that it seemed not to belong to the place at all. With scarcely room enough to turn around in they had been compelled to pay $5.50 per month in advance."

There were to be sure many private charities, philanthropists, and immigrant societies trying to help such people, but the tidal wave of misery that crested during that winter of 1894 overwhelmed them. In its 1895 annual statement, the Christian Aid to Employment Society lamented: "Our treasury is empty . . . our work has been sadly crippled by the scarcity of employment, as our income depends very largely upon subscriptions from employers for services rendered."

As a result, the society said, it had to turn many needy people away. Since December 1894 it had accepted 1810 applications, after investigating to see if they were deserving. "Many [of the 1810] have been shelterless and hungry before employment came. Others have fallen ill for the lack of the necessaries of life, and some have died who might have lived, if a helping hand had been extended in time."

Nathalie Dana, the daughter of a minister, lived in a house on East Seventy-first Street. On a nearby vacant lot camped a family of Irish squatters. Nathalie watched them milking their goats and heard their frequent rows and beatings. Her attitude toward the poor was typically middle class: "It was generally assumed that [they] were not in the same category as our friends, and, like the animals, had less sensibility. . . . The misfortunes of such people were of their own doing, the result of drink and lack of moral fibre."

The ragged bums, redolent or not of whiskey, were the chief face of misery on the streets that winter of 1894–1895. William Dean Howells was deeply troubled by "the sodden tramps whom I meet now and then, looking like . . . forlorn wild beasts." While sitting on his favorite bench in Central Park, the novelist noticed the idle workmen shuffling along the walks and thought such men "must wonder why the city cannot minister to his need as well as his pleasure. . . . If it can give him this magnificent garden for his forced leisure, why cannot it give him a shop where he can go in extremity, to earn his bread." He eavesdropped on the con-

*John Paul Dreiser in the
1890s, wearing the full
beard he sometimes affected.*
(UP)

*Sarah Schänäb Dreiser in
her fifties. "No one ever
wanted me enough, unless
it was my mother."*
(IU)

*The Sullivan Wool Manufactory,
reliquary of the ashes of
John Paul Dreiser's ambitions.
(Sketch by Frederick Booth
for* A Hoosier Holiday.*)*

*The IU freshman, seated
third from right; apparently
a student spelunking club.*
(IU)

The St. Louis reporter, aged twenty-two, in full sartorial cry. "I have a semi-Roman nose, a high forehead and an Austrian lip, with the edges of my teeth always showing."

(IU)

"TD's home in Chicago where his mother died."
(Snapshot taken in the 1920s by Helen Dreiser.)

(UP)

His fiancée, Sara Osborne White (Jug),
in 1894. "An intense something . . .
that was concealed by an air of
supreme innocence and maidenly reserve."
(IU)

Dreiser in the 1890s, taken in Chicago,
perhaps during his 1893 visit to
the "dear old World's Fair where
I learned to love you."
(IU)

Paul Dresser at the zenith of his Broadway celebrity. His songs "bespoke a wistful, seeking, uncertain temperament, tender and illusioned. . . . He was generous to the point of self-destruction, and that is literally true."

(UP)

TD's sister Theresa, *"a shadowy, self-effacing girl,"* who died when struck by a train while wheeling her bicycle across the tracks. *"Poor Theresa, her life was not a sunny one."*
(EU)

Rome, the *"family Nemesis."* He liked to join the other *"dudes"* outside the Terre Haute House, a toothpick in his mouth as though he had just eaten dinner inside.
(EU)

Sister Emma Dreiser, prototype of Carrie, "vain, silly, childlike, beautiful, a nerve harp to be played upon by every wind of circumstances."

(Courtesy of Vera Dreiser)

Claire, one of the "triumvirate" who followed Sarah to Vincennes and Sullivan; the most conventional of the Dreiser sisters.
(EU)

Ed, the youngest, shown in his first acting job—a song slide of "The Baggage Coach Ahead." He is holding the baby.
(UP)

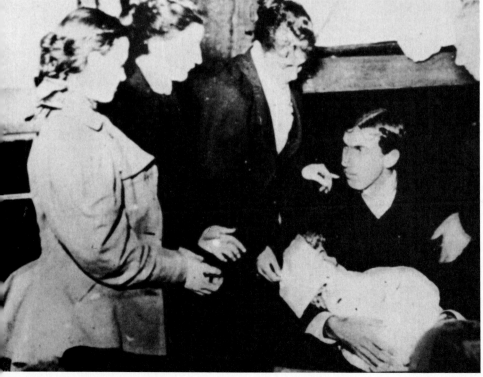

versation of a married couple, both of them shabbily but decently clad. The man patiently explained to his wife why "he had no permanent place in the economy. . . . He blamed no one; he only blamed the conditions."

The park was a landscaped, tree-lined microcosm of the city, where the poor watched the parade of carriages on the mall. The rich made a vulgar display, Howells thought, and lacked the "wicked grace" of Old World aristocrats. Dana remembered her nanny's condemnation of a lady riding past in an open victoria, wearing a garish feathered bonnet and a cumbersome velvet dress. One Fifth Avenue family sent its poodles out for a daily drive in a carriage, attended by a coachman and a footman. The dogs rode regally in the back seat.

When Howells rambled the New York streets, he noted the scraps of paper and straw and fruit peels; the choking dust in the air in summer consisted of pulverized horse droppings. He was repelled by the irregular buildings—a mélange of shapes and styles that reminded him of "a horse's jawbone with the teeth broken or dislodged at intervals." At night, Broadway was illuminated by a blaze of "fire signs"—electric lights, "each trying to shout and shriek each other down." As he passed the luxury hotels, with their great plate-glass windows revealing the diners in their opulent cafés, he wondered why New Yorkers made no protest at "the perpetual encounter of famine and of surfeit."

During Crane's two-day experiment in misery, he had joined the benchers in City Hall Park. Like Theodore, he gazed up at the lofty newspaper offices of Park Row, and the *World*'s shining gold tower like the minaret in an old Persian painting. Crane had been shaken by a sudden vision of the great gulf between him and those buildings. They were "emblematic of a nation forcing its regal head into the clouds throwing no downward glances; in the sublimity of its aspirations ignoring the wretches who may flounder at its feet."

Theodore too was seeing the city from the bottom up, with the eyes of one of the city's itinerant poor. Dorothy Dudley writes, "In adversity his father was growing into him, superseding, undermining the 'pagan' mother, so much adored." He came to understand better Paul's nights in those lonely rooms while he was away from his family, and the blow to his pride and manhood of being out of work. Spencer's Unknowable had superseded his father's harsh God. "Life was desolate, inexplicable, unbelievably accidental—luck or disaster," he told Dudley.

As the winter wore on, Theodore realized he was sinking into the undifferentiated mass of nameless, tattered men, scarecrow arms flapping against the cold. After submerging so far, you reached a depth from which there was no return. You acquired a permanent air of defeat; your eyes were hunted, feral, your gait shuffling and weary. The bums had been pushed down by the iron hand of conditions. Theodore had always fancied that his plight was only temporary, that his destiny would eventually summon him, but now he wondered if he had plummeted too far.

He still had a few dollars saved. When those ran out, he pawned some of his belongings. Perhaps he found some temporary work or sold a few paragraphs to one of the newspapers. At any rate, the more hard up he became, the more reluctant he was to seek help from Howley, Haviland. Paul was on the road with a show, but even if he had been in the city, Theodore's pride would have prevented him from intruding on his older brother's glittering Broadway world. He might have imagined himself lurching out of the snowy night into the glare of the fire signs to accost Paul emerging from the stage door. The humiliation would have been too much.

At one point, reduced to sleeping in flophouses, Theodore found his own experience in misery more than he could bear. Now he was one of those anonymous men, hearing them groan in their sleep, smelling their reeking bodies. One bitter cold night, he later said—perhaps apocryphally—he walked down to the wharves by the East River, intending to hurl himself into the frigid waters. As he picked his way along the pier, he half-tripped over a bulky object, hard yet yielding. It was a sack of potatoes. He was hungry; he hadn't eaten all day. Collecting some small sticks and boards lying about, he made a fire and cooked them. The fire warmed him until they were done. The food restored him; the find was an omen that his luck would turn, that his destiny held.

If the idea for the character of Hurstwood, the tragic saloon manager of *Sister Carrie*, came to him that day in City Hall Park, it acquired stronger outlines during his sojourn on the Bowery. A number of influences converged on him—the spectacle of the bums in Chatham Square, the smells of the flophouses, the thoughts of suicide, the cold and the hunger, the recrudescent fears of poverty and his father's failure—the lean days in Terre Haute. Even in the chance enounter with Mark Twain, dapper in his fur coat and top hat but stalked by the specter of bankruptcy, Dreiser saw an old writer who had been cast aside. What if a man tumbled from the golden coach into these mean streets?

Out of such thoughts as these and the sights around him came the tragic last act of *Carrie,* and a number of urban sketches that he would write around the time he wrote the novel, describing the sweatshops, the life in the tenements, the men in the breadline, lining up at the flophouse, the benchers, the chairwarmers who if they looked respectable sneaked into a good hotel to experience vicariously the comfort and leisure of the guests (as Theodore had done in Cleveland).

But he could not write those things yet; no one was interested and he hadn't the courage to breach the wall of indifference. Instead, he cowered in his lair until spring blew in, trailing scudding white clouds. The change of the seasons signaled the return of summer—and Paul.

19. The One-Man Band

n May Theodore went to the Howley, Haviland office to see if Paul had returned (he hadn't) and while there overheard Pat Howley and Fred Haviland talking about starting a song magazine. Oliver Ditson's, the song publishing house where Haviland once worked, had profitably published the *Musical Record* since 1878, and there were others. They contained the words to numerous songs and were aimed at the trade—music shops, teachers, students, and performers. Howley, Haviland had something of this sort of publication in mind, but one that would advertise their songs to a nonprofessional audience.

The firm now had some songs to push. Within a year or so it had grown from a moonlighting operation to a full-time business. At first the partners had held on to their old jobs (Howley was with Willis Woodward and Company), and they brought out their first sheet music under the pseudonym George T. Worth and Company. Most of those early efforts sank without a trace, but their rent was low and they had no employees to pay. The office consisted of a single large room about twenty feet by twenty, with a tryout piano in one corner, a long table covered with stacks of music, another for correspondence, and wooden bins along the wall in which the firm's entire back stock was stored.

Paul had published some forgettable numbers under the Worth imprint, including "He Loves Me, He Loves Me Not" and "I Told Her the Same Old Story," but in 1895 he wrote a modest hit for the company called "Take a Seat, Old Lady." Based on a scene Paul had witnessed in Terre Haute, it told the poignant tale of a weary old lady who sits in a chair "in front of a building grand," but is ejected by a haughty clerk. A young newsboy brings her a chair, and years later his good deed is rewarded when she "dies without kin" and "leaves all her thousands to him."

But the song that had launched the firm was "The Sidewalks of New York," an infectious waltz about street life written by an actor named Charles B. Lawlor and a hat salesman named Jim Blake. It was a perfect number for the ubiquitous Italian organ grinders who soon were playing it on every corner, just as the verse had said: "While the 'ginnie' played the organ on the sidewalks of New York." That success was followed by another, "I Can't Tell Why I Love You But I Do," written by a teenage prodigy named Gus Edwards, who would become one of the top song-writers of the early 1900s. With profits starting to roll in, Howley quit his job, and Haviland joined him after his employer got wind of what he was doing and fired him.

The sheet music business was undergoing a rapid transformation from cottage industry to mass-production operation, and Howley, Haviland was in the vanguard of the young Turk publishers who were operating out of their hats but determined to cut a slice of the huge profits that could be made. In addition to cheaper printing made possible by the rotary press and photoengraving, a nationwide distribution network for sheet music was in place. No longer were songs peddled at intermissions of minstrel shows and in a few specialty shops. Now they were sold in department stores and music shops in every city and large town. Thousands of copies, retailing for fifty cents each, could be shipped by rail and reach these outlets in a matter of days, should the demand arise.

Techniques for stimulating that demand had also improved, and *Ev'ry Month* was designed to be a cog in the promotional machinery. Not so long ago, popular songs endured for years, slowly piling up sales. But in the 1890s came the phenomenon of the "hit"—a song that sold several hundred thousand copies within the space of a year or so. The most famous of these was Charles K. Harris's "After the Ball," the rage of the Chicago fair, which sold more than seven hundred and fifty thousand copies. Howley, Haviland employed all the usual promotional techniques—paying off singers to plug a song, bribing the padrones of the organ-grinder brigades to play it *ad nauseam*, distributing copies to political clubs and the like—but now they were going a step further. With *Ev'ry Month* they were invading the parlors of America, making a direct appeal to the consumers, giving them a magazine they could read as well as play.

And so there they were, on a day in May, sitting pretty and bubbling with plans for the future. Hearing their talk about issuing a song magazine, Theodore immediately nominated himself as its editor and proposed that they publish a real magazine as a wrapper for their songs. In this fashion, they would attract readers who would play the songs for others, inducing them to buy the sheet music. Any profits from sales of the magazine would be gravy. Pat and Fred liked his idea and hired Theodore at ten dollars a week until the first issue was out, and fifteen dollars a week thereafter. Probably Paul had put in a word or more on his "genius" brother's behalf, wanting to give him a hand. Since Theodore would work cheap, Pat and Fred were willing to take a chance on him, while not alienating their top composer and outside man. They were song publishers, however, not magazine men, and probably envisioned the magazine as a shoestring operation, serving primarily as a vehicle for the firm's songs. Theodore, however, had his own ideas, which would become more visible as time went on.

He had all summer to plan his premier number, scheduled to make its debut in September, after people returned from their summer vacations. He took as his model the ten-cent magazines like *Munsey's,* which he had read so avidly in Pittsburgh and which appealed to the aspiring young urban middle class (of whom he was one, after all). Frank Munsey had pioneered some money-saving innovations that made his low cover price possible. He used photographs lavishly because the development of the halftone engraving process made them cheaper than woodcuts. He also created departments on topics that appealed directly to readers (theater, society, fashion, and the like). They were written by anonymous free-lancers, enabling Munsey to avoid competing for high-priced authors, who in the case of a Rudyard Kipling or a Robert Louis Stevenson commanded as much as thirty-five thousand dollars for a book-length serial.

Theodore borrowed those ideas, and the dime cover price as well, and took further inspiration from the British magazine *The Strand,* which chronicled the doings of London celebrities, and from the theatrical weeklies of New York, though not their risqué aspects. The name *Ev'ry Month* was perhaps inspired by *The Atlantic Monthly's* weekly offshoot, *Every Saturday,* or even *Every Other Week,* the name of the magazine edited by the hero of Howells's novel *A Hazard of New Fortunes*, which was based loosely on the author's move to New York City to edit *The Cosmopolitan*.

That Dreiser was aiming at more than a song magazine was evident early on. Initially *Ev'ry Month* was billed as "An Illustrated Magazine of Popular Music and Literature," but after a few issues it became "An Illustrated Magazine of Literature and Popular Music," which reflected the priorities of the editor—or rather the "editor arranger" as he was identified on the masthead. By the June 1896 issue he had finally targeted his readership. A note inside announces: "EV'RY MONTH having obtained control of THE WOMAN'S MAGAZINE its excellent features will hereafter be combined with this magazine." *The Woman's Magazine* was probably one of several mayfly fashion publications devoted to what Richard Harding Davis called "the New American Girl." Perhaps it had folded and *Ev'ry Month* took over the name, becoming "The Woman's Magazine of Literature and Music."

That was more like it. The chief buyers of sheet music—and popular magazines for that matter—were young women. The upright piano was becoming a standard fixture in the parlor of every middle-class home, supplanting the bulkier and more expensive organ, with its paneled mirrors and elaborate carvings. Thousands of young women dutifully added piano playing to their attainments and performed the latest tunes for family and beaux (Jug had impressed Theodore in this fashion during their courtship days in St. Louis). *Ev'ry Month* was about the size of a piece of sheet music and could be spread out on the music rack.

The average *Ev'ry Month* reader probably bought the magazine for the two or three songs contained in each issue, which cost her only ten cents, compared to fifty cents for a copy of sheet music. So one of them informed the editor-arranger at any rate:

> Thee I wish you would send me and Ed every
> month regular as Ed plays the violen [sic] and
> I would like it for the music there is in it.
>   Sister Emma

His sister's letter did not deter Theodore from his vision of a kind of junior *Munsey's*, full of fiction, articles, departments, and illustrations. At first, though, he was hard pressed for material, and he wrote most of the contents of the early issues. With little advertising, he had to come up with copy to fill thirty-two pages. He had no assistants, so he also had to write begging letters to his literary friends, wangle free illustrative material, edit and proofread copy, and oversee layout and production. Not surprisingly, the early issues were speckled with errors, typographical and grammatical. In the case of one story by a literarily inclined young man named Richard Duffy, who soon gave up selling insurance to become an editor at *Ainslee's* magazine, several pages were dropped and only the conclusion printed. Duffy forgave Theodore and they became friends.

To give the illusion of numerous contributors, Theodore adopted several noms de plume. In the Christmas issue, he was "The Prophet," who signed the "Reflections" column, an editorial grab-bag of notes and philosophical observations that led off the magazine. He was also "The Cynic," the author of an essay called "The Gloom Chasers" (a reworking of a humorous article he had written for the Pittsburgh *Dispatch); "*Edward Al" (a combining of two of his brothers' first names), who conducted "The Literary Shower"; "S. J. White" (a wave to Jug), who wrote the article "We Others"; "Th.D.," the play reviewer, and probably the anonymous author of the column on flowers in the back of the book. In the August 1896 issue his first published short story (aside from the youthful "Return of Genius") appeared. Entitled "Forgotten," it was an amalgam of Paul's song "The Letter That Never Came," telling in prose the sad story of the quiet man lying in a hospital bed asking each day if there is a letter for him, and "Hospital Violet Day," the *Dispatch* piece about flowers and dying in a hospital. Theodore also clipped short poems from other magazines as fillers. He wrote Jug that they had been selected as love poems just for her.

Eventually Theodore's friends responded to his calls for help. From St. Louis Peter McCord contributed fiction, verse, and humorous pieces under his own name and pseudonyms like "James McCord," "J. Rhey McCord," and "The Enthusiast" (a counterbalance to "The Cynic"?). Dick Wood sent some romantic fiction and Decadent verse. Later, William Marion Reedy was represented with an obituary of Joseph McCullagh. (The taciturn editor had committed suicide by jumping from the window of an upper story of his house. Aloof to the end, he left no note.) And Arthur Henry, who had quit his job with the Toledo *Blade* to become a free-lance writer and publicist, offered some poems and philosophical effusions. There were also occasional articles on political issues. John P. Altgeld, the progressive governor of Illinois, for example, was represented by an attack on the misuse of the injunction in labor disputes.

In time, as the magazine began to generate some revenue, Theodore was able to buy fiction and commission articles by New York City writers, paying them a penny a word. George C. Jenks, an out-of-work Pittsburgh newsman who had moved to the city, took over "The Literary Shower." The title was a steal from *Town Topics*'s "The Literary Show," conducted by avant garde critic Percival Pollard. Virginia Hyde wrote a series on well-known contemporary women calculated to appeal to *Ev'ry Month*'s feminine readership. Others were recruited to write on fashions, society, and the theater. Glenn Willets, a scion of an old New York family, specialized in stories and articles about society; bearded Morgan Robertson contributed sea tales. Theodore also purchased syndicated stories by better-known writers, such as Stephen Crane's "A Mystery of Heroism" and Bret Harte's "A Night in the Divide." But his staple was romantic fiction designed for his feminine readers.

At first he depended almost entirely on publicity stills and boiler-plate illustrations, but when the magazine's balance sheet improved he bought original art. He commissioned William Louis Sonntag, Jr., son of a famous illustrator, to do a Christmas spread called "A Christmas With Captain Kidd." Sonntag, a young painter of great promise, introduced Theodore to New York's *vie de bohème*, a world of bearded painters and exotic studios with hangings and "Turkish corners." He painted realistic street scenes that caught the colors of an oily puddle in the gutter or the looming shape of the El. But none of those pictures appeared in *Ev'ry Month*. The editor-arranger did not dare publish any of Sonntag's realistic drawings, which anticipated the urban scenes painted by the Ash Can School. His idea of a cover was a young woman looking pensively at a book or attired in furs and haloed by swirling snowflakes. She was always ethereal, demure, and very proper—a suitable face for the parlor piano.

As time went on, women's features came to dominate *Ev'ry Month*. There were columns that purveyed household hints or discussed fashions and needlework, and series like "American Women in Art." Virginia Hyde (who in feminist fashion signed herself V. D. Hyde) branched out to professional women, e.g., "Portia Come Again," a profile of the lawyer Clara Shortridge Foltz.

But if *Ev'ry Month* had become a women's magazine, Theodore edited it with one woman in mind—Sara Osborne White. He wrote her out in Missouri that she was the magazine's "mascot," and promised that her name would be smuggled into every issue. She insisted he use S. J. W. as a pseudonym because S. O. W. was too personal. And in another letter he tells her that a passage in the "Reflections" column expressed his loneliness for her. Theodore apologized for his neglect, but said he was dedicating himself to the task of making the magazine a success and quotes a poem called "Renouncement":

> I must not think of thee; and, tired yet strong,
> I shun the thought [that] lurks in all delight
> The thought of thee. . . .

He was not always successful, though. "All of the literary people I meet here tell me I'm the most easygoing editor in town," he confessed, "and I think I must be. Here in my office I do more thinking about you than I do about my various duties and frequently I abandon all details and announce myself 'out' to all comers just so I may have an hour's peace in which to write you." Still, "Like Dinah's meals in Uncle Tom's Cabin 'Ev'ry Month' comes out of chaos all o.k." In November 1896 he boasted that it was "forging to the front very rapidly." Later, he tells Sara that he may hire an assistant so that he will be able to spend more time with her after they are married; still later, he writes that someone has offered him an editorship, "but a new magazine would kill me sure." He complains of insomnia and a constant feeling of tiredness, symptoms he had experienced in St. Louis when he was overworked. He could feel a night of sleeplessness coming on—"turning and turning," "painful nervousness"—and would take a teaspoon of brandy to quiet his nerves. Bothered by a nervous stomach, he went to a doctor, who prescribed pepsin, a digestive.

After only a year, circulation rose to sixty-five thousand and the magazine grew to forty-four pages, with advertising up from three pages to nine. The products represented included Quaker Oats, Beecham's Pills, *The Housewife* magazine, Crown Violet perfume, *The Encyclopedia Dictionary*, and Cleveland's Baking Powder. A full-time advertising representative was hired, and Theodore had his own "editorial stationery" printed up on blue paper.

Despite circulation gains, however, his future as an editor was increasingly shaky. *Ev'ry Month* was not a moneymaker, at least in the eyes of Pat Howley and Fred Haviland. Haviland claimed in later years that the firm dropped a total of fifty thousand dollars on it, a considerable loss. The song publishing business being a literally hit or miss affair, the steady drain of *Ev'ry Month* must have assumed outsize proportions in their minds, causing them to nag their editor-arranger to economize. What the financial problems were, Haviland never made clear, but it is possible that even though readership had increased, advertising rates were fixed too low to meet rising production and distribution costs. And the shortfall could not be made up through increased subscription revenues, for *Ev'ry Month* had a limited audience. It lacked the mass impact of a journal like *Munsey's* because it was still basically a song magazine, and Pat and Fred did not wish to make the necessary editorial investment to give it wider appeal. And so it remained something of an anomaly and very much a one-man journal. The "Reflections" column had become Theodore's personal sounding board, a podium from which he propounded his moody observations and pessimistic philosophical musings, laced with Bryanish Populism and at times radicalism—all of which could not have pleased Pat and Fred.

In a typical column, "The Prophet" might dilate for six thousand words on subjects such as the possibility of life on Mars (much in the news because of the astronomer Percival Lowell's sightings of canals); the belief of "a western fruit grower" that plants are sentient ("Cut them and they bleed. . . . Disturb them and they fade and droop, and show every evidence of discouragement"); working conditions in the sweatshops; yellow journalism (with some pointed swipes at his old employers, the *World*); morganatic marriages between European nobility and the daughters of American robber barons, which were also much in the news; and the plight of the city's poor.

Looking over the shoulder of "The Prophet" were his mentors, Herbert Spencer and Charles Darwin. Dreiser had taken up the latter in earnest, and in November 1896 wrote Jug that he had just finished reading a chapter in which the Master explained why the male courts the female. Acknowledging his fiancée's opposition to the doctrine of evolution on religious principles, Theodore boasted that *he* was "firmly grounded in the belief" and gained "as much satisfaction from observing the truth of it, as some would in observing the nearness of a novelist's fiction to actual life," betraying his literary as well as his scientific values.

He did not share with his readers his insights into mating habits, preferring to lecture them on gloomy topics like the neglect of young geniuses in the city (he thought American heiresses should help them rather than marrying European dukes), suicide (he embroidered a brief newspaper item on a young man's leap into the East River with an imaginary account of the suicide's last hours, which was actually a paraphrase of a similar scene in Balzac's *The Wild Ass's Skin*), and man's insignificant place in the universe: "Man is the sport of the elements: the necessary, but worthless dust of changing conditions and . . . all the fourteen hundred million beings who swarm the earth after the manner of contentious vermin are but one form which the heat of the sun takes in its protean journey towards dissipation."

And in another passage he writes: "We are born, struggle and die . . . the lever that moves the Universe is pain."

Such effusions reflected Theodore's own state of mind. The cosmic

chill of Spencer's impersonal universe was seeping into his bones. He
had written to Jug about thoughts of suicide. He was one of those neglected young geniuses. When he wrote of the survival of the fittest ("This
is the law, cold, hard, immutable . . . the law of self-preservation and
upon it all must take their stand and press forward or die"), Theodore
was thinking of his own desperate ambition and the struggle to survive
in the city.

Yet Spencer was also the great apostle of Progress, and "The Prophet"
proclaimed that men must put themselves in harmony with his "beautiful
laws" which "place splendid powers in his hand and assist him to rise . . . to
the highest point of physical and mental power." Though all creatures
great and small are vulnerable to chance and the "onslaught of superior
forces," they are governed by the same eternal laws, "and this, if nothing
more, would indicate that over all rules a Being, and that in his wondrous
superiority, He is not unmindful of the least of his creatures." His eye
is on the sparrow—or rather genus *Spizella*.

Perhaps because he took the doctrine of the survival of the fittest so
personally, "The Prophet" was ambivalent about it. "Everyone is pushing the other for place," he writes, "is training that he may crowd the
other out of the way, shove him back, put him below—that he may be
first and free to go farther." But what of those who fail—and what of the
moral effect on those who shove the weaker ones aside? "Speed is well,"
"The Prophet" writes in the same column, "but it leaves no time to look
about when others cry for assistance, nor will it permit a halt when someone has been trampled on." Those who survive "have been preserved . . . to do . . . what good we can." And then there is the problem
of the trusts, which seemed to exemplify Spencer's teachings that a higher
form will triumph, though actually they reversed the evolutionary process
from simplicity to complexity. Again, Theodore equivocates. As a follower of Bryan he is against them. And so he has it both ways. If trusts
are truly a higher form, he writes, they will indeed prevail; but the people
have the right to defend themselves against their depredations, and in
the end, he suspects, it is the people rather than the trusts that will prevail.

He is, like Spencer, opposed to direct government action to help the
victims of the powerful ("the man is wrong who cries for the State to do
something for the unfortunate. . . . The State cannot legislate brains into
people and therefore it cannot relieve their lack of shrewdness nor make
them successful. It can only offer a free field and encourage enterprise").
New York's poor suffer and die in their dark tenements: it is the im-

mutable law. And yet, unlike Spencer, Dreiser refuses to say that their misery is due to improvidence, alcoholism, or bad character. The true cause of their plight is environment, lack of education and equal opportunity: "They were never taught, never had the time." He calls for improved public education and predicts technological progress will lift the onerous burden of toil from working people's shoulders.

Nor did he share completely Spencer's views that wealth was the reward for natural superiority. In one column he scorns the "money-desire" and the "evil of American rapacity," as evidenced by a recent financial panic in the West. The "money changers (and they are not Jews nowadays)" were behind it, and they "may soon learn that it is evil to crave immense prosperity." In another he equates conditions in the factories with slavery, writing: "[Do] you think slavery is abolished? Read New York State's factory inspector's report on conditions in the 'sweaters.' "

He also finds the success ethos inimical to community: "Our age is largely successful from a commercial view, and it is largely friendless." While he can compare the city to "a sinful Magdalen," decked out in splendor and wealth, he also sees the queer lives of its ordinary people: "The only ones rightfully dwelling in cities are men with knitted brows, and scowling countenances and women with tired, weary eyes. They seem to have a right to dwell in these strange tall hives with narrow doors, and to hurry through these narrow streets, picking their way among wagons and cable cars. . . ." All people are not created and treated equally, and in that truth was the wellspring of compassion. "There are grim forces," he writes, "at work day after day, warping and moulding our brothers, and making them queer creatures, and in this realization our sneers will melt to sympathy." What is to be done? We must "simply obey our code and commandments. Don't lie, don't steal, don't be wilfully cruel to any living creature. For all else a man is still a man however often he may fail."

Fred and Pat's economy lectures made little impression on Dreiser, for he asked for a raise and a share of the profits, which he apparently believed were cascading in. He was thin-skinned and oversensitive, aloof and solitary. The location of his office was symbolic of his place in the firm: he occupied a tiny aerie above the main room, which was reached by a narrow flight of stairs. Like the German professor in Carlyle's *Sartor Resartus*, Theodore saw himself as "watching . . . from a high mental tower . . . making notes of sights most pitiful, most beautiful and most ludicrous." He sat in his tiny cell, with only room enough for two chairs and a desk piled high with manuscripts and newspapers, scrawling his reflections on half sheets of foolscap, viewing the moil of commerce down below.

Max Dreyfus, who later became a famous song publisher and who was working for Howley, Haviland as an arranger at this time, remembered Theodore as "aloof." Mai Skelly, a pretty young singer whom Paul took under his wing in 1897, remembered him as always going off by himself. And Theodore himself complained to Jug, "I am practically alone, month after month." He admits this might be his fault: "I know I am terribly selfish, have a high opinion of my own importance and often place it disagreeably in evidence." Because of his unconventional views, he told her, "They say here that I am a perverted cynic." Although his bosses were "plutocrats and cantankerous goldites," he assured her that "I stand quite alone, but unterrified." But he was pushing his luck by resorting to Populist rhetoric. Paul, a Democrat, might have sided with him politically, but Theodore's relations with Paul were not the best, and he proceeded to further alienate his brother by publishing an article by Arthur Henry which was critical of Paul's style of comedy.

It appeared in the April 1897 issue under the head "It Is to Laugh: A Little Talk on How to Write a Comic Opera." Henry sarcastically enumerated the secrets of success in the genre—including maudlin songs and slapstick pratfalls by fat comedians. If the references to the kind of songs Paul wrote and the kind of humor he practiced were not pointed enough, the article was illustrated with a scene from *Lost, Strayed or Stolen*, a farce in which he had starred. The picture showed the cast, including Paul, who was wearing a fright wig, in various outlandish poses. The caption noted sarcastically: "Here is presented the delicate humor of three gentlemen, in search of a lost infant, inquiring in the wrong home. A jealous Cuban lover's sudden return causes them to assume strange roles and mirthfully smash furniture in the imitation of laborers. Uproarious applause."

In early 1897 Henry visited New York to talk about his article on the theater and other possible contributions to the magazine. After a stint as publicity man for a magician called Hermann the Great, Henry had been living the life of a free spirit and had written two philosophical opuses called "The Doctrine of Happiness" and "The Philosophy of Hope," in which he had pronounced his disenchantment with the rat race. He had come to New York with the avowed purpose of being a poet, leaving Maude to look after their daughter and the mortgage payments on their manse on the Maumee.

Henry arrived in the city, he later wrote, with "nothing but my ticket, a night-dress, eight dollars, a pipe and a poem. . . ." He headed for East Twentieth Street in hopes of selling his two philosophical works. Theodore accepted them, wrote him a voucher for fifteen dollars, and took him to lunch. As they passed through the bustling office, Henry asked Theodore the meaning of all the hubbub. Those people were "succeeding," Dreiser explained with lofty disdain. "And you?" Henry asked.

"I am drawing a good salary. The things I am able to get the boss to publish that I believe in are very few," Theodore replied. "The rest must tickle the vanity or cater to the foibles and prejudices of readers. From my standpoint I am not succeeding."

Over lunch, Henry told him he should be writing novels, poetry, plays. Under the spell of his friend's charm (he once described Henry as "a lover of impossible romances which fascinated me by their very impossibility"), Theodore began to envision greener pastures. Not long after their lunch, in the summer of 1897, Dreiser was fired, as he probably wanted to be. Fred and Pat had already killed "The Prophet"; in the May issue the "Reflections" column is no more. In its stead (though in the back of the book) was an unsigned editorial, obviously by Theodore, on the struggle to succeed. Many try, he wrote, "but no one is going to help them. They are going to encounter enmity, the foremost characteristic of the ambitious, the moment they try."

He left in August, after preparing the September issue, which featured Henry's "Philosophy of Hope." Despite its stormy ending, his *Ev'ry Month* experience had been a valuable one. It had given Dreiser absolute freedom, for a time, to speak his mind, and he had "got it through [his] skull what a magazine was." He left the table while still ahead of the game.

20. Broadway Paul

While cynics might refer to the little simple melodies [I write] as trash and the words as maudlin sentiment, to me with apologies to none the grandest word in the English or any other language [is] Mother.

— Paul Dresser (1897)

aul undoubtedly took Pat and Fred's part in the dispute with Theodore. Push Paul too far, as Theodore had done, and his customary geniality faded. The imbroglio over the conduct of *Ev'ry Month* led to a coolness between the brothers that was mainly on Theodore's part. For Paul, family ties transcended everything. "But she's your sister" or "he's your brother" was his ultimate verdict on all the squabbles he adjudicated.

After Theodore's departure, Paul became more directly involved in the affairs of *Ev'ry Month*. In the fall of 1897 he told a St. Louis newsman that he had come to town to solicit advertising and would "hereafter devote his time to writing songs and in building up his new magazine Ev'ry Month." Paul had all but retired from the stage. "I'm tired of the theater, as it is a dog's life at that," he wrote Mary South, a young Terre Haute friend.

Paul had come to regard himself as a shrewd businessman, entitled to a share of the profits, as well as royalties from his songs. He boasted to a Terre Haute reporter, "You see, I am a publisher as well as a composer and own a big printing establishment in New York." (Howley, Haviland had a printing plant in New York, but Paul certainly didn't own it.)

Pat Howley and Fred Haviland apparently didn't think as highly of Paul's business acumen as he did. Paul's name was not added to the letterhead until 1900—probably at his insistence, for by then he was beginning to feel his contributions were not being adequately rewarded. Paul left a considerable proportion of his royalties in the coffers of Howley, Haviland, and when he needed walking-around money (and he needed a lot of that; his daily progress up Broadway alone cost him several "Vs"), he would simply write a voucher and draw an advance. He probably regarded the sums he left in the firm as an investment, since he fully trusted Howley and, to a lesser extent, Haviland. As a result, Paul had only a vague accounting of all the money he earned during his peak period, between 1895 and 1900, when he was one of the most successful writers of popular songs in America.

Thanks to Paul's talent, the money was rolling in. His two biggest hits appeared in 1895 and 1897: "Just Tell Them That You Saw Me," based on an encounter Paul had with someone he knew from Terre Haute who when asked if he has any message for the home folks, speaks the words of the title; and "On the Banks of the Wabash." Each song sold more than five hundred thousand copies, meaning a total of eighty thousand dollars for Paul and an equal amount in profits for the firm—huge sums in that era. But it also meant the end of the low-overhead days. In 1898 Howley, Haviland moved to larger quarters at Broadway and Thirtieth Street. The new office was much showier, with several tryout rooms, rugs, couches, rocking chairs, pianos, imitation palms, and framed photographs of singers on the walls.

If Theodore had stuck around a bit longer, he might have shared in the new prosperity. It seems doubtful, though, that more money would have made him happy. He later ruefully described his attitude toward Pat and Fred as one of snobbish superiority. He felt the same way about Paul, but his resentment had deeper, more complicated emotional roots than he let on.

Take Arthur Henry's article. It was a bit of hypocrisy, for Theodore had a sneaking affection for much of the theatrical fare of the day, whatever he wrote about it when wearing the mantle of "The Prophet." His letters to Jug are peppered with references to evenings at the theater, and in one he reports that he saw the comedians Charles Evans and Bill Hoey in *A Parlor Match* for the "umpty-steenth time . . . and laughed as much as ever." He also was smitten by Anna Held performing her gyrations to "The Champagne Song." But he loyally adds that her "large fine eyes" and her "wealth of light (not blonde) hair" reminded him of his sweetheart. He was less impressed by John Philip Sousa's latest operetta, *El Capitan*, even though it drew nine curtain calls. Such demonstrations, as far as he was concerned, were reflective of the theatergoing public's taste for "showy, bombastic operas." He preferred the composer's *An Artist's Model*, a "truly delicate and humorous" piece. He even mentions seeing *Lost, Strayed or Stolen*, and makes no comment on it other than to urge Jug to buy "Dreaming," a song from the show.

As for Paul's songs, Theodore probably liked them more than he let on. Certainly he had a fondness for a lot of popular music (from spending so much time around a music publishing house, he formed a lifelong habit of humming popular tunes and had a large repertoire). In a letter to Jug, he describes a pleasant scene at the Howley, Haviland offices on a warm summer evening, listening to his friend Theo Morse, a young composer, playing his latest songs, "Baby" and "I Want You My Honey." The music lulled him into reveries of her.

It is true that Paul's kind of sentimental ballad was slated for obsolescence when ragtime and other more sophisticated music took hold in the 1890s. To Theodore, Paul—thirteen years older than he—was almost a member of another generation. But he was moved by the pathos and melodrama of Paul's lyrics more than he cared to admit. Around this time he wrote a poem that sounds like one of Paul's lyrics. Called "The Old 10:30 Train," it tells of a lonely man listening to a mournful whistle in the night, which reminds him of the train he heard as a boy. He wishes he were a boy again "with Mother near/Me praying on her knee." His interest in songwriting extended to rewriting lyrics for Howley, Haviland.

Theodore's most successful job of lyric writing was for Paul, though it came about in such a casual way as to seem almost inadvertent. As Dreiser recounts it in his story "My Brother Paul," published twenty years after the event, one fine Sunday afternoon he, Ed, Paul, and a few others were lounging about at the office. Paul was noodling on the piano, trying out various melodic fragments that popped into his head. Unable to come up with anything, he asked his brother to give him an idea, and Theodore suggested that he compose something about a river, as Stephen Foster had done with the Suwannee. Paul liked the idea; he greatly admired Foster. But which river? Why not the Wabash? Theodore asked. After all, Paul had played along its banks as a boy in Terre Haute. Dubious, Paul proposed that Theodore write the verse, a story on which to hang a chorus.

Theodore took a pencil and paper and retired to a corner, grumbling that he knew little and cared less about writing a song. After about a half hour he returned with a rough draft of what would be the verse of "On the Banks of the Wabash":

> Round my Indiana home there waves a cornfield,
> In the distance loom the woodlands clear and cool.
> Often times my thoughts revert to scenes of childhood,
> Where I first received my lessons, nature's school.
> But one thing there is missing from the picture,

Without her face it seems so incomplete.
I long to see my mother in the doorway,
As she stood there years ago, her boy to greet.

He also planted the germ of a chorus, basing it on the title of his unwritten play, *Along the Wabash*. His effort didn't give Paul a lot to go on.
For one thing there was really no story or situation, as in "Take a Seat,
Old Lady" or "Just Tell Them That You Saw Me." What was happening
along the Wabash? Some generalized poetic sentiments, a yearning for
home, were called for, but Paul was no poet. Shouldn't there be a girl
in there, waiting for her wandering lover? Something like that: a story.
And of course he needed a melody, the most important element of all.
Paul wrote both the melody and the words for nearly all his songs and
found it difficult to tailor his tune to another man's rhymes. Still, Theodore's idea appealed to him; it tapped his nostalgia for the old home place,
where Mother was standing in the doorway waiting for her boy to return.

As Theodore tells it, Paul sat down at the piano, plinked out a suitable
melody, rewrote the chorus to fit, and was finished in a matter of hours.
According to an article Theodore wrote in 1898, "the words of 'On the
Banks of the Wabash' were written in less than an hour of an April Sunday
afternoon, and . . . the music did not require a much longer period."
Although he did not mention his own role in the song's composition, he
noted, "I know whereof I speak."

That account appeared in *Metropolitan Magazine*. In a letter to Jug earlier that year, Theodore boasted, "Yes, dearie, I wrote the words as I
said, of 'On the Banks of the Wabash.' " And years later Ed Dreiser told
his daughter, Vera, that it had happened much as Theodore had said it
did. Paul, however, never publicly acknowledged his brother's contribution in the various versions he gave the press of how "The Wabash"
came to be written.

The most accurate journalistic account was the one that had Paul writing the song in Chicago in May 1897, after "thinking of his happy days
on the Wabash." Although the item omits the song's inception, it does
jibe with the recollection of Max Hoffman, an arranger with the Witmark
Music Publishing Company, who worked with Paul when the latter was
visiting Howley, Haviland's branch office in Chicago. Hoffman remembered being summoned to Paul's hotel room in June 1897 and finding
him laboring over a melody on his portable organ. Paul told Hoffman he
wanted him to make a piano arrangement for a new song. He had the
tune, but was still working with a dummy lyric. First, Paul had Hoffman

play the melody over and over while he tinkered with the words. By the time he had finished, the dummy lyric was completely changed. Hoffman was struck by the beauty of one of Paul's new lines, "Thro' the sycamores the candle lights are gleaming," and thinking it must have been inspired by the lights reflected on the dark waters of Lake Michigan.

This account does not necessarily conflict with Theodore's. The dummy lyric was probably his, and Paul's main concern was coming up with a chorus that would fit his basic melody, which entailed considerable expansion on his brother's idea. What he produced was superb:

> Oh, the moonlight's fair tonight along the Wabash,
> From the fields there comes a breath of new mown hay.
> Thro' the sycamores the candle lights are gleaming,
> On the banks of the Wabash, far away.

For insurance, he added a second verse with a story about a girl named Mary, someone's childhood sweetheart who is now sleeping by the river. With its sentiment of yearning for lost childhood days ("I loved her but she thought I didn't mean it / Still I'd give my future were she only here"), it is pure Paul, and the story in Terre Haute was that he once courted a girl named Mary O'Brien. But the first verse is clearly by Theodore; it has a poetic quality and a literacy that Paul never attained in his lyrics, which tended to be either crude or florid.

"On the Banks of the Wabash" had its tryout in a vaudeville show playing at the Alhambra Theater in Chicago. Charles K. Harris, author of "After the Ball" and a friend of Paul's, recalled that it received an ovation, and Paul wired Howley, Haviland to rush the song out. After a few months it began to build, and in September Paul reported to the song's dedicatee, Mary South: "The 'Wabash' is going fine. I have sold over five thousand up to date. Had an order for 300 from Lyons Healy Chicago in this morning's mail." A year later he wrote: "The 'Wabash' is still the great hit of the day. Our sales this week up to date have reached nearly 10,000 copies." He meant, of course, that ten thousand copies had been sold within a week. He added, "So you see that as much of a Chestnut as it really is, the song is selling just the same."

Paul's "Chestnut"—an old-fashioned song—went on to sell well over a half million copies and to place his name among the select number of composers of popular songs that have become a permanent part of the American musical vernacular. Not only did it bring Paul bags of money, it won him fame in his hometown, something that meant a lot to him (in 1913 it was chosen as the Indiana state song). All his life Paul lived in hotels, but when he signed the register he always gave Terre Haute as his permanent address, which was accurate: the city was the only roots he had, and his songs frequently told of wandering boys or girls. The small towns they left behind were superior to the city:

> There were no brownstone mansions
> No gilded halls of fame,
> There were no silks or laces rare,
> All tarnished o'er with shame.

The displaced country boys and girls were tempted by, and sometimes followed, "the path that leads the other way." They appeared in the city crowds, shabby and down at heels, saying bravely, "Just tell them that you saw me." When they grew lonely in the big city, they recalled their mother's parting words: "When friends desert, remember/That I'm still your mother dear," and took comfort in the knowledge that "every night there's a light shining through the windowpane" to lead them home. Amid the deceits and temptations of the city, they had a single litmus test for truth: "I believe it for my mother told me so." In his most autobiographical song, "Calling to Her Boy Just Once Again," Paul cried out for the simplicities of childhood:

> I'd give up all the future hope of Heaven,
> Eternally to live in endless pain.
> To see my mother at the east end window
> Calling to her boy just once again.

Working this sentimental lode in the latter part of the 1890s, Paul scored hit after hit. Although he also turned out love songs, patriotic airs, religious anthems, and "coon songs," he was remembered along music publishers' row as the champion of the "heart ballad," the "home song," and, above all, the "mother song." The New York *Sun* called him "the only composer who has been able to strike the popular fancy with this grade of music," and Paul had a monopoly on it for as long as the taste for pathos and melodrama lasted.

Part of the reason he was so successful was that he sincerely believed in what he wrote. "When he sat down to write a song his heart and soul were in it," said Charles K. Harris. "Money meant nothing to him."

Tears rolled down Paul Dreiser's plump cheeks when he was composing. He was proud to write songs that touched people's hearts. "I write for the masses, not the classes," he often said. "On the Banks of the Wabash," his biggest seller, was one of the greatest home, heart, and

mother songs ever written: authentic in its emotion, with a simple, wistful melody that carries an ineffable yearning. "The Wabash" flows through
the heartland of the American psyche like the river that inspired it.

Why did Paul fail to acknowledge Theodore's role in "On the Banks of
the Wabash"? The answer is that by the time he had finished it, the break
with Theodore had occurred. Out of a mixture of pique, ego, and pro-
tectiveness toward his reputation, Paul appropriated the song.

He also felt it was a matter between brothers—family sharing as it were.
And, with his reputation as a man who wrote his own lyrics, Paul did not
want to divide the credit on this, his most famous song. Moreover, he
knew that writing a lyric was no great task; he received hundreds of them
every year from neophytes who wanted him to dash off a little tune to
go with them, making them both rich.

Paul found he wrote best when he was using a true situation rooted
in his own past. Also, he was a professional, a craftsman. He could crank
out dozens of nonce songs or bathetic ballads, but he knew what was
good, and when he was on to it he sweated and wept, trying to achieve
the ideal melding of sentiment, words, and music. Working on "The
Wabash" in that hotel room in Chicago, the magical fusion had occurred,
and he felt—rightly—that the credit belonged to him. With inadvertent
prescience Theodore had summed up the matter in a poem, "Words and
Music," published in *Ev'ry Month:*

> I being but the words and not the song;
> > None cares to hear,
> Till wedded unto music sweet and strong
> > Divinely clear.

In addition to whatever rancor Theodore felt over Paul's appropriation
of "The Wabash," there were temperamental differences between them.
He disapproved of his brother's free-spending ways and his numerous
affairs, most of them with tarts or actresses. When "The Prophet" thundered against shallow metropolitan success, he had Paul in mind. Smugly
engaged to Jug, he wrote to her that Paul "loves all women too well generally to love anyone in particular for long. He is fickle, fat and forty and
worse than ever."

But envy tinged those sniffy words. Mai Skelly remembered Theodore
eyeing her at the *Ev'ry Month* offices in a hungry way that she found
unpleasant. Theodore would see his brother sweeping her off (Mai's mother

in tow as chaperone) to Sherry's or Delmonico's and be reminded again of Paul's superior attainments as a lady's man. Ironically, the more handsome Ed, who had moved to the city in 1897 and whom Paul was helping become an actor, stole Mai from his oldest brother. They fell in love at a party given by the playwright Clyde Fitch, at which Mai sang "On the Banks of the Wabash." Ed won a role in Richard Harding Davis's play *Soldiers of Fortune,* and, with Paul's blessing and financial help, Ed and Mai were married in June 1899 at St. Patrick's Cathedral.

If Theodore was jealous of Paul's association with Mai, he deplored his brother's other women, whom he regarded as flashy and fast. Paul also had a penchant for married women, which repelled Theodore on moral grounds. (Once Paul's friends concocted an elaborate practical joke. They engaged an actor to storm into the Howley, Haviland office and accuse Paul of sleeping with his wife. Paul hadn't the slightest idea who the man's wife was, but he was thrown into such a state of terror by the plausibility of the accusation that he almost had a heart attack.) And Paul's frank carnality offended the Puritan in Theodore. When he and Ed shared a hotel suite with their older brother, Paul would parade around nude every morning with a towel draped over his matutinal erection. This practice so disgusted Theodore that he moved out.

Such were the differences between them, poisons that erupted in pustules of jealousy on Theodore's part. But antibodies of love flowed in their common blood. Sarah's "psychic chains" still held.

21. A Season of "Success"

I had made the amazing discovery that I could write a rather
hack type of magazine article, [and] I ran into Orison Swett Marden, in the editorial offices of the *Christian Herald,* the most successful all-around Christian paper of its day.

—Dreiser (1932)

Nothing is more fascinating than the romance of reality in worthy achievement under difficulty, than contrasting pictures of
obscure beginnings and triumphant endings, than stirring stories of strenuous endeavor and final victory.

—Orison Swett Marden (1901)

nce again Theodore was on his own hook, but he was better
prepared to survive than when he first arrived in the city.
He decided to try the life of the free-lance writer again. After
editing other writers for two years, he felt able to turn out
a salable article and had gained confidence in his ideas. He
had also made useful acquaintances among editors, writers, and artists.
Lastly, he had material in hand—an article he had written for the series
on women artists running in *Ev'ry Month.* It appeared in the November
Puritan under the title "Our Women Violinists."

He also had pieces in the November *Truth* and in the *Metropolitan,* the
latter signed "Theodore Dresser." Possibly he was thinking of adopting
Paul's Americanized (and more famous) spelling of the family name, as
Ed had done. The effort for the *Metropolitan* described Lawrence Park,
a literary and artistic colony in the semiwilds of Bronxville. This enclave
of quaint mansions, he wrote, was located "within half an hour of the
heart of New York City . . . where dainty little brooks trip in and out
among the wild flowers, and great ledges of magnificent rock are bright
with nodding columbines." Here was a new class to aspire to: "Most of
us have a fixed idea in our minds as to how the rich live, and how also
the exceeding poor, but not all are familiar with a third class, the middle

artistic and literary, who occasionally live in colonies after the fashion of the millionaires of Newport, and are, to a certain extent, exclusive." But the article also contained a hint of disapproval at the artificial paradise these successful artists had created for themselves.

For his November harvest of stories, Theodore received two to three hundred dollars, and his career as "specials" writer was launched. For the next two years he sailed ahead, with awesome energy and prolificacy. "I have an easy pen," he boasted to Jug. The magazinist's life was an insecure one, but there was a plethora of new publications hungry for material, aside from magazines like the *Century*, *Harper's*, and *The Atlantic Monthly*, which seemed as exclusive as Lawrence Park. An estimated five thousand people earned a living of sorts as writers, though most barely scraped by. The author of a survey on magazine contributors published in 1893 observed, "It is quite possible for a man to achieve a national reputation for literary work by faithfully devoting his whole time to it and still earn less than a thousand dollars a year"—about what a clerk took home. The ten-cent magazines like *Munsey's*, *Truth*, *Frank Leslie's*, *Ainslee's*, *Cosmopolitan*, and *McClure's*, paid on the average five dollars a column or a half cent a word. The prestigious monthlies paid at least twice that.

To make a good living, the magazinist had to produce in volume. Here Theodore's newspaper experience, which had taught him to write rapidly under pressure, was an advantage. He was used to letting the copy editors clean up his stories, however, and magazines put much of the burden on the free-lancer, so the prose in his early efforts was cliché-ridden and crude.

The free-lancer's best course was to gain entrée at a few journals and build up a reputation as a reliable contributor. Eventually, he or she might become a columnist or contributing editor, drawing a regular stipend. For a time Theodore had a working relationship with *The Cosmopolitan;* in 1899 he became contributing editor to *Ainslee's*, where his friend Richard Duffy was an editor. In exchange for articles and ideas, he was guaranteed seventy-five dollars every other week.

A chance encounter in the fall of 1897 gained Dreiser his most steady outlet and eased him over the bumpy transition from *Ev'ry Month* to the free-lance life. He was contributing unsigned squibs to the *Christian Herald*, and at its office in Bible House on Eighth Street he met opportunity in the person of Orison Swett Marden. Marden was a friend of Louis Klopsch, publisher of the *Herald*, who had taken over the failing paper a few years before and turned it into a moneymaker, and himself into a millionaire. Klopsch, a German immigrant, raised millions of dollars for famine relief in India, China, and other countries through his paper.

Marden wanted Klopsch to back a new magazine that he hoped would bring him an equivalent fortune from the religion of success. After making and losing several modest bundles in the hotel business, Marden had decided his mission in life was not to do but to teach—to inspire others to climb the golden ladder. He wrote—or rather compiled—several books with inspirational titles like *Winning Out, Pushing to the Front, The Secret of Achievement,* and *The Hour of Opportunity.* On his talent with the shears and paste pot, a reviewer commented, "Mr. Marden's labors of the excerpting and arranging order, must have been something really appalling; and one is glad to reflect that his method was one which relieved him from the additional strain of severe and continuous thought." If Dr. Marden (as he liked to be called; he held five degrees) was more scavenger than author, his public didn't mind. *Pushing to the Front* was a huge seller in 1894, eventually going through two hundred and fifty editions. Sensing that the formula of stories about eminent achievers whose lives exemplified the Marden credo—"Unceasing struggle in adversity brings triumph"—would be equally lucrative in a magazine format, he decided to found a weekly called *Success.*

Klopsch agreed to back the new publication and assigned *Christian Herald* managing editor George A. Sandison to help get it started. Sandison suggested Theodore as a potential contributor and introduced him to Marden. Together they came up with a list of subjects for interviews, which included obvious names like John D. Rockefeller, Andrew Carnegie, Marshall Field, and Thomas Edison, and also literary figures like William Dean Howells and Mark Twain. For each profile Marden said he would pay one hundred dollars, a fee that looked munificent to Theodore, who had come to Bible House hoping to sell a squib on Dana of the *Sun* for ten dollars. His first assignment was a profile of the corporation lawyer Joseph H. Choate for the January issue.

Dreiser quickly established himself as a reliable *Success* peddler, and over the next three years contributed about thirty articles and a poem to the magazine. A man who got value on the dollar, Marden published every word Theodore wrote, using leftover scraps as fillers. And when he found that Theodore's copy needed editing, Marden informed him, in the spirit of the sweatshop operator who deducts for ruined materials, "By the way, we shall have to charge you about ten dollars on each article for editing the manuscript." Marden's literary ethics were not the highest. He took sixteen of Theodore's pieces and used them, without permission or credit, in a series of *Success* anthologies, including *How They Succeeded, Little Visits With Great Americans,* and *Choosing a Career.*

Of course there was some irony in the idea of Theodore Dreiser, who had expressed contempt for the moneygrubbers at Howley, Haviland, writing for a magazine that extolled succeeding. Hadn't "The Prophet" written, "Everyone is pushing the other for place . . . that he may be first and free to go farther. . . . That is the character of ambition. It throttles its competitors"? When his biographer Robert Elias asked him how he could praise rich men like Carnegie, Dreiser replied, "If you will look at the magazine you will understand why a denunciation of Mr. Carnegie would have lost me $100." Obviously Marden did not hire Theodore to brood over the sins of the plutocracy, as he had done in *Ev'ry Month,* so Theodore played the game. What is surprising is the extent to which his private attitudes crept into the articles. While praising success, he questioned its premises. Moreover, in his choice of subjects he was able at least to reflect his artistic interests.

The articles themselves are stilted, reverential; each pompous maxim is recorded stenographically. Carnegie on thrift: "It is the first dollar saved that tells." Carnegie on starting at the bottom: "If by chance the professional sweeper is absent any morning do not hesitate to try your hand at the broom." One suspects that some of the interviews were conducted by letter, or even cobbled together from various public pronouncements. At times the hyperbole is numbing. "No more significant story," Dreiser began an article on department store owner Marshall Field, "none more full of stimulus, of encouragement, of brain-inspiring and pulse-thrilling potency has been told in these columns." In the office of the meat-packing magnate Philip D. Armour "a snow storm of white letters [fell] . . . thickly upon a mass of dark desks." There was something awesome in this "mobilization of energy to promote the private affairs of one man."

Dreiser dutifully elicited the data Marden wanted: the hero's boyhood poverty, his early struggles, the virtues that helped him climb the ladder, his tips for the young man who wanted to emulate him, his views on the importance of money (most success cases deprecated money—perhaps because they had so much of it), and his sermons on the virtues of hard work, thrift, opportunity, and so on.

But one senses an underlying ambivalence (Theodore suggested half-seriously to Elias that some of the pieces might be taken as satire). And in the interview with Choate, his questions seem to reflect his private agenda more than Marden's. Dreiser opens their conversation by asking,

"I wish to discover whether you believe special advantages at the beginning of a youth's career are necessary to success."

After gruffly demanding to know his interrogator's definition of advantages ("money, opportunity, friends, good advice, and personal popularity," was the reply), Choate denies that a head start in the race is crucial—certainly it was not in his case. Later he says flatly, "I never met a great man who was born rich." At this point the reporter blandly interpolates, "This remark seemed rather striking in a way because of the fact that Mr. Choate's parents were not poor in the accepted sense. The family is rather distinguished in New England annals." Choate, he notes, graduated from Harvard, and "Influence procured him a position in a Boston law office."

Theodore pressed on: "If equally valuable opportunities do not come to all hasn't an individual a right to complain and justify his failures?" Choate agreed that some men were less fortunate than others, but if such inferior individuals should demand the privileges of their betters, they must prove that they are worthy of them. The interlocutor then wonders if some youths might not overestimate their abilities. He was probing another hole in the success credo: if it instills in young people the illusion that they might succeed, what happens when that illusion is shattered by reality? Doesn't such an overreaching contain the seeds of tragedy? Theodore's fear that he might not achieve his own ambitions was a painful one. The previous year he had written Jug that he was haunted by the thought that "nature had made me a mind fitted above my station." A very American tragedy indeed.

In an interview with the novelist Anthony Hope, Dreiser returns to the question of unrequited ambition, this time in an aside: "I, myself, have heard struggling literary men roundly berate those peculiar workings of nature which could give to one every advantage of physique, natural talent and high aspiration and to many others only burning aspiration without either strength or other qualities to satisfy it."

In other interviews, the subjects themselves sometimes tell him that there is more to success than resolute determination against great odds. From Thomas Edison, Dreiser came away with the idea that some people were born with a gift for certain work—tinkering with electricity, in the case of the Wizard of Menlo Park—and they pursued this bent out of an inner compulsion to the exclusion of all other interests. Armour provided him with an object lesson in the importance of luck, of being at the right place at the right time: he had arrived in Chicago when the city became a railroad hub and when the government needed pork for its soldiers in the Civil War. Carnegie had perceived Pittsburgh's potential as an iron and steel center early on. But although those men had had the wit and courage to seize on their opportunities, thousands of their contemporaries had not. They had lacked shrewdness and boldness in their makeup. And a further point: such opportunities were limited. Only a handful could profit from them, while the rest were failures or ignorant workers who survived on the crumbs from Dives's table.

In the panegyric to Carnegie, the alert reader might have caught an allusion to a development that had further shrunk the field of opportunity—the rise of the large corporation. Carnegie hailed the opportunities for advancement in such enterprises, but his implication was that it was no longer possible to build a business empire from scratch as he had done. In a talk with the fiery Chicago preacher Reverend Frank Gunsaulus, this point emerged more clearly. "The modern young man is more or less discouraged by the growing belief that all things are falling into the hands of great corporations and trusts, and that the individual no longer has much chance," Gunsaulus said. When Gunsaulus was growing up, he had a father who believed that "the dice of life are loaded," and a mother who accepted the Calvinist doctrine of predestination. He was compelled to overcome those beliefs and "convince myself that we are what we choose to make ourselves." Gunsaulus's sermons on the rich man's duty to share his wealth had convinced Philip Armour to set up his institute to educate worthy but poor young men, and he had chosen the minister to head it.

Theodore's deepest sympathies probably lay with Gunsaulus, whom he had heard preach five years earlier when he was living in Chicago, and who was also a literary man—a published novelist, and the "saint" of Eugene Field's literary coterie, the Saints and Sinners. In 1898, after visiting Jug in Missouri, Theodore had gone on to Chicago to interview Armour and others, and he wrote his fiancée expansively that Gunsaulus had told him, "You gave me a look and I feel it all through me—as though you really were worth while." It was as though the preacher had sensed his visitor's sense of destiny. Gunsaulus accompanied Dreiser on the train to New York, talking intensely of life and philosophy.

Yet he had not rid himself completely of the success virus. His letters to Jug from Chicago are full of references to his meetings with the high and mighty, and in addition to impressing her, he seems quite pleased with himself. He boasted that a "millionaire furniture dealer" named Alexander H. Revell, possibly a friend of Paul's, had extended him the courtesies of the Athletic Club for two weeks and provided him with let-

ters of introduction to Armour and Marshall Field. He also met Robert
Todd Lincoln, son of the president and now head of the Pullman Company. He wrote a flattering piece about the company, not mentioning
George Pullman's harsh labor policies which had provoked the great 1893
strike.

But the businessmen he really admired were the emerging successors
to the robber barons, men with a social conscience like John H. Patterson,
president of the National Cash Register Company, who provided his
workers with schools, hobby shops, gymnasiums, and sermons. And most
of all he preferred interviewing artists or writers like the naturalist John
Burroughs, whose life in a mountain hut he had built with his own hands
exemplified the lesson that "all success is not material" that mere dollars
are nothing, and that "the influential man is the successful man, whether
he be rich or poor."

Actually, the majority of his articles were about artists or writers like
William Dean Howells, though he focused on their climb from humble
beginnings, rather than discussing their works. Howells rose from a small-
town boyhood in Ohio to editorship of *The Atlantic Monthly*. Writing about
the American prima donna Lillian Nordica, he stressed the sacrifices she
had had to make for a career. Nordica had "no time for balls and parties,
very little for friends and less for carriage rides and pleasant strolls." He
also praised the idealism of the artists, making an implicit critique of the
businessmen. At the close of an article on the sculptor Paul Wayland Bartlett, for example, he contrasted the successful carver of public monuments with the artisan whose work is too fine for parks and buildings:
"The latter must languish in penury if he does not chance upon a wealthy
lover of the beautiful who will be his patron and look to it that he does
not want while he employs his time in this, to him, unprofitable task, as
the world of business takes it—not unprofitable in reality, however, but
the very best of profit for his own mind and heart, and of incalculable
advantage and profit to the world."

But Dreiser was not, after all, saying anything radical or daring (and
the artists he interviewed were all establishment figures). A reaction was
setting in against the robber barons of the Gilded Age. Carnegie's doctrine of philanthropy was one facet of it; Patterson's employee-welfare
programs another; and the recognition that art was "good" was still another, as the recent emergence of art-collecting, museum-endowing millionaires attested. Marden was probably aware of those trends and had
no objection to articles reflecting them in a muted way. That Theodore
also muted his own opinion is shown when he wrote an article on Choate

for the April 1899 *Ainslee's*. While he extolled Choate's legal acumen, he comes down hard on the lawyer's lack of public spirit, observing "when all is said and done, it can only be concluded that he has done for himself nobly, not for others."

A glimpse into his true state of mind was provided by Myrta Lockett Avary, who was working for Klopsch when Dreiser was contributing to *Success*. One day Theodore stopped at her desk to talk about a picture layout and they fell to chatting. Avary was a widow from the South who had come to New York to make her way, and she felt a sympathetic current flowing from Dreiser: "the ugliest man I ever saw, but also the most interesting." The talk came around to the work she was doing, and he told her: "You should make your name here." He paused significantly, then added, "If they'll let you." Thinking back on it, Avary realized he had meant, "They *won't* let you."

22. The "Specials" Writer

> Man's ingenuity finds many contradictory channels for its expression. The labor to perfect those sciences which tend to save human life goes on side by side with the labor to create new and more potent methods for its destruction.
>
> —Dreiser, "Scenes in a Cartridge Factory" (1898)

> One lies down near Appomattox,
> Many miles away,
> Another sleeps at Chickamauga,
> And they both wore suits of gray.
> 'Mid the strains of "Down in Dixie,"
> The third was laid away,
> In a trench at Santiago . . .
>
> —Paul Dresser, "The Blue and the Gray" (1900)

he connection with *Success* was an augury; Dreiser's magazine career was soon flourishing. By February 1898 he bragged to Jug that with his present "standing and ability," he should be able to average $5000 a year. He appended a brief financial report: As of February 23, four magazines owed him $670, which he should collect by June 1. Of that amount, $270 represented expenses, leaving him a net of $400 earned in the year to date. While illness over the winter had slowed him down (probably bronchitis, which became a chronic complaint with him), he expected to work full blast for the remainder of the year if his health held up. His health was a continuing worry, and Theodore spoke of his "long-since shattered constitution" and delivered a lengthy lecture on why Jug should not visit a friend who was ill with tuberculosis, providing clinical details of how germs are transmitted. His sister Claire was consumptive, and Theodore apparently feared he might be susceptible to the disease. He and Jug constantly complained of poor health; she had a rheumatic heart complaint. He moaned about overwork, but it was all to make enough money so they could marry. They were officially engaged now; he had sent her a ring in June 1896.

As it turned out, 1898 was a boom year for the firm of Th. Dreiser & Co. He sold nearly fifty articles and poems, and easily cleared $5000, as he had predicted. He was doing solid hackwork, learning the ropes fast, attempting to make as much money as he could. His market continued to be the ten-cent magazines—*Cosmopolitan, Ainslee's, Demorest's, Truth, Metropolitan*—which were hungry for straightforward pieces on science, industry, agriculture, and cultural topics. Ray Stannard Baker, who was then a writer for *McClure's*, said of the new journalism, "The immediate creative impulse was an extraordinary sense of newness in the world— fresh interest in world affairs, the thrill of new discoveries and inventions, the 'new prosperity' and in it all and through it all, an awakening sympathy for the world's downtrodden and oppressed." With the twentieth century fast approaching, futuristic pieces on the brave new world of technology were in demand. Interurban trolleys, for example, were still enough of a novelty for Dreiser to recount his experiences on a journey from New York to Boston. In "The Horseless Age" for *Demorest's* he prophesied that motor-powered buses would take a clerk all the way from his office in City Hall to his flat in Harlem at an average speed of ten miles an hour and a cost of only ten cents. Industry fascinated him, though initially at least not in any strongly reformist way. He was primarily interested in the lives of the workers themselves and in the strange beauty of these dark, smoky, hulking factories. Even as he regurgitated a stream of facts on the building of the Chicago drainage canal, he paused to observe that at night "it glows beneath the lamps and sky like a stream of silver."

Another part of him was drawn to nature and scenic areas like the Brandywine River, which he proposed to Jug as a honeymoon destination; historic places, such as Germantown (where his mother's ancestors had first settled) and Tarrytown, or literary sites like Nathaniel Hawthorne's Salem and William Cullen Bryant's home. Despite his fascination with the new, Theodore found romance in old places and called for their preservation. The progress that would tear them down in favor of commercial structures was "reprehensible" and "shameless." In "The Harlem River Speedway" he advocated planting grass and trees along a new urban roadway, and in "The Haunts of Nathaniel Hawthorne" he criticized the trolleys and electric lights in Salem that "glared upon and outraged its ancient ways."

He composed about the same ratio of articles on the arts for the general magazines as he did for *Success*. Eschewing critical analysis, he focused on personality and technique. Few of the artists Dreiser profiled achieved any lasting stature, and he tended to stick to contemporary celebrities or unusual practitioners, such as lady harpists. He sought out classical sculptors like John Quincy Adams Ward, president of the American Sculpture Society, who called for more public statuary of "inspiring and instructive figures in our history." Nevertheless, when on occasion Dreiser wrote about the new in art, he revealed an affinity to realism. His appreciation of Sonntag's city street scenes has already been mentioned, and in *Ev'ry Month* he had written, "Let those paint classics who will. . . . [Those who] insist upon shutting their eyes and their hearts to the sentiment and beauty in every day life . . . their punishment shall be oblivion. . . . In painting and sculpture we must have the truth, though it be, as in literature, told as 'fiction.' " He paid tribute to the pioneering comic-strip artist Richard F. Outcault, a friend of Paul's who had created "The Yellow Kid." He profiled another newspaper artist, also Paul's friend, the political cartoonist Homer Davenport, writing that he takes an "X-ray glance at the impressive bearing of a great public character, and then draws for you the skeleton of it—the miserable qualities of ambition, greed, and other qualities by which too often it is strung together." Referring to a caricature of Mark Hanna, Theodore notes, "The lines of Davenport's pen crack like swishing whips on the backs of the naked."

Dreiser showed himself sensitive to the artistic potential of photography in an article on Alfred Stieglitz, the first ever done on him. At that time Stieglitz was experimenting with a mass-produced Kodak Detective on the theory that if he rid himself of clumsy paraphernalia—the heavy box camera, the tripod, the hood, the glass plates—he might better record city scenes. In the developing process, Stieglitz discovered, one could crop a picture and highlight the central point of interest. Theodore marveled that "by purely photographic methods" Stieglitz had succeeded in conveying "the impression produced by the original scene . . . the clear crowning reality of the thing." He decided that Stieglitz's "Winter on Fifth Avenue," a dramatic portrait of a cabdriver in a snowstorm which caused a sensation when it was first exhibited, "had the tone of reality. . . . The driving sleet and the uncomfortable atmosphere issued out of the picture with uncomfortable persuasion."

On occasion, a glimmer of description shines through in Theodore's own photographic prose, as though he had suddenly seen things with his own eyes rather than with those of the conventional-minded readers for whom he usually wrote. In the trolley article, for example, he watches some millworkers clamber aboard: "Girls in stained gingham dresses, with hats more or less aged and shoes well worn; men and boys in grease-soiled hats, coats and trousers from which all semblance to Sunday shapeliness had departed. This shop-street was ill paved and lined with blear-eyed stores." In a tidal river he sees geese "spattering about, burying their long necks in the slime and smacking their bills prodigiously."

Such glints were rare; usually he stuck to ladling out a thick gruel of facts. Whatever emotion he had left over after the daily grind of article writing he decanted into an occasional poem. His notes during this period, containing lists of facts and possible article subjects, are occasionally interrupted by a poem. In the middle of a summary of a Tiffany lamp designer's career appears: "The moon looks down with sheenful ray/On Egypt's sands, on Khartoum's walls."

He was writing too fast, though, to speak in his own voice, and had adopted a sort of general droning vivacity. One imagines him lucubrating at the Salmagundi Club on West Twelfth Street, where as a nonresident member he had the use of the study, or at the Bible House, where Marden gave him desk space, filling half sheets of yellow foolscap with his crabbed reporter's script. Dreiser was a writing machine; his speed and ability to sustain it for hours at a time accounted in part for his fecundity. But he also learned to use his material thriftily, plagiarizing from himself, expanding or rewriting previously published pieces and reselling them, reheating leftover research.

The "Talk with Choate" for *Success*, was completely recast as "The Real Choate" for *Ainslee's;* the Chicago River flowed naturally into the Chicago drainage canal; the Brandywine coursed through two articles; the women violinists performed an encore in another venue. He made good use of his *Ev'ry Month* pseudonyms, Edward Al and Herman D. White.

Yet recycled material makes up only about one-fifth of his production during 1898 and 1899. Apparently no editor ever found one article identical to another. Duffy did send him a panicky note saying that a profile of the sculptor Henry Shrady, which was going to press, had turned up in identical form in the Sunday supplement of the *World*. It seems unlikely that Theodore would have resold the article under Duffy's nose; perhaps it was all a misunderstanding. At any rate, he continued to write for *Ainslee's* and, as mentioned, became a contributing editor.

One of his worst sins was overshooting space limitations. J. C. Brill at *Munsey's* wrote him that a five-thousand-word article he submitted must be cut to three thousand, and an editor of *The Cosmopolitan* told him, "We would also like permission to materially change or rewrite and condense the manuscript." How much other editors rewrote him is not known; probably Theodore bears the lion's share of the blame for his pedestrian prose, but it may be that some of it was interpolated by other hands. Some of his freshest pieces appeared in *Ainslee's*, where his friend Duffy seems to have given him his head. Duffy was one of the first of his contemporaries to recognize that Theodore was destined for something better than special writing.

Some of the complaints Dreiser received were the fault of the magazine. For example, after the article on the sculptor J. Q. A. Ward appeared, Duffy dispatched a telegram: WARD DENYING SCULPTURE ARTICLE. WANTS RETRACTION BY US. COME DOWN TOMORROW.

Ainslee's had run an article on Ward—but it was under the sculptor's byline. The original manuscript shows that it was written as an interview with Ward, consisting largely of his statements interspersed with occasional questions in Dreiser's *Success* formula. Duffy had apparently removed the quotation marks, condensed it, and run it under Ward's byline. Perhaps he hadn't obtained permission, or perhaps the cuts angered Ward. Some mildly controversial observations praising nude statuary and criticizing the rage for heroic replicas of Admiral George Dewey had been excised.

More damaging were the complaints about factual errors from sharp-eyed readers. One claimed that the route Theodore had followed on his trolley trip from New York to Boston was geographically impossible. Another said an article on the Winchester Arms Company for *The Cosmopolitan* contained "matter copied bodily without credit from the catalogue" of the firm.

The pressure Dreiser was working under partially explained the lapses. In the case of the Winchester article, it could even be said that he was meeting wartime demand—the Spanish-American War had begun in April 1898. A blast of frenetic patriotism, fanned by William Randolph Hearst's *Journal*, swept the land. The sinking of the battleship *Maine* in Havana Harbor was the casus belli, but the war for Cuban independence was popular, appealing to the idealism as well as the chauvinism of the time. The Boys of '98 were eager to fight because they believed they were helping to lift the yoke of oppression from little Cuba's shoulders and because they saw the Spanish as tyrants and Old World meddlers.

Joining the rush to the colors were reporters and artists like David Graham Phillips, Frank Norris, Richard Harding Davis, Stephen Crane, Frederic Remington, and Louis Sonntag, Jr., who signed up as correspondents or combat illustrators and shipped out for Tampa, Florida, the staging area for the upcoming invasion of Cuba. Theodore, however, did not join them, for reasons unknown. Perhaps he believed his health was not sufficiently robust; also, he was twenty-seven, somewhat older than most of the volunteers, and had an increasingly impatient fiancée out in Missouri. Nor did he share the urge to prove himself and the valor of the Anglo-Saxon "race" exhibited by the likes of Davis, Crane, and Norris. He was coming to realize that Anglo-Saxon "blood" was considered bluer than the Teutonic strain. The German-language press in the United States was generally opposed to the war; some papers on socialistic grounds, others because of U.S. designs on German Samoa. Imperialistic sentiments—"manifest destiny" and "trade follows the flag," to mention two— were in the air, while military strategists like Admiral Alfred T. Mahan preached of the new, expanded navy's need for coaling stations.

Yet Theodore did share the patriotic sentiment, and regarded the invasion of Cuba as alternative aid to an "oppressed" people. He joined the chorus with a war poem that appeared in several newspapers and was later collected in an anthology of patriotic verse. Called "Exordium," it begins:

> Right with naked hands hath beaten
> At the haughty gates of crime;
> She hath for their freedom battled
> With all nations, through all time;
> She has marched through snows of Winter
> With her blood-stained feet—sublime.

And so on, for six stanzas. The poem is stirring but rather abstract. No mention is made of swarthy Spaniards or poor Cuba. Even war sounds rather sanitized, a long way from the young novelist Frank Norris's discovery that it was "nothing but a hideous blur of mud and blood." "Right" is a merciful warrior: "By her slaughter brings she healing;/Bringeth love unto the land./She is tender, without error,/And her dead wake to her hand." Other stanzas evoke the Civil War—"the broken line at Shiloh" and "the clouds at Lookout." The meter of the poem is the familiar marching beat of "The Battle Hymn of the Republic."

Remembrance of the Civil War was much in the air at the time; to many people, the idea of lads from North and South fighting together under Old Glory symbolized a healing of the old wounds. Paul capitalized on this theme in a song called "The Blue and the Gray," which became his biggest hit since "The Wabash." "The Blue and the Gray" appeared after the Cuban War was over, however. In 1898 and 1899, he emitted a stream of superpatriotic ballads, including one with the memorable title, "Your God Comes First, Your Country Next, and Then Your Mother Dear." (As Broadway wiseacres pointed out, it was probably the only time in his career that Paul had relegated Mother to third place.) Howley, Haviland fired off "a Fusillade of Patriotic Hits" keyed to the war news, and Paul led the charge with the vigor of Teddy Roosevelt storming San Juan Hill. War had hardly been declared when Paul was reassuring Havana that the Yanks were coming: "We bring food and ammunition/You shall not want very long." And when Admiral Dewey decimated the timid Spanish fleet in the battle of Manila Bay, Paul joined the presidential boom for the hero of the hour with "Come Home, Dewey, Come Home."

Such flag-waving quickies were a dime a dozen. The most popular Spanish-American War song with the troops was the old camp-meeting rouser, "There'll Be a Hot Time in the Old Town Tonight." Paul was gratified to hear that homesick soldiers also liked to sing "The Wabash" around the campfire, so he wrote a new verse and titled it "On the Shores of Havana Far Away." "The Blue and the Gray," which he wrote in 1900, was a stirring stage number, with snatches of "Dixie" and "The Battle Hymn of the Republic" woven in.

Compared to the dozen or so songs Paul wrote, Theodore's contribution to the home front morale was minuscule, consisting of "Exordium" and four articles he wrote in the span of a month on wartime subjects—carrier pigeons, a shipyard where battleships were built, a cartridge factory in Bridgeport, and the Winchester Arms Company. His attitude toward the fray in these pieces was more philosophical than patriotic. For example, in the article on the Winchester company, he reports that he left the plant thinking that the deadly weapons made inside were the enemy of war, because they make it "so swift and decisive, that after a while there may be no longer need of war."

The reader who complained about his cribbing from the catalogue was probably right. The article becomes bogged down in tedious detail on the manufacture of pistols. Yet, in a letter to Jug, Theodore reports that he spent a day at the plant, talking to workers and taking a tour.

He had had a busy week. One Monday, he told her, he looked into clam-digging at Oyster Bay for *Frank Leslie's Monthly*. Tuesday he spent in Roslyn, New York, with a photographer taking pictures of William Cullen Bryant's home to illustrate a piece for *Munsey's;* Thursday he looked over the Union Metallic Cartridge Company in Bridgeport, Connecticut; Friday it was Stamford and an old soldiers' home; Saturday and Sunday mornings he worked with a photographer on illustrations for the last three articles. "Now," he writes, "I have a weeks writing before me—all the hours I can stand in a day in order to put my material in shape." While it is doubtful that he finished all five articles in a week, the fact that he was contemplating doing so gives an idea of the pace he maintained. One can imagine he gave about a day to writing the Winchester article. Pressed for time and with technical data coming out of his ears, Theodore took a shortcut by lifting a description of the manufacturing process from the catalogue.

His conventional support for the war may have given way to confusion when the imperialistic spoils were collected. The issue of expansionism came to a head in the Senate debate on the peace treaty with Spain, signed at the end of 1898, annexing the Philippines. His hero, Bryan, while favoring ratification, thought the United States should free the conquered territories. In 1900 the Great Commoner ran for president as an anti-imperialist, appealing to a small but growing sentiment in the country that enlisted writers and intellectuals like Howells, Mark Twain, and William James. Whether Theodore shared those sentiments is unclear, for he made no comments on the war in his articles. In 1899 he blandly reported the white-man's-burden views of Chauncey Depew, president of the New York Central Railroad. "With regard to the territorial expansion of the United States . . . there is no reason why it should not result in the larger civilization of the world."

When he interviewed former House Speaker Thomas B. Reed at his home in Maine, in September 1898, Dreiser managed an off-the-record gibe that did not appear in his article but which he reported to Jug. Reed, whom he thought resembled Paul physically and in his clownishness, had grown disillusioned with the imperialist sentiments of the Republican Party and resigned as speaker. When they talked about the war, Reed said, "Think of all the hundreds of men who lost their lives in the recent war." Theodore replied, "Oh, but think of the thousands and thousands who have lost their opinions," a reference to Reed's desertion of his party because of its support of the war. Theodore explained to Jug, "This was a direct shot at his conservatism." Actually, imperialism was a young man's game—espoused by political comers like Roosevelt and Senators Henry Cabot Lodge and Albert J. Beveridge, so Theodore may well have cast Reed as an old fogey.

He was too busy chasing success to think much about the war or the question of American imperialism, however, though he did mourn the death of his acquaintance Louis Sonntag, Jr. While in Cuba drawing pic-

tures of ships for Hearst, Sonntag had contracted malaria, as did so many
of the Boys of '98, and died. Here was a vibrant, promising young life
snuffed out. The tragedy reminded Theodore of his own onrushing mor-
tality (he had written Jug on her birthday in May that life was "a great
chase to old age and death"), and of the fragility of youthful dreams. In
his grief he composed a poem dedicated to Sonntag that was published
in *Collier's* and picked up by several newspapers. Called "Of One Who
Dreamed," it was crude in language but heartfelt:

> Lord! one whose dreams were numerous has gone,
> Who living loved and toiled and blessed each dawn.
>
> . . . .

What was the meaning of this pointless death? He demanded an answer from the Unknowable:

> Lord in thy law some good must balance pain
> Else were this all too much—a struggle vain.

23. I'll Have You
No Matter What

I lived in my love for you and my letters. . . . I was cursed, I thought because my imaginings could not be made real. . . . I dwell in my imagination and you who came into my life were admitted to it.
—Dreiser to Sara O. White (1896)

Of all letters, the love-letter should be the most carefully prepared . . . they are the most thoroughly read and re-read, the longest preserved, and the most likely to be regretted in after life.
—*Hill's Manual of Social and Business Forms* (1873)

reiser sometimes feared he was engaged in a struggle vain. All his work now, article after article, was consecrated to becoming a success so they could marry—yet that goal seemed to recede before him.

Their formal engagement had stretched into two years, and they had had an "understanding" since he lived in St. Louis, four years ago. Yet since he had quit the *Republic* they had met only twice. In the intervening months he made love by post to a fantasy Jug, building "silvery castles" about her, he wrote. His objective was a "little quarter of our own with you and pretty furniture in it to make it lovely. I want money to buy you rich dresses and soft luxurious lingerie and best of all I want you with me in a warm voluptuous embrace for nights and nights unending." He longed for the time when

> Your little shoes and my big boots
> Are under the bed together.

His ardent sentiments did not comport with the rules for writing courtship letters in Professor Hill's *Manual*, and they disconcerted the small-town Methodist in Jug. She complained frequently that he was being indiscreet, at one point warning him that someone at the post office was steaming open their letters. Theodore refused to bowdlerize, complaining, "I hate to be careful. It's like being made to mind."

Years later, Jug had her way retroactively. To Dreiser's discomfiture, she had kept his courtship letters, written from 1896 through 1898. She— or someone else—blacked out sentences and destroyed entire pages. There is little question that the main purpose was to remove erotic passages. To which he might have replied that if his sexual feelings had exceeded the bounds of decorum, he couldn't help himself. As he wrote in one of those letters, "Nature . . . has given me a cross of passion."

After Theodore visited her in the spring of 1896, their first meeting in twenty-one months, parting was such a painful wrench that it left him in a state of "almost fainting misery." When his train passed Forest Park in St. Louis, where they had strolled in the early days of their courtship, he was filled with longing for Jug and prayed that love "might be torn from my heart" so that he might be spared "the horror of parting." Back in New York two days later, he wrote her that once he had thought love would be endless delight, but now he had learned that it "is suffering . . . but suffering which one only too gladly endures, like He who took his cross and kissed it."

During that visit she had reciprocated his physical passion up to a point. "What a lover you are. You are Sapphic in your fire," Dreiser exulted. In June he sent her a ring. Perhaps at their last meeting Jug had let him go "too far"on the strength of his promises and felt compromised, though he reminds her that it wasn't entirely his fault: "You abetted me with love and sentiment."

However passionate their lovemaking, Theodore had not let it get out of hand. As he told her later, there were times when she had been "helpless" and would have "succumbed" if he had persisted in his "tender urging." But sex without marriage would have been empty. "I want you— and not your physical virtue . . . the other without you could only have brought me misery." Unspoken was his realistic but almost neurotic fear that she would become pregnant—or even feign pregnancy.

After that visit, Jug pressed him to set a date. Theodore, preoccupied with making *Ev'ry Month* a success, put her off. This led to a crisis in their relationship in the summer of 1896. Jug played a desperate game, flaunting her independence, hinting that others found her attractive, and, finally, not writing him. Apparently she was sufficiently confident that

he loved her to risk this, and she probably knew intuitively what a powerful aphrodisiac jealousy is. Also, she had other beaux, like Bob Rogers
in Mexico, Missouri, with whom she was still friendly.

By mid-August she had reduced the flow of her letters to a trickle, and
he complained she had written him only twice, compared with twenty-
seven times during May and June. When she ignored his pleas for a letter, he threatened to "do something desperate" if he didn't hear from
her. He begged her to "write and complain or write a long accusation,
anything, only write. Don't grow apathetic. Don't change and deceive
yourself into believing that you are not changing."

He suspected that she had found someone else. When Jug went to
Colorado to visit her brother he warned her, "Everything in such soft and
languorous climate appeals to you. . . . In such a time there might come
another, and then where would be I." Worrying about her inconstancy
has made him "nervous and disquieted," he complained. "You have too
much of my heart." He was experiencing for the first time the torment
of being the lover but not the loved. It was agony.

When she described the rushing mountain streams, he replied that he
was reminded of his boyhood in Warsaw, when he used to lie beside the
Tippecanoe River and stare for hours at the eddying waters:

> I love the still peaceful currents, where clear water flows silently, over yel-
> low sand, or long green grass . . . should some overwhelming sorrow take
> from life its natural delight I would love to seek that quiet nook and lie
> down to rest in that crystal sepulchre and pillow my head upon the grass
> and shining sand. There would be peace at last for the flesh. There would
> be quiet and beauty unmarred by sorrow and wearisome longing.

(It was around this time he had written the little essay on suicide in the
"Reflections" column.) He quickly repudiated such gloomy thoughts,
saying all he wanted was a home with her, a retreat where he could find
peace and contentment.

Jug seems to have sensed his vulnerability and twisted the knife, hinting of flirtations . . . that she had been "reckless." He begged her to tell
him if she had changed, but clung to the last shreds of self-respect: "I
do not want you if you have been, as you say, reckless." Alluding to the
necessity of earning enough money to support her, he moaned, "It is one
of the misfortunes that overtake ambitious young men who have not inherited a competence. I left you that I might eventually draw you in-
separably to me and it would be but another fine irony of my fate if my
venture should prove my loss of you."

He suggested that he come to Missouri to talk over their problems, but she discouraged him. He accused her of toying with him: "You think you can coquette and still twine me about your fingers . . . that you can repel me and then bring me back at your leisure; your pleasure. You are making a fool of me and none could realize it better than I." He couldn't sleep, and fretted about her night and day. He contemplated a blissful *Liebestod*: "It seems as if I could take your life and yet I should want you in my arms, close to my heart, to do it; so that your last sigh might be mine, for I do love you."

Soon afterward Jug relented, and in Dreiser's letter of September 11 he mentions rereading her last letter "so many times that I almost know it by heart." He praised her "siren hair" and asserted, "When your hair is down about your forehead and ears you always look so much just like one of Rossetti's maidens," though she is not meek and sorrowful like them. He couldn't live with a girl like that and is "awful glad to have a sweetheart who is gay and aggressive." Recovering his self-respect, Theodore can write of the possibility of her meeting other men. She was free to do so, so long as she did not "accept introductions where a love match is hoped for."

As the days of separation turned into weeks and then months, Dreiser's fantasy life grew in lush profusion. He complimented her on her resemblance to a picture of Cleo de Merade, the Parisian chanteuse who became the mistress of the king of Belgium. He enclosed the picture, and it is a close likeness. De Merade has the same pensive expression that Jug wore in some of her photographs, and her hair is down, framing her oval face. Jug reminded him of a "repentant Magdalen," though only "Magdalenic in sentiment," he quickly added.

She must have been irked as well as flattered by his romantic effusions, for they always drowned out practical questions. He must give her "elegant clothing, a few splendid jewels and suitable surroundings. . . . I have a desire to make your garments elegant not only that you may be pleased but that I may gloat over my *prize*." He is determined to gain "access to the pleasures of your love through splendid trappings. There is a sort of luxurious nourishment in elegancies." He imagines being alone with her in a chamber "warm with light and soft, full hangings and rich with the odour of flowers." His nature is "voluptuous," he boasts, and his "temperament that of an idler."

At Christmas he begged Jug to send him a glove and one of her slippers instead of a present. Feminine clothes pulsed with erotic energy. Wealth and sexuality mingled in dreams of musky, gaslit chambers with opulent scarlet hangings and thick Persian rugs. While passing the *Century* Magazine building (a citadel he yearned to penetrate) in Union Square, he had a fantasy of Jug standing nude on a marble pedestal, and he mentally arranged her in various "classic attitudes." She is both angel and repentant Magdalen; saint and sinner. Her face had a "sacred modesty," a "saintlike beauty," but she was also his "divinely formed madonna," his "little red-halo-ed Venus." Those reveries were tinctured by his earliest erotic stirrings in Warsaw, when he was drawn to sensuous blond earthy girls like Cad Tuttle and to ethereal, saintly maidens like Myrtle Weimar. In the idea Jug, the sensual and the saintly had coalesced.

It was an unstable compound. At times Dreiser had an urge to desecrate her purity. He spoke of wanting "to despoil your saintlike beauty. Like a bouquet of thornless roses you tempt me to crush you to withering in my arms. . . . Can you have such as me?" Another time he quoted Oscar Wilde's "Endymion" and visualized her in moon-drenched landscapes, where nymphs and satyrs amorously cavorted. Caroline Duer's "Nocturne" was also a favorite, and he underlined phrases that echoed the "love madness that seems to hold us":

> When the summer moon in her midnight madness
> Breaks through the clouds that would veil the night,
>
> .   .   .   .
>
> Riot, O wind, in the meadow's green tresses,
> Ripple the pools with the rush of your wing.
> Wake the white land with your wanton caresses,
> For this is the hour when love is King.

He all but confessed that his fantasies led to autoerotic activity. He described himself lying in bed late one morning with only his pillow to embrace, thinking of her. And then "the imagination becomes all powerful and I grasp with a tremor of passion at nothing and bury my face in my pillow with despair." He sought to implicate her in his fantasies. From the rear window of his hall bedroom at 232 West Fifteenth Street, he watched women in the apartment across the courtyard undressing. They reminded him of the risqué dances on the Midway at the Chicago World's Fair. If Jug were with him, he would draw the curtains and "my own girl would engage me with her beauty as no one else can—ever has before."

But he realized the hollowness of fantasy, telling Jug that he wanted her "not in moonlight alone but always and ever." And he worried that "in ordinary life I suppose I will have my cobweb fancies rudely swept aside the more as you become familiar with me. If so then my dreams will have been the richest and the best and I will go back to them then as I go back from them now to you, and think that they are not so delicious as the real may be and that my true pleasure is yet to come."

The real Jug behind the veils of erotic illusion continued to press him on the question of when his big boots and her little shoes would end up under the bed. Theodore was held back by his procrastinating nature and his absorption in becoming a success. "I think on advancement," he told her, but rationalized that he was doing it all for her. "My pride and egotism . . . seem to justify themselves in that they represent both you and I." Repeatedly, he assured her that he would "repay" her for her wait, that he would "atone in all ways I know how," that "all on earth that I can attain shall be yours."

In February 1898 he was feeling more prosperous and discoursed about flats they might rent. In the "fashionable quarter" on Fifth Avenue an apartment fetched $150 a month, but in other parts of the city a nice one with six or seven rooms could be had for $35 per month. But he quickly tired of "miserable matter-of-fact details." "Write me a love letter, Honeygirl," he said, "after you answer this one seriously."

Whenever Jug tried to get him to talk about the actual ceremony, Dreiser became a quivering wreck. Marriage "seems like wandering into a state absolutely blind"; he wished there were "houses already furnished for lovers and a book to buy which would tell husband and wife just what to do." The thought of standing up before dozens of Arch White's friends and neighbors in a Methodist church in Montgomery City struck terror in his heart. Public displays of affection were repugnant to him; people who did it were "like animals." As a way out of his anticipated misery, he lobbied for an elopement, offering to pay her way to New York if she would agree. He also proposed a kind of trial marriage.

In June he visited her, and when they parted his agony at the prospect of another separation was greater than it had been two years before. He had gone to the station, he told her, in a catatonic state. As the train bore him away from her, he wrote a poem to her. Then: "As the hurrying engine sped onward marking each new village with a long cry of steam and each farther main road with four lonely shrieks, I sped ever backward through the far night to my Jug. . . . It was on and on for my body but my heart has not come. . . . Love, my love—idol of my life—oh thou living shrine of my devotion. . . . I am yours wholey [sic] unquestioning until death, forever."

In April he had promised they would be married in September. In August he swore he would come for her within "the next forty days."

Neither pledge was honored. In Dreiser's autobiographical novel, *The "Genius,"* Angela Blue, the heroine, is subjected to similar delays and becomes ill. Her sister—the fictional counterpart of Rose White—finally writes to the hero, saying his fiancée is pining away. She scolds him for worrying about amassing sufficient money to provide Angela with luxuries.

He also wrote in *The "Genius,"* and said as much to his biographer Dorothy Dudley, that he had had affairs with other women during the long engagement. For someone with Dreiser's strong erotic drives, that seems plausible—except that there is no evidence of such affairs. Perhaps he did find release with some casual acquaintances (and there were always the pleasures of the Tenderloin), but one doubts, for example, that he engaged in the pagan alfresco revels with a glamorous singer he describes in the novel. She could as well have been imaginary—perhaps based on the diva Lillian Nordica, who was older than he and married.

If Theodore did dally, he remained true to the ideal Jug. "You have my every passionate physical thought," he swore, "and more I cannot give. If I shared the latter with others in this state of extreme love for you, you would be wronged, but I do not. . . . When I take you in my arms as my own you can know for certain that since my lips first touched yours they have never touched another in either affection [remainder of sentence expurgated]."

Those words were written in 1897; and throughout 1898, his protestations of love grew. He longed for their wedding night, "when nothing shall be withheld from me. . . . We will unite, close, final, perfect—mingle our very beings—sigh exhausted and repaid."

On a riverboat to Buffalo, where he was going to gather material for an article, Dreiser watched a couple enter their cabin and then eavesdropped on their "sighs and light laughter," wishing that Jug were there and that they could go to their own cabin. In August he assured her, "I'll have you no matter what."

October came and still they weren't married. The letters Jug preserved break off in September. But up to that point he is a young man eagerly anticipating the physical bliss they had so long denied themselves, acutely conscious of time slipping by: "It seems as if something dinned into my aching ears all the time the cry 'Losing time, losing time.' . . ."

Perhaps because she too was panicked by the rush of time (she was nearly thirty; he was twenty-seven), she agreed to an elopement. They were married on neutral ground, in Washington D.C., on December 28, 1898. Rose, and perhaps her brother Richard Drace White, were the only others present; it was probably an informal wedding in a Methodist minister's study. For Jug it was the culmination of four years of waiting, living at home like a spinster (she had given up teaching). For Theodore, it was the actualization of a dream that had sustained him during those years on the road, in lonely hall bedrooms and boardinghouses in Cleveland and Pittsburgh and New York.

He seems to have kept the ceremony secret. Ed did not learn about it until the following March. As he wrote Sylvia, "To say that I was surprised to hear that Theo was married is putting it mildly. All though [sic] I had a faint idea he was going to be married when he went away from New York last [June], well I am glad to hear it."

Where they went on their honeymoon is not recorded. Perhaps Annapolis, where Dick was a midshipman, then to Virginia or another southern state where they might find in December the June climate that Theodore thought so salubrious for lovers because of the "languorous quality of the nights and the sunny sensuousness of the days." By the description in *The "Genius,"* marriage tapped reserves of thwarted sexual passion in Jug. They were both ardent but inexperienced. When he was in his sixties, Dreiser confessed to his niece Vera, "It is true that my first marriage was not as happy as it should have been. I was not the most successful sexually of young men when I married Jug." And what woman could live up to his dream Jug, in her silvery cottage? Reality tarnishes, and perhaps the discoloration began to set in during the honeymoon. There is a hint of that in Theodore's assertion to Dorothy Dudley that the only novel by William Dean Howells he ever liked was *Their Wedding Journey*, an odd choice even at a time when Dreiser had sternly repressed his earlier admiration of the man. The book was, after all, Howell's first novel, a charming but slight account of a young couple's honeymoon trip. Dreiser, however, extolled it: "not a sentimental passage in it, quarrels from beginning to end, just the way it would be" (an inaccurate description incidentally). Perhaps Dreiser was confusing it with Howells's *A Modern Instance*, which is about a divorce.

But Dreiser's best-known verdict on his marriage was his claim at the end of *Newspaper Days* that he had wed Jug when "the first flare of love had thinned down to the pale flame of duty." In view of his love letters to her, to say he married her out of duty is stretching matters. True, he had doubts; true, too, he had private reservations about the vows he took, particularly the one that went "forsaking all others." But his later protestation that if convention had not stopped them and they had had sexual relations before marriage, he would not have been trapped, was history soured by disillusionment. (Curiously, he makes that claim in his autobiography. In *The "Genius,"* his and Jug's counterparts do consummate their desires that summer in Missouri—and Eugene, the hero, complains that his wedding night was not as blissful as it should have been because they had done so.) The truth was that Theodore's own desires trapped him, and his need for Sara was strong and more than just physical. The words he wrote in *Sister Carrie*, in a passage about Hurstwood's love letters that was cut from the published book, were a more apt description of Dreiser's state of mind at the time: "Under the influence of a contagion as subtle, expansive and pervasive as love, the mind is above the normal in its power of imagination. . . . Things said or written under such circumstances should have no more significance attached to them than is attached to a ripple of laughter or a burst of song. . . . In a true comprehension of life a man may not be bound by these."

24. Summer on the Maumee

Married! Married! The words were as the notes of a tolled bell.
—Dreiser, "Rella" (1929)

If nothing interfereth in the early June time. . . . I will hie me to your nook on the Maumee.
—Dreiser to Arthur Henry (1897)

heir first home was not in the "fashionable quarter." They took an apartment at 6 West 102nd Street, in a new five-story building. The Upper West Side was a predominantly middle-class area, just emerging from the pioneer stage. New brick and brownstone row houses and new apartments, like the Dakota (an elegant castle in the urban Badlands when it was built in 1884), along Central Park West (which was fashionable), were mingled with vacant lots, shanties, and even a few farmhouses. The neighborhood was an enclave of upward strivers and "respectable" workingmen and their families. Six-room flats could be rented for $35 a month. A new place like the one Theodore and Jug moved into had the latest conveniences: a dumbwaiter in which garbage was lowered to the basement, a speaking tube connected with the front door, a call bell for the janitor, steam heat, and hot and cold running water. Despite his reluctance to deal with practical details before marriage, Theodore had been able to secure a decent flat.

Save for Sylvia, who was keeping company with a Japanese photographer named Hidi Kishima, there were no other sisters or brothers around to welcome Jug into the family. The Dreiser clan had entered another of its centrifugal phases. Emma lived in Bayonne, New Jersey, Sylvia moved to Brooklyn after her marriage in 1900, and Mame and Austin Brennan were in Chicago, as was Claire, who worked as a teacher until she had a flare-up of tuberculosis. Ed was on the road much of the time, and Paul, the Broadway boulevardier, made frequent trips to Howley,

Haviland's Chicago office and was otherwise embroiled in business affairs. Theodore saw them rarely, and the coolness between him and Paul continued, although they wrote each other occasionally. Al was still in Chicago, working at demeaning jobs. Rome, as usual, was wandering and drinking heavily; with Sarah no longer around, his postcards from exotic places stopped coming.

A Christmas reunion in 1896, at which Paul and Theodore passed out the gifts and Brennan passed out from overeating, had been the last major family gathering. But scattered as they were (and as fractious as ever), they were still bound by Sarah's invisible hooks of steel. Paul, the eldest, who most resembled her physically, had assumed Sarah's role to a degree. He had several needy cases to take charge of. The ethereal Theresa had married her sweetheart, the scenery painter Ed Davis. It was a real love match, but Davis's mother resented her new daughter-in-law and made life hell for her. Theresa told Theodore she dreamed that her mother-in-law was dead, a portent she took seriously, being a Dreiser. The premonition was a double-edged sword. Mrs. Davis did die. But in October 1897, while wheeling her bicycle across the tracks of the Lake Shore and Michigan Southern Railroad in Chicago, Tres was struck by a train. Death was instantaneous, Paul wrote his friend Mary South. He had come to the city on business and ended up burying his sister—or, rather, temporarily placing her body in a mausoleum until he could take it to Rochester, New York, where, having no say in the matter, Tres was laid to rest beside her mother-in-law. "Poor Theresa," Sylvia wrote in what could be an epitaph. "Her life was not a sunshiny one."

Another sister who had lived through heavy weather was Emma, but in her case the clouds had temporarily lifted. Three years after leaving Hopkins, she married John Nelson, whose occupation is unknown but who had trouble finding employment in it, whatever it was. They lived in Bayonne for a time, and Emma was obliged to take in boarders. In a letter to Theodore, she portrayed herself as having been wronged by Mame and cut off from Paul's largesse. Mame "talked about us all, even you," and Paul said he "had no use for me as I only rooked him for money but that he would do anything for Mame. I don't care but I will never write him or see him again."

Mame and Brennan were looking after Father Dreiser and little Carl, who was no longer little and who had been shunted around from one sister to another, a leftover stray from Sarah's time. In 1898, on a visit to Chicago, Paul reported to Theodore that he found Carl "in rags" and had to provide money so the boy could go to school. Carl was apparently a troubled boy. He must have suspected that his position in the family was an anomalous one; probably he knew by now that Sylvia, his real mother, had abandoned him. (A few years later, barely out of his teens, he committed suicide.)

On the same trip that he found Carl in a state of neglect, Paul also discovered a seriously ill Claire. Not long after taking a tuberculosis cure, she had hemorrhaged, and Paul gave her the money she needed to return to the sanatorium. The "same tale of woe—wow—" he told his brother. Claire dreaded a "slow, miserable" death from consumption, she wrote Theodore from Arizona. She was not afraid of dying, but prayed that the end would come quickly.

Such was the family Jug had married into. Although in 1899 she may not have met any of her new brothers and sisters, she must have gained enough of a general idea from Theodore to sense the glaring contrast with the White clan. Jug's brothers and sisters were now grown and off pursuing their lives, but theirs was the normal moving-on of small-town young people who have been sheltered in the pod until ready. Theodore's family, by contrast, had been blown apart. John Paul Dreiser, battered by the industrial storms, was now a beached hulk, while Arch White, though not wealthy, was a solid citizen.

The city must have been a cultural shock to Jug, whose only previous experience of urban life had consisted of visits to St. Louis and a trip to the Chicago World's Fair. In addition to acclimating herself, she had to adjust to a new husband and a new home. She would spend lonely days in that apartment on West 102nd Street, with no friends or neighbors to talk to, no mother down the street, as a small-town bride would have had. She had entered a fast-moving urban world in which the streets swarmed with strangers.

But, like most women of her time, Jug had oriented her entire life around the goal of being a good wife. She was an excellent cook (her biscuits became famous among Theodore's friends), sewed her own clothes, and looked after her husband's wardrobe assiduously, darning his socks, laying out his underwear. Theodore soon became happily uxorious. She helped him with his writing, correcting his grammar and spelling and making fair copies of manuscripts. Sometimes, in the middle of an article, he would tire, but rather than stop, he would dictate passages to her, then take up the pencil again when he was rested.

And so they passed the winter, Jug making the apartment into a home and Theodore writing articles. It may well be that his failure to tell others about the marriage resulted in some awkward moments when his city friends called and were surprised to find a wife installed. Did Theodore's reticence betray a lack of pride in Sara, as he later wrote in *The "Genius"*? Perhaps, but Jug seems to have become friendly with people like the sculptor J. E. Kelly, a fan of her biscuits, and later she would grow close to several of the Dreiser sisters and Ed's wife, Mai.

By June 1899 he had saved enough money to take up Arthur Henry's long-standing invitation to visit him and Maude at their "nook on the Maumee." The House of Four Pillars was an old, rambling affair, exemplifying the lavishness of space and republican simplicity of an earlier day. Located in the village of Maumee, it had fourteen airy rooms that provided cool refuges from the baking Ohio sun. The Greek revival pillars and veranda looked out on an apron of grassy lawn sloping down to the unpretentious, meandering river, beside which ran an abandoned barge canal with overgrown towpaths, moss-laden rocks, and rusting gears. Henry had fixed up a study in the basement, which had wood-paneled walls, a fireplace, bearskin rug, and a rocking chair for Theodore with wide arms that could serve as a writing desk. His plan was that they would work side by side.

Maude and Jug were assigned the housekeeping and the cooking chores, respectively. Appetites sharpened by the country air, the men ate voraciously, and Jug prepared farmhand meals with fresh local produce. In time, the food bills mounted to alarming proportions.

But it was a healthy life. Each morning they took a dip in the river and at night they would sit on the bank, concocting Indian legends and singing in the moonlight, Theodore in a rocking chair, "chewing slowly and meditatively with closed eyes . . . singing a bit in a hoarse voice," as Maude Henry remembered.

Marriage undoubtedly contributed to the mellowness of Theodore's mood. Also, he had reached a pleasant upland meadow in his career where he could pause and take satisfaction at how far he had climbed. In only two years he had become a successful specials writer, as he had predicted to Emma Rector he would. Concrete recognition had recently come in the form of membership in the Indiana Club and a listing in the first edition of *Who's Who in America*: "Dreiser, Theodore, journalist-author . . . connected with daily papers, Chicago, St. Louis, Pittsburgh, 1891–5; editor Every Month [sic], musical magazine, 1895–7; then in sp'l work for Cosmopolitan magazine, contributes prose and verse to various periodicals. Author, Studies of Contemporary Celebrities, Poems. Residence, 6 W. 102nd St. New York."

The entry was accurate save for the "author" credits: neither of the books listed had been published. *Studies of Contemporary Celebrities* was to have been a collection of interviews from *Success* and other magazines. A Cincinnati house had offered him an advance of $500, but the firm went bankrupt.

Although he had accumulated enough poems to make a slim volume, no publisher had taken them. Nevertheless, he had told an interviewer from McClure's Syndicate that William Dean Howells had "expressed a hearty liking" for them and that the Dodd, Mead Company "had the book in hand." There is no evidence that Howells ever praised Theodore's verse publicly or privately. He may have expressed his thanks for the *Success* interview and Theodore had taken advantage of the entrée to send him a batch of poems, knowing his generosity to young writers. As for the mention of Dodd, Mead, that may have meant only that it was considering the book. No book of poetry by Theodore Dreiser was ever published by that firm—or by any other at that time. Whatever Howells's verdict, Theodore was in need of a sponsor for his verse.

The obvious patron was Edmund Clarence Stedman, who was to young poets what William Dean Howells was to fledgling novelists. One might well suspect that Theodore first sought to smooth his path to the great man with a little flattery, for in the March 1899 issue of *Munsey's* appeared an idolatrous article entitled "Edmund Clarence Stedman at Home" by Theodore Dreiser. It contains a purported description of the poet's Lawrence Park abode—in the same artists' enclave about which Dreiser had written one of his first magazine pieces—as well as quotations of his verse and a bit of biographical data. But there is no interview with Stedman, though by a verbal *trompe l'oeil*, the reader almost believes that one took place.

What is interesting about the piece is that a substantial section of it is plagiarized—doubly plagiarized, one could say. At first remove it draws on an article Theodore wrote for *The New York Times Illustrated Magazine* the year before; that article—and to a greater degree, the one in *Munsey's*—borrowed almost verbatim from one by Ann Bowman Dodd in *The Critic* in 1885. True, Theodore does say that the writer who comes on Stedman "at this late day . . . must be content . . . to leave the account of the poet's long active life as it has been written down by other pens." But no credit is given to Dodd. What is more, the house Dodd described was the one Stedman lived in in New York City, not in Lawrence Park.

Apparently, though, Theodore was eager to put his praises of the Wall Street versifier on the record, and the reason for his eagerness may well have been that he hoped Stedman would give his collection of poems a boost with a publisher. In April he wrote the bard of Lawrence Park to ask permission to submit some poems; the reply was favorable. Months passed, however, before the verdict came down. On June 9 Ella Boult, a secretary, wrote Theodore that while Stedman found his "characteristic and best mood the contemplative, exemplified in such pieces as 'Compensation,' " he did not think the poems sufficiently "above the average" and "it is impossible for verse to succeed in book form unless it is distinctly above the average." Also, Theodore's work was too "lacking in dramatic or lyric quality" to appeal to the present generation.

To this polite dismissal, Theodore replied arrogantly that he did not need to be told his poetry was unlikely to sell. "A critically admired volume stands more as an exponent of a man's mental calibre than as a source of revenue or general fame." His bravado showed he was developing a prickly literary ego. "Possibly Mr. Stedman will be interested in knowing that these [poems] will be published in the fall," he wrote, an allusion to the phantom Dodd, Mead volume.

Philosophy and emotion wrestled in Dreiser's poetry, with the latter usually winning out. In some the influence of Spencerian doctrine was apparent. When in "Bondage" he wrote of the "ceaseless drag of all desire," he meant desire as Spencer did, as the prime mover within each individual:

> And this thing hunger—ceaseless, yearning pain—
> Its slave you are. Denying is so vain.
> Some one hath touched you saying: "Feel desire."
> His will you do—you run, you run, aspire!

But the philosophy is a backdrop to the poem; in the foreground are reflections on his own life—his desire for Jug and his race for success, the compulsion to run, aspire. As Theodore had shown in *Ev'ry Month*, he interpreted Spencerianism in a personal way, using it to make sense of his life, as one draws on a popular self-help guide. He ended another poem on a straightforward didactic note:

> Yea, through each throbbing heart of man
> There runs a plan, there runs a plan.

—and sounded neither poetic nor fresh.

Much of his poetry reflected the sensibility of a romantically gloomy young man. The language was often halting and clumsy, though heavy with sincerity. Death and the passage of time were his favorite subjects. In "Resignation," for example, Dreiser wrote of kissing the "cool, damp soil/The door, I hope, to peace, to God." We have a "few bright days, a few brief years . . . and lo, the end appears." Then nature takes us, "As tho' it never yet had been."

Although Stedman's letter did not shake Theodore's belief in his poetic talent, the rebuff came at a timely moment, pushing him to other forms of expression. The poems had served to unlock a storehouse of feelings inside him for which he had found no outlet within the constraints of the magazine article format. The words of the interviewer from McClure's Syndicate were more perceptive than perhaps he realized: "Mr. Dreiser's poetical temperament proves itself not a little in his way of life; allowing for the compliance inseparable from earning even the most modest living, he adheres to his own will and impulse with a quite exceptional independence, and manages to reserve a large share of his mind, most of the time, for his own fancies."

Dreiser could count himself a success in the eyes of his peers, but he still seethed to express himself. It was Arthur Henry who gave him the needed push that summer at the House of Four Pillars. His temperament was the catalyst, and his chipper optimism and Quixotic bohemianism counteracted Theodore's gloominess and inclination to drift. The "fine fancies" and "impossible romances" he hawked like a medicine-show salesman were just the potions Theodore needed. Henry spoke of art and poetry in the same way he did of happiness: they were "more accessible than the light at noonday."

Henry wanted to write a novel, but was reluctant to undertake it unless his friend was working on one too, at his side. Theodore also had an idea for a novel, but lacked the confidence to try it. So Henry nagged him to try some short stories as finger exercises. Sitting in his wide-armed rocking chair in the basement of the big house, Theodore began writing his first attempt: "It was a hot day in August. The parching rays of a summer sun had faded the once sappy green leaves of the trees to a dull and dusty hue."

After each paragraph, he considered giving it up, he later told H. L. Mencken. Theodore thought it "asinine," but Arthur Henry praised his efforts and kept him at it until he finished.

As the story—called "McEwen of the Shining Slave Makers"—opens, McEwen is sitting on a park bench in the heart of a large city, a green island of calm in the tossing urban sea. Suddenly, he is transformed into an ant, forced to survive in the Darwinian world of nature. He becomes embroiled in a great battle between his tribe, the *Sanguineae* (a species of black ant; the naturalistic details of the story were drawn from John

Lubbock's *Ants, Bees and Wasps*), and a marauding party of red ants. Mortally wounded, McEwen is on the verge of death when he is suddenly restored to human form. He gazes at the ant battle on the ground, a ferocious, no-quarter contest, and has a vision of life as "strange passions, moods and necessities . . . worlds within worlds, all apparently full of necessity, contention, binding emotions and unities."

In other words, the "God-damned stinking, treacherous game" that Maxwell had said it was in the newsroom of the *Globe* in Chicago; that it was in New York City in 1894. Like McEwen, Theodore had been thrown in it to live or die. But he did not see it entirely in Darwinian terms. The vision of a bloody struggle was tempered by a Tolstoyan recognition of humane values—"binding emotions and unities." McEwen experiences cruelty, but he also acts altruistically, risking his life for his comrade, Erni, and experiences kindness from members of his own tribe. And the story has a vision of nature within the city: two separate yet indivisible spheres, "worlds within worlds," each a metaphor of the other.

"McEwen" was the first of five stories Theodore wrote that summer. In the second he shifted from allegory to realism, drawing upon his own family experiences. Entitled "Old Rogaum and His Theresa," it tells of the daughter of a German butcher in Greenwich Village who seeks to escape from her stern Old World father, a carbon copy of John Paul Dreiser. Like Theodore in Chicago, Theresa Rogaum is drawn to the street, "with its stars, the street lamps, the cars, the tinkle and laughter of eternal life." She walks out with a young man from the neighborhood, a reputed "masher," as Sylvia and Emma had done in Warsaw. Old Rogaum beats and berates her and finally locks her out—as old Paul threatened to do to Sylvia and Emma.

Later, the butcher discovers the body of a young girl on his doorstep, and for a heart-stopping moment thinks it is his Theresa. But she turns out to be a young prostitute who has committed suicide. Rogaum has had a glimpse of what Theresa might become if he continued to lock her out (a policeman tells him that the dead girl's father had done the same). And so when his daughter returns—she had been with her boyfriend— he forgives her. The conflict between youthful desire and paternal authority is dramatized, and Rogaum's tyranny is considered monstrous while his daughter's innocent longing for love is natural. Yet Rogaum loves his daughter, as Theodore was coming to see that old Paul had loved Emma and Sylvia.

The next story he wrote, "Nigger Jeff," drew on the lynching of the young black man who raped two women that Dreiser reported for the St. Louis *Republic*. The details follow the newspaper account closely, though to make the rapist more sympathetic, he is not a psychotic, as his real-life counterpart evidently was, but a victim, too, in a way. A reporter who believes life's rewards and punishments are justly meted out watches as the mob besieges the jail where the suspect is being held, outwits the law-abiding sheriff, and carries off the trembling, pleading prisoner. The reporter passively records the lynching, but the ground opens up beneath him: His Sunday school morality has crumbled. He visits the cabin where the corpse is laid out (noting the "bar of cool moonlight lay just across the face and the breast," as he had done in his article); the mother is weeping in the corner, just as the real-life mother had been. He comprehends that life is a muddle of beauty and pain. As he leaves, the sound of the mother's weeping in his ears, the reporter sorts out the elements of the scene, its color and pathos, "with the cruel instinct of the budding artist that he already was." He suddenly understands that "it was not so much the business of the writer to indict as to interpret." It was not his function to condemn the rape or the lynching but to *show* what happened, to convey his own emotional interpretation of the events, his sympathy with the victims of justice, rather than the journalistic facts.

The story transcends social considerations to focus on the tragic *mise en scène*—the dead boy, his face lit momentarily by the cold bar of moonlight, and the Pietà-esque figure of the mother. They stand for pity and mercy, qualities absent from justice, legal or otherwise. As he leaves, the reporter silently vows, "I'll get it all in! I'll get it all in!"

"Nigger Jeff" shows that Dreiser made a decisive leap that summer in his development as a writer. One need only compare it with a draft he wrote a year or so earlier, entitled "A Victim of Justice" (he never mentioned this maiden effort, preferring to leave the impression that the stories sprang miraculously to his pencil that summer in Ohio). The central event—the lynching—is roughly the same, but the narrator in "A Victim of Justice" is more remote from it, and the language is more stilted. The narrator is not sent to cover a hanging, he is "commissioned to examine into the details of one of those hasty illegalities not uncommon throughout the South." Much of the story is taken up with his dreamy meditations on death while standing in a country cemetery. The earlier work shows Dreiser's inability to make the transition from his meditative essays in *Ev'ry Month* to the short story form. Writing for the magazines had trained him to quell his tendency to philosophical ruminations.

*   *   *

Dreiser wrote two more stories that summer. One, called "The World and the Bubble," a fantasy, has been lost, but a hint of the idea that may have animated it can be found in "The Bubble of Success," an unpublished essay. In it he declares that "deluded selfishness" is the source of all progress. Youths are impelled by illusions of a more glamorous life, but when they achieve their goal, they are disillusioned. Success seen from the outside is a pretty bubble, but once inside, it is not what it seemed or what the world said it was. Human progress is a great bubble chase: "The planner of this curious existence has set before men's eyes a rainbow and at its end a misty pot of gold beyond the distant hillside in order that all humanity may run on and on, achieving, accomplishing but never enjoying." (About the same time, Dreiser described his sole antidote to disenchantment: "I think sometimes that nature is the only thing in life that has not changed for me, the one thing that did not begin as an illusion and conclude as a fraud.")

The fifth story was a fantasy called "When the Old Century Was New," an attempt to write something appropriate for the approaching debut of the twentieth century. He had done an earlier draft of this idea too, which he called "New Year's Bells." The draft does not survive, but Duffy rejected it, finding the language too flat. He urged Theodore to rework the whole idea in "your 1898 style." Duffy, who was as familiar with Theodore's writing as anyone, must have sensed the metamorphosis Dreiser was undergoing.

Whatever the problem with the earlier draft, Theodore's Maumee version was a parody of the popular historical romances of the time, with their detailed allusions to quaint dress and manners. His conceit was to show New Year's Day in New York in 1800. Walton, the central figure, goes about his daily rounds, happily discussing marriage with his fiancée and encountering historical figures such as John Adams and Thomas Jefferson. But Dreiser injects in the story a sense of foreboding, of dark clouds gathering on the horizon. Walton is a sleepwalker, oblivious to foreshadowings of problems that will flare up at the century's end— primarily industrialism and the widening gap between rich and poor. Walton uncomprehendingly notes "the aristocracy, gentry and common rabble forming in separate groups." A ground base of social realism grows increasingly insistent under the dominant romantic theme, and the story closes with a reference to Walton's blindness. He cannot see "The crush and stress and wretchedness fast treading this path of loveliness."

*   *   *

That summer on the Maumee was an immensely important breakthrough for Dreiser; half-formed moods and thoughts coalesced in fictional form. His vision of the city as urban nature, for example; his sense of the artist's duty to see life whole and record it unjudgmentally; the discovery of his family, particularly his sisters and father, as a subject for fiction; the rejection of romanticism for realism. And he also revealed prophetic intuition of the dark underside of progress: *pace* Spencer, society was not necessarily turning out for the best. Life was the unending pursuit of illusion, a rainbow chase. He had also tapped a new source of power within himself. When he returned to New York, he would no longer be content just to write articles and lugubrious poems.

While he was in Ohio, Theodore had received a letter from *Demorest's* requesting "something particularly striking and significant for a leading article for November." The article he wrote would be different from anything he had previously done and take him another step in his pursuit of the bubble of literary fame.

25. Curious Shifts
of the Free-lance

Genius struggles up. Talent often lingers and wears itself out in
journalism unheard of.
　　　　　　　　　　　　　　　—Dreiser, "The Literary Shower" (1896)

reiser returned to New York that September poorer but with
five short stories in his trunk. Henry, who had more confidence in their salability than he did, urged him to send
"McEwen of the Shining Slave Makers" to the august *Century*.

The *Century* submission was a long shot, and Theodore needed to restore his savings after a summer of idleness. So it was back to the life of
magazine journalism for him, and for Arthur Henry too. They formed a
literary partnership, collaborating on articles and sharing the fees fifty-
fifty. Their objective was to make enough money to enable them to work
on their novels. During their extended stay that summer, the Dreisers
had literally eaten the Henrys out of house and home. Theodore had
lent Arthur two hundred dollars. Not to be outdone in generosity, Henry
signed over to his friend a half interest in the second-mortgaged house,
meaning that Theodore took over the mortgage payments. The three of
them returned to New York, leaving Maude to hold the bag, as she later
put it bitterly.

Henry moved in with Theodore and Sara at the flat on West 102nd
Street, and, working together and separately, they lined up assignments
from various editors and divided them. Each had certain areas of ex-
pertise: Henry, for example, specialized in municipal government, and
Theodore fancied himself an authority on education and natural sciences.
But they worked on any ideas they could sell, and collaborated inter-
changeably on the research and writing. Arthur was the better editor of

the two, and polished Theodore's copy; the latter was a far more prolific writer. Henry might do all the research and Theodore the writing. Sometimes they cut several articles out of a bolt of research. If one got stuck midway, the other would tackle the conclusion.

Each would also act as the other's agent. In a letter to Richard Watson Gilder, editor of the *Century*, in December 1899, for example, Theodore proposed a story on "Country legislatures" and enclosed a synopsis of "an idea of Mr. Arthur Henry's which he would be pleased to have you consider. . . . I believe he would write something which would have broad intellectual significance, as well as much human interest."

This practice occasionally caused mixups. Once Theodore sold Woodward at *Pearson's* an article on peach growing that had been rejected by *Munsey's*. Then, a week or so later, Henry strolled into *Pearson's* editorial chambers. When Woodward told him he was desperate for material, Henry hurried home and dug out the peach article. Woodward recognized it as Theodore's idea, and Henry explained (he wrote his partner, who was summering in Missouri) "that some time ago you and I had investigated the subject of American Food products and finding that it was a very important and prolific field had divided it up between us." That was good enough for the copy-hungry Woodward, and Henry offered him a cornucopia of fruit articles—"Grapes and Wine, Oranges and Lemons and Melons." That was overdoing it: the editor told Henry "he didn't think that he would care to use the whole series for fear they would be too much alike." Theodore chided his friend for treading on his heels, but Henry told him that Woodward was not at all concerned about who wrote what and was "anxious to have all the stuff from both of us that we can turn in to him."

They were manufacturing yard goods, so it was no wonder their stories sounded alike. In a letter from the Catskills, where he had fled for some fresh air, Henry reported that between restorative tramps in the mountains, he had finished five articles, but only with great difficulty. He'd had to struggle to "bring out a different phase in each of them."

Sharing out of a common pot was a good idea, since their money dribbled in so irregularly that one—usually Henry—might be insolvent while the other was flush. But it also kept their joint finances in a constant muddle, and neither was businessman enough to straighten them out. An idea of their casual bookkeeping emerges in a letter Henry wrote to his partner: "You owe me $26.19 out of the fruit article. Had you got the check for the song article you would have owed me one half of that, plus the $29.20. Sorry you didn't get the song article check. If you can spare it send me $70.19 out of the fruit article and keep all the money for the song article when it comes."

But they were bohemian brothers now, as close as Sandy, Taffy, and Little Billee in *Trilby*, and the *ménage* on West 102nd Street was, platonically at least, *à trois*. As Henry characterized their relationship, "up to a certain point" they "had share and share alike" in Jug. He writes while on a research trip that he is "homesick for the flat" and in another letter, when the Dreisers were in Danville: "Tell Jug I shall be glad to see my half of our wife again." He admired Jug's beauty—her "girlish figure and glorious mass of red hair," as he wrote once, and regarded her as "a complex combination of child and woman, a being of affectionate impulses and stubborn fidelity, devoted to the comfort of her husband and managing in some mysterious fashion to reconcile her traditional beliefs with his unorthodox thoughts and ways."

Arthur's friendship with Theodore was almost feminine in its tenderness. During Theodore and Jug's sojourn in Danville he wrote, "I too wish with all my heart that we could be constantly together, walking, talking and writing of what seems great and worthy to us. I am not able to get either inspiration or comfort from others I meet. . . . The fact is that you are the only inhabitant of the same world with me." And in his letters Theodore spoke with equal affection. It was Henry, and Henry alone, who encouraged him in the idea that he could write something "great and worthy" and was ceaselessly "ding-donging" him to write a novel.

Theodore continued to procrastinate, but his feet were on the path leading to *Sister Carrie*. Some of his articles reveal a subconscious drift, and hint at themes that he later developed in full measure. One of those was "the song article" Henry mentioned in his accounting letter—"Whence the Song," as it was finally titled in *Harper's Weekly*, where it appeared in December 1900. Richard Duffy remembered that Theodore planned a novel about the music business with a hero "in whom success operated as a virus," and "Whence the Song" may well be a scenario of that novel. The central figure is a Broadway type, "the successful author of the latest popular song." With his "high hat and smooth Prince Albert coat," his "ruddy boutonniere," walking stick, vest "of a gorgeous and affluent pattern," and pearl-gray spats, he is, sartorially at least, the spitting image of Paul. He is also a representative figure of a world that "might well engage the pen of a Balzac or that of a Cervantes." The mention of Balzac was a signal that Dreiser had a novel in mind.

The songwriter's career traces a rising and falling trajectory. In the beginning, he is romping in the summertime of success, "a great man [a nod to Balzac] at last and the whole world knows it." Then comes the decline. His song's popularity fades and the inspiration for another won't come. He has in the meantime flung away his money and is reduced to sleeping on a charitable publisher's carpet: "The lights, the laughter; the songs, the mirth—all are for others," the author observes, sounding like a Paul Dresser ballad. The songwriter becomes ill, is hospitalized. And then: "One day a black boat steaming northward along the East River to a barren island and a field of weeds carries that last of all that was so gay, so unthinking, so, after all, childlike of him, who was greatest in his world."

In describing the Broadway milieu, Theodore brings in bits of color and remembered incidents from the Howley, Haviland days. A publisher is called Pat, after Pat Howley, and a feckless Negro songwriter named Gussie appears to be based on Gussie Davis, author of "In the Baggage Coach Ahead." Davis had died broke that year at the age of thirty-six, and Theodore believed Davis's career exemplified the sad case of the hit-writer who sells his songs outright rather than collecting royalties.

Among the types who appear is a young singer:

a rouged and powdered little maiden, rich in feathers and ornaments of the latest vogue; gloved in blue and shod in yellow; pretty, self-assured, daring and even bold. There has gone here all the traditional maidenly reserve you would expect to find in one so young and pleasing, and yet she is not evil. The daughter of a Chicago butcher, you knew her when she first came to the city—a shabby wondering little thing, clerk to a music publisher transferring his business ease, and all eyes for the marvels of city life.

There are traces of Theresa Rogaum in her, a bit of some secretary Theodore had known at Howley, Haviland perhaps, and a hint of himself as a wide-eyed arriviste in the city. But Dreiser drops her after this description and some show-business banter; she remains merely a type. The songwriter is also a type—a term emphasized by realists who believed characters should represent a class of persons whom one met in certain walks of life and whom readers would immediately recognize. But he is also Paul blended with other Broadway figures whose rapid rise and fall were common gossip along the Rialto. The fate Theodore ascribes to the songwriter reflects his fears that Paul would dissipate his royalties through high living.

In addition to Davis, Theodore may have heard of Charles Graham, author of two hits, "Two Little Girls in Blue" and "The Picture That

Is Turned Toward the Wall," who died in abject poverty. Like Davis, Graham had sold the rights to "Two Little Girls in Blue" for $35 and the publisher made $60,000 on it. "The Picture" was the same—marked down for $15; publisher gets rich. Or of Monroe Rosenfeld, whose "With All Her Faults I Love Her Still" sold 280,000 copies in sheet music and whose other numbers, like "Take Back Your Gold" and "The Wedding Bells Shall Not Ring," did almost as well. He made $75,000 from his songs, it was said, and lost $74,000 at the racetrack.

But Paul wasn't like that. He was no "Gussie," who is a stereotyped shiftless black, constantly wheedling advances of "twenty-five bones" because "it's rent day up my way." Theodore may have *believed* Paul had no business sense, but Paul would have disagreed with him. Paul had learned from bitter experience not to trust publishers. Indeed, he was now a publisher himself, with two partners who were "God's own white men." He had been turning out hits for a decade and was at the peak of his powers. In a contemporary newspaper story, the reporter relates the sad story of Charles Graham, then mentions Paul, as though in contrast: "He is a very thrifty fellow and a businessman too." Paul was charitable to a fault with his relatives and the out-of-work actors who touched him along Broadway, and was a high liver, a gourmand who regularly partook of Diamond Jim Brady–style feasts at Sherry's or Delmonico's. But he was probably making thirty or forty thousand a year and leaving the surplus in the business.

Theodore's portrait was tinged with jealousy. And deeper down, his attitude was shaped by the child within—the fearful little boy who secretly believed that disaster was always around the corner; who was convinced that the provider (and Paul was his father figure now) would inevitably fail. Resentment and fear coalesced, and Theodore composed a wish-dream version of Paul's end: an unmarked grave in potter's field. With Paul "dead" he could then write a laudatory epitaph, the tribute to the creators of the songs a nation sings, with which the story closes.

Another story he completed around this time, probably just after he returned from Ohio, was the "particularly striking and significant" lead article for the November 1899 issue of *Demorest's*. A significant departure from Theodore's hackwork, it was called "Curious Shifts of the Poor" and represented his first venture into New York local-color realism, in which descriptions of life in the Bowery were de rigueur.

Stephen Crane, in the sketches he wrote for the New York *Press* around 1892, had been among the first to discover the Bowery. Two years later, Hamlin Garland, a practitioner of local-color writing in his own Middle

Border stories, moved to New York and aided the penniless Crane. He
sent two of Crane's latest Bowery sketches to George O. Flower, editor
of a popular radical magazine called *The Arena* to which Garland had contributed, and patron of young realists. One of them was published as
"The Men in the Storm," and in 1897 Elbert Hubbard's artsy-craftsy little
magazine, *The Philistine*, had reprinted it. That was where Theodore
probably read it, and George C. Jenks, who conducted the "Literary
Shower" column in *Ev'ry Month*, praised it in his review of Crane's novel
George's Mother. Although Theodore had reviewed *The Red Badge of Courage* favorably, calling it "strong, incisive, bitter and brilliant," like Jenks
he had reservations about Crane's writing about a war he hadn't experienced, and preferred realistic novels like *Maggie*. On another occasion
Dreiser compared Crane unfavorably with Mary Wilkins Freeman, whose
stories of small-town life in New England placed her squarely in the local-
color movement.

   He seems also to have harbored feelings of rivalry toward Crane (they
were after all the same age) and was envious of Crane's sudden fame
after the publication of *The Red Badge of Courage* in 1895. In one article
he called Crane "a metropolitan success," chastised him for "writing night
and day" and implied that Crane owed some of his renown to the laudatory English reviews of *The Red Badge of Courage*, which carried undue
weight in America. Also, Dreiser may have regarded Crane as one of those
slumming Ivy League journalists like William Graham Phillips and Richard Harding Davis, who made the Bowery, the Tenderloin, and the Jefferson Market Courthouse their beats.

   He was wrong on all counts. The fact that Crane had three novels
appear in a bit over a year did not mean he was grinding out copy at a
too-rapid rate. Actually, *Maggie* was first published in 1893 by a medical
book company—at the author's expense—and only a handful of copies
were sold. As for the excessive influence of the British reviews, Crane
had received generally good notices in the United States, too. Finally,
Crane was no socialite reporter. The son of a minister and a dropout from
Syracuse University, he began writing for small-town newspapers as a
teenager, then came to New York City, where he experienced spells of
poverty worse than Theodore's. For a time, he lived in the Art Students
League on East Twenty-third Street, sleeping on the floor and subsisting
on bread and sardines. Later he moved in with some artist friends and
worked on *The Red Badge of Courage*.

   Crane took it to Garland one day in 1894, the manuscript rolled up in
the capacious pocket of his worn ulster. In his laconic way he asked the

older man if he would read it. Garland was bowled over: "Every page presented pictures like those of a great poem, and I experienced the thrill of the editor who has fallen unexpectedly upon a work of genius." When Garland asked where the rest of the manuscript was, Crane allowed that the typist was holding it because he owed her money. Garland lent him fifteen dollars to reclaim the script and asked Flower of *The Arena* and other editors he knew to help the young man.

However wrongly based Theodore's envy of Crane's metropolitan success had been, it was outweighed by admiration. Here was a writer of his own generation who saw the city with a cynical newspaperman's eyes. Dreiser must also have sensed in Crane a kindred Darwinian who regarded life without idealism.

In "The Men in the Storm," Crane describes the bums on a bitter-cold February day lined up outside a lodging house that offered rooms for five cents a night. The story stuck in Theodore's mind; Crane was painting with words what artists like William Louis Sonntag, Jr., William Glackens, and Everett Shinn were painting with their brushes and Stieglitz with his camera. They saw the city in its many guises and moods like a force of nature; they saw the life around them, rather than painting classical subjects. In "The Men in the Storm" Crane describes the crowds hurrying home to their warm dinners as a blizzard "began to swirl great clouds of snow along the streets, sweeping it down from the roofs and up from the pavements until the faces of the pedestrians tingled and burned as from a thousand needle-prickings." A glimpse of the wagon drivers, "muffled to the eyes . . . erect and facing the wind, models of grim philosophy," evoked an image reminiscent of the cabdriver in Stieglitz's "Winter on Fifth Avenue" (which Dreiser would later transmute into a painting by the artist-hero of *The "Genius"*). The natural storm was a metaphor for the economic storm that battered the poor: a looming, palpable presence in the 1890s.

When Theodore wrote "Curious Shifts of the Poor," he had Crane's story in mind. He too depicts a line of ragged, shambling men at a soup kitchen run by the Sisters of Mercy Convent near Emma's old place on West Fifteenth Street. He even noticed similar phenomena—for example, the way the snow piled up, unheeded, on "the old hats and peaked shoulders" of the men. (Crane had written: "It was wonderful to see how the snow lay upon the heads and shoulders of these men, in little ridges an inch thick perhaps in places.") Both resorted to natural imagery in describing the urban scene. Crane harked back to his small-town upbringing ("Occasionally one could see black figures of men busily shovelling the white drifts from the walks. The sounds from their labor created new recollections of rural experiences which every man manages to have in a measure"), while Theodore evoked animals (the men watched the closed door "as dumb brutes look, as dogs paw and whine and study the knob") and the sea ("In the great sea of men here are these little eddies of driftwood").

Other haunts of the homeless are described in "Curious Shifts": Madison Square when theatergoers are heading home and the fire signs blaze and a man known as the Captain collects money for derelicts; the breadline at Fleischmann's Vienna Model Bakery at Tenth Street and Broadway—all scenes he had observed during his Bowery days. But Theodore brought out the humanity of the bums, their pungent talk, while Crane saw them as an undifferentiated mass.

The story showed that Theodore was compelled to write something at once more personal and more objectively truthful than his usual magazine articles. With it he announced himself a follower of the realists—Crane, Garland, and William Dean Howells.

26. Mr. Howells's America

"Is it so hard to rise in the literary world?"
"About as difficult as any other field. There seems to be almost invariably a period of neglect and suffering. Every beginner
feels or really finds that the doors are more or less closed against
him."
                        —Interview with William Dean Howells (1899)

Theodore had a long-standing assignment to do an article on the "Dean of American Letters" for *Ainslee's*. The idea may have been Richard Duffy's, for in March 1899 Duffy had written: "Don't forget the Howells essay. If you're in the vicinity of his apartments just sound him out on the matter." For some reason, perhaps the press of other assignments, Dreiser put off doing it. In June, before he left for Ohio, he requested copies of three poems by Howells that had appeared in *Harper's Monthly*. In November Theodore revived the idea; by then he had probably started *Sister Carrie* (according to Maude Henry he began it at the house on the Maumee). At such a turning point, a renewal of an acquaintanceship with a man who could launch a young novelist's career with a single favorable review must have been uppermost in Theodore's mind. He saw in Howells a literary father—another of those Horatio Alger mentor figures who helped worthy young men to rise.

For nearly a decade Howells had been waging the "realism war" against the forces of romantic idealism. This literary campaign had been launched in the "Editor's Study" column which Howells conducted in *Harper's Monthly* in the 1880s. As America's foremost critic, he had championed European writers, particularly the Russians Turgenev and Count Leo Tolstoy, his personal idol, as well as Americans who seemed to follow in their footsteps. By "realism," Howells meant that a novel should represent life accurately; the artist should employ the objective eye of the scientist, preferably drawing upon his or her own experience as "data."

When in his novel *Annie Kilburn* he tried to show the point of view of poor people, he violated his own rule, writing about a subject of which he had no direct knowledge.

That failure led Howells to write perhaps his best novel, certainly the one with the broadest social panorama: *A Hazard of New Fortunes*. The story is told through the eyes of Basil March, his fictional alter ego, who appears as the young husband in *Their Wedding Journey*. March and his charming wife, Isabel, earnest, thoughtful liberals, are comic figures, unable quite to comprehend the social upheavals of the day, which are dramatized in the streetcar strike that forms the book's centerpiece. Howells intended the character of Basil March as an ironic commentary on himself, on his own inability to act on the injustices he felt in his bones—beyond his courageous protest against the unjust conviction of the Haymarket anarchists in 1886—and his love of comfort that kept him writing novels suitable for young ladies. In an article appropriately titled "The Business of Literature," he advised any aspiring novelist "to make up his mind that in the United States the fate of a book is in the hands of the women." And in 1888 Howells wrote his good friend Henry James: "After fifty years of optimistic content with 'civilization' and its ability to come out all right in the end, I now abhor it, and feel that it is coming out all wrong in the end unless it bases itself anew on a real equality. Meantime, I wear a fur-lined overcoat and live in all the luxury my money can buy."

There was plenty of money. By dint of his long-standing connection with the conservative firm of Harper & Brothers, his talent for writing commercial one-act farces for the theater, and other profitable piecework, Howells was the best-paid writer in America save for his friend Mark Twain, who had gone into bankruptcy as a result of his publishing venture and pouring money into a linotype machine that he hoped would make him even richer. Howells's income averaged $10,000 a year—or well over $100,000 in present-day money.

Perhaps his boldest critical stroke was championing Crane's *Maggie*, so daring for its time that Richard Watson Gilder, who took a paternalistic interest in Crane, could only mumble about excessive adjectives and split infinitives, causing Crane to blurt out, "You mean the story's too honest." The novel tells of a slum girl who is casually seduced and abandoned and becomes a prostitute. Even so, the proprieties are served in the end when she leaps into the river.

Even a rebel like Crane knew the score. He had allowed Ripley Hitchcock, his editor at Appleton, to bowdlerize *The Red Badge of Courage*. His generation was pushing at invisible bounds of propriety that were well guarded by middle-class reviewers, churchwomen, older publishers like the Harper brothers, and professional crusaders like Anthony Comstock, head of the Society for the Suppression of Vice. Young Frank Norris out of San Francisco had in *McTeague* presented a gamy portrait of sexual obsession and cupidity, and Frank Doubleday, a member of the younger generation of bookmen and partner of the magazine pioneer S. S. McClure, had published it. But Doubleday (or someone at the firm) had insisted that Norris withhold *McTeague* until Doubleday had published a lesser (and tamer) novel, a conventional sea tale called *Moran of the Lady Letty*.

That strategy did not appease the moral sentinels. A scene in *McTeague* in which a little boy wets his pants at the theater provoked such a storm that it was cut from the second edition. Moreover, Norris was an avowed disciple of Zola, whom he had read in the original (he had learned French while studying art in Paris). To many American critics the name Zola was synonymous with the Parisian sewers. Although the characters' unnatural lusts were only implied, *McTeague* was too strong for most reviewers. The *Argonaut*'s critic wrote that Norris "riots in odors and stenches" and that he should have subtitled his book "A Study in Stinks." The novel sold 4000 copies in hardcover and 28,000 in a cheap edition, compared with 502,000 for Edward Westcott's folksy *David Harum*, which appeared the same year. Norris could not find a publisher for his first novel, a precocious study of a dissolute college student who regresses to lycanthropy, which he had written while attending Harvard. It was not published until 1914.

Howells had met Norris when the latter arrived in New York City in 1898 to work for the McClure Syndicate. When *McTeague* appeared, Howells rose to the occasion in his review, saying the novel posed important questions about the direction of American fiction:

> Whether we shall abandon the old-fashioned American ideal of a novel as something which may be read by all ages and sexes, for the European notion of it as something fit only for age and experience, and for men rather than women; whether we shall keep to the bonds of the provincial proprieties, or shall include within the imperial territory of our fiction the passions and the motives of the savage world which underlies as well as environs civilization . . .

But fiction at the turn of the century was bound up in such tight editorial stays that Howells was considered a voice of liberalism. What Gilder of the *Century*, Henry Mills Alden of *Harper's Monthly*, or Edward L. Bur-

lingame of *Scribner's Magazine* would permit to be published in their magazines as an article they would not allow in a story. A feature on prostitution
in London, say, was permissible both because it was nonfiction and because it was about London rather than America, but the fictionist could
not write about ladies of the evening. Graphic words like "rape" or "vomit"
or "breast" or "sweat" were proscribed. When *The Rise of Silas Lapham*
was being serialized in the *Century*, Howells cut, at Gilder's behest, a
reference to poor people dynamiting the mansions in Back Bay Boston.
The editor thought the very mention of the word dynamite was dangerous in a time of social unrest. And a fallen woman (i.e., any woman
who disposed of her virginity outside of marriage) must always be punished in fiction. By the same token, a virtuous woman must reject a suitor
who has had an affair with another woman.

The establishmentarians of the *Century*, *Harper's*, and *Scribner's* rationalized these views by saying that the reader of a book is self-selected,
while among a magazine's subscribers are impressionable females. To the
younger generation, if not to Howells, this was hypocrisy. With the boldness of one who was not trying to make a living in the New York literary
marketplace, Norris wrote in the San Francisco *Wave*:

> Why is it that the best magazines should fail to publish the best class of
> stories? Why are not the names of Kipling and of Arthur Morrison and Ste-
> phen Crane seen in *Harper's* and in the *Century* and in *Scribner's* as often
> as these old familiar standbys, the veterans, the "steadies," Brander Mat-
> thews, Octave Thanet, Charles Dudley Warner, Thomas Janvier . . . and
> so many other "magazinists"? . . . The great merit of the stories of these
> "magazinists"—the one quality that endears them to the editors—is that
> they are, what in editorial slang is called "safe." . . . They can be "safely"
> placed in the hands of any young girl the country over. . . . It is the "young
> girl" and the family center table that determines the standard of the Amer-
> ican short story.

Brave words, but for the professional author the price of defiance of
the editorial conventions was failure, even ostracism—as the remarkable
and gifted novelist Kate Chopin discovered following the publication of
her novel *The Awakening*. The heroine, Edna Pontellier, searches for fulfillment in adulterous affairs, and in the end commits suicide. But this
dénouement was clearly not authorial retribution. Edna is trapped by desires that are in conflict with convention. Nature, her friend Dr. Mandelet
tells her, drives men and women to procreate the species but "takes no
account of moral consequences, of arbitrary conditions which we create,
and which we feel obliged to maintain at any cost." The book, which

was published by Herbert S. Stone, the avant garde Chicago publisher and founder of *The Chap-Book*, was resoundingly condemned by the critics, and the library in Chopin's home city of St. Louis banned it—primarily because it was written by a woman. "She was broken-hearted," her son recalled, and wrote little in the remaining five years of her life.

Under the unwritten Protection of Young Ladies Act, much in language and deed was censored by editorial blue pencils and even more self-censored by honest and serious writers. Frank Norris had called for greater openness on the "sex question." The novelist, he wrote, must probe "the unplumbed depths of the human heart, and the mystery of sex, and the problems of life, and the black, unsearched penetralia of the soul of man." But after *McTeague* he abandoned the fight.

The obsession with protecting young women's virtue reflected middle-class anxiety about the growing independence of women, who in the 1890s had begun to leave the sheltered life of prenuptial idleness to work in the cities. Such independence carried with it the threat of freer sexuality, which in turn threatened traditional male domination as codified in the double standard. It was left to married women, the keepers of the cultural flame, to enforce the taboos.

In his witty history of the 1890s, *The Mauve Decade*, Thomas Beer made the strong female figure he dubbed "The Titanness" the villain of literary gentility. She was the churchlady of the small towns and the "advanced" socialite-reformer of the big city who devoted her copious spare time to saving working girls from "immorality" while ignoring the wage system that made prostitution the only alternative for them. But, then, to question such a system would have been to question her businessman husband's way of making a living.

By the decade's end, the tide of the realism war was turning against Howells and his army. Although a number of novels dealing with social problems from conservative, progressive, and radical points of view had been published in the 1890s—perhaps two hundred of them—romances were more popular by far. As early as 1894, Howells had sensed the way the tide was running, as had his protégé Stephen Crane. In an interview with Howells for the New York *Times*, Crane asked if he had "observed a change in the literary pulse of the country within the last four months? Last Winter, for instance, it seemed that realism was about to capture things, but then recently I have thought that I saw coming a sort of counter wave, a flood of the other—a reaction in fact."

"What you say is true," Howells replied. "I have seen it coming. . . . I suppose we shall have to wait."

Soon the bookstores would be inundated by escapist romances, sparked
by the success in the mid-1890s of Anthony Hope's *The Prisoner of Zenda*
and George Du Maurier's *Trilby*. Maurice Thompson, author of *Alice of
Old Vincennes*, led the counterrevolution. Speaking, appropriately, to students at the Hartford Theological Seminary in 1893, he scored realists
like Tolstoy, Flaubert, Whitman, and Ibsen: "They boast of holding up
a mirror to nature; but they take care to give preference always to ignoble
nature. . . . Have you thought out the secret force which . . . always keeps
its votaries sneering at heroic life, while they revel in another sort of life,
which fitly to characterize here would be improper?"

He apostrophized a woman who praised *Hedda Gabler:* "Woman, you
have taken Ibsen's arm and have gone with him into vile company. . . . The smack of hell is sweet to your lips, as it was to those of
new-made Eve."

The romantic idealists were in the saddle as the century turned, steep-
ing their stories in the jingoism of the Spanish-American War and the
brutality of the Philippines campaign against the guerrilla fighters under
Emilio Aguinaldo, and the complacent piety of the pro-business administration of the lovable William McKinley. Thus the heroes of George B.
McCutcheon's *Graustark* and Charles Major's *When Knighthood Was in Flower*
were handsome, tall Americans striding on to the international stage as
were their countrymen. In his interview with Howells, Crane had been
prescient: "a counter wave . . . a reaction" had crashed against the
American shores, and was seeping into the foundations of American literature.

Theodore Dreiser probably had not enlisted in any particular camp of
literature before 1900, but he was a born realist, not a self-made one like
Frank Norris. His family's struggles with convention, his exposure to the
underside of urban life as a reporter, his "conversion" to Darwinism and
Spencerism, his love of Balzac, his view of society as a reflection of nature, his fascination with city scenes in which he found beauty in ugliness, his sexual initiation in the bordellos and boardinghouses of the Middle
West—one could go on; Dreiser was simply naturally inclined toward
writing about life as it was rather than as the idealists thought it should
be.

Although, in the book reviews Theodore wrote for *Ev'ry Month*, he did
not proclaim himself a follower of Howells or Garland, he was aware of
them, as his use of the term "local color" showed. That, of course, was

a phrase introduced by Garland in his realist manifesto, *Crumbling Idols*, published in 1894. Dreiser may not have read Garland's tract, but he was aware of it and had read *Main-Traveled Roads*. He probably missed Howell's critical broadsides from the "Editor's Study" but was familiar with the broad outlines of the argument. Although he had not read Zola, he was cognizant of the European movement called naturalism, which as Zola defined it meant writing novels that illustrated scientific laws and analyzed the extremes of human behavior in terms of heredity. In 1897 Theodore planned an article on the French poet Jean Richepin, one of the "new naturalist school of writers in France which had produced such singular work in prose and fiction."

Actually, Dreiser was an inconsistent realist, retaining a strong streak of the romantic idealist though not one that would lead him to set his fiction in far-off duchies or take him on eccentric byways of life like the Decadents (whom he disliked). In a tribute to Balzac in *Ev'ry Month*, he took care to note that in Balzac's novels "romance and realism blend and become one." (Curiously, Norris, Zola's American disciple, insisted that the master was a romantic because he eschewed Howellsian teacup tragedies for grand passions—such was the imprecision of literary labels.)

As early as 1896, in a caption to a photograph of the novelist Abraham Cahan in *Ev'ry Month*, he had lightly referred to Howells as a "literary Columbus." But in his review of the book the photograph accompanied, Cahan's *Yekl*, a gritty novel of immigrant Jewish life on New York's Lower East Side, Dreiser had complained about the author's excessive use of dialect, thus flouting both Howells' judgment and Garland's definition of local color. (Perhaps he was worried about the young ladies who read his magazine.)

Dreiser was attracted more to Howells the "literary Columbus" than to the theorist and critic. The disparity of their backgrounds was underscored when, in the interview for *Success*, Howells recalled working briefly for a newspaper in Cincinnati, but "one night's round with the reporters at the police station satisfied me that I was not meant for that kind of work." And so he had returned to book reviewing, missing the newsroom internship that had been such a formative influence on Theodore.

Howells apparently approved of the *Success* interview and was hospitable when Theodore paid a visit to his apartment on Fifty-seventh Street in November 1899. Although their talk was brief, Dreiser immediately drew the older man into an earnest discussion of life and death. Howells amiably fell in with him, observing stoically, "Life seems at times a hope-

less tangle. You can only face the conditions bravely and take what befalls."
Theodore characterizes Howell's views on Conditions as "social-
prophetic," speaks politely but superficially of his utopian novel,
A Traveler from Altruria, a critique of capitalism, and quotes the older man's
tribute to Tolstoy. A hint of condescension creeps in when he comments
that Howells has no "modest theory of improvement" to offer. Dreiser
tacitly scolds Howells for reaching "the conclusion that life is difficult and
inexplicable without really tracing the various theories by which it is syn-
thetically proved"—a private allusion to Spencer's *Synthetic Philosophy*.
There is also a hint that Howells is remote from real life. After Howells
comments on the overcrowded city, in which men and women are
"scheming and planning, and sometimes dying of starvation," Theodore
puts a question in the form of a statement: "You have had no direct experience of this great misery." Howells agrees that he has not; he has
only observed it.

Although the tone of Theodore's report on his talk with Howells is
respectful, it is full of allusions to death, as if he were prematurely writing
Howells's obituary (he had similarly written off Spencer two years before
in *Ev'ry Month*). Howells was sixty-three, but had more than twenty years
to live. He makes Howells a monument, praising him for his kindnesses
to young writers, calling him a "literary philanthropist": "It does not matter whether Howells is the greatest novelist in the world or not, he is a
great character. . . . His greatness is his goodness, his charm, his sincerity." Theodore recalls that at their "last meeting" he had mentioned
a certain "young man in the West" who had written a novel, and Howells
had immediately asked to read it and done all he could to help the author
get it published. Now here he was, another young man from the West
with a novel in embryo, and Dreiser hoped for similar treatment.

The two parted that afternoon as the shadows lengthened in Central
Park where, finding the urban equivalent of his pastoral Ohio boyhood,
Howells liked to sit on a favorite bench and observe the grand parade of
arrogant wealth and dismaying poverty. As they mumbled the usual courtesies at the door, Theodore must have fancied that the warm benevo-
lence of Howells's patronage was enveloping him.

A year or so before their meeting, Howells had visited the breadline at
Fleischmann's Bakery and written a self-conscious little essay about it.
He told of watching the hungry men from his carriage, "a dim and solemn
phalanx . . . slouched close together, perhaps for their mutual warmth,

perhaps in an unconscious effort to get near the door where the loaves were to be given out, in time to share in them before they were all gone." Howells was so entangled in the irony of himself observing the scene, a plump, benevolent-looking man with a white mustache, bundled up in a warm fur coat, that he did not even claim to have been present, saying he had been given the account by a friend, who had been urged to go to the Bowery by "young newspaper men trying to make literature out of life and smuggle it into print under the guard of unwary editors, and young authors eager to get life into their literature."

In "Curious Shifts of the Poor," Theodore mentions the appearance of a carriage that could have been Howells's. One of the men in line at a flophouse sees it and jeers, "Look at the bloke ridin'," and another sneers, "He ain't so cold." " 'Eh! Eh! Eh!' yelled another, the carriage having long since passed out of hearing." While Crane and Dreiser recorded the men in the storm, William Dean Howells passed out of hearing.

Part Three

SISTER CARRIE

27. She Went to the City

She went to the city, 'twas all they would say,
She went to the city, far, far away . . .
She grew kind o' restless and wanted to go,
Said she'd be back in a few weeks or so,
She went to the city with a tear in her eye, but she never returned.

—Paul Dresser (1904)

In late September 1899 (if not at Maumee), before his visit with Howells, Theodore had sat down at the dining-room table and written in pencil on a half sheet of copy paper the title of a novel—"Sister Carrie." In later accounts he sometimes gave the impression that he had been visited by a divine afflatus. He told Dorothy Dudley that his mind "was blank except for the name. I had no idea who or what she was to be. I have often thought there was something mystic about it, as if I were being used, like a medium." The explanation echoed a passage in his novel. The inventor Robert Ames tells the heroine, an actress, "You and I are mediums, through which something is expressing itself."

To his friend H. L. Mencken, Dreiser later described the genesis of *Sister Carrie* somewhat differently. Arthur Henry, who had begun a novel called *A Princess of Arcady*, wanted company, and began to "ding-dong" his friend about writing one too. Finally, "I took a piece of yellow paper and to please him wrote down a title at random—*Sister Carrie*—and began." And so, it appears from the manuscript, he did. At the top of the first page are the words of the title, and the first paragraph provides the essential information like a good newspaper lead:

When Caroline Meeber boarded the afternoon train for Chicago her total outfit consisted of a small trunk, which was checked in the baggage car, a cheap imitation alligator skin satchel holding some minor details of the toilet, a small lunch in a paper bag and a yellow leather snap purse, containing her ticket, a scrap of paper with her sister's address in Van Buren Street, and four dollars in money. It was in August, 1889. She was eighteen years of age, bright, timid and full of the illusions of ignorance and youth.

Aside from minor editing, page one of the manuscript appears to be just as it flowed out in Theodore's tiny, penciled script, but it seems unlikely that the story popped into his head. Actually, he had been brooding over elements of it—the character of Hurstwood, for example—for some time. Richard Duffy recalled that before Dreiser started writing, he had prepared a "story backbone, showing his characters moving to an inevitable fate." The theme reminded Duffy of Thomas Hardy, "the master Dreiser recognized and venerated."

The two-word title was a mnemonic key that unlocked a private storehouse of memories. Theodore apparently forgot the "sister" part once he was under way, and it was Jug, serving as copy editor, who later inserted a phrase explaining that "Sister Carrie" was a "half-affectionate" nickname. The true origin of the title lay in family history. Theodore had a sister Carrie, who alone of his sisters always closed her letters to him:

> I remain your
> Sister Emma

The two words at the top of the half sheet of pale yellow copy paper were a private incantation, summoning up the story he intended to tell, the story of Emma absconding from Chicago with her lover, L. A. Hopkins. Knowing few details of Emma's 1883 flight from Sullivan, he was forced to invent, making Carrie a more universal figure, the country girl "venturing to reconnoitre the mysterious city and dreaming wild dreams of some vague, far-off supremacy which should make it prey and subject, the proper penitent, grovelling at a woman's slipper." He also unconsciously fell into the accents of the popular genre of cautionary novels about girls who left home. In those stories, of which Theodore had been an avid consumer as a boy, the heroines were the distaff version of the Horatio Alger hero. They negotiate a minefield of temptations in the urban world, and after fighting off several nefarious seducers, marry honest workingmen or scions of wealthy families. The most popular practitioners of the genre in the 1890s were Laura Jean Libbey and Bertha M. Clay, who specialized in working girls and "society" novels respectively.

The first chapter of *Sister Carrie* echoes the moralizing tone of such books with a pious passage about the fate of girls in the city: "Either she falls into saving hands and becomes better, or she rapidly assumes the cosmopolitan standard of virtue and becomes worse." But Theodore identifies the city itself, not an unscrupulous man, as the seducer, and, in doing so he breaks the bonds of conventional morality. Metropolis has its "cunning wiles," and "The gleam of a thousand lights is often as effective, to all moral intents and purposes, as the persuasive light in a wooing and fascinating eye."

Carrie differs from the popular-novel heroines in other ways. On the first page, she is revealed to be suspiciously lacking in strong ties to Columbia City, Wisconsin, and sheds only a brief tear as "the threads which bound her so lightly to girlhood and home were irretrievably broken." Later, when the possibility of returning to her hometown arises, she cringes at the thought of the "dull round" of rural life, which seems infinitely inferior to the city.

The popular novelists' heroines clung to the past, the old democratic, religious, morally upright village. Theodore remembered no such place: in the four Indiana towns he had bounced among, the Dreisers had been poor or social outcasts. In Sullivan, his mother was, as William Dean Howells wrote of a character in *A Modern Instance*, "that pariah who . . . cuts herself off from hope by taking in washing." Paul, who had not shared in the family's harried odyssey, could idealize Terre Haute as his hometown and sentimentally imagine it as the archetypical rural village where the old folks kept a light burning in the window. But when Theodore recalled his parents, he thought of his father in the grimy, oily mill and of old Paul's mingled shame and pity. Theodore—and his alter ego, Carrie—were city-bound. They looked forward rather than back. They were representative of the thousands of young Middle Western men and women who had left the farms and villages for the arc-lit gaiety of Chicago.

In another departure from the sentimental conventions, the author shows Carrie allowing herself to be befriended by Charlie Drouet, the genial traveling salesman, "masher," and eventual despoiler of her virginity. Though she is on her guard, she does not send him packing as her more virtuous dime-novel sisters would have done. "The instincts of self-protection and coquetry" vie within her. By the time the train pulls into Chicago, she has given him her address. To the naive Carrie, the flashy Drouet seems the acme of urban sophistication. Like the more worldly little soubrette in "Whence the Song," Carrie is "all eyes for the marvels of the city." The kinship between the two women in the author's subconscious is revealed by an inadvertent similarity in their attire. The singer is "gloved in blue and shod in yellow," anticipating an outfit of Carrie's: "On her feet were yellow shoes and in her hands her gloves." And in

her later rise to theatrical success—largely through the benign intervention of chance—Carrie resembles Paul's protégée, the singer Louise
Dresser, born Louise Kerlin and daughter of an engineer he knew while
working as a candy butcher on the Evansville and Terre Haute Railroad.
After hearing her sing "The Wabash," Paul introduced her as his sister
and got her started on a successful vaudeville career.

Carrie is the prototypical young woman of her times, alive to the promise of love and excitement. She was a girl Theodore encountered on a
train in 1898 while traveling on a magazine assignment. As he described
the scene to Jug, he had noticed her staring at him and "took advantage
of her uncomfortable position to help her arrange her seat, and so began
a talk, which lasted from 12:30 midnight to 5 A.M. . . ." His interest had
been piqued by her resemblance to his fiancée. But the similarity was
only physical; the girl in the parlor car was "wholly untrained and quite
of the shop girl order." This leads him to speculate that "better parents
and an intellectual home would have made a refined and lovely creature
of her altogether. Her instincts were all right but her language and de-
portment poor."

The chance meeting provided the inspiration for the scene on the
Chicago-bound train in his novel. He put a bit of his younger, sartorially
resplendent St. Louis self into the character of Drouet (rhymes with *roué*).
Both he and the salesman were "mashers"—fops who hope to attract
women by their finery. During that stage of his life he had met another
girl on a train—Sallie White, one of a party of schoolteachers bound for
the Chicago World's Fair.

Rather than draw on these real-life incidents, however, Theodore did
a curious thing: he spliced in a passage, slightly paraphrased, from a story
by George Ade, "The Fable of the Two Mandolin Players and the Willing Performer." The excerpt described the masher's parlor-car technique
and was the first of several instances in which Dreiser interpolated doc-
umentary material—want ads, news stories, dialogue from plays, and the
like—into his manuscript to give verisimilitude. He also used the real
names of places, buildings, theaters, restaurants, and theatrical figures.
In this case, however, Dreiser chose Ade's fiction for "documentation":
he plagiarized. Could it be he feared that Jug, who was reading the script
as he went along, would object to his drawing on experience? (At the end
of Chapter 3, Jug announces her presence in notes appended to the manuscript, a series of questions on the accuracy of various details, such as
the date of Chicago's first skyscraper.)

In a way Carrie was Jug's rival. There is a strong undercurrent of eroticism in Dreiser's writing. The name "Carrie," which he wrote automatically at the head of his manuscript, tapped his earliest sexual memories. One of the girls in Warsaw who had figured in his fantasies was named Carrie Tuttle—"Cad" for short. "Cad" is Drouet's pet name for Caroline Meeber. This tawny-maned grade-school temptress was one of the first objects of Theodore's awakening sexual desires.

Carrie Meeber also embodied the other side of his pubescent erotic fantasies: the ethereal, unattainable Myrtle Weimar. The kinship to Myrtle is visible in Carrie's most characteristic facial expression—a kind of sadness communicating unfulfilled desire. Her "mouth had the expression at times, in talking and in repose, of one who might be upon the verge of tears," and her eyes have shadows about them, which make her seem even more pathetic. Not that she was inwardly sad; it was simply an accident of nature.

The Middle Western madonnas whom Theodore had adored—Myrtle in Warsaw and the schoolgirl in Bloomington—wore that sweet, sad expression. And, later, he found another pre-Raphaelite beauty who *was* attainable, a "repentant Magdalen," whose eyes were "meek" and "sorrowful," who resembled the French soubrette Cleo de Merade, paramour of the king of Belgium. That girl was of course Jug, who combined innocence, wistfulness, and the erotic appeal of a "red-haired Venus."

Carrie also personified Theodore's own youthful longings, and many of her first impressions of Chicago were drawn from Theodore's memories of his arrival there in 1884. In his first draft he had set the story in August of that year, but he had second thoughts and changed the year to 1889. This was necessary so that later scenes of Hurstwood's downfall could take place during the depression winter of 1893–1894. But at the beginning of the story, Carrie's "illusions of youth and ignorance" were his own in 1884. (He also gives the population of Chicago as more than five hundred thousand, which it was in 1880, rather than more than a million, which it would have been in 1889.) As was Theodore, she is cowed by the city: "The entire metropolitan centre possessed a high and mighty air calculated to overawe and abash the common applicant, and to make the gulf between poverty and success seem wide and deep." Like a frightened animal, she scurries back to the safety of her sister Minnie's drab apartment on Van Buren Street.

Minnie and her husband, Sven Hanson, are composites of people who lived in the Union Park section, that bastion of middle-class respectability on the geographic and social fringes of which the Dreiser family lived. Sven is a taciturn, frugal workingman, employed at the stockyards, who is saving to buy two small lots on which he plans to build a house. He and his wife are the antithesis of Carrie, who feels the drag of desire pulling her to the fine clothes she sees in the department stores while job hunting. Repelled by the lean and narrow life in the Hansons' flat, she takes to standing at the foot of the stairs where she can watch the street scene, as Theresa Rogaum did, as Theodore did as a boy on West Madison Street.

Carrie's first job is at a shoe factory, operating a machine. Led to her work station by a surly foreman, she sees "a line of girls . . . sitting on a line of stools in front of a line of clacking machines," a scene Theodore drew from a visit to a factory in New Jersey that spring. (The repetitive image recalls Herman Melville's description of female workers in a New England paper mill: "rows of blank-looking girls . . . all blankly folding blank paper . . ." standing "like so many mares haltered to the rack.") The stage is set for Carrie's later "downfall." The work is too hard; the shop is dirty; the workers are exploited; she is not strong enough. The other girls are friendly but common; all they talk about is their boyfriends. The male employees are louts who flirt with her. As she leaves, one of them calls out, "Say, Maggie, if you'll wait I'll walk with you." The allusion to Stephen Crane's Maggie (who works in a factory before becoming a prostitute) consigns Carrie to the same fate. She is like the factory girls Jacob Riis wrote about in *How the Other Half Lives:* "Those in their coarse garments—girls with the love of youth for beautiful things with this hard life before them—who shall save them from the tempter?"

After losing her job when she becomes ill, Carrie halfheartedly begins the demoralizing process of hunting for another one and by chance meets the tempter, Drouet, who takes her to a restaurant. A glutton like Paul, he expansively orders a heavy lunch of sirloin steak, mushrooms, hashbrowned potatoes, asparagus, and a pot of coffee. Drouet serves the huge spread with gusto: "As he cut the meat his rings almost spoke. His new suit creaked as he stretched to reach the plates, break the bread, and pour the coffee." Forlorn and cold, Carrie basks before the cheery blaze of his hospitality. His is the remembered warmth of Paul, arriving at the door of the Sullivan cottage in the dead of winter. As they are about to part, he presses into her hand two soft, green, ten-dollar bills. . . .

Unlike the working girls Riis had in mind, who slip into prostitution rather than toil at below-subsistence wages, Carrie finds a tempter who is a kindhearted sensualist. Drouet "would need to delight himself with Carrie as surely as he would need to eat his heavy breakfast." He flirted with women "not because he was a cold-blooded, dark, scheming villain" but because he was driven by "inborn desire." As for Carrie, though she has qualms, she is drawn tropistically, like a sentient plant, to the drummer's sunny generosity. Like him, she is a sinner only insofar as her conscience rules her, and she has, after all, "only an average little conscience, a thing which represented the world, her past environment, habit, convention, in a confused, reflected way." She is unformed, a creature of emotion, "a harp in the wind." (In an article on the harp, Dreiser had written that this instrument was "the voice of poetry, of sentiment and sorrow.")

The author's attitude toward Carrie and Drouet is coolly scientific rather than moralistic. In the accents of Herbert Spencer and Charles Darwin, he observes: "Our civilization is still in a middle stage, scarcely beast, in that it is no longer wholly guided by instinct; scarcely human, in that it is not yet wholly guided by reason." Rather than deploring Carrie's weakness of character, however, Dreiser calmly proclaims:

> We have the consolation of knowing that evolution is ever in action, that the ideal is a light that cannot fail. [Man] will not forever balance between good and evil. When this jangle of free will and instinct shall have been adjusted, when perfect understanding has given the former the power to replace the latter entirely, man will no longer vary. The needle of understanding will yet point steadfast and unwavering to the distant pole of truth.

And so Carrie is seduced by Drouet, and afterward, she offhandedly wonders, "What have I lost?" With that question, the structure of Victorian morality shudders. Looking in the mirror for the answer, she sees a blooming young woman. On the street, she saw one of the girls from the shoe factory, and "a tide rolled between them." Going back would be impossible; she had no choice. "She was alone; she was desireful; she was fearful of the whistling wind. The voice of want made answer for her."

28. *Under the Gaslight*

The forces which regulate two individuals of the character of
Carrie and Hurstwood are as strange and as subtle as described. We have been writing our novels and our philosophies
without sufficiently emphasizing them—we have been neglecting to set forth what all men must know and feel about these
things before a true and natural life may be led.

—Dreiser, *Sister Carrie* (1900)

Just before the point at which Hurstwood meets Carrie, Theodore found himself blocked. After writing nine chapters rapidly, his momentum ran out. Stumped by the problem of
describing how the manager seduces Carrie, he told Dorothy
Dudley, "It seemed to me the thing was a failure, a total frost."
Rather than stew about it, he put the manuscript aside and went off
to write some articles. His novel very much on his mind, he worked on
an article about workers in the textile mills in Fall River, Massachusetts
(though Henry apparently helped with the research for it). *The Cosmopolitan* found it "a picturesque account of the lives of factory girls," but
rejected it, as did Henry Mills Alden at *Harper's Monthly* and John Phillips
at *McClure's*, though they recognized its power. A study of an industrial
town, the article is more than merely picturesque, and one suspects it
was too strong for editors of the day (it was never published). The workers' drab, joyless lives in "the great stone prisons of work" are contrasted
with the few seaside resorts, condemned by the Baptist minister, yet offering "the one touch of beauty, the one breath of fresh air" in this town
of "gray streets and grayer mills."

Dreiser turned to other serious subjects—science, education, social
problems, and politics. An article called "The Problem of the Soil" carried a social message of which Hamlin Garland, in his radical phase, would
have approved: wealthy speculators have monopolized the best land, and
the small farmers, though hardworking and frugal, cannot survive. Even
a piece on weeds was a defense of the "poor" of the plant kingdom, who

demonstrated "how wonderfully life prevails even in the face of great hardship . . . a weed no less than a man struggles to live and propagate its kind, and . . . will make use of the poorest opportunity."

Theodore had money problems of his own, and demanded $100 from *The Cosmopolitan* for an article on boys' clubs and $75 for one on the need for good roads. The editor, John Brisben Walker, had no recollection of offering those sums and told Theodore through a subordinate to take $75 and $50 or leave it. A *Cosmopolitan* editor suggested that Dreiser come up to Irvington-on-Hudson and talk to Walker, offering a "friendly tip" that the volatile editor would be at home early in the morning and was making no appointments, "being up to his eyes in the horseless carriage business." (Walker had plowed his magazine profits into an automobile company, almost bankrupting himself and the magazine in the process.)

Dreiser also quarreled with the *Century* over its rejection of "McEwen of the Shining Slave Makers." An accompanying note said a reader had found the story scientifically inaccurate. Theodore protested to associate editor Robert Underwood Johnson that the story was based on authoritative scientific information. Also, he objected to "being left to the mercy of a scientific reader, who, to me, must stand as the Editor of *The Century*." Johnson replied starchily that the story had been read by a regular member of the editorial staff, that it had been rejected because the magazine disliked allegory, and that an apology was in order. Theodore replied that he stood corrected insofar as his accusation that the editors of the magazine hadn't read the story, but he had no apologies for his defense of the story's accuracy. Nevertheless, he was conciliatory, assuring Johnson, "I could wish nothing better than to gain your personal consideration for the few things I am trying to do." On this letter Richard Watson Gilder, editor of the *Century*, scrawled, "A soft answer turneth away wrath," to which Johnson riposted: "Yes, and a gentle snub bringeth the young man to his senses."

Despite the apology, Dreiser's stock at *Century* was low. On an earlier query letter to Gilder, the editor scrawled: "[Theodore] Roosevelt could handle such a topic. . . . I wouldn't commit myself to either of these before seeing [them]." Johnson dismissed an article on teacher selection and training in the Providence school system as nothing new, provoking Dreiser to shoot off another contentious missive. The improvement of the American school system "has been the one thing that has aroused and retained my enthusiasm. I firmly believe that the welfare of man in the Western hemisphere depends solely upon the *genius*, the humanity, the Christ-like simplicity of the educators of our country." He assured Johnson he had written the story out of love; it was "the result of an enthusiasm aroused by the sight of so perfect an ideal." He probably had his former Warsaw teachers—May Calvert and Mildred Fielding—in mind when he wrote those words.

Theodore fought for his work in lesser forums too. He chastised Ellery Sedgwick, who had taken over the editorship of *Frank Leslie's Popular Monthly*, for rejecting "A True Patriarch," a sketch about his father-in-law, Arch White. Sedgwick explained that his readers were prejudiced against Missourians; more important, Theodore's contribution lacked a plot. For a magazine that must appeal to a mass audience, Sedgwick needed more "robust" material. That admission set Theodore to inveighing against lowbrows. Sedgwick replied in a friendly manner "that the 'average reader' whom you so much dislike would wonder in reading it where the 'story' was going to begin." This would not be the last time Theodore met editorial resistance because the personality sketches he was writing fell between the traditional editorial stools of fiction and article. But he kept writing them. He was experimenting with a fictionlike treatment of factual material. The technique was not, after all, new with him: in his newspaper days, laziness or impatience with the constraints of journalism had driven him to invent news items.

After a six-week lapse, Dreiser resumed the writing of *Sister Carrie*. The talk with Howells in November may have been a spur, and Henry had kept after him, praising what he had done, empathizing so strongly that he became blocked on his own novel. Theodore's sense of guilt for his friend's plight seemed to turn the trick. Whatever technical or emotional problems had been holding him back vanished, and he plunged into another bout of writing.

Hurstwood's attraction to Carrie flares up over a game of euchre at the Ogden Place flat. The manager regards her with "a mild light" in his eye, and determines that by the Lord, he will have this woman—even if it means euchring his friend Charlie. Hurstwood is nearly forty; in 1900 he would be considered a middle-aged man. In his first draft, Theodore had given Hurstwood's age as thirty, only a year older than himself. He realized, however, that Hurstwood should be older. Always acutely sensitive to the passage of time and the onrush of old age, Dreiser assumed that forty was a turning point in the life of a man like Hurstwood; he is at the height of his powers, yet also trapped in the life he has made for himself. The author also had in mind Emma's husband, Hopkins, "who had turned fifty and come to feel life was done with him and had gotten the best of him." Hurstwood's marriage "ran along by force of habit, by force of conventional opinion. With the lapse of time it must necessarily become dryer and dryer—must eventually be tinder, easily lighted and destroyed. . . . The whole thing might move on in a conventional manner to old age and dissolution. Also it might not."

In Theodore's own marriage the roseate tints of courtship had given way to the pallid light of day. Perhaps he was beginning to wonder if it would also move on in a conventional manner to old age and dissolution and projected his forebodings onto Hurstwood. But he was still as emotionally dependent on Jug as he was professionally on Henry. Jug cooked him good country meals and kept his home in order and satisfied his affectional needs. She called him "Theo" or "Honeybugs" and he called her "Kitten." Although her role in *Sister Carrie* was distinctly minor, Jug regarded herself as a collaborator. Years later, when Dreiser was a financial success and relations between them were embittered because of her pleas for money, she tried to tell him how much she shared his dreams: "As for me, you know [your success] was just as great when Sister Carrie was written—not even published."

In 1900 her only feminine rival was Carrie. Borne along by an erotic subcurrent of desire for his heroine, Theodore identified with Hurstwood's attraction for a girl twenty years younger than himself—identified with it and absorbed it. The character of the manager was becoming solider than the wraith who had appeared in the back of Dreiser's mind that day while he was in City Hall Park. The question, of course, was who had that derelict been? His answer is George Hurstwood, who is placed just below the topmost rung of urban success. He is a combined greeter, maître d', and manager of what Drouet, an admirer, calls a "way-up swell saloon." Hurstwood's psychological antecedents can be traced back through the one-shot songwriter in "Whence the Song" to Paul Dresser, and even further back to Paul Dreiser, Sr. Richard Duffy recalled that Theodore's aborted novel was to be about the songwriter "in whom success operated like a virus." Like Paul, Hurstwood is a flash success, all show. His clothes are of the finest cut; he has a "good, stout constitution" and moves among solid, substantial men (in caricaturing Hurstwood's admirers, Theodore mentions a "rotund citizen whose avoirdupois made necessary an almost alarming display of starched shirt bosom"—the image of a photograph of Paul from this period). When presiding at Hannah & Hogg's saloon, Hurstwood is a bit like Paul working the crowd at the Metropole. Even Hurstwood's business relationship with Hannah & Hogg resembles Paul's with Pat Howley and Fred Haviland (since the saloon was a real one in Chicago, it is perhaps only coincidence that the two sets of partners have the same first initials). Hurstwood is a front man who "lacked financial functions," as was Paul. He has a talent for manipulating others, "an intuitive tact in handling people"—as did Paul.

Of course, there are many differences between the two men; Hurstwood is a powerfully original characterization. Paul was more jovial, an impression his enormous girth and ready smile helped convey. Hurstwood exudes an aura of dignity, probity, and inner strength. The solid citizens with whom he consorts look upon him "as someone whose reserve covered a mine of influence and solid financial prosperity." He was a big wheel in the Elks (Paul intended to join the fraternal organization after the Terre Haute chapter honored him for "On the Banks of the Wabash"), and at one of their gatherings is lionized by his cronies. "He was evidently a light among them. . . . It was greatness in a way, small as it was."

Lastly, Hurstwood is given a social position Paul lacked. He lives an outwardly exemplary life, knowing that a hint of scandal would compromise his stewardship at Hannah & Hogg's, where he is considered a faithful and trusted employee. (It could be said that Paul was a hypocrite in his own way, a patronizer of prostitutes who wrote weepy songs about home and mother.) Hurstwood has a social-climbing wife and two equally ambitious children, owns a fine brick house on the North Side, a horse and a trap, and is worth forty thousand dollars (though most of his property is in his wife's name). He is "altogether a very acceptable individual of our great American upper class—the first grade below the luxuriously rich." Hurstwood pays the bills, with only an occasional grumble, and lives in a high style. But he is not the generous soul that Paul was. When a beggar approaches him as he is emerging from the theater accompanied by Carrie and Drouet, he ignores him. Drouet, who embodies the sensual and sentimental side of Paul, gives the man a dime without thinking twice.

The beggar casts an ominous shadow over Hurstwood's path. In noting Drouet's generosity to him and to Carrie, Theodore drops another portent, observing that the drummer would be in the same position as she was if he lost his position and was "struck by a few of the involved and baffling forces which sometimes play upon man." Drouet the salesman and Hurstwood the boniface are both nourished by the regard of others; take it away and they would starve. If the customers didn't like them, they would be panhandling. They produce nothing but that most intangible of assets—goodwill. (Paul, of course, produced songs, but he too depended on the approval of the masses, and appealed to popular taste, of which Theodore was contemptuous.)

And just as the masher Drouet uses clothes and his salesman's patter to seduce pretty girls, Hurstwood's dress and suave manners confirm his standing. When Carrie invidiously compares Hurstwood's soft calf-leather boots, polished to a dull sheen, to the salesman's shiny patent leathers, she has grasped the class language of clothes. In the city, clothes and manners are signs of wealth, power, and status.

Hurstwood is a master social artificer; in his "black eyes" dwells "a cold make believe" and he feigns bonhomie toward his clientele. He lives a dual life in which "circumspectness" is the byword and getting caught is a cardinal sin ("He lost sympathy for the man that made a mistake and was found out"). He is a secret patron of "those more unmentionable resorts of vice." When he invites Drouet to return later in the evening, the salesman half-jokingly asks, "Is she a blonde?" Hurstwood ignores the question—not because he takes affront, but because he is discreet.

Hurstwood is at the height of his reflected splendor in the yellow glow of gaslight, when streams of pleasure-seekers flow toward the restaurants, the theaters, the "gilded chambers of shame"—in the evening, "that mystic period between the glare and the gloom of the world when life is changing from one sphere or condition to another. Ah, the promise of the night. What does it not hold for the weary. What old illusion of hope is not here forever repeated!"

Into this world of pretense slips Carrie, like a fairy-tale heroine, lured by mirages of "wealth, fashion, ease," seeking "that shadow of *manner* which she thought must hang about her and make clear to all who and what she was." During a carriage ride with a neighbor, Mrs. Hale, along the Lake Shore Drive, she dreams of Aladdinish splendors within the mansions, but the gates are closed. When Carrie arrived in Chicago she was a drab country girl in a worn, plain blue dress with black cotton tape trimmings. In the great department stores, the fine gowns seemed to say to her, cozeningly, "You need me"—like the housewares on the shelves at the Spencer, Hibbard and Bartlett warehouse when Theodore worked there as a stock boy. Carrie is a child of the new age of consumerism, consumed by desires for things.

Under the sun of Drouet's generosity Carrie blooms: she dresses well, keeps her teeth white, her nails rosy. She becomes more sensuous: "Her form had filled out until it was admirably plump and well-rounded. . . . Her dresses draped her becomingly for she wore excellent corsets and laced herself with care."

As she grows more fluent in the city's language, its signs of status, wealth, and power, she is drawn to Hurstwood as someone who holds the key to a richer life; in contrast, the good-hearted drummer seems vulgar. Then Drouet cajoles Carrie into appearing in an amateur production sponsored by his Elks lodge. Acting opens up a potent world of illusion, which can conjure up the life Carrie dreams of; it is a "secret passage" to that finer world. The play she acts in is Augustin Daly's melodrama *Under the Gaslight*, a "society play" about mistaken identity, concealed nobility, and the cruelty of the rich.

Carrie plays the heroine, Laura, whom blackmailers expose as a foundling, the daughter of common thieves. Laura was adopted by a wealthy woman, who passed her off to New York society as her niece. But when Laura is unmasked, her blue-blooded friends turn against her as an "impostor." As her former fiancé explains: ". . . there is something wolfish in society. Laura has mocked it with a pretence, and society, which is made up of pretences, will bitterly resent the mockery."

When the night of the performance arrives, Hurstwood has packed the house with the starched bosoms of his cronies, and Carrie, who has discovered she has a natural talent for acting—or rather, expressing feeling (like Paul Dresser in his songs, she could express pathos, the talent of a popular artist)—is at first nervous and does poorly. But Drouet goes backstage and bucks her up before her next entrance. When Carrie hears the actor speak her cue, the words quoted above, she is filled with an emotional kinship with the character she is playing. For she too is a pretender. Hurstwood calls her "Mrs. Drouet" (though he suspects that she and the drummer aren't married), and Drouet has given her the stage name "Carrie Madenda" because he doesn't want to introduce her as his wife. Carrie is beginning to see that she lives in a mirror house of deception—Drouet pretends he will marry her; Hurstwood will pretend he is not married. So she instinctively fights back with her own illusions. Brimming with emotion, she conveys the pathos at the heart of the melodrama, and the formerly restless audience falls silent.

In Laura's final scene, she nobly renounces her former lover, telling him to marry her best friend. As Carrie speaks Daly's bathetic lines ("Remember, love is all a woman has to give, but it is the only earthly thing which God permits us to carry beyond the grave"), her two lovers in the audience are almost sick with sexual desire. Hurstwood, with his somewhat finer sensibility, feels she is speaking just to him and "could hardly restrain the tears," while Drouet resolves that, "He would marry her, by George. She was worth it."

In these scenes, theatrical illusion and Victorian sentimentality mingle in a cloud of musky sensuality. Shrouded in Laura's chaste white gown, Carrie seduces Hurstwood and Drouet from the stage. The world of gaslight, all shadows, gilt and plush, pink flesh and secret sexuality, becomes a theater of desire.

29. Atoms Amid Forces

> Nature is so grim. The city, which represents it so effectively, is also so grim. It does not care at all. It is not conscious. The passing of so small an organism as that of a man or a woman is nothing to it.
>
> —Dreiser, "The Man on the Sidewalk" (1909)

In the next half dozen chapters, Hurstwood's passion for Carrie is exposed, setting off a chain reaction of confrontations. The scenes shuttle cinematically from one major player to another. Out of Dreiser's thwarted playwrighting ambitions came a skill at staging scenes economically and efficiently to move the action along, and his authorial eye functions like a camera. But the catalytic events are always plausible and never violate the novel's realism.

None of the protagonists really act or choose; all fumble, drift, lash out reflexively—particularly Hurstwood's wife—a "pythoness at bay"—or take halfhearted measures. Hurstwood stews about how to respond to the threatening letter from his wife's lawyers, then throws up his hands and escapes to the gilded gaiety of his "resort." Drouet returns to the flat, intending to persuade Carrie to have another go at living together, but she is out and he leaves, saying in those laconic Middle Western cadences which Dreiser renders with perfect pitch: "You didn't do me right, Cad." (Only George Ade at this time had recorded the speech of ordinary Americans so truly.) If Carrie had been home, things might have turned out differently, for her job hunting was fruitless. So it goes—chance, missed connections, drift, procrastination. The characters blindly follow their instincts; they do not frame their choices in rational or moral terms. They are all flotsam, bobbing this way and that as they are carried along by the current.

These people make up the most realistic gallery of urbanites yet to appear in an American novel, save in Howells's *A Hazard of New Fortunes* or Fuller's *With the Procession*. But Howells had assembled a cast of people from familiar social soil—the South, Boston, Ohio—in the city; and Fuller's affectionate, satirical portrait of a vanishing world was focused on the old New England merchant class. The people in *Sister Carrie* are all arrivistes: they are from no discernible origins and their status is based on money. Hurstwood's social-climbing wife and children crave admission to the Lake Shore Drive set as hungrily as Carrie does, though they are far more sophisticated about it. Dreiser's social yearnings led him to place Hurstwood higher on the social scale than the manager of a saloon probably would have been in real-life Chicago society, but doing so makes the point that in the Gilded Age money was a passport. Hurstwood's wife and his children, Jessica and George, covet the symbols of the upper-class world—expensive clothes, being seen at the right places, an advantageous marriage, the correct *manner*. When Hurstwood seduces Carrie, she does not hear his words—"she heard instead the voices of the things which he represented." He is an "ambassador" from a finer world.

But Carrie is a passive striver; a materialist, not a gold digger. Dreiser could not make her a career woman, for though she does grow to greater independence, she lacks education. Still, Carrie is a sister to a generation of remarkable women carving out a place in the world—Jane Addams, Emma Goldman, Margaret Sanger, Alice Hamilton, and others. Dreiser had considerable sympathy with the career women he knew in New York City, but his deepest emotions toward women remained fixed on the past and his sacrificing mother. As he wrote in *Ev'ry Month* (with Jug in mind): "Most men love a dainty, affable, common-sense little woman, with some vanity and some foibles, who believes trustingly in the promises of her lover and would be heart broken if he were untrue to her, and who further believes in fulfilling the natural capacities of women and not in running after a lot of schemes of reorganizing the world and putting love on a higher basis." Theodore shared to some extent the prevailing double standard, but the experiences of his sisters had taught him that sex was a way women could connect with men of a higher class, though such forays were fraught with the danger of being cast aside.

Hurstwood considers Carrie a higher type of woman than those he usually dallies with. It is her wholesome rural innocence that arouses him, and Carrie is instinctively aware of her power. Half in love with Carrie himself by now, Dreiser lingers fondly over her charms. He sinks to some of his most clichéd prose in describing her (his favorite adjective for her is "little" and she goes "trippingly" down many a path).

But when Carrie allows herself to be seduced, instead of condemning her, Dreiser launches into a solemn discourse on the lack of an adequate scientific basis of morality (despite the "liberal analysis of Spencer and our modern naturalistic philosophers"). The implication is that outmoded contemporary standards will be superseded by superior ones founded on truth rather than convention and hypocrisy.

How could Dreiser justify the little Pilgrim's progress by means which no decent heroine, however needy, would employ? He couldn't, of course, because he was writing a realistic description of the experiences of a young woman in the city, not a didactic tale. When Carrie looks for a job after leaving Drouet, she comes up against the sexual exploitation of working women. The only offer she has is from a picture dealer who hints that her personal services will be required after hours. A horrifying prospect, yet she is so desperate that she almost takes the job.

Of course Carrie struggles against the economic undertow that is pulling her into prostitution, but she intuits that her body, like her labor, is a commodity and she had better barter it to the kindest bidder, who at the time is Hurstwood. A residue of her love for him, as a splendid emissary from the finer world, remains, but she is not walking into the relationship with her eyes shut. She will expect him to keep up his end: to marry her, support her, and buy her nice clothes. Even when Carrie is living with Drouet, she felt stirrings of independence. After her triumph on the Elks stage he notices "a lilt in her voice which was new. She did not study him with eyes expressive of dependence." Carrie is learning, unlike Emma and Sylvia in Warsaw, not to give herself too cheaply, not to become a "plaything" of a man, as she tells Drouet. Carrie remains an old-fashioned heroine in that she "falls," and a modern woman in that she rises in spite of her lapses.

In the climactic Chicago chapters, the shallow, ephemeral nature of human contacts in the city colors the action. Dreiser's vision of city life grew out of his youthful impressions of Chicago, with his adult experiences in New York grafted on. The former are more benign. The Middle Western metropolis is seen as a place of enchantment and wonders, but also as a young giant, growing and flexing its muscles; an adolescent city, in a state of becoming. "Its population was not so much thriving upon established commerce as upon the industries that prepared for the arrival of others. The sound of the hammer engaged upon the erection of new structures was everywhere heard. Great industries were moving in." Out in the new additions, along still uninhabited streets, there were "long, blinking lines of gas lamps fluttering in the wind." The air is charged with talk of the prizes to be won by the man who ran faster than the next fellow.

Dreiser extols Chicago's "vast wholesale district" and "vast railroad

yards" like a civic booster; the city is in constant flux, and he describes
its wonders as though future readers might find the references unintel-
ligible. He underscores the historical importance of the department stores
(though he places their advent in Chicago twenty years later than it in
fact occurred), "should they ever permanently disappear." When Hurstwood wants to know the train schedules, he calls from "a famous drug
store [that] contained one of the first private telephone booths ever erected."

Change was progress, good in itself, but that optimistic view was tempered by Theodore's boyhood insecurities. Change brought technological wonders, new places, a fresh start; but it had also meant uprooting
the family from the safety of the familiar; and in later life it meant leave-
takings, the fear of a new city, the loss of old loves. Carrie "was not one
to whom change was agreeable. . . . She was too uncertain of herself,
too much afraid of the world."

Nevertheless, Carrie has youth and hope; she is a strong green shoot
pushing toward the sun. "A fair example of the middle American class—
two generations removed from the emigrant," she is different from tradition-
bound country people like Howells's Squire Gaylord in *A Modern Instance*,
who suffer a loss of identity in the city and flee it because, "The feeling
that they are not of special interest to any of the thousands they meet
bewilders and harasses them; after the searching neighborhood of village
life, the fact that nobody would meddle in their most intimate affairs if
they could, is a vague distress." The city is Carrie's natural habitat—as
it was Dreiser's. Chicago was a place where your neighbors did not care
who you had been. He remembered how Emma had "divorced" Hopkins by moving to a different neighborhood. When Hurstwood attempts
to persuade Carrie to live with him, she objects that she couldn't do so
while Drouet was in Chicago. "It's a big town, dearest," he counters.
"It would be as good as moving to another part of the country to move
to the South Side."

But the freedom of the city is constrained by iron economic laws, which
are a variant of Darwinian natural laws. As soon as Carrie steps off the
train, she becomes "a lone figure in a tossing, thoughtless sea." As in
"McEwen of the Shining Slave Makers," Dreiser envisions nature as a
powerful, indifferent, pervasive presence. He frequently uses storm or
sea imagery to represent nature's underlying forces, and he portrays the
city as a Darwinian jungle where only the strong, the fit, the lucky, can
survive. Humankind huddles together like the men in the storm in Crane's
sketch, while the bitter wind snaps at them like a pack of wolves.

In showing his characters at the mercy of social forces, "conditions,"
like Crane's men in the storm, Dreiser was only reflecting his times. Many

contemporary observers held a similar view, and they were not all Social Darwinists, those apologists for big business who regarded low wages and high profits as God's plan. Early reformers noted the helplessness of individuals against centralized economic power. Robert A. Woods, a social investigator who surveyed the lives of the poor in Boston and Chicago, much as Jacob Riis had done in New York City, warned: "The real trouble is that people here are from birth to death at the mercy of great social forces which move almost like the march of destiny." Poverty stalks Dreiser's protagonists: first Carrie, then Hurstwood.

But in Dreiser's vision, nature is also creative, fertile. Carrie symbolizes the forces of the sun, youth, generation and growth; Hurstwood represents night, pleasure, ease, age and death. Hurstwood regards Carrie as a flower, then as a lily "which had sucked its waxen beauty and perfume from below a depth of waters which he had never penetrated, and out of ooze and mold which he could not understand." Desire awakens him like the coming of spring, but Carrie's waxen beauty will suck him back to the bottom sediment.

"Words are but vague shadows of the volumes we mean. Little audible links they are, chaining together great inaudible feelings and purposes," Dreiser writes. Brooding behind the scenes was the stage manager of all this, the omniscient author, who viewed his characters as "little human beings . . . playing in and out among the giant legs of circumstances." His novel is like a tiny house enfolded in the unfathomable deep of the universe. And beyond the farthest range of infinity, was the ultimate Author, who brooded over the vain spectacle of life, the blinking constellation of city lights, the little people huddled in bubbles of yellow gaslight. Worlds within worlds . . .

> If it were not for the artificial fires of merriment, the rush of profit-seeking trade and pleasure-selling amusements . . . we would quickly discover how firmly the chill hand of winter lays upon the heart;—how dispiriting are the days during which the sun withholds a portion of our allowance of light and warmth.

The axis of the book was about to shift—from Carrie to Hurstwood, from Chicago to New York City, from summer to winter.

Carrie feels depressed at the onset of winter; the "drag of a gray day" fills her with gloom and self-reproach. The events leading up to Hurstwood and Carrie's flight occur in the summer of 1890, but the novel is moving into a chillier clime. They will flee north, to Canada.

30. Strange, Bitter, Sad Facts

At times, sitting at my little dining table in the flat I then occupied at 102nd Street near Central Park West, New York, I felt very much like Martin Luther must have felt when he stood before the Diet of Worms. "Here I stand. Otherwise I cannot do. God help me."
— Dreiser, "Autobiographical Attack on Grant Richards" (1911)

Dreiser also felt the drag of the gray winter days. The writing of the last part of the Chicago section of *Sister Carrie* consumed December and most of January. At the point in the story where Hurstwood, like Emma's L. A. Hopkins, steals the money from his employers' safe, Dreiser was again unable to continue. He told H. L. Mencken the sticking point: "I couldn't think how to have him do it." To his biographer Robert Elias, years later, he recalled he had wanted to present the crime in such a way that Hurstwood's guilt or innocence was ambiguous.

Perhaps the real sticking point was some psychological inhibition that had nothing to do with plotting. Dreiser realized that his book was entering a darker phase. He was, he told Dorothy Dudley, reluctant to face "the question of Hurstwood's decline, which took me back to the *World* days"—the grim winter of 1894–1895—when he was on the Bowery. He knew that Hurstwood would meet the fate Theodore had feared then.

So he put the book aside and returned to magazine work. With the winter chill much on his mind, he proposed eight articles on the South to Woodward at *Pearson's Magazine*, asking for transportation and two dollars a day for living expenses. The topics included conditions in the "black belt" ("Negroes are worked in droves by overseers and I am told that in some cases the whip is not uncommon"); a "model farm" near Charleston, South Carolina; Delaware's Blue Laws (enforced by "the whipping-post and the pillory"); Georgia chain gangs; rural free delivery (recently inaugurated in Maryland); and peach growing, the topic Arthur Henry later unwittingly suggested to Woodward.

The fact that three of the articles had to do with punishment reveals a curious fascination with the subject that had an indirect relationship to Dreiser's novel in progress. Not that he was researching chain gangs because he planned to have Hurstwood end up in one. Rather, his thoughts were drawn to the larger subject of the transgressor of society's fundamental rules.

He was also brooding about another matter that related to his story: Hurstwood's psychology, and, specifically, the mental laws of dissolution that bring him down. This may have been Theodore's subconscious motive for proposing a story about the inventor Elmer Gates, "our foremost American investigator," from whom he confidently expected to obtain material for "six striking specials." Gates had made a number of useful discoveries, including a magnetic gold separator and an electric loom. He also dabbled in accoustics and meteorology—and the workings of the mind. With the profits of his inventions he had founded a facility for pure research called the Elmer Gates Laboratory of Psychology and Psychurgy, in Chevy Chase, Maryland, and was conducting experiments into learning, perception, and the physiological effects of the emotions. Of German extraction (real name Goetz) and from the West, he was a self-made man, one of those eccentric businessmen like Orison Swett Marden whose minds were perpetual motion machines turning out panaceas that would save the world and make a fortune besides.

Evidently they hit it off, for on March 3, not long after Theodore's visit, Gates wrote him a friendly note, mentioning Theodore's interest in "taking up experimental psychology" and suggesting further reading. He later wrote two articles on free will for *Success*, which Theodore may have promoted or even ghostwritten. The wizard of Chevy Chase drew a distinction between will and volition. He regarded will in the traditional sense of moral or rational choice; volition, however, "is not intellection; it is not emotion, it is not organized feeling, and, finally, it is not the power to choose." A chain of neuromuscular responses constituted a purposive act, an act of volition. Such a theory could explain Hurstwood's theft scientifically: he acted out of volition, not will.

Of more interest to Theodore were Gates's ideas on the chemical changes in the body produced by emotions. Gates propounded the theory that positive emotions and truthful thoughts engender "anastates," which make the brain healthy and help the organism adapt to its environment. False ideas or evil emotions produce poisons called "katastates," which "slowly destroy the structure in which its memory is enregistered." A katastate "prevents normal and sane judgments and consequently prevents successful adaptation to environment and therefore tends to destroy or limit the life of the organism in which it is embodied." Such ideas represented the ultimate in materialism. Good and evil, virtue and vice, health and sickness—all could be ultimately analyzed in a test tube. The ideas also provided Theodore with intellectual support at a crucial time.

He needed Gates's help because Arthur Henry was no longer in residence on West 102nd Street. He was off on a dalliance. While delivering some manuscripts to a typing service that Theodore patronized, Henry had met the owner, a woman named Anna Mallon. He was lonely, and Maude was in Ohio. She was tall, intelligent, literarily inclined, and six years older than he. And she ran a successful business. In Anna's office on lower Broadway, twenty or so young women at rows of desks clattered away, with Anna seated at the front of the room like a teacher. This arrangement reminded Henry of a classroom, so he dubbed the typewriter girls "the Infants," or "Infantas," a play on the "Infant Class." He nicknamed their boss "Sister Anna" because she had attended a convent school; also, there was a nun in his novel. And then there was "Sister" Carrie.

Although he was in his early thirties, Henry's peaches-and-cream complexion made him still boyishly handsome. And he was still the spinner of artistic dreams and spouter of fine-sounding ideals. Such an appeal must have touched a soft spot in Anna Mallon that she had kept under wraps on her way to business success. Henry had been enough of a man of affairs himself—newspaper editor, publicist, and the like—to speak her language, but he had abandoned commerce for literature. One can imagine him serenading the practical businesswoman with the sweet sounds of the Doctrine of Happiness: a blend of poetry, moonbeams, and the heady scent of the lilies of the field. The well-educated Anna was probably starved for a literary soul mate and fell for him.

She was a good catch. Not only was her typing service thriving; she came from a wealthy family and stood to inherit a considerable sum. Standing in the way of Henry's claiming it, however, were Maude and Dorothy, back in Maumee. So Henry conducted his wooing decorously, staying with Anna at her parents' home for appearance's sake. When he later told Maude about his new love, she seems to have agreed to an amicable divorce, though Henry waited until she was established in her own career, selling real estate.

Preoccupied with Anna, Henry absented himself from the flat for several months. His temporary withdrawal from the literary partnership added to Theodore's financial insecurity at a time when Dreiser was investing his energies in the unremunerative venture of writing a novel. Without Henry's share of the rent, the expensive flat on West 102nd Street became a burden, providing an additional incentive for Theodore to concentrate on hackwork. But he missed Henry's emotional support more than his financial contribution. They were so close that Theodore resented his friend's abandonment of him and morally disapproved of his abandonment of Maude. This resentment would fester until a later time.

Upon his return, Henry read what Theodore had written, assured him it was wonderful, and chided him for ever doubting himself. Moreover, he could point to a dividend of his friendship with Anna: they would receive cut-rate typing services, which would come in handy since *Sister Carrie* and *A Princess of Arcady* would have to be typed for submission to a publisher.

Confidence restored, Dreiser tackled the crucial scene in which Hurstwood steals the money. When he told Mencken that the problem had been "how to have him do it," he really meant that he was reluctant to show Hurstwood "doing it" as Hopkins had done it. Dreiser didn't want a straightforward theft. He had from the start envisioned Hurstwood as a more prepossessing type than Emma's lover, and while he saw the hollowness of Hurstwood, he wanted to judge him sympathetically. And of course the act must be made plausible; after all, the manager was a worldly man who had in the past always acted coolly and with circumspection.

The simplest solution was to portray Hurstwood's folly as a temporary aberration, the result of great strain. Moreover, Hurstwood takes more whiskey than is his wont, so by the time he goes to his office to total the day's receipts he is a bit tipsy. (Emma had told Dreiser that Hopkins was drunk when he took the money, though, as we have seen, contemporary newspaper accounts strongly suggested that the crime was premeditated.) Still, it would not do to have Hurstwood drunk; that would denude the act of any moral significance. And so he is presented in a heightened state, in which his normal inhibitions are weakened but still present. He "trembles in the balance between duty and desire"; the "ghostly clock of the mind" alternately ticks "thou shalt" and "thou shalt not." Here Dreiser recalled his own youthful lapse when he pocketed the money he had collected for the novelty company in Chicago and bought a new overcoat with it. The power of temptation over "the individual whose mind is less strongly constituted," he writes, addressing the moralists directly, may not be apparent to "those who have never wavered in conscience," but it is very real—as he proceeds to demonstrate with Hurstwood. He had justified Emma's fall by showing the pressures and temptations whipsawing Carrie; now, in a veiled way, he offered an apologia for his own transgression by showing the manager succumb.

Hurstwood covets those green bills—more than ten thousand dollars' worth, as he has determined. Since all his property is in his wife's name, the money means freedom. But then he thinks of the awful danger—of becoming a fugitive, of losing his fine place. Unable to choose, his will becomes paralyzed. But his conscience, like Carrie's, is weak: "the true ethics of the situation never once occurred to him." At this point, Elmer Gates's ideas on the separation of will and volition may have been in the back of Dreiser's mind. He was seeking a way to have the manager *do it* and yet *not do it*.

Hurstwood continues to procrastinate. He puts the money back, realizes it is in the wrong place, takes it out. Finally, his mind lurches to a decision of sorts: "There was something fascinating about the soft green stack. . . . He felt sure now that he could not leave that. No, no. He would do it." But doubts again paralyze him, and at that moment the lock accidentally clicks shut. He has procrastinated so long that chance has taken the decision out of his hands. Now there is nothing for it but to take the money and flee. *"Did he do it?"* Society would say yes, but those privy to the manager's mental debate cannot be so sure. Later, after he has tricked Carrie into fleeing to Montreal with him, when he has time to think about what he has done, Hurstwood realizes the magnitude of his blunder—that it has shut him out from Chicago, his old life, and condemned him to a future that is "dark, friendless, exiled." He is outside the gates. But he also thinks, after seeing the stories of his defalcation in the papers, that society's view is not right either. For it sees "but a single point in a long, cumulative tragedy. All the newspapers noted but one thing, his taking the money. . . . All the complications which led up to it were unknown. He was accused without being understood." *Understanding*—the final plea of the criminal, the exile, and the only absolution society can give. He cannot plead innocence; he can only beg forgiveness and ask that the verdict be set aside because of the circumstances. Earlier, Dreiser had written that "the sentinels of life are forever pacing," ready to shoot down anyone who attempts to break society's rules; later he would cut that passage. For his sympathies had shifted from Carrie to Hurstwood.

*   *   *

In the second, the New York section, of *Sister Carrie,* winter seems to have set in permanently. Events are lit by the cold, washed-out rays of a winter sun or the crimson glow of a Broadway fire sign. New York is different in other ways. It is an imperial city; Chicago is a country town. (Carrie is impressed by the absence of green lawns and houses in New York; she does not like it much.) In this sea full of whales "Hurstwood was nothing."

The atmosphere is charged with the energy of great schemes; it is an opiate enslaving the newcomer to "dreams unfilled—gnawing, luring, idle phantoms which beckon and lead, beckon and lead, until death and dissolution dissolve their power and restore us blind to nature's heart." Seeking to underscore the point, he invokes Gates, comparing the city's air to a "chemical reagent." But Dreiser's science is confused. Rather than registering the emotions, he has it coloring them—the opposite of what a reagent does. In Carrie's book, city lights lead a young girl astray; in Hurstwood's, the spectacle of great wealth undermines a man's confidence. Thus, Dreiser returned obsessively to the vision of the city he had first set down in his "Prophet" essays in *Ev'ry Month.* He saw it as something greater than its "dash and fire," its wealth of sights and colors, its hurrying crowds. It was a dynamo generating a magnetic force which drew people, and a place where "men may starve at the base of cold, ornate columns of marble, the cost of which would support them and many like them for the remainder of their earthly days," as he wrote in *Ev'ry Month.*

New York's dreams are more destructive because they are more remote and unattainable than Chicago's. A young man is vulnerable to them, but he has "the strength of hope" to sustain him through the inevitable setbacks. A man Hurstwood's age is less prone to illusion but, lacking hope, more susceptible to disappointment because he sees more keenly the contrast between his present and his desired state. Shortly after he arrives and he and Carrie take a flat on West Seventy-eighth Street, Hurstwood begins to feel hedged about by the niggling economies necessary to preserve his small capital (he has returned all but thirteen-hundred dollars of the money)—as does Carrie, though she is ignorant of their financial state. He manages to make a start by buying a third interest in a respectable saloon down on Warren Street, but he misses the celebrities, the warmth, and the glitter of Hannah & Hogg's. Regret and "nostalgy" for the old days begin gnawing at his morale, and aging works its wasting ravages. Here, in diagnosing Hurstwood's state, Dreiser resorts to Gatesian psychurgy invoking "certain poisons in the blood, called katastates," generated by remorse, which "eventually produce marked physical deterioration."

More to the point was the prosaic phrase that follows this diagnosis: "He was given to thinking, thinking, thinking. . . . He was left to brood." Here Dreiser exhumed the qualities in himself he knew were destructive. He had no need of Gates's pseudo-psychiatry. Years later, he set down the true diagnosis of Hurstwood's sickness: "a deep and cancerous sense of mistake which ate into his energy and force."

Once, Hurstwood had been inside the bubble of success; it seemed so easy, so natural there. But now that he is outside, he understands that there is a city within the City: "Men were posted at the gates. You could not get in. Those inside did not care to come out to see who you were. They were so merry inside there that all those outside were forgotten, and he was on the outside."

As for Carrie, she adapts to her new circumstances, living quietly as a young matron known as "Mrs. Wheeler" (Hurstwood's pseudonym), passing idle hours with trashy novels, supervising her maid at the housework, or cooking dinner for her husband. But Hurstwood begins to draw away from her. He makes friends of his own and devotes more of his evenings to playing poker. His old habits reassert themselves: "He began to look again into the eyes of women and to take cognizance of the pleasures of the tenderloin." Carrie does not complain; she has sunk into a kind of dormancy.

Then she meets a neighbor, a smart urbanite named Mrs. Vance, who awakens her old melancholy, her old desires. They go to the theater and afterward join the Broadway fashion parade. Carrie feels dissatisfaction with her clothes as she is raked by the supercilious eyes of splendidly dressed men and women. Her discomfiture is like that described in the popular song "What Right Has He on Broadway?" It tells how on the Bowery "You can make a front, / In a suit of hand me down," but on Broadway "There you must look the part, . . . / If you're not dressed complete, / They'll say what right has he on Broadway."

Awakened, Carrie looks at Hurstwood with a more critical eye. She has long since lost her awe of him. She is loyal and affectionate enough, but there is little love between them. And when Mrs. Vance takes her to Delmonico's, she meets a man who opens her eyes to a higher sphere, just as Hurstwood did when she was living with Drouet. He is Bob Ames, an inventor from Indianapolis. What Ames invents is not made clear— something to do with electricity, and he was inspired by Thomas Edison, whom Theodore interviewed for *Success* and whom he admired because

Edison was more interested in contributing useful innovations than in making money. But Ames is also the closest thing to a spokesman for Dreiser's ideas in the novel. It is Ames who comments on the high prices at the restaurants, evincing disapproval of the conspicuous consumption of the Gilded Age. He is an intellectual; he deprecates Bertha Clay's *Dora Thorne*, which Carrie had found only "fair" herself (it is the story of a poor girl who marries a rich young man and—like Laura in *Under the Gaslight*—is rejected for living above her station). Alone, rocking in her flat, Carrie dreams of finer things and remembers her moment of glory on the stage. Ames had told her it was a fine thing to be an actress. . . .

And so Carrie and Hurstwood bemoan their separate states, but each is set on a different trajectory—Carrie's upward, Hurstwood's downward. When he and his partner lose their lease on the Warren Street place, Hurstwood begins trudging the streets looking for a new opportunity, but he did not receive enough money for his interest in the old saloon to buy a comparable place. Reduced to seeking an ordinary job, his applications are rejected because he is either too old or looks too important for the position. When winter sets in, he holes up in the flat, huddling by the radiator's warmth, rocking and reading his papers, lost in their "lethean waters." He takes charge of the household after Carrie, with his acquiescence, lands a job in the chorus line in a comic opera. Now his manhood is slipping away.

Once, after her caustic remarks become too much for him, he bestirs himself to get a job as a scab motorman in Brooklyn. And when he reads about the strike his heart is with the strikers—an identification the old George Hurstwood would not have felt. But he adds: "They can't win. They haven't got any money." The corporation's strength is superior. Still, he needs something and takes the job for a day. He even feels a little of the old superiority, saying, "Poor devils," about his bedraggled fellow scabs. When, despite police protection, the strikers seize him and throw him to the ground, the last raiments of the old, resplendent George Hurstwood are stripped away; he is one of the poor devils. He hurries back to his warm room, where he can read about the strike in the *World*. (Dreiser, however, drew on clippings from the New York *Times* for details.)

Carrie, meanwhile, continues her adventitious rise. This "apt student of fortune's ways" advances to a small speaking part after the comedian happens to make a remark to her and she responds with a pert ad lib that brings down the house. She moves on to a bigger role in another show. The director dresses her as a Quakeress and orders her to frown throughout the comedian's routine. Again, she somehow piques the audience's fancy and is a hit. As the critic of the *Evening Sun* writes: ". . . the vagaries of fortune are indeed curious."

Resuming the stage name of Madenda, which Drouet had conferred on her, Carrie becomes a featured player and is boosted to a salary of one hundred and fifty a week, more than she can possibly spend on clothes. She moves to a lavish apartment, paying a special low rent because the management wants celebrities living in the building. Stage-door Johnnies besiege her. One writes: "I love you and wish to gratify your every desire." But she is not interested in men—or men of that kind. "It does not take money long to make plain its impotence, providing the desires are in the realm of affection." Ames (as in "aims") points her to that realm, urging her to make more of herself, to act in comic dramas—the term for serious plays—but she drifts.

After Carrie walks out on him, Hurstwood sells the furniture—his final stake—and heads for the Bowery, where in a shabby hotel room he reads the paragraph in the *Sun* recording Carrie's latest success and thinks: "Ah, she was in the walled city now. Its splendid gates had opened, admitting her from a cold, dreary outside. She seems a creature from afar off—like every other celebrity he had known.

" 'Well, let her have it,' he said. 'I won't bother her.'

"It was the grim resolution of a bent, bedraggled but unbroken pride."

Throughout the month of March Theodore wrote in one long sustained burst. His self-doubt had dissipated, the tragedy was marching inexorably to its foreordained end, and his writing grew leaner, more telling. In the handwritten manuscript, the revisions—by himself and by Jug and Henry—are sparse. There are also fewer philosophical asides to impede the narrative. A further aid to composition was the availability of the Bowery scenes from "Curious Shifts of the Poor," which he spliced in to show Hurstwood's life when he sinks to the bottom sediment of nameless men. The insertions were almost seamless; sometimes all he had to do was to put verbs in the past tense and replace the reference to "a man" with "Hurstwood." What had been a powerful impressionistic portrait thus acquired an emotional center, a figure against the ground, which it had previously lacked.

Richard Duffy was the only witness to the writing of *Sister Carrie* outside the trio at West 102nd Street. He used to receive periodic progress reports from the author. "Every few days," Duffy recalled, "he would make the breezy announcement that since he last came on view he had written as many as 20,000 words." This had been Theodore's way throughout the writing of the book—tremendous bursts followed by fallow periods when he grew discouraged. His intensity and concentration could be sustained only in relatively short bursts, after which his invention flagged, leading to idleness and doubts. At the beginning of his career, he had only magazine scutwork to escape to during those times.

Symptomatic of the pressures he was working under was the return of his insomnia. At nights he would pace the floor, and Jug would get out of bed and sleepily match his steps. His mood swings during those six months he worked on *Sister Carrie* must have worn a trench between the poles of elation and despair. Like Carrie, he found solace in rocking—a soothing regression to cradle rhythms. Dreiser had acquired another habit—folding and refolding his handkerchief. As Duffy remembers him at this time:

> He always sat in a rocking chair, if he could find one, and he sat in it to rock, his long frame crouched at the shoulders, while he folded a handkerchief into the dimensions of a postal stamp with the slow patience of a Japanese drawing a maple leaf. If he was not talking he would be humming the refrain of "On the Banks of the Wabash" or of some other popular song. He had hundreds in his head.

Describing Hurstwood and Carrie's careers in New York brought Dreiser squarely up against the unpleasant memories of the *World* days. He too had come to the city trailing a small celebrity as the star feature writer and traveling correspondent of the St. Louis *Republic*. He too had discovered that this bigger sea was full of whales, and that he was nothing. He too had stood outside the gates, gazing at that city within the City. He too had gone "on the Bowery," not quite down and out, saved because he had youth and hope, but seeing down-and-out men—many of them victims of the 1893 depression—in Chatham Square.

He remembered working into the night at the dining-room table in his flat: "Something prompted me while I was writing to write sincerely. I would come to strange, hard, bitter sad facts in my story . . . and I would say shall I put that down and something within the very centre of my being would say, 'You must! You must! You dare not do otherwise!' "

A Broadway fire sign apotheosizes Carrie's celebrity. Hurstwood, shambling through the dirty snow, a muttering, ragged, subhuman figure, hesitates before a poster of her and moves on. He stops at the window of a luxury restaurant and gazes at the gleaming napery, the steaming dishes, framed in the glass that barred him from this world (his old world) like a poster advertising the grand life. "Eat," he mutters. "Eat. That's right eat. Nobody else wants any."

While Carrie and her friend Lola sit in Carrie's new suite in the Waldorf, a warm and brightly lit bubble, Hurstwood shambles to his destiny. A heavy snow is falling, and Lola wonders if they can go sleighing. Carrie, who is reading Balzac's *Père Goriot* and is sorry for the old man's suffering, worries about the people out in the cold. Lola sees a man fall in the snow and laughs merrily. "How sheepish men look when they fall, don't they?"

In a hotel lobby in the city, Charles Drouet, in town on business, runs into a comrade of the road and proposes to introduce him to a "couple of girls over here in 40th Street." . . . And on a train bound for New York the former Jessica Hurstwood, now married well, pushes away her hand of euchre and looks haughtily about. An appreciative stare from a man passing through, a banker's son from Chicago, secretly excites her. She looks demurely away and then asks if the storm in New York will delay their sailing. Her husband assures her it won't. In two weeks they will be in Rome. The third member of the party, Jessica's mother, Julia, smiles proudly.

At the door of the Bowery flophouse, Julia's former husband moves in a crush of shabby men, one of them with a face "as white as drained veal," another's as red as brick. At long last the door opens and the crush of men jams up "and then it melted inward, like logs floating, and disappeared."

George Hurstwood pays his fifteen cents and goes to his allotted cubicle. Leisurely, like a man with all of the time in the world, he stuffs his overcoat in the crack beneath the door and carefully lays down his cracked old hat. He stands under the gaslight a moment, then turns on the jet without igniting it. He stands there a moment as the fumes, the sweetish aroma of dead lilies, insinuate themselves into his nostrils. Then, "hidden wholly in that kindness which is night" ("Ah, the promise of the night. What does it not hold for the weary. . . . It is the lifting of the burden of toil"), he lies down, saying, with finality, "What's the use." In the stately dignity of that scene, one of the most moving in our literature, Hurstwood, brought low, becomes great—a man who played the game and lost, dying with a bent but unbroken pride. Four years earlier Theodore had foreshadowed the theme of his book when he wrote in *Ev'ry Month*, "A man is still a man however often he may fail."

Seated at his dining-room table, a pile of yellow half sheets before him, Dreiser wrote:

"The End. Thursday, March 29—2:53 P.M."

Part Four

THE NOVELIST STILLBORN

31. At the Outworks of the City

After it was done considerable cutting was suggested by Henry
and this was done. I think all of 40,000 words came out.
—Dreiser to H. L. Mencken (1916)

ven as Dreiser was writing the final chapters, Anna Mallon's
typists were working on the earlier ones. Eventually, they
outran the author. When they finished Chapter 49, in which
Ames and Carrie converse at a dinner party and a current of
attraction flows between them, the young women had become so caught up in Carrie's story that they sent Dreiser an impatient
note:

> Dear Mr. Author:
>   We have finished the last iniquitous chapter of Sis-
> ter Carrie, and are now ready for something hot and siz-
> zling. So please send her down.
>   Impatiently,
>   THE INFANT CLASS

Anna Mallon was also enthralled and wrote to Dreiser to compliment
him on the scene, saying she would "impatiently await the closing chapter." The fact that the young "typewriters" found Carrie's tale "iniq-
uitous"—meaning risqué—should have sounded a warning bell to the
trio at West 102nd Street. These were the young women whom the "obscenity" laws were designed to quarantine from the virus of immorality.
That they enjoyed the story was a testament to how outmoded those laws
had become.

But the editorial team paid little heed to this portent; they were working hastily. Henry read through the manuscript but made few changes.
Jug was more conscientious, but her only qualification for the task of copy
editor was that she knew grammar, a subject Dreiser had learned first
from German-speaking nuns and failed in public school. Most of her

changes were minor—correcting the words her husband habitually misspelled; adding question marks, to which he was averse, and improving
a few awkward phrases. For example, she changed the backward-running
sentence "On her feet were yellow shoes and in her hands her gloves,"
to "Her brown shoes peeped occasionally from beneath her skirt. She
carried her gloves in her hand."

Jug also served as technical adviser on matters of feminine dress (those
yellow shoes had to go). But this role merged with that of censor when
she deleted the intimate references to Carrie's keeping her body sweet
and wearing "excellent corsets." She also prettified Carrie's speech to
make her more ladylike. Thus, rather than charging that Drouet had "lied"
to her, the little pilgrim says he "deceived" her. Such locutions subtly
changed Carrie's personality, making her a trifle more genteel than the
raw country girl from Columbia City Dreiser had in mind.

Years later, Dreiser characterized Jug's editing as taking out "what she
called the 'bad parts,' " but at the time he was willing enough to delegate
to her minor matters of propriety. Rather than write "bitch," he has
Hurstwood call his wife a "confounded _____." Jug filled in the blank
with "wretch," and he accepted the substitution. When he wrote "bas-
tard" he let it stand.

Nor did she seek to excise the slang that was used so prolifically.
Expressions like "You're a daisy," "rounder," "swell," "grip" (for suitcase), "truly swell saloon," "It's up to you," "nobby," "spruced about,"
and "suspicioned" stayed. Nor, for that matter, was any attempt made
to banish the poetic words of which Dreiser was so fond—"lightsome,"
"airy grace," "fine feather," and the like.

Such terms clashed with Dreiser's journeyman style, learned in a half-
dozen Middle Western newsrooms and honed on scores of magazine specials. His big boots sometimes got tangled up in sentences; or rather, his
thoughts proceeded deliberately, toward their goal in Spencerian periods,
draped in qualifiers and subordinate clauses. In a self-conscious attempt
to soften his inelegance, he would festoon passages with "lightsomes"
an "halcyons."

But Dreiser's utilitarian prose was his great strength; it conveyed the
subject matter honestly. The journalistic writing of the day had this to
say for it: it was attuned to the facts of the contemporary world and it
was more compatible with common speech than the genteel style. If it
lacked the psychological nuances of Howells's style, or that of the master,
Henry James, it was well adapted to conveying a sense of the contemporary urban scene—society, environment, above all, ordinary speech—

and the manners and customs of turn-of-the-century Americans. In contrast, the genteel style was designed to evade vulgarity—to muffle, idealize, or euphemize it. When Dreiser fell into genteelisms himself—when he had Carrie walk "trippingly," for example—his mind was in never-never land; his true voice was speaking when, describing the fresh-from-the-country Carrie, he writes, "her feet, though small, were set flatly."

If his prose was also set flatly, rather than running trippingly, he generally avoided the trap many later realists fell into of telling a humdrum story tediously, resulting in novels that ran on as drearily as a small-town Sunday afternoon. The humdrum details were there, to be sure, most tellingly in the delineation of the breakup of Hurstwood and Carrie's marriage, when they quarrel over the price of steak and his small economies grow into an obsession. The manager's dwindling bankroll, meticulously audited, becomes an account book of his life slipping away.

Structurally, the shifting urban scenes, from Broadway to the Bowery, from flophouse to Waldorf Hotel, are like the shuttles of the loom of destiny. Dreiser's mind worked in dialectic fashion; he showed reality by contrasts: Carrie contrasts the Hansons' flat with her meal with Drouet in a luxurious restaurant; Hurstwood contrasts his sterile marriage with the renewed youthfulness of his love for Carrie—and on and on. Through this interweaving of antitheses, life is presented in the round. Ultimately Carrie will ascend to her suite at the Waldorf while Hurstwood will be borne to an unmarked grave in potter's field. The author's brooding eye records both fates without moralizing. Accorded equal stature and dignity, the three commonplace protagonists become larger than life.

After the hectic events of the Chicago scenes and the hollow dazzle of Carrie's rise on the New York stage, the pace of the novel becomes like the rhythmic tread of a ceremonial procession. The earlier action is slowed by the philosophical digressions characteristic of the Victorian novel—though in Dreiser's case the models were Balzac and Hardy, the best ones. Also, many of these passages are integrated into the bone and tissue of the book. And they are juxtaposed with scenes of great force and economy, told almost entirely in dialogue and gesture (for example, the scene in the restaurant which climaxes with Carrie's acceptance of money from Drouet), anticipating the techniques of later novelists like Ernest Hemingway and F. Scott Fitzgerald. Like Carrie, the book is a mixture of the old and the new—a bridge between the nineteenth-century novel and the twentieth. For that matter, the pervasive pessimism underlying the story, its assumption that desire and selfishness are the motive forces of most human behavior, that chance and inscrutable forces rather than ethics or Providence control human destiny, would also become dominant themes in twentieth-century literature.

The chief flaw in *Sister Carrie* is Dreiser's penchant for abstractions, his godlike pose of applying fundamental laws. He becomes like the Spencerian Unknowable—an almost inhuman intelligence. There is a corresponding chilling lovelessness in his characters that is true to their natures but which the author does not entirely comprehend. At the same time, Dreiser's great strength is his empathy with his characters, which reaches its peak in the final scenes about Hurstwood. In the supreme effort to make believable the climactic downfall of this, the most strongly imagined figure in the book, Dreiser *became* Hurstwood, producing his every thought, his every emotion, from inside himself.

The published version of *Sister Carrie* closes with a kind of epilogue, or rather a coda reprising the themes of the book, added after Dreiser had written "The End." His only explanation of the new ending came in an interview, seven years later, with a reporter from the New York *Herald:* "When I finished it I felt that it was not done. The problem was . . . to lead a story to a point, an elevation where it could be left and yet continue into the future. . . . I wanted in the final picture to suggest the continuation of Carrie's fate along the lines of established truths." Nothing occurred to him immediately, so he hiked to his favorite spot on the Palisades, the sheer cliffs across the Hudson from Manhattan, and lay down beneath a shelf of overhanging rock. "Two hours passed in delicious mental revery. Then suddenly came the inspiration of its own accord." He reached for his pencil and scribbled the new ending in his notebook. Finis.

Casting a bit of cold water on this romantic account is the existence of thirteen pages of notes with the original manuscript. Except for the beginning, which was written by Dreiser, the notes are in Jug's hand. Apparently he started to jot down some ideas, became tired, and dictated the rest to her. The notes are a rough outline for the coda that ultimately appeared in the published book. Similar phrases occur in both—for example, "the mind that reasons and the mind that feels" (Carrie being an example of the latter) and "a harp in the wind." Carrie is lured by distant gleams of beauty that disappear when viewed close up, like glints of sunlight on trees: "You approach and it is gone—only to be found on the next more distant tree." (In his article on Stieglitz Dreiser had written of the "spirit of beauty which ever dances before us, across hills and fields, but is so rarely captured and made our own.")

The notes show that Dreiser was, as he suggested to the interviewer, attempting to bring his book full circle, back to Carrie. Rather than state what happens to her, though, as Balzac did in his epilogues, he summarizes her character to foreshadow her future. She is driven by feeling, rather than reason; "beauty," rather than desire for fine things or even sex, as one might have thought, lures her on. Dreams call her; she will always be dissatisfied with present reality. In some ways she has changed: she is "no longer walking the street and looking with wonder and longing—on the outside—every doorway a bar—a sealed entrance to the garden of delight." Now she is inside the garden: the secret passage of the theater has taken her there. But she finds no satisfaction in the things that would appeal to a "Lillian Russell type." Ames has instilled in her a new ambition—acting in a comedy drama; she has become "the old mournful Carrie—with the unsatisfied longing." Ultimately, she can only be happy sitting in her rocker and dreaming: "Dream boats and swan songs—such joys as never were."

Those jottings, considerably reworked, found their way into the new ending. As Chapter 49 was originally written, the reader would expect that Ames and Carrie fall in love, perhaps marry, but a strong theme in Dreiser's dictated soliloquy was the need to dash that expectation. "Ames is not a matrimonial possibility," he says flatly. "That is not his significance." And so he rewrote the Ames-Carrie tête-à-tête to eliminate all hints of warmth between them. In the new draft the inventor tells her bluntly that she should use her gift for conveying emotion and pathos in serious drama; if Carrie continues to live solely for herself, she will lose this gift. She must live for others through her art—use her talent to express their feelings. Ames's final words to her are brusque and commanding: "If I were you, I'd change." And he walks out of her life. Ames's "significance" is thus as a bearer of the author's message, and nothing more.

In the original scene between Ames and Carrie, Ames forgets his reservations about "the moral status of certain types of actresses," and when he bids Carrie farewell, he is "wide awake to her beauty." The "blind strivings" passage that follows suggests that even if Carrie does enter into a relationship with Ames, "the light is but now in these his eyes," and tomorrow it will be someone or something else. Perhaps Dreiser did not intend it so, but a censorious reader might interpret the phrase to mean there would be other men for her. Dreiser had written himself into a moral trap. The only way to get out was to eliminate Ames as a possible husband, alter the passage beginning "O blind strivings of the heart," which closes the scene between him and Carrie so that it carries a note of disapproval for Carrie's past conduct, and transpose it to the end of the novel.

The point of the new version is that Carrie has moved beyond her attraction for the false "representations" of beauty and finer things—Drouet, Hurstwood, the stage, applause, success—none of which made her happy. Now she awaits "that halcyon day when she should be led forth among dreams become real." The coda ends with Carrie sitting in her rocking chair, dreaming. On her first night in Chicago, Carrie had sat in the Hansons' flat, rocking and fantasizing of the pleasures of the city. Now those pleasures have proven false; she must long, alone; happiness will always elude her.

Carrie is left in a kind of stasis that is out of keeping with the realism of the rest of the novel. In her rocking chair, she moves yet goes nowhere. Is it some Spencerian state of equilibrium beyond desire, when all motion stops? But deprived of the Ames possibility, the author throws up his hands, leaving his heroine as a kind of nun of desire, cloistered from further contamination by the world.

The epilogue carries more than a hint of Arthur Henry's views on desire in "The Doctrine of Happiness" (it leads to dissatisfaction). Did he influence Dreiser to revise the book along more philosophical lines? (Dreiser claimed he wrote the final chapter to *A Princess of Arcady* when Henry got stuck.) Jug put her hand in too. Making a fair copy, she added small but significant changes. For one thing, she cut a description Dreiser had written of the new Carrie: "Her honor she kept decently." Was Jug fearful that any reference to Carrie's virtue at this point might make it seem that the author was protesting too much? And she also changed the final apostrophe to Carrie in her rocking chair. Originally the sentence had read, "In your rocking-chair, by your window, shall you know such happiness as you may ever feel." But Jug altered "know" to "dream" and "ever" to "never." The changes add a nuance of finality: Carrie may only dream, she may never feel.

The apologia for Carrie is complete. When she came to the city, she was "poor, unsophisticated, emotional." The "drag to follow beauty" was so strong that she abandoned "the admired way, taking rather the despised path leading to her dreams quickly." But who shall cast the first stone? "Not evil, but goodness more often allures the feeling mind unused to reason." Such thoughts were not opposed to Dreiser's beliefs, but were they true to Carrie's temperament?

*   *   *

The new ending was dispatched to the Infants, and by early April 1900 the typescript of *Sister Carrie* was done. Again the editorial team sharpened its pencils and fell to. Now Henry began to take charge in a more visible way. At first his contributions were stylistic. He worked hard at making Dreiser's sometimes tortured sentences rest easier on the page. But as Jug had done in a different way, he occasionally ignored the awkward power of Dreiser's style and substituted something slicker and blander. Theodore let himself be edited, but he was not sitting by idly. Contrary to his later reputation as a careless writer, Dreiser tinkered with many clumsy sentences. He seemed determined to make his prose correct.

After this final polishing, Carrie was ready to go out into the world. Dreiser decided to aim high: he chose Harper & Brothers, still a leading house despite its recent reorganization in bankruptcy by J. P. Morgan, and still the publisher of Mark Twain and William Dean Howells. Might Howells be disposed to intercede on behalf of another young novelist from the West now that Dreiser's article about him had appeared in the March *Ainslee's?* Another consideration was that Henry Mills Alden, the editor of *Harper's Monthly*, had been sympathetic to his nonfiction work.

Alden gave the manuscript a quick reading and told Dreiser that, while he liked it, he thought it unlikely that Harper's would publish it. But at the author's behest he forwarded the script to the parent firm with some favorable words appended. On May 2 the novel came back. The accompanying reader's report called *Sister Carrie* a "superior piece of reportorial realism" with excellent touches of local color, particularly the rendering of "below-the-surface life in the Chicago of twenty years ago." But, it continued, the author's touch was "neither firm enough nor sufficiently delicate to depict without offense to the reader the continued illicit relations of the heroine. . . . I cannot conceive of the book arousing the interest or inviting the attention . . . of the feminine readers who control the destinies of so many novels." Those words may have produced consternation at West 102nd Street. Dreiser may have prepared a heated mental rebuttal to the criticisms, but he desperately wanted his novel out.

With Dreiser lacking sufficient detachment to make the necessary adjustments, Arthur Henry took command: "[Henry's] weakest and most irritating trait was a vaulting egotism which caused him to imagine, first, that he was as great a thinker and writer as had ever appeared; second, that he was at the same time practical, a man of the world, a man of affairs."

Or so Dreiser later characterized his friend in an embittered recollection. At the time he probably welcomed Henry's worldly advice. Henry

went through the entire typescript, lightly penciling brackets around suggested cuts. Dreiser followed him with a soft-leaded pencil, drawing heavy
black lines through sentences and paragraphs, where he agreed. He accepted nearly all of Henry's suggestions, and they were fairly extensive—
more than thirty thousand words came out. Some of these were arguably
surplusage—several philosophical passages, for example, that were awk-
wardly worded; chunks of dialogue from *Under the Gaslight*. Their excision
speeded up the story.

But the majority of the trims homed in on phrases that could be con-
strued as "immoral"—passages that cast doubt on the sanctity of marriage, for example, or that alluded to sexuality even in an indirect way.
Thus, the section about Carrie's experiences looking for a job after Drouet
has left her—being ogled by prospective employers—was dropped, as
was her tentative decision to take the job at the picture-frame store. A
passage describing Carrie's answering warmth to Hurstwood's amorous
pleas was extirpated, lest there be the slightest doubt about her innate
chastity. References to Drouet's philandering while he was living with
Carrie also had to go—as did the words "living with." Although the book
was strong enough to stand the cuts, something was lost—the social comment on the plight of the working girl in the job-hunting section, for
example. The removal of references to Carrie's feelings about Drouet
and Hurstwood made her seem more frigid in her liaisons; but her pangs
of conscience after Drouet seduces her were also dropped, making her
even more of a cipher. Hurstwood becomes a man who has remained
faithful to his wife all those years, despite his coolness toward her. Some
of the subversive cynicism had gone out of Dreiser's book. Yet in his—
and Henry's—defense it should be said that their surgery should be judged
by the literary mores of the times. By those standards, they were merely
removing tasteless references.

Now, it would seem, *Sister Carrie* had been scrubbed of all blemishes.
Surely she was ready to make her debut in polite society. Her next destination, it was decided, would be the firm of Doubleday, Page, a new
house formed only the previous year by Frank Nelson Doubleday and
Walter Hines Page.

32. A Novel Amid Forces: The Spendings of Fancy

I had the definite and yet entirely illusory notion that because [*Sister Carrie*] was considered excellent by a number of personal and critical friends it must sell and sell well. All one had to do was to take it to a reputable publisher and get it published. Presto—fame and fortune.

—Dreiser to Fremont Older (1923)

Every great publishing house has been built on the strong friendships between writers and publishers. There is, in fact, no other sound basis to build on; for the publisher cannot do his highest duty to any author whose work he does not appreciate, and with whom he is not in sympathy.

—Walter Hines Page (1903)

t thirty-eight, Frank Nelson Doubleday had spent more than half his life in publishing. He started with Charles Scribner's Sons when he was fifteen, and put in twenty years there, during which he founded and edited *The Book Buyer* and served as manager of *Scribner's Magazine*. In 1897, after a disagreement with the incumbent Scribner, he left the firm to work for S. S. McClure, who needed someone to run his new publishing house. The two men soon clashed, however; McClure had met his ego match. Doubleday really wanted to run things, and McClure's trusted associates, John Phillips and Albert Brady, disliked him. McClure later told Phillips that hiring Doubleday had been one of his worst blunders. "He cant [sic] help forcing himself into your place & mine & he cant help trying to make himself not only first but the only one."

Doubleday departed in 1899, taking with him Page and Frank Norris, who had been working as a reader. The firm he left behind continued under the name McClure, Phillips with fair success, though later in the decade S. S., a magazine genius but an erratic businessman, had to sell it—to Frank Doubleday, who paid half what it was worth. As Doubleday once told Samuel Hopkins Adams, "When I make a deal with a man, if I don't feel later that I got the better of it, then I feel cheated." When Christopher Morley, then one of his editors, demanded a raise, Doubleday asked him how much he was presently receiving. Morley told him, and he said coolly, "Yes, there must be something wrong if you haven't made yourself worth more than that." (Later Morley got the raise.)

Handsome, mustachioed, with a Barrymorean profile, Doubleday could be enormously charming, and his kindnesses to authors he favored were legion. He had sat with Rudyard Kipling night and day when Kipling was ill with pneumonia in New York City. The British author became his friend for life, nicknamed him "effendi," a pun on Doubleday's initials, F.N.D., and wrote *Just So Stories* for his children. But it was as a businessman that Doubleday shone, and within a decade he made Doubleday, Page one of the largest publishing houses in America. He was the most prominent of the new breed of "commercial" publishers who reached out to a wider, more unsophisticated audience, just as McClure, Munsey, and others were doing in the magazine field. And if this meant placing a lowest-common-denominator appeal over literary worth, so be it. Morley called Doubleday "really the first of a new era in book publishing—which he visualized foremost as a business, not merely as a dignified literary avocation. . . . He was inexhaustible in fertile schemes for larger distribution. . . . The idea that publishing should be essentially an intelligently conducted commerce, not a form of aesthetic bohemianism, appealed strongly to his authors." George H. Doran, who became Doubleday's partner in the 1920s, recalled acerbically, "In the Doubleday economics of publishing the auditor-in-chief and not the editor-in-chief was the final arbiter of publishing policy."

Walter Hines Page was definitely a junior partner (in 1903, when the firm incorporated, he was made vice president). While he was editor of *The Atlantic Monthly*, Sam McClure had lured him from Boston to New York at three times the salary. A mild progressive, Page specialized in books by public figures, for example, the autobiographies of Booker T. Washington and Helen Keller. Doubleday parked him as editor of a magazine founded under the firm's auspices in 1900 called *World's Work*, which reported on business, labor, inventions, and industrial trends, and busied himself with developing such best-selling authors as Thomas Dixon, Jr., and Gene Stratton Porter. But Doubleday also backed Frank Norris (who gave the firm its first best seller, *The Pit*, in 1903), Ellen Glasgow,

Upton Sinclair, and Joseph Conrad, as well as printing anything Kipling wrote.

Though primarily interested in public affairs, Page did have literary views. He was, for example, a strong advocate of a genuine American literature. The best writing, he said, sprang from the native soil, from the common people and common speech. "Any subject is a good subject," he once wrote, "that has an abiding human interest." That meant, he wrote to the journalist Elia Wilkinson Peattie in 1897, tackling "the strongest material of modern life," including "the one central tragedy," which was "the wreck of womanhood." Page admired Frank Norris, who had a "larger conception [of American life]—a conception that included its vast economic significance—perhaps than any other writer of fiction."

Norris was now launched on the first volume of his projected Trilogy of Wheat, *The Octopus* (which he jocularly called "The Squid"). As the author of the controversial *McTeague*, he would, of course, be an ideal reader of *Sister Carrie*. The members of the firm steered realistic fiction to him, though Frank Doubleday had reason to be skeptical of Norris's judgment, given the young novelist's indifference to commercial appeal. (Norris once wrote, "To make money is not the province of the novelist.")

Norris's presence may well have influenced Dreiser's decision to send *Sister Carrie* to Doubleday, Page. As it happened, Rose White arrived for a visit in April while Theodore was revising *Sister Carrie*. She had come across *McTeague* and was praising it to the skies. On her recommendation, Dreiser read it and found it a revelation—"the first real American book I had ever read," he told H. L. Mencken years later.

Norris sat up all night reading the manuscript of *Sister Carrie*. A few days later, he announced to a visiting writer, Morgan Robertson, "I have found a masterpiece. The man's name is Theodore Dreiser." Robertson said he had known Dreiser as the editor of a small-time song sheet called *Ev'ry Month*. Well, whatever he had been, Norris said, he had written a great book which Doubleday, Page *must* publish, and he intended to convey his personal feelings to the author immediately. Norris did so on May 28:

> My Dear Mr. Dreiser:
>   My report of *Sister Carrie* has gone astray and I cannot now put my hands on it.
>   But I remember that I said, and it gives me pleasure to repeat it, that it was the best novel I have read

in M.S. since I had been reading for the firm, and that
it pleased me as well as any novel I have read in any
form, published or otherwise. . . .

Of course, Norris quickly added, he was only one member of the firm. He had passed the manuscript to Henry Lanier, and after him Page would read it. Then the three of them would have a "pow-wow" and come to a decision. Norris promised to "do all in my power" to shepherd it to the promised land. In view of subsequent events, it should be noted that Norris apparently thought that the three of them, and particularly Page, had the power to make a final decision. At the time, Doubleday was in Europe and not expected to return until mid-July.

On June 8 Norris invited Dreiser to come to his rooms at the Angelsea Hotel at 60 Washington Square South, an establishment popular with artists and bohemians of the paying sort, and told him the book was officially accepted. What else they talked about can only be conjectured, but they probably hit it off. Dreiser must have felt a kinship with the tall, slender Californian with the prematurely graying hair. Both had fallen under the sway of Darwin and both regarded the city as the great subject for modern novelists. Although Norris wrote of the West, he proclaimed the traditional Bret Harte mining camp setting outmoded: "The novel of California must be now a novel of city life." Both saw human beings as battlegrounds on which primitive instincts and reason struggled for mastery. The dentist McTeague, like Hurstwood and, even more, Drouet, was a creature of instinct. They also shared a contempt for fine literary style. Aside from Norris's worship of Zola (whom Dreiser still had not read), their great difference was that of class: Norris, of "good stock," believed in the superiority of the Anglo-Saxon "race" and, like Zola, believed that heredity determined character, while Dreiser, the immigrant's son, pitied the downtrodden and could not accept invidious distinctions based on class or race.

The day after their meeting, Page had written to offer his congratulations on "so good a piece of work." However, Norris's enthusiasm for *Sister Carrie* outstripped Lanier's and Page's. Lanier was opposed to the presentation of such low types in a novel. "People are not of equal significance," he explained to Dorothy Dudley. But he agreed with Norris's estimation of the book's power and integrity. Page also had reservations about the characters; apparently not all subjects were suitable for fiction after all. Still, he called it "a natural" and agreed it must be published. When he met with Dreiser to discuss terms, Page voiced his reservations and urged him to fictionalize all the names and places. An oral agreement was made on the spot. Publication was scheduled for the fall.

With his novel accepted, Dreiser could feel that he had, in the words of Richard Duffy, "scaled the outworks of the walls of the City." He was rapidly spinning illusions of literary fame, if not fortune, and planned to make his living as a novelist—"to join the one a year group." A couple of subjects were fermenting in his brain, and he scraped together some money, planning to head for Montgomery City, where he could live off his in-laws' hospitality while Jug had a "good old visit with her folks," as Henry put it.

In the meantime, he shared the tidings of his success with friends and editors he knew. Elmer Gates offered to arrange for him to deliver a lecture at the Players Club in the fall; Page had promised him a banquet. The word spread, and congratulations flowed in—from William Belmont Parker, the assistant editor of *The Atlantic Monthly*, from old newspaper pals in St. Louis, and, of course, from various members of the White clan. The patriarch, Archibald, had taken an interest in his son-in-law's writings since the *Ev'ry Month* days, when he cheered on the pro-Bryan effusions of "The Prophet." The lively Rose had a literary bent, and Jug's brother Pete was a fan. The good opinion of these conservative small-town folk was crucial to Dreiser.

In Missouri he set to work on a novel he would call *The Rake*. He had delegated to Arthur Henry the task of handling any problems that might arise in his absence, and Theodore's friend hovered over the book as though it were his own. On July 14, Henry wrote that he had had a discussion with Lanier about the use of real names. When Lanier insisted that all of them be changed, they had a "warm argument," Lanier contending that Dreiser was "straining after realism." He implied that unless the changes were made, the book would not be published. Henry agreed that the name Hannah & Hogg ought to be altered because the theft took place there, but insisted that all the others were necessary. Lanier also wanted a new title—something more "pretentious." Henry urged Teddie not to back down, but said he should make a decision on all these matters quickly.

When Henry's letter arrived, Dreiser took it as confirmation of a premonition he had had two days earlier "that there was something in the wind that boded ill to me." He even asked one of the blacks who worked for Arch White where the local "Old Mammy"—the fortune teller—lived, but for some reason could not bring himself to consult her. Then he fell into "a deep gloom" and that night suffered a "physical derangement of the nervous system" and was unable to sleep. By morning the fit of depression had passed. "There is a tenth sense stirring in the minds of men. . . ." he wrote Henry in explanation of his premonition. Four days later another letter from Henry arrived:

> Dear Teddie:
>   It has dazed me. I am amazed and enraged. Doubleday has turned down your story. . . .

Doubleday had returned from Europe. After hearing Norris's enthusiastic endorsement, he took the manuscript to his home in Oyster Bay, Long Island, to read over the weekend. Monday morning, we may fairly presume, he stormed into the office and summoned Page. A stunned Frank Norris described his reaction to Henry, who relayed it to Dreiser: " 'Doubleday,' [Norris] said, 'thinks the story immoral and badly written.' He don't make any of the objections to it that might be made [i.e., those raised by Page and Lanier]—he simply don't think the story *ought* to be published by anybody first of all because it is immoral."

Norris's initial reaction was to advise Dreiser to seek another publisher. He offered to try to place it with Macmillan, and told Henry if they acted at once, there would still be time to get *Sister Carrie* out in the fall. In a note to Henry before their talk, Norris makes no mention of Doubleday's opposition other than to assure Henry that "Page—and all of us— Mr. Doubleday too—are immensely interested in Dreiser and have every faith that he will go far."

The following morning Henry returned to the publisher's offices at 34 Union Square and raised the question of whether the firm had a legal obligation to publish the book because of Page's oral agreement with Dreiser. Norris agreed that it probably did, and suggested Henry see Doubleday, who was unclear as to whether there was an agreement or not. When Henry described Page's representations, Doubleday admitted that he could be forced to publish, but said that it would be a great mistake for Dreiser to insist, since "[Doubleday] would make no effort to sell it as the more it sold the worse he would feel about it."

After Henry left, Doubleday apparently conferred with Page, and they decided to try to talk Dreiser into withdrawing the book. In a letter dated July 19, which he sent to Dreiser c/o 6 West 102nd Street, Page asked "to be released from my agreement with you." What had happened, he explained, was that the more everyone at the firm thought it over, the more strongly they believed that "the choice of your characters has been unfortunate. I think I told you that, personally, this kind of people did not interest me, and we find it hard to believe they will interest the great majority of readers." Also, the problem of the use of real names seemed even more serious than was originally thought. Of course the firm stood ready to "make amends" if Theodore felt injured in any way, but really, it would be harmful to his future as a writer (for which the firm had the highest hopes) for him to make so controversial a debut.

Only a year later, Page wrote Virginia Frazier Boyle that a novel she had submitted, which he called "an unrelieved study of the most distressing form of disease" (apparently insanity), was too controversial. He advised her not to publish it until "after you have put forth several other books and shown an orderly and progressive development of your literary career with other material." Presumably, an established author could better stand the obloquy that might be heaped on her or him. Such advice was common at that time, and always it was given for the writer's sake. No mention was made that the publisher was saved from the risk and possible embarrassment of launching an unpleasant book by an unknown writer.

Doubleday's thunderclap had caused Page to execute a graceless somersault. Initially, according to Arthur Henry, Page had planned simply to return the script with a polite letter saying the firm had changed its mind. He had postponed sending it, however, until after Doubleday had talked to Henry, then changed his tack. The others covered themselves. Lanier suddenly found his objections to the characters looming large. Norris was more equivocal, sincerely proclaiming his admiration for *Sister Carrie*, but trying to stay in Frank Doubleday's good graces. He was loath to jeopardize his relationship with the firm, which had allowed him to support his new wife while undertaking the most ambitious project of his career, the Trilogy of Wheat.

Curiously, none of the principals would cast Doubleday as the main villain. Dreiser's initial attitude toward him was that "he must have ample reasons"* for his objections.* Henry reserved his fire for the other editors; he called Doubleday "sincere" but "mistaken." Page, however, was not sincere; he "is more suave than honest." Lanier "is a good deal of a cad," who knew nothing of real life; he was "shallow" and "conceited." Even Norris came in for some raps: he too was shallow and, moreover, not

---

*Dreiser's later opinion of Doubleday was expressed in a letter to H. L. Mencken in 1916: "I like Doubleday. He is such a big husky incoherent clown."

much of a writer. Henry had read some chapters of *The Octopus*, which the Infantas were typing, and found them "crude" and "overdone"— the kind of bad writing he and Teddie might fall into "if we worked alone."

As for Norris, he seems to have snatched at a scrap of rumor that would let Doubleday off the hook. Sometime after Dreiser returned from Missouri, Norris told him that Mrs. Doubleday had actually raised the fuss. Where he got that information is unknown, but it lent support to Norris's theory that Effendi would come 'round once the critics hailed the book as a work of genius. Thus began the legend that Neltje Doubleday had torpedoed *Sister Carrie*, a story that Dreiser in later years retailed to Mencken and others and to his biographer Dorothy Dudley, who transformed Neltje into a veritable Titaness, a stand-in for all the snobbish, meddling, do-gooding clubwomen who sought to tame the new realism. As Dudley envisioned it, Mrs. D had strolled into Frank's study while he was perusing the manuscript, read it herself, reached for the smelling salts, and demanded that the book not be published.

Dudley could find no confirmation for this tale, however. Henry Lanier told her flatly, "It was Frank who made the trouble. He hated it enough without other influence, called it 'indecent,' and begged us at once to break the contract." Neltje Doubleday was a much admired woman, and her main interest was in writing books about birds and gardening, which her husband published and which sold well. Her favorite charity was the Red Cross, not "purity leagues" or rescuing fallen women, as Dudley implies. When Neltje died suddenly in Hong Kong in 1918, Frank Doubleday was prostrated by grief, and the literary gossip about his wife's suppressing *Sister Carrie* became a painful slur on her memory. When a scholar asked him about the matter in 1931, he replied that he wished the subject could be dropped. As best he could remember, Neltje never saw *Sister Carrie*, and he was positive that "she expressed no opinion about it which affected the treatment of it by the publishing house." The British publisher William Heinemann, who published an abridged edition of *Sister Carrie* in 1901, told Dreiser that same year that he had quarreled with Mrs. Doubleday about the merits of the book, which she vehemently attacked. All that anecdote proves, however, is that Neltje backed her husband in his distaste for *Sister Carrie*.

Neither Dreiser's nor Arthur Henry's letters at the time mention the lady. Dreiser's are dominated by concern about the personal embarrassment he would suffer if the book did not come out. In a letter dated July 23, he equivocates, telling Henry that if he and Norris think it best to submit the book to Macmillan—well and good. However, if the manuscript is returned to him by Doubleday, Page, he will refuse to accept it, and he thinks it should remain with the house until the "matter has been adjudicated."

Despite the setback, Theodore feels his career is secure—"Not that, after all, it is essential that I should have a career," but his views "are needed by society and will work for its improvement—the greater happiness of man." He plans not to tell Jug about the contretemps, and asks Henry not to either. And he forwards a handwritten reply to Page, asking Henry to have it typed before sending it. He closes with a warm embrace: "Surely there were no better friends than we. . . . You are to me my other self a very excellent Dreiser minus some of my defects, & plus many laughable errors which I would not have. If I could not be what I am, I would be you."

In the attached letter to Page, Dreiser writes that if the book is not published, the setback to his literary career "will work me material injury." The words material injury would alert any lawyer to a possible suit; furthermore, Dreiser speaks of the reputation of the house of Doubleday, Page—a "keen and honorable conception of justice and duty is I believe the pre-requisite of every great publishing firm." Honor required that the agreement be carried out. Let readers be the final judge of the book's quality: "The public feeds upon nothing which is not helpful to it. Its selection of what some deem poison is I am sure wiser than the chemistry of the objectors. Of what it finds it will take only the best, leaving the chaff and the evil to blow away."

In his earlier letter to Henry, however, Dreiser had not been so lofty. He had said that should Doubleday persevere, he would "make known this correspondence, every scrap of which I have" and then "the house of Doubleday would not shine so brightly." And he said twice that if Henry could somehow get the loan of the MS, he should take it to Macmillan for a quick opinion—something he did not tell Page. If that was not a double game, it was a hedging of his bets.

Henry had meanwhile come to a new view. In a letter Dreiser received three days after he had dispatched his reply to Page, Henry said simply, "Hold Doubleday and Page to their agreement." Norris, he added, shared that opinion, saying, "Doubleday will soon get over his kick and that it will be a great seller," and promising that he would send out copies to reviewers and otherwise "strain every nerve" in behalf of the novel.

And when Henry received the draft of Dreiser's July 23 letter to Page, he wrote, "We arrived at exactly the same conclusion. . . . I will not take the MSS from them even as a loan for fear they would think we might weaken. And then too it would give them the chance for an argument that they do not have now with the book still in their possession." But in his accompanying letter Dreiser had proposed that the Macmillan route be explored if possible.

Henry's role at this stage was crucial, and he was not entirely disinterested. He had had a similar experience with his first novel, an incident he apparently never told Dreiser about. Nearly ten years before, he had written a book called *Nicholas Blood, Candidate*. It was a violently racist political novel almost as scurrilous as Thomas Dixon, Jr.'s, *The Leopard's Spots* or Dixon's more famous novel *The Klansman*, on which D. W. Griffith based *Birth of a Nation*. Probably *Nicholas Blood* was a youthful indiscretion Henry now preferred to forget, but at the time he had badly wanted it published. His publisher had set type for the book, and then had second thoughts and canceled their agreement. Although Henry found another house—probably publishing the book at his own expense—the novel had flopped. Not surprisingly, when his friend fell into a similar predicament, Henry urged him to stand on his original contract.

In early August he urged Dreiser to return to New York; delay, he warned, worked to Doubleday's advantage, enabling him to postpone the book until spring. By that time Dreiser might have finished his second novel, which the firm would insist on publishing first. Given this intelligence from the front lines, and Dreiser's own stubborn belief in the merit of his book, all hope of compromise was dashed. It became a matter of principle—stubbornness, rather—that Doubleday publish *Sister Carrie*. Frank Doubleday's candid warning that he would do nothing to sell the book passed them by.

Page sent a second slippery, avuncular letter on August 2, in which he mentioned for the first time the firm's concern about the "financial return from the novel." He also noted that James Lane Allen had finished a novel a year ago that was postponed in favor of another book. If a popular writer like Allen could delay a book, why couldn't Dreiser? Page dangled the possibility of doing some articles for *World's Work*, which would be launched shortly.

In his reply, Dreiser conceded nothing and showed how far he had traveled on the road to becoming a serious novelist since writing *Sister Carrie*. Regarding Page's contention that Dreiser could postpone without harm to his career, he observed: "I do not have much faith in the orderly progression of publication as regards novels. A great book will destroy conditions, unfavorable or indifferent, whether these be due to previous failures or hostile prejudice aroused by previous error. Even if this book should fail, I can either write another important enough in its nature to make its own conditions and be approved of for itself alone, or I can write something unimportant and fail, as the author of a triviality deserves to fail."

He reaffirmed his belief in the overall merit of what he had written, despite its imperfections: "I feel and I know . . . that the world is greedy for details of how men rise and fall. In the presence of a story which deals with the firm insistence of law, the elements of chance and sub-conscience direction, men will not, I have heart to feel, stand unanimously indifferent."

That was a sound statement of the theme of *Sister Carrie*. Even the pre-Freudian slip—"sub-conscience" for "sub-conscious"—suggests he was aware that he had broken through the pack ice of convention to dark psychological waters. He placed his faith in ultimate critical vindication.

Too late, Page, in a letter written August 15, named five publishers, including Macmillan, that he would be willing to try to interest in *Sister Carrie*. Dreiser did not reply; perhaps by then he had returned to New York, where at last he confronted Page and Lanier in person. The latter remembered him as "crushed and tragically pathetic" during their fifteen-minute talk. Lanier tried to persuade him that it would be unfair to his book to let the firm issue it when the head of the house was so staunchly opposed. Crushed or not, Dreiser did not waver. He gave the two editors an ultimatum: if they did not publish, he would take legal action.

The junior members met with Doubleday, who called in the firm's lawyer, Thomas H. McKee. McKee, who thought Dreiser had a good case, advised Doubleday that he was legally bound to publish *Carrie,* and that the minimal criteria for publication included printing copies and filling orders from bookstores, if any. Frank Doubleday was a man of his word; he would honor a promise made by his partner as though it were his own. But he would also make good his threat to discourage the book's sale.

Years later, Dreiser wrote that his first inclination had been "to take the book under my arm and walk out," but that Norris and Henry had persuaded him to stand on his contract—"of all silly things."

33. A Novel Amid Forces: Fortune's Way

> You would never dream of recommending [it] to another person
> to read. Yet . . . as a work of literature and the philosophy of
> human life it comes within sight of greatness.
>
> —Seattle *Post Intelligencer* (1901)

O n August 20, 1900, Doubleday, Page signed a contract with Dreiser for the publication of a book called *The Flesh and the Spirit;* however, Dreiser penciled "Sister Carrie" underneath the typed line. Had Doubleday insisted on a "pretentious title" per Lanier's suggestions? If so, Dreiser resisted. Nor is it clear if the publisher proposed the chapter titles that Dreiser and Henry concocted at the last; probably it was their idea—an attempt to make the book more pretentious, that is, more ornately literary. The dedication was to "Arthur Henry whose steadfast ideals and serene devotion to truth and beauty have served to lighten the purpose and strengthen the method of this volume."

Those gestures show that Dreiser had returned to the city ready to fight for his book, even though the summer almost past had been the unluckiest of his life. It had started so propitiously, too, with Norris's letter and Page's offer. And, buoyed by the triumph of his hopes, he had plunged into his second novel, *The Rake,* writing ten chapters or so in an initial burst. Although the manuscript has been lost, it is known that *The Rake* was about the adventures of a young newspaperman named Eugene. So autobiographical was it that Dreiser later spliced one of the scenes into the MS of *Newspaper Days,* merely changing the hero from third to first person.

Then the trouble with Doubleday darkened the horizon like a summer squall, and he had to abandon the novel and return to New York. Looking back, Dreiser could have decided that his run of bad luck started on the journey out when he lost his wallet; followed in short order by the premonitions and Arthur Henry's letter confirming them. Henry, in one of his bulletins from the front, had advised Theodore to come home at once: "That region seems to be your country of calamity. You had better get out with what money and skin you have left." If Dreiser had returned he probably could have avoided some of the trouble, but he had fallen into an oddly detached, fatalistic mood, as though he didn't fully grasp the seriousness of the threat. Then he became angry. As he wrote Henry, "Fortune need not forever feel that she must use the whip on me."

He continued to fight even as the book was readied for the printers, and it is quite possible that his manner further irritated the autocratic Doubleday, who was used to having his own way. In September the publisher (who seems to have taken over the editing of the book) wrote him under the frosty salutation "Dear Sir," curtly agreeing to the title *Sister Carrie* and demanding that real names be changed, that all the "profanity" be removed, and that certain passages be altered. Dreiser began his reply on a conciliatory note, saying he had changed several of the names per request and had struck out sentences that were considered "suggestive." But he quickly got his back up. Some of Doubleday's demands he could not agree to. A reference to Delmonico's had been questioned; Dreiser thought the restaurant was sufficiently well known to remain. After all, Richard Harding Davis frequently referred to Delmonico's; why couldn't he? Why had Doubleday removed a reference to a book by the American writer E. P. Roe, while leaving in Balzac's *Père Goriot?* Was there a double standard for foreign authors? (Dreiser was actually alluding to an old grievance of his—editors allowing foreign authors to say things that American authors could not.) As for alleged profanity, "Since when has the expression 'Lord Lord' become profane. Wherein is 'Damn,' 'By the Lord,' and 'By God.' "

The ways of the censor were indeed capricious and arbitrary. Names like the Waldorf, the Broadway Central, and Charles Frohman, the producer, which Dreiser said he had changed, appeared in the final book, while others were altered. For obvious reasons, Hannah & Hogg's became Fitzgerald & Moy's; several actors' names were fictionalized, others were not; as a general rule, only the names of businesses mentioned negatively were fictionalized. All "by Jesus"es and "by the Lord's" were excised, others were not. The great to-do about the names petered out in a confused flurry of trivialities.

Still, a pair of sharp eyes belonging to someone at the publishing house continued to vet *Sister Carrie* for risqué bits until the book was on the presses, and emendations were made even after Dreiser had returned the corrected author's proofs (which he had had Richard Duffy read as a check). For example, the timing of the pro forma marriage of Carrie and Hurstwood in Montreal was changed so that it occurred before they consummated their "complete matrimonial union"; instead of counting his money in a "dingy lavoratory" Hurstwood counted it in a "dingy hall"; Hurstwood's patronage of "those more unmentionable resorts of vice" and Drouet's query "Is she a blonde?" were jettisoned. Now the much-laundered Carrie was spotless.

For her debut she was outfitted in the drabbest possible garb, lest anyone be allured by her. The cheap-looking, dull brick-red binding and plain-black title lettering (in those days books did not have dust jackets) would have been more appropriate on a plumbing manual. As Dorothy Dudley wrote, it was "an assassin's binding." Nor did the size of the first printing bespeak much enthusiasm on the publisher's part—1000 copies, of which 450 remained unbound, pending orders. To discourage the latter, the title was not listed in the Doubleday, Page catalogue, though Zola's *Fruitfulness* was (in a bowdlerized translation and described as an exposure of "an evil . . . which is sapping the vitality of France" but full of "clear, sound healthy feelings"), as well as *Bob Son of Battle* and *Spencer and Spencerism*. Henry's *A Princess of Arcady* is praised as a "charming idyll," "a delicate romance," and a "striking contrast to the strenuous and often unpleasant fiction which is so common today." The firm's salesmen probably made no effort to cry up *Sister Carrie*. No advertising was taken. The price was $1.50, the standard charge for a novel at the time.

At least one story Dreiser told in later years, crediting it to Frank Norris and Thomas H. McKee, was not true—that all copies were stored in the basement at the Doubleday, Page offices. Orders from wholesalers were filled, and copies did appear in the stores. Painfully few of them, though: only 456 volumes were sold between November 1900 and February 1902, netting Dreiser $68.40 in royalties, a return not calculated to encourage him to join the one-a-year club.

The only bright spot in the picture was Frank Norris. True to his word, he sent out copies to reviewers—more than one hundred of them—accompanied by personal letters. Isaac Marcosson, a young book columnist for the Louisville *Times* and an admirer of Norris's, recalled receiving one, and his review—highly favorable—was the first to appear after the official publication day, November 6. Other reviewers followed suit, in a somewhat desultory fashion, and *Sister Carrie* was fairly widely reviewed, for which Norris deserves the major share of the credit.

What is more, the reception was generally favorable; even the most hard-shell moralists could not find any specific obscenities to complain about. The precensors, from Jug and Henry to the unknown blue penciler at Doubleday, Page, had done their work well. The minions of Anthony Comstock did not raid any bookstore; Frank Doubleday was not hauled from his Oyster Bay home and clapped in jail.

Of course there was some clucking over Carrie's fall and rise. For example, *Life*, at the time a humor magazine, found nothing funny about her career and warned: "Such girls, however, as imagine that they can follow in her footsteps will probably end their days on [Blackwells] Island or in the gutter." The reviewer for the Newark *Sunday News* (recruited by Dreiser's friend Peter McCord, who was working on the paper) correctly noted that "after having yielded up that which woman holds most precious . . . this strange heroine feels but the lightest pangs of remorse or shame" and faulted the author for his "failure to appreciate the power and depth of certain feminine instincts." But that was one of the few sour notes in a review that went on to hail Dreiser's "great talent—possibly genius."

Another seeming censure when taken out of context were the observations of the Chicago *Tribune* that *Sister Carrie* was "a presentation of the godless side of American life" and "Not once does the name of the Deity appear in the book, except as it is implied in the suggestion of profanity." But the point being made was that a novel dealing with this segment of society "has been waited for through many years." People like Drouet and Hurstwood existed, so they should be shown. What is more, the book contained a "spiritual lesson" in that each character was responsible for his or her own fate and "self-discipline and well grounded morals would have avoided every evil."

What was mainly complained of was the unrelenting unpleasantness of the realism, the absence of edification or idealism, the plethora of slang and the lack of a "literary" style. For a few reviewers the book was too somber, but many others praised this quality, though remarking that it would doom it to unpopularity. Typical of the latter was Wallace Rice of the Chicago *American*, who noted at the end of his review, "the utter truth of portions of the book will keep it from attaining any very wide popularity." Such statements recurred and became, in effect, self-fulfilling prophecies. And so many reviewers felt duty bound to discuss the book's morality that it acquired a sort of guilt by association.

Marcosson was among the few reviewers who celebrated *Sister Carrie* as an exploration of new fictional territory. "Out in the highways and hedges of life you find a phase of realism that has not found its way into many books," he began. "It reeks of life's sordid endeavor; of the lowly home and the hopelessly restricted existence. Its loves, its joys, its sorrows, are narrow. There is little sunshine. It is plain realism." At last, here was a book about the "other side of the social scale." Unlike the critics who were baffled by the title, he found it apt; it suggested "a plain woman, plain in the sense of being of the great common people." This was the sort of fiction "which must be read and which we must have." The Chicago *Tribune* agreed: "America needs enlightenment rather than indiscriminate flattery if the present rate of advance is to be maintained."

Also perceptive was the anonymous reviewer for the *Commercial Advertiser*, a lively New York paper sympathetic to new movements in the arts, to which some of the young rebels of the turn of the century gravitated, including Norman and Hutchins Hapgood and Lincoln Steffens. The *Advertiser*'s critic took the eighteenth-century French economist Turgot's maxim that "Civilization is at bottom an economic fact" as his text and traced its working-out in the story of Hurstwood. We have all known such men, he wrote, suave, well-fed, and successful. But the case of Hurstwood illustrates Turgot's rule: if the economic pilings on which their lives are built are swept away, they will sink into destitution, loss of self-respect, moral squalor. It was astute recognition of Dreiser's sense of the economic tragedy at the heart of American life.

And out in St. Louis the iconoclastic William Marion Reedy was so excited by the book that he wrote Dreiser to tell him so: "I have just finished reading 'Sister Carrie'—in one sitting. It is damned good. I shall say so as emphatically as this in the *Mirror*. I thank you for the treat I've just had."

Reedy (whom, it will be recalled, Dreiser never met during his St. Louis stint) was as good as his word. He found in *Sister Carrie* a major step forward: "its veritism out-Howells Mr. Howells and out-Garlands Mr. Hamlin Garland." Despite its photographic truth, the novel had "an art about it that lifts it often above mere reporting" and "there lurks behind the mere story an intense fierce resentment of the conditions glimpsed." Yet it was a moral tale despite its directness, which, Reedy correctly noted, "seems to be the frankness of a vast unsophistication. . . . The story, as a whole, has a grip that is not exercised upon any unwholesome taste." (Reedy wrote Dreiser he had discussed the book's morality in hopes of stimulating readership.) Like many other reviewers, he was enthralled by the evocation of Hurstwood's downfall "in a kind of narcotic procrastination touched with fitful gleams of paretic, puling pride." Carrie he found a bit "shadowy," but the character of Drouet "you have met often, and liked, with a touch of contempt." *Sister Carrie* was about the "commonest kind of common people, yet the spell is there. . . . You find yourself trying . . . to analyze the charm away. But you cannot."

The review was the beginning of a long comradeship on the literary battleground. Dreiser had found an eloquent champion, and they began corresponding. He gained other converts, though pitifully few of them—Marcosson; Edna Kenton of the Chicago *Daily News*, a young woman who had migrated to the city like Carrie; Alfred Stieglitz, who gave copies to friends; George Horton of the Chicago *Times Herald;* H. L. Mencken, a fledgling Baltimore reporter; and a few score anonymous reviewers in places like Hartford, Detroit, Albany, Indianapolis, and Seattle. Most of the book's discoverers were young and on the fringes of the literary world, newspaper men and women many of them, who had passed through the same tank towns and Middle American cities that Theodore had on their flight from conventional small-town upbringings, and who hungered for writers who were as true to American life as Tolstoy was to Russian and Hardy to English. And there were a few others, anonymous souls, scattered across the arid cultural plains of the nation, who read his book in small-town frame houses and city hall bedrooms in the watches of the night and thought, *I am not alone.*

In all, about thirty reviews straggled out over the course of a year. Some, like the one by McCord's friend at the Newark *Sunday News*, were not published until well into 1901. Fewer than five could be characterized as downright negative, and about ten were mixed. Although the positive reviews probably did not win over the consumers of light popular fare who made up the great majority of the book-buying public, surely there were more than 456 readers for *Sister Carrie* in the United States. After all, Norris's *McTeague* had sold in excess of four thousand copies in hardcover. Why didn't Dreiser's novel reach a similar number?

Reedy had a hunch as to the explanation, which he noted at the beginning of his review: *Sister Carrie* "has been neither extensively advertised by its publishers, Doubleday, Page & Co. nor enthusiastically reviewed, if, indeed, it has been reviewed at all, in any of the journals of criticism." A few other reviewers also noted that the book had slunk out like a freed convict, and Horton wondered why the publisher of *Sister Carrie* would spend a good deal of money pushing a trivial work like *An Englishwoman's Love Letters* when it had the real thing. Horton was a friend of Henry's from the latter's Chicago days, so a bit of logrolling was involved; however, he genuinely admired the novel. When Henry told him the full story of Doubleday's hostility to the book, Horton replied: "I am not at all surprised at your version of the Doubleday-Dreiser story. I had fancied something of the kind. 'Sister Carrie' is a work of genius and Doubleday belongs to that species of long-eared animals which are not hares."

More than a year after publication day, Reedy published an inquest on *Sister Carrie*'s corpse by John H. Raftery, a Chicago newsman. Raftery noted that the novel did attract considerable interest, and several reviewers "went to great trouble to 'give away' to various publications careful reviews." But the editors of those journals were not receptive, and Raftery quotes a publisher on the reason why: "In this country the popularity of a book depends upon 'judicious advertising.' Half the so-called 'literary editors,' who cannot see anything unless illuminated by the great white lights of the advertising pages, failed to discover any great merit in the book." The lack of advertising also influenced the booksellers. The almost universal opinion in the trade was, "It is a 'dead one' from the shopkeeper's point of view" because the publisher did not back it up. That of course is a common fate for first novels; still, a less hostile publisher might have, on the strength of the reviews, taken out some advertising. A rather pretty garland of quotes could have been woven, though again one cannot say for a certainty that such an ad would have made a dent on the wall of indifference *Sister Carrie* met.

But the good reviews were too scattered in time and geography to have much of an impact on readers and certainly not on Frank Doubleday. Few New York dailies noticed *Carrie*, and many of the most important literary magazines (the "journals of criticism" Reedy referred to) were conspicuous by their silence. The *North American Review*, *The Atlantic Monthly*, and *Harper's Monthly* (where were Parker and Alden?), *The Critic*, *The Arena*, *Literary Digest*, *Current Literature*, *Century*, and *The Nation* either ignored *Sister Carrie* or merely listed it in their "books received" column. Where, above all, was William Dean Howells?

Moreover, the favorable reviews (save for Reedy's and Marcosson's) failed to convey that intangible something—a sense of excitement, a sense of a new fictional era dawning—needed to lift a book out of the ruck of titles. A strategically located notice by a fellow realist like Garland or Fuller might have helped, but both were hors de combat in the realism war. Garland had married, and he was worried about supporting his family. Perceiving the way the literary winds were blowing, he had abandoned his stark tales of the Middle Border and his crusading Populist single-tax novels and turned to writing romances of the West. When he did read *Sister Carrie* in 1903, he wrote in his diary: "Relentless, plodding, powerful book not unlike Norris's 'McTeague'—a serious, well-intentioned book but wholly in the French school of Zola. It has no grace, no evidence of cultivation, but it has verity. The author is unknown to me. From his name I take him to be the son of a German." He decided he did not like the book enough "to become an advocate of it."

Fuller would also have been a sympathetic reader. His two Chicago novels had anticipated Dreiser in their emphasis on the importance of money and class in human affairs. But the fusillade of criticism Fuller's two realistic novels had drawn sent him into retreat, and now he was writing elegant travel books and romances set in medieval Italy when he could spare time from managing (more in the janitorial than in the executive sense) his inherited tenements. The rise of newspapers and popular magazines with articles on interesting individuals, high and low, had usurped the realistic novelist's field, Fuller wrote in 1899, and the novelist would be well advised to turn to biography if he or she sought readers. Thus Fuller congratulated Garland on signing up to do a biography of Ulysses S. Grant for S. S. McClure. One must march with the procession or walk alone.

The dominance of romantic and historical fiction was now a cultural fact. *When Knighthood Was in Flower* and *Richard Carvel* were best sellers. Maurice Thompson, champion of idealism and foe of realism, had a popular success in *Alice of Old Vincennes* (though he did not live to enjoy it). "Local color" had arrived, to the extent that people were no longer reading folksy, cheerful Scottish or English novels; they were reading folksy, optimistic American ones like *David Harum* and Irving Bacheller's *Eben Holden*.

The earnest reformist novels that had a mild vogue in the 1890s were giving way to romances of business, a variant of the historical romance. Ironically, Frank Norris pioneered this approach (though he was miles above the other authors in the genre) in *The Octopus*, which had good sales when it appeared in 1901. Its readers probably appreciated the novel more as a saga of California than as a study of the power of the railroads—and in a way they were right. For Norris backed off from indicting anyone;

the railroad, like the ripening wheat and the ranchers who grew it, were all embodiments of higher Forces, out of whose struggles emerged a greater good. At Doubleday's request, Norris had, in the course of his researches, interviewed C. P. Huntington, baron of the Southern Pacific Railroad. The result was to shade the historical facts, leaving the impression that the railroad was a neutral engine of progress rather than the promoter of rapacity and political corruption that it had been.

Borne into the twentieth century on a rising tide of economic prosperity, their armies and navies victorious in Cuba and the Philippines, Americans were indeed turning to the "taradiddles" of historical romances, which William Dean Howells had deplored in his first "Easy Chair" column for *Harper's Monthly* in 1900. The Era of Good Feeling under McKinley and Mark Hanna would give way to the middle-class progressivism and big-stick diplomacy of Theodore Roosevelt, who called upon Americans to feel "the mighty lift that thrills 'stern men with empire in their brains.' " The prevailing orgy of Anglo-Saxon race pride represented a backlash among the old American stock against the waves of immigrants imported by the money barons to work in their Pittsburgh mills and Lower East Side sweatshops. In such a climate, who would notice a novel about a chorus girl, a drummer, and a saloonkeeper written by the "son of a German"? Like Carrie walking the streets of Chicago, Dreiser was still an outsider looking in the windows.

Not long after his novel came out, Dreiser ran into Howells at the Harper offices. "You know," the Dean said, "I didn't like *Sister Carrie*," and hurried off. At that moment the generational fault-line cracked open. To endorse a woman like Carrie Meeber would have run counter to Howells's deepest instincts; let the next generation admit her into literature— he had gone as far as he could. The seeds of free expression Dreiser had planted must lie dormant for another decade.

In 1898 Harold Frederic, author of *The Damnation of Theron Ware*, which had also been too strong for Howells (though the two later became friendly), had died in London at the age of forty-two. In 1900 Stephen Crane died in Germany, where he had retreated to fight a last battle with tuberculosis. His constitution had been weakened by the malaria he contracted covering the Spanish-American war in Cuba, and his will to live had been vitiated by financial worries. Deeply and foolishly in debt, Crane had turned to writing romances for quick money. Asked by a friend why he had abandoned realism, he replied, "I get a little tired of saying, 'Is it true?' "

In October 1902, Frank Norris would die suddenly of peritonitis, his resistance to infection also undermined by the malaria he had contracted in Cuba. As Dreiser had written in 1898 about another victim of that war, William Louis Sonntag, Jr., "Lord! one whose dreams were numerous has gone."

Part Five

DOWN HILL AND UP

34. *Losing the Thread*

Similarly, any form of social distress—a wretched, down-at-heels neighborhood, a poor farm, an asylum, a jail, or an individual or group of individuals anywhere that seemed to be lacking in the means of subsistence or to be devoid of the normal comforts of life—was sufficient to set up in me thoughts and emotions which had a close kinship to actual and severe physical pain.
— Dreiser, *Dawn* (1931)

By mid-December 1900 it must have become clear to Dreiser that his brave hopes of critical and public vindication had been wildly optimistic. Like Hurstwood, he began to brood. The many good reviews seem not to have assuaged the pain of failure. By his testimony ten years later, they might have been about someone else's book. Asking himself if he had believed the reviewers who hailed him for writing a work of genius, he answers, "I'm quite sure I didn't. I was the most surprised man—or boy, for I was a boy in mind, all the same, that you ever saw." His conscious mind hadn't fully absorbed the subconscious streams the writing of *Sister Carrie* had tapped. And he was still bruised by Frank Doubleday's verdict of "immoral." That seemed the critical judgment that mattered most deeply; it worked under his skin like a splinter and festered.

In an interview with a reporter from the St. Louis *Post-Dispatch* in December 1901 (the only one he gave on the book), Dreiser felt compelled to defend himself against the charge. He said he did not see anything immoral about "discussing with a clean purpose any phase of life . . . from a philosophic standpoint. If life is to be made better or more interesting, its conditions must be understood. No situation can be solved, no improvement can be effected, no evil remedied, unless the conditions which surround it are appreciated." William Dean Howells had said as much many times. But such lofty sentiments were somewhat hollow, however sincerely offered; they did not remove the chancre of self-doubt eating at him from within.

The blows of rejection by the world reopened the old Warsaw wounds. Dreiser must have confused Doubleday's view with the public's indifference. Even if he did not share the censure, it hurt him. Indeed, he seems to have exaggerated it all out of proportion; Dreiser's fears about the damage to his career became a self-fulfilling prophecy. He believed he had become, as he had predicted to Page, a literary pariah, shunned by editors, friends, and relatives alike.

Possibly the first manifestation of this self-doubt was his abandonment of the novel he was working on, *The Rake*. The title alone suggests that Theodore was sailing into perilous moral waters again, perhaps writing about his youthful amours. After the Doubleday shock, he may have grown doubtful that he would find a publisher for such material. Then he became preoccupied with the problems associated with his first novel. By the time he could return to *The Rake*, the buoyant mood in which he had started it was gone. It was a summertime book, about a young man searching for a place in life. When he resumed in the fall, his mood was more somber. He had been thrown off stride.

In January 1901 he abandoned it completely and began a new book. The inspiration for its heroine, whom Dreiser called Jennie Gerhardt, was another of his sisters. Something had impelled him to sift the ashes of his earliest memories in Terre Haute. That something could only have been the death of John Paul Dreiser on Christmas Day 1900, at the age of seventy-nine. Theodore received the news in Montgomery City, where he and Jug were spending the holiday. Paul was living with Mame and Brennan in Rochester when he died. He spent his last days peacefully, tending the Brennans' garden, going to early Mass daily. A picture of him at the time shows a frail, tanned, bearded old man dressed in a black ulster, holding a cane in one hand and a hat in the other. Sylvia's abandoned Carl was living with them too, though Carl would now have been sixteen or seventeen and probably was about to strike out on his own. Evidently the idea of his father living with Mame—the daughter who had disgraced him in Terre Haute with her affair wih Colonel Silsby—struck Theodore as the seed of a novel. A stern, Old World father who had disowned his daughter in her youth spends his final days in her care; presumably he has forgiven her, as she has forgiven him (perhaps Mame had even told him as much).

John Paul Dreiser's death was the catalyst that turned Theodore urgently to the story of Jennie, for he began writing it on January 6, 1901, less than two weeks later. His credo of the ruthlessness of the writer, set down in "Nigger Jeff," had not been puffery. But Theodore's haste did not mean he was indifferent to his father's passing. A hint of his feelings toward the old man survives—an inscribed copy of the first edition of *Sister Carrie*. The inscription reads:

> *To my dear father*—with a sort of inheritance proviso by which I manage to inscribe it also to *Mame and Austin*. If any of you fail to read and praise it the book reverts to me. With love (according to precedence)
> Theodore

Apparently Theodore had not sent the book to his father before old Paul's death, and he may have been glad that he hadn't. The testamentary language he jocularly used turned out to have been prophetic—cruelly so, since aside from the clothes on his back, his father would have had nothing to leave Mame and Brennan but that book. Theodore had that curious way of prematurely consigning to death father figures in his life. He had done it with Howells and Spencer, and he had done it again with his real father, whether by pure chance or subconscious compulsion. Underlying their reconciliation lay a substratum of deep-seated anger at old Paul—resentment of his failure to provide for the family and of his authoritarian ways.

John Paul Dreiser's copy of *Sister Carrie* also became, in a curious way, a symbolic link between Theodore's past and future. For at some point he began making corrections in the book—mainly grammatical and stylistic improvement. Though he gave up after about seventy pages, this was the beginning of what would become a grand obsession—a new edition of *Sister Carrie*.

Of course it was a trifle callous-seeming for Theodore to use his father's copy for the corrections—as though he were saying, well, *he* won't need it any longer. It is possible of course that he felt little grief at his father's passing. Theodore never wrote about its effect on him, while his descriptions of the impact of his mother's death are extravagant. The latter was a loss, the former . . . a gain. On the other hand, in a letter he wrote to Richard Duffy only a day or so after his father died, some of Theodore's grief must have showed through. In his reply, dated December 30, Duffy expresses concern about his mental state: "I am very sorry to hear of the bereavement you have suffered in the death of your father. . . . I hope you will force yourself to bear this trial with fortitude, the more so, since it has seemed to me that you are lately inclined to ponder sadly.

Ponder and weigh life's bundle of waste, I know you must. It is the heritage of your philosophic Teutonic ancestors."

Duffy must have noticed depressive tendencies in Dreiser in New York, and he now feared that the latest blow might intensify them. Duffy also sensed that Dreiser had been brooding about the poor reception of his book, and he makes reference to *Sister Carrie*'s encouraging reception, meaning the laudatory letters Dreiser has received, rather than the reviews.

Disregarding his friend's advice that his next book contain "a truly humorous character," Dreiser plunged into the Jennie Gerhardt story, which begins with scenes of cold and hunger in Terre Haute, memories of gathering lumps of coal along the railroad tracks. He wrote with considerable speed, finishing five chapters in six days and ten by February 3. Clearly, he was seized by the story of Jennie; the first ten chapters were also the ones most directly grounded in his childhood.

Back in New York City after the holidays, Theodore was confronted once again with the problem of making a living. It must have been clear by then that he could expect little in the way of royalties from *Sister Carrie*. As a belt-tightening measure, he and Jug moved to a cheaper apartment at 1599 East End Avenue, along the East River. From his window Dreiser could see Blackwells Island, where were located the city's prison, insane asylum, and charity hospital.

The island held a morbid fascination for him; it was a dumping-ground for the unfit, the unlucky, and the immoral. As far back as 1896 he had written about it in *Ev'ry Month:* "It is bleak, dismal and isolated—a spot at once mournful and grewsome. . . . The storm beats about it some nights, the moon floods about it on others, but always it is forsake like, always sad. There are iron bars in the windows, idle guards in the court, and far over the water, you can see the lights of the city, gleaming and blazing and soft over the tide you can hear the murmur and the gayety and life that is there."

He told the story of a young rake named Weber, heir to a piano company fortune, who ruined his health in dissipations and ended up in the island's insane asylum. And while Dreiser always had pleasant associations with the Hudson—crossing it with Paul on his first visit to the city, picnics on the Palisades—the East River appeared in his writings as an urban Styx. He had contemplated ending his life in its black, frigid waters after leaving the *World* in 1894. In "Whence the Song" the composer ends up on "a black boat steaming northward along the East River to a barren island and a field of weeds." In the revised ending of *Sister Carrie*, brief mention is made of Hurstwood's body being carried away on a "slow, black boat setting out from the pier at Twenty-seventh Street upon its weekly errand . . . to the Potter's Field."

Now the gloomy island confronted him daily, and "the sight had a most depressing effect on me," he said. But that must have come later. The first winter Arthur Henry joined them to re-create briefly the old *ménage à trois*, and he probably kept Dreiser's mind off the view. Henry had envisioned a "cozy winter" in which both of them would work on their novels (he was also starting another one). First, of course, they would churn out some articles and lay up sufficient money to finance their next literary ventures.

So all went well in the new flat during those first months. Dreiser pushed ahead on his novel, completing nearly forty chapters. He had thirty of them typed by the Infant class, with the idea of showing them to a publisher and obtaining an advance to live on while he completed the book. He decided to query George P. Brett, head of Macmillan, who had written him that he liked *Sister Carrie*. (Did Dreiser once again kick himself for holding Doubleday to his contract?) But in his letter, in which he pledged a finished manuscript by midsummer, Theodore confessed that "an error in character analysis makes me wish to throw away everything from my fifteenth chapter on and rewrite it with a view to making it more truthful and appealing." Doubts had begun to set in. Brett showed interest but said the firm never advanced money on an uncompleted book.

The reception at other houses was even less hospitable. At the Century Company the manuscript was returned to him by a secretary without even a form rejection; at A. J. Barnes a reader was so shocked that he threw it into his fireplace; and John Phillips, of McClure, Phillips, successor to Doubleday, McClure, told him that if that was his idea of literature, he should go into another line of work. Dreiser later wrote that Phillips had warned him he was becoming a "social pariah." But as the editor who had summoned young Frank Norris to New York and the champion of *McTeague* at Doubleday, McClure, Phillips could not have been entirely out of sympathy with *Sister Carrie* or its author. Indeed, he had encouraged Dreiser to contribute to *McClure's Magazine*.

Dreiser was also circulating copies of *Sister Carrie* in the hope that someone might give his aborted child a miraculous second life. His idea was that he would offer a publisher the rights to both his novels. He made a preliminary inquiry to Doubleday, Page about buying the plates and unsold stock not long after he returned to the city. A statement prepared by the publisher in February puts the value of what is on hand at about

seven hundred fifty dollars. It concludes with the following cryptic statement: "New royalty arrangement might be made more favorable to [sic]
publisher—author is sick. Sell for cost less 15%."

Apparently the idea was that Dreiser would buy the plates out of his
royalties. What his sickness was is not known. It could have been a particularly debilitating case of the flu or bronchitis.

Then came an upswing in *Carrie*'s fortunes. In May the London publisher William Heinemann asked for permission to bring out a British edition of *Sister Carrie* (Frank Norris had sent him a copy) in his Dollar Library
series, which was devoted to publishing young American writers. There
was one problem: the price of books in the series was fixed at four shil-
lings (the equivalent of a dollar), and Dreiser's novel was too long to sell
at that price. Could he condense the first two hundred pages to about
eighty? Already a bit punch-drunk from cuts and changes, Dreiser was
queasy about wielding the shears once more. Fortunately, Arthur Henry
volunteered to undertake the job. He accomplished it with dispatch,
compressing Carrie's story and making a new, tighter book in the process,
one that probably should have been called "The Death of Hurstwood,"
since the manager becomes the focus. Heinemann was pleased and bent
all efforts to have his edition out in late July.

If this news cheered Dreiser, the effect was only temporary. For his
other literary affairs were not prospering. He was not selling articles at
his old pace. In 1898 he had published almost fifty articles, poems, and
stories; in the year and a half after he finished *Sister Carrie*, he sold only
thirteen. And several of them had been researched before or during those
miraculous six months in which he completed his novel. He began to
think that a conspiracy of rejection had formed against him, not only among
book publishers but among magazine editors.

The truth of the matter was that Dreiser was no longer able to grind
out "specials"; he had lost touch with the market—possibly by choice.
His antipathy to magazine writing could be traced back to the summer
on the Maumee, only two years before. That discovery of untapped powers, followed by the brief, heady glory of being a novelist, had permanently disqualified him for hackdom. He was, he thought, a literary man
at last.

That was a very inconvenient thought, for he still had to earn a living,
and he had Jug to support. Apparently he tried to turn out some articles,
but found himself blocked. He would sit at his desk for hours with no
result, and finally walk the streets, worrying about what he would do.
The only thing he was capable of writing was the kind of impressionistic

sketches (e.g., one called "Hell's Kitchen") and short stories he had begun in the summer and fall of 1899. A few of the latter he sold, but it was a slow business. It had taken him two years of continuous effort to get "McEwen" and "Nigger Jeff" published, and it was Duffy who finally took them for *Ainslee's*. Reedy ran "Butcher Rogaum" in the *Mirror*, and "A True Patriarch" was taken by John Phillips for *McClure's*, after some haggling over the price—Dreiser, obviously out of need, had demanded more than the hundred dollars Phillips offered. Phillips explained patiently that since the author hadn't initially fixed a price, he assumed Theodore had left that to the magazine.

By June Dreiser still had no publisher to back his second novel and faced the task of recasting almost two-thirds of what he had written. He had sold nothing in months, and his money was dwindling. Then Arthur Henry breezed in from a sojourn with Anna, under her parents' watchful eyes, and invited him and Jug to spend the summer at Dumpling Island, a few hundred feet off the coast of Connecticut. His sweetheart owned the island, and Henry intended to settle in there for some writing. Though the cast of characters had changed (Anna in place of Maude), it must have seemed an opportunity to renew the fellowship and productivity of that summer on the Maumee. Dreiser accepted, with Jug planning to join them in July, after a stay with her family. It would be like old times, helping each other on their novels, the best of comrades.

35. *Nancy, Ruth, Tom and I*

In all the world, there is no lovelier retreat than this island, where
Nancy, Ruth, Tom and I were together for a month. And yet, we
became more and more unhappy as the days passed.
—Arthur Henry, *An Island Cabin* (1904)

rthur Henry's novel probably did little better than Dreiser's,
but he did not fall into a similar gloomy state. He was full
of talk of their working together and excited about his next
effort. He had made a trip to upstate New York to research
the setting. Henry never wrote the novel; instead, he turned
to autobiographical back-to-nature books which were then in vogue—
perhaps as a reaction against too-rapid urbanization.

The idea for the first of these came that summer in 1901; he would
call it *An Island Cabin*. It would tell about two couples—Ruth and Tom,
Nancy and himself—who escape to the perfect retreat and spoil it because they have brought their city troubles along.

The serpent of discord slithered into Henry's Eden simultaneously with
Dreiser's arrival. When Theodore debarked from the small sailboat used
to haul water and supplies, he saw a large, unpainted saltbox house surrounded by sand, rocks, and tangled scrub growth. Henry, who had thought
his friend would love the rugged natural beauty of the setting, was shocked
to hear him complaining. The place was filthy; Henry was a sloppy
housekeeper; the dishes were greasy and the knives rusty; the floor needed
scrubbing; the bedding was damp; the food atrocious. Henry had vowed
to live on two dollars a week and was subsisting entirely on a diet of fish,
potatoes, and onions. Dreiser was in no mood for Thoreauvian simplicity
and thought the back-to-nature regimen a pose. Since the island was only
a few hundred feet offshore, however, they were hardly roughing it.

But he was in a jumpy state; greasy dishes and damp bedding touched
off depressing resonances in his psyche. In addition, he missed Jug. She
had spoiled him, he confessed to Henry. "She makes me so comfortable

in a thousand ways that I'm lost now. . . . If she were here, I could stay forever. I cannot do housework. I cannot look after my things."

Gradually, however, he responded to the beauties of rocks, sand, and sea. Henry watched him gazing at a sunset and thought: "There is no one more sensitive to the world about him, more deeply sympathetic with it." Although the sea had always fascinated Theodore, he became uneasy when a storm sent angry waves crashing against the island. When they went out in the boat, Dreiser's fear of the water was apparent. It was embedded in childhood memories of a boat ride with Rome on the Wabash, and of the time he had almost been swept away by the Ohio River in Evansville. But when Henry took the tiller, he sat back docilely, even when the sea was rough. Henry noticed that, "relieved of responsibility or the need for action, he could face danger, whether real or fancied, with at least an outward quiet."

Rather than relaxing and reverting to primitivism like Henry, Dreiser devised schemes for making their life more civilized. He proposed clearing away the natural growth and putting in a lawn. He suggested filtering seawater through sand so they wouldn't have to make frequent trips to the spring on nearby Mystic Island. Then he suggested it would be easier to tow the partially filled barrel behind them rather than placing it in the boat. Removing the rudder, they attempted this and almost came to grief. In the confusion, Henry assumed the role of captain and barked orders at Dreiser. The latter rebelled and shouted back. They yelled at each other in the heeling boat until Dreiser broke into tears. "Come now, let's not quarrel," he said. "My God, man, shall we let a worthless barrel break up our friendship." And they clasped hands emotionally.

Waiting for Jug and Anna to arrive, they spent most of the time in loafing, talking, or reading. They held long philosophical colloquies under the stars, Dreiser in a rocker that was providentially among the sparse furnishings, and Henry stretched out on a blanket and pillow. One night they argued about the nature of the universe. Henry thought it "wise, generous and tender," tending toward "harmony, beauty and order." "Men rob and murder and deceive," he said, "and yet the sum total of their conduct from the beginning until now is progress toward a loving fellowship."

Dreiser scoffed. Rocking in the darkness, he opined that the universe might be an individual, like President McKinley or Chancellor Bismarck, or J. P. Morgan or John D. Rockefeller—but he doubted it had the strength of purpose of such great men. It might well be John L. Sullivan, the prizefighter, "good-natured enough when sober, mellowed by a little liquor, made maudlin by more, and ugly by too much." Or "it might be a crab or a leaf or an atom of the air, and man but a minor subdivision in its make-up." It didn't matter, really. "Any conception of life is good if held in reverence," he said. "Reverence is man's salvation." But modern man lacked an object of reverence. He had outgrown traditional religious beliefs; science had toppled the old gods and left nothing in their place. So much for Spencer's reconciliation of the two.

Those unguarded words, uttered in the solitude of Dumpling Island under the star-seeded heavens, were signs of a spiritual crisis. Many turn-of-the-century Americans faced a similar one, a mental dislocation caused by rapid industrialization. It produced the same ferment that the economic one of the eighties and nineties had, and a similar multiplicity of novel doctrines vied for converts—*Yellow Book* Decadence, the crafts movement, medievalism, the flight to Oriental exoticism, the strenuous life, the warrior mystique, the back-to-nature cult, Christian socialism, and so on. To all of these Dreiser had been exposed in varying degrees, or at least was aware of. But all had this in common: they were reactions against the Prospero of science and the Caliban of industrialism. The naturalist John Burroughs, whom Dreiser interviewed for *Success,* was one of the many who tried to define the contemporary loss of faith.

> How the revelations of science do break in upon the sort of private and domestic view of the universe which mankind have so long held! To many minds it is like being fairly turned out into the cold, and made to face without shield or shelter the eternities and infinities of geologic time and sidereal space. We are no longer cosily housed in pretty little anthropomorphic views of things. The universe is no longer a theater constructed expressly for the drama of man's life and salvation. The race of man becomes the mere ephemera of an hour, like the insects of a summer day. . . . We feel the cosmic chill.

Dreiser knew this ephemeral feeling. "We are insects produced by heat and wither and pass without it," he had written in *Sister Carrie* in another context. The chill of gray days plunged him into gloom; the chill of the cosmic winds affected his inner weather. Stripped of self-esteem by the collapse of his inflated ambitions, he was as vulnerable as Hurstwood after his fall from Chicago celebrity. And he felt himself sinking into that state of apathy and drift he feared and that had given rise to the dark, fictional alter ego.

At last Jug came. They were late meeting the train and found her sitting on her luggage, pouting—at which, Henry reports, Dreiser "pulled her from the trunk and beat her publicly that all men might know he was the master of his house," a description Henry probably intended figuratively but which accurately reflected his own psychological treatment of Maude and, later, Anna.

Her presence was like the return of the sun. She enjoyed the boat ride, loved the island, thought the floor of the cabin perfectly clean, and found the living conditions ever so jolly. Immediately establishing herself in the kitchen, she cooked mouth-watering dishes with the materials at hand. Dreiser proudly made over the kitchen to suit her. When Anna Mallon arrived, he told her, "I found a lot of your trash around here and threw it in the sea. When [Jug] is in a place two minutes, it begins to look like home."

Anna's reaction is not recorded, but this was the first of many such flare-ups between Dreiser and her. He was full of "half-playful, half-cynical jibes and railleries," Henry recalled, and Theodore's sharpest thrusts were aimed at Anna. It was becoming clear that he had hoarded a resentment against her for taking Henry away that winter when he was struggling to write *Sister Carrie*. Jug did not entirely approve of Anna either; she had liked Maude. It was the familiar aftermath of a divorce, when old friends find themselves torn between the new and the discarded partner.

Relieved at least of the housekeeping worries, Dreiser relaxed a bit and made trips to Noank, where he sat on the docks listening to the local fishermen's gossip. One day he heard them talking about a saintly man named Charlie Potter, who was considered a true Christian in that, although he had a family and little money himself, he managed to provide food for the poor. Dreiser was fascinated and sought the man out. In a sketch he wrote not long after, he has Potter explain, "Most men are so tangled up in their own errors and bad ways, and so worried over their seekings, that unless you can set them to giving it's no use. They're always seeking, and they don't know what they want half the time." To Dreiser, Potter represented the epitome of the practicing Christian—undoctrinal, devoted to visiting the sick and comforting the afflicted, like Arch White, like his mother. Here was a man who had discovered the true meaning of life: helping others.

But back on Dumpling Island, the summer visitors were embroiled in most un-Christian bickering. Not only did Anna have to bear Dreiser's caustic attacks, she quarreled with Jug, who must have disapproved strongly of her relationship with Arthur on moral grounds (as did Dreiser, for that matter; after all Maude was a *mother*). At one point Anna and her maid, Brigitte Seery, a pretty Irish immigrant girl who did double duty as chaperone, flounced off to the city. After her departure Dreiser gave Henry his heartfelt apologies and offered to leave. There were tearful self-recriminations all around, and Dreiser promised to stop demanding boiled fish for supper and to eat it fried, as Anna liked it. For his part, Henry begged their forgiveness for his overbearing ways and tiresome preachments on the simple life.

When Anna returned the next weekend, she and Henry had a bruising quarrel that brought buried tensions to the surface. She was angry with him for idling away the summer, doing no work on his novel. She had been supporting him with loans and was afraid he had been corrupted. Henry denied the charge and shouted that he was leaving her. In a poisonous mood, they went sailing, with Anna at the tiller and Henry berating her incompetence, driving her to tears. A storm came up. Weeping and angry, Anna clung to the tiller, vowing to take them back. Henry sat hunched in the bow, fighting his urge to interfere. She succeeded in landing the boat, and, in the aftermath, purged of their anger, they became lovers again—in a chaste way. For Henry was ostentatiously platonic with Anna. Dreiser wondered at their relationship—the "marked absence of that salt of desire and especially that intense avidity for exclusiveness which is the mark sterling of all true passion. . . . He did not enough want to be alone with her."

Of course they had to be cautious, for among the other bizarre goings-on that summer, Anna's mother had come to Noank and maintained a daily vigil of Dumpling Island through a telescope. And she was not alone; a Greek chorus of townspeople joined her, presumably in hopes of seeing the bohemians from the big city disporting themselves in pagan revels. They were probably disappointed.

Henry's attitude toward women was congenitally idealistic, and though he was always carrying on affairs, which he told Maude about, he was not overly interested in the sexual side. He seemed to be seeking in them the innocence of boyhood. In *A Princess of Arcady* the hero, based on himself, has for thirty years kept the torch burning for a youthful sweetheart who broke off the engagement to become a nun. They meet; she is an old woman, beyond all desire. He vows to keep loving the girl he once knew, not the white-haired lady she has become.

At the end of July the Dreisers returned to the city. The differences between Arthur and Theodore had apparently been patched over, but Dreiser, at least, nursed a wound that would not heal. Once again his feckless friend had betrayed him—for a woman. The odd emotion of jealousy Anna aroused in Theodore must have been troubling. He saw in himself feelings for another man that had disturbing implications. He had, in his way, loved Henry more than any other human being save Jug and his mother; now he was wondering if he had made a fool of himself, or worse. Even if there were no homoerotic overtones to his attraction, he had fallen totally for an illusion. As Maude wrote many years later, "It was inevitable that Dreiser should come under the benign influence of the calm, clear gray eyes, the idealism, the reasoning mind of Arthur Henry . . . always ready for adventure, for gay laughter, for hard work when necessary, but ingrained with the . . . fairy-taled happenings of early youth." Now the enchantment was broken, leaving Theodore hurt and angry, betrayed and abandoned.

As for Arthur and Anna and Maude, their three-way relationship also came to a dénouement that summer. Maude, whose tolerance was considerable, knew about Anna, but Arthur assured her that he was no more in love with Anna than he was with his grandmother. So, at Anna's behest, Maude came out from Toledo with Dorothy to join them on the island. One day while Maude was relaxing in a hammock and Anna was sitting cross-legged on the floor sewing, Arthur sprang up from his writing desk and announced that he thought he ought to marry Anna. Maude told him she would not object, but what about Dorothy? Arthur said distractedly, "Lord, I'll take her or you can." "No, Arthur, you will not take her," Maude replied. She could not help remarking that this was an unexpected development, given his protestations that he wasn't in love with Anna. "Well, I'm not," Arthur explained, "but her mother is sitting over there at Noank trying to watch this island with a telescope, and I feel I ought to marry her."

Having pried as much sense out of him as she was going to, Maude went out to talk to Anna, who had fled the cabin. Deeply embarrassed, Anna said wildly, "I wouldn't have Arthur for a million dollars if you want him." Maude said she didn't want him, but warned her about Arthur's casualness when it came to money and his marriage vows. That made no impression on Anna, who wanted Arthur very badly, enough to risk being disinherited by her disapproving mother (which is what eventually happened).

Thus ended the summer on Dumpling Island. An amicable divorce was arranged by Henry's old Chicago journalistic friend Brand Whitlock, who lived in Toledo, practicing law and writing a novel about politics.

After the brief *pro forma* proceedings, Arthur gave Maude a big kiss and told her he deeply loved her for all she had done. He even dedicated his next novel to her—an interesting wrinkle, since Henry had dedicated *A Princess* to Anna three years earlier. He and Anna were joined in a civil ceremony in March 1903 in New York City. Arthur was thirty-five, Anna was forty-one, and she often spoke of him as her lost lamb, her little boy.

36. *Journeys to Altruria*

It is quite true that to the victor belongs the spoils, and to the strong the race, but at the same time it is sad to think that to the weak and vanquished belong nothing.

—Dreiser, "Reflections" (1896)

It may be necessary that some should drudge and slave, and others walk in elegance and conduct the more honored affairs of life, but it certainly makes a grind of things. The drudges are so numerous. It looks so often as though they were held down by lack of advantages and that men might do more for them. They have to struggle so hard for bread. They have to wear such wretched clothes. Their days are all toil, and their nights weariness.

—Dreiser, *Ev'ry Month* (1897)

ack in New York City, his money running low, Dreiser returned to magazine writing, but not to salable articles about lady harp players and trolley trips. He and Henry had exhausted the fruit crop, and in any case they were working separately now. Henry was hatching his book and Dreiser was writing out of a personal vision.

As a measure of how far he had come, Dreiser sold three articles on the down-and-out for, to all places, *Success*. One of them was a spin-off from "Curious Shifts of the Poor," focusing on the character of the Captain, who conducted his nightly auction in the theater district to raise money for the city's legions of Hurstwoods. Another was an inspirational tale about a cripple, and the third described how the lives of tenement dwellers had become twisted under the never-ending pressure of economic survival. Although such stories were somewhat downbeat, Orison Swett Marden published them, billing the one about the Captain as a "distinct commentary on the social conditions of our day." The old success-peddler was sensing the winds of change. The national mood was increasingly progressive; a popular backlash against big business was

building, and in a year's time S. S. McClure would launch the muckraking era in popular journalism.

As for the change in Dreiser, it stemmed, as already mentioned, from
his desire to write serious stories with a social or ethical moral; he was
seeking to divine the emotional springs of altruism. But it also rose out
of the inversion of his fortunes, which concentrated his mind on poverty.
The elastic had gone out of his youthful ambition; the golden prizes that
he had once pursued—money, fame, artistic glory, the love of women—
had vanished like a dream. Now, even the path to a modest literary respectability (let alone glory) seemed barred. And so he increasingly identified with the poor, the victims of the "economic fact." Not coincidentally,
the novel he was working on had immersed him in memories of his own
childhood poverty, and the upwelling pity—for himself, for his mother
and sisters—spilled over to the huddled masses in their tenements and
sweatshops.

Brooding as always about religion, Dreiser sought answers to social
questions in the nondoctrinal sphere of social Christianity, encapsulated
in the verse from St. James that he quoted in at least two stories he wrote
at this time: "Pure religion and undefiled before God and the Father is
this. To visit the fatherless and widows in their affliction, *and* to keep
himself unspotted from the world." Such ideals were not new with him.
He had written of the duty of the wealthy to help the poor, the culls and
discards of the industrial system, of whom his father had been one. In
his last years old Paul had been cared for by his family; if Mame and
Brennan hadn't taken him in, he might have gone to the poor farm. But
Dreiser was beginning to wonder if perhaps society had an obligation to
care for such people.

The two sketches he wrote upon his return from Noank show a renewed preoccupation with the apolitical Christian socialism that Howells
advocated. One was Charlie Potter's story, which he called "The Disciple of Noank." Potter is regarded as something of an eccentric by the
townsfolk, a truly good man but impractical, since in a competitive world
you must "look out for Number One." Dreiser searched out Potter in
order to hear his philosophy. Plying him with the same kind of leading
questions he used in his *Success* interviews, Dreiser discovered that Potter
had found in altruism the secret of happiness. When Potter told him that
charity leads to greater human brotherhood and proclaimed, "All the misery is in lack of sympathy one with another," the interlocutor let slip a
brief aside: "Yes, I thought, looking down on the mills and the driving
force of self-interest—on greed, lust, love of pleasure, all their fantastic
yet moving dreams." Charity fosters the spread of human brotherhood,

*John Paul Dreiser in his
seventies, at the home of his
daughter Mame and son-in-law
Austin Brennan in Rochester,
New York, where he died on
Christmas Day 1900. Soon after,
Dreiser began* Jennie Gerhardt.

(EU)

*Louise Dresser (née Louise
Kerlin), Paul's adopted sister,
a vaudeville headliner when she
introduced "My Gal Sal," and
later a movie actress. Her rapid
rise under Paul's tutelage provided a model for Carrrie's career.*

(Courtesy of Vera Dreiser)

The cover of Ev'ry Month, *the song magazine
for which TD was "editor-arranger" and wrote
his Spencerian "Reflections" as "The Prophet."*
(UP)

*TD as a free-lance writer,
in the late 1890s.*

(IU)

*Jug as a young matron,
circa 1906.*

(Courtesy of Vera Dreiser)

*"Taken bout the time I wrote
Sister Carrie—1900."*

*Dumpling Island, just a few
hundred yards off the shore
in Noank, where Arthur and
TD spent the summer of 1902.
Here the Henrys' marriage
went on the rocks; later, after
the publication of* An Island
Cabin, *so did Dreiser and
Henry's friendship.*

*Anna Mallon (left), who lured
Henry away from Dreiser at
a crucial time. Her Infant
Class typed* Sister Carrie.
(Courtesy of Donald T. Oakes)

*Arthur Henry, who encouraged
Dreiser to write* Carrie. *"You
are to me my other self a very
excellent Dreiser minus some
of my defects. . . . If I could not
be what I am, I would be you."*
(Cornell University)

*The House of Four Pillars in
Maumee, Ohio, where Theo
and Jug, and Arthur and Maude
Henry, spent a halcyon summer
in 1899. According to Maude,
Dreiser began* Sister Carrie *here.*
(Courtesy of Donald T. Oakes)

Memorandum of Agreement

Theodore Dreiser Esq., of *New York* —

hereinafter called "the author," being the author and proprietor of a work entitled *"The Flesh & the Spirit" or Sister Carrie*

hereby grants and assigns to Doubleday, Page & Co. the above mentioned work, and also all rights of translation, abridgment, dramatization, selection, and other rights of, in, or to said work. Doubleday, Page & Co. shall also have the exclusive right to take out copyright for the said work, and to obtain all renewals of copyright and to hold said copyrights and renewals, and to publish said work during the terms thereof.

No payment shall be made by Doubleday, Page & Co. for permission gratuitously given to publish extracts from said work to benefit the sale thereof ; but if Doubleday, Page & Co. receive any compensation for the publication of extracts therefrom, or for translations, abridgments, or dramatizations, such compensation shall be equally divided between the parties hereto.

The author guarantees that the work is original, and in no way an infringement upon the copyright of others. Also that it contains no libelous statements. And that the author and __his__ legal representatives shall and will hold harmless the said Doubleday, Page & Co. from all suits and all manner of claims and proceedings which may be taken on the ground that the said work is such violation or contains anything libelous.

Doubleday, Page & Co., in consideration of the rights granted, agree to publish the work at their own expense, in such a style or styles as they deem most advisable, and to pay the author, or __his__ legal representatives, a royalty of ten per cent. on the retail price, cloth style, on all copies sold ~~after until 1500~~ copies have been sold; 12½% on the next 1000, and 15% ~~on all subsequent copies~~ ~~over 3000~~

It is understood and agreed that no royalty shall be paid on any copies given away, or destroyed, or sold at a price below cost. Also that but half royalty shall be paid on copies sold in foreign countries, at special edition prices.

Expense of author's corrections exceeding ten per cent. of cost of composition shall be charged against the author's account, and it is agreed that the author shall furnish an index, if required, at __his__ expense.

Statements of sale shall be rendered semi-annually, in the months of February and August, and settlement thereof shall be made in cash four months later.

It is agreed that Doubleday, Page & Co. shall furnish to the author free of charge ten copies of the work as published ; and should the author desire any more copies for __his__ own use, they shall be supplied at one-half the retail price. It is understood and agreed that any copies thus purchased shall not be sold again.

It is further understood and agreed that after a lapse of two years should the work, in the opinion of the said Doubleday, Page & Co., become unsalable, the said Doubleday, Page & Co. may then melt up or destroy the plates. It is understood and agreed that in this case the author may purchase the said plates at cost should __he__ desire to do so. In case the author buys the plates under this provision he shall not have the right to use any illustrations furnished by Doubleday, Page & Co. without special agreement between the parties hereto.

This contract may be assigned by either party, but only as a whole, and no part of their respective interests shall be assigned by either party. No assignment of the author shall be valid, as against Doubleday, Page & Co., unless and until they shall have received due evidence thereof in writing.

Executed this *Twentieth*

day of *August* 19*00*

Theodore Dreiser

Witness :

Frank Norris

Doubleday Page Company

e contract for The Flesh and *Spirit between Theodore Dreiser d Doubleday, Page, witnessed Frank Norris. The author has ned in* his *title*—Sister Carrie.

Two views of TD during his editing career.

(IU)

Jug and Theo in their new apartment, around the time he became editor in chief of The Delineator.

(UP)

which in turn would counteract the exploitation in those mills. Yet Dreiser also recognizes the power of those "moving dreams."

In the second Noank story, "A Heart Bowed Down," he tells of another charitable man, once a rich and respected figure in the community, who has been eclipsed by a rival, the owner of the local shipyard and other businesses. Now reduced to operating a general store that is dusty and cluttered with junk and flyspecked merchandise, he has become a religious crank, a virtual hermit embittered by the loss of his former eminence and obsessed with the idea that all the townspeople who deserted him for his rival must ask his forgiveness. Into this figure Dreiser poured some of his own loneliness and bitterness. Ostracized for his beliefs, the old man is a victim of the power of money and respectable society—like the artist who stubbornly clings to his independence.

The artist is the hero of another story written around this time, a portrait of William Louis Sonntag, Jr., who was not a victim of an intolerant society—indeed, he was on the verge of brilliant success—but of the caprices of fate. Nonetheless Dreiser identified with him as a symbol of youthful promise cut short—as his own seemed to be. The story closes with an elegiac image of a lamp being dimmed and a threnody to youthful hopes: "We toil so much, we dream so richly, we hasten so fast, and, lo! the green door is opened. We are through it, and its grassy surface has sealed us forever from all which apparently we so much crave—even as, breathlessly, we are still running." He reverted to the image of death as a door; on the other side was the agonizing ineffable mystery.

He sold two of these stories with no trouble. The faithful Duffy took "The Disciple of Noank" for *Ainslee's*, changing the title to the more "scriptural" "A Doer of the Word." John Kendrick Bangs, the humorist who was also editor of *Harper's Weekly*, accepted the Sonntag story, titling it "The Color of Today" and asking Dreiser to send him more material. Only "A Heart Bowed Down" failed to find a home, probably because of its technical shortcomings. If Dreiser had become a "pariah," as John Phillips predicted, the word still hadn't reached every editorial office.

The only politically controversial article he wrote was "A Mayor and His People," a profile of the socialist mayor of Bridgeport, depicted as an honest and enlightened public servant who is cast out by powerful economic interests he has offended. He sent it to *McClure's*, which had accepted "A True Patriarch." Lincoln Steffens, who was acting as managing editor, wrote a detailed critique of the piece and recommended that the author "make it over into what we want." That touched off an exchange of letters, with Steffens insisting that Dreiser must make his story "either a definite account of the facts or a fiction story. . . . As it stands it is neither one nor the other." Dreiser did a bit of fiddling with the piece but stubbornly ignored Steffens' instructions. The latter returned it, saying, "it is plain that . . . anything of yours is to be taken as left, not changed."

At that time, Steffens was about to begin the investigations for a series of articles on municipal corruption that ran in *McClure's* as "The Shame of the Cities" and caused a sensation, so he favored the reportorial approach. Dreiser, however, saw reform as part of the great Spencerian dialectic of action and reaction, bubbling up out of the seething caldron of conflicting self-interests. He was not interested in writing exposés. He supported the worthy end of "municipal socialism," as practiced by Mayor Sam Jones of Toledo and others, but he had come to regard art as separate from politics. If Dreiser contemplated politics at all, it was as a corrupt, Darwinian spectacle. The mayor was an exemplar of the fate of all idealists rather than a hero in the cause of clean government, and municipal ownership of trolley lines, water and gas companies. As the mayor says, "People are not so much interested in me or you or your or my ideals in their behalf, as they are in strength, an interesting spectacle. And they are easily deceived. These big fighting corporations with their attorneys and politicians and newspapers make me look weak—puny. So the people forget me." And Dreiser concludes that the mayor failed because "The fates did not fight for him as they do for some, those fates that ignore the billions and billions of others who fail." And he adds a personal note: "Yet are not all lives more or less failures . . . ? We compromise so much with everything—our dreams and all."

In later years, Dreiser, reminiscing to Dorothy Dudley about his career as a specials writer, explained, "I did not want to fritter life away over magazine articles. The best a publicist could hope to become would be an Ida Tarbell, a Ray Stannard Baker, a Lincoln Steffens." And so the muckrakers lost a recruit to their ranks, and Dreiser put more distance between himself and current trends in the magazine world.

In an effort to revive his own compromised dream, he again inquired of Doubleday, Page what it would charge him for the plates and unsold stock of *Sister Carrie*. Ripley Hitchcock, an editor at Appleton, wrote him to praise *Carrie* and suggest that if Dreiser could write another story that was "less drastic," he would be interested in publishing it; then his firm would reissue *Carrie*. (Hitchcock had a precedent for this approach. He had turned down Stephen Crane's *Maggie: A Girl of the Streets* in manuscript but published a trade edition after the success of *The Red Badge of*

Courage, which he also handled.) For some reason Hitchcock could not follow through on the offer, but his interest made Dreiser think more seriously about the possibility of a reincarnation for *Carrie.* Doubleday was not cooperative. The company asked $500 for plates and unbound books. As J. W. Thompson of the firm informed Dreiser in a letter dated September 23, 1901, even that price represented a loss to the company of between $150 and $200.

Dreiser, who had nothing like $500 in the bank, talked about taking out a note for the amount, which was agreeable to Thompson if Theodore could find a financially reputable individual to cosign it. Then fortune's wheel took another spin. Rutger B. Jewett, trade book editor at the J. F. Taylor Company, a young house, was interested in publishing Dreiser's second book and then reissuing *Sister Carrie.* "I believe in you and in your work," Jewett wrote him, "and intend to make it possible for you to finish that second book by advancing enough for you to live on while you do it." Dreiser leaped at the chance. Under the contract signed September 30, J. F. Taylor agreed to buy the plates and unsold stock of *Sister Carrie* from Doubleday for $500. It also undertook to reissue the book "either for the coming winter or spring trade, whichever seems the more advisable, under the same name or some suitable title." In return Dreiser gave the company an option on his next novel—the story of Jennie Gerhardt, of which he had supplied a synopsis. In a separate letter of agreement, dated November 6, Taylor promised to pay Dreiser $100 a month on account for a year.

Taylor had founded his firm in 1898, primarily to reprint European and American classics, but he had recently formed a small trade department, headed by Jewett. Though Jewett was most interested in *Carrie,* Taylor, a cautious businessman, was worried that Doubleday had "killed" the book. As Jewett explained, Doubleday, Page had sprinkled enough copies in the stores so that booksellers would say, "Well, we gave it a trial, and still have the books we ordered." And so Taylor suggested a title change to make the book seem to be a new one.

In the wake of the agreement with Taylor, Dreiser received some heartening news from abroad. The reviews of the Heinemann edition surpassed his wildest imaginings. What is more, they came out together, an authoritative, nearly unanimous chorus of yeas. Nearly all of the major literary organs were represented. The *Spectator* praised the "really powerful" study of Hurstwood and called *Sister Carrie* "an engrossing and depressing book." The *Academy* found it "thoroughly good, alike in accurate and synthetic observation, in human sympathy, in lyric appeal and in dramatic power." The London *Daily Mail* eschewed British understatement: "At last a really strong novel has come from America; a novel almost great because of its relentless purpose, its power to compel emotion, its marvelous simplicity."

The most impressive review, though, was by the novelist and poet Theodore Watts-Dunton in the *Athenaeum*. *Sister Carrie*, he writes, is "a broad, vivid picture of men and manners in middle-class New York and Chicago" and "a thorough and really masterly study of the moral, physical and social deterioration of one Hurstwood." And he summed up: "it strikes a key-note and is typical both in the faults of its manner and in the wealth and diversity of its matter, of the great country, which gave it birth." Readers of *Sister Carrie*, he said, will find a "permanent place upon their shelves for the book beside M. Zola's 'Nana.' "

For the first time, a critic, British or American, recognized the plain, authentic voice of America in Dreiser's novel—sensed the extravagant energy of its cities and the commonplace yet poignant hungers of its people. Here at last, a London critic said, was a true American novel, one whose awkward style faithfully mirrored the country it described.

The British reviews, as Dreiser later wrote, have "done me proud." But they were far too late to resurrect *Sister Carrie* in America. And although the Heinemann edition got off to a fast start in the stalls, it ended up selling only about one thousand copies and earning the author some eighty dollars in royalties.

So Jug added the London clippings to her *Sister Carrie* scrapbook, to yellow and fade like the rose Theodore once sent her and which she saved all her life. Dreiser turned his restless eyes southward. He decided to flee winter's spirit-deadening chill for the Blue Ridge Mountains and dig in for a siege of writing. After receiving his first monthly check from Taylor in early November, he closed his apartment, packed Jug off to her family, and headed for Bedford City, Virginia, near Roanoke.

Sometime before he left, he must have opened his door to a representative of the *City Directory*, preparing the listings for the 1902 edition, which covered the period from July 31, 1901, to July 31, 1902. Dreiser's occupation was not given as "author," as it had been in previous directories, but as "clerk." Was it a joke? Had he taken a temporary job? Whatever his motive, Dreiser had stripped himself of the epaulettes of authorship and slunk away in the drab anonymity of a clerk—Melville's Bartleby the Scrivener reincarnate—to begin what would be a year of flight from his personal Furies.

37. The Crannies of the World

Here I be, full of glee—rich as, rich as—rich can be, or something to that effect. Oh you ought to breathe in this sweet thin air. Lord a' mighty it's great.

—Dreiser to Mary Annabel Fanton Roberts (1901)

nce he was out of New York, the reliable drug of change took effect and Dreiser's spirits soared. Bedford City was "home like, southern and high and dry," he wrote J. F. Taylor. He found a good boardinghouse, and his room had a view of the mountains, a great improvement over Blackwells Island. Mrs. Clayton, his landlady, set a bountiful table, and his appetite was sharp. On November 14 he wrote to Mary Annabel Fanton Roberts, who was editing the MS of the Jennie Gerhardt story, that he was considering abdominal surgery to increase his capacity for the steaks, biscuits, waffles, and other delicacies Mrs. Clayton served up. He noted approvingly that a mild winter was promised and rhapsodized over the mountains—"great towering lonely figures with a blue haze always hanging over them." In such a setting, he felt certain that his "malarial feeling" would be replaced by a "desire to work."

The reference to malarial feeling is Dreiser's first to the general sense of debility that would dog him for the next year. There is no evidence that he actually had malaria; perhaps it was the aftermath of a serious case of flu. He was trying to give a medical label to a cluster of complaints—apathy, aches and pains, and increasingly frequent bouts of insomnia, that old nemesis.

But in Bedford City, the illness, whatever it was, went into remission. The spectacular scenery of the Blue Ridge Mountains and the pristine air intoxicated him. As though to make himself psychologically at home, however, he painted in a bleak Dreiserian backdrop in a letter to Mrs. Roberts: "the deep blue blacks of the dome, picked out with millions and millions of stars. How they do glisten. Underneath is this little town, its cottages hugging the ground and the soft glow of the windows seeming to struggle in a feeble way against the immensity of the blind universe without. —Oh the little lamps, the wee little humans! How they struggle between the crannies of the world."

Jauntily he told her to send him the manuscript she was working on "heavily edited. . . . Pull it together close—everything can go except the grip. That I must have in it." Part of his reason for egging Mrs. Roberts on was that he was already getting some gentle prodding from his new publishers. A letter from Jewett had arrived almost as soon as Theodore did, passing along some suggestions of Taylor's regarding the novel. This was followed a week later by another from Jewett containing an additional advisory from his boss, relating to the proposed new edition of *Sister Carrie*. Dreiser replied directly to Taylor on November 25. He told the publisher that his spirits were high, that he had regained his "full interest in the idea" of his novel, and that he was determined "to live up not only to the letter but the spirit of our agreement. I want to complete a good novel on time and there you are."

He must have felt like he was reliving a bad dream when he read this sentence in Jewett's first letter, however: "To the majority of readers some moral coloring seems essential. One of the criticisms for instance which some of the women readers have brought against your story of Carrie is that it points no moral." Taylor was concerned that Dreiser would not play up sufficiently the reasons for the Kane family's rejection of Jennie when they learn she is Lester's mistress. Or, as Jewett had put it: ". . . the man's family treated the woman as they did . . . because, from their point of view, they could do nothing else. . . . She had transgressed social law and therefore must be made to feel her sin. . . . As you sketched your second story to me, the moral was on every page but the reading public needs a certain amount of explanation."

There is no reason to think that Dreiser was dissimulating when he assured Taylor that the idea that Lester's family would reject Jennie "accords with my own exactly." The Kanes were, after all, respectable Cincinnati gentry. But Taylor seemed to be saying their voice should be the author's. Also, the fact that Taylor raised the point shows he apprehended that Dreiser would create another Carrie—one who rises by falling. So, while Taylor's "suggestion" could be regarded as sensible enough, it could have planted in Dreiser's mind the worry that his supposedly liberal new publishers were Frank Doubledays under the skin. Such fears could not have been helpful at this stage, when he needed to regain his original enthusiasm, pick up the dropped thread of the story, and follow it wherever it led. With no Arthur Henry to serve as a sounding board, no Elmer Gates to provide supportive "scientific evidence," Dreiser was thrown back on his own self-doubts.

Not that Taylor was issuing ultimatums. He was, he wrote on December 4, merely offering a suggestion, and he assured Dreiser that "in every case [we] would leave the final decision in your hands." But Taylor revealed how conventional his literary taste was: "It seems to me that in writing such powerful books as you do, the book should be written with some purpose other than merely giving a picture of life, for the reason that the books are bound to have in time a tremendous influence. This suggested to me the idea of pointing a strong moral in your second book." Underscoring a moral was not Dreiser's way; he believed that a true picture of life was in itself moral. Experience was the teacher; life must be shown in all its messy, plethoric complexity—not poured into moral molds. Taylor's real concern was for the feminine audience that "controls the destinies of so many novels." From the standpoint of a publisher still living in the Victorian era, that attitude made good business sense, but the suggestions were ill-timed, raising doubts when Dreiser needed encouragement.

Then there was the matter of *Sister Carrie*. Taylor felt, Jewett reported, that the relationship between Carrie and Ames should be developed into a love story in order to "win a much warmer audience" for the book. In a "thoroughly womanly way," Jewett explained, Carrie would confess to Ames that she loved him and suggest marriage. But Ames would turn her down because of her past. Cruel, perhaps, but "it is exactly the position that 99 men out of every 100 would take." Not that Jewett approved of such a view, but it was the way of the world—"simply the damnable result of a dual code of ethics, one for woman, another for man." The change would be a "little" one, which would not affect the main outline of the book, and the outcome would be the same: "Carrie would not marry the man just as you do not allow her to, only more would be made of the situation . . . and vital color given to the picture."

Dreiser replied noncommittally that while the suggestion was "equally potential" with that regarding Kane's family, he was unable to attend to it at present because he was "straining every nerve—bending every energy" to complete his second novel. "No one could be more open to thoughtful suggestions than I am," he assured his publisher. "I try to steer my course by the light that I can get from all sources."

Jewett must have scented evasion, for he returns to the proposal in a subsequent letter. This time, however, he envisions Carrie nobly refusing to marry Ames "because of the mistakes of her past life. That her experiences, shame, suffering, and empty triumphs could have made her big enough for this sacrifice is not only possible but probable. In fact, I know it to be the case with just such a woman on the New York stage to-day." While the revision seemed only a minor change to Jewett, Dreiser could not have seen it that way.

In his letter of December 4, Taylor also suggested postponing publication of *Sister Carrie*. Jewett had led Dreiser to believe that the new edition would be out the following spring. Now Taylor was telling him that "our experience has taught us that it is almost impossible to bring out a book that has once been on the market, unless something has occurred in the interim which would insure the success of the reissue." Applying this principle to *Sister Carrie*, he thought they should hold off until after the new novel had "made a success," creating a demand for Dreiser's earlier work. Shades of Walter Hines Page!

Taylor had in effect introduced a new condition into their agreement—that Dreiser's second novel be a success. Though Theodore's reply has been lost, it must have shown flashes of his old truculent self, for Jewett felt compelled to write soothingly, "I do not wonder after your experience with Doubleday that you feel suspicious of possible unfair treatment in the case of this book. We want however to do what is perfectly square and honorable with you." The firm stood ready "to issue the book again in its present form for you this spring if you wish," but in view of reports from the company's salesmen, it would be best not to republish *Sister Carrie* without the requested changes, including a new title.

Shaken by the rumblings from New York, he made little progress on his novel in Bedford City. His initial optimism rapidly dissipated; he also missed Jug. He was so lonely that he became friendly with a black tailor and dry cleaner named J. E. Bowler. Actually, Bowler was a remarkable man, so if loneliness drew Dreiser to him, it was soon replaced by liking and respect. Intelligent and ambitious, Bowler was a strong supporter of civil rights in the Booker T. Washington sense of self-improvement—without overstepping the color line and presuming he was as good as a white man.

Their acquaintance flowered into a sporadic correspondence that continued over the next decade. (In one of those letters, Bowler notes that it was the first time he had ever written to a white man on matters having nothing to do with business.) Bowler found Dreiser to be a man of "large sympathy." They talked of philosophy (what else with Dreiser?) and of Bowler's fierce ambition to better himself. Seeing in his new friend his own youthful drive to succeed, Dreiser encouraged him, telling him (as Bowler later recalled), "you would be disappointed in me, if in the future you didn't hear of some good achievement of mine," and offering to help him obtain a tailor's apprenticeship. Though Dreiser's troubles deterred him from being of any assistance on the latter score, he sent Bowler uplifting books and continued to cheer him on.

After a month of futile effort in Bedford City, Dreiser fled to Missouri to spend the holidays with the White family. During a stopover in St. Louis he was interviewed by a reporter for the *Post-Dispatch*, and it was then that he made his first public mention of Neltje Doubleday's alleged role in suppressing *Sister Carrie*. He did not, however, cast her as the sole villain of the piece. Rather, he told the reporter only that Neltje had taken "a violent dislike to it." Her husband then read the MS, agreed with her, and sought to rescind a "signed" contract. Theodore described the critical reception of *Sister Carrie* in America as favorable. The friendly reporter, anxious to help one of the brethren, laid it on thick: "The newspapers, in fact, hailed Dreiser as the producer of a masterpiece of naturalism." Then, of course, came the English reviews: "At this point Mr. Dreiser's triumph really began." And, as already mentioned, Dreiser defended his book against charges of immorality, which had occurred "in America (not in England)." He did not mention—at least the reporter did not—the reissue of *Sister Carrie*, or, indeed, the new novel he was writing. Was he now having doubts that he would finish it?

At any rate, the puff probably went down well in Montgomery City. From Dreiser's description of Arch White in the semifictional "A True Patriarch," his father-in-law had little use for fame or riches; still, he must have felt paternal concern about his daughter's welfare. Good reviews were nice, and an article in the *Post-Dispatch* even better; but Dreiser's financial prospects could not have looked too secure at this point. He no longer even had a permanent address, and Jug was forced to live at home. Such things a father could understand, while glowing British reviews and contracts for future books were a distant urban fantasy. Dreiser's increased moodiness must also have given Archibald cause for concern.

Still, in the warmth of the White family circle at Christmastime, Dreiser cheered up and sent Duffy a description of the festivities as well as thanks for a copy of Walt Whitman's *Leaves of Grass* and a testament of friendship. He also passed around to his in-laws the Christmas issue of William Reedy's *Mirror*, which contained his story "Butcher Rogaum's Door." And the previous week Raftery's article had appeared, providing chapter and verse for Theodore's claim that his book had not had a fair chance.

Undoubtedly he paid the *Mirror* offices a visit; he had much to thank Reedy for. The corpulent editor had not only written the most perceptive contemporary review of *Sister Carrie;* he had done some strenuous literary logrolling for it. Even though he had not been surprised that the book was a commercial failure, Reedy constantly sought to reassure Dreiser that the novel was a great one and would eventually win the recognition it deserved.

In one letter, for example, Reedy claims he knows at least fifteen people who thought it a "tip-top novel." He adds that he heard an old lady denounce the portrayal of Drouet because she had seen "just such drummers . . . doing just such things," and told Dreiser he should take that as a compliment. When the first English reviews came out, Reedy took note of them in the *Mirror* and proudly reminded readers that he had been one of the first to praise the novel. And when Dreiser continued to write him gloomy letters, he dispatched a prescription of optimism (at a time of personal tragedy—his wife was mortally ill): "If life wears the aspect you endeavor to reflect in your letter . . . the whole thing is hardly of enough importance to worry about it. Everything is for the best, as we come to find out as we grow a little older. At least I am not able to look at the matter in any other way."

Richard Duffy also continued to write Dreiser letters full of positive thinking, accompanied by books he thought his friend would like and newspaper articles. In response to the Christmas letter he noted, "One does not often get so much of a purely personal statement from you" and proceeded to ramble on about how both of them looked far afield in the world but always returned to the old friends. In an earlier letter, however, Duffy may have unwittingly stirred up bad feelings between Dreiser and another old face—Arthur Henry. Henry's account of the summer on Dumpling Island was being serialized in the New York *Post,* and Duffy enclosed a clipping of the first installment. Henry had told Dreiser the previous August that John Phillips had encouraged him to make a book out of the island experiences but probably did not convey how fully he intended to record them.

In February he and Jug struck out on a restless odyssey through the South, searching for a pleasant place to work while absorbing the therapeutic benefits of travel, that "boon to the weary and distressed . . . which, because of its boundless prodigality of fact and incident, causes the mind to forget," as he had written in *Sister Carrie.* Dreiser was looking for another kind of therapy as well. From Red Sulphur Springs, West Virginia, he reported to Duffy that the water "is supposed to be good for insomnia. Hence my presence." They had been traveling so much that he received two of Duffy's letters at once. Dreiser wrote that he was "interested" in Henry's "Island Cabin" story and wondered if McClure would bring it out as a book. "Hen has rather gone out of my life recently and so a bit of news now and then would be welcome." Duffy was Dreiser's only New York connection now. The novel was "proceeding slowly but proceeding."

Duffy had cheered him with a sheaf of Thomas Hardy's poems, which Dreiser found "rousingly beautiful." Hardy was "the greatest figure in all English literature," an appreciation that confirms the suspicion that the Wessex chronicler was one of the major influences on Dreiser's poetry, along with William Ernest Henley and A. E. Housman. Most prescient of all was Dreiser's judgment on Whitman: "Time will put him above all other American poets up to now."

Duffy's next letter, dated February 10, 1901, shows the Dreisers had not found the great good place as yet, for he asks how the "one night stand regimen" was agreeing with them. Duffy comments enviously on the "bully kind of life" they must be living which provided the constant changes of scene the artist needed. Why, he opined, Dreiser must be "pretty near easy in mind" by now. Any other news? Oh yes, Henry's "Island Cabin" articles would definitely be published as a book by McClure, Phillips.

Jug's comments on their bully life go unrecorded. After a few weeks of jerking about, they landed in Hinton, West Virginia, a town near another hot springs. Perhaps Theodore's mysterious malaise could be cured by some magic waters. He persisted in believing his troubles were physical. But what if they were not?

38. The Wild Ass's Skin

I wandered here & there in Virginia & West Virginia, unable to write. My mood made worse by the fact that the money that was being sent me was being used up & I was getting no where.

—Dreiser, "Down Hill and Up" (1920)

he Dreisers remained in Hinton for about seven weeks. Now gloom pervaded his reports to Jewett, and the editor wrote him on March 17, "The last time I saw you I told you that if you did not learn how to laugh some times just for the sake of relief you would go crazy, or die of grief."

What provoked Jewett's good advice was a small misunderstanding which reveals the pressure Dreiser was working under. In his last letter Dreiser had sought to explain his slow progress and alluded cryptically to "a very sad period of entanglement" he had been going through for the past three weeks, adding that he was now "beginning to see the light." Jewett had replied breezily, "What is the trouble? Your character in the novel, or real life?" The touchy author was annoyed by his editor's bantering hint that he was neglecting his book for an amorous entanglement when it was a literary one and huffed that he was devoting all his efforts to completing his book on time. Jewett replied that if he had been dissatisfied with Dreiser's progress he would have told him so without resorting to "innuendo." When Dreiser mentioned an entanglement, he had naturally asked, "like the French judge . . . 'Well, who is the woman?' "

What Jug would have thought of Jewett's little joke, had she seen the letter, is another matter. Devoted as she was, her life was getting no easier, as her husband grew more restless and moody. He soon tired of the charms of Hinton and moved on to Lynchburg, Virginia, leaving her behind. Not liking it there, he continued to Charlottesville. Thinking he was still in Lynchburg, Jug sent him a postcard there saying she would arrive on the No. 4 train and that he should meet her at the station. Either he had forgotten to tell her of his move or his letter doing so crossed her card in the mails. In any case, she must have had some anxious moments at the Lynchburg station. It may be that Dreiser did have a seizure of temporary amnesia about his wife—that he was subconsciously abandoning her. Jug was a solace to him but a financial burden. To put it bluntly, one could live more cheaply than two. At any rate, she returned to Missouri not long after this, leaving Dreiser to fight it out alone in Charlottesville for two more months.

Thrown back on himself, Dreiser's distrust of his publisher flared up anew when he read the March issue of the trade publication *The Bookman*. A gossip column carried several items of direct interest to him. The first, a "blind" story that mentioned no names, was clearly about the suppression of *Sister Carrie* and its ultimate vindication by the English reviewers. The account blames Mrs. Doubleday more directly than the version Dreiser gave to the reporter from the *Post-Dispatch*, but it adds that Frank Doubleday "was heard to say" that although he knew the book would succeed critically, he "preferred that the stigma of its success should not rest upon his house." Since that anecdote echoes what Doubleday told Arthur Henry at their first confrontation in the summer of 1900, Dreiser must have guessed that his former partner was the informant. The next two items confirm such a surmise since they are about Henry. One recounts the difficulties Henry had publishing his first novel (the deplorable *Nicholas Blood, Candidate*, though the title is not mentioned), and the second is a puff for his forthcoming book, *An Island Cabin*, due to appear shortly.

The final item, however, could have come only from Jewett. It reports that *Sister Carrie* would be republished in the spring by J. F. Taylor & Co. "in more attractive form, and, let us hope, under a new and more significant title." Furthermore, the author intends to make some changes in it; specifically, he will expand the role of the third man in the book with whom Carrie is involved, "whose path crosses her own at the close of the book, but in an abortive manner, which leaves an impression of artistic incompleteness and faulty observation."

Replying to Dreiser's query, Jewett confirmed that he had indeed talked to *The Bookman*'s stringer, "Cooper of the Commercial Advertiser," whom he described as an admirer of *Sister Carrie* "very keen to strike a blow for the book wherever and whenever opportunity opens." Jewett fed Cooper a story about the changes, making it appear that they were the author's idea. Since Dreiser hadn't agreed to make the changes, he must have found the promise of them disturbing. He was also anxious to know when Henry's book would appear, wondering what Arthur would write about the disastrous summer on Dumpling Island.

Dreiser told Jewett in early April that he could expect the novel's opening chapters shortly. Jewett replied that production of the book must begin in June if it were to be out in September; any later in the fall would mean lost sales. He prodded Dreiser to come up with a title, but when Dreiser suggested *Jennie Gerhardt,* Jewett requested something more "abstract" and accused his author of having a fatal fascination for heroines with diminutive first names. If he did use her in the title, he should use her formal first name, Jane. Thus, he might call the book "Jane Gebhardt."

The misspelling detonated another minor explosion in Charlottesville, and Jewett was obliged to reassure his thin-skinned author that it was an innocent typo. Again he begged Dreiser to erase the Doubleday past: "You have a mind . . . that needs filtering to remove the taint of old suspicion." Dreiser cooled off and suggested that the novel be called *The Transgressor,* which Jewett liked, perhaps because it had a strong moral ring to it.

Under normal circumstances, those minor outbursts by Dreiser would have meant a return to his old form as gadfly of editors and publishers. But his were the plaints of a deflated, rather than a swollen ego; their origin was in his persisting fears that his publisher would find his book immoral and his growing doubts that he could meet his deadline. He was using Jewett as a dartboard for his anxieties.

The obligation to finish his new book in time for fall publication was becoming more onerous with each passing day. To keep Jewett temporarily happy, Dreiser set in motion a small deception. He gave his editor the impression that the opening chapters were new, or at least a complete reworking of an earlier draft. Actually, the ten chapters he forwarded at the end of April were those Anna Mallon's employees had typed the previous spring. Following his quarrel with Anna that summer, Dreiser had engaged a new typist, a New York woman named M. E. Gordinnier, but had not sent her anything. Under the impression that the ten chapters he had received were newly typed material, Jewett advised him: "Edit your chapters before sending to the typewriter; it will save time in the long run." Nevertheless, he had finished reading chapters one through ten with "a strong sense of eagerness for chapter 11. Chapter 3 is a gem!"

It also appears that Jug did the cutting on those chapters. More than twenty years later, she recalled her role in editing *The Transgressor:* "Every word was so precious to me that I wanted to add as an addenda every paragraph that I cut out of it down in Virginia that spring."

But she did little on the first ten chapters, written in January 1901, which had flowed from Dreiser's pencil as rapidly as the initial chapters of *Sister Carrie.* The trouble, the "error in character analysis," he had mentioned to George P. Brett, came later in the story. *The Transgressor* is a novel about a poor girl from Columbus, Ohio—Jennie—who meets the distinguished Senator Brander, a somewhat Bryanesque figure, while she and her mother are working as cleaning women at the principal hotel in Columbus.

Brander, a man of fifty, is attracted to the eighteen-year-old Jennie's wholesome beauty and takes pity on her family, which is suffering severe poverty because the father, William, a German immigrant glassblower, is out of work. Brander begins taking her out, and, despite the great difference in their ages, he proposes marriage. The neighbors, however, are critical. They "saw only a family, in the Gerhardts, given to making mistakes"—like the Dreisers in Warsaw. Gerhardt, a strict Lutheran under the thumb of puritanical Pastor Wundt, is ashamed. He berates his wife for her moral laxity in bringing up the children ("Such a wife! Such a home! Such a family! . . . She would make streetwalkers of them all!") and forbids Brander to see Jennie again.

But Sebastian—"Bass"—the oldest son, who is working as an installment-payment collector à la Theodore, and in his off hours playing the dude à la Rome at the Columbus counterpart of the Terre Haute House, loses sixty dollars of his employer's money in a poker game. Fearing he will be fired, he begs Jennie to go to Brander that night and borrow the money. To save her brother, she does and Brander seduces her.

At this point, Dreiser began rewriting and discarding and changing the order of events. For example, in an early draft, after Brander loses his bid for re-election, he wangles an appointment as ambassador to Brazil and sails off, without a word about sending for Jennie. Apparently, Dreiser decided that version made Brander seem too callous, for he scrapped it, and resorts to his favorite deus ex machina—chance. The senator promises to marry Vennie but dies of a heart attack before he can so.

When Gerhardt learns Jennie is pregnant, he expels her from the house. Bass, Jennie, and her mother hatch a plan whereby Bass will go to Cleveland and get a job and the family will follow. Gerhardt, meanwhile, sells the mortgage-encumbered house, pays off his debts, and moves to Youngstown, Ohio, where there is an opening in his craft. Bass finds employment, and the mother and the other children join him in Cleveland. Jennie, who in the meantime has given birth, goes to work in a factory, but the combined family income, even with old Gerhardt contributing most of his paycheck, is barely enough for them to survive. When the father is badly burned in an accident, he is unable to work and needs constant medical attention.

With overdue bills piling up and the family facing eviction, Jennie is accosted on the street by Lester Kane, the handsome, rakish son of a wealthy Cincinnati carriage manufacturer. Overcome by his charm, she shyly describes her family's troubles and accepts ten dollars. Kane persuades her to sup with him at a fancy hotel that provides private dining rooms to patrons interested in seduction. After much soul-searching, Jennie decides she will keep the assignation, reasoning that since she is already "ruined," no man will marry her and she might as well convert her good looks into a commodity. "The lesson Brander's action had taught her was coming back. . . . The world would buy beauty. It could be induced to pay something for her soul." At the hotel, though, she loses her nerve and breaks into tears (as Emma had done in Evansville under similar circumstances). Kane takes pity on her and sends her home with forty dollars. As far as he is concerned, he is merely postponing his pleasure.

Kane is a charming bachelor in his mid-thirties, much in demand socially, who travels around representing the family business interests (something like the role assigned to the jovial, pleasure-loving Austin Brennan). Marriage is a fine institution, Kane thinks, but not for him. The next time he is in Cleveland he asks Jennie to meet him, and they go to lunch. In a scene strongly reminiscent of Drouet's seduction of Carrie (this was not the only time Dreiser reflexively harked back to his first novel), he urges her to go to New York City with him. He will provide for her family—even buy them a new house. Jennie hesitates, but she feels a "drag of affinity." He will be kind, she thinks, and while she realizes a man in his position will not marry her, she will at least be able to pose as his wife. Perhaps in time he will relent and do the right thing. Lester sweeps away her last shreds of compunction by taking her to a fancy dry-goods store and buying her an expensive wardrobe, as Drouet had done with Carrie.

Screwing up her courage, she explains to Mrs. Gerhardt that a Mr. Kane wants to help them and has invited her to accompany him to New York. Her mother promptly asks, "Will he marry you?" Yes, Jennie replies, "the lie falling like a leaden weight from her lips to her heart."

Jennie's motives are an unstable mix of selfishness and altruism. Dreiser is incapable of showing a normal attraction between her and Kane. On the one hand, she sacrifices her virtue for her family; on the other, she is attracted to Lester and dazzled by the world of luxury he has introduced her to. In New York, she is stirred, Carrie-like, by the fashion parade on Broadway. As for Lester, his attraction to Jennie is that of the strong for the weak, which Dreiser regards as a law of life. He is a man who takes what he wants: "The Macheavellean [sic] manner in which

Lester thus complicated Jennie's sense of consideration for her mother with the need of yielding to him while at the same time destroying any illusions as to the nature of his feeling for her, was calculated to upset and undo that little wanderer—to make her feel the helplessness of her portion."

When the little wanderer returns from New York, her brothers and sisters ooh and aah over her resplendent new wardrobe and handsome carriage. Mrs. Gerhardt has told her husband that she is married, but he is suspicious. His relationship with Jennie is still cool because of her child, Vesta, though he attended the little girl's baptism. In the final scene of Chapter 30, Jennie talks with the old man. There is still an abyss between them, "a sort of voiceless non-understanding of one another as if two voids had met." He asks her solemnly if she is indeed married. When Jennie says she is, he says, "Well . . . I hope for the good of your soul that is so." She is readmitted to the family—on probation.

The story continues with Lester moving to Chicago and setting up Jennie in an apartment, where his sister discovers by accident his illicit relationship.

There the original manuscript ends. It should be apparent why, two years earlier, Dreiser (or was it Jug and Henry?) had misgivings about its publishability and the "appeal" of his characters.

Lester is an unattractive figure—a rake, a rich Drouet, without the latter's saving goodheartedness. Jennie doesn't love him, so what can she possibly see in him but his money? She nobly sacrifices her virtue for her family, but Dreiser can bring no emotional poignancy to that theme. Her decision to sell herself is presented so tentatively, as though he had grave misgivings, that it lacks conviction. He shows her reveling in her new luxuries, and seems to half-approve of the masterful way Lester overcomes her resistance. And William Gerhardt seems a long way from forgiving his daughter, who has lied to him as well as to her mother. If the theme of reconciliation between father and daughter had initially attracted Dreiser, his unresolved hostility toward his own father (of whom Gerhardt is almost a carbon copy, down to the year he stepped off the boat at Castle Garden) prevented him from effecting one: the old man remains suspicious. There is a chilling finality to that scene in which Jennie and William Gerhardt meet in "voiceless non-understanding" like "two voids."

Unable to attain the necessary detachment from his material, still stuck in his first book, Dreiser began flailing about and lost the thread. He desperately tried to rewrite and rearrange, but when he patched here the story became unraveled there. The facts of Mame's life stubbornly refused to yield to imaginative flights; they remained inert, sordid.

On top of his writing problems, Dreiser had to cope with loneliness in a strange city with no J. E. Bowler to talk with. His isolation is fore-shadowed in the words he had written for *The Transgressor*: "Man's tend-ency appears to be away from the immaterial, the nothingness of poverty, toward a greater materiality. Busy with the earth he is happy, as if he were long over-surfeited with the spirit. Out yonder where lie the cold, the blackness, the intense currents laboring immensely he is unhappy. Here under the low roofs, within the dome of life he finds content in little things, peace and enjoyment."

And he goes on to say: "Perhaps this is why the lone herder goes in-sane; why the incoming wanderer views the twinkling home-lights of the valley with exultation, why the cities swell with an ever increasing tide of population. Man does not want to be alone." He must have felt a bit like that lone herder.

He slogged on, and in early June sent Miss Gordinnier the first batch of manuscript. Unable to stay in Charlottesville any longer, he set out on a tramp northward. He hoped that the exercise would calm his frayed nerves, but there was an element of panicky flight in his trek—almost a fugue state; he needed to put distance between himself and the book and the other worries that were tormenting him. (He later told an in-terviewer, Isaac Goldberg, that he was seized by "an aching desire to be forever on the move.") As each month passed, his debt to his publisher mounted another hundred dollars. Dreiser had wished for freedom from financial pressures so he could write, and magically Jewett had appeared and offered it to him. But in his present depressed state, the boon was coming to resemble the wild ass's skin in Balzac's novel. The more Theo-dore used it, the more it shrank and the more he suffered.

A gauge of his state of mind is a letter he wrote to Howells not long before leaving Charlottesville. In a review of a biography of Longfellow in the April *Harper's*, Howells had written that the beauty of the poet's work was more apparent to a man in his later years, "when impartial chance decimates the rank in which he stands, and leaves him safe only till the next round at best. Those who fall become the closer friends to those who remain untouched."

After quoting this passage, Dreiser writes, "There is something so mel-low, kindly and withal so lonely about it that I venture to offer, if I may, a word of fellow feeling and appreciation ere the 'next round' take you and it be too late." In the "fitful dream" that is life, he is heartened by the "mental attitude" of the three writers he most admires—Hardy, Tol-stoy, and Howells. And he closes with an unconsciously morbid flourish:

If the common ground is to be credited with the flowering out of such minds as yours I shall not be disturbed to return to the dust. There is enough in the thought to explain the wonder of the night, the sparkle of the waters—the thrill of tender feeling that runs abroad in the odours and murmurs and sighs. Buried Howells and Hardys and Tolstoys shall explain it to me. I shall rejoice to believe that it is they who laugh in the waters—that it is because of such that the hills clap their hands.

What Howells thought of this communication is not known, since he never replied. A student of psychological subtleties, he had surely perceived and resented the implication that he was an aging has-been in Dreiser's earlier "tribute" in *Ainslee's*. Now he was laid in the grave and given a funeral oration. But Howells could not have known about the death of Dreiser's real father—or that this letter, with its allusions to "tender, sorrowful doubt" and (quoting approvingly one of Howells's lines) "the wisdom of the man humbled to the universal conditions," was a reference to Dreiser's own state.

Before leaving Charlottesville, Dreiser heard from another voice from the past. Arthur Henry laid his tangled financial affairs on Theodore's doorstep. He would have written sooner, Henry said, but he didn't know Dreiser's address and "hesitated to inquire from those who might know as I do not wish anybody to think we might not be good friends." He was worried that Dreiser had fallen behind on his share of the payments on the House of Four Pillars and offered to take them over, promising to reimburse Theodore later "with interest." As if he longs to revive the old partnership, Arthur asks how his friend's book is coming, says he plans to start a novel, and signs himself "Affectionately."

The Maumee house was encumbered by back taxes and overdue mortgage payments and had been damaged by Halloween vandals. Dreiser evidently demanded to know just what he owed on his half share, and Henry was a bit vague himself. Dreiser must have written bluntly that he wanted his money back. Henry's letter of May 15 is simply signed "Arthur." In it he reports that the second-mortgage holder, a man named Hiett, had made him an offer, and he has decided to sell because he can't keep up the payments. He says, however, that Dreiser can have the house by paying $300 to Maude. That of course was out of the question, and when Henry in another letter asks if he might pay Dreiser his share of the proceeds of the sale that winter (he is short just now and still owes Anna $500 of the $1000 he borrowed from her last summer), Dreiser put his foot down. In June Henry gives in: "I have written to Hiett to pay the balance to you"—a matter of perhaps $100 but badly needed.

To Dreiser that summer in Maumee when they were brothers must have now seemed just another of Henry's airy dreams, as implausible as the Doctrine of Happiness.

By early June Dreiser had walked as far as Rehoboth Beach, Delaware, where he settled temporarily. As soon as Jewett learned his address, he fired off an urgent query: "What and where is the delay?" The firm had made up a dummy of *The Transgressor* for its salesmen and was anxious to have the book. His back to the wall, Dreiser confessed the truth: he could not possibly finish in time. On June 20 Jewett bowed to the inevitable: "If the book cannot mature in time for September publication it will be better to postpone the issue until the following February. . . . Do not get discouraged."

Actually, Miss Gordinnier was just finishing up another batch of manuscript—about twenty thousand words in all—and she forwarded it to Delaware when she learned of Dreiser's whereabouts. She had enjoyed Jennie's story, she reported: "Am sorry I did not have the first chapters . . . the story having great interest for me, it being so truly everyday and human. It is a surprise to me that a man can so comprehend the minute details of household life as you have."

That was the first simple human response he had had to the novel from a stranger, but Dreiser was not so charmed that he forgot his innate frugality. He paid her bill but complained about errors and, as he had done with Jewett, accused her of deliberately changing words—even substituting new phrases. Also, he wanted her to put more words on a page. Gordinnier refused to be bullied. Their agreement the previous fall, when she gave him a special low rate, was for an average of two hundred words a page, she pointed out. She was a businesswoman, not a housewife working for "pin money." The low rate did not include checking typed copy against the MS, which in any case was so hard to follow that "the brain dances polkas, and the eyes see polka dots."

Dreiser could not stay angry at spunky Miss Gordinnier, and soon she had completed another one hundred pages. She thanked him for entrusting her with the work. As the Infants had done with *Carrie*, she identified with Jennie, and like them she provided an ingenuous warning: "Unless Jennie reaps the proverbial whirlwind in the closing chapters I fear me that the issue of your book . . . will break up the typewriting profession, not to mention other employments."

39. The Ache of Modernism

I was hard up, and everything seemed futile. . . . Life seemed an endless chain without meaning.

—Dreiser to Dorothy Dudley (1932)

[My] thoughts seem to flow on in a continuous and wearying chain and I rise so sore in the brain that I fairly ache.

—Dreiser, Diary Entry (1902)

One day . . . he was seized with a particular nervous disturbance. . . . It was though his nervous system had given way at every point and division. For the time being he was intensely frightened, believing he was going crazy.

—Dreiser, *The "Genius"* (1915)

hen Miss Gordinnier's letter reached him in early July, Dreiser's wandering had landed him in Philadelphia, where he had taken a room at 3225 Ridge Avenue, toward the outskirts of the city. Why Philadelphia? Perhaps he did not feel ready for New York. Also, his friend Peter McCord had been living in Philadelphia, and had worked for the *North American* (the town's "yellow sheet," he told Dreiser). Although he had recently jumped to the Newark *News*, McCord pulled strings to enable Dreiser to do some unsigned pieces for the *North American*.

J. F. Taylor's check in June was the last because of Dreiser's failure to meet the deadline. He now owed the publisher seven hundred dollars unless he could somehow finish *The Transgressor*. But first he must bail out his sinking financial ship, and the free-lance seas seemed hostile at this point. Henry Mills Alden returned his story "A Samaritan of the Backwoods" with a curt-sounding note: "It is not the kind of material we want in whatever shape it may be put."

The *Harper's Monthly* editor was probably not banishing Dreiser from his pages; he was merely closing the door on the semifictional genre, of which he was not an admirer. His colleague at the *Weekly*, John Kendrick Bangs, asked Dreiser to write a piece on "Christmas in the Tenements" for the appropriate December issue. Managing editor R. C. Penfield cautioned, "We do not want too much 'misery' in the story, but I don't know that you know too much of it, for publication at least . . . a Christmas number should be bright and cheerful and you can find much in this line among the tenements, I am sure, to write about." Dreiser must have had a bitter laugh over the imputation that he knew nothing about poverty.

The usually hospitable Duffy rejected "The Mayor and His People," explaining that *Munsey's* was now mainly in the market for light, amusing material. Convinced there was a conspiracy of rejection against him, Dreiser sent "Samaritan" to *The Atlantic Monthly* under McCord's name. Years later he told Dorothy Dudley that the magazine had informed him he was "morally bankrupt" and wanted nothing more to do with him. *The Atlantic*, a conservative publication, may have closed its doors to him, but those at other editorial chambers were still ajar. Dreiser's problem continued to be his insistence on writing stories like "Samaritan," rather than the factual articles which Alden and others expected of him.

To cap it all, Jewett was somewhat less than enthusiastic about the last batch of chapters of *The Transgressor*. "You elaborate certain parts of the narrative to excess," he wrote, mentioning the section dealing with the Gerhardts' problems of economic survival in Cleveland; "the reader becomes confused and weary." Nothing incurable, but obviously Dreiser was floundering—and in need of an Arthur Henry to advise him. But by this time Henry's *An Island Cabin* had appeared, with its unflattering portrait of the querulous and eccentric Tom. The average reader would not know who Tom was, of course, but his real-life counterpart could picture New York editorial insiders laughing at Theodore Dreiser over seidels at Pfaff's Saloon.

"Christmas in the Tenements" would be the last full-length magazine article Dreiser wrote for many months. It was also one of the best of his urban sketches in the vein of "Curious Shifts of the Poor." Amid dogday heat he conjured up holiday scenes of ragged children at shop windows gazing longingly at the cheap baubles with "an earnest, child-heart longing which may never again be gratified if not now." He had a personal understanding of a child's cravings. If they are left unfulfilled, or, worse, denied by a hard, puritanical father, he believed, the child's life is permanently warped. He also tried to show that at Christmastime "sympathy, love, affection and passion" were just as prevalent in the slums as they were on Fifth Avenue—that the child's desires were the "indissoluble link which binds these weakest and most wretched elements of society to the best and most successful." It was a Howellsian-Tolstoyan message with a Dreiser twist: desire, not love, as the solvent of class barriers.

The picture of Dreiser sweating over Christmas visions in August skews the truth somewhat. He had difficulty completing the piece, and was still at it in October, long past the deadline. Penfield finally wrote him that the magazine would set aside two pages for him, and he would have to cut the galleys to fit—"or we will." By this time writing had become an onerous labor. Dreiser had difficulty concentrating; his ideas scattered like a flock of startled birds at the least disturbance. "I found that consecutive thought and close reasoning is very difficult for me," he later wrote. "I do not get very far before I question the order and merit of what I am doing and find myself utterly confused as to what is best and interesting."

Jug had joined him in September and became a helpless onlooker to his increasingly futile struggles. All Dreiser's efforts at self-cure having failed, he decided to seek professional help. On October 22 he called at the offices of Dr. Louis Adolphus Duhring, two blocks from the University of Pennsylvania Hospital. Among Dreiser's medley of symptoms were various skin disorders, ranging from a burning sensation on his fingertips to eczemalike rashes and itching feet.

Duhring, a prominent dermatologist, was interested in the neurotic condition popularly known as neurasthenia, perhaps because he had suffered from it himself. As Dreiser recited his symptoms, the doctor fixed him "with a heavy, deprecatory gaze." In addition to the skin disorders, Dreiser complained of chest pains and headaches, that he was losing his hair, had an abnormally large appetite, and couldn't sleep. He said at times he felt exhausted and down in the depths.

When Dreiser had finished, Duhring told him he was suffering from "nervous exhaustion"—neurasthenia. What Theodore had described were the classic symptoms. Although problems arising in the nervous system were difficult to deal with, Duhring had a theory that certain drugs could alleviate them. To be sure, this was a controversial regimen, and most specialists in nervous diseases would not agree with him. If Dreiser wished to undergo the still-experimental therapy, Duhring would administer a course of several different nostrums that the patient must take in sequence. He must also avoid being alone too much, seek "amusing and

companionable society," and go to the theater. The doctor's first prescription was a mixture of antipyrine (an analgesic) and sodium bromide
(a sedative), for which he collected eight dollars.

Duhring also recommended that his patient keep a diary of his symptoms, and this Dreiser did religiously, noting everything from bowel
movements to his mental state. Based on what he wrote, a modern diagnosis would be a moderate to severe case of depression. Dreiser exhibited nearly all the textbook symptoms: apathy, chronic fatigue, insomnia,
procrastination, abnormally large appetite, guilt, remorse, anxiety, a fear
of depleting his resources (in his case sexual), and various physical complaints (headaches, dyspepsia, constipation).

In the past, as we have seen, he had demonstrated a tendency to mel-
ancholia, often accompanied by bouts of insomnia. When Duffy in his
Christmas letter warned of his friend's "Teutonic" tendency to brood,
he inadvertently alluded to a less romantic truth: Dreiser may well have
inherited his depressive tendencies from John Paul Dreiser, who alter-
nated fits of rage with spells of apathy and withdrawal. Theodore himself
was aware of the possibility. "There is an access of gloom, a brooding in
me over long periods, so like him," he told Dorothy Dudley. His bouts
of elation and despair while working on *Sister Carrie*, though not abnormal
for a creative writer, suggest the classic manic-depressive cycle; and an
entry in the medical diary shows his mood swings continued: "My chief
complaint at this time concerns a certain nervousness of temper over enthusiasm [sic] tending to mental wildness coupled with a permanent and
sometimes noticeably disturbing form of brain ache. It seems to move
about in the head like flashes of sheet lightning round a summer sky."
And in later entries he rides an emotional roller-coaster.

The onset of symptoms like these, along with various physical ailments
and a general feeling of debility that had no discernible organic cause,
was very disturbing. Dreiser's fear that he had contracted malaria—or
something worse—was still with him in Philadelphia: "I have an unaccountable drowsiness and achyness both in body and mind which reduces
me to the necessity of lying down a great deal. Malaria might be a reason
for it. Some inherent blood affliction also."

At the same time, he thought his problem might be hypochondria—
"confusing physical opposition to labor with illness," or else, "I am in
a much depressed mental state." But he concludes that he is probably
suffering from "purely mental exhaustion from past excesses both of sexual passion and mental labor."

His mention of sexual excesses probably referred only to his relations with Jug. For all the external troubles bedeviling their marriage, they continued to be sexually active, and she became more demanding, hungrier for affection. After the separation over the summer they would have sought to make up for lost time, and Dreiser formed the idea that overindulgence had weakened his system, a hangover from the sexual traumas of his adolescence. He still seemed to believe in a kind of Malthusian theory of libido. If one overdrew on the available supply, one was left mentally and physically debilitated.

He notes that "my tendency to overindulge in thoughts concerning the sexual relation, as well as in the relation itself" caused a "nervous ache in the region of the genito-urinary organs." He tried total abstinence, but was not always successful: "*Wednesday, Nov. 19th* Rose at seven after having foolishly taxed myself by copulating with Mrs. D. but I could not control my desire."

Curiously, the words "but I could not control my" were written in Jug's hand. Either Dreiser had used a crude phrase which she later cleaned up or she had been the one who could not control her desire. As mentioned, she was ardent, and it could be that she chafed under Dreiser's self-imposed regimen. But proper young women did not admit such behavior, and she probably assumed that Duhring would read the diary. Having arrogated to herself a permanent right of veto over intimate references to her in Theodore's work, she excised it.

Since Duhring put his faith in drugs, he was not much help in easing the sexual anxieties that were the origin of Dreiser's idea that he was suffering from overindulgence. A decade later Sigmund Freud would take up the phenomenon of neurasthenia, or "modern nervousness," and conclude that its primary cause was "the undue suppression of the sexual life in civilized peoples (or classes) as a result of the 'civilized' sexual morality which prevails among them." While Dreiser was certainly not sexually deprived, he was probably suffering a kind of sexual dissatisfaction Freud described—that of a man who has followed the conventional course of abstinence before marriage and finds that the marital relationship does not live up to the anticipation.

In blaming his troubles on carnal overindulgence, Dreiser repressed his loss of sexual desire for Jug, which became associated with the shame and guilt learned from the antimasturbation propaganda he read as a boy. Like many Victorian males, he had put his love object on a pedestal; his respect for Jug's social superiority roused the sleeping incest taboo. As Freud noted, "whoever is to be really free and happy in love must have overcome his deference for women and come to terms with the idea of incest with mother and sister." Jug's aggressiveness in the sexual relation would only have repelled Theodore more, reinforcing his feelings of inadequacy.

Of course the lifelong bachelor Dr. Duhring could not have had much understanding of sexual problems. His treatment was, as he said, unconventional; most experts on neurasthenia advised against using drugs. The standard cure called for months of absolute bed rest accompanied by frequent meals. Another growing body of opinion called for vigorous exercise. Dr. J. H. Kellogg, who operated a famous sanatorium in Battle Creek, Michigan, thought most cases of neurasthenia were caused by "chronic toxemia" due to an accumulation of food wastes in the system. He recommended, among other things, a vegetarian diet and bowel movements after every meal.

Neurasthenia had become a vogue ailment by the turn of the century. In his book *American Nervousness* (1881), its discoverer, Dr. George Miller Beard, had called it the "American disease." Beard found that the symptoms appeared most frequently among members of the upper and middle classes. In 1900 Dr. William B. Pritchard wrote that they afflicted "bright intellects . . . leaders and masters of men, each one a captain of industry." Among the causes Pritchard cited were overwork, worry, stress and anxiety. The malady was said to be largely prevalent among urbanites, leading to the hypothesis that the novel pressures of city life and rapid technological and social change were also to blame.

In short, neurasthenia was a manifestation of what Thomas Hardy called "the ache of modernism." Dreiser showed his awareness of the impersonality and anomie of urban life in *Sister Carrie*. And he takes them up more directly in a passage in his second novel:

> The tremendous and complicated divisions of our material civilization, the multiplicity and variety of our social forms, the depth, subtlety and sophistry of our mental cogitation, gathered, remultiplied and phantasmagorically disseminated as they are by these other agencies, the railroad, the express and post office, the telegraph, telephone, the newspaper, and, in short, the whole art of printing and distributing, has so combined as to produce what may be termed a kaleidoscopic glitter, a dazzling and confusing show-piece which is much more apt to weary and undo than to enlighten. We weary of it, our brains grow tired, it produces a sort of intellectual fatigue by which we see the ranks of the victims of insomnia, melancholia and insanity recruited.

In the story of Jennie Gerhardt, he had staged a battle between old and new. On one side were arrayed tradition and religion, embodied in

Gerhardt; and on the other youth and sexuality, personified in Jennie. But her compromised position brings her into conflict with a new set of forces, which Dreiser saw as more puissant than the family and the church— "society," money, convention, represented by the Kane family and their set. Yet those were the forces Taylor had wanted Dreiser to placate by giving his book a moral.

Taylor and Jewett were not reactionaries, but here was a novel in which the heroine's immoral career leaves her comfortably ensconced in a pleasant Chicago flat, her every wish granted. Such a career, the moralists would say, encourages other young women to go forth and do likewise. Miss Gordinnier's jest that the story would break up the typing profession tended to confirm their fears. Why be a respectable working woman if you could be Jennie?

On November 10 Dreiser makes his last mention of his inability to work on the book. Then he complains of "mental wildness" and "brain ache"— and of being haunted by a "disturbing sense of error." Five days earlier, Jewett, sensing something was wrong, made what turned out to be a final plea: "Open the door and sweep out the rubbish of distrust. . . . I know that when the book is finished it will be good." He also returned "the papers and chapters which you desire." The reason Dreiser wanted the manuscript became clear in his next letter. He notified Jewett that he was sick, unable to finish *The Transgressor*, and that he had burned the manuscript. He would try to pay back the money he owed them someday. Jewett sent him a kindly reply: "Brace up, stop worrying, and rest your head as well as your body. You exaggerate greatly the obligation under which you think you are staggering. I gambled on a manuscript and when the manuscript is finished I believe that the result will justify my plunge."

It would be more than seven years until Dreiser seriously took up the story of Jennie Gerhardt again, ten before it was published. Much later he explained that he had lost interest, that it had become no longer "vital" to him. There was some truth in that; Jewett and Taylor were not entirely to blame, for Dreiser was himself dissatisfied with the novel and because of other worries and the psychochemical imbalances that triggered his depression, he could not rekindle his enthusiasm for it. But his near paranoiac suspicions of Taylor and Jewett, coupled with the fear that the book would be denounced even if it were published, also sapped his energy and self-confidence.

On November 14, four days after his final attempt to work on *The Transgressor*, Dreiser undertook a magazine assignment that enabled him to express his true feelings about morality and immorality in fiction. It was a four-hundred-word editorial for a new publication called *Booklovers Magazine*. The editor, Seymour Eaton, had advertised for "short, pungent, vigorous" editorials for his magazine, "anything which hits the nail on the head." He promised to "pay cash and good prices," which probably brought Dreiser to his door in hopes of making a few quick dollars. So crippling was his writer's block, however, that it took him more than a month to complete the squib.

Entitled "True Art Speaks Plainly," it was a despairing protest against censorship. The only guide to morality in art, Dreiser wrote, could be expressed in three words: "Tell the truth." The artist must express what he or she sees, "honestly and without subterfuge: this is morality as well as art." Censors were not really worried about "the discussion of mere sexual lewdness, for no work on that basis could possibly succeed." What they feared were books that challenged the status quo. The censors' claimed motive of protecting people from obscene literature was a pretense. Censorship sought to suppress the subversive truth: "Immoral! Immoral! Under this cloak hide the vices of wealth as well as the vast unspoken blackness of poverty and ignorance; and between them must walk the little novelist, choosing neither truth nor beauty, but some half-conceived phase of life that bears no honest relationship to either the whole of nature or to man."

The cry of immoral literature "has become a house of refuge to which every form of social injustice hurries for protection . . . the objection to the discussion of the sex question is so great as to almost prevent the handling of the theme entirely." He could have been speaking of his own inability to handle it in *The Transgressor*.

A single sentence in his diary was almost as eloquent: "Ah me—Ah me, who is it that tells the truth and is happy."

Duhring apparently never read the medical diary he had suggested his patient keep. But his assignment gave Dreiser a license to indulge his tendencies to hypochondria and introspection, noting and thereby magnifying even the most transient physical symptoms, worrying about the slightest mental anomaly. Nor did Duhring offer any practical advice beyond that proffered at the first visit; he contented himself with prescribing various drugs and "tonics" in response to the latest reported symptoms, physical and mental. Dreiser confided to his diary that his mind seemed to move in obsessive patterns, endlessly repeating the same series of thoughts. He reports, for example, being "irritated some by a thread of ideas which my will cannot cut off" and that he "Couldn't stop thinking." What he was thinking about, what the nightmares and "annoying dreams" that murdered his sleep were, he did not record. His insomnia continued to torment him, and it assumed the classic pattern of depression: fitful sleep early in the evening, followed by wakefulness from about 3:00 A.M. until morning. At one point he wrote despairingly, "I do not believe I have had one real sound nights rest since my first going to Duhring."

That was not quite true, but the good nights were rare. Duhring had prescribed bromides in low doses, and when they failed to promote sleep he gave his patient scopolamine, a drug of the belladonna family, and chloral hydrate, a pre-barbiturate sedative and the traditional ingredient in Mickey Finns. He was also prescribing the aspirinlike drugs antipyrine and phenacetin, and, for lethargy, a standard tonic of the day, a cocktail of small amounts of arsenic, strychnine and quinine, which were supposed to stimulate the blood.

Thus, over a period of two months, Dreiser swallowed a medicine chest full of drugs, some of them capable of producing bizarre mental reactions when taken in sufficiently large amounts. Scopolamine, for example, can induce "twilight sleep," hallucinations, and a psychoticlike state. Arsenic and strychnine in nonfatal doses produce similar effects. And bromides, which tend to accumulate in the system, can produce the condition known as "bromism," with symptoms that include skin rash, headaches, and constipation, all of which Dreiser mentioned in his diary. The dosage he was taking was not a large one, but bromide's action is unpredictable; some people are more sensitive to the adverse side effects than others. Also, in cases of depression these might be worse. (A contemporary pharmacology textbook states: "Bromide has no rational place in the management of patients with depression.")

Dreiser also writes that his weaker eye, the one with the cast, pained him and was not accommodating properly to light—a characteristic toxic reaction to scopolamine, which dilates the pupil. He sometimes strayed from his doctor's instructions as to dosages (which were in the normal range); for example, he mentions taking one and one-half and one and three-quarters teaspoons of the scopolamine preparation, rather than the one teaspoon called for.

Even if he did not abuse the drugs, they could have accounted for the turn for the worse Dreiser's condition took in Philadelphia. Some of the odd physical and mental symptoms he recorded in the diary could have been caused by the drugs, and his obliviousness to their origin made them all the more disturbing. He was a little like the "jay" who has been slipped a Mickey Finn and wonders why the world is suddenly spinning out of control.

40. In His Steps

[Hurstwood] buried himself in his papers and read. Oh, the rest of it—the relief from walking and thinking. . . . So he read, read, read, rocking in the warm room, near the radiator and waiting for the dinner to be served.
—Dreiser, *Sister Carrie* (1900)

This morning after breakfast I bought a paper and strolled down to the water works and back reading it. Then I came home the moment I thought my room was made up and sat down in it, a feeling of cowardly content holding me, as if here at least I was safe. Then I read, rocking and dreaming, the interesting life the novel pictured being a sort of salve to my distress.
—Dreiser, Medical Diary (1903)

D uhring's advice that he seek "amusing and companionable society" was ignored, though not by choice. Theodore and Jug knew almost no one in Philadelphia and had little social life. They lived quietly at a boardinghouse at 210 Spruce Street. Once he took her to the theater to see Henrietta Crosman in *The Sword of the King,* and when Jug's brother Dick and his wife visited for a few days, she accompanied them to a football game. Jug also became friendly with Mrs. Lillian Fulton Scott, who was one of the tiny coterie of admirers of *Sister Carrie.* She had written to Jug to propose that since Theodore's style had so much in common with Frank Norris's, he should write the final volume of the *Trilogy of Wheat,* which Norris had died before completing.

A few friends from New York came to call. Duffy arrived in November, and the anticipation of his visit was enough to put Dreiser in a "nervous condition." Duffy viewed his friend's mood swings as the artist's *Sturm und Drang.* ("I understand now better than ever before how much you suffer and enjoy. One complements the other.") They tramped about Manayunk, an industrial suburb near the Dreisers' boardinghouse, en-

gaging in a philosophical debate. The verbal joust put Dreiser in an
overwrought state, and he noted in his diary that day: "Find that I suffer
from a peculiar illusion as to the necessity of varying the progress of an
idea—changing the direction of my thoughts—which is purely a result
of mental overwork."

When it was time for Duffy to catch a train to New York, Dreiser accompanied him to the station and stood at the gate until he was gone—
a forlorn figure, one imagines. Later, Duffy suggested he read John Stuart
Mill's account of his nervous breakdown in his autobiography. Of more
concrete help was the fifty dollars Duffy sent him "on account" for future
work, along with the news that *Ainslee's* would use three of Dreiser's poems.
The money was, in effect, a loan. "I should have been vexed had I been
unable to manage this now," Duffy wrote. Whenever Dreiser felt like
doing something for the magazine, fine, but Duffy reiterated that "our
aim now is almost wholly to amuse." Another caller was Charles D. Gray,
a friend who worked in the collection department of the Jewelers Association and who had picnicked with Jug and Dreiser in happier times.
Gray spent Christmas day with them, talking over old times and over-
indulging in seasonal fare, for which Dreiser was later punished by in-
digestion. Gray was welcome in another sense: he paid back part of the
thirty-five dollars he owed Dreiser.

But those visits were about the extent of their social life, and Jug must
have had a good deal of time on her hands. She devoted herself to nursing
her husband, bathing his forehead when the "brain aches" came on, rub-
bing his chest with Chicago Oil when he had a cold, reading to him, and
correcting his manuscripts. There was precious little copy editing for her
to do, however, even after Dreiser abandoned his stalled novel and tried
to write some shorter pieces.

He managed to finish two stories, but one of them was a rewrite of an
earlier piece, "The Investigations of Mr. Buckley, Reporter," and the
other he seems not to have thought much of, for he did not send it out.
He became briefly excited about writing an article on working conditions
in the mills at Manayunk, like the one he had done on Fall River, but
got no further than requesting an interview with a factory inspector and
commenting in his diary on a view of them in the rain, "so squalid, so
poor, so suggestive of all that is artistic and grim in toil."

His sympathies for labor gushed forth again one night at dinner in his
boardinghouse. The talk was about the hearings being held on the long
and bitter anthracite coal miners' strike in Pennsylvania before a commission appointed by Theodore Roosevelt. That day, Clarence Darrow,

a radical lawyer from Chicago who was representing the mineworkers, had made a speech in which he called for decent wages and an eight-hour day. When the woman sitting next to him said she would like to slap Darrow for what he had said, Theodore defended the miners, thinking of their "grimy, narrow lives." Later, his lack of money to fill a prescription for medicine for his bad eye made him reflect on "the lot of the poor who sometimes under such circumstances have no resource in their own intellect, and speculating on how hard it must be." But of course, he still regarded himself as having the resource of intellect, and of being different from them and from the coal miners whose plight had so saddened him.

At the factory in Manayunk he had an encounter with a rude Irish policeman that brought out Theodore's Tolstoyan thoughts on nonviolence. The cop blocked his way, telling him he must obtain a pass if he wanted to walk through the mill property. Dreiser flared up at his insolent manner, and they argued. As he turned on his heel and walked off, the cop called after him, in a more moderate tone, asking him where he wanted to go and then gave him directions. In the aftermath, Dreiser wished he had been more conciliatory and exercised Christian forgiveness: "Why not always, as Christ said, gentle and kind. 'If any man compel thee to go with him a mile, go with him twain.' "

When he was not at his desk futilely trying to herd wayward thoughts into line, Dreiser spent the time walking, exercising, reading, and making the editorial rounds. In early December he called at the offices of the *Times* and the *Record*, but they were not hiring. Nor was the *Evening Bulletin*, to whom he applied by letter under the name R. D. White (i.e., his brother-in-law Richard Drace White). Was he buffering himself against rejection? Was he too proud to petition for a lowly reporter's job under the name of the novelist Theodore Dreiser? Why use Jug's brother's name?

The new year arrived, but for Dreiser it meant being wakened by bells and whistles at midnight and restlessly tossing until dawn. He noted in his diary, "The whole question of recovery seems to have narrowed down to one of sleeplessness." Sometimes he thought he detected an improvement in his condition. He marveled that he was "still subject to the most halcyon and delightful moods. One would fancy now that, being sick and weary as I am, I would have no heart for anything save the wretched contemplation of my mood, but I am not thus steadily afflicted at all." But for the manic-depressive, happiness is a fling with a fickle mistress.

On January 26 Jug returned to Montgomery City. He could no longer afford her keep. He did not even have enough money to pay for her ticket and asked Joseph Coates, editor of the progressive *Era* magazine, for an advance on the fees for two articles he had sold him—"The Problem of the Soil" and "A Mayor and His People." After seeing Jug off, Theodore returned to his room and brooded over his loss. Now he was alone, and he had no hope of her returning until he could make some money. But he wrote little. Instead, using Coates' library card, he borrowed books and sat in his room reading.

He chastised himself for sinking into a Hurstwood-like torpor and felt "doomed to rot." But the next day found him in a euphoric mood, and he wrote, "I might as well use my time to improve my knowledge of current novels since I shall want to be writing another one myself some day." He had set himself a program of reading all the contemporary realists, beginning with Howells's *The Rise of Silas Lapham* and John Hay's *The Bread-Winners*, and proceeding through books by Garland, Harold Frederic, Robert Grant, Brand Whitlock, and Henry B. Fuller.

The next afternoon his psychic barometer dropped sickeningly: "All the horror of being alone and without work, without money and sick swept over me and I thought I should die." He was so homesick for Jug he almost wept. He even thought of asking Coates to send him the balance due on the two articles so he could go to Missouri. "I must get something to do something for a change or I will utterly go mad," he wrote.

But all he accomplished the following day was to visit the University of Pennsylvania's Free Dispensary, a charity facility which he hoped would take his case. At first Dreiser was so ashamed of being seen among the needy that he was unable to enter. Finally, after a great effort of will, he went in and was relieved to find that the place was closed for the weekend.

On Sunday, February 7, his mood graph curved upward. He attended Mass at a Catholic church in Manayunk, and was soothed by the cool darkness, the sonorous beauty of the music, the starburst of candles on the altar, and the ritual itself. He returned to his room and read Ida Tarbell's biography of Lincoln, which enthralled him. He identified with the president's early years of poverty and struggle and was drawn to the Christ symbolism in his martyrdom. "Lincoln and Christ," he wrote, "somehow these two are naturally associated in my mind. They were both so kind, so tender, so true. Oh that we could all be great, noble and altogether lovely." The sacrificial death of these two figures reminded him of the good side he discovered in his father—Paul's toil for his family and his fanatical yet saintly belief in God. Dreiser's pent-up grief and guilt welled up when he read the story of a man whose martyrdom redeemed the Union dead, as Christ's did the suffering of all humankind.

In the ensuing days, his mood remained fairly good and he slept reasonably well. Perhaps it was no coincidence that the improvement came at a time when he was no longer taking the drugs Dr. Duhring prescribed. Dreiser had money enough to refill only one of the prescriptions—for phenacetin. At his last visit, he had asked Duhring if he could continue the treatments on credit. The doctor was displeased, but put him on his honor to send the money in a few days.

Now Theodore was unable to do that. The awareness that his funds would cover his board and room for just one more week strangely elated him: a decision was being made for him. Intimations of impending changes infused him with fresh hope. With the fifteen dollars Gray still owed him and thirty-five to forty more from Coates, he could go to New York. When he could actually obtain the money was uncertain; he was reluctant to dun Coates, and Gray's check might arrive too late for him to pay his next week's board. If it did, Dreiser resolved to throw himself on the mercy of the streets. That would be better than prolonging his stay in Philadelphia. Like Hurstwood, he was drifting with the current, but he was relieved rather than worried.

The same day he visited Duhring, he thought of applying for manual labor, but decided against it because he believed he was destined to do "literary and socialistic work and that very shortly I would be able to do it." Rather than asking Coates for the money that day, he decided to try a charitable society which provided free meals in exchange for chopping wood. But the place was in a "very poverty-stricken neighborhood" and the "idea of an appeal was too painful." On another day, he went to the streetcar barns to ask about a conductor's job, as Hurstwood had done, but was relieved to find the employment office closed.

Pride and shyness, abetted by false hope, conspired to keep Dreiser from getting a job; even the decision to go to New York enabled him to postpone the matter. He had half convinced himself that his health was improving and that he would soon be on his feet again, "writing articles and finishing my story." His mind was teeming with ideas that he was sure he could convert into magazine specials. He promptly entered a Horn & Hardart restaurant and ordered a fifteen-cent bowl of mock turtle soup, leaving him only thirty-seven cents. While dining, he fell into talk with a follower of Henry George and became excited about the idea of doing two articles on the single-tax movement in Philadelphia.

A few days later the weather turned fine, and he walked, singing to himself for joy, feeling that life was so beautiful that he could not remain poor always. He would grow strong and be able to write. And, "Love was to come back and play its part in my life again." He wrote that shortly after being plunged into grief by Jug's departure. He was hopelessly torn: he wanted her, he wanted a new love.

On February 14, while strolling along Wissihickon Creek, he met a Negro cook who in season worked at a resort. The man shocked him by talking of the wealthy guests, especially the "immoral" women (Dreiser felt it improper for a person of color to talk so freely of white people); nonetheless, visions of beautiful women sipping champagne and flirting with unattached gentlemen set him thinking again of the disparity between his dream and his present deprived state. "I am homely and backward," he decided, "with no art of impressing women. . . . Some men have so much. I have had so little." Nature had eliminated him from the sexual struggle; he was one of the unfit.

All he can do now is wait for his dreams to materialize, but the thought is hard to bear: "Not now. Not now. Somehow now is almost always commonplace. We see when we return that we have to wait. To be alone, to live alone, to wait, wait, wait, that is the lot accorded us and only the dreams are real. The substance of them is never with us—never attainable."

By a circuitous route he had come full circle to the coda of *Sister Carrie:* "Tho' often disillusioned, she was still waiting for that halcyon day when she should be led forth among dreams become real." In his rocking chair, reading, he could only dream of a better life, waiting wearily for this storm to pass. Dreams were the only certainty, but fulfillment lay beyond the next hill, and when you got there you were inevitably disappointed. Meantime, new dreams rose up to disconsole you. But this dilemma suggested a way out: in a work of imagination, of art, dream and reality fused in timelessness. Then, if your dreams were the right ones, success followed.

Instinctively, Dreiser was groping his way out of the cave; his desire to write was the guiding thread that would lead him to daylight. After Jug's departure his diary changes, as though a burden had lifted. The hypochondriac's querulous litany gives way to shards of narrative. With Jug no longer peering over his shoulder, he presupposes a general reader: "You know how it is when you are going downhill temporarily, nothing seems right." His ordeal was being transmuted into literary material: ". . . thinking how I would write all this. What a peculiar story my life would make if all were told."

Another sign that his mind was groping toward health were the poems he wrote—chinks in his writer's block. As far back as November, he had been dashing them off. After taking a walk, Dreiser "felt lonely and wrote a little poem." It survives. Scrawled on the back of an envelope, it is about an old man "tottering in ugliness . . . muttering in despair." His springtime is over, and "it is now winter." But out of the earth come the flowers: "Life of the world springs up from dead life/Have faith and go in peace if you would be born again." He was searching for comfort in Spencer's philosophy—the idea that decay produces life. Yet there was a religious symbolism too.

Years later, telling Dudley about this period in his life, Dreiser blamed his depression in part on brooding about the cosmos: "Here was this immense system about us, chaotic, meaningless, as far as we could find out . . . and you personally were nothing. . . . I got to thinking that there was no answer and that depressed me." But he did not tell Dudley about the recrudescence of his religious instincts. Nor would it be the last crisis in his life when Dreiser reverted to the faith of his youth. Shattered by fears, his mind clutched for wholeness in the symbolism of religion, if not its dogma, at the Catholic service in Manayunk and at other churches he attended while in Philadelphia. He expressed this emotion in another poem (never published):

> To thrill with the touch of cool water
> To walk the good earth singing, singing
> To breathe deeply, think tenderly
> In no way to treasure bitterness
> But to feel that life is good and so proclaim it
> This shall be for a prayer unto your maker
> It shall be for a testament that
>   he hath made you whole.

On February 10 he overcame his reluctance to ask Coates for the rest of the money *Era* owed him. Coates agreed to give it to him in a few days, and they talked for a while about *The Transgressor*, which Coates had just read. He found the writing overwrought in places, but when Dreiser told him the story in his own words, just as he had it, fully formed, in his mind, the editor was enthusiastic. "We will hear more of you yet," he said.

Friday, February 13. With only six cents left he walked five miles to the center of the city *("The beauty, the comfort, the affection of the world. How the sign of it or its semblance pricks the soul in want.")* Coates told him he would have to wait until Monday for his money, since Stoddard, the bookkeeper, was out. Footsore and anxious that he not miss supper at his boardinghouse, he walked back as fast as he could. *("Me. Theodore Dreiser. A man who has ideas enough to write and to spare and walking for want of a nickel.")* He made it in an hour and twenty minutes.

That weekend he watched a funeral procession go up to the door of a house where only the day before he had seen a black dog howling—an omen of death, he remembered his mother telling him.

Monday, February 16. Again he walked to town. Coates informed him that Stoddard was out, but agreed to authorize a check. However, the man who signed the checks was absent. Would it be all right if he mailed it?

> *I said very well and came away, but oh me it was not very well. To walk so far, not to be sure of getting it after all, to have to face a weekly room rent and board overdue and probably very much expected.*

Tuesday, February 17. The check from Coates arrived, but it was election day and the banks were closed. After recording this latest reversal, he writes:

> *Though one has neither houses nor lands, nor affection nor companionship he can still live. It isn't pleasant I'll admit but it can be done. How I am trying to tell you.*

Then, with the words "I wish those who are doubtful about the" the diary breaks off. But his experiment in misery had more time to run.

41. Touching Bottom

There was no light anywhere. Only a storm of evil and death . . . his troubles with Angela, the fact that he could not work, the fact that he felt he had made a matrimonial mistake, the fact that he feared he might die or go crazy, made a terrible and agonizing winter for him.
—Dreiser, *The "Genius"* (1915)

A world or given order was passing. . . . For days and weeks and months and years I seemed absolutely alone with a vast sea that urged and persuaded without explaining. I was to change, but I could not see why. The wonder of it, the indifference of it, the inexplicableness of it, seized me as with an icy hand. I was afraid. I did not want to die.
—Dreiser, *An Amateur Laborer* (1904)

Men and women get to living as if in a cave like criminals, outcasts, mad people. Then waters well up, the crust gives way, the cave is gone. You see them alive again in a new medium. I believe life holds such revaluations, a breaking down, a welling up of strange waters.
—Dreiser to Dorothy Dudley (1932)

"In the chill glow of a dying February day," with thirty-two dollars in his pocket, Dreiser arrived in New York City. He took the ferry across the East River to Brooklyn. The tidal flood was like a moat separating him from the gleaming skyline of Manhattan. But in Brooklyn he could live more cheaply. He intended to tour the editorial offices and collect some assignments, sound out employment possibilities, then return to his hideout and write. When he had made enough money he would send for Jug and take an apartment in Manhattan.

Although Paul, Sylvia, Ed, Mame and Brennan, and Emma lived in and around the city, he did not call on them. Too proud to ask for their help, he was also too ashamed of his present state; he, the novelist, reduced to this. Besides, when had he ever helped them?

After debarking from the ferry, he wandered the streets of the Williamsburg section, looking for lodgings. He kept to the waterfront streets as though magnetically drawn to the urban Styx. Eventually he came upon a neighborhood of shabby tenements, factories, livery stables, and a few large brownstones that had seen better days but had sunk to the level of boardinghouses. The place was redolent of failure.

He found a small, four-story brick tenement at 113 Ross Street, a downhill thoroughfare near the Brooklyn Navy Yard and the Wallabout Channel. The landlady, a Mrs. Curry, tall and angular with piercing eyes that matched her black dress, led him up creaking stairs to the top floor, where there was a single room furnished with a rocking chair, a black walnut bookcase filled with religious tracts, and a highboard bed. It was clean and only $2.50 a week. Dreiser took it. If he rationed his money carefully, eating at a boardinghouse nearby, walking rather than taking trolleys and ferries (though it was a long way from his dwelling to the Brooklyn Bridge), he could hold out for several weeks.

Shortly after his arrival, a letter from Ripley Hitchcock caught up with him. Hitchcock had read part of *The Transgressor* in manuscript the previous spring. Having recently resigned from Appleton, he planned to join another house, A. S. Barnes, and was writing to "bespeak an opportunity of seeing your next novel." Dreiser replied that "a long illness—quite a year and a half of nervous prostration—has completely destroyed all my original plans." He said his novel was about three-quarters done, adding more accurately that he had "no immediate prospects of finishing it this spring, as I hoped." He was still "down in the dumps in regard to 'Sister Carrie,' " despite the excellent notices it received in England. He concluded on an optimistic note: "I seem to be just emerging from a long siege of bad weather and am only now looking to my sails again."

Perhaps his fortunes *had* changed: he had hardly been in the city a week and opportunity had sniffed him out in Brooklyn. He set up a meeting with Hitchcock and scaled down his claims as to *The Transgressor*, saying he could show him only a fragment of the story, the same material Hitchcock had perused more than a year ago—that is, the chapters typed by Mallon's typists. He was making "radical changes" in the MS. Moreover, there were "certain things relating to this story which make it impossible for me to offer any hope that we can come to any arrangement concerning it." He was probably referring to his contract with J. T. Taylor.

Hitchcock was a rising young man on the turn-of-the-century publishing scene. As Stephen Crane's editor on *The Red Badge of Courage* at Appleton, he had performed some cosmetic surgery. He had also suggested some strategic cuts of a different nature in the MS of Edward Westcott's *David Harum* that helped transform it into a best seller in 1898. Obviously, Hitchcock was attuned to the popular taste of the day, yet sympathetic (up to a point) to the new realists.

Nothing much came of their discussion, but they kept in touch. A few weeks later Dreiser brought along Peter McCord to another rendezvous at the Harvard Club to discuss a novelette McCord had written. Hitchcock would continue to help Dreiser in any way he could, encouraging him, telling him he would write more books as good as *Carrie*, and keeping a benign eye on his literary career. The possibility of Barnes reissuing *Sister Carrie* came up, for Dreiser later asked Jewett what sort of job Barnes would do.

Carrie was homeless again. Because Dreiser had not finished his second book, Jewett and Taylor were unwilling to reissue it. But they generously authorized him to place it elsewhere if he could. Another publisher, Rand, McNally, had expressed interest, but nothing came of that. Dreiser's reference to the English reviews in his letter may have been calculated to soften up Hitchcock for an appeal that he adopt the little wanderer, but Hitchcock had not changed his view that a second, "less drastic" novel should pave the way for *Carrie*'s rehabilitation. Since *The Transgressor* still belonged to Taylor, that course was an impossibility, and Hitchcock was in no position to commit his company to buy out Dreiser's contract.

The friendly interest from Hitchcock was the last Dreiser received from a publisher. He tried to sell his two-book package to one other house, but the proposal was coldly rejected by the editor in chief, who had known him as a magazinist. "I myself saw the wretchedness of the proposition after I made it," Dreiser later recalled. Who would be crazy enough to stake him in his present state? Defeated, he walked all the way back to Ross Street via the Brooklyn Bridge to save seven cents.

That was his last sortie to publishers row for a while. Theodore collected a few magazine assignments but no job offers. He also tried Park Row but found nothing. Lowering his sights, he called on some local papers in Brooklyn. One editor told him flatly he was overqualified for the staff opening; another promised him a job as the paper's Long Island correspondent for fifteen dollars a week but later reneged.

A sign of his desperation was that he asked Arthur Henry for help. Henry, whom Hitchcock was also interested in publishing, had originally put the editor in touch with the wandering Dreiser, and Henry later wrote Dreiser asking if "something definite could not come from Hitchcock's desire to be of use to you and to get you to work with him." Henry made inquiries of friends at *The Nation* and *The Outlook*, but they were not hiring.

Gradually, Dreiser gave up and withdrew into his little room on Ross Street. He was a writer, so he must keep writing rather than take a temporary job to tide him over (a mistake, he later realized). All he had to do was ride out the storm. He tried to write at the little leaf-table in his tiny room, but it was useless. He spent most of the time staring at an evil brown stain on the peeling wallpaper where the rain had leaked in. His nights were riven by insomnia. "Day after day," he remembered, "I rose to a futile effort to produce some literary article which I might sell and night after night I lay down to a sleepless couch, the ravages of worry and brooding keeping me wide awake."

He was able to complete only one essay during his ordeal in Brooklyn, a syrupy paean to the joys of being poor and a pathetic effort, one suspects, to overcome the depression into which he was sinking. There were many compensations, he declared, for a person without money in the city. He could go to the library, visit a museum, watch the "tortuous, tideful rivers that twist among great forests of masts," gaze at sunrises and moonsets and moonrises. Not that a truly poor person could find recompense in such things, but for him "they are substances of solace, the major portion of all my wealth, or possible wealth, in exchange for which I would not take a miser's hoard."

Those sunrises and moonsets and moonrises suggested the nightly vigils of the insomniac; his insistence on the blessings of poverty was the dissimulation of one who increasingly feared the specter of Hurstwood at his side. Daily, Theodore confronted the gray economic facts, and no afterglow of sunsets could gild them.

Most days his pencil could produce nothing, and he would walk the streets. Guilt and self-recrimination, the depressive's companions, matched his strides. Why hadn't he taken better care of himself—avoided overwork and sexual excesses? Why hadn't he saved his money when he and Jug were first married? Instead, he had purchased fifteen hundred dollars worth of furniture and given her a generous housekeeping allowance so she might keep an ample table. He had even bought himself a frock suit and a silk hat. He had failed as a husband, all but broken off with his best friend, and bungled his opportunity to write the great book that would, as he had once boasted to Page, "destroy conditions, unfavorable or indifferent."

Always inclined to fatalism, he was drowning in it. Dreiser believed his troubles had been "foreordained—worked up by invisible and adverse powers." That such a belief directly contradicted his self-reproaches for past mistakes did not occur to him at the time, but a mind in the grip of depression is impervious to logic. There was neurotic security in fatalism: one simply drifted, waiting for the tide to deposit one safely on the distant shining shore of health.

He conceived the theory that "all life—animal and vegetable—was bound up, so far as their individual conditions were concerned, in a great overruling Providence—fate, power or star, under which they were born, by which they were protected, with which they were compelled to suffer or prosper accordingly as this particular force, Providence or star was successful in the larger universe of which it was a part." Now his star was having a bad time, and he must wait until the plot in the vast sidereal drama took a more favorable turn.

The god Science had forsaken him. He feared omens of death like the howling black dog he saw in Philadelphia; he half believed that the 13 in his house number was the cause of his ill-luck. And Dreiser's theory that his troubles were due to an unlucky star was a kind of sanitized astrology, in which he had more than a casual interest. Just over a year ago, when his downward slide was beginning, he had had his horoscope prepared by one Jeremiah MacDonald, MD, PhD, who told him that Uranus was his ruling planet, that he had a strong love nature ("with you to love is to worship"), and advised him never "to do business in big cities." Theodore's principal fault was "the too strong determination to rule and dominate" others, but, MacDonald added, he had "a strong will and cannot be kept down in the world." (The soothsayer also prophesied inaccurately that in 1902, after some "quarrels and losses through risk," Dreiser would "change with benefit and have a successful year financially.")

But whatever solace he found in astrology, superstition, religion, or sunsets was only temporary. Dreiser was cursed with a pessimistic vision too profound for any of the traditional spiritual nostrums to work. As he wrote later, "It seems as if my mind had been laid bare, as if by a scalpel, to mysteries of the universe, and that I was compelled to suffer blood-raw, the agonies of its weight." His state of mind was like that expressed in Stephen Crane's poem:

> Should the wide world roll away
> Leaving black terror,
> Limitless night,
> Nor God, nor man, nor place to stand. . . .

Nights were the worst. Insomnia clamped him in its jaws. His bed was a torture rack. Sleep, sleep; he remembered how as a child sweet drowsiness would swoon him as soon as his head touched the pillow. Now he lay in the insomniac's half-world between unconsciousness and wakefulness until the watery early light filtered through his dirty window. The days were almost as bad; he sat at his desk or walked the streets in a semistuporous state.

Hurstwood-like, he nursed his dwindling funds. His only expenses were his weekly rent of $2.50 and another $4.50 for board. Premonitions of impending disaster would periodically jerk him out of his apathy, and he would mutter, "I must do something!" But only manual labor was available. He would slink by the factories, offices, and warehouses in the area, eyeing them furtively. On the few occasions when he was able to nerve himself to enter, he would be struck by a "cold fear of inability" and hurriedly retrace his steps. He thought himself superior to the work. Once, when he started to join a group of men in an employment line, rough, healthy laborers all, he sensed their curious stares forming a wall against him and scuttled off. He imagined they were asking, What is this frail intellectual doing here?

In his eerie state of hyperselfconsciousness, dealing with clerks and other functionaries was painful. He was sure they laughed at him behind his back. If only he could talk with the company president. After all, he had conversed on an equal plane with Joseph Choate, Andrew Carnegie, and Philip Armour. He would tell the tycoon that he was going through a temporary bad spell and thought a stint of physical labor might do him good. The president would nod gravely and offer him something to do. When he applied again—in Hurstwood's steps—for a motorman's job at a trolley company, he was buoyed by this fantasy as far as the chief's secretary, who politely suggested that he obtain an application at the hiring office around the corner. To his relief, it was closed.

When his money was almost gone, Theodore decided to try a private charity. "I have done my share towards sustaining society, both by working, giving in alms and paying my taxes. Why should not society do something for me?" he told the president. The charity head patiently explained that what little money he had to distribute must go to the desperately needy. All he could do was to give Theodore letters of introduction to places that provided temporary jobs. Once he was outside, Dreiser tore up the letters and threw them in the gutter. The letterhead of the charitable society would stigmatize him as a beggar wherever he presented it, and his pride could not bear that.

Then he received a ten-dollar check for a poem he had dug out of his trunk and sent to a magazine, and when that sum was almost gone, he remembered an old debt and collected it. He moved into a smaller room that had just become available in his lodging house. It cost only $1.25 per week, and he gave up eating at the boardinghouse, taking his meals at cheap restaurants in the area. By this resort, and by eating little, he cut his food expenses to two dollars a week.

His new room was a six-by-eight hall bedroom, furnished with a chair, a tiny table, and a grimy oil stove. It had a single narrow window overlooking the street; a chintz curtain hanging on one wall served as a wardrobe. It was the meanest room at 113 Ross Street save one: a tiny alcove formerly used as a closet where an old lady dwelt. He sometimes caught a glimpse of her floating like a ghost through the dark, dingy hall, or sitting in the chair that was her only furniture, her hands cupped in her lap, her eyes transfixed by some inner vision. She had been worn down by the urban seas to a thin, translucent shard. Her room was the end of the line.

His money played out like a lifeline through his hands. He cut his meals down to a bottle of milk and half a loaf of bread a day, supplemented by an occasional apple or potato he picked up in the gutter at the Wallabout market. He was emaciated-looking; his weight had dropped to 130 pounds. (Hurstwood's, after his bout with pneumonia, had fallen to 135.) He began to have hallucinations. At night, he felt a sensation that Something was coming; he could hear its footsteps in the hallway and then feel it beside his bed. The hairs on the back of his neck would stand up as a hand groped toward his head on the pillow— Then he would jump up and light the lamp and confront his empty room.

He was also subject to queer distortions of perception. He imagined that lines and angles were slightly off plumb, and twisted his chair in a full circle, attempting to realign himself with the universe. Out of doors he noticed a similar phenomenon—streets, trees, curbs, all looked out of kilter. And when he read a newspaper, the columns slanted maddeningly. He shifted the paper around, vainly trying to straighten them.

Those perceptual distortions probably had a medical explanation. Dreiser's weaker eye, which had not been accommodating properly in Philadelphia because of the drugs he was taking, had now lost its adjustment to the stronger one. Normally, images seen by his stronger eye dominated, but because of the mental stress he was undergoing, he began seeing through the weaker astigmatic one (which he had seen the doctor in Philadelphia about, without receiving treatment), precipitating perceptual distortions. His symptoms resembled those of the condition called cyclophoria: floors seem slanted, right angles become obtuse, houses appear to be leaning over. Experiencing these bizarre visions is very disorienting to the sufferer and can exacerbate the original mental distress.

Persons in this state sometimes regard these optical phenomena as "visions." Abraham Lincoln, who had a weaker eye, once had a double perception of himself in the mirror, and interpreted it as a prophecy that he would be elected to two terms, though he would not complete the second one. While Dreiser may have had schizophrenic tendencies (his niece Vera thought so), sleeplessness and fasting seem to have been the other contributing factors in his hallucinations. (He could also have been taking excessive amounts of one of Dr. Duhring's sleep draughts to combat his maddening insomnia, though he doesn't directly mention doing so and could hardly have spared the money to purchase them.) In Theodore's case they took the form of an out-of-body experience. He saw himself as another person—or rather two persons. One was "a tall, thin, greedy individual who had struggled and thought always for himself and how he should prosper." And the other was a silent, philosophical creature who was watching him with aloof detachment, "taking an indifferent interest in his failures."

Rather than the mystic's telescopic vision of God, he had an X-ray view of himself as a quivering bundle of nerves, appetites, desire, ambition, selfishness, ego, and dread—qualities he had personified in Drouet, with his piggish sensualism; Carrie, with her selfish desires; and Hurstwood, with his apathy and terror of life. This self, Dreiser perceived, was "now in a corner and could not get out." The other self—he called it his "oversoul," in the Emersonian sense of a higher, universal consciousness— was the philosophic Dreiser, the creator of Carrie and Drouet and Hurstwood, the detached, self-conscious artist who must "get it all in." But his oversoul did not seem so terrible. True, it was indifferent, cold, and remote. It contemplated him as if he were a fly stuck in flypaper or the moths that danced around the lamp in his room. Yet his oversoul was not malignant: "He was very wise and sane and I had great faith in him. . . . In all probability he would bring me through. Something would happen."

In *Ev'ry Month* Dreiser had once written about the people who perished during a bitterly cold New York winter: "They are too shy to complain openly, too thin-skinned to endure pity, too fearful of public opinion to seek refuge in a workhouse, and too timid and weak-bodied to risk seizing what is not their own." Now in the direst straits he had exhibited all those traits. He had refused charity and avoided workhouses; he had been too proud to ask family or friends for help and too respectable to steal. Yet here he was, still alive; he could still live. He had been reduced to a speck of urban dust blown about by capricious winds, yet he believed "something would happen." When all his outer defenses were peeled away, a faith in life remained. As he had written of Carrie: "She was saved in that she was hopeful."

Later, he wrote: "You cannot move in the crowd and not feel the ancient faith of the world that life is good and something comes of this opportunity of existing. What is it, who can say. You only feel it, and it renews your youth."

42. Just Tell Them That You Saw Me

"I long to see them all again, but not just yet, she said,
'Tis pride alone that's keeping me away.
Just tell them not to worry, for I'm all right don't you know,
Tell mother I am coming home some day."
— Paul Dresser, "Just Tell Them That You Saw Me" (1895)

A great provision against would be suicides here was the open
condition of the rooms. . . . There was no chance to turn on the
gas here because there was none.
— Dreiser, *An Amateur Laborer* (1904)

he dual sense of himself recurred as he dragged about the
Brooklyn streets in his stuporous state, but it continued oddly
to hearten him. Not that he had much cause for optimism.
He was down to his last few dollars; he felt dragged out and
looked terrible—as his sister Mame told him when he appeared
on her doorstep one day.

He had somehow summoned up the resolve to have still another try
at finding an editorial job in Manhattan, and after a day of fruitless rounds,
he found himself on Fourteenth Street near Union Square, only ten blocks
from the Brennans' apartment on Washington Square. He was pricked
by a desire to see his sister, despite their strained relationship in recent
years. Perhaps writing *The Transgressor* had reminded Theodore of her
hard life, which made him more sympathetic toward her.

When Mame opened the door, she was shocked and insisted he stay
for lunch, which turned out to be a five-course spread, since Brennan
was a dedicated trencherman. Dreiser wolfed down his portion, his first
decent meal since he gave up eating at the boardinghouse. In response
to his sister's anxious questions, he said he had been going through a

session of neurasthenia but was feeling better. When she invited him to join them on a country outing, he declined, too proud to tell her that he could not afford the rail fare.

The Brennans' apartment was by no means luxurious, but with its drapes, pictures, and heavy carpets it seemed a palace. To live like this, to have plenty to eat, to sleep in a soft bed! A longing for material comforts filled him with a rush. Shelter and food—a mind unmoored in them was adrift in a storm. When he parted from Mame and Brennan, he gave her a false address. He knew she was in touch with Paul. If Paul learned where his younger brother was, he would seek out his shabby lodgings.

On his way to the Twenty-third Street ferry, he stopped at Fourth Avenue to inspect the excavations for the new subway. The wind suddenly picked up and whipped his hat away, whirling it down somewhere in the inky depths. The loss upset him. He was now down to exactly three dollars and thirty-one cents, and a new one would cost him at least two dollars. Not only did it keep his head warm in the cold wind, the hat stood for respectability, dignity, status. He had resisted pawning an engraved gold watch which he had bought in St. Louis. That and his frock suit, his overcoat, and a silk topper, which were stored in his trunk at Ross Street, were the last vestiges of his former status.

But if he did buy a new hat, he would not have enough for food, for his room rent was due tomorrow. He stood in the dark, lashed by the cold winds, at the brink of the shadow-pooled pit. Never, he later wrote, had he felt so keenly "the vastness, the indifference, the desolation of the world" as he did that night. He could only resign himself to the workings of fate. It would either save him or finish him off; he was powerless to affect the outcome. He walked along Fourteenth Street until he found a hat store, where he bought a cheap brown woolen cap for fifty cents— a workman's cap, but at least it would keep his head warm.

The next day he paid Mrs. Curry the $1.25 he owed for rent, leaving him one dollar and fifty-six cents. He figured if he cut out lunches and lived on milk and bread, he would finish the week with a bit over a dollar. That he would use to go to Manhattan, where he would put his trunk in storage and wander the streets until he found some kind of charitable institution that provided free beds. The time had come to break out of his depressing cubicle. But Dreiser found himself reluctant to go. He was like an old convict who is afraid to leave the safety of his cell. And how could he survive in Manhattan with practically no money?

A few days later, a navy steward came to the house with an invitation from Dreiser's brother-in-law Dick White to have dinner on his ship, the battleship *Indiana*, which had just tied up at the Brooklyn Navy Yard. Theodore told the messenger he would come, but with all his troubles, he worried that he had no dress suit, and, worse, no decent hat. He still owned a threadbare business suit, which would serve for the occasion, but his only other hat, the topper, would look ridiculous with it. All he had was the cloth cap—the universal symbol of a laborer, proclaiming his fall from middle-class grace.

Yearning for a decent meal settled the debate. Dick tactfully made no comment on Theodore's appearance when he arrived, introducing him to his fellow junior officers, a collection of golden youths who were pursuing a socially acceptable career. Dreiser could not help thinking how little these trim, clean young men knew of cold or hunger.

Dick was not the only one to track him to his hideout on Ross Street. Earlier that month Dreiser had received a letter from a New York architect named Wilson Potter, who had somehow heard that he was down and out and offered him a job as a gardener at his summer home in Connecticut. Dreiser replied that he was interested; after all, Dr. Duhring had advised him to try light manual work. But Potter was out of town when Theodore's reply arrived, and when he did try to locate Dreiser, the latter had moved away.

Another letter came that week from Paul, who had written to the fictitious address Dreiser had given to Mame. The number was in the same postal district, and an efficient clerk redirected it to the correct location. Paul's letter was full of josh and tender concern. He demanded that Theo come to see him, or else he would go to Brooklyn. Dreiser did not reply.

As his final day at Ross Street drew near, he felt a slight lift of spirits. Surely nothing worse could happen to him now. Emanations of Paul and Mame's affection pulsed from the city. Not that he would ask *them* for help, but *someone* knew he was alive. Saturday morning he ate half of the loaf he had bought the night before, packed his trunk and his grip, stuffed some letters from publishers in his pocket to use as references, and walked out of his room and the house at 113 Ross Street. For eight weeks he had lived there, and now, on a warm spring morning in April, he was leaving it and the old lady in the end room and Mrs. Curry in her funereal black dress. He took the ferry across the East River.

He stood at the rail watching a cloud of sea gulls swooping down to snatch bits of garbage floating on the choppy green waters. Fighting, eating, going hungry—emblems of nature's blind profligacy. And on the far side, amid the shining buildings of the city, the teeming crowds in the streets, all of them scrabbling for subsistence like the gulls. He decided that the questions of who succeeded and who failed had little to do with the Darwinian concept of fitness. Some were born with money; others beauty. He had been born with a gift to write; it was not something he had acquired or studied for. It would have been better to be born with money or beauty, but he must accept his lot.

Leaving the ferry, Theodore walked along Twenty-third Street. Now he must deal with the urgent question of where he would sleep that night and the nights to come until he found a job. He thought of the New York Charitable Societies, which had their offices at Twenty-third and Fourth Avenue. He walked in the back entrance of the building, still debating whether to ask for help. Before he could make up his mind, it was closing time.

He strolled on, mulling over what to do next. Then he remembered a journalist friend who had worked for the New Haven Railroad as a conductor following a nervous breakdown. He had heard that George Henry Daniels, the general passenger agent of the New York Central, had literary inclinations. Why not make his case as he had so often imagined himself doing? The New York Central employed thousands of people; surely it would have a menial or clerical job for him. And, after all, Theodore had published an interview with the company's president, Chauncey Depew, in *Success*.

Impelled by this desperate hope, he walked up Fourth Avenue to the Grand Central Depot, a red-brick edifice with three tall clock towers on Forty-second Street; inside, were the administrative offices of the railroad. Resuming his identity as a literary man had a tonic effect. The airs he unconsciously assumed got Theodore through the outworks to the office of the passenger agent's secretary. After he had described his plight, showed his letters from publishers, and made some allusions to his last meeting with Depew, the secretary was impressed. Daniels was out, but could Dreiser come back in an hour? He could and did and found awaiting him a letter signed by Daniels himself asking the chief engineer of the railroad to extend all courtesies to the bearer.

Elated, Dreiser allowed himself to be bucked down the chain of command until he ended up with the engineer of maintenance of way, A. T. Hardin, who had charge of thirteen thousand employees who performed roadwork on the Central's far-flung empire. Hardin listened patiently as Dreiser, encouraged by a sympathetic listener of his own kind, poured out his story. After all, neurasthenia was a respectable complaint—the American Disease, afflictor of overworked dynamos in business as well as the arts. Hardin said he used a Whitely Exerciser when the pressures of overcivilization became too much for him, or retreated to his country place. He admired Dreiser's determination to take the physical-labor cure, but thought the job of track worker too strenuous. He would ponder the matter over the weekend.

Intoxicated by the heady air at the corporate summit, Dreiser bowed himself out. Now he had hope. There was one small problem, though. He had no money for food, and he had left his half loaf of bread on a windowsill outside the chief passenger agent's office. When he went back for it, it was gone. Then he remembered his watch. He had once written about the Provident Loan Association, which had been set up by some enlightened citizens to extend loans to poor people who brought in trinkets that conventional pawnbrokers would not accept. He went there, and to his surprise, the clerk offered him twenty-five dollars.

He could live for weeks on that! It would enable him to survive until his first railroad paycheck came through. He treated himself to a full-course meal and decided to spend the night at the Mills Hotel, another enlightened institution for the poor, which rented clean rooms for twenty cents a day. But first he felt an urge to luxuriate in the spring sunshine and decided to take the Hudson ferry to Fort Lee and hike along the Palisades. He joined the afternoon fashion parade up Broadway, intending to buy a decent hat at a shop he knew on Forty-second Street. What he was wearing might provoke a chorus of "What Right Has He on Broadway?"

As he was approaching the Imperial Hotel on Thirty-second Street, Dreiser noticed two men emerge from a hansom cab. One was a small hunchback; the other a tall, fat man elegantly turned out in a Prince Albert coat, gray pants, and white spats. He recognized them immediately. Ducking his head, he tried to hurry past, but a familiar voice pulled him back.

"Hello, Paul," he said. The old resentment welled up, and he replied sullenly to Paul's barrage of anxious questions.

But Paul would not be brushed off. He was appalled by his younger brother's appearance. "Look, old man," he said. "I'm going away tonight. I've got to go to Buffalo, but I want you to let me loan you something until I come back."

And he reached into his pocket and extracted a fat roll of bills. "I know you're in hard luck. We've all been that way from time to time." Paul tried to press the money into Theodore's hand, but the other brushed it away. It became a ridiculous scene, Theodore insisting angrily that he didn't want the money, Paul pleading with him to take it.

"Please," Paul begged. "For God's sake don't let your pride stand between us. You can get along, but don't let me go away worrying about you. Take it and you can pay me when you choose."

Dreiser looked into those blue eyes that were so like his mother's. He was on the verge of tears and would have thrown his arms around Paul if there hadn't been so many people around. He stuffed the roll in his pocket, muttering that he would not spent a penny of it.

Paul made him promise to come to the hotel the following Monday. Then he was gone. Theodore strode along Broadway, thinking that a world with Paul in it could not be such a hard place. He had the twenty-five dollars, Paul's money, *and* the prospect of a job that would restore him to health. The sudden windfalls had transformed him from an urban cipher to a semblance of his normal self.

He merged with the Broadway throng, then entered a drugstore and had a prescription filled, immediately regretting the outlay because he intended to pay back Paul's loan on Monday. Then he took the elevated down to Bleecker Street, where the Mills Hotel was located. It was an imposing nine-story structure of cream-colored brick set in a neighborhood of run-down tenements, a monument to the philanthropy of Darius O. Mills, who had built it as a refuge from Bowery flophouses.

Once inside the handsome doors, which would not have looked out of place on one of Paul's Broadway hostelries, Theodore found himself among the same cast of bums, down-and-outers, and lost souls that one saw along the Bowery. There were some young workingmen, living here to save money until they could move somewhere better, but for many this was a way station on the familiar road that led to Blackwells Island and the boat on the East River. He noted that the walls of each cubicle were raised on jacks above the floor, and reached to within three feet of the ceiling. It would be impossible to commit suicide in this room. There was not even a gas jet.

He spent a restless night amid the constant hubbub created by the men in neighboring cubicles who cried out in their sleep or talked to themselves while their neighbors cursed them and shouted, "Chop it off!" The next day, to escape this bedlam, he took the elevated train to 125th Street and caught a ferry to Fort Lee. Warmed by the sunshine, he felt the stirrings of returning life. He was still young; he still hoped. He vowed he would die before he would return to the horror of his life in Brooklyn.

Monday came, and as he walked up Broadway to keep his appointment with Paul, the streets seemed fresh and clean in the bright sunlight. The trees in Madison Square Park were stippled with young leaves and the fountain plashed. In the Fifth Avenue Hotel across the way, the chair-warmers were opening their morning papers; atop the tower of Stanford White's Garden the golden Diana was poised on her pedestal, aiming her bow. The theater signs proclaimed new stars, new pleasures within. The dudes on the corners eyed the passing women.

He walked toward Paul's hotel, emerging from a chrysalis, hatching plans. He must get back his health and then earn a living. He must have some money—"Enough to be clean and decent and mentally at rest." He must never again be poor. As he entered the ornate portals of the Imperial (one likes to imagine), the shadowy figure following him, a man in a shabby overcoat and a battered hat, hesitated, turned away, and shambled off. Soon, Hurstwood was swallowed up by the crowd.

Part Six

THE LOST DECADE

43. The Way Back

> After a long battle I am once more the possessor of health. That
> necessary poise in which the mind and body reflect the pul-
> sations of the infinite is mine. I am not overconscious. I trust
> I am not under so. All that is, now passes before me a rich,
> varied and beautiful procession. I have fought a battle for the
> right to live and for the present, musing with stilled nerves and
> a serene gaze, I seem the victor.
>
> —Dreiser, *An Amateur Laborer* (1904)

Dreiser wrote those somewhat smug words in 1904 after his
chance encounter with Paul on Broadway. He exaggerated
the depth of his recovery, but he had clearly won the right
to live. He did not do it alone, of course. The help, material
and psychological, of Paul was crucial. At the nadir of his life,
his older brother had pulled him out of the abyss. Paul's first move was
to bundle Theodore off to a sanatorium he regularly visited. Its official
name was the Olympia Hygienic Institute, but most of its habitués called
it simply Muldoon's after the former wrestling champion William Muldoon who owned it. Nestled in the gently rolling Long Island hills, it
drew a wealthy clientele who were run down from overwork or debilitated
by the excesses of the flesh. Muldoon, who had been a saloon bouncer
on the East Side, exhibition opponent of "Strangler" Lewis on the
vaudeville circuit, foe of Charles Whistler in an epical match that lasted
eight hours and ended in a draw, and trainer of John L. Sullivan, badgered and hectored them back to health.

His cure consisted of regular exercise sessions with the medicine ball
(which he had invented), simple food, fresh air, long walks, and horse-
back rides. But the chief therapeutic agent was Muldoon himself. Now
sixty but still in peak physical shape, he was omnipresent, bullying fat
businessmen, shattering their pompousness, forcing them to think again
of their bodies, if only by way of their aching muscles. Austin Brennan,

who had been there and called the ex-wrestler "Bulldoon," claimed he had "endured more pain during the three weeks I spent there than at any period of my life."

Under Muldoon's regime, Dreiser's health steadily improved, and he began to know what a normal night's sleep was like. After only a month's stay, he had resumed negotiations with Hitchcock on a new edition of *Sister Carrie* and had written an article about the sanatorium, "Scared Back to Nature," which appeared in the May 16 *Harper's Weekly*. Perhaps because he was still under Muldoon's lash, Dreiser speaks of the "marked strain of autocracy" of the host and "a certain helpless servility" among the guests. Yet he must have felt Muldoon's authoritarian methods were good, for he quotes him approvingly as saying they were designed for "wresting a man's mental control from him in order to increase his mental energy. If his will has nothing to do with the arrangement of his day, his mind is much more likely to contemplate nature and to rest." Dreiser later credited the hazing and strenuous exercise with taking his mind off himself and checking his morbidly introspective tendencies.

After two months at the sanatorium, he was sufficiently recovered to go to work for the New York Central, remaining there from early June until Christmas day 1903. Theodore was an unlikely railroad hand, not strong enough to do heavy labor, eagerly engaging his perplexed co-workers in philosophical discussions, insisting on his superior status as a recovering neurasthenic. He was first put to work in the carpentry shop at Spuyten Duyvil, north of New York City, sweeping up shavings, sawdust, and other scraps. After only a week of this, he applied to R. P. Mills, the supervisor of buildings, for a transfer and was assigned to inspect a pile-driving operation at the Tarrytown freighthouse. He liked this supervisory role and remained at it a few weeks before the job ran out and he was transferred to a section gang back at "the Spike." A month later he again requested a transfer, invoking friends in high places: "I was given to understand by Mr. Hardin that a change could be had if I desired and I now think one would be beneficial to me." On September 1, after demanding and receiving a pay raise from fifteen to seventeen and a half cents a day, he was assigned to a masonry crew under a tough Irish foreman named Mike Burke, and there he remained for the remainder of his railroad stint. Theodore made himself useful to Burke by performing various clerical chores, such as filling out requisition forms, which the foreman loathed doing.

He retained a foothold in the middle-class world by boarding in Kings-bridge with a cultivated widow named Mrs. Hardenbrooks, who had been impressed by his literary credentials, and her family, which included a widowed daughter. Dreiser told Dorothy Dudley that he had an affair with an unnamed woman around this time, and in his autobiographical novel, *The "Genius,"* written in 1911, the hero, Eugene, does take up with the landlady's daughter, a well-off, unconventional beauty named Car-lotta, who is married to an absentee gambler. The real daughter was rather plain, and Dreiser mentions no affair in *An Amateur Laborer,* an unpub-lished nonfiction account of his railroad experiences written in 1904. A local mystery woman who lived in Kingsbridge with her father, whom he saw driving by in a carriage, seems more like Carlotta, but Dreiser did not even speak to her. Possibly the woman in the novel is a composite of the two. Eugene does greet Carlotta with the same phrase Dreiser describes using with the Hardenbrooks' daughter, but there the resem-blance ends. Whatever real-life dalliance he was engaging in was ended with the arrival of Jug in August, and by then he had moved out of the Hardenbrooks home. (In *The "Genius"* Eugene's wife finds out about the affair and their marriage is shaken; he promises her that he will give up his philandering.)

The life of an amateur laborer was beginning to pall. "I saw that I was as unfitted to be a hewer of wood as I was to be president of the railroad," Dreiser recalled. In addition to providing timely financial aid, Paul sent his brother a stream of encouraging letters. When Theodore groused about his work with the tie-laying crew, Paul wrote, "Suppose you have those spikes driven so d———d deep that in the ages to come they will be . . . looked upon, as the great sticks of macaroni used by the monsters who lived in 1903—."

When his brother sounded blue, Paul wrote, "Now that depressed *ga-gerino* . . . must be cut out. Remember the future of the great New York Central system must not weaken." Or he composed mock aphorisms: "The wicked flee when none pursues" and "Woman, like tea, some-times is weak."

Occasionally Paul's deep concern for Theodore's welfare would break through the clown's mask. In August, perhaps because Dreiser had moved and Paul lost track of him, he shot off a telegram: WHAT IS THE MATTER THEODORE ARE YOU ILL ANSWER QUICK. Occasionally he would enclose a "V" for spending money, or invite him to have dinner in town. Although *Sister Carrie* was probably the only serious work of literature Paul had ever read, he continued to regard his brother as a genius. When he heard that

Theodore had written a long letter outlining his philosophical views to a Utah reader, Paul reprimanded him: "Now you cut out giving opinions and views to every rube who writes and wishes to know something about God, Jeff Davis and Roosevelt — You have been working long and hard to get yourself in condition to write. So when you do write let it be on your book. Don't waste gray matter on anything but your life's ambition."

There were others cheering him on as well. Duffy, of course; Coates, whom Theodore had known only while he was in Philadelphia, but who was obviously impressed with him; J. E. Bowler, the tailor, who, when he learned of Dreiser's illness, expressed "sincere sympathy" and said he was "glad to see from your letter that you are bearing it so patiently & philosophically." Jewett had sent him buck-up letters at Muldoon's, and when he learned Dreiser was working on the railroad, he applauded: "Good for you. Health is bound to come to you through some strenuous channel. Keep a stiff upper lip, and you will come out all right." Despite Dreiser's outstanding debt, he also forwarded a royalty check from Heinemann for British sales of *Sister Carrie.*

His railroad experience did provide Dreiser with a firsthand view of the "labor question," just as his stay at Muldoon's had yielded an unglamorous view of the ruling class. In the space of seven months he explored both sides of the Great Divide in American society. Previously he had expressed a Populist disapproval of great wealth while sometimes envying its privileges. As for the working class, it was beneath him. After seeing both classes close up, he found little to admire in either. The Muldoon's crowd was grasping, money obsessed, and self-indulgent, while the workers were beaten down, conniving, with a "sour, pugnacious view of life." Yet he envied the physical strength and dexterity of the workers and came to see that they deserved more help from society. Their lot was a grim one, an unending round of toil enforced by the lash of economic necessity; they created wealth for others—the overindulged patients at Muldoon's; their tasks were fragmented, mind-deadening, and uncreative, and their lives were haunted by economic insecurity. In "The Toil of the Laborer," a long essay he wrote not long after leaving the railroad, Dreiser seemed to call for economic security for all: "That none should suffer, that none should want! This after all seemed the worthiest thought that sprang at the sight of the toil-weary man."

A more immediate consequence was that he gave up the free-lance life and became an editor again. Paul was instrumental in his return to the magazine world. He was writing a farce called *Boomerang* with Robert H. Davis, managing editor of the New York *Daily News*, which was starting a Sunday supplement, and Paul asked his collaborator to take his brother on staff. One suspects Paul would have supported Theodore had he wanted to resume working on his novel. He could certainly afford to. Now a full partner in the renamed Howley, Haviland and Dresser, Paul was still turning out hits—"Mr. Volunteer," "The Voice of the Hudson," "Where Are the Friends of Other Days?" and "The Boys Are Coming Home To-Day"—though none of them was as big as "On the Banks of the Wabash" and "The Blue and the Gray."

In October 1903 Paul wrote an impatient Theodore that Davis "will do something for you after January 1." On the strength of that offer Theodore left the railroad just before Christmas. He and Jug took their furniture out of storage and moved to a modest apartment at 399 Mott Avenue in the Bronx—with the help of a fifty-dollar check from Paul. Jug's brother Pete White also aided them with a loan, telling them not to worry about paying it back.

In January 1904 Theodore began the job on the *Daily News*, turning out feature stories on lurid or sentimental topics such as "The Love Affairs of Little Italy" and "The Cradle of Tears" (a New York foundling home). It was while he was at the *News* that he began "The Toil of the Laborer." After finishing it, he took up the more ambitious *An Amateur Laborer*, working on it at the office in his spare time. He had increasing amounts of that. In June the Sunday supplement was canceled and he was unemployed. After a few months' idleness, during which Paul may have tided him over, for he sold few articles, he secured an editorial post at the Street and Smith pulp fiction factory through Duffy.

And so Dreiser gradually emerged from his nightmare. But it left scars. He still considered himself a writer, but now he had all but resigned himself to giving up his novel. He wanted no more of the horror and privation he had known during those eight weeks at Ross Street. Although his nerves were still not one hundred percent, his writer's block had completely thawed. His labor experiences had provided him with a rich vein of material, which he worked assiduously. In Philadelphia he was thinking about the "peculiar story" his life would make, and the article about Muldoon's had set him off.

As so often happened in Dreiser's writing career, after the initial burst he ran out of steam on *An Amateur Laborer*. He could never decide whether to make it autobiographical, which was how he initially wrote it (with a subtitle "The Case of the Author"), or to recast it as a novel. Ripley Hitchcock, who read the thirty-odd chapters Theodore finished, favored the novelistic approach, while Joseph Coates, editor of *Era* in Philadelphia, advised him to stick to a factual account, in the tradition of Jacob Riis's exposés. "People like true things," Coates wrote him; a " 'true story' told as you can tell it, with all your keen insight and power and sympathy ought to have a good chance of its value being recognized." Coates, the progressive, saw the book as an important document on the condition of labor, while Hitchcock, one guesses, thought a novel would be more commercial.

An Amateur Laborer, which describes Dreiser's bout with neurasthenia, contains passages of great power and unrelenting gloom that echo Melville's *Pierre* or Dostoevsky's *Notes From the Underground.* One cannot imagine that it would have been popular, though if Dreiser could have found and sustained the proper form, it would have been one of his greatest works. But that is only speculation. *An Amateur Laborer* remains a fragment for literary anthologists.

What he wrote in 1904, when the events were still fresh in his mind, remains the truest account of his breakdown; in later years Dreiser expurgated or embroidered the record he set down. For example, in "Down Hill and Up," an essay written in the 1920s, and in a letter to H. L. Mencken, he told of seriously contemplating ending it all in the "icy cold and splashing waters" of the East River, only to be diverted by an interloper—an Erie Canal boatman in one version and a jovial drunken Scotsman in another. Although Dreiser undoubtedly had suicidal thoughts during this period, there is no mention of an attempt in *An Amateur Laborer.* And when he drew upon his railroad experiences in his autobiographical novel, *The "Genius,"* he toned down the hardship aspects considerably.

He quickly learned that there was no market for grim stories like "The Toil of the Laborer," which was widely rejected and not published until 1913 in the New York *Call,* a socialist paper. In search of salable material, he carved out incidents and characters from the *Laborer* and expanded them into shorter pieces—one on the Mills Hotel and a humorous sketch called "The Cruise of the Idlewild." Rather than drawing social morals, he focused on personalities like Mike Burke, whom he transformed from the brutish despot who appears briefly in "Toil" into a heroic leader, so devoted to his men that he sacrifices his life for them. (The real Burke died no such noble death; he makes his last appearance in Dreiser's life when he refuses to let a New York *Daily News* photographer take his picture to illustrate the article about him.) Similarly, he fleshed out the one-dimensional portrait of Muldoon in *Harper's Weekly* in a sketch called "Culhane, The Solid Man," which defends the ex-wrestler's methods more unequivocally than he did in the initial account. (Muldoon didn't like the sympathetic portrait, however, claiming it exaggerated his methods, and avenged himself in his autobiography, claiming that Dreiser had spent only a day at the sanatorium and then fled to the city. That account is belied by his bill for an eight-week stay, which Paul had paid.)

Although the passing of time mellowed Dreiser's recollections of his bout with neurasthenia, it was a watershed in his life. The helplessness and humiliation of his poverty lacerated his soul, leaving a fresh scar over the old ones from Terre Haute and Sullivan days. He had engaged in a bout of nihilism that had endangered his health and sanity. He was worried for months afterward that the damage was permanent: "To be maimed as an insect. To get a hurt that would not heal." Henceforth, he would strive to live with the paradox that nature was cruel and profligate and blind, yet to be alive was good.

He had felt the lash of social prejudice that falls on the helpless sufferer of mental torments. The mentally ill person, he wrote in *An Amateur Laborer*, is "debarred . . . from broad and pleasant social contact. He is injured. Therefore he is not morally whole. Let him go forth and wander by himself. He does not any longer belong to the sane and healthy order of society."

He also learned that the truth teller is often cast outside the walls of the city. When he wrote *Sister Carrie*, Dreiser had held the idealistic belief that the interests of artists and society were harmonious and that one who told the truth performed a socially useful act. He had not sought wide popularity, but he had supposed that presenting an honest picture of "conditions" would gain him honor and recognition—if not urban celebrity, at least admission to the prestigious colonies of literary fame, inhabited by a Stedman or a Howells. Now he realized that the times were out of joint for his kind of book. As he had written despairingly in Philadelphia, "Ah me—Ah me, who is it that tells the truth and is happy." Censorship was no mere harmless condemnation from backwoods pulpits; it was no quaint local ordinance like one against spitting tobacco in the street. Censorship was used by the dominant class to banish truth by branding it an obscenity. "Immoral" meant politically and socially suspect. He who was deeply opposed to mixing politics and art had learned that art had political consequences.

Theodore did not relish being an outsider—neither the ultimate isolation of madness nor that uniquely urban loneliness he had experienced in Brooklyn. While living at Mott Avenue in the Bronx, he wrote a short sketch entitled "The Loneliness of the City" that articulated a longing for human fellowship. It described the anonymous lives of his fellow tenants in the building, who chase after wealth, fame, and pleasure. Only in times of calamity do they recall "the importance of the individual relationship . . . friendship, affection, tenderness." The sketch closes with this admonition: "After all is said and done, we must truly love one another or we must die—alone, neglected despised and forgotten, as too many of us die."

When the Genius of Dreiser's first published story for the Chicago *Globe* renounces the protection of the gods and decides to go out in the world, he hesitates, remembering all the terrors and uncertainties of life that he had sought to escape. At that moment, a voice whispers in his ear: "In thine own hand is the power—the strength. Achieve thine own glory. It is for thee and thee alone to do this. In effort, will thy genius be sharpened. Aid from the gods would but destroy thee."

Unlike his Genius, Dreiser had placed his faith in the voices of praise and the good fortune that forever smiles on young men. Wiser and more bitter now, he could see that there was no aid from the gods (or the Stedmans and Howellses), and that forces which were quite ordinary and human, ones within himself and outside himself, could destroy him. And so he must armor himself, shore up his defenses against the economic storms, and cultivate allies inside the gates, a fifth column as it were, while toughening himself mentally and spiritually. He exercised regularly, followed Muldoon's regimen of calisthenics, taking a bath and drinking several glasses of hot water upon rising—"work and cleanliness," the old wrestler had stressed. And he toughened his mind by reading philosophy—Schopenhauer, Kant, and others.

He must change, Dreiser told himself in Brooklyn. It would not happen in a day, or a week, or a year, but he set his life on a new course. As he had written at the time of the *Sister Carrie* debacle, "Fortune need not forever feel that she must use the whip on me."

44. The Best of Brothers

But still I think of him . . . on Broadway between Twenty-ninth and Forty-second Streets, the spring and summer time at hand, the doors of the grills and bars of the hotels open, the rout of actors and actresses ambling to and fro, his own delicious presence dressed in his best, his "funny" stories, his songs being ground out by the hand organs, his friends extending their hands, clapping him on the shoulder, cackling over the latest idle yarns.

—Dreiser, "My Brother Paul" (1919)

But remember that fame in many cases is but the last few throbs of a broken heart.

—Paul Dresser (1905)

Where are the friends of other days,
Friends that I loved so well;
Friends that I never turned away,
Is there no one to tell?

—Paul Dresser, "Where Are the Friends of Other Days?" (1903)

B
etween 1900 and 1911 Theodore Dreiser published no novels, and he almost disappears from the pages of American literary history. Yet his "silent decade" was not a time of withdrawal or prostration. Those years were marked by ambition and a strong attraction to power and money. Being Dreiser, he never pursued those two goals with the single-minded zeal of a *Success* subject, but there was a good deal of the bourgeois in him, and during these years that side of his nature was in the ascendant. The writer, the bohemian, the nonconformist, were accordingly eclipsed—though, as his various employers (some of the most neurotic dynamos in the American success-worship pantheon) soon learned, he remained prickly and independent. Exposed to the rough game of commerce, Dreiser found he liked it; the vulnerable, failed novelist of the post–*Sister Carrie* days developed a tough hide.

But he still clung to his dream of being a novelist, and to his obsession with reissuing *Sister Carrie*. His bitterness toward Frank Doubleday (and wife), exaggerated as it was, was like adrenaline to an athlete, energizing him in a single-minded fight to win justice for his book. Hamlin Garland was struck by this fixation when he had lunch with Dreiser in February 1904, writing in his diary, "He was bitter over his treatment by Doubleday and disposed to take the world hardly." Also present were Henry Blake Fuller, the quondam Chicago realist, and Irving Bacheller, author of the best-selling *Eben Holden* and founder of the newspaper syndicate that had first published *The Red Badge of Courage*. Garland had recently written Dreiser to tell him of his admiration for *Sister Carrie*, saying he was impressed by its "power and verity," which reminded him of Norris's *McTeague*. Dreiser replied gracefully, recalling his pleasure on first encountering *Main-Traveled Roads* in the Carnegie Library at Pittsburgh and adding, "Your kind wish to know more of me is reciprocated, though in a public way I seem to know much of you already."

The luncheon might have been the beginning of a mutually beneficial friendship; instead, Garland took an instant dislike to the author of *Sister Carrie*. In his diary he noted disapprovingly that Dreiser talked incessantly of his struggles: "He became a bit tiresome at last and we were glad when he went back to his work as a boss of a gang of excavators." Since Dreiser had left his railroad employ the previous December, Garland must have been confused; perhaps Dreiser ran on so volubly about his experiences (which he was in the midst of writing about) that he gave the impression he was still hefting ties. Garland found him "tall, thin, ugly and very uncouth" and of a "serious not to say rebellious turn of mind."

Garland's antipathy was a straw in the wind: Dreiser was not invited back, as it were, and he disappears from Garland's diary, the definitive social calendar of the New York literary world in the early 1900s. While Garland was a clubman par excellence, Dreiser never belonged to any of those cozy sanctums frequented by literary gentlemen: the Metropolitan, the Lotus, the Century, the Players. Nor was he in attendance at the various social events at which Garland was a regular: the Sunday literary soirées held at the home of Brander Matthews; the Medicean banquets given by Andrew Carnegie at his Fifth Avenue mansion for prominent figures in business and the arts; the gastronomic Festschrifts for Howells and Mark Twain contrived by Colonel George M. Harvey, J. P. Morgan's man at Harper and Brothers. Years later, Dreiser recalled that Walter Hines Page's promise to give him a banquet "brought about very ponderous notions as to my own importance." And the prospect of delivering a lecture at the Players in the fall, dangled before him by Elmer Gates, had influenced his decision to stand up to Frank Doubleday. But the inflated hopes of those days were in storage now, like the unsold copies of *Sister Carrie*.

That book, it should be said, lived on in a kind of limbo, the flame of its reputation kept flickering by a handful of critical champions such as William Marion Reedy and a few score intelligent readers who passed their dog-eared copies among friends. One of the younger generation who remembered was Edna Kenton, now a Chicago book critic. In 1905 she wrote Dreiser out of the blue to express her continuing admiration of him for having written "the strongest, best biggest novel of American life that so far has been printed," and to ask if there were any plans to reissue it. Dreiser told her *Carrie* was still in the doldrums, but he was looking for a publisher with courage enough to bring it out. "Maybe—the gods providing—when I take up my pen again, the world will be a bit more kindly disposed," he concluded. "I am older now, a little bit wiser and not so radical I was going to say, but it wouldn't be true—simply sorrowful and uncertain." Kenton replied, "Surely a courageous publisher is not entirely nonexistent, though Americans indeed are not yet at that stage in their art life where they relish the Slavonic [sic] touch in the native novel. But I . . . cannot lose faith in that book and its ultimate great success."

But the country was changing. A rebellious minority of the younger generation was about to put its stamp on American culture. They were the ones to whom the legend of *Sister Carrie*'s suppression would become a manifesto in the battle for freer expression in literature and in morals and manners. A transitional group between Dreiser's and the cynical rebels of the 1920s, they were imbued with Victorian idealism and moral seriousness. But they were also alive to the whisper of desire: the "sex question" would become prominent on their social and literary agendas.

This was a generation that, as the critic Randolph Bourne said, rebelled at the monotonous daily fare of "classics" served up in the literature classes at freshwater universities and Ivy League institutions alike and raided the library shelves for sustenance—Hardy, Tolstoy, Flaubert, Turgenev, Meredith, Moore, and the other modern writers who were not taught in their courses. The realism wars of Howells's day were as remote from them as the Peloponnesian Wars; they took as axiomatic the proposition that literature should represent the truth about life. The "daring" French writers like Zola and de Maupassant, while not widely available, were no longer exotic cultural contraband. In theory at least, the young people saw no reason why American writers could not tackle the same subject matter. Indeed, Zolaesque novels like Norris's *The Pit* and Upton Sinclair's *The Jungle*, as stomach-turning as *l'Assommoir*, were best sellers in the early 1900s, riding the wave of reform of the progressive era. The muckrakers, who were enjoying a tremendous vogue, made the daring social and political subject matter of the "economic novels" of the nineties—political corruption, big-business chicanery, exploitation of workers—familiar reading matter for a mass audience.

The young intellectuals also repudiated the saccharine romantic view of life purveyed in the popular fiction of their day. Ludwig Lewisohn, trying to make a living as a writer, dutifully read the magazines and found them full of "Dishonest, sapless twaddle, guided by an impossible moral perfectionism . . . and strung on a string of pseudo-romantic love." And Dorothy Dudley recalled, "Young people were tired of vicarious romance. They must have experience themselves . . . and have it quickly." They wanted novels that held the mirror up to life. They poured into the cities, questing, eager, not yet sexually "emancipated" like the bohemians of the twenties (the young women among them still believed in chaperoned introductions leading to engagement and marriage), but in rebellion against American "puritanism" that stifled freedom and experimentation in the arts.

In 1905 the movers and shakers of this generation were still cocooned in universities, small towns, or newspaper city rooms. The physically deformed but spiritually luminous Randolph Bourne, who would become its leading critical voice before his untimely death in 1918 at the age of thirty-two, was working for a piano-roll maker in Bloomfield, New Jersey; Dorothy Dudley, daughter of an old Chicago family, was matriculating at Bryn Mawr; Henry L. Mencken, another 1900 reader of *Sister Carrie* and now the twenty-five-year-old managing editor of the faltering Baltimore *Morning Herald* had discovered George Bernard Shaw's plays and critical essays; and Ludwig Lewisohn was at Columbia reading German poets and finding that they wrote about *life*, in contrast to the English department's demigods—Wordsworth, Tennyson et al.—who "had no sense for reality at all, only for pseudo-reality." In a decade's time those four young people would become Dreiser's critical champions by their various lights; they were carriers of the virus of the New, infected in part by Dreiser. In his essay "The History of a Literary Radical," Bourne wrote of the impact the modern novelists had on him (referring to himself in the third person): "His orthodoxies crumbled. He did not try to reconcile the new with the old. He applied pick and dynamite to the whole structure of the canon. Irony, humor, tragedy, sensuality, suddenly appeared to him as literary qualities in forms that he could understand. They were like oxygen to his soul."

The young people would turn on establishment authors like Longfellow, Whittier, Holmes, Lowell, and, through guilt by association, Howells. Pick and dynamite in hand, they set out to clear away the "crumbling idols" as Garland had done in his day (and Howells in his and Longfellow in his). In 1905 most of the revered ancients were either dead, living off the annuity of their reputations, or unread. Many of the tottering survivors had been translated into living monuments as members of the recently founded American Academy of Arts and Letters, of which Howells was the inevitable first president and Garland a member and eager booster.

Similarly entrenched were the guardians of purity in literature, led by the indefatigable smut-smiter Anthony Comstock. In 1906 Comstock and his vigilantes at the New York Society for the Suppression of Vice raided numerous publishers and vendors of allegedly obscene books and attempted to close the Art Students League in New York because nude models were used. The annual report of the society for that year claimed that one thousand pounds of obscene books and stock had been impounded and destroyed.

And the contemporary censorship movement was alive on other fronts as well. The New York Public Library put its copy of Shaw's *Man and Superman* on special reserve because of the controversial ideas advanced in the work; Shaw's play about a former prostitute, *Mrs. Warren's Profession*, was widely attacked as immoral in a campaign orchestrated by Comstock (prompting Shaw to coin the term "Comstockery"); *Tom Sawyer* and *Huckleberry Finn* were snatched from open shelves in the children's room of the Brooklyn Public Library because they set a bad example to young people; Havelock Ellis's *Studies in the Psychology of Sex* could be purchased only by licensed physicians; the New England Watch and Ward Society banned performances of Oscar Wilde's play *Salome;* copies of Swedenborg's *Amor Conjugialis*, a prototypical marriage guide, was seized by U.S. postal authorities on the grounds that it was prurient.

Still, there was a growing resistance to Comstockery. The attacks on Shaw's play had the predictable effect of creating long lines at the box office. Art lovers, who saw nothing wrong with nudes, rallied to the support of the Art Students League. And censorship was not monolithic; there were quirky cracks in the façade. For example, the critic James Huneker noted that the Metropolitan Museum of Art did not use fig leaves on its statuary, though the Louvre and other great museums in Europe followed that "needlessly offensive custom." And Ellis's book had, after all, been published in America, while being banned in England. There was a growing upper- and middle-class constituency, not for pornography but for serious art, and the heavy brogans of Comstock and his Dogberrys were trampling on their cultural flower beds.

As for Dreiser, he continued the hunt for a "courageous" publisher. He made his first breakthrough while working at Street and Smith, the dime novel and mass magazine empire ruled by the brilliant, cultivated Ormond C. (Million Dollar) Smith, who is supposed to have said, "The worse the swill, the more the public will buy." Dreiser's first job was editing *Diamond Dick* and the Jack Harkaway stories, a popular series of boys' adventure yarns written in the 1870s, which Street and Smith was reissuing.

His task on the latter, he recalled, involved "cutting them in two and tacking an end to the first half and a beginning to the second, thereby doubling the output for the firm." Not quite doubling; Harkaway's creator, an Englishman named Bracebridge Hemyng, had written twenty-two of the novels, which were converted into twenty-eight titles by Dreiser and others and republished between 1905 and 1913. As well as cutting, the chore involved writing new transitions and expositions and updating or Americanizing Hemyng's Britishisms.

For example, in place of a passage containing a pre–Spanish-American War allusion to Cuba, Dreiser substituted a discussion of a perennial political issue of his day—high tariffs. The result was a distinctly populist version, for the American character points out that the tariff wall "has its drawbacks. You see, it prevents competition from foreign nations, and a lot of wealthy fellows can get together and form a trust, and they have the people at their mercy." Dreiser, who may have read the Harkaway stories as a boy when they first appeared in *Frank Leslie's Weekly*, retained the perfervid prose style that the genre's young devotees expected—as this passage shows: " 'Monday,' said Mr. Mole, ex-schoolmaster and supposed proprietor of a tea garden in China, 'if there is a heart capable of thankfulness throbbing beneath your dusky skin let it respond to my feelings of satisfaction at having escaped the savage Pisangs.' "

The irony of Dreiser's refurbishing the hackwork of another while his own powerful novel languished in obscurity probably did not escape him, but he seems to have been enjoying himself. And his faith that he would someday be doing better things remained strong. When he did finally achieve a measure of fame, Charles DeCamp, one of his co-workers at

Street and Smith, wrote to remind him of "the days we used to walk up town from 7th Av & 15th St and how confidently you predicted what you have done. I used to believe you too—about the only time I ever did believe a man predicting about his work."

Another admiring co-worker on the Street and Smith assembly line was Charles Agnew MacLean, who had read and liked *Carrie*. Both men had ambitions beyond rewriting dime novels, and they hatched the idea of forming a publishing company, buying the plates and stock of *Sister Carrie* from the J. F. Taylor Company, and issuing it as the first title on their list. Dreiser was making only fifteen dollars a week and was in debt, so MacLean had to come up with the necessary five hundred dollars. The deal was consummated in January 1905, and Jewett wrote to congratulate MacLean: "You are purchasing one of the best American books ever written."

But starting a publishing company required far more capital than the two junior editors could raise, and Dreiser was impatient. In February he was again offering *Carrie* and *The Transgressor* to Hitchcock at Barnes. Hitchcock declined, saying the firm did not believe *Carrie* would sell. He probably also doubted that Dreiser would ever finish *The Transgressor*, having had the unfinished MS of *An Amateur Laborer* in his office for more than a year.

Thinking to evade the New York publishers, Dreiser submitted the package to James Poll and Company, a small Boston house, with a covering letter that recited the familiar story of Doubleday's suppression. By now the legend had acquired a commercial twist. Dreiser argued that Doubleday had aborted the book—that it had never been published at all. Poll was not impressed; a subordinate informed Dreiser in February that while his employer did not think the book immoral, he was "dubious of its selling qualities."

Dreiser had a financial motive for reviving *Sister Carrie*. He still owed J. F. Taylor seven hundred fifty dollars, representing the advance on *The Transgressor*, plus interest. Not that Taylor was dunning him, but he did invite Theodore in for a discussion of their contract. The upshot of this meeting was an amicable agreement that Dreiser would attempt to sell the rights to *Carrie* and his second novel to another publisher and reimburse Taylor out of the proceeds. A year later Taylor was still inquiring about Dreiser's plans to repay him; eventually he did, but it took Dreiser another year to find a publisher.

The nebulous partnership between Dreiser and MacLean was dissolved after they quarreled. Dreiser later told Dorothy Dudley that

MacLean had been jealous of his rise in the company and worked behind his back to undercut him. Actually, both men rose. Dreiser was made editor of a new "home" magazine called *Smith's,* and MacLean was given the job of resuscitating *Popular Magazine,* a wobbly yearling in the company's large stable (O. C. Smith founded and killed magazines with blinding rapidity). MacLean transformed his charge into a hairy-chested man's magazine, using then-unknown writers like Zane Grey and John Buchan, who later wrote the classic mystery *The 39 Steps,* and increased the circulation from 70,000 to 250,000 in two years.

Dreiser did a similar job on *Smith's,* starting from scratch. His first issue appeared in April 1905, with a publisher's note promising not to "tamper with the higher education or attempt to alter the present formation of the universe"—which seemed safe enough—and to render the reader "some assistance in enduring the little sorrows and tragedies of life." *Smith's* was said to be aimed at "the every-day reader who seeks entertainment" and would not be a "class" magazine. Or, as Paul would have said, it was for the masses and not the classes—and at no time for the asses. Paul, not surprisingly, gave Theodore's premier issue a glowing review: "Great— fine, exstatic [sic]—imperishable genius art thou."

Although he sounded his usual jovial self, Paul was having business worries. He and Pat Howley had a falling out with Fred Haviland, for reasons that are unclear but probably arose out of squabbles over money. Haviland's wife, Mabel, later recalled that the three partners had "made lots of money but none of them held on to it." And Haviland himself told the music publisher Edward B. Marks that Paul had started the trouble. A friend in Buffalo had convinced Paul that he was too great a songwriter to split the profits with the others, and Paul became unpleasant. Having left a portion of his royalties in the business, he apparently felt he had been cheated when the money vanished.

He and Pat bought out Haviland for $8000 and tried to make a go of it with a company of their own, but went bankrupt in 1905 and had to sell their song catalogue at a distress price. (A year later Howley bought it back for peanuts.) Then Paul founded his own firm, using money lent to him by Ed Dreiser and by Mai and her mother. Ed served as president of the company, although he had little experience in song publishing. He was supposed to be a check on the profligate Paul, who was given a twenty-five-dollar weekly allowance and told to closet himself with his portable organ and write more hits.

But the hits didn't come. Tastes had changed; ragtime, which Paul deplored, was having a vogue. The day of the "mother" song had passed.

Also, Paul now had loftier aims. In an interview with the New York *Sun* in mid-1905, while he was still technically Pat Howley's partner, Paul complained that although he had a trunkful of good songs—"genuine songs of feeling that ought to stir the heart"—the music-buying public wanted only junk. The man who had once said that a nicely broiled steak and plenty of bread and butter were all the monument to genius he needed, told the reporter that to the "true artist" financial success wasn't sufficient: he must know that he was doing his best work, like a painter or a novelist. At a time when his genius brother Theodore was working on magazine row, Paul was talking like an avant garde poet. He had become a captive of his popularity and was trying to break out.

A sign of his rebelliousness was that he was composing socially significant songs. He was not an anarchist, he assured the reporter from the *Sun*, but he was appalled at how "the rich of this country are getting richer and richer, and the poor are getting poorer and poorer." Then, heaving his monstrous bulk to the piano (he weighed over three hundred pounds), Paul played and sang the chorus of a song he had written:

> The People, the People are marching by
> The cry of the downtrodden, far and nigh
> Is heard in the homes where the weary sigh
> The People, the People are marching by.

Paul's social conscience was emerging at a bad time. He needed to write more "junk"—or rather he needed to recover his faith in the songs he did best, which, sentimental as they were, derived from his honest emotions. But the row with Haviland had embittered him, and he had grown disillusioned with the Broadway crowd that plucked him like a golden chicken. It was said that he had fifty thousand dollars in outstanding loans that he could not collect. He had let the money slip through his hands like water, peeling a V or two off his fat roll whenever a needy actor with a sad tale stopped him along Broadway. All those Vs had added up. And there were women too, expensive women, and Lucullan feasts at Delmonico's and Sherry's, and rounds of drinks at the Metropole bar. When the interviewer asked him if he was a sentimentalist, Paul replied, "If you lived most of your day . . . on the road between 34th Street and 59th Street on Broadway, right in the heart of the Rialto, you would soon cease . . . being a sentimentalist. There are the greatest lot of grafters and cutthroats in this place that could be."

And so, while Dreiser's star was now on the rise, Paul's had entered a dangerous phase. The Paul Dresser Publishing Company quickly flopped

(Ed later wrote Theodore, "the business in 28th Street was a failure from the start"), leaving Mai's parents and Ed out twenty-five hundred dollars. Paul's financial affairs were in a hopeless tangle; he had lost the song-writer's only asset, his catalogue. In May, even before the interview with the *Sun*, he had written Austin Brennan, who cosigned some notes for him, "I am going through bankruptcy now and clean up. I've been getting the snotty end of the stick for a long time, so I am going to use it on some of the others." By then he had quarreled with Pat Howley too. In a letter to Brennan in August, Paul mentions a man who was arrested for pirating songs, adding, "Howley is mixed up in it and is as big a crook as Haviland."

His only hope was to compose another "Wabash," and, surprisingly, despite all his troubles, he did succeed in writing the big one—"My Gal Sal." But the pardon came too late. He persuaded his former protégée Louise Dresser, now a vaudeville headliner, to introduce it, and he put her picture on the cover. Her renditions were well received, but for a time "Sal" remained what was known in the trade as a "stage hit"—one that pleases audiences—rather than a "selling hit." Eventually it would earn a lot of money, but not in Paul's lifetime.

Disillusioned, bitter, and alone, Paul had let his thoughts roam back to the Evansville days, and Sallie Walker. She was Sal—"a wild sort of devil, but dead on the level"—perhaps the only woman other than Sarah Dreiser whom Paul ever loved. The millions of people who played the song in parlors all over America and heard it in vaudeville theaters never knew that its inspiration was the madam of a high-class Evansville brothel.

By late 1905 Paul was broke, and he had to ask Emma, now living on West 106th Street, to take him in. The old quarrels were forgotten. Despite her own troubles—her remarriage had been an unhappy one—Emma welcomed him. Paul was given a small room, in which he set up his portable organ and tried to compose. He was drinking heavily and his health was poor. To economize, he took his meals at the home of Mai Dreiser's Aunt Kate. He was suffering from pernicious anemia, rheumatism, dropsy—accumulation of fluid in the tissues—and had a bad heart. Sensitive about his girth because sometimes women laughed at it, he went on crash diets, taking nothing but milk or orange juice and losing forty or fifty pounds in the course of a few weeks. The diets, followed by eating binges, surely overtaxed his heart. And his fall from Broadway celebrity depressed him. "Where Are the Friends of Other Days?" concealed his bitterness in poignancy. He "emanated a kind of fear," Dreiser recalled.

After work, Theodore would visit him. They would reminisce about the old days, and Paul would urge him to take notes and write a book about him. In December 1905 Paul seemed to be feeling better and sent Mame a jocular note referring to her as "Mary Queen of Scots" and to Brennan as "Gluefoot Bill—the terror of the trail to the bottom of the hill." At the close, he reports, almost in passing, "I've been a little ill recently but nothing to amount to anything." But he had premonitions he would die, and worked on a lugubrious religious song called "The Judgment Is at Hand." Theodore had identical presentiments. One day a co-worker at Street and Smith found him kneeling in his office, fingering a rosary and weeping. The anecdote is suspect. It comes in the middle of a highly inaccurate paragraph about Dreiser in a book by Quentin Reynolds, *The Fiction Factory*, and its credibility is not enhanced by the fact that Theodore is said to be praying for his dying mother. Nevertheless, the story has a symbolic truth.

On January 29, 1906, a wire from Ed announced the dreaded news: PAUL IS DYING. Dreiser hurried up to Emma's place and found his good brother laid out on the bed, "his soft hands folded over his chest, his face turned to one side on the pillow, that indescribable sweetness of expression about the eyes and mouth—the empty shell of a beetle." He was forty-eight.

Although Paul had told Emma there would be enough for everyone, he died penniless. Unlike the songwriter in "Whence the Song," however, he did not end up on a boat bound for potter's field. The White Rats, an organization of vaudevillians, volunteered to pick up the tab. The New York *Telegram*, a theatrical paper, commented in its obituary, "He made two or three fortunes solely from his compositions" but did not elaborate. Perhaps the rounders at the Metropole shook their heads sadly and lifted their glasses to good old Paul, and friends in the music business suddenly remembered they had been planning to help him get back on his feet or pay back that loan or whatever. Charles Harris later wrote that he and Paul had agreed to be partners a few days before he died.

Tout Broadway turned out for the funeral, which was held at St. Francis Xavier church on West Sixteenth, not far from where Emma lived when Theodore first arrived in the city. Paul had been a parishioner there, and in his homily Father Van Rennselaer (who, when Paul skipped Mass, would hunt him down like the Hound of Heaven), said that Paul had been a good Catholic who, no matter how far he strayed, always returned home to the Church. The light, one wants to add, was always burning in the window. Then the priest read the lyrics of "The Judgment Is at Hand," its first and only public performance:

> And then came an angel, majestic pure and grand,
> Calling "Arise, Ye" Judgment is now at hand.
> "As ye have sown, so shall ye reap,"
> Just as the Master planned
> Arise ye all, seek not to hide
> The judgment is at hand.

A week or so later the *Telegram* reported that Paul's "sister," Louise Dresser, who had heard the news of his death just before she was to go on stage and cancelled her performance, had contributed money for funeral expenses. Apparently the two hundred and fifty dollars the White Rats put up was not enough to bury him. A friend of Paul's also wrote the *Telegram* that a benefit was being planned, as "the family have no money . . . at present the body lies in a receiving vault."

No benefit was held; Broadway's memory is short. Mai's mother, Margaret Skelly, came to the rescue and arranged that Paul be buried in the family plot. But Mame thought he should lie in Chicago in St. Boniface's cemetery, next to Sarah and John Paul, Sr. A year later, forging Mrs. Skelly's name, she had the body exhumed and shipped there. The Skellys were furious when they learned what had happened, and Mai, though she was a good Christian woman, was a long time in forgiving Mame for that stunt. Ed, who had dropped one thousand dollars of his own money on the song publishing company, was forced to live off his mother-in-law for a time, which galled his independent spirit. "If I don't do something soon to put myself where I can hold up my head," he wrote Theodore, "I'll go crazy."

Meanwhile, the surviving Dreisers quarreled in their usual fashion over the funeral bills and who would be executor of the estate—"if you can call it that," Theodore wrote Mame, after he had taken the job to keep peace in the family. He hired Thomas McKee, the former Doubleday lawyer who was now a colleague, to unsnarl Paul's copyrights. McKee reported that "the gang that has the songs come pretty close to the line of highwaymen, and I have grave doubts of your getting satisfaction, let alone money."

45. The Gates of the City

Ah, she was in the walled city now. Its splendid gates had opened,
admitting her from a cold, dreary outside. She seemed a creature afar off—like every other celebrity he had known.
—Dreiser, *Sister Carrie* (1900)

Success may be the worst failure and failure the best success.
—Hall Caine, quoted by Dreiser (1905)

Paul's death closed a chapter in Dreiser's life. He was now at
the age—thirty-five—when he could look back on the New
York of the 1890s, Paul's New York, as a vanishing era. Paul
had been a dominant presence then; a sun whose warmth and
gravity Theodore felt even when they were estranged, a com-
bustion of fame, money, and desire that had burnt up too quickly. His
memories of Paul's New York were tinted by its afterglow—his first walk
up Broadway with his brother, the Sunday night at Manhattan Beach,
the *Ev'ry Month* days, the stockboys bundling up copies of "Just Tell
Them That You Saw Me," the organ grinders playing it on every corner. . . . Those sweet memories would waft back to him over the years
like a whiff of flowers on a summer night.

The legal ownership of Paul's songs was eventually untangled—but
in any case they could earn something only if a publisher brought them
out in sheet music. Most of them were as dead as the era that spawned
them, save "On the Banks of the Wabash," "My Gal Sal," and a few
others. Ed was able to lease the selling rights of "Sal" to a publisher on
a 5-percent royalty basis. The song started slowly, but gradually caught
on, and Ed earned a good sum out of it over the years, so perhaps Paul
had paid back the borrowed money after all. It was the least he could
do.

There were other severances with the past. His feud with Arthur Henry
over the unflattering portrait in *An Island Cabin* erupted. The occasion

was the reissue of that book by A. S. Barnes in 1904, along with Henry's new book, *The House in the Woods*. Not long after Dreiser left the New York Central and took the apartment on Mott Street, a letter from Henry arrived. The tone was friendly but a bit defiant. Henry said he could understand why Dreiser would nurse ill will toward him, but he could not resist challenging him to "prove you can face *all* the facts and that you are not simply nursing a grudge and come down here this evening. Hitchcock and I want to see you about your future work and mine."

Dreiser was infuriated and sent a scorching reply:

> Here is the way to face all the facts. If your feelings have undergone no change and [sic] I accuse you of flagrant abuse of those unchanged feelings in 'An Island Cabin.' Let the book be brought out, not at a dinner or in the presence of those who do not know, but here in my own rooms, between us, and where those others [Jug] who do can be quickly gathered. If there is no evidence of this flagrant abuse how long do you suppose I will be delay [sic] in taking you to my ~~arms~~ [sic] heart again. And if there is, how long can you honestly refuse to acknowledge it and to make me the amends a wrong demands.

Henry persisted, requesting a meeting "to see if it is not possible to come to a friendly and affectionate understanding again." Apparently they did meet, but Dreiser was his usual obdurate self. When all efforts had failed, Henry wrote a preface to the new edition, in which he denied, rather unconvincingly, that the character of Tom had anything to do with Dreiser: "Tom as I have depicted him could not be the author of *Sister Carrie*. . . . He is a shadow of no value, except to enforce the moral I used him for."

Dreiser could not have been placated and must have objected that the preface only made matters worse by identifying him. Still, Henry had not intended to hold him up to ridicule in his book. Dreiser was thin-skinned—especially in 1902 and 1903, when his ego was badly bruised by the failure of *Sister Carrie*. He never really forgave "Hen," and in the story "Rona Murtha," written in the 1920s, he paid back his former soulmate with a cruel portrait of Henry's relationship with Anna, making him out to be a sponger. He probably had told Henry as much, and there was nothing the latter could do to convince him otherwise.

After Dreiser vetoed the conciliatory preface, Henry wrote him: "It is very clear to me that this book is not responsible for the interruption of our friendship. That was doomed before the book was written." He accused Dreiser of listening to gossip about him and Anna and making accusations to her that "should have come directly, and at once, from you to me." Henry denied that he was after her money, pointing out that Anna's parents disinherited her after she married him; moreover, she had given up her lucrative typing business and helped him to build a house in the Catskill Mountains with her savings. He concludes, "I had no idea of the extent of the evil elements in you, and I can't yet believe that you will not still eliminate them before they have perverted your whole being. . . . Independent of that, my heart is filled with affection for you." In time the anger between them cooled, but only the ashes of their former friendship remained.

The old world was breaking up and a new order was forming. Even Theodore's brother Al—who, Theodore always said, had more talent than any of them—was in trouble. While she was in Chicago seeing to Paul's reinterment, Mame found Al in a down-and-out condition and wrote Theodore, "Poor dear All [*sic*], he is having a hard time and oh how I wish we could help him—he had a great heart and so full of love—" Not long afterward, Al vanished forever, a wandering boy who never came home.

In different ways and degrees, Dreiser had been dependent on Paul, Al, and Arthur Henry, but now he no longer needed them. Under his editorship, *Smith's* was prospering. In the June issue, the editor proclaimed that all periodicals must live by the law of the jungle: *"Success is what counts in the world, and it is little matter how the success is won. It is a hard, cold fact with little comfort in it for the unsuccessful, but it is still a fact that we must recognize."*

Fortunately, *Smith's* was one of the fit. Out of a stockpile of memories of the magazines that had fueled his dreams of New York and his experiences at *Ev'ry Month* and as a free-lancer Dreiser had patched together a periodical with instant popular appeal, aimed at young married couples (this was the "home" part). The first issues tended to be lightweight, emphasizing slick fiction with alternating masculine and feminine appeal, and features like "Art Studies" (photographs of beautiful, fashionably dressed actresses); "The Passing Hour," an illustrated chronicle of the doings of Society and European royalty; and "The Out-of-Town Girl in New York," a fashion column aimed at the Carrie Meebers among his readers.

With the magazine's future presumably assured, the editor proclaimed in the June issue that henceforth *Smith's* would shoulder its social responsibilities. In the July number he criticized his countrymen's pursuit of the "Almighty dollar," though he admitted that this unseemly chase had made America the richest nation on earth and announced "a change in the spirit of the American people." The wage earners, the bone and sinew of the Republic, were demanding that "modern conditions be at one with moral health and national honor." They were calling for "the *right* use of national wealth, for integrity and civility in public office, for honesty and fair-dealing in the business world, for sanity and liberality in schools and colleges, and for kindness and humanity everywhere."

Thus did Dreiser align *Smith's* with the progressive sentiments abroad in the land, which he shared despite his lingering Social Darwinism. In subsequent issues he presented an article by Cleveland's reform mayor Tom Johnson, an old hero, on municipal socialism, and one by Kansas Governor E. W. Hoch recounting his battle with Standard Oil's lobbyists in his state. He also published articles on "The Public and the Post Office," "Wanted: A Parcels Post," "How Our Railroads Regulate Us," and "The Coming Socialism."

None of this was radical at the time. For a brief moment in American history socialism was seriously discussed in popular journals like *The Saturday Evening Post*, the businessman's Bible. Even the old success salesman, Orison Swett Marden, had joined the muckrakers. Ever since *McClure's* had caused a great public stir in 1902 with its articles by Lincoln Steffens, Ray Stannard Baker, and Ida Tarbell on corruption in the sanctums of corporate and government power, muckraking had become good business as well as good citizenship. If there was anything unique about *Smith's* approach, it was a more popular emphasis. The editor promised lively, not-too-demanding analyses of social problems. "It is not necessary," he wrote, "that an article on a topic of real public importance be dull and heavy."

But he lightened the editorial mix with dollops of "service" features, fashion articles, and popular fiction to hold the allegiance of readers interested primarily in entertainment. Thus, in August Dreiser announced with some typographical fanfare that he had signed exclusive contracts with the "Three Most Popular Authors in the World"—Mary J. Holmes, Mrs. Georgie Sheldon, and Charles Garvice, whose books had had an aggregate sale of *"ten million copies."* In later issues, the editor expounded his tastes (Dreiser was nothing if not confessional with his readers). He was looking for stories with a "personal human element," he writes in one issue, and for authors who see life vividly, he says in another, "with the eyes of a child" and "hold the thing up to us as fresh and interesting as it actually is." He vowed to publish only stories that "reflect American manners and customs, thought and feeling," but also confessed to a predilection for tales that depicted a character's rise from rags to riches. One of these, by Charles Fort, with whom Dreiser became friendly, was "The Aspirations of Mr. Lannigan."

While not serious literature, the stories occasionally touched the lives of *Smith's* readers and featured plausible heroes and heroines with whom they could identify. They could hardly be said to reflect Dreiser's literary tastes, but they did not totally belie them. He was not being a cynical exploiter of the masses; as he did at *Ev'ry Month*, he showed an evangelical desire to uplift and educate. He never abandoned his boyhood faith in ambition and self-improvement, and it cost him little enough to share it with his readers, however much he might brood on the profounder currents beneath life's raging seas.

Those darker preoccupations he vented in occasional short sketches like the one on loneliness in the city. In another *pensée* published in 1905 in *Tom Watson's Magazine* (to which Duffy had migrated) and called "A Lesson From the Aquarium," he indulged his naturalistic vision. Observing how some fish guard their eggs from predators, how the hermit crab will evict another of its species from a shell it covets, and how suckerfish attach themselves to sharks for protection, Dreiser points to analogues in the human world. Capitalists who control a franchise would love to emulate the fishes' skill in driving away predators; real estate sharpers would envy the crab's success in acquiring the property it covets, and, "What weakling, seeing the world was against him, and that he was not fitted to cope with it, would not attach himself, sucker-wise, to any magnate, trust, political or social (we will not call them sharks) . . . ?" He concludes: "The very air we breathe seems to correspond to their sea, and as for the tragedy of it—but we will not talk of the tragedy of it. Let us leave the Aquarium." In his intellectual cosmos Darwin was in the ascendant, and Tolstoy in decline.

In January 1906 he cut out an editorial in the New York *Tribune* entitled "The Materials of a Great Novel." Commenting on the recent death of Charles T. Yerkes, the "traction king," the editorialist noted the fight over Yerkes' estate, estimated to be worth more than twelve million dollars and now carrion for the legal jackals. Yerkes' story would indeed make a great novel, the editorialist continued, though not one suitable for a William Dean Howells or a Henry James: "The tale is too intricate and various and melodramatic for any kind of living novelist . . . by divine right it is the property of Balzac." Balzac was, of course, dead, but his American acolyte, Theodore Dreiser, filed away the clipping for future reference.

The antibusiness climate must have seemed hospitable to a muck-

raking book on a financier like Yerkes. Then too, it would be an opportunity to write about this corporate buccaneer and evoke the pillage
of America in the furnace years of capitalism. Here was a man with syba-
ritic tastes, a connoisseur of art and beauty, an inveterate womanizer,
whose mistress lived opulently in a mansion not far from his Fifth Avenue
palazzo (linked by a tunnel, the gossip writers reported). With an im-
perious disdain for public opinion, Yerkes had indulged desires that burned
in Dreiser's secret heart. How bully to write about a man of power and
wealth rather than fallen women and men in the storm!

Dreiser's nerves were attuned to the moneymaking energies in the air;
he was beginning to enjoy the success game, though he could stand off
and contemplate it philosophically. In the dissolution of Yerkes' fortune,
he saw the final dissipation of Motion that Spencer had said was the ultimate equilibrium. And, in a more personal way, he was applying the
bitter lessons of Ross Street, associating his weakness with the feminine
side of his nature, turning to an admiration of strength and physical or
business prowess—a psychological change signaled by his interest in Mike
Burke and Muldoon as heroic figures. No more did he write about Tolstoyan altruists. A novel about their antithesis, the egoistic Charles Tyson
Yerkes, began to take form in his mind.

Another newspaper story that year—this one about a sensational murder—interested him. On July 12 the body of a young woman named Grace
Brown was discovered under seven feet of water in Big Moose Lake in
upstate New York. A few days later Chester Gillette, who had been her
lover, was arrested and charged with drowning her. As a stack of letters
police found in Gillette's room indicated, Grace had been pregnant and
had pleaded with him to marry her. Gillette, however, was tired of her,
and, not wanting to tie himself to a poor shopgirl (they both worked at
a skirt factory owned by Gillette's uncle), he lured her out in a boat, hit
her with a tennis racket, and pushed her into the water. That at least
was the prosecution's theory, and the jury agreed. (Gillette claimed she
had jumped into the lake and drowned after he refused to marry her).
In 1908 Gillette was electrocuted, like Red Bulger, whose fate Paul had
anticipated in his song "The Path That Leads the Other Way."

The Grace Brown case interested Dreiser because it involved a young
man who murders a girl with whom he was once in love but who stands
in the way of his social advancement. Dreiser had known of several such
cases while he was a reporter and collected clippings on others, including
the sensational Roland Burke Molineux trial in 1899. (Molineux, a New
York socialite, was convicted of poisoning a woman who had taken

cyanide-laced Bromo-Seltzer intended for a man with whom Molineux had quarreled. He also supposedly poisoned a rival for the hand of a wealthy woman he wanted to marry.) As an ambitious young man dreaming of wealth, Theodore had often fantasized about marrying a rich woman, and had written in *Ev'ry Month* that American heiresses should patronize young geniuses (like himself) rather than marrying effete European royalty.

This idea—success through marriage—would merge with a more obscure desire to write a novel about a murderer. He had discussed the latter with Duffy and with Frederick Booth, an artist friend. Booth later recalled their agreeing that murder was the most dramatic act a person could commit and the ultimate subject for a novel. But how, Dreiser had asked, could the novelist understand what was going through a murderer's mind if he had not killed anyone? He would succeed only if he could "be brave enough to imagine himself in the clothes and skin of a murderer." He did not feel himself capable of doing this as yet, but someday he would be.

Dreiser would find a clue in his own marriage, which was becoming a torment to him. Like modern urban couples who repair to the analyst's couch, he and Jug became interested in Christian Science and paid regular visits to a practitioner. Dreiser's sexual desires, which demanded variety, were thwarted by the constrictions of monogamy. He was finding Jug small-townish and censorious. As he had written in (and deleted from) *Sister Carrie*, speaking of Hurstwood, "When a man, however, passively, becomes an obstacle to the fulfillment of a woman's desires, he becomes an odious thing in her eyes." He saw Jug as an obstacle to his sexual fulfillment. Not that his interest in the Gillette and Molineux cases reflected a desire to murder her—at least a conscious one. But in his desire to be free of Jug lay the beginnings of an understanding of Clyde Griffith's feelings toward Roberta in *An American Tragedy*. She was a barrier to his great chance for money and love with Sandra. Dreiser's marriage provided the psychic key that would admit him to the forbidden place—the mind of a murderer.

Meanwhile, as a rising magazine editor, he demanded and got an increase in salary to sixty dollars a week. His place in the Street and Smith factory seemed assured, but, as he had done at *Ev'ry Month*, Dreiser made enemies in the upper reaches of management, MacLean among them. Some sort of infighting was touched off. Perhaps Dreiser demanded a more royal budget; perhaps it was his innate stubbornness and rebelliousness.

As he admitted to Dorothy Dudley, "I was always difficult to deal with." Possibly, too, he sought to make *Smith's* a more serious magazine; more reflective, within limits, of his tastes, and O. C. Smith feared that Dreiser had higher ambitions than a magazine aimed at the everyday reader seeking entertainment. Later, a columnist for *The Standard & Vanity Fair* wrote cryptically that "before the house had acquired the asset of a brain, the lesser organs in the establishment combined to prevent the disruption of the nincompoops' union. But Dreiser executed a masterly flank movement of securing another job before the blow fell."

The escape hatch was the editorship of *Broadway Magazine*, a "white-light" monthly, the term for publications that reported on lurid doings in the theatrical quarter. Under Roland Burke Hennesey, who founded it in 1898, it had achieved a flash success by featuring pictures of women in tights and racy gossip of the demimonde by a columnist called The Red Soubrette. Hennesey had sold out, however, and after his successor cleaned it up, the paper fell on hard times. Its circulation now stood at an anemic twelve thousand.

As chance would have it, the present publisher was Thomas McKee, the former Doubleday lawyer. Dreiser's work at *Smith's* caught his eye, and McKee remembered him as a brilliant, if stubborn young man. So, in April 1906, even as his enemies at Street and Smith were whetting their dirks, Dreiser received a letter from Caleb L. Litchfield, who seems to have been acting editor, asking if he would like to discuss his ideas for improving the *Broadway*. What Litchfield and McKee had in mind was more than minor tinkering with format. They wanted a moral face-lift. The *Broadway* was to shed its disreputable image as a white-light monthly and, while keeping its New York orientation, become respectable enough to be displayed on the center table in the average God-fearing American's parlor.

That evening Dreiser sketched his ideas for rehabilitating the faded soubrette. He proposed a department that would cover celebrities; regular articles about the "play of the month"; and coverage of the art world, including halftone reproductions of paintings of beautiful women ("a careful supervision to be exercised as to merit and purity"). There would be articles on subjects like "The City of Crowds" (the title of a piece he had already written for *Smith's*), "The Richest Ten-Acre Field in the World" (Manhattan real estate), "The Greatest Buildings in the World, "The Greatest Terminal Problem of the Age" (the new Grand Central Station), "Our Underground Life" (subways), "Sorting Three Million Letters" (the post office), interviews with "any personality which makes a real stir in the city," and portraits of society hostesses like Mrs. Stuyvesant Fish. The magazine should also cover current fads like the bolero, "the new Italian peasant dance . . . being practiced by the wealthy." Such an article might appropriately be "illustrated in pretty poses by a good looking girl."

Possibly realizing he was laying on the feminine pulchritude a bit thick, Dreiser quickly added that the magazine should publish regular symposiums on "the big questions . . . where these can be handled without top-heaviness." And of course there would be fiction, selected by the sole editorial criterion of telling a good story. He deliberately omitted the need for a wholesome moral. Those hastily cobbled ideas won him the job. His salary would be sixty-five dollars a week to start, rising to one hundred dollars if circulation reached one hundred thousand.

Not long after he was hired, the magazine was purchased by Benjamin Bowles Hampton, a young dynamo from Illinois who had made a fortune in the advertising business. The trajectory of Hampton's career coincided with the growing importance of advertising in the magazine world. He had started out by buying Irving Bacheller's literary syndicate and, using its periodical outlets, converted it into a lucrative advertising agency. But, as a student at Knox College, Hampton had nursed journalistic ambitions. Now that he had made some money he could indulge them, and *Broadway Magazine* was to be his playpen.

When Hampton took over, he retained McKee as publisher and Dreiser as editor. Years later, when Dreiser was a major literary figure, Hampton told Dorothy Dudley, "The minute I set eyes on him, I figured the man was a genius. I said to myself, 'Jesus, here's a wow.' " Hampton may have embellished his memories, but during the first months of Dreiser's tenure he was preoccupied with affairs at his ad agency and gave his editor a free hand.

Amid piles of lumber and the sound of carpenters' hammers at the magazine's new offices on West Twenty-second Street, Dreiser hired a staff. Hampton was throwing fistfuls of money into the enterprise, so Dreiser could engage writers and artists at eighteen to twenty-five dollars a week. A cloud of out-of-work journalists gathered like flies on a cow pat, including Charles Fort, who shared Dreiser's fascination with the cosmos and offered some bizarre metascientific speculations of his own. As assistant editor and manuscript reader he hired an intelligent young woman named Ethel M. Kelley, late of Bryn Mawr College. She thought her boss a commercial hack—until she read *Sister Carrie* and became a worshiper.

Another of Dreiser's discoveries was a cynical young man from the West named Harris Merton Lyon, who casually agreed with Dreiser that a piece he had done for the previous editor stank. They talked, and Lyon revealed his ambition to be a serious writer. Dreiser admired his brashness, his disdain for sham, and his intoxication with the city. (Lyon once told him, "God, how I hate to go to bed in this town! I'm afraid something will happen while I'm asleep and I won't see it!") Seeing in Lyon the young arriviste in the city he had once been, Dreiser took a paternal interest in him, perhaps the closest to fatherhood he ever came. (Although Jug wanted children badly, Theodore did not, probably fearing they would be another chain binding him to her. Also, he needed to be the exclusive object of her mothering; even as he was eyeing other women, he was reluctant to give up the stable home she provided.)

The presence on staff of young people like Kelley, Lyon, a "bohemian" art director, and others made the *Broadway* offices an after-hours gathering place of their peers with literary and artistic ambitions. Dreiser had a rapport with them, and they helped him keep *au courant*, providing tips on the tenor sensation from Italy who was giving a recital at Aeolian Hall or the next avant garde exhibition at Edward Steichen's 291 Gallery. Lyon also proved to be an asset. He wrote polished vignettes on urban life that caught the sophisticated tone Dreiser was seeking in the magazine and contributed brilliant, ironic short stories in the vein of his idol, de Maupassant.

Within a year Dreiser had earned his bonus: circulation had risen above the hundred-thousand mark. He had transformed *Broadway* into a mirror of the glamorous side of New York life, with occasional excursions into its more grim or exotic byways. In its way it was a city magazine, a prototype of *Vanity Fair* and *The New Yorker*. It served as a bridge from the scandalous white-light magazines that catered to the outlanders' view of New York as Sodom-on-the-Hudson, to those that viewed the Rialto and the city in which it was set through worldly, unmoralizing eyes. Dreiser's achievement was, in the words of the columnist for *The Standard & Vanity Fair:* "the prettiest piece of transformation work seen in New York for many a day. He turned in a river of good literature and snappy special articles, changing the magazine completely except in name. People began to sit up and take notice of the *Broadway*. Instead of sneaking around the corner to read it, they carried it in the sunlight and were proud of it."

As a result of his raise, he and Jug were able to move to a larger apartment in Morningside Heights and live in bourgeois comfort. Life might have continued in this more or less pleasant vein but for Ben Hampton, who began taking a more active role as publisher. With his restless energies and robust ego he could not be happy in the countinghouse; he hankered for some editorial glory. Also, his sublimated journalistic juices were flowing. He had grand ideas of making the *Broadway* into a muckraking organ and increasing circulation in the bargain. He could not have helped but notice how Thomas Lawson's series "Frenzied Finance," a sensational exposé of Wall Street, had boosted the circulation of *Everybody's* to one million copies in 1904. Dreiser had done a good job, but Hampton regarded him as too literary.

This time it was Hampton who exercised the masterful flanking maneuver and Dreiser who was outflanked. Realizing that staff members were intensely loyal to Dreiser, Hampton set about wooing them, plying them with lavish dinners, promising them bonuses and other emoluments when his plans for a new and bigger *Broadway* jelled. Perhaps his cruelest cut, from Dreiser's standpoint, was corrupting Lyon. As Dreiser told it, Hampton infected Lyon with the success virus. Soon the youthful American de Maupassant was writing stories with happy endings! Lyon also took to wearing English tweeds, drinking ale out of a pewter mug at Keen's Chop House, and other decadent practices. Like a father whose son has grown away from him, Dreiser privately mourned his loss.

In the mellowness of time, Ben Hampton said he always regarded Dreiser as a fine editor with "a marvellous objective mind; however, Dreiser had an even more admirable subjective mind—in other words, he was a creative artist. Also, though Hampton didn't say it, Dreiser was disorganized and inefficient (a charge McKee had laid against him in several crotchety memos). He had been miscast as editor of *Broadway Magazine*—"Christ in Hell," as Hampton put it with an ad man's hyperbole.

When Hampton shared those memories with Dorothy Dudley in 1930, *Hampton's Magazine* had long since gone under—a victim, said Upton Sinclair, of the Wall Street bankers, who denied Hampton a loan at a critical time in order to silence his crusading journalism. Others, however, blamed the magazine's demise on poor management. Hampton had run it deep into debt and made it a poor credit risk. But it had its moment in the sun, with circulation rising to four hundred and fifty thousand and each issue "hammering at conditions as they really are," according to Sinclair's postmortem. "There was not one great and powerful interest in America that [Hampton] had not antagonized."

Dreiser, however, always remembered his employer acerbically, as a hustling, insensitive, albeit charming businessman. As though he could not forgive Hampton's changing the magazine, Dreiser never gave him credit for challenging the trusts. Moreover, several members of his staff, which Hampton had supposedly been subverting, followed Dreiser when he left. The two men often heatedly disagreed about what constituted good fiction, with Hampton calling for "virile and lifelike" stories but insisting that they appeal to the general reader and be *clean*. Dreiser, who was publishing fiction that reflected his own tastes to a greater degree than he had been able to do at *Smith's*, found Hampton's criteria mutually exclusive.

By Dreiser's account, Hampton's final maneuver was to form an editorial advisory committee headed by himself and made up of his loyalists on the staff. Dreiser was effectively bypassed; no longer did the magazine reflect his tastes. It was time to move on again. He had by now acquired the reputation of being a magazine doctor, the man to call in when the patient was failing and heroic remedies were needed.

The Delineator, a ladies' magazine owned by the Butterick Company, which sold tissue-paper patterns of the latest fashions, was just such an invalid. The magazine's main function was to sell patterns, but the company's president, George W. Wilder, realized that to do that, the "Del" needed bright editorial matter to attract readers. His last editor, who had also served as art director, had committed suicide over an unhappy love affair with a society woman, and Wilder needed a replacement immediately.

And so, in June 1907, even as Ben Hampton was putting into effect his editorial plans, not the least of which was changing the magazine's name to *Hampton's*, Dreiser received a letter from Wilder (who with lofty unconcern misspelled his name "Dreyser") informing him, "If you would call at this office to see me tomorrow (Friday) morning at or about eleven o'clock you would be doing me a courtesy that I would very much appreciate." Actually, Wilder had learned from John O'Hara Cosgrave, editor of *Everybody's*, in which Wilder was a silent partner, that Dreiser wanted to jump Hampton's ship.

Dreiser boarded the Sixth Avenue elevated train to Spring and MacDougal streets, where the Butterick Building loomed up, its three-planed front commanding a magnificent view of the southern tip of Manhattan. He took the elevator to Wilder's office on the fifteenth floor, where, amid trappings of corporate splendor, he was offered the editorship of *The Delineator* and the two other members of the Butterick trio, *The Designer* and *New Idea Women's Magazine*, at a starting salary of seven thousand dollars a year, with bonuses keyed to increasing circulation. He accepted Wilder's offer. The gates had been opened; he had attained the inner city.

46. A Pirate Selling Ribbons

> From now on it shall be the NEW DELINEATOR—new in hu-
> manitarian energy; new in serviceable tenderness; new in will-
> ingness and desire to aid and to see that idea of the fathers that
> has come down to us from the times of the Pilgrims shall not
> be brought to nothing.
>
> —Dreiser, "Concerning Us All" (1908)

*T**he Delineator* was, as mentioned, regarded by the Butterick
Company as primarily an advertising vehicle for its wares. In
the average issue the first fifty pages were devoted to detailed
drawings of various styles, which the reader could purchase
as a Butterick pattern for ten or fifteen cents each. In an age
of muckraking and progressivism, the thirty-five-year-old Del, the flag-
ship publication, seemed old-fashioned. It was the kind of magazine
mothers would recommend to their daughters as they did Butterick's conservative dress styles ("Safe fashions for home people"). Arthur Sullivant
Hoffman, who served as managing editor under Dreiser, described it as
"a fashion sheet with an omelet of magazine material poured loosely on
and around it."

As it happened, Dreiser was as intimately acquainted as any man could
be with the dreams of the young women from the villages and farms who
joined the rush to the cities beginning in the 1880s. *Sister Carrie* was testimony to that. He understood that, though their interests were mainly
centered on home and family, they had to live in a hard world; they were
affected by social conditions impinging on the domestic sphere. The audience for the Butterick trio consisted largely of rural and small-town women
(including their displaced sisters in the city), and Dreiser had grown up
in small towns in the Middle West. Frances Perkins, then a writer and
social reformer, who tried unsuccessfully to sell him an article, thought
Dreiser was the first to use the phrase "west of the Mississippi River"
to refer to a state of mind and level of sophistication as well as to a geo-

graphical region. So, whatever impelled George Wilder to anoint the author of the "immoral" *Sister Carrie* as the savior of the prim Butterick magazines, he had made a shrewd choice.

After cleaning out his desk at the *Broadway*, Dreiser moved into a large office on the twelfth floor of the Butterick Building. In this edifice two thousand employees toiled at putting out the magazines and paper patterns that were the company's stock in trade. The building resembled the prow of a great ocean liner, and one might imagine the basement, where great presses clanked and thundered (the world's largest printing plant), as the engine room, manned by grimy stokers. On the bridge, the fifteenth floor, Wilder and his corporate lieutenants held forth, while down on the eighth were the hard-eyed quartermasters of the business department.

What the captain's quarters were like can only be conjectured; Dreiser's (when the interior decorators had finished) were merely opulent. He had picked up the idea somewhere in his magazine travels that decor was power—the more lavish, the better for the executive image. William C. Lengel, who in 1910 came to be interviewed for the job of secretary to the great man, remembered the reception room as an awesome expanse, perhaps a hundred feet long and forty feet wide. "Hardwood inlaid floors with oriental rugs, the walls and ceiling paneled in white pine. Large Louis Seize chairs set about massive library tables and against the walls." Guarding the gate to the inner sanctum was a pretty receptionist whose sole job was to usher in callers and to answer the bell on the editor's desk when he had messages for his subordinates. Once admitted, the twenty-one-year-old Lengel gawked at the thick drapes and massive pictures, chosen to harmonize with the color scheme of green and bronze, which conveyed solid, understated luxury. Dominating the room, rather like a potentate's throne, was a massive black desk on a raised platform, which Dreiser later confessed he had positioned to give him the psychological advantage of looking down on visitors. Behind it sat a hulking figure who continued writing for five minutes before deigning to notice Lengel.

He was a tall man—six feet one inch, to be precise—who wore a gold pince-nez attached to a black ribbon and was dressed in heavy professorial tweeds with a contrasting vest. A young reporter named Sinclair Lewis, who interviewed Dreiser around this time, observed his bulging waistline (Dreiser weighed a prosperous 180 pounds) and decided he looked like a "wholesale hardware merchant." He was not handsome—some called him ugly. The novelist Fannie Hurst—then a young writer just in from St. Louis with a batch of short stories under her arm—remarked on his "strange lantern of a face," which gave no sign of greeting. The features beneath the high, sloping forehead and unruly hair the color of wet straw were puffy as though molded from putty. His sensuous lips were parted over even, prominent teeth, and the cast in one eye made it difficult to tell if he was looking at you or not. Hurst had the impression that Dreiser was "regarding me without seeing me, focusing on somewhere in an area between, rather than into, my eyes." Others who had audiences with him remembered him alternately looking down and peering sharply at them through his pince-nez. On first meeting, Dreiser seemed gruff and autocratic, but those who knew him best agreed that his manner was partly for show; that he was a shy, often kindly and emotional man, a bit uncouth and incapable of small talk.

Everyone who met him was intrigued by his nervous habit of pleating his handkerchief; few realized the habit was the only outward manifestation of a highly nervous temperament. Nina Carter Marbourg, a frequent contributor to the magazine, sensed this inner unease, calling him "the most nervous man I ever saw in an editorial chair." Frances Perkins also thought him "queer"—that is, neurotic.

Yet, his quirks and tics aside, Dreiser was clearly in charge. He presided over editorial meetings impassively, a kind of Buddha figure, speaking briefly, quick to praise, slow to censure. In a worshipful portrait, Charles Hanson Towne, who was his fiction editor, pictured Dreiser as a "dominating personality" and a decisive executive, a rock of strength in a tossing sea of ringing telephones and harried editors. "People moved in and out of his presence, and he settled the problem they presented to him in the briefest possible language. He never quibbled; his mind was made up immediately." Lengel, however, remembered sub-editors coming out of his office swearing and women subeditors emerging with tears in their eyes. He was known to tear up an issue at press time in order to get in a compelling story. Writers complained of the magazine's sitting on articles for six or nine months, and Dreiser explained to one irate author that he and his staff had been unable to decide what to do with his piece. When Dreiser gave orders, Lengel said, he tried to be jovial, but his "curious eyes and that twisted mouth made his attempted lightness seem arrogant and dictatorial. What he intended as joviality was mistaken for sarcasm." He was called a slave driver who badgered his subordinates mercilessly, demanding ideas, ideas, ideas. On one of his nervous prowls he happened into the office of Sarah Field Splint, head of the children's department, and told her, "You can stay on as long as you have ideas. But once you stop you'll have to leave. I don't want any hard feelings." "There won't be any hard feelings," replied Splint, on the verge of tears. Nearly every morning Dreiser brought in a sheaf of notes for stories and features, which his secretary copied meticulously on special forms for presentation at weekly editorial meetings. "He was exceedingly tolerant at the criticism of his offerings, and, at these meetings at least, never showed any impatience or raised his voice," Lengel wrote.

The tyrant image was largely dissipated by familiarity. The younger members of the staff found that once they broke through his autocratic crust, Dreiser listened to their ideas or problems. They in turn admired his novel. A woman on the staff had disliked and feared Dreiser until she read *Carrie*. Then she felt a strong loyalty to him because he had written "the one big serious true American novel with blood in it—not ink." Even those who had not read the book came to respect his ability and his professionalism. Ray Long, who succeeded him at *The Broadway*, said he learned the editor's trade by reading copies of Dreiser's letters to contributors in which he outlined story ideas. The humorist Homer Croy, one of several Missourians Dreiser hired (Lengel was another), because his wife was from the state and he had been a newspaperman in St. Louis, wrote, "In Philadelphia there were two great names—George Horace Lorimer and Edward Bok. In New York—Dreiser." Perhaps the comparison to the legendary editors of *The Saturday Evening Post* and *Ladies' Home Journal* was a little strained, but it was not far off the mark.

Ensconced in his luxurious office with a view of the East River, he sometimes gazed out the window, lost in thought. Towne wondered if he was dreaming of a new book. Lewisohn was reminded of a line from *Carrie*: "Who would not dream on a golden chair." Elia W. Peattie, one of his editors, thought him wildly miscast, later calling him "a pirate selling ribbons."

Out of a kind of *nostalgie de la boue*, he liked to walk in the Italian slums from which the Butterick Building jutted up like an alien monolith. He inhaled the color, the noise, the jostling humanity. Lengel remembered him each evening walking with a rolling gait along MacDougal Street to the elevated train, humming spirituals or popular tunes of the nineties.

When Lengel asked Dreiser why he wasted his time editing a women's magazine when he could write a novel like *Sister Carrie*, Dreiser shrugged and said, "One must live. Don't you know the story of that book?" Later, he told him. A sad story, but one that, ironically, had had a happy ending.

47. Sister Carrie Redux

—And what is your Mr. Dreiser doing these days?
—Dreiser?
—The author of *Sister Carrie!* . . . Americans do not know
that England looks on *Sister Carrie* as the finest American novel
sent over in the last twenty years and to Dreiser as the biggest
American novelist who has sent us anything . . .

—William J. Locke, British novelist in an interview
on arriving in New York City (1908)

When you wrote *Sister Carrie* there was just one way in which
to write the novel about a woman. It was to prove that as
a matter of Christian sin, not even cause and consequence, . . . the woman was punished. . . . You cleaned up the
country and set the pace for the truth and freed the young, and
enlightened the old where they could be enlightened.

—Edgar Lee Masters to Theodore Dreiser (1939)

en Hampton told Dorothy Dudley he had deeply admired
Sister Carrie and always wished he had been the one who put
up the money for its republication in 1907. Probably he had
been too busy consolidating his control to notice that Dreiser
had succeeded in finding a new publisher on his own. Knowing of her boss's desire for a new edition, Ethel Kelly gave it to a friend
named Flora Mai Holly, who was starting out as a literary agent, to try
to sell. Holly was herself a true believer and familiar with the book's history. At the time *Sister Carrie* came out, she had been working for *The
Bookman* and had heard the trade gossip about *Carrie*'s abortive publication.

The times were right for *Carrie*. Even John Phillips, Sam S. McClure's
literary editor, who in 1903 lectured Dreiser that his fiction was immoral,
had recently told him he thought it should be published. To avoid any
lingering traces of old prejudices, however, Holly placed the book with
a new firm, B. W. Dodge and Company. Dodge was a shrewd, uncon-

ventional publisher who was looking for a way to launch his company with a big splash and was willing to take a chance. He had been a salesman for Dodd, Mead and worked up to an editorial position before quitting to found his own house. His business affairs were disorderly, but Dodge was ebullient and full of schemes for making money ("stunts" he liked to call them). He also had a talent for charming wealthy people—"moneybags"—into backing his ventures. His only major weakness—a fatal one as it turned out—was a considerable thirst for hard liquor. He was, in Dreiser's words, "a lovable alcoholic." Ludwig Lewisohn described Dodge as "an intelligent, hearty, generous, bearded fellow with a slightly rowdy flavor of an older America about him," who was "fast drinking himself to death."

Something of a free spirit, Dodge had no moral qualms about publishing *Sister Carrie*. His disagreements were with conservative people like his previous employers, the Dodd family, who were all "very pious Presbys." He had a junior partner, Charles H. Doscher—"canny, suburban, church-going," in Lewisohn's words—who, as it happened, had formerly worked for Doubleday, Page. Though Dodd later said Doscher's opinion "didn't count"—that he had decided to publish *Carrie* "all by my lonesome"—Doscher did read it and found it "an absorbing story," a little "risqué perhaps for Victorian times but not for 1907."

Ben Dodge was precisely the kind of publisher Dreiser needed—brash, hustling, and willing to launch the book with a suitable "stunt." He also moved quickly. Holly set up a meeting between author and publisher in late January 1907, and by early March they had agreed on a contract. Dreiser would receive 10-percent royalties on the first three thousand copies sold and 15 percent on all copies thereafter—standard terms for that day. A new wrinkle was that the author agreed to buy fifty shares of stock in B. W. Dodge and Company at $100 a share. Dodge had talked Dreiser into underwriting his own book. He was to pay $1000 down, which would cover production costs and leave something over for advertising and promotion. The remaining $4000 would be deducted from royalties.

In return, Dreiser became a director of the new firm, entitled to a share of its profits, if any. As subsequent events showed, he intended his stock purchase as a serious investment and hoped to make money out of it. He took an active role in the company's affairs, both to protect the value of his shares and to have a say in the publication of his novel. Where he found the $1000 is another matter; perhaps he had saved it, for he and Jug lived frugally.

Dreiser and Dodge devised a two-pronged strategy for Carrie's reha-

bilitation which called for advertising the novel's literary merits and pub-
licizing the story of its "suppression" so the public would think of it as
virtually a new book. If people caught a whiff of the risqué, well, so be
it; the first part of the strategy would pre-empt any charges of pandering
to the public's appetite for sensation.

Proceeding on the first front, Dreiser wrote letters to Carrie's prominent admirers informing them that Carrie was at long last being resurrected and asking permission to use a quote in the advertising brochure.
To Reedy, he boasted that the new edition would be a deluxe job with
color plates, and its advent in the stores would be heralded by posters.

On the other front, Dreiser wrote a long account of the Doubleday
story, mentioning no names. Although intimating that Doubleday's attempt to back out had been "a coarse bit of commercial conduct," he
immediately softened the aspersion by tacking on the phrase to the effect
that there had been "considerable justification on both sides" for what
occurred—referring to his own pigheadedness, no doubt. Dreiser advanced the theory that, despite favorable reviews, the book "fell flat"
because reorders were not filled. That was a bit of an exaggeration. As
John H. Raftery's inquest into the death of *Carrie* for Reedy showed, the
booksellers did not reorder because sales were minuscule and because
the publisher had not advertised it; Doubleday had considered himself
bound to fill orders.

Thus, the latest version of the Doubleday Legend, which would undergo
further coats of gloss in later years. Though he did not mention Mrs.
Doubleday by name in his 1907 account, Doscher's wife remembered
Dreiser's coming to their house for dinner and spending the entire evening talking bitterly about the publisher's wife. He was a bit unbalanced
on the subject, she thought. Neltje Doubleday had been caught up in
an actual "realism war," not one fought from an editor's study, and truth
was the first casualty.

Dreiser's account was not used in the brochure that Dodge eventually
disseminated among booksellers. It was too long, and Dodge may not
have wanted to stir up trouble with a publisher as prominent as Frank
Doubleday. Instead, he indulged in a tease: "This book was accepted
by a leading American publisher, but strangely enough immediately with-
drawn; meantime an English edition was published and had an instantaneous success. As its suppression in this country was our gain, we have
no comments to make, but again ask you to read the comments of others
who can fairly be supposed to be unprejudiced judges."

There followed a ten-page compilation of blurbs, leading off with the powerful endorsements by the British critics in 1901. After those came quotes in smaller type from American writers and critics such as Frank Norris, Garland, Whitlock, Albert Bigelow Paine, Edna Kenton, Reedy, and others, taken from letters to Dreiser. There were almost no quotes from the American reviews. The brochure concluded with "A Bit of Literary History"—an edited excerpt from the 1903 article in *The Bookman* that Dreiser had unexpectedly read in West Virginia. Dropped, however, is the implication that Doubleday hoped the book would not succeed.

While all the laudatory quotes from American literary celebrities were accurate, the prominence given to the English reviews seemed to be an example of the Stephen Crane Ploy, or Literary Colonialism Revisited. The publisher also fibbed a little when he said that most of the American celebrities had "heard of the book from the English edition," which was not exactly the case but was presumably intended to emphasize the book's nonappearance in the United States. In other words, a few independent-minded American litterateurs had heard the news from England, boarded ship immediately, and bought a copy on Charing Cross Road.

And so *Sister Carrie* made her second debut on May 18, 1907. Dodge and Dreiser had made certain that this time the little knight did not venture forth half-equipped. No assassin's binding for the new model: she was decked out in bright red cloth of good quality, and the title was stamped in gold letters. There was only one illustration, a full-color frontispiece in which Carrie, looking pert in her "little Quaker" costume, is shown curtsying before the curtain. The warm dedication to Arthur Henry had been removed, however, as had the borrowed passage from George Ade.

To supplement the promotional brochure, which was aimed at booksellers, Dodge took out advertisements in the newspapers. Here, his huckstering was more uninhibited. He trumpeted the book's uniqueness ("The Curtain Raised on a Generally Unwritten Phase of Life"), its power ("Startling in reality"), and, not least, its daring ("Sensational revelations"). The respectable literati were cued ("The realism of a Zola without the faults. One of the most remarkable novels in literature . . ."), but the general public was not neglected ("and everybody is going to read it").

Not everybody did by any means, but sales got off to a brisk start. In the first three months after publication, more than 4600 copies were sold, and eventually the total reached about 8500—small in comparison to the 200,000-copy sale that year of Robert W. Chambers's society novel *The Younger Set*, or the even higher sales of *The Lady of the Decoration* by Frances Little, in a Century Company dollar edition—but respectable. In 1908, after sales had cooled down, Grosset and Dunlap brought out a cheap edition of 10,000 copies, taking the excess stock off Dodge's hands. Doscher recalled that *Sister Carrie* launched the firm, and he was able to sell his interest at a profit. More to the point, the book's critical reception established Dreiser's reputation as an important American novelist, even though he had published nothing for seven years.

This time the reviews came out in a single authoritative wave, rather than intermittent ripples. This time he won the approval of critics for the mainstream papers. The Washington *Evening Star*'s reviewer wrote that the novel was "one of the most important books of the year"; Agnes Repellier of the Philadelphia *Public Ledger* called it "literature of high class"; the Los Angeles *Times* described it as "somber, powerful, fearlessly and even fearfully frank"; and the New Orleans *Picayune* averred it was the "strongest piece of realism we have yet met with in American fiction."

There were dissents, of course, and the moralists fulminated. The *Ohio Journal*, for example, warned, "Such books are to be shunned . . . there is so much in the world that is fresh and clean, elevating little stories . . . that are worth telling." The Chicago *Advance* warned, "The book is not a good or wholesome one for women to read." In the heart of Watch and Ward Society country, the Boston *Transcript*'s reviewer found it "a matter for regret that [the author] should devote his creative energy to a woman and two men who never quicken our nobler impulses." And *The New York Times Saturday Review* prissed: "We do not, however, recommend the book to the fastidious reader, or the one who clings to 'old-fashioned ideas.' It is a book one can very well get along without reading."

Yet, the *Times* notice was on the whole favorable, albeit delivered through clenched teeth. Similarly, the *Transcript*'s reviewer said that Dreiser had succeeded in investing his sordid characters "with the dignity of psychological insight and literary perception, and with an interest—often rebellious—which never flags." She made it clear that the book did not appeal to prurient tastes, and as a feminist she was not puzzled by the title. It stood for "the sisterhood of woman: her temptations and her opportunities, her wrongs and her rights, her obedience to the ordinary demands of the moment, her responsiveness to the appeal of sex, her power to develop out of and above it into independence of thought and action." Perhaps too polite to say it, she meant that this was no portrait of a lady. Carrie Meeber Wheeler Madenda was a modern woman.

The New York *Evening Sun*, coming at the male-female issue from the perspective of the censors' claimed solicitousness for young girls' sensibilities: "Amid the thousands of anaemic novels that come out like a flood, written by ladies, for ladies of both sexes, here is a book written by a man, obviously intended for men, and without a thought of that everlasting nuisance, the young person."

The times were changing. Other reviewers excused the author for choosing disreputable protagonists. As the *Evening Sun*'s reviewer pointed out, if the propriety of a novel's characters were the issue, then many classics, from Defoe's *Moll Flanders* to George Moore's *Esther Waters*, should not have been published.

There was much more of this kind of sociological analysis, but it took a member of the younger generation—a literary radical—to recognize the transcendant cultural issue involved. Writing in the Houston *Post*, the reviewer saw in *Sister Carrie* "one more evidence of a broader American intellectual freedom." He continued:

> Possibly the day may come when George Moore's *Memoirs of My Dead Life*, will not have to be expurgated as if for children, when it is issued in the United States. No wonder England, no wonder France, no wonder Germany look patronizingly down upon us—a nation of grown men and women for whom publishers must expurgate books before they are allowed to read them! "The land of the free," "freedom of the press"—the words are empty. . . . The time is coming some day—I care not whether it is within twenty-five years or within a century—when the United States will have to "stand for"—if it comes to the point of compulsion—an American Tolstoi, Turgenieff, Flaubert, Balzac, Nietzsche, Wilde, de Maupassant.

The reviewer was Harris Merton Lyon. If his pocketbook was now in Ben Hampton's camp, his soul was still with Dreiser. In his choice of an intellectual son, Dreiser could not have done better.

In an interview with the New York *Times* after *Sister Carrie*'s successful second debut, Dreiser said he was too busy editing *The Delineator* to write novels. He spoke of the dramas of ordinary life, and the twists and turns of fate. Here he was, surely, at the summit of success, making money and basking in the light of critical admiration. Yet, he told the reviewer, "The mere living of your daily life is a drastic drama. . . . The banquet of tonight may crumble to the crust of the morning."

Perhaps he was thinking that, only four years ago, he had been a beggar; now, he was an invited guest at the feast. From his office on the twelfth floor of the Butterick Building he could see all the way to the southern tip of Manhattan, where the two rivers converged—the East, river of the nameless dead, and the Hudson, river of power and dreams. Two streams in his life had also converged: his constant struggle for money and power and his idealistic battle for art, expression, and truth. Beyond their confluence lay the open sea, awaiting further voyages.

"I simply want to tell about life as it is," he told the interviewer. "Every human life is intensely interesting . . . the personal desire to survive, the fight to win, the stretching out of the fingers to grasp—these are the things I want to write about—life as it is, the facts as they exist, the game as it is played!"

Epilogue

"Behold, the sea is ever dancing or raging," he would write seven years later, in the coda of his novel *The Titan*. The currents that had plunged him to the bottom had bobbed him to the surface and borne him safely to the shining sands. But all was change and flux; the seething tides raged on. . . .

Would he remain in his baronial office at *The Delineator*, like McEwen, high above the city's warring ants? Would he, like Carrie, rock and dream, a restless prisoner in the bubble of success? The storm clouds were gathering. He would have rivals who would stir a witches' brew of enmity. George Wilder, on the fifteenth floor, was watching him. As long as the magazine progressed, Wilder would bide his time. But hoving into view was one Erman Ridgway, editor of *Everybody's Magazine*. In 1908 the Butterick Company would buy *Everybody's* in an exchange of stock so cozy that Thomas Lawson might have used it in the next episode of "Frenzied Finance."

Forsooth, the mutterings of thunder could be heard by those who had ears to hear them. The sky would darken with fulgurous clouds; the sea would rage. By 1909 Ridgway would be publisher of the Butterick trio and a year later Dreiser would be out. But that is another story . . .

And what of the flower-faced young girl of eighteen named Thelma Cudlipp, with whom Dreiser would fall in love, adding further winds of scandal to the storm whirling around him? Poor Jug, his loyal Kitten— she would at last put her foot down and demand an end to his philandering. Life was a tragedy, Dreiser said, forgetting that it was sometimes a domestic farce in which angry wives pursue husbands to the sound of slamming stage doors. ("My God! ma, is that you!")

The errant husband is ejected from the corporate sanctum and lands with a thud behind his writing desk. Can he make a go of it, he asks his young protégé H. L. Mencken. He will write four novels and see. In a tremendous burst, he does: *Jenny Gerhardt* (*The Transgressor* resurrected and rewritten), *The Financier*, *The Titan*, *The "Genius"*—and, in his subconscious, his greatest novel, *An American Tragedy*, is germinating. The seeds of these books had been planted in the fallow soil of his silent decade, and the storm brought rain and, lo, the earth bore fruit.

The improbable life of Dreiser—a meandering, twisting river that ever flowed toward its destiny—what can one make of it? What inscrutable author conceived and wrote it? Let him answer:

> Each according to his temperament—that something which he has not made and cannot always subdue, and which may not always be subdued by others for him. Who plans the steps that lead lives on to splendid glories, or twist them into gnarled sacrifices, or make of them dark, disdainful, contentious tragedies? The soul within? And whence comes it? Of God? . . .
>
> In a mulch of darkness are bedded the roots of endless sorrows—and of endless joys. Canst thou fix thine eye on the morning? Be glad. And if in the ultimate it blind thee, be glad also! Thou hast lived.

He had lived to fight another day. If he had gone under, as so many of his literary generation went under, Dreiser would still have been remembered for a single book: *Sister Carrie*. But if he had not waged his lonely battle to vindicate that book, had not republished it at a key moment in history, it might have lain forgotten like Henry Adams's *Education* or Herman Melville's *Billy Budd*, to be discovered in the 1920s. Perhaps our cultural history would have been no different in the event, but it was better that Dreiser was there to pass on the torch to a new generation. And even better still that he was able to resume and continue his work, carrying on his stubborn fight against the censors, the moralists, and the academic superpatriots, stubbornly telling the truth as he knew it, writing about the game as it is played.

ACKNOWLEDGMENTS

First, for the most priceless gift of all, time, I wish to express my gratitude to Victor Navasky and Hamilton Fish, editor and publisher of *The Nation*, for allowing me time off from my editorial duties to work on this book. Thanks also to my capable replacements, Zachary Sklar and Kirkpatrick Sale, and to my other colleagues at the magazine who filled in for me at various times. Helping in another way were the researchers—Sheila Dillon, Dana Seligman, Amy Singer, and Vania Del Borgo by name—who saved me long stints at the library by unearthing various hard-to-find articles and publications. Thanks also to Lynn Nesbit, my agent, and to Phyllis Grann of G. P. Putnam's Sons, who hatched this project; to my editor, Faith Sale, for putting up with a procrastinating and dilatory author, and to her assistant, Ben McCormick, for helping assemble the manuscript. Finally, my respects to Shirley Sulat and Denise Auclair, who typed various drafts of the manuscript.

While this book is not intended as a scholarly work and is aimed at that cherished patron of serious writers, the general reader, it draws upon the work of many scholars. My hope has been to provide a thorough, factual treatment of Theodore Dreiser's life in the context of literary and social history and some critical assessment of his place in American literature; but also to provide a readable narrative for the aforementioned GR. Consequently, I have kept the usual scholarly apparatus out of the body of the book—not only footnotes, but attributions of the "As Professor So-and-So says" variety. Credit is given in the Notes and the Bibliography. The latter is not intended to be an exhaustive list of my reading or a survey of the "field" of Dreiser studies, which has yielded an abundant harvest of books and monographs; it is, rather, an informal list of the editions from which I have quoted. Students who wish further information on a source that seems inadequately identified should write me care of the publisher.

"Where did you get that?" Dreiser often said to conscientious biographers trying to verify this or that fact. Since he can no longer make such remonstrances, the inquiring reader will have to depend on me as a pale and far-removed stand-in. Not that Dreiser himself was always the most accurate source. Memory sometimes played tricks even on him, the author of some of the most honest auto-biographies ever written in this country.

Of course, I am fortunate in having the works of previous biographers as a solid foundation. Dorothy Dudley, a young woman who knew Dreiser in the 1920s, was the first to attempt the job, and her *Dreiser and the Land of the Free* (as the second edition is called), while as much cultural study and sounding board for her own ideas as biography, does provide useful interviews with the subject as well as his contemporaries. Robert H. Elias was next in line and the first to attempt a serious study of life and works in his *Theodore Dreiser: Apostle of Nature*. Elias had the advantage of knowing Dreiser for more than a decade. His book came out in 1949, and he has since published an emended version containing an invaluable survey of the state of Dreiser knowledge as of 1970.

In 1965 came W. A. Swanberg's *Dreiser*, which draws copiously on interviews with contemporaries, many of whom are gone. While not the study of Dreiser's art and thought that Elias's book is, Swanberg's is more emancipated from the constraints of space and time that kept Elias from portraying fully the human side of the writer. Some have felt that Swanberg perhaps emphasized the "human, all too human" Dreiser at the expense of the great writer. But if that is true, it was perhaps inevitable, given his focus on the life rather than the works.

Certainly, there has been no shortage of full-length critical studies of Dreiser, the artist, beginning with H. L. Mencken's in one of his *Prefaces*, and Burton Rascoe's slender volume written in the 1920s, both of which effectively defended Dreiser against his critics before he had written the novel that certified his great-ness, *An American Tragedy;* and on through essays and books by such effective champions as Alfred Kazin, Irving Howe, Van Wyck Brooks, Charles Shapiro, Maxwell Geismar, F. O. Matthiessen, John J. McAleer, Philip Gerber, Ellen Moers, Richard Lehan, Yoshinobu Hakutani, Donald Pizer, Robert Penn War-ren, to name some of the most prominent.

I have built on these foundations, though it would be presumptuous of me to claim that they served as pillars on which I erected a grand, overarching su-perstructure. Not at all. Rather they have been guides and companions to me in my own quest for an understanding of Dreiser the person and Dreiser the writer. This book is simply one edifice among several, reflecting, as all books do, its author's temperament and inclinations. It seeks to create Dreiser anew for readers of the 1980s and I hope beyond. In addition to a fresh eye, I can offer some more solid scholarly coin—new materials that have come to light since pre-vious books, or, as in the case of the letters Dreiser wrote to his then fiancée, that have been "cleared" for quotation. There is also the new loam thrown up by scholarly plows, notably the series of books either published or in preparation for the University of Pennsylvania Press, which has already given us the "re-stored" *Sister Carrie*, the unpublished diaries, and a book version of *An Amateur Laborer*. These works, along with others placing various facets of Dreiserana "between boards," have been of considerable assistance, not the least of which is giving the researcher the leisure to peruse materials rather than spending frantic hours of hand-copying letters and other documents like a medieval scribe in reading rooms across the nation.

More specifically, I would like to mention Robert Elias's three-volume edition of Dreiser's letters; Donald Pizer's book of heretofore uncollected or unpublished Dreiser prose, as well as his researches into the writing of various Dreiser works; Richard Lehan and the late Ellen Moers's investigations of the sources of various Dreiser texts; Richard W. Dowell's editing of *The Dreiser Newsletter*, which has published a good deal of new material, and his researches in conjunction with the University of Pennsylvania Edition of *An Amateur Laborer*. Mention should also be made of James L. W. West, III, who has demonstrated the importance of the bibliographer's craft to biography; Thomas P. Riggio, who has contributed fresh facts and interpretations in his introduction to the Dreiser diaries and in his researches in collateral areas; Larzer Ziff's study, *The American 1890s*, a model of literary history; T. D. Nostwich, who generously shared with me his cache of Dreiser's journalism, the product of Lord knows how many eyestraining hours poring over old newspapers; Yoshinobu Hakutani for *Selected Magazine Articles of Theodore Dreiser* (the first of a three-volume set); and Jack Salzman for relieving me of the burden of locating the reviews of Dreiser's books in newspapers and magazines. None of these authorities, of course, are responsible for any errors in this book.

I must also express gratitude to Donald T. Oakes, who has let me draw upon his inquiry into the life of Arthur Henry—a labor of love by that vanishing breed, the dedicated amateur scholar—which he plans to publish with a reissued version of Henry's little nature classic, *The House in the Woods*. And to Gupton and Grace Vogt my thanks for helping me locate information on Sara White Dreiser. Gupton Vogt also generously and properly opened up to scholars the aforementioned courtship letters from Dreiser to Jug, and he introduced me to Louise Graham, who shared with me her memories of her Aunt Jug, as did Mrs. Graham's daughter Mary Lou Ahmann.

Returning to the Dreiser side of the family, I must express my deep gratitude to Vera Dreiser, who tirelessly answered my questions about her Uncle Theodore, about whom she wrote a valuable and insightful book that brings to bear her firsthand knowledge of family history and her training as a psychologist. And to her daughter, Tedi, who with her husband, Joel Godard, has provided warm hospitality, including, on one memorable evening, an impromptu living-room concert of several Paul Dresser ballads.

Finally, my list of credits would not be complete without mention of the various librarians who eased my path through various thickets of Dreiserana. Preeminent among these is Neda M. Westlake, a familiar name in this section of books on Dreiser. Until her retirement in 1984, she served as curator of special collections at the Van Pelt Library, University of Pennsylvania, where the Dreiser Collection resides. A Dreiser scholar in her own right, she has guided, I would hazard, hundreds of seekers through its riches. Her knowledge is, of course, invaluable, but the inspiration of her friendly, encouraging presence should also be recognized. Following her retirement, Daniel G. Traister, the present curator, and Kathleen Reed, assistant curator, have extended to me several courtesies and assistances. I must also thank Saundra Taylor at the Lilly Library, Indiana University, for her help. Other librarians have aided me in ways large and small, and I thank them *en bloc*.

The various collections drawn upon are mentioned in the appropriate citations, but I must specifically thank the custodians of the Dreiser Collection, Van Pelt Library, University of Pennsylvania; the Lilly Library, Indiana University; the Ellen Moers Collection at the Butler Library, Columbia University; the Manuscripts and Archives Division of the New York Public Library; the Mencken Collection at the Enoch Pratt Free Library, Baltimore; the Robert H. Elias Collection, Cornell University Library; and the Clifton Waller Barrett Collection in the Alderman Library, University of Virginia, for granting me access to Dreiser letters, notes, diaries, manuscripts, photographs, and other materials. Unless otherwise noted, and with the exception of the courtship letters of TD to SOW (Sara Osborne White), which are at the Lilly Library, all letters cited are in the University of Pennsylvania Dreiser Collection. The libraries from which material was obtained are denoted as follows:

ColU—Columbia University Library, New York City
CorU—Cornell University Library, Ithaca, New York
EUL—Emory University Library, Atlanta, Georgia
EvL—Evansville Public Library, Evansville, Indiana
IHS—Indiana Historical Society, Indianapolis, Indiana
IU—Lilly Library, Indiana University, Bloomington, Indiana
MCHS—Montgomery County Historical Society, Montgomery City, Missouri
StLML—St. Louis Mercantile Library, St. Louis, Missouri
SuL—Sullivan County Library, Sullivan, Indiana
THL—Emeline Fairbanks Library, Terre Haute, Indiana
UP—University of Pennsylvania Library, Philadelphia, Pennsylvania
UVa—University of Virginia Library, Charlottesville, Virginia
VCHS—Vigo County Historical Society, Terre Haute, Indiana
WaL—Warsaw Public Library, Warsaw, Indiana

I am indebted to the following for the photographs:

Theodore Dreiser Collection, Department of Special Collections, Van Pelt Library, University of Pennsylvania, for the photographs of Theodore Dreiser, circa 1893; John Paul Dreiser; the Dreiser home in Chicago; brother Paul Dresser; brother Ed, the actor; Theo and Jug; the cover of *Ev'ry Month*; the contract for *The Flesh and the Spirit*; and Dreiser during the writing of *Sister Carrie*.

Lilly Library, Indiana University, for the photographs of Sara Schänäb Dreiser;

426 *Acknowledgments*

Theodore Dreiser, the freshman; Dreiser in St. Louis; Sara Osborne "Jug" White; Dreiser in Chicago; Dreiser, the free-lance writer; and two views of Dreiser, the editor.

Special Collections Department, Robert W. Woodruff Library, Emory University, for the photographs of sister Theresa; sister Claire; brother Rome; and John Paul Dreiser at seventy.

Vera Dreiser for the photographs, from her private collection, of sister Emma; Paul's adopted sister, Louise Dresser; and Jug as a young wife.

Donald T. Oakes for the photographs, from his private collection, of Anna Mallon; the House of Seven Pillars; and Dumpling Island.

Cornell University Library for the photographs of Arthur Henry.

NOTES

Chapter 1.

"I will not say" "Dawn" (holograph), ch. I.

It was an ancient town Information on Mayen and German Dreisers from Dr. Renate Schmidt-von Bardelben, "Dreiser on the European Continent," *The Dreiser Newsletter*, Fall 1971.

"I have never met" Henry Dreiser to TD, Dec. 23, 1900.

"There is no real" Carmel O'Neill Haley, "The Dreisers," *The Commonweal*, July 7, 1933.

Paul Dreiser obtained a job Robert H. Elias, *Theodore Dreiser: Apostle of Nature*, 6. Information on Paul Dreiser's early career in America obtained from the following: Pamphlet, "In the Year of 1850 in the Village of Connersville," Markle file (THL); H. W. Beckwith, *History of Vigo and Parke Countys* [sic], 142; *History of Montgomery County, Ohio*, 51, 58.

Sarah Mary Schänäb Information on Sarah Dreiser's background: Dr. Hale T. Schenefield, "A Personal Memoir of Theodore Dreiser. With the relations of the Dreiser, Arnold and Parks Families" (WaL); Shari Dreiser Scott to Ellen Moers, Jan. 31, 1965, EM Coll, Box 8, "Mother and Religion" (ColU); "In Memory of Rev. H. A. Snepp," St. Joseph Conference Minutes, Sept. 4–8, 1895, Plymouth, Indiana, ibid.; Undated, unsigned letter to Helen Richardson Dreiser re Esther Ann Snepp, ibid.

"madly in love" *Dawn*, 4.

moved to Terre Haute Edwin Ellis (George's son) to TD, Feb. 6, 1906: "I have known Paul [Jr.] since his birth. His father came with my father from Ohio to this city. . . ." George Ellis came to Terre Haute in 1853, as mentioned. Actually there were two Ellis mills; Terre Haute histories variously refer to the Riverside Mill, which seems to have been George's and which ran continuously until his death, and the Wabash Mill, which Edwin seems to have managed or owned. Paul Dreiser, Sr., worked in both places.

three children Photostat in EM Coll from "Dreiser Family Bible" says that the children, James George and Havery [?] died in Terre Haute in 1854 and 1855. In *Dawn*, 5, TD writes that the children were "all boys and all taken within three years."

The story of three babies and other superstitions are recounted in *Dawn*, 6–9. See also Mary Frances Brennan ("Mame," TD's sister) to A. R. Markle, Jan. 12, 1941, Markle file (THL).

In 1857 Sarah John Paul Dreiser, Jr. (Paul Dresser) was born on April 22, 1858. A. R. Markle, "Some Light on Paul Dresser; His Anniversary Is This Month," Terre Haute *Sunday Tribune*, April 14, 1941, Markle file (THL).

the Reverend Merrick A. Jewett A. R. Markle to Robert H. Elias, July 19, 1947 (CorL). Mame's recollection was that Rose backed the Jewetts. Brennan to Markle, Jan. 12, 1941. Markle says that Rose "was always the real owner of the property." *History of Greene and Sullivan Counties, State of Indiana*, 613.

"employed as a foreman" Sullivan County *Democrat*, May 21, 1864. See Thomas P. Riggio, "The Dreisers in Sullivan: A Biographical Revision," *The Dreiser Newsletter*, Fall 1979.

Jewetts' venture Dr. Maple's Scrapbook, 13, 15 (SuL).

three-story brick building Richard W. Dowell, "Ask Mr. Markle?" *The Dreiser Newsletter*, Spring 1977.

"ruined the business" Brennan to Markle, Jan. 12, 1941.

Paul did not endow the church Riggio, "Dreisers in Sullivan."

kindly and intelligent TD, "Sarah Schanab," MS, Box 92A (UP).

"a little house" "The Home of My Early Childhood," Brennan to Gertrude [Nelson], copy in Markle file (THL). All quotes from this letter.

"the large family" Rachael Harris, "Personal Recollection of the Dresser [sic] Family," Sullivan *Daily Times*, June 14, 1937.

"one of the best" Quoted in Riggio, "Dreisers in Sullivan."

"withdrawing from the firm" Sullivan *Democrat*, April 15, 1869.

"pay all indebtedness" Ibid.

"Highest Cash Price" *Democrat*, June 2, 1870. Clipping, Dr. Maple File, 30 (SuL).

"wool manufacturer" Census Roll, enumerated Aug. 30, 1870 (SuL).

a storm Riggio, "Dreisers in Sullivan"; Dowell, "Ask Mr. Markle?"

"WOOL" *Democrat*, May 12, 1871. Ad is dated May 10.

Deed records Dowell, "Ask Mr. Markle?"

"Yankee treachery" Brennan to Markle, Jan. 12, 1941.

"laborer" Markle file (THL).

"He was a good" Quoted in Riggio, "Dreisers in Sullivan."

TD's birth date Baptismal record, Church of St. Benedict, Sept. 10, 1871. Markle to Robert H. Elias (CorU). Record also in Markle file (THL).

Chapter 2.

"All this industry" H. W. Beckwith, *History of Vigo and Parke Countys* [sic], 482.

Terre Haute at this time Historical material from Beckwith; William F. Cronin, ed., *An Account of Vigo County From Its Organization;* Loren Hassam, *A Historical Sketch of Terre Haute, Indiana;* C. C. Oakey, *Greater Terre Haute and Vigo County;* H. C. Bradsby, *History of Vigo County, Indiana, With Biographical Selections.*

"that sacred little spot" Quoted in Nick Salvatore, *Eugene V. Debs: Citizen and Socialist,* 3, 21, 22.

Dreiser children The names appear in family records various ways, but Dreiser gives the original German versions in the holograph MS of "Dawn."

the pull of Mayen In a letter from Mrs. Johann Dreiser, TD's cousin, May 3, 1922, she refers to her last communication from Paul, Sr., in the 1890s: "He mentioned the names of his children. They were mostly the names which his sisters in German also bore. It seems that in his heart he stayed true to his native country."

"puny beyond belief" *Dawn*, 7.

"I was always" Ibid, 19.

"velvety hand" "Sarah Schanab" (UP).

"My mother was" Mary Frances Brennan to A. R. Markle, Jan. 13, 1941.

"enfolding her legs" *Dawn*, 17.

so wrought up Vera Dreiser, *My Uncle Theodore*, 33.

"Oh years later" *Dawn*, 17.

"Long after I had" "Dawn" (typescript), ch. XXVI, 236.

"form of brooding" Ibid.

"charm and seductivity," "disassociated implements" Vera Dreiser, *My Uncle*, 33.

"I am convinced" Ibid, 31.

"Aren't you sorry" *Dawn*, 19.

"Are you going," "Oh, work" "Dawn" (holograph), ch. I.

"That was the birth" *Dawn*, 19.

"the little wise-looking" Carmel O'Neill Haley, "The Dreisers," *The Commonweal*, July 7, 1933.

"Give me God!" Ibid.

Chapter 3.

"At the same time" *A Hoosier Holiday*, 390, 391.

"The more I think" Ibid., 391.

"laborer," "spinner," etc. "Dreiser Notes," Markle file (THL).

"As we utter" Quoted in Alan Trachtenberg, *The Incorporation of America*, 71.

"a great business" C. C. Oakey, *Greater Terre Haute and Vigo County*, 368.

"he could have," "by now he" "Dawn" (typescript), ch. XV, 8.

"All the woolen" *HH*, 412.

Industrialization had transformed See Arthur Harrison Cole, *The American Wool Manufacture*, 112, 166, 167, 211, 212.

"long, dreary" *Dawn*, 23.

"to devote his" Mary Frances Brennan, "My Brother Paul," with MFB to TD, July 5, 1906. Box 190.

leading to the study Catherine C. Etienne, registrar, St. Meinrad Seminary to author, June 9, 1982. The school had no record of Paul's attendance between 1873 and 1878; records prior to that time were destroyed by fire. Probably he attended the school when he was around twelve, ca. 1870.

Paul, Jr., lasted The account of Paul's peregrinations is drawn from "Paul Dresser" by Max Ehrmann, a pamphlet in the Markle Coll (THL); the Reverend F. Joseph Mutch, letter to *The Commonweal*, Aug. 18, 1933; Indianapolis *Journal*, Sept. 25, 1899, clipping in PD Scrapbook, Box 392 (UP).

"vainglory, indifference" Quoted in Ellen Moers, *Two Dreisers*, 220.

"mental vaguery" "Dawn" (typescript), ch. III, 30.

"You have the damndest" Ibid., 3.

"vain, silly" Ibid., ch. XIV, 102.

"wornout clothes" *Dawn*, 349.

" 'I don't know' " Quoted in *Dawn*, 69.

"They fought over" "Dawn" (typescript), ch. III, 28.

"a grave, thoughtful," Ibid., ch. VI, 38.

"seemed even then" Ibid.

"It was during" Ibid., ch. V, 30.

"Now we are about" Quoted, Vera Dreiser, in *My Uncle Theodore*, 35.

the "Evansville Biography, Paul Dresser" file, Evansville Public Library; Markle file (THL); and the PD Scrapbook (UP).

"The festive dudelet" John W. Grant to TD, Sept. 16, 1931.

"Let me introduce" Lyric quoted in Sigmund Spaeth, *Read 'Em and Weep*. Account of Paul singing "Lardy Dah" from Roy L. McCardell, "Theodore Dreiser, Master of the Matter of Fact," *Morning Telegraph Sunday Magazine*, Dec. 28, 1919, PD Scrapbook (UP).

"I'm General Grant" Phil M. Hacker to TD, March 28, 1921 (UP).

"You can't get" Quoted in "Proposed Memorial of Interest to Many Here," Evansville *Journal*, Oct. 15, 1922 (EvL).

"You hardly ever" Quoted in "The Dresser—Marking One-Time Home of Noted Song Writer," Evansville *Courier*, June 1, 1952 (EPL).

"it looks as if" Quoted in John H. Mackey to TD, April 27, 1923 (UP).

"No mah deah," "MR. PAUL DRESSER" Quoted in undated clipping, Terre Haute *Daily Tribune*, PD Scrapbook (UP).

"the sensational comique," New York *Dramatic Mirror*, Feb. 10, 1906, Vera Dreiser file (UP).

Chapter 4.

"Over the hill" Thomas E. Hill, *Hill's Manual*, 366.

"lightning rod agent" "Dreiser Notes," Markle file (THL).

"Where the Orange Blossoms Grow" Terre Haute *Mail*, Sept. 28, 1878, Markle file (THL). Clipping in Dresser Scrapbook (UP). The story of Paul's first song is confirmed in "Public Memorial Proposed to Memory of Paul Dresser," Terre Haute *Tribune*, March 5, 1911. The song is called "And I'm Going Back to Dixie Where the Orange Blossoms Grow" (VCHA).

"musician" Markle file (THL).

"she would look" *Dawn*, 67.

"Perhaps you will" Ibid., 75.

"Observation proves" *Hill's Manual*, 108.

"like the sun" *Dawn*, 113.

For a time, he travelled The account of Paul's early career is drawn from clippings in

Chapter 5.

"In 1889 Chicago" *Sister Carrie*, Pennsylvania Edition, 15.

"[Theodore] would do" Edward Dreiser, "My Brother Theodore," *Book Find News*, March 1946.

"guttural" "Dawn" (typescript), ch. VI, 39.

"I could not view" *Dawn*, 28.

"yellowish," "deep enough," "an intense sense" "Dawn" (typescript), ch. VI.

"Hear me, Lyman Treadwell" Quoted in Mark Sullivan, *Our Times: The Turn of the Century*, 210.

records show . . . rented to Paul "Proposed Memorial of Interest to Many Here," Evansville *Journal*, Oct. 15, 1922 (EvL).

In the two decades Statistics from James DeMuth, *Small Town Chicago*, 6.

"It is the only" Henry B. Fuller, *With the Procession*, 203.

"Tush! It's the" Quoted in Philip L. Gerber, "The Financier Himself: Dreiser and C. T. Yerkes," *PMLA,* Jan. 1973.

Male office workers Richard Sennett, *Families Against the City* (a sociological study of the Union Park section from 1872 to 1890), 38.

"But I must go back" Quoted in DeMuth, *Chicago,* 14.

The neighborhood where the Dreisers lived See Sennett, *Families,* 44–59.

"were selling themselves" "Dawn" (holograph), ch. XXI; *Dawn,* 173.

Chapter 6.

"I was raised" TD to Richard Duffy, Nov. 10, 1901 (IU).

"From contemplating" *A Hoosier Holiday,* 113.

The population was then Description: author's visit. Historical details: George A. Nye, *Warsaw in 1885 and 1886,* unpublished MS (WaL). *Biographical and Historical Record of Kosciusko County, Indiana.*

"simple, conservative" *Dawn,* 188.

Augusta Phillipson et al. "Dawn" (holograph), ch. XXXIII.

"some phase of" *Dawn,* 198.

"legs, breasts" "Dawn" (holograph), ch. XXXVIII.

"elite of the seventh" Ibid. ch. XXX.

"money, daring" *Dawn,* 250.

"I never had much" Edward Dreiser, "My Brother Theodore," *Book Find News,* March 1946.

"A kind of," "in a kind of" "Dawn" (typescript), ch. XLVIII.

"What are you" Ibid.

"the large expenditure" Quoted in Steven Marcus, *The Other Victorians,* 22.

"as soft and pleasing" *Dawn,* 271.

"Shameless creatures," "You are too rough" Ibid., 229, 231.

"A scandal hung" "Dawn" (holograph), ch. XXXVI.

"She watched" Chicago *Mail,* Feb. 17, 1886. Quoted in Donald Pizer, ed., *Sister Carrie,* Norton Critical Edition, 375, 376.

"A Woman in the Case" Ibid., 375 ff.

"I was more" "Dawn" (holograph), ch. XLI.

"a keen rivalry" Ibid., ch. LIII.

"I would not give" Edward Dreiser, "My

Brother Theodore," *Book Find News,* March 1946. Dating questionable; this poem appeared in *Broadway,* August 1906, when TD was editor, under the title "The Poet's Creed."

"In the old brick" Nye, *Warsaw,* Book 13 (WaL).

"We knew Dreiser" Quoted in Dorothy Dudley, *Dreiser and the Land of the Free,* 53. I have been unable to locate this quotation, described by Dudley as being from a review of *A Hoosier Holiday* in *Winder's Travel Magazine* (which existed).

"Ma, I'm going" *Dawn,* 194.

Chapter 7.

"Ah the horror" "Dawn" (holograph), ch. LIX.

a shadowy self-effacing Ibid., Ch. XXX.

"sissy sons" *Dawn,* 330.

"The shadows" Ibid., 332.

"inured to a lean," "morbidity that" "Dawn" (holograph), ch. IX.

"You need me!" *Dawn,* 339.

"a shambling man" Ibid., 342.

"My gott" Ibid., 343.

"Mind and mind" Ibid., 344.

"extensive knowledge," "Never resulted," "I had been," "the habit" Christian Aaberg to TD, Oct. 19, 1921.

"buzzing dreams" "Dawn" (holograph), ch. LXXXI.

"How beautiful" Ibid., ch. LIII.

"enormous red brick house," "dressed in" Dorothy Dudley, *Dreiser and the Land of the Free,* 61.

She would pay his In a letter to Richard Duffy, Nov. 18, 1901, Dreiser says that he paid half his tuition, but one wonders how he could have saved the money. His pride was speaking.

"I am glad" *Dawn,* 372.

Chapter 8.

"I attended the state" TD to Richard Duffy, Nov. 18, 1901.

"a charming place" Ibid.

He did not get off TD's grades at I.U. in Joseph Katz, "Theodore Dreiser at Indiana University," *Notes and Queries,* March 1966.

"I never learned" *A Hoosier Holiday,* 484.

He joined Philomathean Club Katz, "Theodore Dreiser."

"belligerent attitude" TD to Emma Rector, March 1, 1894 (IU). In Richard W. Dowell, "You Will Not Like Me, I'm Sure," *American Literary Realism*, Summer 1970.

"Never in my life" *Dawn*, 398, 399.

"several years" TD to RD, Nov. 18.

"Those dear old" TD to Rector, March 1.

"You know," "Oh, ma," "You think" *Dawn*, 509.

"Well, that's" Ibid., 513.

Chapter 9.

"It always seemed" *Dawn*, 91.

"I can't cry" Ibid., 516.

Dreiser's earlier versions "Dawn" (holograph), ch. LXXI.

"asking cool" Ibid.

"Theodore Dreiser, through" Quoted in Joseph Katz, "Theodore Dreiser at Indiana University," *Notes and Queries*, March 1966.

"The palls of heavy" *Newspaper Days*, 19.

" 'Theodore,' he said" *Dawn*, 583.

"I done the best" *Newspaper Days*, 31.

"Well might I" "Dawn" (holograph), ch. LIX.

Chapter 10.

"I seethed to express" *Newspaper Days*, 3.

"We are dealing" "Newspaper Days" (holograph), ch. III.

"Why did you pick" *Newspaper Days*, 39.

"Very good!" Ibid., 50.

"CLEVELAND AND GRAY THE TICKET" Chicago *Globe*, June 21, 1892.

"Cut the gentle con" *Newspaper Days*, 59.

Chicago journalists John Demuth, *Small Town Chicago*, which characterizes Field, Ade, and Dunne; John J. McPhaul, *Deadlines and Monkeyshines;* Emmett Dedmon, *Fabulous Chicago.*

Arthur Henry Maude Henry (Arthur's first wife) told Robert H. Elias that her husband and Dreiser first met in Chicago. MWH to Elias, April 2, 1945 (CorL).

"nosing and speculative tendency" *Newspaper Days*, 65.

"From surrounding basements" *Globe*, July 24, 1892.

"Maybe you're cut out" *Newspaper Days*, 67.

"A cheap coffin" *Globe*, Sept. 11, 1892.

"The daily newspaper" Quoted in Larzer Ziff, *The American 1890s*, 150.

"whose younger years," "glory and an," "In thine own," "Achieve thine own" *Globe*, Oct. 23, 1892. Donald Pizer, ed., *Theodore Dreiser: A Selection of Uncollected Prose*, 33.

"Dorse, I think" "Dawn" (holograph), ch. LXXI.

"though I ejaculated," "the religionist who" "Newspaper Days" (holograph), ch. IV.

"buzzing dreams" Ibid.

"You don't care" *Newspaper Days*, 86.

Chapter 11.

"I went into" TD to Mencken, May 13, 1916. In Robert H. Elias, *Letters of Theodore Dreiser*, I, 211.

"What reporters don't" Quoted in Larzer Ziff, *The American 1890s*, 153.

"Ambitious" TD to Emma Rector, March 1, 1894 (IU). Richard W. Dowell, "You Will Not Like Me, I'm Sure," *American Literary Realism*, Summer 1970.

"Um yuss!" *Newspaper Days*, 104.

"I despised St. Louis" TD to Rector, Dec. 13, 1893.

"intensely uxorious," "feminine ministrations" "A Book About Myself," Part II, holograph MS, ch. XXIV.

"flushed like a" "Newspaper Days" (holograph), ch. XII.

Reedy had been a See Max Putzel, *The Man in the Mirror: William Marion Reedy and His Magazine;* Clarence E. Miller, "William Marion Reedy: A Patchwork Portrait," *Bulletin of the Missouri Historical Society*, Oct. 1960.

Office rumor had it Miller, "William Marion Reedy."

"The enduring novel" Quoted in Yoshinobu Hakutani, *Young Dreiser*, 68, 69.

"a splendid writer," "Though you sent him" Quoted in Henry Burke, *From the Day's Journey*, 167.

"Men set up before themselves" "Theosophy and Spiritualism," St. Louis *Globe-Democrat*, Jan. 20, 1893.

"Olney Wade," "books and fine," "If you

want," "realistic and" "Dreiser Clipping File,"
microfilm, reel 1, folder 9 (UP).

"Worldly experience," "the gorgeous sun,"
"I never get up," "of a gloomy," "When you
look" TD to Rector, March 1, 1894.

"Many forms," "eyes that were,"
"Someone will," "To those inquiring," "I'm
blind," "a loving mother," "Burned to
Death," *Globe-Democrat*, Jan. 22, 1893.

"It's hell" *Newspaper Days*, 163.

"the skin of his hand" *Globe-Democrat*, Jan.
22, 1893.

"BURNED TO DEATH" Ibid. And see
also "SIXTEEN DEAD," January 23, 1893.

"You called for me" *Newspaper Days*, 167,
168.

Chapter 12.

"I went to" TD to Sara Osborne White,
June 30, 1898.

"a world of unreality" *Newspaper Days*, 179.

"Those who are" Quoted in Robert H.
Elias, *Theodore Dreiser: Apostle of Nature*, 54.

"brings back visions" "The Black Diva's
Concert," St. Louis *Globe-Democrat*, April 1,
1893.

"the colored lady," "fervid tribute," "A
Great Editor and 'Black Patti,' " St. Louis
Chronicle, April 1, 1893. This and subsequent
stories located by T. D. Nostwich.

"The African temperament," "Music and
Musicians," St. Louis *Republic*, April 2, 1893.

"he is even better" *Globe-Democrat*, "The
Theaters,"May 1, 1893.

"dallied with the 'black bottle,' " "so
carelessly" "John L. Out for a Lark," *Globe-
Democrat*, Feb. 28, 1893.

"[McCullagh] is becoming" *Chronicle*, May
1, 1893.

"Remember Zola and Balzac" *Newspaper
Days*, 211.

"brute," "demon," "THIS CALLS FOR
HEMP"*Republic*, January 17, 1894. Quoted in
T. D. Nostwich, "The Source of Dreiser's
'Nigger Jeff,' " *Resources for American Literary
Study*, Fall 1978.

"distorted," "wailing more like," "with a
swish," "Through the broken," "came to his
death," "TEN-FOOT DROP" *Republic*, Jan.
18, 1894. Quoted in Nostwich, "Nigger Jeff."

"Mr. Joy said" *Republic*, June 20, 1893.

"Mere humor, such as" *Newspaper Days*,
415.

"the hot river" Ibid., 283, 284.

"the best dressed" Quoted in Harry Burke,
From the Day's Journey, 168.

"a genius for overdressing" Quoted in
Burke, *Journey*.

"parvenu" "Dawn" (holograph), ch. XLVI.

"an intense something" *Newspaper Days*,
242.

Sara's hair color and other information on
Sallie White: Interview with Mrs. Louise Graham (niece), St. Charles, Missouri, Nov. 1985.

"work up a big" Quoted in Daniel Lowe,
Lost Chicago, 150. See also Alan Trachtenberg,
The Incorporation of America, 208, 234.

"It is too ideally" Florence Adele Sloane,
Maverick in Mauve, 72.

"to be swept" *Newspaper Days*, 249.

"One can understand" Quoted in Guy
Szuberla, "Dreiser at the World's Fair: The
City Without Limits," *Modern Fiction Studies*,
Autumn 1977.

"beautiful as a," "in the silence" Quoted
in Howard Mumford Jones, *The Age of Energy*,
250.

"a massive," "in droves," "They made
one" Quoted in Szuberla, "World's Fair."

"who sweat," "aggressive," "eat cold"
Quoted in Larzer Ziff, *The American 1890s*, 104.

"If you marry now" *Newspaper Days*, 343.

"Your habit of walking" H. B. Wandell to
TD, Oct. 2, [1893]. (Letter in possession of
Mr. and Mrs. Gupton Vogt.)

"New York's the place" TD to Rector,
Dec. 13, 1893. In Richard W. Dowell, "You
Will Not Like Me, I'm Sure," *American Lit-
erary Realism*, Summer 1970.

Chapter 13.

"I was of the wandering" TD to SOW,
Sept. 21, 1896.

"I was far more" "Newspaper Days" (holograph), ch. L.

"hollow as a dream" Ibid.

"brushed around" TD to Rector, April 4,
1894. In Richard W. Dowell, "You Will Not
Like Me, I'm Sure," *American Literary Realism*, Summer 1970.

"all the surging" *Newspaper Days*, 319.

He personally shepherded Arthur Henry

to Dorothy Dudley, quoted in *Dreiser and the Land of the Free*, 104.

sympathies were with the workers "The Strike To-Day," Toledo *Blade*, March 24, 1894. In Donald Pizer, ed., *Sister Carrie*, Norton Critical Edition, 416–423.

Ibid., 423.

Henry's wife, Maude MWH to RHE, April 12, 1945 (CorU), Donald T. Oakes, unpublished MS, Afterword, 11. See also Helen Dreiser to RHE, Feb. 19, 1945: "Mr. Dreiser . . . does not think he wrote most of the strike articles" (CorU).

"If he had been" *Newspaper Days*, 373.

"hurrys [sic] along" TD to Rector, April 4, 1894.

Chapter 14.

"Just about then" "Now Comes Author Theodore Dreiser Who Tells of 100,000 Jennie Gerhardts," Cleveland *Leader*, Nov. 12, 1911. In Donald Pizer, ed., *Theodore Dreiser: A Selection of Uncollected Prose*, 186.

"The City of Pittsburgh" "At the Sign of the Lead Pencil," *The Bohemian*, Dec. 1909. Pizer, *Uncollected Prose*, 171.

"They were talking" Quoted in Jeremy Brecher, *Strike!*, 73.

"Higher up the tenement" Quoted in Joseph Frazier Wall, *Andrew Carnegie*, 580, 581.

"was to think and" *Newspaper Days*, 395.

"I'd rather have" Ibid., 406.

"Peace on Earth" Quoted in Paul Boase, ed., *The Rhetoric of Protest and Reform, 1878–1898*, 18.

"the general unrest" "Reed Just as He Stands," Pittsburgh *Dispatch*, April 28, 1894.

"After working twelve hours" Quoted in Wall, *Carnegie*, 580.

"a suicide by" "The Last Fly of Fly Time," *Dispatch*, Oct. 3, 1894.

"Hospital Violet Day" *Dispatch*, May 12, 1894.

"stowed away with heartaches" "And It Was Mighty Blue," *Dispatch*, May 15, 1894.

Chapter 15.

"Your home which I" TD to SOW, Sept. 21, 1896.

"New York . . . had" *Newspaper Days*, 452.

"a man of some" *History of St. Charles, Montgomery and Warren Counties, Missouri*, 707.

"aristocrats" Interview with Billy Joe Auchly, Montgomery City, Missouri, Nov. 1985.

"What's that got to" "A True Patriarch: A Study from Life," *McClure's*, Dec. 1901.

"moderately successful," "not a man," "few men" *History of St. Charles*, 707.

"He believed that" *McClure's*, Dec. 1901.

"a very successful and good" "Life and Influence of Danville and Danville Township," undated clipping, Montgomery County Historical Society, Montgomery City, Missouri.

"never had two nickels" Interview with Mrs. Louise Graham (Jug's niece), Nov. 1985.

he carried her to her room "Newspaper Days" (holograph), ch. LXVIII.

"Don't you know" Ibid., ch. LXVII.

TD's walk up Broadway, Taken from *Newspaper Days*, 439, 447, and Stephen Jenkins, *The Greatest Street in the World*.

"I have never lived" "Newspaper Days" (holograph), ch. LXII.

"Sometime you ought to" *Newspaper Days*, 449.

Chapter 16.

"To understand," "For every religion" Herbert Spencer, *First Principles*, 19, 39, TD's Library (UP).

"in the furnace stage" *Newspaper Days*, 375.

"left the country" Ida Tarbell, *The Nationalizing of Business*, 2.

"There are really but" Quoted in Paul Boase, ed., *The Rhetoric of Protest and Reform, 1878–1898*, 8.

"an ambitious young man" TD to SOW, Aug. 14, 1896.

"quite blew me" *Newspaper Days*, 457.

"His conclusions never" Quoted in William Irvine, *Apes, Angels and Victorians*, 109.

"Spencer's idea of" Ibid., 30.

"I remember that" Quoted in Richard Hofstader, *Social Darwinism in American Thought*, 45.

" 'All is well' " Ibid.

"personal ends must be" Quoted in James G. Kennedy, *Herbert Spencer*, 69.

"At the Approach" "Reflections," *Ev'ry Month*, Feb. 1897. In Donald Pizer, ed., *Theodore Dreiser: A Selection of Uncollected Prose*, 107.

"the Alexander" "Literary Notes," *Ev'ry Month*, May 1896. Ibid., 59.

marginalia in *First Principles* Most of the marginalia in TD's copy are in pencil, though some are in pen and perhaps were added at a later date. I am only conjecturing that this is the copy that TD read in Pittsburgh, and that he added the marginalia at this time. One note reads sarcastically, "Only god can make a tree," a reference to Joyce Kilmer's poem, which was published in 1914. The comments are clustered in certain sections; the chapter on the "Unknowable" is relatively free of carping.

Chapter 17.

"Some transition is needed" Honoré de Balzac, *Lost Illusions*, 161.

"If you have it" "The Literary Shower," *Ev'ry Month*, June 1896. In Donald Pizer, ed., *Theodore Dreiser: A Selection of Uncollected Prose*, 72.

"This desire to attend" "Reflections," *Ev'ry Month*, Oct. 1896. Ibid., 96.

"the idea of Hurstwood was born" *Newspaper Days*, 464. In the MS, TD adds the qualifier "if ever."

"Paul says you can" Ibid.

"This young man" Ibid., 466.

"How to Improve" "Better Tenements Wanted," New York *World*, Dec. 13, 1894.

Dreiser seems not to See Allen Churchill, *Park Row*, and Isaac Marcosson, *David Graham Phillips and His Times*, 177.

"Terseness" Quoted in Churchill, *Park Row*, 39.

"a dropsical eagle" Ibid., 227.

"Mrs. Moriarity" New York *World*, Dec. 24, 1894.

"What was the trouble?" *Newspaper Days*, 488, 489.

"waiting for something" "Newspaper Days" (holograph), ch. LXXXI.

"He had turned fifty," "suffering from the same" Ibid., ch. LXV, 62. I used photocopies of this part of holograph MS in Moers Coll, "Two Dreisers," folder 10 (ColU).

By another account Vera Dreiser, *My Uncle Theodore*, 96.

Chapter 18.

". . . the Bowery" "Mark Twain: Three Contacts," MS (UP). Published in *Esquire*, Oct. 1935.

"Did He Blow Out" New York *World*, Feb. 16, 1895. There is no evidence that Dreiser wrote this story.

"Old stuff!" "Three Contacts."

"I'm not to be" Ibid.

"felt his liver" Stephen Crane, "An Experiment in Misery," New York *Press*, April 22, 1894. In R. W. Stallman and E. R. Hagemann, eds., *The New York City Sketches of Stephen Crane*, 37.

"the vilest part" Quoted in Ellen Moers, *Two Dreisers*, 24. Moers provides an illuminating discussion of "Bowery journalism."

"A room perhaps" Jacob Riis, *How the Other Half Lives*, 53.

"in the attic with" Ibid., 36.

"Our treasury is empty" *The 1895 Annual Statement of the Christian Aid to Employment Society* (NYPL).

"Many [of the 1,810]" Ibid.

"It was generally assumed" Nathalie Dana, *Young in New York: A Memoir of a Victorian Girlhood*.

"the sodden tramps" Quoted in Moers, *Two Dreisers*, 26.

"he had no permanent" William Dean Howells, *Impressions and Experiences*, 240.

"a horse's jawbone" Ibid., 265.

"each trying" Ibid., 270.

"the perpetual encounter" Ibid., 272.

"emblematic of a nation" Crane, in *New York City Sketches*, 43.

"In adversity his father" Dorothy Dudley, *Theodore Dreiser and the Land of the Free*, 135.

"Life was desolate" Ibid., 134, 135.

One bitter cold night Clara L. Jaeger, unpublished MS, 42–44; CLJ to author, Oct. 26, 1984. In the early 1930s, when Mrs. Jaeger worked for TD as a secretary, he told her of his life on the Bowery and thoughts of suicide. He also claimed that he seriously contemplated ending it all in the East River in 1903, while he was down and out in Brooklyn, only to be saved by a chance intervention. The latter story is suspect, since he gave at least two versions of it, yet did not mention it in his most complete account of that period, *An Amateur*

Laborer. The story TD told Mrs. Jaeger includes some plausible details, and I am inclined to believe there is some truth in it, that he was at least considering suicide at this time.

Chapter 19.

"It becomes not only" "Reflections," *Ev'ry Month,* Sept. 1896.
"A western and rather" "Reflections," *Ev'ry Month,* Jan. 1897. In Donald Pizer, ed., *Theodore Dreiser: A Selection of Uncollected prose,* 104.
"in front of a building grand" "Take a Seat, Old Lady," words and music by Paul Dresser. © 1894 by Howley, Haviland & Co. Reprinted in *The Paul Dresser Songbook,* 3.
"While the 'ginnie' " Quoted in Mark Sullivan, *Our Times: The Turn of the Century,* 254.
That D was aiming For the fullest account of TD's *Ev'ry Month* career see Joseph Katz, "Theodore Dreiser's *Ev'ry Month,*" *Library Chronicle,* Winter 1972; John F. Huth, Jr., Theodore Dreiser: Prophet," *American Literature,* May 1937; and Ellen Moers, *Two Dreisers,* 32–43. I have consulted the incomplete files of *Ev'ry Month* at the University of Pennsylvania and in the Ellen Moers Coll, Columbia University. A number of TD's "Reflections" notes and book reviews articles in the magazine are reprinted in Pizer, *Uncollected Prose.*
"EV'RY MONTH having" Quoted in Katz, "Dreiser's *Ev'ry Month.*"
"Thee I wish you" Emma Dreiser Hopkins to TD, ca. 1896.
He was also Pseudonyms listed in Katz, "Dreiser's *Ev'ry Month.*"
her name would be TD to SOW, Oct. 18, 1896. He addressed her in letters sometimes as "S. Jug White," and occasionally used "Sallie Joy White" as a pseudonym. In a letter to her dated Sept. 11, 1896, answering her complaint about the use of SOW, he explains, "I intend to use SOW to indicate less familiarity."
"I must not think" Quoted in TD to SOW, Oct. 18, 1896, in which he tells her he is choosing poems for her.
"All of the literary" TD to SOW, July 10, 1896.
"Like Dinah's meals" Ibid.

"forging to the front" TD to SOW, Nov. 4, 1896.
"but a new magazine" TD to SOW, Jan. 20, 1897.
The products represented *Ev'ry Month,* Dec. 1896.
dropped a total of $50,000 Fred Haviland told Edward Marks. Marks, with A. J. Liebling, *They All Sang,* 122.
"Cut them and they" "Reflections," *Ev'ry Month,* June 1896. In Pizer, *Uncollected Prose,* 62.
"firmly grounded in" TD to SOW, Nov. 4, 1896.
he embroidered a brief newspaper item The story appeared in "Reflections," *Ev'ry Month,* June 1896.
"Man is the sport" "Reflections," *Ev'ry Month,* Sept. 1896. In Pizer, *Uncollected Prose,* 89.
"We are born" "Reflections," Aug. 1896. Ibid., 85.
"This is the law" "Reflections," June 1896. Ibid., 62.
"place splendid powers," "onslaught," "and this" "Reflections," Sept. 1896. Ibid., 93, 94.
"Everyone is pushing," "Speed is well" Unsigned, *Ev'ry Month,* May 1897. Ibid., 115, 114.
"have been preserved" "Reflections," *Ev'ry Month,* Feb. 1897. Ibid., 111.
problem of the trusts "Reflections," March 1897. Ibid., 113.
"the man is wrong" "Reflections," *Ev'ry Month,* Feb. 1897, Moers Coll (ColU).
"They were never taught" Unsigned, *Ev'ry Month,* May 1897. 115.
"money changers" "Reflections," *Ev'ry Month,* Feb. 1897, Moers Coll (ColU).
"[Do] you think" Ibid.
"The only ones" Quoted in Moers, *Two Dreisers,* 35.
"There are grim forces," "simply obey" Ibid., 35, 36.
"watching . . . from a high" "Reflections," *Ev'ry Month,* Jan. 1896. In Pizer, *Uncollected Prose,* 16.
he sat in his tiny cell Arthur Henry, *Lodgings in Town,* 81.
"aloof" Max Dreyfus to Vera Dreiser, April 13, 1960, Box 384A (UP).

going off by himself Vera Dreiser, *My Uncle Theodore*, 79.

"I am practically alone" TD to SOW, Dec. 1, 1896.

"I know I am" TD to SOW, Oct. 18, 1896.

"It appeared in the" Richard W. Dowell, " 'On the Banks of the Wabash': A Musical Whodunit," *Indiana Magazine of History*, June 1970.

"Here is presented" Caption and picture in Vera Dreiser, *My Uncle*, 76.

"nothing but my ticket" Henry, *Lodgings*, 23.

"And you?" Ibid., 82, 83.

"a lover of impossible" "Rona Murtha." In *A Gallery of Women*, II, 567.

"but no one" Unsigned, *Ev'ry Month*, May 1897. In Pizer, *Uncollected Prose*, 115.

"got it through" Quoted in Dorothy Dudley, *Dreiser and the Land of the Free*, 142.

Chapter 20.

"While cynics might" PD to Mary South, Nov. 5, 1897 (IU).

"hereafter devote his time" Undated clipping, Dresser Manuscripts (IU).

"I'm tired of the theater" PD to MS, Aug. 2, 1897.

"You see, I am" Undated clipping, Paul Dresser Scrapbook (UP).

Each song sold The standard composer's royalty was 4 to 8 cents a copy. A clipping in the Paul Dresser Scrapbook, "Popular Songs and Their Writers," by Caroll Fleming, reports that "The Wabash" netted Paul $20,000 on 500,000, and "Just Tell Them That You Saw Me," $16,000 on 400,000. Paul told one writer that "The Wabash" sold 750,000, and another that he made $30,000 on the song. As a partner in the firm, he may have been credited with a higher royalty than the normal songwriter.

"umpty-steenth time," "large, fine eyes" TD to SOW, Oct. 16, 1896.

"showy, bombast," "truly delicate" TD to SOW, Sept. 12, 1896.

In a letter TD to SOW, May 18, 1896 (IU).

"The Old 10:30 Train," "with Mother" Dreiser Clipping File, microfilm, reel 1 (UP).

"Marion Drace" (pseudonym), *Tom Watson's Magazine*, March 1905.

As D recounts it "My Brother Paul." In *Twelve Men*, 76-101.

"Round my Indiana home" "On the Banks of the Wabash, Far Away," words and music by Paul Dresser. *The Songs of Paul Dresser*, 72.

Paul wrote both the melody and the words Charles K. Harris testifies in his autobiography, *After the Ball:* "[Paul] couldn't write a lyric to anybody else's music; neither could he set music to any other one's lyric, as he often told me. Because the combination would not fit, although he once said: 'I tried it several times, Charley.' " Quoted in Richard W. Dowell, " 'On the Banks of the Wabash': A Musical Whodunit," *Indiana Magazine of History*, June 1970.

"the words of" "The Birth and Growth of a Popular Song," *Metropolitan*, Nov. 1898.

"Yes, dearie" TD to SOW, May 15, 1898. To assuage Jug's apparent jealousy, TD adds that the second verse about Mary was not his idea, and that he knows no girls of that name.

Ed Dreiser told Vera Dreiser, *My Uncle Theodore*, 75, 78.

"thinking of his happy" Undated clipping, Paul Dresser Scrapbook (UP).

Hoffman remembered being summoned Isadore Witmark and Isaac Goldberg, *From Ragtime to Swingtime*, 170, 171.

"Oh, the moonlight's" *Songs of Paul Dresser*, 72.

once courted a girl Quoted in Dowell, "Banks of the Wabash."

received an ovation Ibid.

"The 'Wabash' is going" PD to MS, Sept. 6, 1897.

"The 'Wabash' is still" PD to MS, Aug. 11, 1898.

"There were no brownstone" "The Town Where I Was Born," in *The Songs of Paul Dresser*, 250; "The Path That Leads the Other Way," 86; "Every Night There's a Light," 108; "I Believe It for My Mother Told Me So"; and "Calling Her Boy Once Again," 176.

"the only composer" PD Scrapbook (UP).

"loves all women" TD to SOW, March 24, 1897.

This practice so disgusted Vera Dreiser, *My Uncle*, 74.

Chapter 21.

"I had made" Unpublished MS (UP). Quoted in Donald Pizer, *Theodore Dreiser: A Selection of Uncollected Prose*, 273, 274.

"Nothing is more" Quoted in John F. Huth, Jr., "Theodore Dreiser, Success Monger," *The Colophon*, Winter 1938.

"within half an hour," "Most of us" Theodore Dresser [sic], "New York's Art Colony: The Literary and Art Retreat at Bronxville," *Metropolitan*, Nov. 1897.

"It is quite possible" Quoted in Frank Luther Mott, *A History of American Magazines*, IV, 40.

For a time Theodore He mentions the *Cosmopolitan* connection in his entry in the 1900–1901 *Who's Who*. Richard Duffy to TD, Jan. 30, 1899. *Ainslee's* to TD, Sept. 22, 1899 (UP).

"Mr. Marden's labors" Quoted in Irvin G. Wyllie, *The Self-Made Man*, 128. Other information about Marden from this book and *Dictionary of American Biography*. See also Pizer, *Uncollected Prose*, and Huth, "Theodore Dreiser."

"By the way" Quoted in W. A. Swanberg, *Dreiser*, 91.

"It is the first dollar" "A Monarch of Metal Workers," *Success*, June 3, 1899. Reprinted, unsigned, in O. S. Marden, ed., *Little Visits With Great Workers*, 51. (Many issues of *Success* are not available at NYPL, so I have drawn from *Little Visits*.)

"No more significant" Quoted in Robert H. Elias, *Theodore Dreiser: Apostle of Nature*, 99.

"a snow storm" Ibid.

"I wish to discover" "A Talk with America's Leading Lawyer," *Success*, Jan. 1898. In Pizer, *Uncollected Prose*, 119.

"money," "I never met," "This remark," "If equally" Ibid., 120, 122.

might be taken as satire TD to Robert H. Elias, April 17, 1937 (CorU).

"nature had made me" TD to SOW, Aug. 14, 1896.

"I, myself, have" Quoted in Huth, "Theodore Dreiser."

"The modern young man," "the dice of life" Marden, *Little Visits*, 435.

"You gave me" TD to SOW, Feb. 7, 1898.

"all success is not" "Fame Found in Quiet Nooks," *Success*, Sept. 1898. In Yoshinobu Hakutani, ed., *Selected Magazine Articles of Theodore Dreiser*, 50.

"no time for balls" Marden, *Little Visits*, 557.

"The latter must languish" Quoted in Huth, "Theodore Dreiser."

"when all is said" "The Real Choate," *Ainslee's*, April 1899. In Hakutani, *Selected Magazine Articles*, 156.

"You should make your" Quoted in Myrta Lockett Avary, "Success—and Dreiser," *The Colophon*, Autumn 1938.

Chapter 22.

"Man's ingenuity finds" "Scenes in a Cartridge Factory," *Cosmopolitan*, July 1898.

"One lies down" *The Songs of Paul Dresser*, 176.

"standing and ability" TD to SOW, Feb. 23, 1898.

"long-since shattered" TD to SOW, May 15, 1898.

he had sent her a ring "I mailed you a memento of our promises—the ring." TD to SOW, June 12, 1896.

"The immediate creative impulse" Ray Stannard Baker, *American Chronicle*, 92.

"The Horseless Age" *Demorest's*, May 1899.

"it glows beneath the lamps" "The Smallest and Busiest River in the World, *Metropolitan*, Oct. 1898. Quoted in Yoshinobu Hakutani, ed., *Selected Magazine Articles of Theodore Dreiser*, 34.

"glared upon and outraged" "The Haunts of Nathaniel Hawthorne," *Truth*, Sept. 21, 1898.

"inspiring and instructive," "gives so much more latitude" "J. Q. A. Ward," MS (UVa). It is interesting to contrast this discussion with that of Hamlin Garland with the sculptor Laredo Taft, in which Garland calls for "original" sculpture, meaning of common people. Taft, however, complains that there are already too many "cast-iron soldiers in badly fitting belted jackets and baggy pantaloons. . . . Sculpture should not illustrate life, it should only symbolize it." (Garland, *Roadside Meetings*, 264.)

"Let those paint classics" "Reflections," *Ev'ry Month*, Jan. 1896. In Donald Pizer, *Theodore Dreiser: A Selection of Uncollected Prose*, 44.

"X-ray glance," "The lines of" "A Great

American Caricaturist," _Ainslee's_, May 1898. In Hakutani, _Selected Magazine Articles_, 223.

"by purely photographic," "the clear crowning" Quoted in Ellen Moers, _Two Dreisers_, 12, 13.

"had the tone" "The Camera Club of New York," _Ainslee's_, Oct. 1899.

"Girls in stained," "spattering about" "Herman D. White" (pseudonym formed from TD's middle name, initial for his last name, and Jug's maiden name), "From New York to Boston by Trolley," _Ainslee's_, Aug. 1899.

"The moon looks down" Miscellaneous Notes and MSS file (UVa).

Virginia D. Hyde Some Dreiser scholars suggest that this is a pseudonym, but there is a letter from Hyde to TD at UP.

"We would also like" J. C. Brill to TD, April 29, 1898.

"WARD DENYING SCULPTURE ARTICLE" RD to TD, Oct. 17, 1899.

Some mildly controversial Comparison of the MS version of the Ward article (UVa) with the published version.

"matter copied bodily" H. J. Miller to _Cosmopolitan_, Aug. 3, 1898. Quoted in W. A. Swanberg, _Dreiser_, 94.

"oppressed" TD to Clarence S. Howell, May 17, 1910. Copy of letter in Dreiser Manuscripts II (IU).

"Right with naked hands" In Sidney A. Witherbee, ed., _Spanish-American War Songs_, 276, 277. The poem was also syndicated and a copy is among the miscellaneous papers in the Dreiser Manuscripts II file (IU).

"We bring food" Words and music by Paul Dresser, "We Are Coming, Cuba, Coming," © 1898, PD Coll, Box 391 (UP).

"so swift and decisive" "The Making of Small Arms," _Ainslee's_, July 1898.

"I have a weeks" TD to SOW, April 4, 1898.

"With regard to the" "Life Stories of Successful Men—No. 11, Chauncey M. Depew," _Success_, Nov. 1898. See MS, "What the New Century Offers," 24, 25 (UVa).

"Think of all," "Oh, but," "This was" TD to SOW, Sept. 16, 1898.

"a great chase" TD to SOW, May 5, 1898.

"Lord! one whose" Clipping in Dreiser Manuscripts II (IU).

Chapter 23.

"I lived in my" TD to SOW, Sept. 21, 1896.

"Of all letters" Thomas E. Hill, _Hill's Manual_, 104.

"little quarter of our" TD to SOW, July 10, 1896.

"Your little shoes" Ibid.

"I hate to be" TD to SOW, Aug. 28, 1898.

"Nature . . . has given" TD to SOW, June 25, 1896.

"almost fainting," "might be torn," "the horror" TD to SOW, May 1896.

"is suffering . . ." TD to SOW, May 4, 1896.

"What a lover" TD to SOW, May 1, 1896.

"you abetted me" TD to SOW, Oct. 18, 1896.

"I want you" TD to SOW, June 30, 1898.

"do something desperate" TD to SOW, Aug. 20, 1896.

"Everything is such soft," "You have too" TD to SOW, Aug. 19, 1896.

"I love the still" TD to SOW, July 10, 1896.

"You think you can," "it seems as if" TD to SOW, Sept. 1, 1896.

"so many times" TD to SOW, Sept. 11, 1896.

"awful glad," "accept introductions" TD to SOW, Oct. 10, 1896.

"repentant Magdalen" TD to SOW, Oct. 4, 1896.

"elegant clothing," "gain access" Ibid.

"warm with light" TD to SOW, Oct. 31, 1896.

"voluptuous," "temperament" TD to SOW, Oct. 4, 1896.

"sacred modesty," "saintlike beauty" TD to SOW, June 25, 1896.

"divinely formed" TD to SOW, July 3, 1898.

"red-halo-ed Venus" TD to SOW, Jan. 24, 1898.

"to despoil your saintlike" TD to SOW, June 25, 1896.

"love madness," "When the summer" TD to SOW, March 24, 1897.

"the imagination becomes" TD to SOW, July 29, 1898.

"my own girl" Ibid.

"not in moonlight" TD to SOW, Sept. 15, 1896.

"I think on advancement" TD to SOW, Oct. 18, 1896.

"all on earth" TD to SOW, Dec. 26, 1896.

"miserable," "write me a love letter" TD to SOW, Feb. 23, 1898.

"seems like," "houses already furnished" TD to SOW, Feb. 1, 1898.

"as the hurrying engine" TD to SOW, June 20, 1898.

"the next forty days" TD to SOW, Aug. 15, 1898.

"and more I cannot" TD to SOW, March 24, 1897.

"when nothing shall be" TD to SOW, July 3, 1898.

"sighs and light laughter," "I'll have you" TD to SOW, Aug. 15, 1898.

"It seems as if" TD to SOW, Aug. 31, 1898.

"To say that I was" Ed Dreiser to Sylvia Dreiser, March 10, 1899.

"the languorous quality" TD to SOW, March 24, 1897.

"not a sentimental passage" Quoted in Dorothy Dudley, *Dreiser and the Land of the Free*, 143.

"It is true that" Quoted in Vera Dreiser, *My Uncle Theodore*, 192.

"the first flare" *Newspaper Days*, 502.

"The desire to write" *Sister Carrie*, Pennsylvania Edition, 610, 611.

Chapter 24.

"Married! Married!" "Rella." In *A Gallery of Women*, II, 103.

"If nothing interfereth" TD to Arthur Henry, May 20, 1897.

Six-room flats Description based on the flat Carrie lived in when she first moved to New York City. *Sister Carrie*, Pennsylvania Edition, 307.

A Christmas reunion Described in TD to SOW, Dec. 26, 1896.

Death was instantaneous Paul Dresser to Mary South, Nov. 1, 1897 (IU).

"Poor Theresa" Sylvia Dreiser to TD, Nov. 7, 1897.

"Mame talked about us" Emma Dreiser to TD, undated.

Carl's suicide Interview with Vera Dreiser, Dec. 15, 1982, tape (EUL).

"same tale of woe—wow—" Paul Dreiser to TD, undated.

"slow, miserable" Claire Dreiser to TD, Jan. 24, 1898. Dreiser manuscripts II (IU).

sculptor J. E. Kelly Kelly to Jug, Sept. 18, 1900[?].

"chewing slowly and meditatively" Quoted in W. A. Swanberg, *Dreiser*, 103.

"expressed a hearty," "had the book," "apt" The clipping is in Dreiser Manuscripts II (IU). TD also mentions the interview and his "forthcoming" book of poems in a letter to Jug, July 27, 1898. See also Ellen Moers, "New Light on Dreiser in the 1890s," *Columbia Literary Columns*, May 1966.

plagiarism See Edward Mercur Williams, "Edmund Clarence Stedman at Home," *The New England Quarterly*, June 1952.

"at this late date" "Edmund Clarence Stedman at Home," *Munsey's*, March 1899. In his otherwise definitive article, Williams does not mention this admittedly vague qualification—which did not excuse TD for the literary misdemeanor of using the precise wording of the Anna Bowman Dodd article.

"characteristic and best," "above the average," "it is impossible," "the present generation" Quoted in Moers, "Light on Dreiser."

"A critically admired," "Possibly Mr. Stedman" Ibid.

"ceaseless drag," "And this thing" *Ainslee's*, April 1899.

"Yes, through each" *Ainslee's*, Jan. 1898.

"cool, damp soil" "Resignation," clipping in Dreiser Manuscripts II (IU).

"Mr. Dreiser's poetical" Ibid.

"more accessible than" Arthur Henry, "The Doctrine of Happiness," *Ev'ry Month*, Oct. 1897.

"It was a hot day" "McEwen of the Shining Slave Makers." In *Free and Other Stories*, 54.

He thought it "asinine" TD to Mencken, May 13, 1916. In Robert H. Elias, *The Letters of Theodore Dreiser*, I, 212.

details of the story Moers, *Two Dreisers*, 144.

"strange passions" "McEwen." In *Free*, 75.

"with its stars" "Old Rogaum and His Theresa." Ibid., 207.

"a bar of cool moonlight" "Nigger Jeff." Ibid., 110.

"with the cruel," "it was not so much" Ibid., 111.

"I'll get it" Ibid.

"The planner of this" "Little Essays on Great Problems: The Bubble of Success," unpublished MS (UVa).

"your 1898 style" Richard Duffy to TD, Oct. 8, 1898.

a parody of the popular historical romances See Joseph P. Griffin, " 'When the Old Century Was New': An Early Dreiser Parody," *Studies in Short Fiction*, Summer 1980.

"the aristocracy, gentry" "When the Old Century Was New." In *Free*, 356.

"the crush and stress" Ibid., 369.

"something particularly" *Demorest's* to TD, Aug. 4, 1899.

Chapter 25.

"Genius struggles up" "Edward Al," *Ev'ry Month*, June 1896. In Donald Pizer, *Theodore Dreiser: A Selection of Uncollected Prose*, 73.

"an idea of Mr." TD to Richard Watson Gilder, Dec. 9, 1899, Century Coll (NYPL).

"that some time ago" Arthur Henry to TD, undated.

"he didn't think," "anxious to have" Ibid.

"bring out a different" Henry to TD, undated.

"You owe me $26.19" Henry to TD, June 19, 1900.

"up to a," "had share" Henry, *An Island Cabin*, 193.

"homesick for the flat" Henry to TD, 1899.

"Tell Jug I" Henry to TD, 1900.

"girlish figure," "a complex combination" Henry, *Cabin*, 193.

"I too wish" Henry to TD, July 9, 1900.

ceaselessly "ding-donging" TD to Mencken, May 13, 1916. In Robert H. Elias, *Letters of Theodore Dreiser*, I, 213.

Richard Duffy remembered Theodore planned a novel, "in whom success" Richard Duffy, "When They Were Twenty-One, Part II," *The Bookman*, Jan. 1914.

"the successful author," "ruddy boutonniere," "of a gorgeous," "might well" "Whence the Song." In *The Color of a Great City*, 242.

"a great man," "The lights" Ibid., 254.

"One day a black" Ibid., 258.

"a rouged and powdered" Ibid., 243.

"He is a very thrifty" New York *Sun*, undated clipping, Paul Dresser Scrapbook (UP). (This article also discusses Rosenfeld and Graham.)

"strong, incisive, bitter" "Edward Al" (pseud.), "Literary Notes," *Ev'ry Month*, May 1896. Pizer, *Uncollected Prose*, 57.

"a metropolitan success," "writing night and day," laudatory English reviews *Ev'ry Month*, Sept., Nov. 1896; Feb. 1897. See Ellen Moers, *Two Dreisers*, 36-38. Other scholars have also noted Crane's influence on Dreiser.

"Every page presented pictures" Hamlin Garland, *Roadside Meetings*, 196.

"began to swirl great" *The Arena*, Oct. 1894. In R. W. Stallman and E. R. Hagemann, eds., *The New York City Sketches of Stephen Crane*, 91.

"the old hats and peaked shoulders" "Curious Shifts of the Poor," *Demorest's*, Nov. 1899. In Pizer, *Uncollected Prose*, 138. See *Sister Carrie*, Pennsylvania Edition, chs. 45-47.

"Occasionally one could see" Stallman and Hagemann, *NYC Sketches*, 91.

"as dumb brutes," "In the great sea" Pizer, *Uncollected Prose*, 137, 139.

Chapter 26.

"Is it so hard" "The Real Howells," *Ainslee's*, March 1900. In Donald Pizer, *Theodore Dreiser, a Selection of Uncollected Prose*, 143.

"Don't forget the Howells" Duffy to TD, March 1899.

In November Theodore revived the idea of a Howells interview In a note to "The Real Howells," 142, Pizer points out that "newly re-issued" edition of Andrew Lang's *Homeric Odes*, which the two discussed, was published in Nov. 1899. Thus I conjecture the interview took place in that month, though it could have been later. The point is that Dreiser had *Sister Carrie* on his mind, and probably in the works, and may have asked Howells if he would read it when it was finished.

"After fifty years of" Quoted in Kenneth Lynn, *William Dean Howells*, 8.

"You mean that the story's" Quoted in Thomas Beer, *Stephen Crane*, 86.

"riots in odors," "McTeague: A Study"

Quoted in Franklin Walker, *Frank Norris*, 224. Walker provides the publishing history of *McTeague*.

"Whether we shall abandon" Quoted in Walker, *Norris*, 226.

graphic words like "rape" Thomas Beer, *The Mauve Decade*, 236.

mention of the word dynamite Lynn, *W. D. Howells*, 280.

"Why is it that the best" Quoted in Walker, *Norris*, 146.

"takes no account of moral conse-quences" Kate Chopin, *The Awakening*, 147.

"She was broken-hearted" Quoted in Larzer Ziff, *The American 1890s*, 305.

"the unplumbed depths" Quoted in Walker, *Norris*, 80.

perhaps 200 of them Walter F. Taylor, *The Economic Novel in America*.

"observed a change," "What you say" "Howells Fears Realists Must Wait," New York *Times*, Oct. 28, 1894. In R. W. Stallman and E. R. Hagemann, eds., *The New York City Sketches of Stephen Crane*, 90, 91.

"[They] boast of holding up," "Woman, you have taken Ibsen's" Quoted in Ziff, *American 1890s*, 88.

"literary Columbus," review of Yekl "Literary Notes," *Ev'ry Month*, Sept. 1896.

the Decadents, whom he disliked "Reflections," *Ev'ry Month*, June 1896. In Pizer, *Collected Prose*, 66, 67. TD dismisses Aubrey Beardsley, "the weird and obscure in litera-ture" and Oscar Wilde (called the "preacher of higher knowledge") as fads, and says that artists like George du Maurier and Charles Dana Gibson and writers like Kipling, Hall Caine, and Hamlin Garland will endure.

"romance and realism blend" "Reflec-tions," *Ev'ry Month*, May 1896. In Pizer, *Collected Prose*, 59.

"one night's round with the reporters" "How William Dean Howells Climbed Fame's Ladder," *Success*, April 1898. In *American Lit-erary Realism*, Fall 1973.

"Life seems at times," "deep reasoner," "the conclusion that," "scheming and plan-ning," "You have no," "observed it" "The Real Howells." In Pizer, *Collected Prose*, 143.

"literary philanthropist," "It does not matter," "young man in the West" Ibid., 146.

"a dim and solemn phalanx" Howells, *Literature and Life*, 156.

"young newspaper men trying" Ibid., 154.

Chapter 27.

"She went to the city" "She Went to the City," words and music by Paul Dresser, *The Paul Dresser Songbook*, 240. Ellen Moers notes the connection between this song and *Sister Carrie* in *Two Dreisers*, 99. Since the song was written in 1904, one wonders if Paul had his brother's novel in mind.

"was blank" Quoted in Dorothy Dudley, *Dreiser and the Land of the Free*, 160.

"You and I are mediums" *Carrie*, Penn-sylvania Edition, 405.

"I took a piece" TD to Mencken, May 13, 1916. In Robert H. Elias, *Letters of Theodore Dreiser*, I, 213.

"story backbone, showing his," "the master" Richard Duffy, "When They Were Twenty-One," *The Bookman*, Jan. 1914.

"venturing to reconnoitre the" *Carrie*, Pennsylvania Edition, 4.

popular genre of cautionary novels Cathy N. and Arnold E. Davidson, "Carrie's Sisters: The Popular Prototypes for Dreiser's Hero-ine," *Modern Fiction Studies*, Autumn 1977.

"The gleam of a thousand lights" *Carrie*, 4.

"the threads which bound" Ibid., 3.

"that pariah who . . . cuts" William Dean Howells, *A Modern Instance*, 64.

"the instincts of self-protection" *Carrie*, 5.

"On her feet were yellow" Ibid., 147.

"took advantage of her uncomfortable," "wholly untrained," "better parents" TD to SOW, Sept. 2, 1898.

Carrie Tuttle—"Cad" for short See Thomas P. Riggio, "Notes on the Origins of 'Sister Carrie,' " *The Library Chronicle*, Spring 1979.

"mouth had the expression" *Carrie*, 144.

Theodore's memories of his first arrival In the holograph MS of "Dawn" (ch. XXVIII), TD writes that ch. II of *Carrie* was drawn from his first impressions of the city and expressed "a faint inkling of what I thought."

changed the year to 1889 John C. Berkey

and Alice M. Winters, Historical Notes, *Carrie*, Pennsylvania Edition, 558.

"The entire metropolitan centre" *Carrie*, 17.

"a line of girls" Ibid., 36. Changed by Henry for published version to eliminate repetition. Dreiser's article on the sweatshops: "The Transmigration of the Sweat Shop," *Puritan*, July 1900.

"rows of blank-looking girls" Quoted in Adrienne Siegel, *The Image of the American City in Popular Literature*, 77, 94.

"Say, Maggie, if you'll" *Carrie*, 41. See Duane J. MacMillan, "*Sister Carrie*, 'Chapter IV': Theodore Dreiser's 'Tip-of-the-Hat' to Stephen Crane," *The Dreiser Newsletter*, Spring 1979.

"Those in their coarse" Jacob Riis, *How the Other Half Lives*, 123.

"As he cut the meat" *Carrie*, 59.

"Drouet would need to" Ibid., 75.

"not because he was" Ibid., 63.

"only an average little conscience" Ibid., 89.

"Our civilization is still" Ibid., 73.

"the voice of poetry" Quoted in Robert H. Elias, *Theodore Dreiser: Apostle of Nature*, 97.

"We have the consolation" Ibid.

"a tide rolled between them" Ibid., 79.

"She was alone" Ibid., 90.

Chapter 28.

"The forces which regulate" *Sister Carrie*, Pennsylvania Edition, 119.

"It seemed to me" Quoted in Dorothy Dudley, *Dreiser and the Land of the Free*, 162.

Henry apparently helped with the research Telegram, Henry to TD, Aug. 28, 1899. Henry tells TD when he will return from Fall River. The unpublished MS of "Fall River" is vividly and powerfully written, as though Dreiser had been there. TD used a few paragraphs from this article in an editorial for *1910* (no. 5) entitled "The Factory." In Donald Pizer, *Theodore Dreiser: A Selection of Uncollected Prose*, 175.

"a picturesque account of the lives" *Cosmopolitan* to TD, Nov. 2, 1901; H. M. Alden to TD, Oct. 24, 1899; *McClure's* to TD, Oct. 11, 1899.

"how wonderfully life prevails" TD, "The New Knowledge of Weeds: Uses of the So-Called Pests of the Soil," *Ainslee's*, Jan. 1902.

"friendly tip," "being up to his eyes" *Cosmopolitan* to TD, Oct. 10, 1899.

"being left to the mercy" TD to Robert Underwood Johnson, Jan. 9, 1900, Century Coll (NYPL).

"I could wish nothing better," "A soft answer," "Yes, and a gentle snub" TD to RUJ, Jan. 16, 1900, Century Coll.

"[Theodore] Roosevelt could handle" TD to RUJ, Dec. 12, 1899, Century Coll.

"has been the one thing," "the result of an enthusiasm" TD to RUJ, Feb. 8, 1900, Century Coll.

"robust," "that the 'average' reader" Ellery Sedgwick to TD, Oct. 19, 1900.

his age as only 30 James L. W. West, III, Textual Notes, *Carrie*, Pennsylvania Edition, 639.

"who had turned fifty" "Dawn" (holograph), ch. LXV.

"ran along by force of habit" *Carrie*, Pennsylvania Edition, 87.

"As for me, you know" Sara White Dreiser to TD, Jan. 19, 1926.

"success virus" Richard Duffy, "When They Were Twenty-One," *The Bookman*, Jan. 1914. "It was designed to show the career of a writer of popular songs, in whom success operated as a virus. As he mapped it out, it promised to have both the qualities of success and novelty."

"good stout constitution" *Carrie*, 43.

"rotund citizen whose avoirdupois" Ibid., 179. (And see photograph of Paul in photo section of this volume.)

"lacked financial functions" Ibid. 179.

"an intuitive tact" Ibid., 178.

"as someone whose reserve" Ibid., 178.

"he was evidently a light" Ibid., 180.

"altogether a very acceptable" Ibid., 44.

"struck by a few of the involved" Ibid., 63.

"black eyes," "a cold make believe" Ibid., 45.

"He lost sympathy for the man" Ibid., 85.

"those more unmentionable" Ibid., 44.

"Is she a blonde?" Ibid., 48.

"that mystic period between the glare" Ibid., 10.

"that shadow of manner" Ibid., 23.

"Her form had filled out" Ibid., 146.

"secret passage" Ibid., 177.

". . . there is something wolfish" Ibid., 184.

"Remember, love is all a woman" Ibid., 192.

"could hardly restrain," "He would marry her" Ibid., 193.

Chapter 29.

"Nature is so grim." TD [unsigned], "The Man on the Sidewalk." In "At the Sign of the Lead Pencil," *The Bohemian*, Oct. 1909. In Donald Pizer, *Theodore Dreiser: A Selection of Uncollected Prose*, 165, 166.

"You didn't do me right, Cad" *Sister Carrie*, Pennsylvania Edition, 26.

"she heard instead the voices" Ibid., 118.

"Most men love a dainty" TD [Edward Al], "The Literary Shower," *Ev'ry Month*, July 1896. In Pizer, *Uncollected Prose*, 79.

"liberal analysis of Spencer" *Carrie*, 87.

"a lilt in her voice," "plaything" Ibid., 198.

Carrie as old-fashioned heroine and modern woman See Sheldon Grebstein, "Dreiser's Victorian Vamp," *Midcontinent American Studies Journal*, Spring 1963. In Pizer, ed., *Sister Carrie*, Norton Critical Edition, 541, 551. See also Larzer Ziff, *The American 1890s*, 278, 341.

"Its population was not," "long, blinking lines" *Carrie*, Pennsylvania Edition, 16.

"should they ever permanently" Ibid., 22.

"a famous drug store" Ibid., 271.

"was not one to whom change" Ibid., 207.

"The feeling that they are of not special" William Dean Howells, *A Modern Instance*, 241.

"It's a big town," "It would be as good" *Carrie*, 149.

"a lone figure in a" Ibid., 12.

"The real trouble is that people" Quoted in Frederick Lewis Allen, *The Big Change*, 61.

"which has sucked its waxen" *Carrie*, 146.

"Words are but vague shadows" Ibid., 9.

"little human beings . . ." Interview with TD, "Author of *Sister Carrie*," St. Louis *Post-Dispatch*, Jan. 26, 1902. In Pizer, *Uncollected Prose*, 149.

"If it were not for the artificial" *Carrie*, 90, 91.

"drag of a gray day" Ibid., 91.

Chapter 30.

"At times, sitting at my little" TD, untitled MS, "Autobiographical Attack on Grant Richards," ca. 1911 (UVa).

"I couldn't think how" TD to Mencken, May 13, 1916. In Robert H. Elias, *Letters of Theodore Dreiser*, I, 211.

Hurstwood's guilt or innocence was ambiguous Elias, *Theodore Dreiser: Apostle of Nature*, 107, 108.

"the question of Hurstwood's decline" Quoted in Dorothy Dudley, *Dreiser and the Land of the Free*, 162.

"Negroes are worked in droves," "the whipping-post" TD to W. Arthur Woodward, Spring? 1900? Elias, *Letters*, I, 47, 48.

"our foremost American," "six striking specials" TD to Woodward, Elias, *Letters*, I, 48, 49.

"taking up experimental psychology" Elmer Gates to TD, March 3 and May 29, 1900.

"is not intellection" See Ellen Moers, *Two Dreisers*, 167, 168. Moers was the first to investigate Gates's influence on TD; however, I feel she overstates it a bit. Mainly, TD received encouragement, though he certainly borrowed superficially some phrases and was confirmed in his own thinking by Gates's ideas on free will. But he could have written the sections in which Gatesian concepts appear without having met the inventor.

"slowly destroy the structure," "prevents normal" Gates to TD, Nov. 11, 1901. Here Gates presumably repeats what he told Dreiser at their meeting more than a year previously.

"Sister Anna" attended convent See Donald Oakes, MS on Arthur Henry, Afterword, 43.

"the individual whose mind" *Carrie*, Pennsylvania Edition, 269.

"There was something fascinating" Ibid., 271.

"dark, friendless, exiled" Ibid., 287.

"but a single point" Ibid., 299.

"The sentinels of life" Ibid., 132.

"Hurstwood was nothing," "dreams unfilled" Ibid., 305.

"men may starve at the base" "Reflections," *Ev'ry Month*, Oct. 1896. In Donald Pizer, *Theodore Dreiser: A Selection of Uncollected Prose*, 96.

"certain poisons in the blood," "eventually produce" *Carrie*, Pennsylvania Edition, 339.

"He was given to thinking" Ibid.

"a deep and cancerous sense" TD to John Howard Lawson, Oct. 10, 1928. In Donald Pizer, ed., *Sister Carrie*, Norton Critical Edition, 476.

"Men were posted at the gates" *Carrie*, Pennsylvania Edition, 339.

"He began to look again" Ibid., 316.

"You can make a front" "What Right Has He on Broadway?" words by Harry Dillon and music by Nat Mann (1895). Ibid., 568.

". . . the vagaries of fortune" Ibid., 448.

"I love you and wish" Ibid., 455.

"It does not take money" Ibid., 457.

"Well, let her have it" Ibid., 449.

"Every few days" Richard Duffy, "When They Were Twenty-One," *The Bookman*, Jan. 1914.

"He always sat in a rocking" Ibid.

"Something prompted me while" "Attack on Grant Richards."

"Eat. Eat" *Carrie*, Pennsylvania Edition, 493.

"How sheepish men look" Ibid., 495.

"couple of girls over here" Ibid., 496.

"as white as drained," "and then it" Ibid., 499.

"hidden wholly in that kindness" Ibid.

"A man is still" "Reflections," *Ev'ry Month*, June 1896. In Pizer, *Uncollected Prose*, 65.

Chapter 31.

"After it was done" TD to Mencken, May 13, 1916. In Robert H. Elias, *Letters of Theodore Dreiser*, I, 214.

"Dear Mr. Author": James L. W. West, III, John C. Berkey, and Alice M. Winters, Historical Commentary, *Sister Carrie*, Pennsylvania Edition, n. 15, 537.

"Her brown shoes peeped" Ibid., 509. Most of my information on the editorial changes in the MSS comes from the above cited historical commentary to the Pennsylvania Edition of *Carrie*. Also helpful was James L. W. West, III, *A Sister Carrie Portfolio*.

"what she called the 'bad parts' " Quoted in Dorothy Dudley, *Dreiser and the Land of the Free*, 163.

Rather than write "bitch" West, *Carrie Portfolio*, Historical Commentary, 509.

Jug concentrated her efforts Stephen C. Brennan, "The Composition of *Sister Carrie:* A Reconsideration," *The Dreiser Newsletter*, Fall 1978. See also Jack Salzman, ed., *Sister Carrie*, Appendix B, by Neda M. Westlake.

"her feet, though small" *Carrie*, Pennsylvania Edition, 4.

"When I finished it," "Two hours passed" New York *Herald*, July 7, 1907. In *Sister Carrie*, Norton Critical Edition, 432.

"the mind that reasons," "You approach" Notes at the end of "Carrie," holographic MS (NYPL). For a transcript of these at times illegible notes, see West, *Carrie Portfolio*, 36, 39.

"spirit of beauty which ever dances" "The Camera Club of New York," *Ainslee's*, Oct. 18, 1899, Moers Coll (ColU).

"no longer walking the street," "Lillian Russell type," "the old mournful Carrie," "Dream boats and swan song," "Ames is not a matrimonial" "Carrie," holograph.

"If I were you" *Carrie*, Norton Critical Edition, 356.

"wide awake to her beauty," "the light is but now," "O blind strivings" *Carrie*, Pennsylvania Edition, 487.

"That halcyon day when" *Carrie*, Norton Critical Edition, 369.

she cut a description *Carrie*, Pennsylvania Edition, 654, 658.

she also changed the final apostrophe Ibid., 655, 659.

"poor unsophisticated," "drag to follow," "the admired way," "Not evil" *Carrie*, Norton Critical Edition, 367, 368.

substituted something slicker *Carrie*, Pennsylvania Edition, 513, 514.

Alden gave the manuscript a quick reading . . . he forwarded Vrest Orton, *Dreiserana: A Book About His Books*, 14.

"superior piece of reportorial realism," "below-the-surface life," "neither firm enough" Quoted in *Carrie*, Pennsylvania Edition, 519.

"His weakest and most irritating trait" "Rona Murtha." In *A Gallery of Women*, II, 567.

[Henry] went through the entire typescript . . . Dreiser followed West et al, Historical Commentary, *Carrie*, Pennsylvania Edition, 522.

the majority of the trims Ibid.

Chapter 32.

"I had the definite and yet" "Down Hill and Up" (unpublished MS), 4 (UP).

"Every great publishing house" Quoted in Charles A. Madison, *Book Publishing in America*, 161.

"He cant [sic] help forcing" Quoted in Peter Lyon, *S. S. McClure*, 169,171.

Doubleday, who paid half what it was worth Madison, *Publishing*, 276.

"When I make a deal" Quoted in Lyon, *S. S. McClure*, 322.

"Yes," he said, "there must be something" Quoted in Christopher Morley, "The Bowling Green," *Saturday Review of Literature*, Feb. 10, 1934. Morley, of course, intends the anecdote fondly, but it seemed double-edged to me.

"really the first of a new era" Ibid.

"In the Doubleday economics of publishing" George H. Doran, *Chronicles of Barabbas*, 46.

"Any subject is a good subject" Quoted in Burton J. Hendrick, ed., *The Training of an American: The Earlier Life and Letters of Walter H. Page 1855–1913*, 286, 187.

"the strongest material of modern life" Ibid., 293.

"larger conception of American life" Ibid., 316.

"To make money is not" Quoted in Franklin Walker, *Frank Norris*, 269.

"the first real American book" TD to Mencken, May 13, 1916. In Robert H. Elias, *Letters of Theodore Dreiser*, I, 211. For the record TD adds, "and I had read quite a number by W. D. Howells and others."

"I have found a masterpiece" Quoted in Dorothy Dudley, *Dreiser and the Land of the Free*, 168.

"My Dear Mr. Dreiser": Norris to TD, May 28, 1900. In Donald Pizer, ed., *Sister Carrie*, Norton Critical Edition, 434.

"The novel of California" Quoted in Isaac Marcosson, *Adventures in Interviewing*, 234.

"so good a piece of work" Page to TD,

June 9, 1900. In *Carrie*, Norton Critical Edition, 435.

"People are not of equal," "a natural" Quoted in Dudley, *Land of the Free*, 169.

"scaled the outerworks of the walls" Duffy to TD, July 3, [1900].

"to join the one a year group" TD to Fremont Older, Nov. 27, 1923. In Elias, *Letters*, II, 418.

set to work on . . . The Rake See Thomas P. Riggio, Introduction, *Theodore Dreiser: The American Diaries*, n. 5, 8.

"warm argument," "straining after," "pretentious" Henry to TD, July 14, 1900. In *Carrie*, Norton Critical Edition, 435, 436.

"that there was something," "deep gloom," "physical derangement," "There is a tenth sense" TD to Henry, July 23, 1900. In Elias, *Letters*, I, 53.

"Dear Teddie": Henry to TD, July 19, 1900. In *Carrie*, Norton Critical Edition, 437, 438.

" 'Doubleday,' he said, " 'thinks the story immoral' " Ibid.

"Page—and all of us—" Norris to Henry, July 18, [1900]. In *Carrie*, Norton Critical Edition, 437.

"he would make no effort to sell it" Henry to TD, July 19, 1900.

"to be released from my agreement" Page to TD, July 19, 1900. In Elias, *Letters*, I, 55.

"an unrelieved study of the most distressing," "after you have put forth" In Hendrick, *Training*, 294, 295.

He was loath to jeopardize his relationship with the firm See Jack Salzman, "The Publication of *Sister Carrie:* Fact and Fiction," *The Library Chronicle*, Spring 1967.

"he must have ample reasons" TD to Henry, July 23, 1900.

"sincere," "mistaken," "is more suave than honest" Henry to TD, July 19, 1900.

"is a good deal of a cad," "shallow," "conceited" Henry to TD, July 14, 1900.

"I like Doubleday. He is such a big husky incoherent clown." TD to Mencken, May 13, 1916. In Elias, *Letters*, I, 211.

"crude," "overdone," "if we worked alone" Henry to TD, July 31, 1900.

"It was Frank who made the trouble." Quoted in Dudley, *Land of the Free*, 180.

"she expressed no opinion about it" Frank

N. Doubleday to Franklin D. Walker, May 4, 1931. In Franklin Walker, ed., *The Letters of Frank Norris*, 60; Reprinted in *Carrie*, Norton Critical Edition, 463.

William Heinemann . . . told Dreiser . . . he had quarreled with Mrs. Doubleday Dudley, *Land of the Free*, 182. Dudley seems to believe that this quarrel took place in 1903, and mentions that "Page and Norris were present," which would be impossible since Norris died in 1902. But Dreiser mentions Heinemann telling him of the quarrel in a letter to Fremont Older, Nov. 27, 1923. (Elias, *Letters*, II, 421.)

"matter has been adjudicated," "Not that, after all," "are needed by society," "Surely there were no better" TD to Henry, July 23, 1900. In Elias, *Letters*, I, 52, 53, 54.

"material injury," "a keen and honorable," "The public feeds" TD to Page, July 23, 1900. Ibid., 57, 58.

"make known this correspondence" TD to Henry, [July 23], 1900. Ibid., 52, 53.

"Hold Doubleday and Page to their agreement," "Doubleday will soon get over" Henry to TD, July 26, 1900. In *Carrie*, Norton Critical Edition, 446.

"We arrived at exactly the same conclusion" Henry to TD, July 31, 1900. Ibid., 446, 447.

Henry's role . . . he had written a book called See James L. W. West, III, *"Nicholas Blood* and *Sister Carrie," The Library Chronicle*, Spring 1979.

"I do not have much faith in" TD to Page, Aug. 6, 1900. In Elias, *Letters*, I, 61.

"I feel and I know" Ibid., 61, 62.

"crushed and tragically pathetic" Quoted in Dudley, *Land of the Free*, 182.

The junior members met with Doubleday; McKee advised TD to Older. In Elias, *Letters*, II, n. 11, 420.

"To take the book under my arm" Ibid., 419.

Chapter 33.

"You would never dream" Seattle *Post Intelligencer*, Jan. 20, 1901. In Jack Salzman, ed., *Theodore Dreiser: The Critical Reception*, 11.

a book called The Flesh and the Spirit The contract is in Letters to TD file at UP.

spliced one of the scenes into the MS of Newspaper Days See Robert H. Elias, "Bibliography and the Biographer," *The Library Chronicle*, Spring 1971.

"That region seems to be your" Henry to TD, undated.

"Fortune need not forever feel" TD to Henry, July 23, 1900. In Elias, *Letters of Theodore Dreiser*, I, 54.

"Dear Sir," "profanity" Doubleday to TD, Sept. 4, 1900. Ibid., 63, 64.

"Since when has the expression 'Lord Lord' " TD to Doubleday, undated. Ibid., 64, 65.

appeared in the final book, while others were altered Donald Pizer, ed., *Sister Carrie*, Norton Critical Edition, n. 1, 453.

"those more unmentionable," "dingy lavoratory," "dingy hall," "naked cupid" *Carrie*, Pennsylvania Edition, 527, 528. See also James L. W. West, III, *A Sister Carrie Portfolio*, 62, 67.

"an evil which," "clear, sound," "charming idyll," "delicate romance," "striking contrast" *Catalogue of Books Published by Messrs. Doubleday Page and Company, 34 Union Square, New York, 1900–1901* (NYPL).

"Such girls, however, as imagine" Quoted in Salzman, *Critical Reception*, 2.

"after having yielded up that" Ibid., 17.

"a presentation," "Not once," "has been waited for," "self-discipline" Ibid., 15.

"the utter truth of portions" Ibid., 12.

"Out in the highways," "other side," "a plain woman," "which must be read" Ibid., 1.

"America needs enlightenment" Ibid., 15.

"Civilization is at bottom" Ibid., 4.

"I have just finished reading 'Sister Carrie' " Quoted in Neda M. Westlake, "The *Sister Carrie* Scrapbook," *The Library Chronicle*, Spring 1979.

"Its veritism out-Howells Mr. Howells," "an art about it," "there lurks behind," "seems to be" Salzman, *Critical Reception*, 7, 8.

he had discussed the book's morality Reedy to TD, Jan. 4, 1901. Quoted in Max Putzel, *The Man in the Mirror*, 125.

"in a kind of narcotic," "you have met often," "commonest kind of common people" Salzman, *Critical Receptions*, 8.

"has been neither extensively advertised" Ibid., 6.

"I am not at all surprised" Quoted in
Westlake, "*Carrie* Scrapbook."

"went to great trouble to 'give away,' "
" 'In this country,' " "It is a 'dead one' " John
H. Raftery, "By Bread Alone." *Reedy's Mirror*,
Dec. 5, 1901 (StLML).

"Relentless, plodding, powerful" Hamlin
Garland, *Companions of the Trail*, 210, 211.

[Fuller] congratulated Garland on signing up See Larzer Ziff, *The American 1890s*, 115,
116.

At Doubleday's request, Norris had . . .
interviewed C. P. Huntington See Oscar Car-
gill, Afterword to *The Octopus*, 464, 465.

"the mighty lift that thrills" Quoted in Ziff,
American 1890s, 220.

"You know, I didn't like Sister Carrie"
Quoted in Dorothy Dudley, *Dreiser and the Land
of the Free*, 197. This is Dreiser's account and
may be apocryphal. I have included it because
it expresses at least symbolic truth. If Howells
had not disliked *Carrie* he would have reviewed it—unless he feared for his position at
Harper's if he did so, which seems unlikely.

"I get a little tired of saying" Quoted in
R. W. Stallman, *Stephen Crane*, 499.

"Lord! one whose dreams were numerous" Clipping in Dreiser Manuscripts II (IU).

Chapter 34.

"Similarly, any form of social distress"
Dawn, 107.

"I'm quite sure I didn't" TD, unpublished MS, "Autobiographical Attack on Grant
Richards," ca. 1911, 17 (UVa).

"discussing with a clean purpose" "Au-
thor of *Sister Carrie*," St. Louis *Post-Dispatch*,
Jan. 26, 1902. In Donald Pizer, ed., *Sister Carrie*, Norton Critical Edition, 458.

John Paul Dreiser was living with Mame
Vera Dreiser, *My Uncle Theodore*, 120.

To my dear father This copy is in the
Dreiser Coll (UP).

he began making corrections in the book
See James L. W. West, III, "John Paul Dreiser's Copy of *Sister Carrie*," *The Library Chronicle*, Spring 1979.

"I am very sorry to hear" Duffy to TD,
Dec. 30, 1900.

He wrote with considerable speed TD
dated each chapter. See holograph MS of
"Jennie Gerhardt" (UP). See also Thomas P.
Riggio, Introduction to *Theodore Dreiser: The
American Diaries*, n. 5, 8, and Richard Lehan,
Theodore Dreiser: His World and His Novels, 83.

It is bleak "Reflections" *Ev'ry Month*, Dec.
1896 (UP).

"a black boat steaming northward"
"Whence the Song." In *The Color of a Great
City.*

"slow, black boat setting out" *Carrie*,
Norton Critical Edition, 369.

"had a most depressing effect on me"
"Down Hill and Up" (unpublished MS), Part
I, unpaged (UP).

"an error in character analysis" TD to
Brett, April 16, 1901, Macmillan Coll (NYPL).
Quoted in Preface, Richard W. Dowell, ed.,
An Amateur Laborer, xiii.

"social pariah" "Down Hill and Up" (unpublished MS), Part I, 8, 9 (UP). Quoted in
Dowell, *Laborer*, xii.

New royalty arrangement might be made
Doubleday, Page to TD, card written in pen,
Feb. 27, 1901.

Heinemann edition of Carrie See Historical Commentary, *Carrie*, Pennsylvania Edition, 529, 530. Also John C. Berkey and Alice
M. Winters, "The Heinemann Edition of
Sister Carrie," *The Library Chronicle*, Spring
1979.

The latter explained patiently Phillips to
TD, Nov. 3, 1901.

Chapter 35.

"In all the world, there" Arthur Henry,
An Island Cabin, 213.

"She makes me so comfortable" Ibid.,
181, 192.

"There is no one more" Ibid., 167.

"relieved of the responsibility" Ibid., 191.

"Come now, let's not" Ibid., 186.

"wise, generous and tender," "harmony,
beauty and order" Ibid., 172.

"Men rob and murder" Ibid., 171, 172.

"good-natured enough when sober," "just
an average" Ibid., 171, 173.

"Any conception of life" Ibid., 174.

multiplicity of novel doctrines See Jackson Lears, *No Place of Grace.*

"How the revelations of science" Quoted in Howard Mumford Jones, *The Age of Energy*, 313.

"pulled her from the trunk" Henry, *Cabin*, 193.

"I found a lot of your trash" Ibid., 206.

"Most men are so tangled up" *Twelve Men*, 73.

Chapter 36.

"It is quite true that to the victor" "Reflections," *Ev'ry Month*, June 1896. In Donald Pizer, *Theodore Dreiser: A Selection of Uncollected Prose*, 64.

"It may be necessary that some should drudge" TD (unsigned), *Ev'ry Month*, May 1897. In Pizer, *Uncollected Prose*, 115.

"distinct commentary on the social" Quoted in Robert H. Elias, *The Letters of Theodore Dreiser*, I, 122.

"Pure religion and undefiled" *Twelve Men*, 74, 190.

"All this misery," "Yes, I thought" Ibid., 74.

"A Heart Bowed Down" TD to John Phillips at *McClure's*, Aug. 22, 1901.

"We toil so much, we dream" *Twelve Men*, 360.

"A Doer of the Word," more "scriptural" Duffy to TD, Oct. 18, 1901.

"make it over into what we want" Steffens to TD, Oct. 23, 1901.

"either a definite account" Steffens to TD, Oct. 29, 1901.

"It is plain that" Steffens to TD, Nov. 13, 1901.

"People are not so much" *Twelve Men*, 341.

"The fates did not fight," "Yet are not all lives" Ibid., 343.

"I did not want to fritter life" Quoted in Dorothy Dudley, *Dreiser and the Land of the Free*, 147.

one that was "less drastic" "Down Hill and Up" (unpublished MS), Part I, unpaged (UP).

a loss ... of between $150 and $200 Thompson to TD, Sept. 23, 1901.

"I believe in you and in your work" Quoted in Richard W. Dowell, ed., *An Amateur Laborer*, xv.

"either for the coming winter" Enclosure, Jewett to TD, Sept. 20, 1901.

Doubleday Page had "sprinkled" Taylor to TD, Aug. 14, 1924. Taylor was, of course, recollecting his motives twenty-three years earlier.

"really powerful," "thoroughly good" Quoted in Jack Salzman, *Theodore Dreiser: The Critical Reception*, 20.

"At last a really strong novel" Ibid., 18.

"a broad vivid picture of men and manners" Ibid., 24, 25.

"have done me proud" TD to Ripley Hitchcock, Feb. 27, 1903.

ended up selling only 1,000 copies *Sister Carrie*, Historical Commentary, Pennsylvania Edition, 530.

His occupation was ... given ... as "clerk" Dowell, *Laborer*, xiv.

Chapter 37.

"Here I be, full of glee" TD to Mary Annabel Fanton Roberts, Nov. 14, 1901. In Robert H. Elias, *The Letters of Theodore Dreiser*, I, 66.

"home like, southern and high and dry" TD to Taylor, Nov. 25, 1901. Ibid., 68.

"great towering lonely figures," "desire to work" TD to Roberts. Ibid., 66, 67.

"the deep blue blacks of the dome" Ibid.

"full interest," "to live up not only" TD to Taylor, Ibid., 69.

"To the majority of readers," "... the man's family treated" Jewett to TD, Nov. 13, 1901.

"accords with my own exactly" TD to Taylor. In Elias, *Letters*, I, 68.

"in every case [we] would leave," "It seems to me that" Taylor to TD, Dec. 4, 1901.

"win a much warmer," "thoroughly womanly way," "it is exactly," "simply the damnable," "Carrie would not marry" Jewett to TD, Nov. 22, 1901.

"equally potential," "straining every nerve," "I try to steer" TD to Taylor. In Elias, *Letters*, I, 68.

"because of the mistakes of her past" Jewett to TD, Dec. 30, 1901.

"our experience has taught us," "bad business," "made a success" Taylor to TD, Dec. 4, 1901.

"I do not wonder after your," "to issue the book" Jewett to TD, Dec. 30, 1901.

"large sympathy," "you would be disappointed" Bowler to TD, Oct. 26, 1902.

"a violent dislike to it" "Author of *Sister Carrie*," St. Louis *Post-Dispatch*, Jan. 26, 1902. In *Carrie*, Norton Critical Edition, 456.

"The newspapers," "At this point," "in America" Ibid., 456, 457.

sent Duffy a description Duffy to TD, Jan. 9, 1902.

"Butcher Rogaum's Door" *Reedy's Mirror*, Dec. 12, 1901. The title was changed to "Old Rogaum and His Theresa" in *Free and Other Stories*.

"tip-top novel," "just such drummers" Reedy to TD, Jan. 4, 1901. Quoted in Max Putzel, *The Man in the Mirror*, 126.

"If life wears the aspect you endeavor" Reedy to TD, Oct. 24, 1901. Ibid., 127.

"One does not often get" Duffy to TD, Jan. 16, 1902.

"boon to the weary and distressed" *Carrie*, Pennsylvania Edition, 290.

"is supposed to be," "Hen has," "proceeding slowly," "rousingly beautiful," "Time will" TD to Duffy, Feb. 2, 1902. In William White, "Dreiser on Hardy, Henley, and Whitman: An Unpublished Letter," *English Language Notes*, Dec. 1968.

"one night stand regime," "bully kind of life," "pretty near" Duffy to TD, Feb. 10, 1902.

Chapter 38.

"I wandered here & there" "Down Hill and Up" (unpublished MS), Part I, unpaged (UP).

"The last time I saw you" Jewett to TD, March 17, 1902.

"a very sad period of entanglement," "beginning to" Quoted in Jewett to TD, March 17, 1902.

"What is the trouble?" Jewett to TD, March 12, 1902.

"like the French judge" Jewett to TD, March 17, 1902.

Jug sent him a postcard Sara Dreiser to TD, March 26, 1902. "Forwarded to Charlottesville, Va. (Lynchburg) General Delivery, March 28, 1902."

At any rate See M. E. Gordinnier to TD, May 23, 1902; W. A. Swanberg, *Dreiser*, 119; Richard W. Dowell, ed., *An Amateur Laborer*, xv.

"was heard to say," "preferred that the stigma," "in more attractive form," "whose path crosses" Quoted in James L. W. West, III, "*Nicholas Blood* and *Sister Carrie*," *The Library Chronicle*, Spring 1979.

"Cooper of the," "very keen to strike" Jewett to TD, March 21, 1902.

he might call the book "Jane Gebhardt" Jewett to TD, April 9, 1902.

"You have a mind" Jewett to TD, April 16, 1902.

ten chapters he forwarded . . . were those The typescript of "Jennie Gerhardt" is stamped "Anna C. Mallon & Co." It bears penciled editing and comment by Jewett, mentioned in his letter to TD of May 27, 1902.

M. E. Gordinnier . . . had not sent her anything Gordinnier to TD, June 17, 1902; postcard, Arthur Henry to TD, Aug. 17, 1901, re Mallon's typing.

"Edit your chapters before" Jewett to TD, May 20, 1902.

"a strong sense of eagerness" Jewett to TD, May 2, 1902.

"Every word . . . was so precious" Sara Dreiser to TD, April 9, 1926.

"saw only a family, in the Gerhardts" "Jennie Gerhardt" (holograph), ch. IX.

"Such a wife! Such a home!" Ibid., ch. XII.

"The lesson Brander's action had taught her" "Jennie Gerhardt" (typescript), ch. XX, 10.

"Will he marry you?" "the lie falling" "Jennie Gerhardt" (holograph), ch. XXVIII.

"The Macheavellean [sic] manner in which Lester" Ibid.

"a sort of voiceless non-understanding," "Well . . . I hope for the good" Ibid., ch. XXX, XXXIII.

"Man's tendency appears to be away" Ibid., ch. XXIX.

"Perhaps this is why the lone herder" Ibid.

"an aching desire to be forever on the move" Isaac Goldberg, "A Visit With Theodore Dreiser," *Haldemann Julius Monthly*.

"when impartial chance decimates the rank" TD to William Dean Howells, May 14,

1902. In Ellen Moers, *Two Dreisers*, 175. (Original letter is at Houghton Library, Harvard University.)

"There is something so mellow, kindly," "If the common ground" Ibid., 176.

"hesitated to inquire from those who might know," "with interest," "Affectionately" Henry to TD, May 8, 1902.

he can't keep up the payments Henry to TD, May 16, 1902. Unpublished MS by Donald Oakes provides further information on TD's and Henry's obligations on the Maumee house, and identifies Hiett as the second mortgagor.

"I have written to Hiett" Postcard, Henry to TD, June 1902.

"If the book cannot mature" Jewett to TD, June 10, 1902.

"Am sorry I did not have the first chapters" Gordinnier to TD, June 12, 1902.

"the brain dances polkas" Ibid.

"Unless Jennie reaps the proverbial" Gordinnier to TD, July 5, 1902.

Chapter 39.

"I was hard up" Quoted in Dorothy Dudley, *Dreiser and the Land of the Free*, 201.

"[My] thoughts seem to flow" Thomas P. Riggio, ed., *Theodore Dreiser: The American Diaries*, 72. All entries from the section called Philadelphia 1902–1903, generally known as the Medical Diary.

"One day ... he was" *The "Genius,"* 257.

the town's "yellow sheet" McCord to TD, July 7, 1900; Aug. 9, 1901.

He now owed the publisher ... $700 Richard W. Dowell, ed., *An Amateur Laborer*, xv.

"It is not the kind of material" Alden to TD, Aug. 1, 1902.

"We do not want too much 'misery' " Penfield to TD, June 24, 1902.

mainly in the market for light amusing material Duffy to TD, July 31 and Aug. 12, 1902.

"morally bankrupt" Quoted in Dudley, *Land of the Free*, 201.

"you elaborate certain parts," "the reader becomes confused" Jewett to TD, Aug. 20, 1902.

"an earnest, child-heart longing" *The Color of a Great City*, 282.

"indissoluble link which binds" Ibid., 282, 283.

"or we will" Penfield to TD, Oct. 8, 1902.

"I found that consecutive thought" Riggio, *American Diaries*, 64.

"I do not get very far before" Ibid., 67.

he complained of chest pains Dowell, *Laborer*, 6.

"nervous exhaustion," "amusing and companionable" Ibid.

nearly all the textbook symptoms See, for example, Nathan S. Kline, MD, *From Sad to Glad*, from which the list was compiled.

"There is an access of gloom" Quoted in Dudley, *Land of the Free*, 25.

"My chief complaint at this time" Riggio, *American Diaries*, 62.

"I have an unaccountable drowsiness" Ibid., 67.

"confusing physical opposition," "I am in a much" Ibid., 66, 67.

"purely mental exhaustion" Ibid., 67.

"my tendency to overindulge" Ibid., 62.

"Wednesday Nov. 19th" Ibid., 65.

were written in Jug's hand Ibid., n. 14, 65.

"the undue suppression of the sexual life" Sigmund Freud, "Sexual Morality and Modern Nervousness." In *Sexuality and the Psychology of Love*, 24.

"whoever is to be really free" "Contributions to the Psychology of Love." Ibid., 65.

most experts on neurasthenia advised against using drugs See "The American Disease," *The American Monthly Review of Reviews*, Oct. 1905.

"chronic toxemia" due to an accumulation See J. H. Kellogg, *Neurasthenia*.

"the ache of modernism" Thomas Hardy, *Tess of the D'Urbervilles*, Bantam Edition, 123.

"The tremendous and complicated" "Jennie Gerhardt" (holograph), ch. XXVI, 3.

"mental wildness," "brain ache," "disturbing sense of error" Riggio, *American Diaries*, 62.

"Open the door and sweep" Jewett to TD, Nov. 5, 1902.

he had burned the manuscript J. W. Taylor to TD, Aug. 14, 1924. Taylor recalls TD's saying he destroyed the MS back in 1902, though there is no mention of this in the Medical Diary.

"**Brace up, stop worrying**" Jewett to TD, Dec. 19, 1902.

he explained that he had lost interest Quoted in Montrose J. Moses, "Theodore Dreiser," *The New York Times Review of Books*, June 23, 1912. In Donald Pizer, ed., *Theodore Dreiser: A Selection of Uncollected Prose*, 194.

"**short, pungent, vigorous,**" "**anything which,**" "**pay cash**" Riggio, *American Diaries*, 63, 83, n. 29.

"**Tell the truth,**" "**honestly and without,**" "**the discussion of,**" "**quiet acceptance**" "True Art Speaks Plainly," *Booklovers Magazine*, Feb. 1903.

"**Immoral! Immoral!**" Ibid.

"**Ah me—Ah me**" Riggio, *American Diaries*, 104.

"**irritated some by a thread,**" "**couldn't stop thinking**" Ibid., 82.

"**I do not believe I have had**" Ibid., 83.

scopolamine, chloral hydrate, antipyrine and phenacetin, small amounts of arsenic, strychnine and quinine Prescriptions are shown in the Medical Diary. Substances prescribed were verified by Donald B. Hayes, registered pharmacist, Crawfordsville, Indiana. All dosages were in "the normal parameters."

"**Bromide has no rational place**" Louis S. Goodman and Alfred Gilman, *The Pharmacological Basis of Therapeutics*, 163. Information on the actions of these drugs from this book and also from Donald B. Hayes, letter to author.

Chapter 40.

"**[Hurstwood] buried himself in his papers**" *Sister Carrie*, Pennsylvania Edition, 354.

"**This morning after breakfast**" Thomas P. Riggio, ed., *Theodore Dreiser: The American Diaries*, 92.

he should write the final volume Ibid., n. 9, 63.

"**I understand now better than ever**" Duffy to TD, Nov. 16, 1902.

"**Find that I suffer from a peculiar illusion**" Riggio, *American Diaries*, 61.

"**I should have been vexed,**" "**our aim now**" Duffy to TD, Dec. 5, 1902.

he paid back part Riggio, *American Diaries*, 76.

requesting an interview Robert Hamilton to TD, Dec. 28, 1902.

"**so squalid, so poor**" Riggio, *American Diaries*, 102.

"**grimy, narrow lives**" Ibid., 108.

"**of the lot of the poor**" Ibid., 101.

"**Why not always, as Christ said**" Ibid., 104.

"**under the name R. D. White**" W. S. McSean to "R. D. White," Dec. 9, 1902.

"**The whole question of recovery**" Riggio, *American Diaries*, 89.

"**still subject to the most halcyon**" Ibid., 92.

"**doomed to rot,**" "**I might as well use**" Ibid., 92, 93.

"**All the horror of being alone,**" "**I must get something**" Ibid., 94.

"**the man of sorrows,**" "**Lincoln and Christ**" Ibid., 110.

"**literary and socialistic work**" Ibid., 96.

"**very poverty-stricken neighborhood**" Ibid., 99.

"**writing articles and finishing my story**" Ibid., 99.

"**Love was to come back**" Ibid., 106.

"**I am homely and backward**" Ibid., 109.

"**Not now. Not now.**" Ibid.

"**You know how it is when you are going**" Ibid., 105.

"**thinking how I would write**" Ibid., 108.

"**tottering in ugliness,**" "**Life of the world**" Envelope in Dreiser Manuscripts II (IU).

"**Here was this immense system**" Quoted in Dorothy Dudley, *Dreiser and the Land of the Free*, 201.

"**To thrill with the touch of cool water**" Dreiser Manuscripts II (IU).

"**We will hear more of you yet**" Riggio, *American Diaries*, 102.

"**The beauty, the comfort**" Ibid., 107.

"**Me. Theodore Dreiser.**" Ibid.

an omen of death, he remembered Ibid., 110.

"**I said very well and came away**" Ibid., 112.

"**Though one has neither,**" "**I wish those who**" Ibid.

Chapter 41.

"**There was no light**" The *"Genius,"* 269.

"**A world or given order**" Richard W. Dowell, ed., *An Amateur Laborer*, 3.

"Men and women get to living" Quoted in Dorothy Dudley, *Dreiser and the Land of the Free*, 482.

"In the chill glow of a dying February" Dowell, *Laborer*, 7.

He found a small four-story Ibid., 7–9.

"bespeak an opportunity of seeing" Hitchcock to TD, Feb. 14, 1902.

"a long illness," "no immediate," "down in the dumps," "I seem to be" TD to Hitchcock, Feb. 27, 1903.

"radical changes," "certain things relating" TD to Hitchcock, March 2, 1903.

brought along Peter McCord to discuss Hitchcock to TD, April 11, 1903.

Barnes . . . came up . . . Dreiser later asked Jewett Jewett to TD, May 1 and May 8, 1903.

another publisher, Rand, McNally Jewett to TD, Dec. 19, 1903.

he walked all the way back to Ross Street Dowell, *Laborer*, 17.

"I rose to a futile effort" Ibid., 11.

"tortuous, tideful rivers," "they are substances" *The Color of a Great City*, 80. See also Dowell, *Laborer*, xvii.

"all life—animal and vegetable" Dowell, *Laborer*, 12.

"with you to love," "to do business," "the too strong," "a strong will" Jeremiah MacDonald to TD, Dec. 14, 1901.

"It seemed as if my mind" Dowell, *Laborer*, 122.

"Should the wide world" Quoted in Maxwell Geismar, *Rebels and Ancestors*, 80.

"I have done my share towards" Ibid., 30.

because of the mental stress he was undergoing this equilibrium had been upset A theory of the reason for TD's perceptual distortions provided by Dr. Byron S. Lingeman, Massachusetts Eye and Ear Infirmary, Boston. See J. Pearlman, *Psychiatric Problems in Ophthalmology*.

"a tall, thin, greedy individual," "taking an indifferent" Dowell, *Laborer*, 25.

"now in a corner and could not" Ibid.

"He was very wise and sane" Ibid., 27.

"They are too shy to complain" "Reflections," *Ev'ry Month*, Feb. 1897. In Donald Pizer, *Theodore Dreiser: A Selection of Uncollected Prose*, 110.

"You cannot move in the crowd" "The City of Crowds," *Smith's*, Oct. 1905.

Chapter 42.

"I long to see them" *The Songs of Paul Dresser*, 12.

"A great provision against would be" Ibid., 136.

When Mame opened the door she was shocked Ibid., 31-34.

"the vastness, the indifference" Ibid., 36.

a New York architect named Wilson Potter Ibid., xix.

He stood at the rail . . . He had been born with Ibid., 44.

"Hello, Paul," "Look old man," "I know you're" Ibid., 53, 54.

"Enough to be clean and decent" Ibid., 59.

Chapter 43.

"After a long battle" Quoted in Richard W. Dowell, ed., *An Amateur Laborer*, 3.

Dreiser wrote those words a year after James L. W. West, III, has demonstrated that TD started writing *An Amateur Laborer* while he was at the New York *Daily News*. See West, "Mirrors and Microfilm: The Dating of Dreiser's *An Amateur Laborer*," *Manuscripts*, Winter 1983.

"I endured more pain during the three weeks" Austin Brennan to Paul Dresser, April 25, 1903.

"a man's mental control from him" "Scared Back to Nature," *Harper's Weekly*, May 16, 1903.

"I was given to understand by Mr. Hardin" TD to R. P. Mills, July 31, 1903.

the Hardenbrooks' daughter Ibid., 107, 108, 138–141.

"I saw that I was as unfitted to be" Dowell, *Laborer*, 160.

"Suppose you have those spikes" Paul to TD, June 16, 1903.

"Now that depressed" Paul to TD, June 22, 1903.

"The wicked flee," "Woman" Paul to TD, July 26, 1903.

"WHAT IS THE MATTER THEODORE" Telegram, Aug. 23, 1903.

"Now you cut out giving" Paul to TD, Oct. 1903.

"sincere sympathy," "glad to see" Bowler to TD, Oct. 25, 1903.

"Good for you." Jewett to TD, June 19, 1903.

"That none should suffer" Quoted in Dowell, *Laborer*, xxx.

"he will do something for you" Paul Dresser to TD, Oct. 18, 1903.

a fifty-dollar check from Paul Dowell, *Laborer*, xvii.

secured an editorial post . . . through Duffy Duffy to TD, Nov. 11, 1904. Duffy writes, "if you will come in at your earliest convenience we will talk turkey," which, I conjecture, refers to a job, not Thanksgiving. Also, Elias says Duffy got him the job. See *Theodore Dreiser: Apostle of Nature*, 133.

Pete White F.V. White to Sara Dreiser, Jan. 5 1903.

"People like true things" Coates to TD, Sept. 28, 1904.

he told of seriously contemplating ending it all "Down Hill and Up," Part I, 14, 15. TD to Mencken, March 27, 1943. In Robert H. Elias, *Letters of Theodore Dreiser*, III, 980, 981.

he carved out characters Dowell details the times of composition, sequence, and fate of these various stories, and shows how TD carved them out of the "Laborer" manuscript and changed the focus over the years. See Introduction to *An Amateur Laborer*, xxix ff.

The real Burke . . . refused to let Ibid., xxxiii.

his bill for an eight-week stay Ibid., 196.

"To be maimed as an insect" Ibid., 124.

"debarred from broad and pleasant" Ibid.

"Fortune need not forever feel" TD to Arthur Henry, July 23, 1900.

Chapter 44.

"But still I think of him" *Twelve Men*, 108.

"But remember that fame" Paul to TD, May 12, 1905.

"where are the friends" Words and Music by Paul Dresser, (1903). In *The Paul Dresser Songbook*, 222.

"He was bitter over" Donald Pizer, ed., *Hamlin Garland's Diaries*, 123.

"power and verity," "Your kind wish" Quoted in Lars Ahnebrink, "Garland and Dreiser: An Abortive Friendship," *The Midwest Journal*, Winter 1955–1956.

"He became a bit tiresome" Pizer, *Garland's Diaries*, 123.

"brought about very ponderous" TD to Fremont Older, Nov. 27, 1923.

"the strongest, best biggest novel" Kenton to TD, May [?] 1905. In Robert H. Elias, *Letters of Theodore Dreiser*, I, 72.

Dreiser told her, "Sister Carrie is still," "Maybe—the gods providing" TD to Kenton, May 6, 1905. Elias, *Letters*, I, 73.

"Surely a courageous publisher" Kenton to TD, June 30, 1905.

"Dishonest, sapless twaddle" Ludwig Lewisohn, *Up Stream*, 158.

"Young people were tired of" Dorothy Dudley, *Dreiser and the Land of the Free*, 215.

"had no sense for reality" Lewisohn, *Up Stream*, 130.

"His orthodoxies crumbled" Randolph Bourne, *The History of a Literary Radical & Other Papers*, 29.

"needlessly offensive custom" Quoted in Van Wyck Brooks, *The Confident Years*, n. 2, 296.

"cutting them in two" Dudley, *Land of the Free*, 206.

"has its drawbacks," " 'Monday,' said Mr. Mole" Quoted in Kenneth W. Scott, "Did Dreiser Cut Up Jack Harkaway?" *The Markham Review*, May 1968. Although no direct evidence exists that TD worked on the Harkaway books, Scott makes a persuasive case that he did. In Box 169 at the UP, there is a note called "Literary Experiences," an outline of an autobiographical volume TD planned to write, to follow *Newspaper Days*. One item reads: "Street and Smith—Diamond Dick."

"the days we used to walk" Charles DeCamp to TD, July 9, 1914.

"You are purchasing one of the best" Jewett to MacLean, Jan. 19, 1905.

having had the unfinished MS of Hitchcock to TD, July 25, Sept. 22, 1904; July 18, 1905. In these letters Hitchcock is clearly referring to "Laborer" (asking whether he intends to make it "narration or fiction"), then saying he wants to publish the book (Feb. 9, 1905), and finally writing that he will hold a package with TD's manuscript in it until Dreiser wants to pick it up.

"dubious of its selling qualities" Poll to TD, Feb. 25, 1905.

A year later Taylor to TD, July 7, 1905; April 19, 1906.

"tamper with the higher," "some assistance" "The Publisher's World," *Smith's*, April 1905.

"Great—fine, exstatic [sic]" Paul to TD, June 1905.

"made lots of money but none" Mabel Haviland to Vera Dreiser, Dec. 10, 1959, Vera Dreiser file, Box 384A.

Haviland himself told Edward Marks Isaac Goldberg, *The Rise of Tin Pan Alley*, 175, 176.

"genuine songs of feeling," "the rich," "will, I'm" "Writes Home and Mother Songs," "But He Is No Sentimentalist Paul Dresser Says—Facts That Contradict Him." New York *Sun*, May 29, 1904, Paul Dresser Scrapbook (UP).

"The People, the People" Unpublished. The lyic is among the papers in the PD Scrapbook.

It was said that he had Charles K. Harris in *After the Ball* writes that Paul had a memorandum book listing all his debtors, but could not collect from one of them.

"If you lived most of your day" New York *Sun*, May 29, 1904, PD Scrapbook (UP).

"the business in 28th Street" Ed Dreiser to TD, Oct. 8, 1906.

"I am going through bankruptcy now" Paul to Brennan, May 19, 1904, Box 392 (UP).

"Howley is mixed up in it" Aug. 11, 1905.

set up his portable organ "My Brother Paul," by Mary Dreiser Brennam [sic], typescript with letter to TD, July 5, 1906. See Mai Skelly Dreiser to Helen Dreiser, Jan. 11, 1947. She recalled: "Poor Paul when he was at Emma's he told them there would be enough for every one when he passed on. The truth was he didn't have a quarter to buy a meal. He ate his meals at my Aunt Kate's."

pernicious anemia, rheumatism, dropsy, bad heart Paul mentioned some of these complaints in letters. In its obituary notice, the New York *Telegraph* mentions "dropsical complaint" and heart trouble. As for Paul's diet-

ing, an undated clipping in the Scrapbook, "Paul Dresser Quite Ill," reports that he had been on a thirty-five-day fast, taking nothing but orange juice and water. When he began the fast he weighed 326 pounds and was gaining a pound a day. After losing sixty-six pounds, he began "making up for the meals he missed and his stomach would not stand the strain."

"emanated a kind of fear" *Twelve Men*, 105.

"I've been a little ill" Paul to Mary Brennan, Dec. 10, 1905.

"PAUL IS DYING" Telegram, Ed Dreiser to TD, Jan. 29, 1906.

"his soft hands folded over" *Twelve Men*, 108.

"He made two or three fortunes" New York *Telegraph*, Dec. 31, 1906.

in his homily Father Van Rennselaer Mary Frances Brennan, in "My Brother Paul."

"And then came an angel" Typescript in PD Scrapbook.

"the family have no money" New York *Telegraph*, Feb. 20, 1906.

forging Mrs. Skelly's name Vera Dreiser, *My Uncle Theodore*, 126, 127.

"If I don't do something soon" Ed Dreiser to TD, Oct. 8, 1906.

"if you can call it that" TD to M. F. Brennan, Oct. 16, 1906.

"the gang that has the songs" McKee to TD, Sept. 1907.

Chapter 45.

"she was in the walled city" *Sister Carrie*, Pennsylvania Edition, 449.

"Success may be the worst" Quoted in *Smith's*, "The Publisher's Word," April 1905.

"My Gal Sal" royalties Herbert E. Marks to TD, July 9, 1932. Box 259 (UP).

"prove you that you can face" Henry to TD, undated. (Letter owned by Mr. and Mrs. Gupton Vogt.)

"Here is the way" TD to Henry, Jan. 12, 1903. (Letter owned by Mr. and Mrs. Gupton Vogt.)

"to see if it is not possible" Henry to TD, Feb. 8, 1904.

"Tom as I have depicted him" Feb. 17, 1904.

"It is very clear to me," "should have," "I had no idea" Ibid.

"Poor dear All [sic]" Mary Frances Brennan to TD, March 22, 1906.

"Success is what counts" TD[?] "A Word to the Public," *Smith's*, June 1905.

"the right use" *Smith's*, July 1905.

"It is not necessary" "What the Editor Has to Say," *Smith's*, June 1906.

"a personal human," "with the eyes," "reflect American" *Smith's*, Aug. 1906.

"What weakling, seeing," "The very air," "A Lesson from the Aquarium," *Tom Watson's Magazine*, Jan. 1906. In Donald Pizer, ed., *Theodore Dreiser: A Selection of Uncollected Prose*, 161, 162.

"The materials," "The tale is too intricate" Quoted in Philip L. Gerber, "Dreiser's Financier: A Genesis," *Journal of Modern Literature*, March 1971.

"be brave enough to imagine" Dorothy Dudley, *Dreiser and the Land of the Free*, 208, 209.

"I was always difficult" Quoted in Dudley, *Land of the Free*, 206.

"before the house had acquired" *The Standard & Vanity Fair*, Jan. 3, 1908.

"a careful supervision," "any personality," "the new," "illustrated," "the big questions" TD to Caleb L. Litchfield, April 10, 1906. In Robert H. Elias, *Letters to Theodore Dreiser*, I, 76-79.

"The minute I set eyes on him" Quoted in Dudley, *Land of the Free*, 109. See also Roy L. McCardell, "Benjamin B. Hampton— Publisher, Publicist and Picture Producer," New York *Morning Telegraph*, April 24, 1921.

"God, how I hate to go to bed" *Twelve Men*, 217.

"the prettiest piece of transformation" *The Standard & Vanity Fair*, Jan. 3, 1908.

"a marvellous objective mind," "Christ in Hell" Quoted in Dudley, *Land of the Free*, 211.

"hammering at conditions" Ibid., 210.

"If you would call at this office" Wilder to TD, June 6, 1907.

Chapter 46.

"From now on" *The Delineator*, Jan. 1908.

"a fashion sheet" Hoffman to Robert H. Elias, Jan. 10, 1945 (CorU).

"west of the" Frances Perkins, Oral History Coll (ColU).

"Hardwood inlaid floors" Lengel, "The 'Genius' Himself," *Esquire*, Sept. 1938. Lengel saw the *Delineator* offices in 1910, after a 1909 renovation. I have found no description of Dreiser's office prior to that time, other than allusions to his large chairs, great desk, and other symbols of power.

"strange lantern of a face," "regarding me without seeing" Fannie Hurst, *Anatomy of Me*, 156, 157.

"the most nervous" Nina Carter Marbourg, "Some of the Editors I Have Met," *Newspaperdom*, Oct. 24, 1907.

"queer" Perkins, Oral History.

"dominating personality," "People moved" Charles Hanson Towne, *Adventures in Editing*, 122, 123.

"curious eyes" Lengel, "Genius."

"You can stay," "There won't" Quoted in W. A. Swanberg, *Dreiser*, 147.

"He was exceedingly" Lengel, "Genius."

"the one big" Quoted in Dorothy Dudley, *Dreiser and the Land of the Free*, 126.

"In Philadelphia" Homer Croy, *Country Cured*, 142. I have added Lorimer's and Bok's first names to the quote.

"Who would not dream" *Sister Carrie*. Quoted in Alfred Kazin and Charles Shapiro, eds., *The Stature of Theodore Dreiser*, 17.

"a pirate selling ribbons" Quoted in Jack Salzman, ed., *Theodore Dreiser: The Critical Reception*, 71.

"One must live" Lengel, *"Genius."*

Chapter 47.

"Mr. Dreiser" Quoted by Dorothy Dudley in *Dreiser and the Land of the Free*, 234.

"When you wrote" Masters to TD, April 20, 1939.

Holly was . . . familiar with the book's history In Flora Mai Holly to James T. Farrell, July 4, 1943.

"an intelligent, hearty generous," "canny suburban" From Lewis Lewisohn, *Cities and Men*. In Alfred Kazin and Charles Shapiro, eds., *The Stature of Theodore Dreiser*, 17.

"very pious Presbys" Dodge to TD, Feb. 13, 1913.

"an absorbing story," "risqué" Doscher to Neda M. Westlake, Aug. 12, 1954.

they had agreed on a contract Enclosure, ibid.

To Reedy, he boasted TD to Reedy, March 19, 1907. In Robert H. Elias, _The Letters of Theodore Dreiser_, I, 80.

"a coarse bit of," "considerable justification" Quoted in Neda M. Westlake, "The _Sister Carrie_ Scrapbook," _The Library Chronicle_, Spring 1979.

talking bitterly about the publisher's wife Doscher to Westlake, Aug., 12, 1954.

"This book was accepted" Quoted in Westlake, _"Carrie_ Scrapbook."

"The Curtain Raised" Quoted in Elias, _Theodore Dreiser: Apostle of Nature_, 137.

sales got off to a brisk start See James L. W. West, III, "Dreiser and the B.W. Dodge _Sister Carrie_," _Studies in Bibliography_, University of Virginia, 1982.

he was able to sell his interest Doscher to Westlake, Aug. 12, 1954.

"uncommon quality," "literature of high class," "somber," "strongest piece of real-

ism" Quoted in Jack Salzman, _Theodore Dreiser: The Critical Reception_, 47, 29, 38, 44.

"Such books are to be shunned" Quoted in Dudley, _Land of the Free_, 216.

"The book is not," "a matter for regret" Salzman, _Critical Reception_, 42, 32.

"We do not" Ibid., 29.

"with the dignity of psychological" Ibid., 33.

"Amid the thousands" Ibid., 31.

"one more," "Possibly the day may come" Ibid., 38.

"The mere living of your daily life" Otis Norman, _The New York Times Saturday Review of Books_, June 15, 1907. In Donald Pizer, _Theodore Dreiser: A Selection of Uncollected Prose_, 163.

"Every human life is intensely" Ibid., 163, 164.

Epilogue

"Each according to his temperament" _The Titan_, 551.

SELECTED BIBLIOGRAPHY

Allen, Frederick Lewis, *The Big Change*. New York: Harper and Brothers, 1952.

Baker, Ray Stannard, *American Chronicle*. New York: Charles Scribner's Sons, 1945.

Balzac, Honoré de, *Lost Illusions*. Penguin Books, 1971.

Beckwith, H. W., *History of Vigo and Parke Countys*. Chicago: H. H. Hill and N. Iddings Publishing, 1880.

Beer, Thomas, *The Mauve Decade*. New York: Alfred A. Knopf, 1926.

———, *Stephen Crane*. New York: Alfred A. Knopf, 1923.

Biographical and Historical Record of Kosciusko County, Indiana. Chicago: Lewis Publishing Company, 1887.

Boase, Paul, ed., *The Rhetoric of Protest and Reform, 1878–1898*. Athens, Ohio: Ohio University Press, 1980.

Bourne, Randolph, *The History of a Literary Radical & Other Papers*. New York: S. A. Russell, 1956.

Bradsby, H. C., *History of Vigo County, Indiana, With Biographical Selections*. Chicago: S. B. Nelson and Company, 1891.

Brecher, Jeremy, *Strike!* San Francisco: Straight Arrow Books, 1972.

Brooks, Van Wyck, *The Confident Years*. New York: E. P. Dutton, 1955.

Burke, Harry, *From the Day's Journey*. St. Louis: William Harvey Miner, 1924.

Cady, Edwin H., *The Realist at War*. Syracuse: Syracuse University Press, 1958.

Carter, Everett, *Howells and the Age of Realism*. Philadelphia: J. P. Lippincott, 1954.

Chopin, Kate, *The Awakening*. New York: Bantam Books, 1981.

Churchill, Allen, *Park Row*. New York: Rinehart and Company, 1958.

Cole, Arthur Harrison, *The American Wool Manufacture*. Cambridge: Harvard University Press, 1926.

Dana, Ethel Nathalie, *Young in New York: A Memoir of a Victorian Girlhood*. Garden City, N.Y.: Doubleday, 1963.

Dedmon, Emmett, *Fabulous Chicago*. New York: Random House, 1953.

DeMuth, James, *Small Town Chicago*. Port Washington, N.Y.: Kennikat Press, 1980.

Doran, George H., *Chronicles of Barabbas*. New York: Rinehart and Company, 1952.

Dreiser, Theodore, *An Amateur Laborer*. Richard W. Dowell, ed. Philadelphia: University of Pennsylvania Press, 1983.

———, *The American Diaries, 1902–1926*. Thomas P. Riggio, ed. Philadelphia: University of Pennsylvania Press, 1982.

———, *Dawn*. New York: Horace Liveright, 1931.

———, *Free and Other Stories*. New York: The Modern Library, 1925.

———, *A Gallery of Women*, 2 volumes. New York: Horace Liveright, 1929.

———, *The "Genius"*. New York: Boni and Liveright, 1923.

———, *Jennie Gerhardt*. Garden City, N.Y.: Garden City Publishing Company, [n.d.].

———, *Newspaper Days*. New York: Beekman Publishers, 1974.

———, *Sister Carrie*. New York: Doubleday, Page, 1900.

———, *Sister Carrie*. New York: B. W. Dodge, 1907.

———, *Sister Carrie*. Norton Critical Edition, Donald Pizer, ed New York: W. W. Norton, 1970.

———, *Sister Carrie*. Jack Salzman, ed. New York: Bobbs-Merrill, 1970.

———, *Sister Carrie*. Pennsylvania Edition, John C. Berkey; Alice M. Winters; James L. W. West, III; and Neda M. Westlake, eds.

Philadelphia: University of Pennsylvania Press, 1981.
———, *The Titan* New York: Thomas Y. Crowell Company, 1974.
———, *Twelve Men*. New York: Boni and Liveright, 1919.
Dreiser, Vera, with Howard, Brett, *My Uncle Theodore*. New York: Nash Publishing, 1976.
Dresser, Paul, *The Songs of Paul Dresser*. New York: Boni and Liveright, 1927.
Dudley, Dorothy, *Dreiser and the Land of the Free*. New York: The Beechhurst Press, 1946.
Elias, Robert H., *Letters of Theodore Dreiser*, 3 volumes. Philadelphia: University of Pennsylvania Press, 1959.
———, *Theodore Dreiser: Apostle of Nature*. Emended Edition. Ithaca: Cornell University Press, 1970.
Exman, Eugene, *The House of Harper*. New York: Harper & Row, 1967.
Freud, Sigmund, *Sexuality and the Psychology of Love*. New York: Collier Books, 1963.
Fuller, Henry B., *With the Procession*. Chicago: The University of Chicago Press, 1965.
Garland, Hamlin, *Companions of the Trail*. New York: Macmillan, 1931.
———, *Hamlin Garland's Diaries*. Donald Pizer, ed. San Marino, Cal.: Huntington Library, 1968.
———, *Roadside Meetings*. New York: Macmillan, 1930.
Geismar, Maxwell, *Rebels and Ancestors*. Boston: Houghton Mifflin, 1953.
Goldberg, Isaac, *Tin Pan Alley*. New York: John Day, 1930.
Goodman, Louis S., and Alfred Gilman, *The Pharmacological Basis of Therapeutics*. New York: Macmillan, 1958.
Hakutani, Yoshinobu, ed., *Selected Magazine Articles of Theodore Dreiser*. Rutherford, N.J.: Fairleigh Dickinson University Press, 1985.
———, *Young Dreiser*. Rutherford, N.J.: Fairleigh Dickinson University Press, 1980.
Hardy, Thomas, *Tess of the D'Urbervilles*. New York: Bantam Books, 1981.
Harris, Charles K., *After the Ball*. New York: Frank-Maurice, 1926.
Hassam, Loren, *A Historical Sketch of Terre Haute, Indiana*. Terre Haute: Gazette Job Rooms, 1873.

Hendrick, Burton J., ed., *The Training of an American: The Earlier Life and Letters of Walter H. Page, 1855–1913*. Boston: Houghton Mifflin, 1928.
Henry, Arthur, *An Island Cabin*. New York. A. S. Barnes and Company, 1904.
———, *Lodgings in Town*. New York: A. S. Barnes and Company, 1905.
Hill, Thomas E., *Hill's Manual of Social and Business Forms: A Guide to Correct Writing*. Chicago: Quadrangle Books, 1971. [Reprint of the 1885 edition]
History of Greene and Sullivan Counties, State of Indiana. Chicago: Goodspeed Brothers, 1884.
History of Montgomery County, Ohio. Chicago: W. H. Beers and Company, 1882.
History of St. Charles, Montgomery and Warren Counties, Missouri. St. Louis: Paul V. Cochrane, 1969.
Hofstadter, Richard, *Social Darwinism in American Thought*. Boston: Beacon Press, 1955.
Howells, William Dean, *A Hazard of New Fortunes*. New York: New American Library, 1965.
———, *Impressions and Experiences*. New York: Harper & Brothers, 1896.
———, *Literature and Life*. New York: Harper & Brothers, 1911.
———, *A Modern Instance*. New York: Penguin Books, 1984.
Hurst, Fannie, *Anatomy of Me*. New York: Doubleday, 1958.
Irvine, Wiliam, *Apes, Angels and Victorians*. New York: McGraw-Hill, 1955.
Jenkins, Stephen, *The Greatest Street in the World*. New York: G. P. Putnam's Sons, 1911.
Jones, Howard Mumford, *The Age of Energy*. New York: The Viking Press, 1971.
Kazin, Alfred, and Charles Shapiro, eds., *The Stature of Theodore Dreiser*. Bloomington: Indiana University Press, 1965.
Kellogg, J. H., *Neurasthenia*. Battle Creek, Mich.: Good Health Publishing Company, 1915.
Kennedy, James G., *Herbert Spencer*. Boston: Twayne Publishers, 1978.
Kirk, Clara Marburg, *W. D. Howells, Traveler from Altruria*. New Brunswick, N.J.: Rutgers University Press, 1962.

Lears, Jackson, *No Place of Grace*. New York: Pantheon Books, 1981.

Lehan, Richard, *Theodore Dreiser: His World and His Novels*. Carbondale and Edwardsville, Ill.: Southern Illinois University Press, 1969.

Lewisohn, Ludwig, *Up Stream*. New York: The Modern Library, 1926.

Lowe, David, *Lost Chicago*. New York: American Legacy Press, 1985.

Lynn, Kenneth, S., *William Dean Howells*. New York: Harcourt Brace Jovanovich, 1971.

Lyon, Peter, *Success Story: The Life and Times of S. S. McClure*. Deland, Fla.: Everett/Edwards, 1967.

McCabe, James D., Jr., *New York by Gaslight*. New York: Greenwich House, 1984.

McPhaul, John J., *Deadlines and Monkeyshines*. New York: Prentice-Hall, 1962.

Madison, Charles A., *Book Publishing in America*. New York: McGraw-Hill, 1966.

Marcosson, Isaac, *Adventures in Interviewing*. New York: John Lane, 1923.

———, *David Graham Phillips and His Times*. New York: Dodd, Mead and Company, 1932.

Marcus, Steven, *The Other Victorians*. New York: Bantam Books, 1967.

Marden, Orison Swett, ed., *Little Visits With Great Americans*. New York: The Success Company, 1905.

Marks, Edward, with A. J. Liebling, *They All Sang*. New York: The Viking Press, 1934.

Moers, Ellen, *Two Dreisers*. New York: The Viking Press, 1969.

Mott, Frank Luther, *A History of American Magazines*, 4 volumes. Cambridge: Harvard University Press, 1957.

Norris, Frank, *The Octopus*. New York: New American Library, 1964.

Oakey, C. C., *Greater Terre Haute and Vigo Countys* [sic], 2 volumes. Chicago: Lewis Publishing Company, 1908.

Orton, Vrest, *Dreiserana: A Book About His Books*. New York: Haskell House, 1973.

Pizer, Donald, *The Novels of Theodore Dreiser: A Critical Study*. Minneapolis: University of Minnesota Press, 1976.

———, ed., *Theodore Dreiser: A Selection of Uncollected Prose*. Detroit: Wayne State University Press, 1977.

———, Dowell, Richard W., and Frederic E. Rusch. *Theodore Dreiser: A Primary and Secondary Bibliography*. Boston: G. K. Hall, 1975.

Putzel, Max, *The Man in the Mirror: William Marion Reedy and His Magazine*. Cambridge: Harvard University Press, 1963.

Reynolds, Quentin, *The Fiction Factory*. New York: Random House, 1955.

Riis, Jacob, *How the Other Half Lives*. New York: Hill and Wang, 1957.

Salvatore, Nick, *Eugene V. Debs: Citizen and Socialist*. Champagne: University of Illinois Press, 1984.

Salzman, Jack, ed., *Theodore Dreiser: The Critical Reception*. New York: David Lewis, 1972.

Sennett, Richard, *Families Against the City*. New York: Vintage Books, 1970.

Siegel, Adrienne, *The Image of the American City in Popular Literature*. Port Washington, N.Y.: Kennikat Press, 1981.

Sinclair, Upton, *The Brass Check*. Pasadena, Cal.: Published by the Author, [1919].

Sloane, Florence Adele, *Maverick in Mauve*. Commentary by Louis Auchincloss. New York: Doubleday, 1983.

Spaeth, Sigmund, *Read 'Em and Weep*. New York: Arco, 1945.

Spencer Herbert, *First Principles*. 5th London Edition. New York: A. L. Burt, [n.d.]

Stallman R. W., *Stephen Crane*. New York: George Braziller, 1968.

——— and Hagemann, E. R., eds., *The New York City Sketches of Stephen Crane*. New York: New York University Press, 1966.

———, *Our Times: America Finding Herself*. New York: Charles Scribner's Sons, 1927.

Sullivan, Mark, *Our Times: The Turn of the Century*. New York: Charles Scribner's Sons, 1926.

Swanberg, W. A., *Dreiser*. New York: Bantam Books, 1966.

Tarbell, Ida M., *The Nationalizing of Business*. Chicago: Quadrangle Paperbacks, 1971.

Taylor, Walter F., *The Economic Novel in America*. New York: Octagon Books, 1964.

Trachtenberg, Alan, *The Incorporation of America*. New York: Hill and Wang, 1982.

Walker, Franklin, *Frank Norris*. New York: Doubleday, Doran, 1932.

———, ed., *The Letters of Frank Norris*. San Francisco: The Book Club of California, 1956.

Wall, Joseph Frazier, *Andrew Carnegie*. New York: Oxford University Press, 1970.

West, James L. W., III, *A Sister Carrie Portfolio*. Charlottesville: The University of Virginia Press, 1985.

Witherbee, Sidney A., ed., *Spanish-American War Songs*. Detroit: S. A. Witherbee, 1898.

Witmark, Isadore, and Isaac Goldberg. *Story of the House of Witmark: From Ragtime to Swingtime*. New York: Lee Furman, 1939.

Wyllie, Irvin G. *The Self-Made Man in America*. New York: The Free Press, 1954.

Ziff, Larzer, *The American 1890s*. London: Chatto and Windus, 1967.

INDEX